THE EU–CHINA RELATIONSHIP
EUROPEAN PERSPECTIVES

A Manual for Policy Makers

THE EU–CHINA RELATIONSHIP
EUROPEAN PERSPECTIVES

A Manual for Policy Makers

Editor
Kerry Brown
University of Sydney, Australia

Imperial College Press

Published by

Imperial College Press
57 Shelton Street
Covent Garden
London WC2H 9HE

Distributed by

World Scientific Publishing Co. Pte. Ltd.
5 Toh Tuck Link, Singapore 596224
USA office: 27 Warren Street, Suite 401-402, Hackensack, NJ 07601
UK office: 57 Shelton Street, Covent Garden, London WC2H 9HE

British Library Cataloguing-in-Publication Data
A catalogue record for this book is available from the British Library.

THE EU–CHINA RELATIONSHIP: EUROPEAN PERSPECTIVES
A Manual for Policy Makers

Copyright © 2015 by Imperial College Press

All rights reserved. This book, or parts thereof, may not be reproduced in any form or by any means, electronic or mechanical, including photocopying, recording or any information storage and retrieval system now known or to be invented, without written permission from the Publisher.

For photocopying of material in this volume, please pay a copying fee through the Copyright Clearance Center, Inc., 222 Rosewood Drive, Danvers, MA 01923, USA. In this case permission to photocopy is not required from the publisher.

ISBN 978-1-78326-454-4

Typeset by Stallion Press
Email: enquiries@stallionpress.com

Printed in Singapore by B & Jo Enterprise Pte Ltd

Dedicated to Chloe Sageman, Angelika Meier and Rosheen Kabraji, for their help and assistance over the last few years during the ECRAN project

Contents

About the Editor	xi
Introduction	xiii
Abbreviations and Acronyms	xxi

Section One China and the EU: The General Context	1
Chinese Internal Views of the EU Gudrun Wacker	3
The Chinese Five Year Programme (2011–2015) and Europe 2020 Roderic Wye	12
China's Green Economy and EU–China Cooperation Jørgen Delman and Ole Odgaard	23
Section Two Chinese Internal Politics and the EU	33
China: The National People's Congress Roderic Wye	35
The Chinese People's Political Consultative Conference (CPPCC): Its Role and its Future Jean-Pierre Cabestan	51
The Role of Chinese Soft Power Anonymous	63
The Situation of Lawyers in the PRC Nicholas Bequelin	71
Cadre Training and the Party School System in Contemporary China Frank N Pieke	82

The Role of Think Tanks in China   88
Nicola Casarini

Public Consultations in China   98
Jasper Becker

Section Three   Chinese International Relations   113

An Assessment of EU–China Relations in
Global Governance Forums   115
Giovanni B. Andornino

China's Response to the US 'Return to Asia' Tour   128
Andrew Small

BRICS: A Cohesive Grouping?   139
Sylvia Hui

China–Pakistan Relations   148
Gareth Price

The Chinese Reaction to the March 2011 Earthquake
and Tsunami and the Nuclear Aftermath   156
Caroline Rose

China–Vietnam Relations on Maritime Borders   165
Marianna Brungs

Patterns of China–Russia Cooperation
in Multilateral Forums   175
Neil Munro

Competing Claims in the South China Sea:
Assessment and Prospects   183
Philip Andrews-Speed

The Impact of the Arab Revolutions on China's
Foreign Policy   201
Ben Simpfendorfer

China and the Democratic People's Republic of Korea   214
Amy Studdart

Reappraising Chinese Engagement in Africa *Ian Taylor*	223
China's Energy Policy Towards Central Asia *Bobo Lo*	232
China and Latin America *Rhys Jenkins*	241
China's 'Non-Policy' for Afghanistan *Bernt Berger*	251
China–Burma Relations *Marianna Brungs*	261
China and Southeast Asia *David Camroux*	274
The Changing Politics of Nepal *Gareth Price*	285
China and Russia's Competition for East and Southeast Asia Energy Resources *Philip Andrews-Speed*	294
Section Four The Chinese Economy	**307**
The Liberalisation of Chinese Financial Markets *Vilem Semerak*	309
Investment Provisions in China's Free Trade Agreements *Christopher M Dent*	327
Bond Issuance by Local Authorities in China *Vanessa Rossi*	337
The Role of Shadow Banking in Chinese Business *Sandrine Lunven*	347
Family Businesses in China *Anonymous*	355
Where does China Stand in the Eurobond Debate? *Vanessa Rossi*	366

Innovation in China — 373
Alice Rezková

Chinese Investments into the EU Energy Sector — 380
Hinrich Voss

Chinese Overseas Acquisitions: The Nokia Siemens/
Motorola Case — 390
Marc Laperrouza

The Chinese Middle Class — 397
Paul French

Tax and Pensions in China — 406
Stuart Leckie and Rita Xiao

Waste Management in China — 416
Anonymous

Section Five   Chinese Social Issues — 429

Social Unrest in China — 431
Jude Howell

The Recent Labour Unrest in China and the Politics
of Handling Collective Mobilisation by the Party-State — 441
Eric Florence

Urbanisation, Rural-to-Urban Migration and Housing
in China — 452
Bettina Gransow

Land Acquisition in China — 465
Staphany Wong

China's Food Security — 477
Robert Ash

Suggested Further Reading — 495

Index — 499

About the Editor

Kerry Brown is Professor of Chinese Politics and Director of the China Studies Centre, University of Sydney and Team Leader of the Europe China Research and Advice Network (ECRAN) funded by the EU. He is also an Associate Fellow of Chatham House, London. He was previously Head of the Asia Programme at Chatham House, London and a member of the British Diplomatic Service from 1998 to 2005, serving as First Secretary, British Embassy Beijing 2000–2003 and Head of the Indonesia and East Timor Section 2003–2005. Educated at the universities of Cambridge (MA) and Leeds (PhD), he is the author of *Purge of the Inner Mongolia Peoples Party* (Global Oriental Ltd, 2006), *Struggling Giant: China in the 21st Century* (Anthem Press, 2007), *The Rise of the Dragon: Chinese Inward and Outward Investment in the Reform Era* (Chandos Publishing Ltd, 2008), *Friends and Enemies: The Past, Present and Future of the Communist Party of China* (Anthem Press, 2009), *Ballot Box China* (Zed Books Ltd, 2011), *China 2020* (Chandos Publishing Ltd, 2011), *Hu Jintao: China's Silent Leader* (World Scientific, 2012), *Contemporary China* (Palgrave Macmillan, 2013), and *The Networked Leadership: China's Fifth Generation Leaders* (Forthcoming).

Introduction

Kerry Brown, Team Leader, ECRAN

The relationship between the EU and China is one of the most important of the 21st century. They are vast trading partners, and enjoy multiple links with each other. Indeed, the complexity of these connections is something that would be hard to map adequately. From regions, to Member States, right up to the EU central administration, there are dialogues across almost every conceivable sector, and which permeate areas as diverse as civil society, sustainability and culture. From a period in the mid-1970s when China was remote to Europeans, and even the act of travelling there arduous and indirect, there are now millions of passengers travelling along direct routes from multiple centres in the EU and China to each other every year. A full comprehension of EU–China relations, in spite of its full richness and complexity, is critical for those who want to truly understand contemporary international politics, security and economy. It is a much misunderstood relationship, and one that does not have the high profile it deserves. The essays in this collection, by some of the world's leading experts on EU- and China-related issues, should help in getting to terms with this relationship.

The chapters here were all commissioned as part of the Europe China Research and Advice Network (ECRAN). This was established in early 2011 after a competitive tendering process, with the remit to supply policy advice, analysis and research to the EU and the Member States. This is the first collection of short papers issued as a result of the project, which was funded by the EU.

ECRAN was built on previous projects which had focused on creating a wider network of advice across the expert communities within the EU with knowledge of China. There was recognition that, in universities, companies, think tanks and other places, people were engaged in multiple areas dealing with China and its contemporary society, economics and political development, and that these groups needed to be better brought together so that their insights and expertise could be readily available for policy makers. With the establishment of the European External Action Service (EEAS) after the implementation of the Lisbon Treaty in 2009, a designated diplomatic service for the European Commission existed and it was necessary to give its officials access to good-quality advice, based on long engagement and first-hand experience.

The study of China in Europe has a history of almost two centuries, with the Sorbonne in Paris and the Universities of Oxford and Cambridge in the UK having some of the earliest sinology departments. The development of Chinese studies has, however, been slow, with clusters of people studying its language, history and culture spread across different departments in universities. Things became even more complicated with the isolation of the People's Republic of China (PRC) after its foundation in 1949, and the subsequent intense politicisation of the study of modern China.

By the second decade of the 21st century, however, with the growth in importance of the PRC's economy and its opening up to the outside world, more and more colleges, schools and university departments across the whole of the EU began to either acquire capacity in some areas of the study of modern China, or to increase and enhance what they already had. Increasing numbers of students started to take an interest in studying China either for reasons of their future career, or for its intrinsic interest. More often than not, they did it for both reasons.

The expanding political and economic engagement between the EU and China also necessitated attempting to create a better bridge between these diverse and dispersed expert academic communities and the policy makers working in Brussels and elsewhere in government in the Member States. One of the main impetuses therefore behind the creation of ECRAN was to fill this unmet need, and to draw together those with expertise in the contemporary politics, society and economy of China. A network of almost 300 throughout the 28 Member States was established, many in major universities or with demonstrable long-term experience and expertise in the research and analysis of trends in modern China. These formed the key component of the project.

From 2011, ECRAN undertook four core activities. The first was to commission, after competitive tendering, long papers of up to 20,000 words on issues ranging from analysis of the 12th Five Year Programme issued in 2011, to research on different types of social unrest within China, and the dynamics of nationalism as it developed in the country. Some of these papers have been published, and many have been made available in a series of books issued in 2013. Over 25 such long papers, some single authored and some joint authored, by internationally recognised experts have been issued, all of them peer reviewed to the highest scholarly standards, breaking new ground in the ways in which they approach subjects and the field research they contain.

The second strand of the project was to undertake special briefings for the EEAS, the Member States and the Directorate Generals within the European Commission. Bespoke briefings deploying key experts in the EU were arranged, mostly in Brussels, which covered issues ranging from prospects for US and China relations, to the Chinese leadership transition in 2012–2013, and the maritime border disputes in the East and South China Seas which had intensified from 2009. In addition to these focused events, the third strand arranged large-scale public events, with annual events held in Brussels, and then subsidiary events covering specific issues held in Ireland, Poland, Belgium, the Czech Republic and the UK with local partners. These helped to inform public engagement and debate about relations between the EU and China, and about how to improve understanding of Chinese politics and economic behaviour. Those in attendance included journalists, policy makers, members of the public and academics.

The final element of the project, and perhaps the most important, was to commission short papers, which were usually an *ad hoc* response to events and where the EEAS and Member States felt there was a need to have an outside expert perspective. A selection of these short papers is contained in this collection. The authors commissioned include some of Europe's most experienced and accomplished experts on China. They come from across the EU family of nation states, from Germany, to Bulgaria, Romania, Italy, France, Sweden and Hungary.

The short briefing papers produced for ECRAN have a specific format, which is worth explaining in order to help to understand fully how the different chapters in this book are presented and structured. They were written for busy policy makers, some of whom had no background in the issues being discussed, and therefore had to avoid as far as possible technical language, and explain any specialist background or context. They had to be succinct, and in a highly user-friendly format, with the executive summary containing everything that was key to the rest of the paper, and serving as 'utterly indispensable things to know' for those too busy to even read the rest of the content. Their content is also very much policy-oriented, and this explains some of the prescriptive language that these reports contain. They are geared towards suggesting ideas and approaches for policy, rather than being solely analytic pieces.

The worlds of academia and policy making, whether in government or other fields, are famously different. For the former, neutrality is important, with the impartial collection and weighing of evidence, and the provision of good analytic conceptual frameworks constituting some of the key elements of their work. For policy makers, however, the main dynamic, especially in foreign policy, is to come up with pragmatic, workable proposals that can guide action. In dealing with China, the challenges are particularly steep in this area. China has a wholly different political system to the members of the EU, it has a different understanding of the role of the state in the economy, and has been developing in ways far more rapid and on a greater scale than that ever seen in Europe, where the processes of modernisation and industrialisation occurred over several decades rather than just two to three. For this reason, framing constructive policy about China for the EU, especially with the challenges of forging consensus on this across the Member States, is hugely complex.

Despite this, or in fact precisely because of it, the necessity of having good policy is great. The option of not having some overarching guidelines for engagement does not exist. The EU, with its High Level Strategic Dialogue with China, and with 56 strategic dialogues in political, economic and social areas, has to somehow devise a workable overarching narrative of its objectives in engagement with China. This tends to be easier in the economic realm (although there, on the issue of market access and subsidies, it can be tough enough) than it is in the political, where the EU enjoys a famously testy and difficult dialogue with China on issues like human rights and the rule of law. These are explored in some of the papers in this collection. Good-quality analysis based on a solid empirical foundation is therefore a massive help for policy makers. It can deepen their understanding of a particular issue, and supply them with bespoke material that gives them context, impartial advice and fresh ideas. The short papers here are examples of such material.

Each of these pieces has to be read in the context of the EU's relation with China from 2011 to 2013. The dominant motifs of this period were the deepening and ongoing crisis in the eurozone, and the immense impact this had on both Europe's economic and political confidence. The word 'crisis' was used densely over this period, with one high-level dialogue with China actually cancelled in late 2011 because of the gravity of the problems within the eurozone. While these problems eased up a little into 2013, it is clear reading through some of the material here, particularly the section on economic relations, that this had a direct impact on the way in which the EU actually related to China. There was a tangible sense as the world's largest single economic area was coming to an awareness for the first time that the fastest-growing emerging economy, and already the world's second largest by this period, was a radically different entity to the one that had existed even a decade or so before. The relationship therefore moved into a period of sharply different dynamics, where the Chinese internal market with its promise of growth was seen as critical for Europe's future success, and the EU market, while still immensely important, as one fated in the coming decades to either stagnate or even to decline in importance.

Europe was still the single most important economic actor in this period, and predictions of its demise were often over stated. Even so, there was a sense in which those engaged as policy makers and observers of the relationship over this period saw a profound underlying change. China was, as some of the contributions on its international affairs make clear, viewed as being more assertive in its attitude to the world outside. On issues from trade to climate change, to criticisms of its own internal rights system, it was far less willing to hear external lecturing and more expectant on being viewed as an equal partner. We can see in these papers therefore a view of a relationship in transition, and of two major parties, the EU and China, undergoing significant and historic internal change.

These papers are focused in particular on the issues that mattered to Europe, and one of the key questions given to all of the authors was to relate the issues they were addressing to Europe, and give a clear indication of where Europe's interests should lie, and what sort of involvement or impact it might seek. Of course, some issues, like the crisis around North Korea, were remote and ones in which the EU had no direct say in beyond being a concerned international player. Others, like the relations between the US and China, were immensely significant to the EU and were observed keenly. Issues of labour or social unrest and development within China related directly to the stability of the country, and to the investment, geopolitical and security interests of the EU. There were few issues in which, at the very least, the EU did not have an interest, even if it had no direct link.

One value in publishing these treatments, beyond the intrinsic merits of each, is that they give an audit — at a particular, critical moment — of the EU's understanding of one of its major trade and political partners. In that sense, more than being simply about China, these are also papers that let the EU see itself more clearly through interaction with a power that is dynamic, changing and often asks hard questions. There are often no easy answers when dealing with China. The clampdown within China that occurred as a result of the Jasmine Revolutions from

2010 in the Middle East in particular threw up unexpected issues, both in the ways in which China responded diplomatically, but also in terms of the ways in which it guarded its own domestic polity. China's impact in Africa also lacked a straightforward pattern, with some seeing it as being a force for good through its developmental impact, and others criticising it for its negative human rights influence. On these issues, the EU had to think hard about its own core values, especially when it was faced by a more complex international situation, and a China that was often less willing to listen to external voices that criticised it and felt emboldened by its own strong growth over this period.

We have here therefore an overview of the core relationship, but also of EU perspectives on it. The authors, from their diverse backgrounds, give voice to often very different treatments of China, and also to different frameworks by which to understand it, and to understand the EU's relationship to it. Some of the treatments here are critical and placed within a clear context in which the EU has absolute values on which it has to stand and where it cannot compromise. Others ask questions about how the EU might do more to internalise and engage with the role that China is playing internationally. These shifting perspectives help us to understand better the complexity and evolving nature of this hugely important but often vexed and mutually frustrating relationship.

It is important to stress here that, while policy briefs, these papers are *not* expressions of EU policy, and should not be read as such. Nor are they formal expressions of policy for any of the organisations which authors are indicated as affiliated to. They were offered by experts on a personal basis, and contain advice and perspectives which were impartial. This disclaimer is important. The EU is often criticised for its approach to China, and to the way in which it frames policy. These papers however should not, and cannot, be used as ammunition for those who want to attack the EU. For this, they will need to look elsewhere. Each of the papers in this collection were written with the clear understanding that they should contain good quality, impartial advice, and that their contents might assist policy makers in their discussions and thinking. But they carry no official mark of approval and are not in any way expressions, or indication, of EU policy.

The ECRAN project divided its work into three core areas — politics, society and economics. I am grateful to the key experts in these areas, who helped in the selection of authors to write specific papers, the articulation of frames of reference and the peer review of the papers once they were completed. For politics, this was Professor Shaun Breslin of Warwick University. For economics, it was Professor Shujie Yao, and for society Professor Lina Song, both of Nottingham University.

I am immensely grateful for their help in this area and for the ways in which they helped to improve the contributions. In collecting these papers, I have created a wider classification, adding international relations and also a broader initial selection of papers that deal with the overall context of the relationship.

There are, of course, differences not only between the traditions of sinology within the Member States, but also between each individual author. So while each author was asked to provide an executive summary, main points, an argument and then policy recommendations, it was also important to maintain the different perspectives, and stylistic characteristics of each author. I hope that comes through in what is written here. It is also extremely important to stress that these pieces are published as they were written, and that therefore some of the information they contain is out of date. The date of their writing is clearly indicated at the head of each piece, and so they should be read as up to date at this time. I have wanted to present the immediacy of the works, and their topicality rather than trying to revise and change them. Nor are they densely referenced. This is once more due to their function as policy briefings, not academic writings, despite the considerable scholarship they are based on. Each of these papers has been produced by people who have extensive experience in their area, and as such is a digest; a distillation of their advice and knowledge on a particular area. For that reason, references have been kept to a minimum, though we have added brief suggestions for further reading at the end which can help explore broader areas beyond the treatments given here.

I am grateful to all of the authors for their work on these papers, but also to Chloe Sageman and Angelika Meier for all they have done for the ECRAN project, and to colleagues at the EEAS and across the Member States who have participated in the ECRAN project and supplied feedback. I am also grateful to Imperial College Press for its assistance in making these important papers available to a wider public. These show the deep and lively engagement throughout the Member States on matters relating to its relations with China, and for that reason deserve a wide audience. It has been a huge privilege to have worked on the ECRAN project and to have had the opportunity to learn from so many accomplished and learned colleagues. I am sure that it has enriched, assisted and deepened policy making thinking and has been of immense service to a relationship that simply has to work and improve in the years ahead.

Kerry Brown
Sydney
July 2014

Abbreviations and Acronyms

ACFIC	All-China Federation of Industry and Commerce
ACFTU	All-China Federation of Trade Unions
ADB	Asian Development Bank
AML	Anti-monopoly Law
AMS	Academy of Military Sciences
APA	Administrative Procedure Act
APEC	Asia-Pacific Economic Cooperation
ARF	ASEAN Regional Form
ASEAN	Association of Southeast Asian Nations
bcn	Billion cubic metres
BIT	Bilateral investment treaty
bn	Billion
BoC	Bank of China
boe/d	Barrels-of-oil-equivalent per day
BRIC	Brazil, Russia, India and China
BRICS	Brazil, Russia, India, China and South Africa
CO_2	Carbon dioxide
CAS	Center for American Studies at Fudan University
CASS	Chinese Academy of Social Sciences
CATIC	China Aviation Technology Import-Export Corporation
CBRC	China Banking Regulatory Commission
CCB	China Construction Bank
CCCWS	China Center for Contemporary World Studies
CCIEE	China Center for International Economic Exchanges
CCP	Chinese Communist Party
CCS	Carbon Capture and Storage
CDB	China Development Bank
CDM	Clean Development Mechanism

CEPRI	China Electric Power Research Institute
CFISS	China Foundation for International Strategic Studies
CFIUS	Committee on Foreign Investment in the United States
CICIR	China Institutes of Contemporary International Relations
CIIS	China Institute of International Studies
CIISS	China Institute for International Strategic Studies
CIRC	China Insurance Regulatory Commission
CIS	Commonwealth of Independent States
CLCS	Commission on the Limits of the Continental Shelf
CMC	Central Military Commission
CNOOC	China National Offshore Oil Corporation
CNPC	China National Petroleum Corporation
CNPCI	China National Petroleum Corporation International Ltd
CNPCIW	China National Petroleum Corporation International Watan
COASI	Asia-Oceania Working Party
COFCO	China National Cereals, Oil and Foodstuffs Corporation
CPB	Communist Party of Burma
CPPCC	Chinese People's Political Consultative Conference
CRF	China Reform Council
CRI	China Radio International
CSES	China Society for Environmental Sciences
CSR	Corporate social responsibility
CSRC	China Securities Regulatory Commission
DFID	UK Department for International Development
DOC	Declaration on the Conduct
DPRK	Democratic People's Republic of Korea/North Korea
DRC	Development Research Center of the State Council
EA	Enterprise Annuity
EAS	East Asian Summit
ECLAC	Economic Commission for Latin America and the Caribbean
ECRAN	Europe China Research and Advice Network
ECS	East China Sea
EEAS	European External Action Service
EEZ	Exclusive economic zone

EFSF	European Financial Stability Facility
EIA	Environmental Impact Assessment
EMU	Economic and Monetary Union
ESM	European Stabilisation Mechanism
ESPO	East Siberia Pacific Ocean
ETIM	East Turkestan Islamic Movement
EU	European Union
EUISS	European Union Institute for Security Studies
EUR	Euro
FALG	Foreign Affairs Leading Group
FAO	Foreign Affairs Office
FATA	Federally Administered Tribal Areas
FDI	Foreign direct investment
FDRA	Federal Democratic Republican Alliance
FIT	Feed-in tariff
FLE	Fundamental Law of Education
FSB	Financial Stability Board
FTA	Free trade agreement
FYP	Five Year Programme/Five Year Plan
GATT	General Agreement on Tariffs and Trade
GCC	Gulf Co-operation Council
GDP	Gross domestic product
GHG	Greenhouse gas
GM	Genetically modified
GSM	Global System for Mobile Communications
GTI	Greater Tumen Initiative
GW	Gigawatt
ha	Hectare
HNWI	High net worth individual
HRZ	Haier-Rube Economic Zone
HW	Hazardous waste
IA	Individual account
IAS	Institute of American Studies at CASS
ICBC	Industrial and Commercial Bank of China
ICJ	International Court of Justice

IES	Institute of European Studies at CASS
IIS	Institute of International Studies at Tsinghua University
IMF	International Monetary Fund
IP	Intellectial property
IPO	Initial public offering
IPR	Intellectual property rights
ISAF	International Security Assistance Force
ISW	Industrial solid waste
ITLOS	International Tribunal of the Law of the Sea
IWEP	Institute of World Economics and Politics
JDA	Joint development agreement
JI	Jamaat-e-Islami
JUI	Jamaat-e-Ulema-e-Islami
KMT	Kuomintang
LAL	Land Administration Law
LFG	Landfill gas
LNG	Liquefied natural gas
m	Million
M&A	Mergers and acquisitions
MCC	China Metallurgical Group
MEP	Ministry of Environmental Protection
MFN	Most-favoured-nation
MNC	Multinational company
MOF	Ministry of Finance
MOFCOM	The Ministry of Commerce of the People's Republic of China
MOFTEC	Ministry of Foreign Trade
MOHURD	Ministry of Housing and Urban-Rural Development
MoU	Memorandum of Understanding
MSDF	Maritime Self-Defense Force
MSI	Motorola Solutions
MSW	Municipal solid waste
NATO	North Atlantic Treaty Organization
NC	Nepali Congress
NDRC	National Development and Reform Commission

NERI	National Economics Research Institute
NGO	Non-governmental organisation
NLD	National League for Democracy
nm	Nautical mile
NOC	National oil company
NOx	Nitrogen oxide
NPC	National People's Congress
NPCSC	Standing Committee of the National People's Congress
NPL	Non-performing loan
NPT	Non-Proliferation Treaty
NPTF	Nepal Peace Trust Fund
NSN	Nokia Siemens Networks
OECD	Organisation for Economic Co-operation and Development
OLA	Office of Legislative Affairs
OSCE	Organization for Security and Co-operation in Europe
PAYG	Pay as you go
PBoC	People's Bank of China
PBSC	Politburo Standing Committee
PCA	Permanent Court of Arbitration
PE	Private equity
PLA	People's Liberation Army
POP	Persistent organic pollutant
PPC	Public Power Corporation
PRC	People's Republic of China
PRD	Pearl River Delta
PV	Photovoltaic
QFII	Qualified Foreign Institutional Program
R&D	Research and Development
REN	Redes Energéticas Nacionais
RMB	Renminbi
ROK	Republic of Korea/South Korea
RRR	Required-reserve ratio
SAT	State Administration of Taxation
SCID	State Grid International Development

SCO	Shanghai Cooperation Organisation
SDRs	Special Drawing Rights
SEPA	State Environmental Protection Agency
SEZ	Special economic zone
SGCC	State Grid Corporation of China
SIIS	Shanghai Institute of International Studies
SINOPEC	China Petroleum and Chemical Corporation
SIS	School of International Studies at Peking University
SME	Small and medium enterprise
SOE	State-owned enterprise
SOx	Sulphur Oxides
SPDC	State Peace and Development Council
SWP	German Institute for International and Security Affairs
t	Tonnes
TAC	Treaty of Amity and Coperation
tce	Tonnes of coal equivalent
TFP	Total factor productivity
TIP	Turkestan Independence Party
tn	Trillion
TPP	Trans-Pacific Partnership
TRADP	Tumen River Area Development Programme
TRIM	Trade-Related Investment Measure
TSF	Total Social Financing
TVEs	Township and village enterprises
UAE	United Arab Emirates
UML	Unified Marxist Leninists
UMTS	Universal Mobile Telecommunications System
UN	United Nations
UNCLOS	United Nations Convention on the Law of the Sea
UNFCCC	United Nations Framework Convention on Climate Change
UNGA	United Nations General Assembly
UNHRC	United Nations Human Rights Commission
UNSC	United Nations Security Council
US	United States of America
USD	US Dollars

USDA	US Department of Agriculture
USSR	Union of Soviet Socialist Republics
WMP	Wealth management product
WTE	Waste to energy
WTO	World Trade Organization

Section One
China and the EU: The General Context

Chinese Internal Views of the EU
(March 2012)

Gudrun Wacker

Senior Associate, German Institute for International and Security Affairs (SWP)

Executive Summary

Chinese leaders and officials follow developments in the EU mainly from the perspective of their possible impact on EU–China relations. Public statements are usually framed in polite diplomatic language and therefore tend to project a positive assessment of the European integration project. They do not necessarily reflect how Chinese leaders or the elite really think about the EU.

China's leaders value the EU as a successful example of economic integration and as a project that fosters peace and stability between its Member States. An economically strong EU that is able to find its way out of the current euro crisis is important to China out of self-interest: as long as China's growth path depends in part on exports, Europe will be an indispensable market for Chinese goods.

Chinese leaders and specialists understand the necessity to foster relations with *individual* Member States. This is seen as a concrete level of economic and other cooperation and is also the level at which China interacts with Europe in international organisations and groupings, like the Security Council of the UN or the G20. From the Chinese perspective, there is generally no clear-cut distinction between Europe, European Member States and the EU.

Despite economic, political and ideological friction, the Chinese elite do not perceive the EU as a competitor in geo-strategic terms (unlike the US). They identify common interests and a wide range of opportunities for cooperation with the EU.

However, Chinese expectations that the EU could develop into a counterweight to the US have been reduced, and not only since the sovereign debt crisis. The Lisbon Treaty is seen as a further step in the direction of a common European identity at the global level, but is yet to prove its actual effect on the EU's relations with third countries.

The EU and its institutions should try to avoid projecting their own internal views on other countries like China; achievements that are considered major breakthroughs from an EU perspective, e.g. the Lisbon Treaty, will not be noticed and acknowledged by Chinese leaders unless they prove to be relevant for Sino–EU relations.

Main Points

- Chinese leaders tend to comment on the EU only when it has direct relevance to China. However, what Chinese leaders say in public is not necessarily the same as what they really think.
- Chinese (academic) publications and informal meetings are less 'filtered' and are thus more informative regarding how members of the Chinese elite really see the EU.
- Chinese views of the EU are often influenced by how Europe is perceived to view China.
- China fosters bilateral relations with many EU Member States. However, both the EU and Europe are very often mentioned as a general framework within which China's relationships with individual Member States are embedded.
- The entry into force of the Lisbon Treaty and the inception of the European External Action Service are considered steps that could strengthen European identity at the global level. However, it is not seen as a watershed event by Chinese leaders.
- Despite economic, political and ideological friction, the Chinese elite do not perceive the EU as a competitor in geo-strategic terms (unlike the US).
- The possibility of the EU forming a political counterweight to the US is seen as a welcome, but unlikely, possibility.

Introduction

The vast majority of Chinese leaders' remarks and comments on the EU have focused on the relationship between the EU and China. Developments in the EU are usually commented upon when a concrete event takes place, such as meetings with representatives from Europe either in China or in Europe. Only a small number of comments and statements related to the EU are published when there is no reference to China.

What Chinese leaders say in public – and this is what usually gets reported by the Chinese (and/or Western) media – is not necessarily the same as what they really think. This is particularly the case with regard to meetings with politicians from the EU or its Member States, when statements have gone through the filter of diplomatic language. Thus, such statements tend to reconfirm the importance of the EU, not only as an economic entity, but also as an actor at the global level.

English-language articles in the Chinese press are usually published in the context of high-level meetings between Chinese and European politicians and are intended mainly for Western audiences in and outside of China. Occasionally, Chinese leaders place an op-ed on Europe in one of the Western newspapers, which is meant as a direct message to the European public (and politicians). So far, such public 'admonishment' of the EU, as seen for example in the article 'Europe needs to learn learning'[1] by Chinese Vice Foreign Minister and former Ambassador to the UK Fu Ying in spring 2011, has been rare.

Chinese (academic) publications and informal meetings are more informative regarding how members of the Chinese elite really see the EU as they usually express their views in a less 'filtered' way. Here, we sometimes see quite a negative view of the EU, although it is important to note that there is not *one* shared opinion on the EU in China, but different views depending on the role and position of individuals and their knowledge of the EU.

The above caveats have to be borne in mind when reading the following summary of Chinese views of the EU. This overview is based on official speeches and statements, media coverage, Chinese academic publications and personal conversations in China.

General Trends

In part, the ways in which the EU and its Member States are seen by the Chinese elite is a reflection of the way that European media and publics are

---

[1] Fu Ying, 'Europa muss das Lernen lernen', Botschaft der Volksrepublik China in der Bundesrepublik Desutchland, 31 March 2011. Available at: http://www.china-botschaft.de/det/sbwl/t811408.htm. Accessed 9 January 2013.

perceived to view China. This was clearly the case before and during the 2008 Olympic Games, for example. During this period, there was a general feeling in China and among Chinese living in Europe, that 'the West' (publics/politicians in the US and Europe) was neither willing to acknowledge China's successes in modernisation nor to welcome China as an equal player in international society. This came in reaction to the criticism of China in the run-up to the Olympics: there were incidents during the torch relay in London and especially Paris, calls from some quarters to boycott the Games, and French President Nicolas Sarkozy's announcement (while France had the EU Presidency) that he might not attend the opening ceremony all influenced how the Chinese elite felt about Europe.

Aside from emotional ups and downs, there are some features that are frequently raised in the Chinese discourse on the EU:

- The EU is the biggest economy in the world.
- The EU is perceived to be a powerhouse of technology and innovation.
- The EU has the potential to become a counterweight to the US in international affairs, but achieving this will require political will. European integration is the best way to enhance Europe's international role.
- The Commission is the central negotiating partner for China on trade policy (including anti-dumping cases), but even in this field, Member States can play an important role.
- Individual European states (with the possible exception of Germany) are weak; their strength comes from joint positions and actions.
- Europe as a whole is in decline due to demographic factors and lack of willingness or ability to adapt to globalisation and its speed.
- China needs an economically strong EU and welcomes a politically strong EU, as long as it does not set out to criticise or undermine China's position and claims.

The EU, Europe and EU Member States

Europe (*Ouzhou*) is used in a broader sense than the EU (*Oumeng*) by Chinese politicians and the elite. Europe includes countries like Switzerland or Iceland, and it is also identified with Western history and civilisation. There is admiration for the philosophical traditions of individual European nations. The Ancient Greek philosophers, the Renaissance in Italy, Enlightenment in France, and logic and rational thinking in Germany were, for example, all explicitly mentioned by Chinese Prime Minister Wen Jiabao in October 2010.

Regarding the EU, its integration as an economic and political space is seen as a necessary way to tackle challenges (like the global financial crisis) and to bring more political weight to the international table. The EU presents the biggest economic entity in the world and as such is an important trading and cooperation partner for China.

Between the EU and China there are many regular high-level and sectoral meetings. However, when Chinese politicians travel to Europe, they usually combine three European countries in one trip and rarely visit Brussels. China is fostering bilateral relations with practically all Member States of the EU because this is seen as important for practical cooperation and investment projects. In this way, China also hopes to gather support from Member States on those issues that must be decided at the EU level, either in the Commission or in the Council (e.g. lifting the arms embargo). However, very often the EU or Europe is mentioned as a general framework in which China's relationships with individual Member States are embedded.

Chinese interlocutors usually list the economic and social strengths of each Member State and raise special areas for cooperation with these countries accordingly. The fact that Germany is the strongest economy within the EU and is China's biggest EU trading partner has made this relationship the most important to China among the European countries. This has been underlined by the Chinese readiness to accept Berlin's offer to establish so-called 'government consultations' between both countries.

Individual EU Member States are not only important for China as bilateral cooperation partners, but some of the bigger states are also relevant because China frequently has to deal with them (and not with the EU) in international contexts such as the UN Security Council, the G8 plus (Heiligendamm) process or the G20. The fact that larger Member States are not willing to give up their respective countries' representation within international institutions and groupings in favour of a joint European seat underlines the importance of maintaining and fostering these bilateral relationships for Chinese leaders.

From the Chinese perspective there are advantages and disadvantages in dealing with European Member States that are divided on many issues: on the negative side, it is more complicated, requires more capacity and makes it more difficult to understand the core interests of the Europeans; on the positive side, Member States can be played off against each other on issues relevant to China, such as human rights.

The Lisbon Treaty

Chinese observers have followed developments closely within the EU including the Constitutional Treaty, its failing in 2005, the inception of the Lisbon Treaty and its problems during the process of ratification. When the Treaty was finally ratified and entered into force in December 2009 (during the global financial crisis) there was much praise from Chinese politicians. It was seen as a further step in the direction of European integration, but also a result of Member States' recognition that the individual states of the EU could only face the crisis together.

The extended European Parliament competencies outlined in the Lisbon Treaty are seen as addressing the EU's lack of democratic legitimacy with its Member States. However, at the same time, a larger role for the European Parliament is expected to be a complicating factor in China–EU relations as, in the past, the European Parliament has been more outspoken and critical on China than the Commission or the Council Secretariat (as are parliaments in the Member States).

The appointments of Lady Ashton as High Representative of the Union for Foreign Affairs and Security Policy and Herman van Rompuy as President of the European Council were officially welcomed by China but were not commented on (abiding by China's policy of 'no interference' in the affairs of other nations). However, one could sense that these choices were seen by the Chinese side as a sign of Member State reluctance to move in the direction of stronger political union. Nevertheless, the entry into force of the Lisbon Treaty and the inception of the European External Action Service are considered steps that could strengthen European identity at the global level (provided the EU is able to overcome the European sovereign debt crisis).

It would be wrong to assume that the Lisbon Treaty is perceived as a watershed event by Chinese leaders. Officials in European institutions should be careful not to project their own concepts, perceptions and institutional logic on to their external partners; what constitutes a major breakthrough from the European perspective does not necessarily have the same significance on the Chinese side, except if this 'breakthrough' also manifests itself in substantive changes in external relations and especially relations with China.

The EU as a Counterweight to the US

In many Chinese academic publications, the topic of the EU as a counterweight to the US is discussed. However, politicians and officials are too diplomatic to come out with direct statements on this issue. Nevertheless, whenever Chinese politicians speak of a 'multipolar world', in which several power centres coexist, this can be viewed as part of the discourse on the EU as a counterweight to the US. In 2003, when the US prepared for the war in Iraq and EU Member States were divided over whether or not to offer their support, there were many voices among China's EU specialists who expressed hope that the EU would develop as an international actor in its own right. This also has to be understood against the background of the impending EU enlargement, the Constitutional Treaty and the first European Security Strategy. The initiative of then French President Chirac and German Chancellor Schroeder to lift the arms embargo against China was interpreted as a further sign of emancipation from the US.

The hope that the EU would develop into a real *political* counterweight to the US received a heavy blow when, from the Chinese perspective, the EU was seen to cave under American pressure and decided not to lift the arms embargo against China in 2004–2005. Some Chinese academics still see this as a European move to try and repair the transatlantic partnership at the expense of China. Notwithstanding the Lisbon Treaty, the expectation of the EU as a counterweight to the US has mostly disappeared in China. Nevertheless, some experts see the US and the EU competing for leadership on certain global issues, for example, climate change. Moreover, the recent Asian 'pivot' launched under US President Obama and predominantly interpreted as an effort to contain China, makes the EU more attractive as a partner with whom China has no strategic conflict. From the Chinese perspective, the possibility of the EU forming a political counterweight to the US remains a welcome, but unlikely, possibility.

While we can still assume that, until very recently, the EU has been seen at least as an *economic* counterweight to the US and as a possible alternative for China in terms of diversifying foreign currency holdings away from the US dollar, the unfolding of the European sovereign debt crisis has now cast some doubts among Chinese experts and politicians. However, since the crisis had its origins in the US and some of the Chinese elite believe that the US is in a process of (relative) decline, the EU is still seen as very relevant in the global economy and as an economic partner.

Even if the EU and its Member States are not able to act as a counterweight to the US, the most important factor from the Chinese perspective is that they do nothing that is seen to undermine Chinese interests *vis-à-vis* China itself (Tibet, Taiwan) and more broadly in the region.

The Global Financial Crisis and the European Sovereign Debt Crisis

The economic (trade, investment) field has dominated Chinese statements on the EU and its Member States for many years, since these issues are the foundation of the partnership. In the last few years, the topic of the global financial crisis and the European debt crisis has been raised frequently in the speeches of Chinese politicians. With regard to the 2008–2009 global financial crisis, Chinese officials and leaders have displayed optimism with respect to Europe's ability to solve the crisis. The initial tenor of Chinese statements on the EU during this period was praise for how Europe had grasped the crisis as an opportunity for deeper integration. There was widespread belief that the EU would be able to deal with the crisis effectively and come out of it stronger politically.

However, when the European debt crisis started to affect more and more countries in the eurozone, Chinese commentators became more focused on the need for political will from members of the eurozone, in order to address the crises in the Member States. The question mark over whether the eurozone can overcome the crisis has become a hotly debated issue in China, alongside discussion of the European expectation that China would come to its rescue. The dominance of this topic can be seen in recent newspaper reports as well as the statements of political leaders during visits and meetings.

Statements that underline China's general willingness to help the EU during its crisis and, conversely, those that explain why China's capability (as a developing country) to support the EU is limited, are about even in number. From the Chinese perspective, there is a clear contradiction between, on the one hand, the EU's appeals to China for help with the euro crisis when, at the same time, there is debate within the EU concerning the desirability of foreign direct investment (FDI) from China.

Because of the euro debt crisis, the EU has lost at least part of its lustre as an economic power and as a model for social security systems. The fact that the EU–China Summit in 2011 had to be postponed due to an emergency EU summit on the euro, signalled to China the severity of the sovereign debt crisis. However, most Chinese experts and officials still expect that the EU will be able to overcome the crisis through deeper integration (e.g. fiscal).

Conclusion and Recommendations

China's leaders value the EU as a successful example of economic integration and as a project that fosters peace and stability between its members. China has self-interest in an economically strong EU that is able to find its way out of the crisis; as long as China's growth path is in part dependent on exports, Europe will be an indispensable market for Chinese goods. There is still some hope that the euro might become an alternative to the US dollar; therefore, China is keen to see the EU act swiftly and decisively to overcome the present crisis.

Despite economic, political and ideological friction, the Chinese elite do not perceive the EU as a competitor in geo-strategic terms (unlike the US). They identify common interests and a wide range of opportunities for cooperation with the EU. Chinese expectations that the EU could develop into a counterweight to the US have been shattered, and not only since the sovereign debt crisis.

Relationships with individual Member States have always been important and have been carefully cultivated through high-level visits and concrete cooperation projects. Despite a new sense of urgency caused by the EU's handling of the debt crisis, Chinese leaders still express confidence (or rather calculated optimism/*Zweckoptimismus*) that the EU will be able to overcome its difficulties. However, for the Chinese elite, global trends confirm a relative loss in the economic and political weight of the West and Europe.

The Chinese Five Year Programme (2011–2015) and Europe 2020

(May 2011)

Roderic Wye

Associate Fellow, Asia Programme, Chatham House

Executive Summary

The Chinese Five Year Programme and Europe 2020 reflect the differing economic, social and political systems that produced them, and the ways in which they articulate their divergent economic challenges. Both see the immediate short-term period as crucial for attaining economic transformation and steady and sustainable economic growth. But Europe 2020 takes a longer (ten-year) and more wide-angled view, while the Chinese Programme is more detailed and comprehensive.

Their economic strategies are different: China is looking to diversify and upgrade its industry in terms of the value chain, moving more towards domestic consumption; Europe is seeking to avoid slipping back to its pre-crisis ways by developing smart, sustainable and inclusive growth.

There are a number of areas where interests and aims overlap. Both are committed to wider international engagement, though Europe notes the threat to its competitiveness from China and other emerging economies. There is a strong emphasis on research and development in each; both, though from differing starting points, put strong emphasis on controlling emissions, energy efficiency and the development of new green technologies. Both recognise the need for changes in the international governance system, but they are also seeking to increase their own influence therein.

The Programme is an invaluable guide to the main lines of Chinese strategic thinking in a wide range of economic and social policy areas. It identifies the key objectives for China over the next five years, and shines light on opportunities for cooperation with international partners. The Programme will form the backdrop, both in the macroeconomic approach and in individual sectors, to the High Level Economic Dialogue with the EU.

In specific priority areas that the Programme sets out, those offering the strongest links to the EU agenda are climate change, green technologies, science and technology, education, development of services, digital technologies and improvements in the legal and regulatory environment. But it also highlights areas such as competition policy and market access where the EU will need to engage China more forcefully. The question remains how.

Main Points

- The Chinese Five Year Programme is a detailed and comprehensive document. It is approved by the National People's Congress (NPC) and has the full authority of the Chinese Communist Party behind it. The European 2020 Strategy is more selective in its priorities and has less directive authority than the Chinese Programme.
- The economic strategies underlying the Chinese Programme and the Europe 2020 Strategy are very different. China is looking to diversify its industry and move towards domestic consumption; Europe's focus is on developing sustainable and inclusive economic growth and avoiding a return to its pre-crisis ways.
- There is a high degree of convergence between the Chinese and European documents in a number of key areas. These include: the transformational role of research and development; an emphasis on green energy and carbon efficiency; education and employment; and governance. There are potential benefits to be gained from better cooperation between China and Europe in these areas.
- EU policy makers should regard the Chinese Programme as a document that informs all areas of Chinese policy. In essence, it gives the clearest insight into consensus within China on key developmental challenges for the next five years. It should form an important part of the strategic background for the EU's Chinese policy making.

Introduction

The 12th Five Year Programme for the National Economic and Social Development of China was adopted by the NPC, China's annual parliamentary meeting, on 14 March 2011. It is the strategic blueprint that sets out the overall goals and guidelines for Chinese domestic policy and, in particular, Chinese economic policy for the next five years. This paper compares the Chinese Five Year Programme with Europe 2020 and the strategic vision for European development set out therein.

Nature of the Documents

The Chinese Programme is a fully comprehensive document which has been worked through at all levels of the Chinese system. It has been approved by both the Party and the legislative/executive systems and has the full authority of the Chinese Communist Party. But, unlike in the past when the Five Year Plan was a binding and directive document, the Programme sets goals and priorities and does not seek to direct every area of economic activity. It has few binding targets and those targets it does list will not necessarily be fulfilled. It is, by its nature, a consensus document with all the provinces and ministries having had a say in its drafting; it is important for the individual parts of the Chinese bureaucracy to have their projects and aims included in the plan in order to attract state funding and support. Its detailed implementation is carried out through annual national plans also approved by the NPC, with authority over the Chinese governmental system. The European 2020 Strategy is more selective, concentrating on three priorities supported by seven flagship initiatives. It is dependent for its implementation on national plans to be formulated by national governments, and has less directive authority than the Chinese Programme.

Economic Environment

The Chinese view of prospects is considerably more optimistic than that of the EU. For China, the next five years are 'a crucial phase in building a well-off society in an all-round way' and a 'highly significant period for deepening the reform and accelerating the transformation of the modes of economic growth'. This is set against a background in which they had addressed the 'negative aspects caused by the international financial crisis and maintained a steady and rapid economic development'. It envisages an annual 7% growth rate over the next five years. In a Chinese context, this is a modest rate; the last Programme set a rate of 7.5% but actually exceeded 11%. It underpromised and overdelivered.

All this stands in stark contrast with the EU, which sees itself as facing a moment of transformation following the crisis that 'has wiped out years of economic and social progress and exposed structural weaknesses in Europe's economy'. The financial system in Europe is still fragile and Europe is above all concerned that it does not slip back into its pre-crisis ways. Europe 2020 calls for collective action as a Union to take charge of its future and turn the EU into a smart, sustainable and inclusive economy delivering high levels of employment, productivity and social cohesion. China is more comfortable with its existing policies, many of which are reiterated in the document, while the Europe 2020 strategy takes as a key theme the need to avoid going back to the previous policy mix.

Challenges

Both documents acknowledge the continuing impact of the international financial crisis. For China, this is more a problem of global economic governance although it is also a major factor influencing global demand and thus its previous pattern of export-led economic growth. But it is not the same level of threat as it is for the EU ('the recent economic crisis has no precedent in our generation') and China does not face the continued pressure on national economies seen in the euro area ('the still fragile situation of our financial system is holding back recovery as firms and households have difficulty in borrowing, spending and investing'). Both approaches recognise the significance of increased globalisation and the need to respond to this. Europe prides itself on having one of the most open economies in the world, but notes intensifying competition from the developing world and, in particular, the newly emerging economies.

For Europe, the problem is being faced with structurally lower growth rates than its main partners, while for China the problem is, if anything, the opposite: controlling growth. Both highlight problems surrounding employment — Europe's employment rates average 69% for men and women aged 20–64. In China, many of the headline targets are concerned with keeping urban unemployment rates down (although the official rate of uneployment is only 4%, there is wide reporting of underemployment). For Europe, there is a set of issues around the demographic ageing of the population, leading to a smaller working population and a higher share of retired people. China has targets for continued slow population growth and, although ageing is mentioned, it does not have the urgency that there is in Europe — yet. Europe 2020 notes intensifying competition from the developing world and from China and India in particular as putting pressure on European industry to remain competitive.

More widely, both documents speak of major transformations of the economic structure. For China, this entails a move towards greater domestic consumption (currently this represents only 38% of GDP, falling from 45% in the late 1990s), with less reliance on the export-driven sectors of the economy. China is looking to 'elevate the core competitiveness of manufacturing industry, improving new and strategic industries' (energy conservation and environmental protection industries, new generation IT industry, biological industry, high-end equipment manufacturing industry, new energy industry, new materials industry, new energy automobile industry), and speeding up the development of the service industry.

Headline Targets and Areas in Common

The table in Annex 1 is based on the main policy priorities and targets set out in China's Five Year Programme, with the headline targets and initiatives from Europe 2020 mapped onto it. Given the comprehensive nature of the Chinese document it is unlikely that there would be some form of matching target for every European priority. Nevertheless, there is a high degree of convergence in a number of key areas, particularly over the transformational role of research and development (both set specific targets in terms of the overall percentage of GDP), the emphasis on green energy and carbon efficiency, education and employment, and governance. There are numerous areas in the Chinese Programme which have no equivalent in the European document, for example chapters on social management, law and order, democracy, military, and transport.

Research and Development

Research and Development (R&D) is a fundamental priority in both documents and an essential underpinning for economic development. Both have specific targets for significant increases in R&D spending expressed in terms of an increased share of GDP (EU at 3% of GDP and China at 2.2%). China sees this as essential to help the economy move further up the value chain ('scientific progress and innovation will support the transformation of the economic system'), while the EU seeks to meet the challenges of developing markets — such as China — which will increasingly compete with European manufacturing.

For both, R&D is part of a wider necessity to develop workforce skills, combined with a strong emphasis on education. The Chinese Programme calls for the development of education at all levels (a number of the headline targets refer to educational aspirations), and seeks to 'nurture the scientific spirit, creative thinking and innovative capacities of students'. Two of the EU's flagship initiatives, 'Innovation Union' and 'Youth on the Move', address this area of concern directly. The key for the EU, however, is not just to spend more but to achieve greater impact through education, training and lifelong learning.

Successful exploitation of new digital technology is another important element that is shared in both documents. China intends to construct a new-generation national information infrastructure based on broadband which can lead to the informatisation of all economic and social activities, more e-commerce and a greater role for e-government. 'A Digital Agenda for Europe' is one of the flagship initiatives to 'deliver sustainable economic and social benefits for a digital single market'.

Green Energy and Environment

The promotion of a more resource-efficient, green and competitive economy is a key element in the European approach. The foundation of the pillar of sustainable growth — an area where Europe is seen as having a lead — gives Europe an advantage in the race to develop new technologies, including green technologies. The document contains headline targets for the achievement of 20/20/20 (reducing greenhouse emissions by 20%, an increase in the share of renewables to 20% and a 20% increase in energy efficiency). The EU calls for 'drastic action' to meet climate and resource challenges, and is more strongly worded in this respect than the Chinese programme. It notes the need for outreach to other parts of the world in pursuit of a global solution to the problems of climate change. 'An energy efficient Europe' is one of the flagship initiatives seeking to decouple economic growth from resource and energy use.

The Chinese Programme stresses the building of a resource-saving and environment-friendly society. The relatively few binding targets among the headlines are all related to emissions control, and there are more of them than previously. China plans for more diversified and clean energy sources and, over the next five years, seeks to provide significant increases in hydro-power (120 m kW), wind (70 m kW) and solar (5 m kW). More nuclear power will be developed on 'a safe and efficient basis' (40 m kW), although the nuclear programme is now under review following the Fukushima disaster in Japan in March 2011. There is a whole chapter on green development, green and low-carbon development ideas, and on how to improve incentives and constraint mechanisms to achieve green goals (such as controlling greenhouse gas emissions, reducing energy intensity and CO_2 emissions). There are sections in the Programme on construction (green building industry), energy conservation, developing recycling as a key feature in the economy and on improving environmental protection. Under 'the principle of common but differentiated responsibilities', China says it seeks a fair and reasonable international system for confronting climate change and will participate in international discussions and seek areas of practical cooperation in research, development and capacity building.

Social Development

For China, 'the fundamental end of economic transformation is to improve people's lives' and the Programme calls (without giving figures) for a 'significant reduction in the population in poverty'. But the main emphasis is on achieving an overall rise in living standards for both the urban and rural populations. This approach involves targets for the annual increase in per capita incomes (7% per annum for both rural and urban incomes), regular raising of the minimum wage (by 13% per annum), significant improvement in the provision of, and access to, welfare services (including medical services and pensions), the provision of employment as a priority, adjustments to tax and income distribution with higher taxes for high earners, and significant improvements to housing (control of the real estate market, provision of 36 million units of affordable housing).

For Europe, there were 80 million people at risk of poverty in the EU prior to the financial crisis (19 m of them children). Europe 2020 calls for this figure to be reduced by 20 m. This is supported by the 'European Platform Against Poverty', designed to ensure economic, social and territorial cohesion to allow those living in poverty to take an active and dignified part in society.

Services Industry

The development of service industries is a key area for China in its effort to move the economy towards domestic consumption and develop new sources of employment. The Programme foresees extensive development of the services sector as part of the reorganisation of industrial structure. Financial services, modern logistics industry, high-tech services, business services (supermarkets etc.), development of tourism, domestic service, sports facilities and cultural industries are all mentioned as areas for development. The Programme promises fair and transparent market access standards, tax reform and better government procurement to support the development of the service industries. For some economies in the EU, this is a key area for future potential cooperation because of the current strength of these sectors. There is, however, the question of how open China plans to make these developments to external actors. This is a key area of dialogue for the EU and China.

Governance

Both see the need to be more involved in global international governance. There is a whole chapter of Europe 2020 concerned with the roles of the various institutions involved in implementing and overseeing the strategy. This would be redundant in the Chinese Programme where the roles of the various state and Party institutions are well-established. But the transformation of government functions and improving government's credibility is a core task for China. This includes wider references to political reform (socialist democracy and the legal system will be improved), but there is also a strong stress on social stability and 'social management' leading to a 'harmonious and stable society' with considerable emphasis on improving social security systems, minimising wealth gaps and developing grass roots (usually Party-controlled) organisations. Fiscal, tax and financial reform is also an important target. The EU notes that stronger economic governance will be required to deliver results, with stress on the need for both EU unity in this endeavour and a regulatory environment that renders financial markets both effective and secure. There is no sign that the Chinese Communist Party will relinquish its monopoly on political power in China; indeed, throughout the Programme, it is clear that the priority remains developing a society where the Party remains in the vanguard.

International Aspects

The Chinese Programme remains strongly committed to the policy of 'opening up'. It aims to open the coastal areas even further, with the development of administrative management systems to achieve international competitiveness, further opening of the service sector, developing an international trade in services, and attracting foreign investment in the sector. Moving up the value chain is a central theme. China seeks to 'stabilise and expand' foreign demand and to compete in future with 'comprehensive advantages' rather than on cost alone. It envisages an increased level of foreign investment (in modern agriculture, high-end technology, advanced manufacturing, energy conservation, new energy and modern service industry). It aims to 'make full use of the attractiveness and influence of China's huge market'. China also sees itself as increasing its operations overseas — through building up its legal and regulatory system, as well as negotiating investment protection and double taxation agreements. It looks to 'expand cooperation with developed countries'. It is looking to increase its influence in international economic and financial organisations; for reform of the international system 'in a more fair and reasonable direction'; to work actively in the G20; and to oppose all forms of protectionism.

For Europe, China is both an opportunity and a challenge, with its investment in R&D putting pressure on some sectors of the European economy to remain competitive, including in the area of green technology. Europe is looking to export more to the developing economies which, to some extent, matches China's willingness to import more consumer goods. Europe is determined to build a 'strategic relationship' with the emerging economies to 'promote regulatory and other cooperation' and to resolve bilateral issues (securing market access and a level playing field for European business). Europe states that it 'adds value on the global scene' but will only be able to effectively deliver results if it acts jointly. Both China and Europe see the need for changes to the international financial system.

Annex 1. Comparison of headline targets and priorities.

Priority Areas	CHINA		EU		
	Headline Target	Policy Priorities	Headline Targets	Flagship Initiatives
Economic development	Steady and rapid, growth of 7% per annum	Growth to be smart, sustainable and inclusive	n/a	n/a
Upgrade of science and technology	R&D expenditure to reach 2.2% of GDP Nine-year education consolidated	n/a	3% of GDP to be invested in R&D, reduce the share of early school leavers to 10% from 15%, and increase the share of the population	A Digital Agenda for Europe Innovation Union Youth on the move
Economic restructuring	Consumption increases, service sector value added, development of strategic emerging sector	n/a	n/a	Industrial Policy for the Globalisation Area
Resource conservation and environmental targets	n/a	n/a	20/20/20 climate/energy targets to be met	Resource-efficient Europe

(*Continued*)

Annex 1. (*Continued*)

Priority Areas	CHINA		EU		
	Headline Target	Policy Priorities	Headline Targets	Flagship Initiatives
Increase in people's livelihood	Annual increases of at least 7% in per capita incomes, rural and urban, 45 m new urban jobs, increased pension and medical insurances, 36 m new low-cost housing units, increase of life expectancy by one year, significant reduction in the numbers in poverty	n/a	Raise the employment rate of the population aged 20–64 from 69% to 75%; reduce the number of Europeans living below national poverty lines by 25%, lifting 20 m people out of poverty	European Platform Against Poverty
Reform and opening up to be deepened	Fiscal, tax and financial reform, government credibility and administrative efficiency to be improved	Stronger economic governance required to deliver results	n/a	n/a
Improvement in social construction	Socialist democracy and legal system improvements, social management, harmonious society	n/a	n/a	n/a

China's Green Economy and EU–China Cooperation

(January 2013)

Jørgen Delman and Ole Odgaard

Professor, Department of Cross-Cultural and Regional Studies, University of Copenhagen; Senior Policy Advisor, Danish Energy Agency

Executive Summary

In recognition of increasingly serious environmental constraints to China's development, the Chinese government has chosen to invest substantially in an ambitious green transformation of the economy over the last two Five Year Programme periods (i.e. from 2005). The most important strategic goals are:

- China's emission of CO_2 per GDP unit (the carbon intensity) shall improve by 40–45% by 2020.
- Non-fossil energy (renewable and nuclear energy) shall account for around 15% of the primary energy consumption by 2020.

There are several factors behind the formulation of these goals:

- China's national security of fossil energy supply is seriously threatened.
- Globally, China is one of the most polluted countries in the world and its biggest emitter of greenhouse gases.
- China cannot copy the Western development model and must embark on a more sustainable development path at an earlier stage.
- China eyes an opportunity to become the leading nation in green technology.

The 12th Five Year Programme (2011–2015), approved by the National People's Congress in March 2011 and its subsequent accompanying measures are part of a long-term effort to pursue these goals. Two key concerns are that:

- Coal still accounts for 70% of China's energy demand and that the share of renewable energy in the total energy demand will increase only modestly despite promises to increase it significantly in the previous Five Year Programme.
- Previously some key targets were not met due to opposition from powerful local sector interests.

The ambition in the present Five Year Programme is to lower the annual GDP growth rate to 7.5% from roughly 10% on average over the last 30 years. Yet China will continue to be the global number one with regard to installed green GW, even with a very small increase in the share of renewables in total energy supply as is the case now. At the same time, China will install so many new coal power plants that it will account for about 50% of the net global increase in coal consumption until 2035. China will produce more CO_2 and emit more CO_2 per capita than any other country before its emissions peak around 2030–2035.

Whereas China's need for more energy is legitimate, the challenges for China and the world are significant. China does the following to address them:

- It has created a comprehensive regulatory framework for green development with associated measurable targets; the monitoring system for energy efficiency and emission targets will be improved.
- The present Five Year Programme puts new mechanisms in place to supplement the traditional top-down decrees to attain the stipulated targets; energy taxes will gain importance and an emissions trading scheme will be introduced on a pilot basis.
- An absolute — but not binding — energy consumption cap has been endorsed.
- Local governments will be pressed to toe the line and implement the requisite policy measures.
- China will continue to be among the top investors in green technology and green development.

China's Green Development is the Key to its Future

China was the first developing country to adopt a national climate change programme in 2007 and in 2010 it communicated its greenhouse gas emissions targets to the United Nations Framework Convention on Climate Change (UNFCCC) in compliance with the Copenhagen Accord from 2009, the outcome of the Copenhagen Climate Change Summit in December 2009. Among the most important targets are:

- China's carbon intensity, i.e. the emission of CO_2 per GDP unit, shall improve by 40–45% from 2005 to 2020.
- Non-fossil energy (renewable energy and nuclear energy) shall account for around 15% of the primary energy consumption by 2020 (see also Table 1).

At its annual gathering in Mach 2011, China's National People's Congress adopted the new 12th Five Year Programme for 2011–2015 which will facilitate the implementation of these targets and their associated sub-targets. The plan promotes a new 'green development' approach, which also embraces 'low carbon

Table 1. Selected targets in the five year programmes (FYPs) and accompanying long- and medium-term plans (%).

	11th FYP Target (2010)	11th FYP Actual Result (2010)	12th FYP Target (2015)	Goal 2020
Share of non-fossil energy in primary energy (hydro, renewables, nuclear)	10 (for renewable energy only)	8.6	11.4	15
Energy consumption per GDP unit (=energy intensity)	−20	−19.1	−16	—
CO_2 emission per GDP unit (=carbon intensity)	—	—	−17	−40 to −45
Target for all four grid corporations: share of non-hydro renewables in total electricity consumption	1	2 out of 4 fulfilled targets	—	3
Forest coverage	20	20.4	21.7	23
Green tech's contribution to GDP	—	5	8	15

* Non-binding target.

development'. There are at least four good reasons that China invests substantial political and financial capital in a greener future:

- China's dedication to lower its CO_2 emissions and improve its energy efficiency reflects concerns for its future energy security. Until 1993, China was a net exporter of oil, while it now imports more than half of its oil. In 2030, this share will reach an alarming 80%. Natural gas will become a major fuel, with 40% of it being imported as well. In 2007, China became a net importer of coal. The share of coal in energy demand is likely to remain above 65% for years to come.
- China has become one of the most polluted countries in the world, not least due to the use of coal. There is an urgent need to lower the consumption of coal and to continue to reduce the emission of sulphur oxides (SOx), nitrogen oxides (NOx) and other traditional pollutants.
- China is the world's biggest emitter of greenhouse gases (GHGs) and will account for 44% of additional global emissions until 2035. China's own environment is suffering considerably from climate change and China acknowledges that it must contribute to cut global emissions.
- China's government is aware that China cannot copy the Western development model and that it has to embark on a more sustainable development path at an earlier stage.

There are still many stumbling blocks on China's road ahead, but the 12th Five Year Programme signals a new step in China's green transformation and its ambition to become one of the world leaders in green development. While the Programme deals with many issues relating to this, the focus here is primarily on energy and climate change since developments in these areas will have the greatest consequences for the EU, in terms of economy, business and global climate.

In 2011, China and the US's renewable energy investments were the highest in the world at USD 55 bn. However, if the EU was viewed as one entity rather than individual states, it would have the highest renewable energy investments worldwide, twice as much as China or US.

Nevertheless, the take off of China's green enterprises in recent years is a wake-up call. In 2011, China was the world's biggest producer of wind turbines, solar PV and solar thermal panels, electrical and hybrid vehicles, nuclear power plants, hydro-power plants, as well as the most energy-efficient coal-fired power plants. From 2004 to 2009, the market share of Chinese wind energy companies in the national market rose from 25% to almost 87%, and they are now moving into the global market. A similar trend is seen for biomass power, and nuclear power is posted to do the same. The quality gap between Western and Chinese technologies is being closed quickly and China's growth in patent rights of energy technology is also catching up with the leading industrialised nations.

Green Energy Targets

Table 1 shows the most important overall green energy targets in the 11th and the 12th Five Year Programmes as well as similar targets in accompanying energy plans. The 11th Programme energy intensity target was almost attained, but the target for renewable energy — one of the most important — was not fulfilled by any margin. Further, the less comprehensive target for green electricity was not met, as China was unable to meet its non-binding 2010 target that the grid corporations should have 1% of electricity demand from renewable energy sources (again, excluding hydro), as two of the four grid corporations did not meet their quota.

The underfulfillment of the renewable energy target does not signal failure for this sector. On the contrary, due to high economic growth, coal-based energy consumption has grown with such momentum that even an almost stagnant market share for renewables would actually represent a sharp increase in commissioned power generation equipment. The annual GDP growth rate was planned at 7.5% in the 11th Five Year Programme, but the *de facto* rate was 11.2%. Therefore, the hydro, nuclear, and renewable energy sectors all grew more than anywhere else in the world, as did coal and oil.

The development of non-fossil power capacity has been impressive. China had 1 GW of grid-connected wind turbines in 2005, which was upped to 30 GW in 2010, the highest in the world, assuming that the EU is regarded as individual countries rather than one entity. In 2015, China has planned to commission at least 100 GW. Nuclear power and solar power have experienced a similar trend. Hydro-power, by far the largest source of renewable energy, expanded from 117 GW in 2005 to 220 GW in 2010, and the Five Year Programme foresees another record level of 290 GW by 2015.

From Worn to Green China Model

The turn towards greener development stems from a growing recognition by the Chinese leadership that the successful and internationally hyped 'China model' is delivering diminishing returns and has become dangerously worn due to soil, water and air pollution, environmental degradation, and man-made climate change as a consequence of GHG emissions.

For example, due to China's fast economic growth, energy consumption has more than tripled in 20 years. China is now the world's largest energy consumer. Almost 70% of the energy consumption is based on coal, and the country is expected to commission so many coal power plants and coal-based industries that it will account for half of the net global increase in coal consumption from 2008 until 2035. China's incremental demand for coal in 2009 and 2010 equals the total EU consumption of coal. During the 12th Five Year Programme, China is expected to increase its coal-based power supply by 45%. By 2035 China's stock of newly installed coal-fired power plants will be more than twice as big as the total capacity of coal-fired power plants in the US, the EU and Japan combined.

In addition to other contributing factors, coal remains critical in creating the negative environmental consequences that are wearing down the China model. China now appears to be facing up to this challenge, both at the national and the international level.

China's Impact on Global Climate Change

While China's new policies will contribute to more green development, it is clear that the absolute level of energy demand and CO_2 emissions will not decline in the coming years. According to World Bank definitions, China has moved from being a lower–middle income country (€755–€2,982) to an upper–middle income country (€2,983–€9,209); a better living standard for its citizens requires more energy, be it green or black. China's energy consumption and CO_2 emissions are therefore forecasted to peak only by 2035–2040 in the business-as-usual scenario.

Since 2000, China has contributed 53% of the net global increase in CO_2 emissions. In 2007, China became the world's largest emitter of CO_2 and its per capita emissions of CO_2 exceed the world average. Still, this is about half of the Organisation for Economic Co-operation and Development (OECD) and thus much lower than the EU. But China now contributes one-quarter of the global CO_2 emissions and its CO_2 emissions are expected to double from 2005 to 2020. If all GHGs are included, China will also double its emission in 2020 compared to 2005. The implication is that by 2015, China will surpass the EU or Japan with regard to GHG per capita emissions, despite its GDP per capita remaining lower.

Even more, China's share of the global emissions will double in 2030 compared to 2000 and by 2035 China will emit more energy-related CO_2 than the US, Canada, the EU and Japan combined.

Therefore, the challenges for China and the global community are both sizeable and tangible. The 12th Five Year Programme points to the reduction of domestic carbon and other emissions as a priority during the planning period and it promises an improved system for monitoring these emissions. This is needed nationally but also to assess compliance with the carbon intensity target and to prepare and consolidate the national greenhouse gas inventories that will have to be reported to the UNFCCC regularly.

Comprehensive 'Green' Efforts

China has developed a comprehensive set of policies, strategies, plans, laws, regulations, incentive packages and mechanisms to stimulate the turn towards green development and they are continuously being refined. Although the targets set in these are voluntary and non-binding in the international context, they are, in principle, binding at the national level, even more so after the approval of the 12th Five Year Programme. Key implementation tools, mechanisms and responsibilities at national and provincial level have been made explicit in subsequent guidelines promulgated by Beijing since August 2011.

The CO_2 emission target, combined with an emissions trading scheme introduced in the 12th Five Year Programme, is now being followed by concrete measures based on pilot testing in recent years. Another important policy will be the adoption of CO_2 taxes on fossil fuels which is expected to be implemented gradually in the present Five Year Programme. The CO_2 tax will use market mechanisms rather than the traditional top-down decrees to attain its purpose.

A notable new idea from 2013 is to institute an absolute cap on energy consumption of 4 bn tonnes of coal equivalent (tce) by 2015. This is 23% higher than in 2010 and should be seen against an estimated need of 4.8 bn tce in 2020 in a business-as-usual scenario. The cap is non-binding and may, at a later stage, be made binding in order to lower the increase in energy consumption effectively. A cap system has the advantage that, if economic growth is higher than expected, the energy intensity must improve beyond the official target in order to comply with the cap. This is a plausible outcome as the GDP rate was underestimated in almost all Five Year Programmes over the last 30 years, but the Chinese growth rates have slowed down in recent years. On the other hand, if the caps are set too high, they may lower the intensity improvements to a level below the targeted rate.

Generally, there is considerable dissatisfaction in China at both leadership level and in academic circles with the national system for monitoring energy saving and GHG emissions. The 12th Five Year Programme implementation measures for energy saving and reduction of emissions from August 2011 propose a number of measures to strengthen this work and they have subsequently been followed up by more detailed regulations at lower levels.

Stumbling Blocks on the Way

The implementation of green energy and climate policies has not been smooth. Statistics in Table 1 show that the contribution of renewable energy was lower than planned in the 11th Five Year Programme period. To make the disappointing result more palatable, China's Statistical Bureau even reduced the original 15% target of standard renewables for 2020 by re-classifying it as 'non-fossil energy', in order to include nuclear power. The reason for underfulfillment is that the high share of coal had not been reduced as planned. When nuclear power is deducted, the share of renewable energy has almost been stagnant from 2005 to 2011. The new target for non-fossil fuels was also included in China's non-binding emission reductions pledge under the Copenhagen Accord.

Further, it may be argued that the lowered ambitions are also reflected in the climate target of 40–45% improved carbon intensity by 2020, since credible calculations show that this target can be attained by the already adopted energy efficiency policies at only marginal incremental abatement costs, if any.

Twisting the Arm of Local Governments

Clearly, China's central leadership has acknowledged the need for more green policies, but dedicated policies do not always work. Common Western assumptions about a strong top-down rule by the Chinese authoritarian Party-state are challenged by the fact that economic reforms and administrative and economic decentralisation since the 1980s have stimulated a quasi-federalist trend. Local governments are often more responsive to local interests at the expense of long-term investments in clean energy and a better environment, and alliances between

Party-state officials and enterprise managers in traditional strategic and highly polluting sectors often set the local agenda despite pressure from above and protests from NGOs and local people.

The central government has thus now decided to make the top government leader in each province responsible for attaining the energy saving and climate change goals within the province. This may help implementation as the central leadership controls the promotion and demotion of local top leaders, who in turn control the leaders at lower levels. However, this requires the effective monitoring of goals; a somewhat risky assumption, according to experiences of the past.

EU Cooperation with China on Development and Climate Issues

In recent decades, a number of important international cooperation programmes have been implemented in the broad field of green development with a variety of countries and international agencies, business partners and NGOs. The EU and its Member States have played a key role in this, and China's central government accords high priority to the continuation of such international collaboration.

China's ability to address its needs differs substantially from most other developing countries. China has the largest foreign currency reserve in the world. China is also the country that has received most support from the Clean Development Mechanism (CDM) which has transferred large quantities of green technology to China in exchange for emissions rights. During the process, China has become a prime mover with regard to production of high-end green technology itself and China's enterprises are now set to become major players in the global markets. Half of China's renewable energy projects have received CDM support and China's CDM projects count for about 60% of all CDM projects worldwide. Other countries have been critical of China's dominance in the CDM arena, and China appears ready to accept a change to the CDM regime in the future, if common consent on a new set of criteria for CDM can be obtained in the international climate change negotiations.

Effectively, China's technology gaps are largely addressed through existing programmes. For example, the EU has entered into cooperation with China on Carbon Capture and Storage (CCS), energy efficiency, methane recovery, transmission technology, etc. China has also proved quite successful in attracting advanced energy technologies from the world market through normal business activities.

Any notion that the EU would have to distance itself from China to win the race to the top in green development would be ill-conceived. On the contrary, the EU must intensify its cooperation with China on its path to a greener economy due to the magnitude of China's challenges from a global perspective, the serious efforts of the Chinese leadership to transform the economy and the opportunities in the huge Chinese market throughout its value chains pertaining to green technology and solutions. The EU should take a stake in this, just like China has taken a big stake in the green technologies and solutions offered by the EU. Alongside these activities the EU should uphold the adherence to international rules pertaining to intellectual property rights and international trade, etc.

Section Two
Chinese Internal Politics and the EU

China: The National People's Congress

(August 2013)

Roderic Wye
Associate Fellow, Asia Programme, Chatham House

Executive Summary

China's parliamentary body, the National People's Congress (NPC), has remained a conservative institution and has not sought actively to increase its authority at the expense of other parts of the political system. The NPC as a whole remains firmly under the control of the Chinese Communist Party (CCP).

It has nonetheless developed over the years into a more effective and professional legislative authority, carrying out a busy schedule of legislative activity. It is also becoming more active in providing formal interpretations of the law. It, or at least the Standing Committee, may need to start meeting more frequently in order to meet growing legislative demand.

The annual meeting of the NPC has become an important platform for the public presentation of the regime's economic and social policies. The NPC is likely to continue the trend of developing its role in consensus building. It will also continue to increase its part in providing formal supervision over the activities of the executive, but it is unlikely to play any significant role in holding the executive to account. There will not be any significant progress towards the development of Western-style multi-party democracy in the NPC or in its electoral processes in the next five years.

The National People's Congress

The NPC is China's national legislative body. In theory, it is the 'highest organ of state power' according to China's current state Constitution, and formally holds powers of appointment and dismissal over the President and the Premier as well as over senior ministers. In practice, it has often been seen as a simple 'rubber stamp', endorsing Party policies and decisions, and providing the formal legal framework for the Party-state to function in the modern age. While it is clear that the NPC cannot fully live up to its billing as the expression of the sovereign power of the Chinese people, it nonetheless occupies an important and significant place in the structure of the Chinese state and is increasingly used both as a platform for announcing major policy directions and as a means for consulting and involving a wide range of interests in the formulation of laws and some key policy documents. By current convention, the Chairman of the Standing Committee of the NPC occupies the third-highest-ranking position in the Standing Committee of the Central Committee of the Chinese Communist Party (CCP) which is an indication of the significance in which the office is held within the system. The current Chairman is Zhang Dejiang.

This paper will look at how the NPC is constituted and what its principal functions are, examine briefly its record under the previous Chairman of the Standing Committee, Wu Bangguo, and speculate upon how the NPC might develop over the course of the next five years.

Meetings and Functions of the NPC

Each NPC is elected (mainly by provincial level People's Congresses through an indirect process described below) for a fixed five-year term. The current 12th NPC was elected in 2013 and will be in office until 2018. It consists of no more than 3,000 deputies (2,987 were elected in 2013), representing China's 32 provinces (including Taiwan), special municipalities and autonomous regions, with special representation from the two Special Administrative Regions of Hong Kong and Macao, and the People's Liberation Army (all of which have separate electoral procedures). The NPC deputies are elected indirectly and serve for the same term as the NPC itself. The NPC's full functions, as provided for in the Constitution, are set out in Annex 1. They cover three main areas: legislation, supervision and personnel appointments for the principal offices of the state.

The NPC meets in full session once a year, in February/March, for about two weeks, during which it typically hears and approves reports on the work of the government (from the Premier), the work of the Supreme Court (from the Chief Justice), the work of the Supreme Procuratorate (from the Chief Procurator), the work of the NPC Standing Committee (from the Chairman of the Standing

Committee), and reports on the annual economic plan and budget. It also may perform some legislative functions as the full NPC is the only body that can pass China's most fundamental or basic laws, although most legislative activity is, in practice, devolved to the NPC Standing Committee. At the first session of each Congress, the NPC formally appoints the President, the Premier, the Vice Premiers and State Councillors, and the ministers of the State Council, who again serve (in theory) for the whole of the term, although in practice ministers are replaced more regularly (which is one of the powers of the NPC Standing Committee).

This annual NPC session has become one of the great set pieces in the Chinese political calendar because of the Report on the Work of the Government in which the Premier summarises the achievements of the administration over the past year and sets out the main policy guidelines and targets for the coming years. Over recent years it has become increasingly open to the press, with greater access given to the deputies and regular press conferences presented by the government spokesperson, culminating in the Premier's press conference at the end of the session. This is one of the few regular occasions at which a senior member of the leadership meets the press, and although it is carefully managed, it does allow for a more human presentation of the Chinese leadership and their policies.

The annual NPC session also hears, debates and approves the annual economic plan and budget. Once every five years, it is also the body to which the Five Year Programme for Economic and Social Development (commonly known as the Five Year Plan) is publicly presented, and it has the authority to approve the Programme. The NPC thus occupies a crucial place in the economic planning system, as the focus for the annual and Five Year Programmes and as the apex of the planning processes. The documents that are presented to the NPC have been worked over both at official levels and through a lengthy consultation process in which representatives of interest groups have their opinions solicited on the emerging draft. In the case of the Five Year Programme, its main provisions are also formally approved in advance by the CCP.

The NPC is an important element for consensus building and in the reconciliation of differing institutional interests within the Chinese system. The formal presentations to the NPC, especially the Premier's work report, are the product of detailed and prolonged drafting exercises that bring together the various interest groups. Much of this goes on behind the scenes, and is carried out before the documents in question are actually presented in public. The documents are then further discussed at meetings of the delegates at the NPC itself. This discussion remains relatively superfluous to the process, although minor amendments to the documents are taken at the Congress. Overall the NPC and its meetings act as an enabler allowing these processes of wider consultation to take place. It is becoming a much more capable and efficient organisation. It has a number of specialist committees, charged with overseeing specific areas of work, such as the Foreign Affairs Committee and the Finance and Economic Committee. Often the committee members of these specialists are distinguished professionals in their field including former ministers and senior officials. But little is revealed of how these committees actually supervise or work in practice. Much of the work is done by their professional full-time staff which has grown considerably over the years.

The Standing Committee of the NPC

A Standing Committee of the NPC is elected by each new Congress at the beginning of its five-year term. The Standing Committee consists of approximately 150 members (all deputies to the NPC), elected by secret ballot at the first session of each new Congress. It also elects a Chairman, currently Zhang Dejiang, and a number of Vice Chairmen. The Chairman is the highest-ranking legislative/parliamentary figure in China. He presides over the meetings of the NPC and of its Standing Committee. The Standing Committee exercises the powers and functions of the NPC when it is not in session and itself meets every two months (usually for about a week), mainly to take forward the legislative agenda, but also to make formal appointments and dismissals of senior government officials, and to conduct other formal but essential business such as the ratification of treaties. The Standing Committee of the NPC regularly hears reports from the State Council (the Executive) on issues of the day. It has the power to request these reports and others are made on the initiative of the government. The Standing Committee also has the authority to make amendments to the annual economic plan when necessary, and can thus give some flexibility to the planning system through an ability to respond to changing circumstances. The NPC Standing Committee meets in closed session, though its deliberations and decisions are reported by the official press. The Standing Committee of the NPC is an active and busy body, as is evidenced by the latest annual report on its work which stated that it had 'deliberated and passed 16 bills and draft decisions on legal issues; listened to and deliberated 13 work reports by the State Council, the Supreme People's Court, and the Supreme People's

Procuratorate; investigated compliance with six laws; conducted investigations and studies on two special topics and made inquiries on three special topics; handled 506 bills submitted by NPC deputies; approved three treaties and accords that China concluded with foreign countries; approved China's accession to an international convention; and made decisions on and approved the appointment or removal of a number of employees in state bodies'.

Deputies to the NPC

The roughly 3,000 deputies to the NPC are required to attend full sessions of the NPC and the attendant group and general meetings of their delegation. When the NPC is not in session they may be called upon to join groups set up for the investigation of specific questions, and have the right to attend meetings of the People's Congress which elected them. But usually they have other jobs and do not serve as full time parliamentarians. Members of the NPC Standing Committee are elected from among the Deputies to the NPC. They are elected on the basis that they will represent (1) the CCP; (2) other political parties and patriotic and democratic personages not affiliated to any political party; (3) social organisations of workers, youth and women; (4) the People's Liberation Army; and (5) ethnic minorities with a population of more than a million. They have more demanding requirements than ordinary deputies; they are expected to undertake their duties on a full-time basis and may not serve in a state administrative, judicial or procuratorial position. They are, however, able to hold Party and other positions — for example the most senior Vice Chairman, Li Jianguo, is also a member of the Politburo and Shen Yueyue, another Vice Chairman, is Chair of the All-China Women's Federation.

The Chinese People's Political Consultative Conference

The Chinese People's Political Consultative Conference (CPPCC) meets at the same time as the NPC, although their set piece events are scheduled separately, and it has a similar five-year term. The CPPCC was established before the formal foundation of the People's Republic of China (PRC) and acted as the legislative body until the NPC was set up in 1954. The CPPCC now has no formal legislative or supervisory powers, and its members are appointed and selected rather than elected.

Composition of the NPC: Elections and Democracy

Deputies to the NPC are elected every five years by an indirect process, whereby they are elected by the People's Congresses at provincial level, which are themselves elected indirectly by the People's Congresses at the next administrative level down. Direct elections to People's Congresses take place only at the lowest levels at which such Congresses exist in counties, districts, townships and towns. These elections occur once every five years, in advance of the process of selecting the deputies for the NPC. They are a carefully managed process, governed by the Electoral Law passed in 1979, and amended several times, most recently in 2010. In nods towards a democratic process, the voting in both direct and indirect elections is held by secret ballot and the law requires that the number of candidates exceeds the number of vacancies (and there are specified proportions for this, to cut down on the possibility of too many candidates presenting themselves). Through provisions for the selection and adoption of candidates, the Party has generally managed to ensure that only those who are politically acceptable are able to stand and be elected for office as a deputy of the People's Congress.

Independent candidates are actively discouraged and are seldom able to stand, let alone be elected. In the elections leading up to the 2013 Congress, a number of independent candidates have tried to put themselves forward as candidates but have met with a very frosty reception from the authorities. Above the basic levels, the processes are even less transparent and more easily manipulated by the Party. It is not a requirement that the deputies elected by indirect election to provincial or higher People's Congresses need themselves be deputies of the lower People's Congress which elects them. There is thus not necessarily any direct linkage between the deputies elected and any mass electorate. Members of the senior leadership are elected by a wide range of provinces with which they have no obvious immediate connection. The final outcome is a group of deputies for the NPC in which members of the CCP comprise about 70% of the total and the body as a whole is largely amenable to the Party's direction. In any case, a further check is added as the Standing Committee of the outgoing NPC is the body in charge of organising and supervising the election of the deputies to its successor.

There was one further amendment made to the electoral process for the current term, to rectify what was becoming an increasingly anomalous position whereby the number of voters in each rural electoral unit was four times the number in each urban unit. The Electoral Law was amended in 2010 to allow for equal representation in legislative bodies to rural and urban people. This was hailed by the Chinese press as being of great significance to the improvement of the People's Congress system and the development of the socialist democracy, as it could better demonstrate equality among people, regions and ethnic groups. The old system could possibly have had some justification when the rural population was 80% of the whole (on the grounds of trying to establish a rough equality between urban and rural interests) — but made no sense at all following the rapid urbanisation of Chinese society in recent years and was resulting in the serious under-representation of the countryside and its interests.

Supervision

Much is made of the important supervisory role of the NPC. In 2006, a law pertaining to the Standing Committee's supervision of People's Congresses at all levels was passed. The law requires Congresses to supervise the work of the people's governments, courts and procuratorates in order to promote administration according to the law and the impartial administration of justice. The main way in which this function is performed at national level is through the annual reports to the Congress submitted by the Premier, the Head of the State Planning apparatus and Minister of Finance, and the heads of the two branches of the judiciary. Although these reports are formally debated by the deputies in the course of the annual two-week session and some minor amendments are often made to the text of the documents, there is no forensic questioning of the content of the report and they are invariably accepted by the Congress in full session. There have been a number of occasions on which there were significant numbers of votes cast against (or abstentions from) some of the reports, and most commonly they were made against the report of the Chief Procurator and were widely interpreted as signs of strong dissatisfaction with the performance of that body particularly over its failure to tackle corruption effectively — which is one of the main tasks of the Procuratorate. But these votes have never been sufficient to reject the report or to bring about either a change in the leadership of the Procuratorate or a major change in policy. In the lifetime of the outgoing Congress, such large-scale demonstrations of dissatisfaction have not really occurred, although the voting on the reports (and on other issues) is never unanimous and contains a varying number of abstentions and votes against.

Opposition at the NPC

The holder of the office of Chairman of the NPC Standing Committee is very much part of the central leadership caucus and has not tended in any significant way to augment the powers and influence of the NPC at the expense of the other organs of state. But this was not always the case. Individual leaders such as Peng Zhen and Qiao Shi in the 1980s and 1990s tried to use the NPC to expand their influence within the state system, and there has been a generalised trend of the NPC seeking to become more active, especially in its monitoring and supervision of government activities. But there has been no real attempt to set the NPC against the other branches of the system. There have been considerable tussles over some pieces of legislation, such as the Property Law in 2006, but these have tended to be part of wider political debate rather than the NPC seeking to assert itself as an independent political actor.

The NPC as a Legal Authority

The NPC has the power, above that of the Supreme People's Court, to interpret the legislation that it passes. This power has been exercised most notoriously in the case of the Hong Kong Basic Law where the NPC Standing Committee has issued a number of decisions and interpretations of the Basic Law mainly in the context of political development in Hong Kong. It has tended to take a conservative and literalist view of the provisions of the law. But it is difficult to judge whether this is the result of the political climate in Beijing, which has always been suspicious of a faster pace of democratic development in Hong Kong, or whether this is a reflection of the jurisprudential approach of the NPC. It has also issued decisions and interpretations on a number of other laws, and normally does so when 'the specific meaning of a provision needs to be further defined' or when new developments 'make it necessary to define the basis on which to apply the law'. It makes these interpretations following a request from an appropriate executive or judicial authority. What the NPC has not been called upon to do is provide interpretations of China's own basic law, the Constitution. There is no constitutional court in China and there have been no legal challenges to executive decisions or actions based on reference to the provisions of the Constitution. The authority to interpret the Constitution is firmly vested in the NPC.

The NPC under Wu Bangguo

Wu Bangguo served two full terms as Chairman of the NPC Standing Committee, being first elected in 2003, following his promotion to the Standing Committee of the Politburo the previous year. Wu's ties and his political inclinations were with the more conservative wing of the Party. He served for many years in Shanghai, alongside Jiang Zemin, and was then a Vice Premier in the State Council, first under Li Peng and then the more reform-minded Zhu Rongji. His predecessor as Chairman of the NPC Standing Committee was Li Peng, a particularly hard-line figure, and Wu generally avoided rocking the boat while continuing to build up the effectiveness of the NPC as a legislative body and trying to make it more responsive to the changing needs of China's governmental system. He set up a comprehensive review of China's legislation in 2009 and 2010, and claimed to have met the political target set by the Party of establishing a comprehensive legal system with Chinese characteristics by 2010.

The NPC, under Wu, deliberately set out to give the impression of a workmanlike and efficient organisation, taking its responsibilities seriously, but without seeking to pose any challenge to the political *status quo*. Unlike some of his predecessors who occasionally tried to use the NPC to further their own political ambitions or to influence the course of the political debate in China, Wu was content to concentrate on efficient administration and on avoiding controversy. While he presided over a period of gradual opening up of the NPC's proceedings and activities to a wider audience, and a greater measure of transparency in its action, he nonetheless ensured that it was not used as any sort of vehicle for voicing comments that deviated significantly from the political mainstream.

His political pronouncements were infrequent, but they all came very much from the more conservative end of the spectrum. He showed no interest in fundamental political reform or in moving the NPC towards a more 'Western' style of democratic behaviour. His two most reported sets of remarks were in 2009 and 2011, both following a very similar line. In March 2011 he said that 'we have made a solemn declaration that we will not employ a system of multiple parties holding office in rotation; diversify our guiding thought; separate executive, legislative and judicial powers; use a bicameral or federal system; or carry out privatisation'.

International Relations

The Chairman of the NPC Standing Committee has a busy schedule of formal visits to foreign countries, which are treated by the Chinese on a par with the most senior visitors and a significant part of its overall diplomatic effort. In addition to meetings with senior parliamentary figures, he invariably seeks meeting with top state and government leaders wherever he travels and speaks with authority similar to that of the President or the Premier. Chairman Zhang Dejiang is also involved in the reception of senior state visitors to China.

Relations between the NPC and the European Parliament have not always been easy. The European Parliament has, on occasion, passed resolutions or taken stances on issues which the Chinese government has found objectionable, such as human rights, Tibet, and the status of Taiwan. These objections have sometimes been voiced by statements issuing from the NPC or its leaders condemning the Parliament's actions. But there is nonetheless a long-established parliamentary exchange with China, which takes place annually on a rotating basis between Beijing and Brussels, and senior visits have taken place regularly in both directions. The current Chair of the NPC's China–Europe parliamentary relations group is Zha Peixin, a former ambassador to the UK and to Ireland.

Future of the NPC

It will probably be difficult for the NPC to develop any major new role over the next five years. The new Chairman of the NPC Standing Committee, Zhang Dejiang, is a man in the mould of his predecessor. He is very much part of the current inner circle of the leadership having been chosen to take charge of Chongqing in the immediate aftermath of Bo Xilai's fall. Since assuming office he has shown no immediate evidence of any desire to shake up the system in any significant way. In early 2013 there was a debate over 'constitutionalism' in China, which appeared to be used by reformers as a way to argue for political reform in China, and might have offered openings for a greater role for the NPC. But the official line emanating from the Party's various mouthpieces has been dismissive of the idea, and Zhang will have no wish to break with that.

Even if no new political role is being sought for the NPC, the trend towards developing more channels for the supervision of the administration is likely to continue. The Chinese leadership is struggling to find ways in which to respond to mounting manifestations of popular dissatisfaction with the way in which systems function: repeated examples of poor or corrupt administration from all walks of life are being reported in the press. Systemic failures like those behind the Wenzhou rail crash in August 2011 do not get fully investigated. There is a potential role here for the NPC, with its carefully controlled and selected membership, and its existing place within the system, to exercise more of a public supervisory role, holding the executive to some form of account but without threatening the system. Despite the political standing of the Chairman of the Standing Committee, the NPC itself has neither the political nor the institutional weight within the Chinese system to direct or supervise the operations of the executive much more closely. But it can give some public expression on areas of concern within a controlled environment such as the annual session of the NPC. This can be a useful safety valve for the regime but it is unlikely to become a focus for concerted opposition to acts of the executive.

Legislation is likely to remain a relatively slow and protracted affair. New laws commonly now have two or more readings at the Standing Committee before they are passed, and the more important laws have to wait for the annual session of the NPC. It may be that the Standing Committee will have to increase the frequency and/or the length of its sittings. As Chinese society becomes increasingly complex and dependent on some form of legal structure to support it, the demand for legislation can only grow. The NPC Standing Committee still performs its functions in a rather stately fashion. Granted much of the work has already been done before any legislation reaches the Standing Committee, but if it is to take its legislative and scrutinising roles more seriously it will need to increase both the care with which it examines and deliberates legislation and the amount of legislation that it passes. Both these are likely to increase demands on the time of the Standing Committee and this is without any consideration being given to its much-heralded role of supervising the executive and calling it to account.

Should the PRC ever move further towards a legally based system in which legal challenges to the executive become more common, the NPC occupies a potentially crucial position as the sole authority to interpret the Constitution, and indeed the other laws that it passes. It is beginning to issue more decisions and interpretations and to take a more active role in the administration of the law.

In the much longer term, the NPC holds a number of seeds of potential political and procedural change. In the past it has been able to be used on occasion as a blocking mechanism for the introduction of controversial new pieces of legislation, and has shied away from others that could have a significant impact on the way in which China operates. There would certainly be scope for a more proactive NPC to take a greater role in the initiation of legislation.

Electoral reform, allowing legislators to be directly elected, would be a major change — but there is no immediate prospect of this happening. While China may undertake more experiments with direct elections in various lower parts of the system, it will be extremely wary of any form of direct election at national level, with all the potential that might have for opening up some form of political opposition to the Party.

Annex I: The Powers and Functions of the NPC and its Standing Committee[2]

ARTICLES 62, 63 and 67 OF THE PRC CONSTITUTION:
Article 62 The National People's Congress exercises the following functions and powers:

(1) to amend the Constitution;
(2) to supervise the enforcement of the Constitution;
(3) to enact and amend basic laws governing criminal offences, civil affairs, the State organs and other matters;
(4) to elect the President and the Vice-President of the People's Republic of China;
(5) to decide on the choice of the Premier of the State Council upon nomination by the President of the People's Republic of China, and on the choice of the Vice-Premiers, State Councillors, Ministers in charge of ministries or commissions, the Auditor-General and the Secretary-General of the State Council upon nomination by the Premier;
(6) to elect the Chairman of the Central Military Commission and, upon nomination by the Chairman, to decide on the choice of all other members of the Central Military Commission;
(7) to elect the President of the Supreme People's Court;

---

[2] Constitution of the PRC. Available at: http://www.npc.gov.cn/englishnpc/Constitution/node_2825.htm. Accessed 28 August 2013.

(8) to elect the Procurator-General of the Supreme People's Procuratorate;
(9) to examine and approve the plan for national economic and social development and the report on its implementation;
(10) to examine and approve the State budget and the report on its implementation;
(11) to alter or annul inappropriate decisions of the Standing Committee of the National People's Congress;
(12) to approve the establishment of provinces, autonomous regions, and municipalities directly under the central government;
(13) to decide on the establishment of special administrative regions and the systems to be instituted there;
(14) to decide on questions of war and peace; and
(15) to exercise such other functions and powers as the highest organ of state power should exercise.

Article 63 The National People's Congress has the power to remove from office the following persons:

(1) the President and the Vice-President of the People's Republic of China;
(2) the Premier, Vice-Premiers, State Councillors, Ministers in charge of ministries or commissions, the Auditor-General and the Secretary-General of the State Council;
(3) the Chairman of the Central Military Commission and other members of the Commission;
(4) the President of the Supreme People's Court; and
(5) the Procurator-General of the Supreme People's Procuratorate.

Article 67 The Standing Committee of the National People's Congress exercises the following functions and powers:

(1) to interpret the Constitution and supervise its enforcement;
(2) to enact and amend laws, with the exception of those which should be enacted by the National People's Congress;
(3) to partially supplement and amend, when the National People's Congress is not in session, laws enacted by the National People's Congress, provided that the basic principles of these laws are not contravened;
(4) to interpret laws;

(5) to review and approve, when the National People's Congress is not in session, partial adjustments to the plan for national economic and social development or to the State budget that prove necessary in the course of their implementation;
(6) to supervise the work of the State Council, the Central Military Commission, the Supreme People's Court and the Supreme People's Procuratorate;
(7) to annul those administrative regulations, decisions or orders of the State Council that contravene the Constitution or other laws;
(8) to annul those local regulations or decisions of the organs of state power of provinces, autonomous regions, and municipalities directly under the central government that contravene the Constitution, other laws or administrative regulations;
(9) to decide, when the National People's Congress is not in session, on the choice of Ministers in charge of ministries or commissions, the Auditor-General or the Secretary-General of the State Council upon nomination by the Premier of the State Council;
(10) to decide, when the National People's Congress is not in session, on the choice of other members of the Central Military Commission upon nomination by the Chairman of the Commission;
(11) to appoint or remove, at the recommendation of the President of the Supreme People's Court, the Vice-Presidents and Judges of the Supreme People's Court, members of its Judicial Committee and the President of the Military Court;
(12) to appoint or remove, at the recommendation of the Procurator-General of the Supreme People's Procuratorate, the Deputy Procurators-General and procurators of the Supreme People's Procuratorate, members of its Procuratorial Committee and the Chief Procurator of the Military Procuratorate, and to approve the appointment or removal of the chief procurators of the people's procuratorates of provinces, autonomous regions, and municipalities directly under the central government;
(13) to decide on the appointment or recall of plenipotentiary representatives abroad;
(14) to decide on the ratification or abrogation of treaties and important agreements concluded with foreign states;
(15) to institute systems of titles and ranks for military and diplomatic personnel and of other specific titles and ranks;

(16) to institute State medals and titles of honour and decide on their conferment;
(17) to decide on the granting of special pardons;
(18) to decide, when the National People's Congress is not in session, on the proclamation of a state of war in the event of an armed attack on the country or in fulfilment of international treaty obligations concerning common defence against aggression;
(19) to decide on general or partial mobilization;
(20) to decide on the imposition of martial law throughout the country or in particular provinces, autonomous regions, or municipalities directly under the central government; and
(21) to exercise such other functions and powers as the National People's Congress may assign to it.

Annex II: The Leadership and Committees of the NPC[3]

CHAIRMAN OF THE STANDING COMMITTEE: Zhang Dejiang

VICE CHAIRMEN OF THE STANDING COMMITTEE:
Li Jianguo	Wang Shengjun	Chen Changhzhi	Yan Junqi
Wang Chen	Shen Yueyue	Ji Bingxuan	Zhang Ping
Qiangba Puncog	Arken Imirbaki	Wang Exiang	Zhang Baowen
Chen Zhu			

SECRETARY GENERAL: Wang Chen.

SPECIALIST COMMITTEES:[4]
Ethnic Affairs Committee: Li Jingtian
Law Committee: Qiao Xiaoyang
Internal and Judicial Affairs Committee: Ma Wen
Finance and Economic Affairs Committee: Li Shenglin
Education, Science, Culture and Public Health Committee: Liu Binjie
Foreign Affairs Committee: Fu Ying

---

[3] See, http://www.npc.gov.cn/englishnpc/Organization/node_2848.htm. Accessed 28 August 2013.
[4] See, http://www.npc.gov.cn/englishnpc/Organization/node_2849.htm. Accessed 28 August 2013.

Overseas Chinese Affairs Committee: Bai Zhijian
Environmental Protection and Resources Conservation Committee: Lu Hao
Agriculture and Rural Committee: Chen Jianguo

WORKING AND ADMINISTRATIVE BODIES:[5]
General Office, Legislative Affairs Commission Budgetary Affairs Commission, Credentials Committee, Hong Kong Special Administrative Region Basic Law Committee, Macao Special Administrative Region Basic Law Committee

---

[5] See, http://www.npc.gov.cn/englishnpc/Organization/node_2850.htm. Accessed 28 August 2013.

The Chinese People's Political Consultative Conference (CPPCC): Its Role and its Future
(August 2013)

Jean-Pierre Cabestan

Professor in Political Science and Head, Department of Government and International Studies, Hong Kong Baptist University

Executive Summary

As its name indicates, the Chinese People's Political Consultative Conference (CPPCC) is a consultative assembly aimed at giving a status, platform and the illusion of influence to the non-administrative elites of the country. The CPPCC includes a National Committee and local committees down to the county level. Their members are not elected but hand-picked by the Chinese Communist Party (CCP). While around 60% of its 2,237 members do not belong to the CCP, the National Committee is chaired by Yu Zhengsheng, number four of the CCP top leadership, and operated on a daily basis by the director of the CCP United Front Department, today Ling Jihua, under the supervision of his predecessor, Du Qinglin, member of the CCP Central Secretariat.[6] Both Du and Ling are CPPCC Vice Chairmen. The CPPCC is therefore an institution whose objective is to both

---

[6] Ling Jihua was transferred in August 2012 to this position from his directorship of the very powerful CCP Central Committee General Office after his attempt to cover up the death of his son with two young ladies in a sports car accident in Beijing earlier that year.

consult scientific, cultural, artistic and now more and more entrepreneurial elites and keep them as faithful to CCP rule as possible. Although every year CPPCC members make thousands of proposals to the government, their impact is minimal. While some CPPCC members take advantage of the softer political environment to air candid criticism about specific policies or decisions, to date none of them has challenged the system. The CPPCC's activities are likely to keep expanding both within China and overseas. But its political influence will probably remain marginal, and its role will continue to mainly legitimise CCP domination.

Historical Background

The Chinese People's Political Consultative Conference (CPPCC) was created by the Chinese Communist Party (CCP) on the eve of the foundation of the People's Republic of China (PRC) (30 September 1949). Echoing the failed Political Consultative Conference set up by the Nationalist Kuomintang in 1946 to prevent a return to civil war, the new CPPCC (180 members) was designed both as a symbol of the 'new democracy' then promoted by Mao Zedong, a more inclusive and accommodating political system supposed to be distinct from both capitalism and socialism, and an instrument of united front, the well-known strategy developed by all communist parties in order to win over and submit non-communist elites.

Then chaired by Mao himself, it included prestigious figures as Mme Sun Yat-sen (Song Qinglin), the writer Guo Moruo and the Dalai Lama (until he fled China in 1959). Fourteen 'democratic parties', small political forces which had split with the Kuomintang, were also represented. Elected for five years, the CPPCC drafted an apparently moderate 'Common Programme' which was regarded as the PRC's first *de facto* state constitution and acted as new China's parliament until the establishment of the National People's Congress (NPC) in 1954. Gradually, local CPPCCs were set up down to county level.

Chaired after 1954 by then Premier Zhou Enlai, the CPPCC (559 members) continued to operate and expand (1,199 members in 1964) until the outbreak of the Cultural Revolution (1966) but its role had already become weaker after the anti-rightist movement in 1957 and the dismissal or arrest of numerous non-CCP figures who dared to speak up during the Hundred Flowers Movement, a short-lived attempt by Mao to give more voice to the intelligentsia and the society in the aftermath of the 1956 Hungarian and Polish uprisings.

The CPPCC system was resurrected in March 1978, one-and-a-half years after Mao's death (1976). Freshly rehabilitated, Deng Xiaoping chaired its National

Committee (the 5th since 1949, 1,988 members) and used this institution as an avenue to rehabilitate many leading cadres who had been persecuted by Mao. In 1983, Deng Yingchao, Zhou's widow, took over the CPPCC (6th, 2,039 members) until 1988 when she was succeeded by Li Xiannian, a semi-retired leader close to Zhou and who had survived the whole Maoist era (7th).

In 1993, as the revolutionary generation of CCP leaders was leaving the stage, the political status of the CPPCCs was stabilised. Since then, its National Committee Chair has been the number four of the CCP Politburo Standing Committee (PBSC, behind the PRC president, the NPC chair and the Prime Minister): Li Ruihuan, one of the few reformists that survived after Tiananmen, from 1993 to 2003 (8th & 9th CPPCC), Jia Qinglin, a Fujian Party secretary close to Jiang Zemin, from 2003 to 2013 (10th & 11th CPPCC) and Yu Zhengsheng (12th CPPCC), a former Shanghai Party secretary, since then. As other top state leaders, the CPPCC chair is now supposed to serve two terms and retire. However, born in 1945, Yu was nearly 68 when he took over this position. As a result, he should be replaced at the next (19th) Party Congress in autumn 2017 from his position in the PBSC and, in March 2018, from his position of CPPCC Chairman.

The CPPCC: Ambiguous Constitutional Status

The CPPCC was not mentioned in the 1954, 1975 or 1978 PRC state Constitutions. It is only referred to in the Preamble of the current 1982 Constitution in the following paragraph:

> In the long years of revolution and construction, there has been formed under the leadership of the Communist Party of China a broad patriotic united front that is composed of democratic parties and people's organizations and embraces all socialist working people, all patriots who support socialism and all patriots who stand for reunification of the motherland. This united front will continue to be consolidated and developed. The Chinese People's Political Consultative Conference is a broadly representative organization of the united front, which has played a significant historical role and will continue to do so in the political and social life of the country, in promoting friendship with the people of other countries and in the struggle for socialist modernization and for the reunification and unity of the country.[7]

---

[7] See, http://english.people.com.cn/constitution/constitution.html. Accessed on 28 August 2013.

And in 1993, the following sentence was added to the preamble:

> Under the leadership of the communist Party of China, multi-party cooperation and the political consultative system will continue to exist and develop for a long time to come.[8]

These political statements make very clear the mission, the role and the composition of the CPPCC. On the one hand, the CPPCC is aimed at representing all of the 'patriotic' forces (as the democratic parties) and individuals, in other words the non-communist and non-administrative elites (e.g. who are not (any more) CCP or government cadres) which accept the leading role of the CCP and endorse its reunification strategy with Taiwan (and then with Hong Kong and Macau). On the other hand, the CPPCC is a major instrument of the CCP's united front work: winning over ever-changing elites and forces, both within China but also overseas. The 1993 amendment was added as a sign of prudent political overture, four years after Tiananmen, in order to emphasise and guarantee the perpetuation of this institutional arrangement.

However, the CPPCC status is not legally defined in the Constitution and in no way can it be compared to an 'upper house' or a senate. The PRC has a unicameral legislature, the NPC, and although the CPPCC has established relations with other countries second chambers (for instance, the French Senate of the British House of Lords), its role, organisation and membership remain very different. As an official Chinese website indicates: 'Cooperative relations between the CCP and other political parties are based on the principle of "long-term coexistence and mutual supervision, treating each other with full sincerity and sharing weal or woe"'.[9]

CPPCC Organisation

The CPPCC is an institution comprising a National Committee (today 2,237 members) and 3,118 local committees (totalling 632,000 members)[10] at the provincial, municipal (or prefectural), and country levels. All of them are now appointed for a renewable term of five years. The National Committee's plenary session is held in

---

[8] *Ibid.*

[9] 'IV. The System of Multi-Party Cooperation and Political Consultation', China Internet Information Center, http://www.china.org.cn/english/Political/29034.htm. Accessed on 28 August 2013.

[10] Latest data end of 2008.http://www.ccppcc.gov.cn. Accessed 26 September 2011 and http://www.chinatoday.com.cn/english/zhuanti/2013-03/04/content_522637.htm. Accessed 12 December 2013.

Beijing every year in March and lasts one week to ten days. As the NPC, it delegates most of its competences to a large Standing Committee (298 members) that meets every two months. Standing Committee members run the CPPCC's nine special committees (among them economic affairs, population, resources and environment, education, liaison with Hong Kong, Macau, Taiwan and overseas Chinese, and foreign affairs). The National Committee has also set up, in the last 15 years, three 'national mass organisations': the China Committee on Religion and Peace created in 1994 and whose international role is growing; set up in 2011, the China Economic and Social Council is engaged in 'research and counseling and service for the promotion of coordinated economic and social development and the promotion of a harmonious society'; and established in 2006, the China Institute of the Theory of the CPPCC, an 'academic organisation', is 'engaged in research and publicity concerning the system of multi-party cooperation and political consultation led by the CCP',[11] in other words in propagating the Chinese model of socialist democracy.

The number of 'groups' officially represented in the CPPCC has gradually increased, up to 34 groups today. Among them, are the CCP and the eight 'democratic parties' reorganised at the end of the 1950s and reactivated in 1978 (see Appendix 1, below), but also several mass organisations, such as the Communist Youth League, the Federation of Trade Union and the Women's Federation, and quite a few professionals regrouped in 'circles' (agriculture, sports, press and publications, etc.).

Chaired by the CCP's fourth-highest-ranking member, the CPPCC National Committee leadership is formally constituted of a large variety of non-communist, ethnic (non-Han) and religious figures (about half of the 23 vice chairpersons and 65% of the Standing Committee members). However, its key leader is the director of the CCP United Front Department, today Ling Jihua, who runs the day-to-day operation of this assembly, with the assistance of secretary general Zhang Qingli, another CCP Central Committee member and former Party secretary of Tibet and then Hebei. The local CPPCC committees replicate this organisational model.

Membership

Officially, CPPCC members are supposed to be 'personnages who represent all areas and sectors of the Chinese society, have social influence and are capable

---

[11] See, http://www.cppcc.gov.cn/zxww/2012/07/03/ARTI1341301498421103.shtml. Accessed on 28 August 2013.

of participating in the deliberation and administration of states affairs'.[12] As a tradition, CCP members have always constituted a minority in the CPPCCs, representing usually one-third of the delegates. At the 11th CPPCC National Committee (2008–2013), they numbered 895 (40%) while non-communists amounted to 1,342 (60%). There were 393 women, accounting for 18%. All of China's 56 ethnic groups are represented and, as a result, minorities are over-represented. Leaders of the major authorised religious groups (67 members), the 8 'democratic parties' (380), members of the intelligentsia (scientists, professors, doctors, writers, artists) as well as compatriots from Hong Kong (124) and Macau (29) also sit in this August assembly.[13]

In the last 15 years, more and more celebrities (for example the movie director Zhang Yimou and hurdler Liu Xiang) and wealthy entrepreneurs have been co-opted into joining what is often described as a 'riches' club (*furen julebu*). In 2011, 20 of the top Chinese executives whose companies are listed on the Shanghai and Shenzhen Stock Exchanges were CPPCC delegates (63 were NPC members), including Yang Chai, President of China Life Insurance, Ma Mingzhe, Chairman of Ping An Insurance and Li Shaode, President of China Shipping Groups. While state-owned enterprise managers remain better represented, private entrepreneurs have become more numerous: 71 of China's 1,000 richest persons, including Li Shufu, President of Zhengjiang Geely Automobile Company, sit on the 11th CPPCC (75 are NPC delegates) side-by-side with the usual Hong Kong and Macau pro-Beijing tycoons. Lately, the top representatives of foreign companies have also joined this 'temple of celebrities' (*mingren tang*), for example, Fang Fang, the China Chief Executive of JPMorgan. Nevertheless, more traditional elites, for example, neo-Marxist Chen Kuiyuan, President of the Chinese Academy of Social Sciences and a fierce critic of bourgeois liberalisation, remain well entrenched in this institution (he is CPPCC vice chairman). And many former and retired CCP and government leading cadres are represented in the national and local CPPCCs. In 2013, 83 billionaires have been reported to have been elected to the new NPC (31) and CPPCC (52), including Robin Li Yanhong of Baidu, Yang Yuanqing of Lenovo and Cao Dewang of Fuyao Glass.[14]

---

[12] See, http://www.cppcc.gov.cn/zxww/2012/07/03/ARTI1341301498421103.shtml. Accessed on 28 August 2013.

[13] See, www.ccppcc.gov.cn. Accessed on 26 September 2011.

[14] *South China Morning Post*, 8 March 2013. Since 2013, 84 (up from 76 previously) delegates to the NPC and 69 (down from 74 previously) delegates to the CPPCC have belonged to the "Top 1000"

The same trends can be observed in the local CPPCCs. Moreover, the membership of different CPPCCs can partly overlap, since leaders of local CPPCCs also belong to the CPPCC of the immediate higher level.

CPPCC members are not elected officially, but are selected by consultation and recommendation from the Standing Committee of the CPPCC of the same level and approved by the Chair's Council (chair and vice chairs) of the preceding CPPCC. In reality, they are recommended by the CCP United Front Department and appointed by the Communist Party Committee of the same level. It is hard for a 'candidate' to refuse such an offer and usually, he or she accepts in order to enlarge his or her network of useful connections. Clearly CPPCC membership is perceived as a status symbol and also, for the CCP, an efficient method to better integrate the new elites. Before he was taken into custody in April 2011, artist Ai Weiwei had been twice offered a CPPCC membership but it is not known whether he accepted or not.

In the last decade an increasing number of CPPCC members have been expelled for corruption, others due to a lack of attendance, or the adoption of citizenship of another country, for example, actress Gong Li (a member of the 9th and the 10th CPPCC). For instance, between 2003 and 2007, at least seven influential CPPCC National Committee members were expelled and later arrested for graft, including Qiu Xiaohua, former Head of the National Bureau of Statistics; Zheng Xiaoyu, former Director of the State Food and Drug Administration; ex-Vice Governors of Sichuan and Henan provinces Li Dachang and Li Debin; former Chairwoman of the Heilongjiang CPPCC Han Guizhi; and former Chairman of the Industry and Commerce Federation of Ningxia Li Pinsan. More recently, in 2010, Huang Yao, also Guizhou CPPCC Chair, and Zhang Chunjiang, former Deputy General Manager of China Mobile were stripped of their CPPCC membership. At the local level, corruption seems to be even more widespread, leading to the fall of Sun Shuyi, Shandong CPPCC Chair (see below), Chen Shaoqi, Guangdong CPPCCC chair in 2009 and of Song Chenguang, Jiangxi CPPCC Vice Chairman in 2011. One of the key drivers of this surge of corruption cases has been the increasing recruitment of and proximity with business people in the CPPCCs.

The CPPCC leadership is aware of the growing corruption of its members but prefers to rely on education rather than repression to solve the problem. In March 2012, Dong Lianghui, a CPPCC member and the daughter of late leader Dong

---

richest people in China. For an updated list of the top 100, cf. "Hurun Rich List 2013", http://www.hurun.net/usen/NewsShow.aspx?nid=1476. Accessed on 12 December 2013.

Biwu, declared that 'corruption can mainly be attributed to a lack of education and values'.[15]

Competences

CPPCCs do not have any legislative powers but enjoy three main functions: consultation, supervision and participation.

- The CPPCCs are consulted before political decisions are made. For instance, at the March 2011 session, the CPPCC National Committee plenary session deliberated on the 12th Five Year Programme and made some recommendations.
- Supervision is usually carried out by groups of CPPCC members who make suggestions and criticism concerning the work of specific government departments. They can also report and expose violations of discipline or laws.
- Participation refers to conducting investigations and studies, reporting on social conditions and popular sentiment, and drafting proposals (*ti'an*). Proposals need to be approved by the CPPCC's Committee for Handling Proposals established in 1991. Every year, the CPPCC National Committee submits a few thousand proposals to the government, the Party of the NPC. Between 2008 and 2013, the CPPCC handled 26,699 proposals (against 23,000 between 2003 and 2008). Government departments are required to address these proposals. Usually, over 90% of the national CPPCC proposals are claimed to be satisfactorily handled. However, in September 2011 Mao Likun, Vice Chair of CPPCC Committee for Handling Proposals, complained that only around 1,000 of the 6,000 proposals approved every year by the CPPCC could actually be carried out by the government's departments.

Indeed, not every CPPCC member's initiative is welcomed. For example, at the 2008 annual session, Sun Shuyi, who was then also Chairman of Shandong's CPPCC (see above), and a number of other Shandong delegates proposed that the government allocate funds to finance the construction of a large 'Chinese Cultural Symbolic City' near Qufu, Confucius' hometown. The high cost of the project (USD 4.2 bn) and its self-serving nature triggered a countermotion signed by 100

---

[15] Wu Linfei, 'CPPCC Member Emphasizes Education to Curb Corruption', Women of China report, 12 March 2012. Available at: http://www.womenofchina.cn/html/womenofchina/report/139131-1.htm. Accessed on 28 August 2013.

other delegates, including Mao's grandson Mao Xinyu. As a result, the proposal was turned down.

The CPPCC activities also serve to publicise the activities of the 'democratic parties' (see Appendix 1). For example, between 1990 and 2006, these groups submitted more than 2,400 proposals on a large variety of subjects (anti-secession law, taxation reform in rural areas, social stability, etc.). However, this represents a small portion of total CPPCC proposals.

The main added value of the CPPCC, in particular at the national level, has been the political stage it offers to the non-bureaucratic elites of the country. It allows them to air their views in a more candid manner than governmental officials, and perhaps also NPC delegates. The political environment of the day has an impact of the degree of openness and pluralism that comes out from the CPPCC. In the last ten years, the renewed blood among members has contributed to turning the CPPCC(s) into a platform for daring criticism; a loudspeaker for China's current problems and social tensions. However, some CPPCC members use it as a platform for non-professional and even irresponsible comments that reflect more their privileges or class bias than a real comprehension of the political issues at stake. But, all in all, most CPPCC members' comments or proposals are viewed as politically correct and, instead of pushing for a genuine political reform, contribute to legitimising the current CCP-led political system.

CPPCC membership does not constitute a full-time job, except for the Chair's Council members. Most members are busy one week a year with this institution and sometimes do not even care to show up at the plenary session (especially at the local level). Standing Committee members are more involved (around six weeks a year) but tend to concentrate on tourism-oriented study tours within and outside of China.

The National Committee of the CPPCC has developed international relations with many countries and upper houses and participates in China's diplomatic activism on the international stage. Between 2003 and 2008, Chair's Council members visited 70 countries and received 46 foreign delegations. Its leaders are used to propagate a more pluralistic and open-minded image of China. In other words, the CPPCC's international activities are aimed at enhancing China's soft power.

Conclusion

Although often presented as one of the 'four leading teams' of Chinese governance (with the Party, the government and the NPC), the CPPCC is the weakest and probably the most marginal. True, the CPPCCs are supposed to provide advice and supervision to China's political leadership. And they help the latter to better communicate with, and win over, the country's non-administrative elites. But the CPPCCs' elitist membership and lack of democratic legitimacy do not really contribute to a more harmonious CCP state–society relationship. CPPCC members are not responsible before voters and, on the contrary, seem mainly interested in their new proximity to power and the opportunities this offers to expand their business and bureaucratic connections. Moreover, their proposals are rarely translated into policies.

Some criticism has been expressed along these lines in China and some have even called for an abolition of the CPPCCs. However, this remains a minority view, or at least an opinion that has few chances to percolate to the upper strata of the CCP system, unless the CCP leadership decides to embark into a meaningful political reform process. Since they took office in November 2012 and March 2013 respectively, neither CCP Secretary General Xi Jinping nor Premier Li Keqiang have given any indication that they would move in that direction; in fact, quite the opposite. As a consequence, it is fair to conclude that in the foreseeable future the CPPCC will stick to its role and probably try to both diversify its membership and better check the government's activities.

A changing membership and the promotion of a growing number of managers and *nouveaux riches* may contribute to enhancing the CPPCCs' influence, especially at the local level. However, the past two decades have proven that China's entrepreneurs are usually politically legitimate, provided that their business interests are not threatened. The ultimate question is whether China's non-elites will continue to observe the CPPCC's annual political theatre silently or whether they will express increasing opposition to it and the PRC's other legitimising but undemocratic institutions.

Appendix 1
China's Eight 'Democratic Parties'

The total membership of the 'democratic parties' (*minzhu dang*) was estimated in 2013 around 893,000 against 710,000 in 2011, 290,000 in 1988 and 80,000 in 1978 when they were reactivated. Their membership has increased regularly in the last 20 years, and even faster in the last few years, but the CCP (85 m members in 2013) makes sure that they do not become too large. Their finances are controlled by the CCP.

The following lists the date of establishment, the sector of society represented, estimated membership and current leader of the eight 'democratic parties':

1) Kuomintang's Revolutionary Committee 國民黨革命委員會(1948)
Ex-Kuomintang, people in relations with Taiwan, dedicated to the unification of the motherland
101,865 in 2012 (42,000 in 1992)
Chairman: Wan Exiang (since 2012)
Number of CPPCC Members: 65

2) Democratic League of China 中國民主同盟 (1941)
Middle- and senior-level intellectuals in the fields of culture, education, science and technology
230,000 in 2012 (100,000 in 1993)
Chairman: Zhang Baowen (since 2012)
Number of CPPCC Members: 65

3) Chinese Democratic Association for National Construction 中國民主建國會 (1945)
Representative figures in the economic field (entrepreneurs, managers and engineers
140,000 in 2013 (40,000 in 1988)
Chairman: Cheng Changzhi (since 2007)
Number of CPPCC Members: 65

4) Chinese Association for the Promotion of Democracy 中國民主促進會 (1945)
Representative intellectuals in the fields of education, culture, publishing and science

133,000 in 2013 (24,000 in 1988)
Chairwoman: Ms. Yan Junqi (since 2007)
Number of CPPCC Members: 45

5) Peasant and Workers Democratic Party 中國農工民主黨 (1930)
Intellectuals of the medical and health sectors
125,600 in 2013 (43,000 in 1988)
Chairman: Chen Zhu (since 2012)
Number of CPPCC Members: 45

6) Justice Party (*Zhigongdang* 致公黨, 1925)
Middle and upper levels of returned overseas Chinese and their relatives
28,000 in 2011 (15,000 in 1993)
Chairman: Wan Gang (since 2007)
Number of CPPCC Members: 30

7) 3 September Society 九三學社 (1944)
Representative middle- and senior-level intellectuals in the fields of science, technology, higher education and medicine
132,000 in 2012 (11,000 in 1983)
Chairman: Han Qide (since 2002)
Number of CPPCC Members: 45

8) Taiwan Democratic Autonomous League 台灣民主自治同盟 (1947)
Representative and upper-level Taiwan compatriots living in large and medium-size cities on the mainland
2,700 in 2013 (1,300 in 1992)
Chairwoman: Ms. Li Wenyi (since 2005)
Number of CPPCC Members: 20

The Role of Chinese Soft Power
(September 2011)

Anonymous

Executive Summary

The Chinese government continues to stress the peaceful development of its society, claiming its growth is non-confrontational and beneficial to everyone. It is therefore not suprising that Beijing has readily embraced the concept of 'soft power' — not only because it is compatible with many aspects of its redefined strategic thinking ('the harmonious society/world'), but also because it offers a ready solution to comfort the uneasiness expressed in various international fora about China's rise (the 'China threat' thesis).

Essentially a state project, the cultivation of Chinese soft power is at the top of the state's agenda. It is commonly believed in Chinese strategic circles that soft power has become an important indicator of a state's international status and influence. The authorities promote a preferred idea of what China is, aiming to permeate international public awareness on the positive outcomes of the country's economic rise. China wants to persuade the international community that its ideas and values are legitimate choices in the Chinese context.

However, the main problem is that the majority of China's soft power messengers are, in one way or another, censored by Beijing. In light of Western standards, China suffers from corruption, inequality, and a lack of democracy, human rights and the rule of law. While that may make the country attractive in authoritarian and semi-authoritarian developing states, it undercuts China's soft power in the West.

Education is one of the principal sources of Chinese soft power. The educational great leap forward intends to transform China into the world's major educational powerhouse on two fronts: first, to continue to raise the level of Chinese universities into the ranks of world-class institutions; second, to project Chinese soft power by promoting Confucius Institutes around the world.

Due to the sensitive nature regarding the perception of China worldwide, the authorities support an enhanced competitiveness in multiple forms of communication. China Radio International, Central Chinese Television's (CCTV) broadcasts and foreign-language editions of the *People's Daily* are used as vehicles to convey the message of China's peaceful development.

Despite the efforts of Chinese strategists to put forward various proposals, it appears that a clear Chinese soft power strategy is still in its embryonic phase. China's soft power approach lacks assertiveness.

Limits of the current Chinese soft power policy include concerns over the legitimacy of its political system (with a unique structure that is poorly understood for much of the rest of the world), and an imbalance of resources and lack of a coherent policy agenda. Nevertheless, trends in Chinese diplomacy suggest a possible pattern of great power politics as reconfigured by non-confrontational competition over soft power.

Introduction

China's development over the past three decades is arguably the most important international development of our era. Impacting the global system in ways we are yet to fully understand, it is continuously posited in commentary and from governments that the country is on its way to becoming 'a responsible major power' (*fuzeren de daguo*). Since the beginning of the 21st century, the People's Republic of China (PRC) has emphasised the peaceful development of its society, which poses no threat to other nations. Chinese officials claim that its growth is non-confrontational, gradual and beneficial to all parties, and they are attempting to substantiate this claim by pursuing a soft approach in the PRC's foreign relations.

Although the Chinese did not coin the concept of soft power, they are keen to leverage it. The political establishment has readily embraced the notion not only because it is highly compatible with many aspects of its traditional and strategic thinking ('the harmonious society/world'), but also because it offers a ready solution to ease the anxieties around the world about China's rise (the 'China threat' thesis), anxieties many in the Chinese elite are acutely aware of.

Soft Power: The Chinese Context

'Soft power' is generally defined as the ability to 'get your way' in world politics without coercion, and rests on a country's attractive resources that enable it to set the political agenda, and so 'co-opt' other countries. Its currency is culture, political values and foreign policies.

The notion was coined more than 20 years ago by American scholar Joseph Nye in his book *Bound to Lead: The Changing Nature of American Power* (Basic Books, New York, 1990). In the preface to the book, he further developed the definition of soft power as the ability to get what you want through attraction rather than coercion or payment. The definition is made by distinguishing soft power from hard power (i.e. economic and military power). However, the concept has come under closer scrutiny due to the ambiguity of its definition and scope, ranging from oversimplification to broad definitions that eventually rendered the concept useless as a means of distinguishing between various types of power.

There are three main schools of soft power in China, each emphasising different structural elements of the concept. Firstly, China is a country which has a long history of civilization. Chinese culture, in this case, is regarded as the essence of its soft power. Secondly, the rapid economic development in the past two decades makes China the new star among developing countries. It is possible for less developed or even industrialised countries to learn from the Chinese success. Thirdly, despite much criticism abroad, China's political system is regarded internally as an important part of the country's soft power and the Chinese economic model is intertwined with/made possible (also) because of the framework offered by the political system.

Key Elements in the Chinese Soft Power Policy

A particular feature of the Chinese soft power system is that it is essentially a state project, actively cultivated and built up. The Chinese Communist Party (CCP) legitimises itself primarily by achieving economic growth and maintains the political stability of the country based on its ability to present itself as a positive unifying force, both over Chinese territory, and over potential political fragmentation. Although this is an argument about domestic politics, a similar one can be made about foreign affairs. China needs a stable international environment to guarantee the inflow of foreign direct investment (FDI), hi-tech machinery and raw materials on which economic performance relies.

Mitigation of the China threat theories that have arisen abroad in some quarters and promotion of positive attitudes towards the country are central to China's national interest. In other words, soft power is at the top of the government agenda, as former President Hu Jintao expressed publicly on many occasions. President Hu often talked about the necessity to build China's cultural soft power to meet domestic needs and international competition. It is commonly believed in Chinese strategic circles that soft power has become an important indicator of a state's international status and influence. It is also believed that soft power has lagged behind, creating an imbalance in its national comprehensive power structure. In the government's vision, China has to transcend the conventional approach that focuses on hard power and instead seek to gain international influence to maintain a soft counterbalance. In other words, Chinese authorities promote a preferred idea of what China is, aiming to permeate public awareness on the positive outcomes of the country's economic rise.

Promoting Chinese culture and language plays a significant role in implementing Chinese soft power and the authorities undertake coordinated efforts to transform China into a major cultural power. Education, in this case, is one of the principal sources used to promote soft power because it plays a role in shaping a country's image internationally. The educational great leap forward intends to transform China into the world's major educational powerhouse on two fronts: firstly, to continue to push dozens of Chinese universities into the ranks of the world's best institutions and to attract more international students to the country; secondly, to carry a new mission to promote Chinese soft power overseas by promoting Confucius Institutes around the world.

Public Diplomacy and Media

One important policy instrument available to the Chinese government for the development of soft power is public diplomacy, which has three elements. The first is news management, which must be reactive and quick. The second is strategic communications, which should be proactive and tactical. The third is relationship building, which is a long-term project. There has been a lot of investment in the third element of Chinese public diplomacy in the past few years. It can be argued that China's public diplomacy is closer to that of France than of the US, insofar as it is based much more on cultural exchange and long-term relationships than on media and strategic communication.

Lack of credibility is a major problem for China's public diplomacy. The state as the major messenger of soft power is seldom trusted. Consequently, the policy focuses on building political trust to positively alter the image of China's political system, its foreign policies and the human rights situation. The role of non-state or independent actors in public diplomacy is still limited.

2004 marked a milestone in the history of Chinese public and cultural diplomacy as it was the first year following the end of the leadership transition process that placed Hu Jintao at the helm of the CCP as Chairman of the Central Military Committee (after the resignation of Jiang Zemin in September that year). Pessimistic interpretations were circulating in the West of how China would either collapse in the near future due to internal contradictions or (in a minority view) become an insatiable expansionist power. Reacting to these prognoses, the Hu Jintao administration adjusted the 'Five Principles of Peaceful Coexistence', that were so important in foreign policy discourse from the 1950s onwards, and remodelled them into the central narrative of a 'peaceful rise' (*heping jueqi*), which was quickly replaced by 'peaceful development' (*heping fazhan*) to avoid the negative implications of the term 'rise'. These slogans have been publicised as part of the first and especially the second elements of China's public diplomacy.

Chinese policy makers pay much attention to the role of the media in boosting or damaging the country's image. Because of deep sensitivity to foreign perceptions of Chinese policies worldwide, the Chinese authorities support enhanced competitiveness in multiple forms of communication, both written and audio-visual. In 2008, Chinese Politburo Standing Committee member Li Changchun called for strengthening China's domestic and international communication capacity in order to promote 'China's cultural soft power'. An announcement of plans to spend USD 6.6 bn followed shortly, with the aim to create a new international news channel that should be able to compete with CNN and the BBC.

Although at present the influence of media in Chinese language may be largely limited to Chinese living abroad, its impact cannot be underestimated. It could potentially help China achieve its objectives indirectly, as more and more Chinese integrate in the host countries and participate in the democratic process. China's growing influence in the US media market is a good example, especially among ethnic Chinese. The trend is to reach the people in their own language, i.e. Cubans watch Chinese TV series through CCTV Espanol. In the early 1940s, even before the foundation of the People's Republic of China, China Radio International (CRI) had been attempting to 'win hearts and minds'. Nowadays, CRI broadcasts in 43 different languages around the world and it is said to be the most comprehensive and far-reaching radio network in the world. CRI, CCTV's broadcasts and foreign-language editions of *People's Daily* are useful vehicles to convey the message of China's peaceful development. However, the media is only credible when it is independent and adheres to journalism codes of conduct. A new generation of Chinese journalists aim to acheive these standards and the government sometimes turns a blind eye to their publications, although these journalists know that they always have to operate carefully and stay within certain political boundaries.

The Confucius Institutes

The Confucius Institutes seem to be the most global and systematic, or at least visible, central government action in public diplomacy. The name is instructive, since for years the CCP asserted that Confucianism had held back China's development. With significant implications for foreign policy and cultural diplomacy, the Hu Jintao government has accelerated the return of Confucianism as a guiding philosophy and ideology of the state, despite the fact that it has not officially linked this new approach with Confucianism. Partly as a move to appease the US government, Hu Jintao distanced his administration from previous President Jiang Zemin's policy discourse of a 'multipolar world' by applying the Confucian concept of 'harmonious society' (*hexie shehui*) as the progression towards 'harmonious world' (*hexie shijie*). The Confucian connotations do not challenge US hegemony directly and evoke the traditional Chinese idiom 'harmonious but different' (*he er bu tong*). The trend (though not entrusted with formal acknowledgement of the state) is to revive the Orthodox tradition of Confucianism, to bring back loyalty to tradition that rejects heterodoxy (meaning at the same time Marxist ideology and Western values). It is about national identity formation but also a superevaluation, and returning to the concept of Chinese exceptionalism with its roots in Confuciucianism.

Confucius was also adopted as the figurehead of the Office of Chinese Language Council International (Hanban), which manages China's version of the British Council or Alliance Française. In 2004, the first international Confucius Institute was inaugurated in Seoul, South Korea. By the end of 2010, according to the organisation's official website, 322 Confucius Institutes and 369 Confucius Classrooms had been established in 96 countries. Based on the list of Institutes cited, it becomes apparent that they have been distributed fairly equally between

Europe, the Americas and Asia. There is a striking symmetry between China's top trade partners and Confucius Institute partners (US, Japan, South Korea, Germany and the UK). It is still too early to assess the extent to which they will become a force in promoting Chinese culture. Their main focus today is to organise Chinese-language classes; increasing numbers of elementary and middle schools across Europe having introduced Chinese to their curriculum and the number of European students learning Chinese (Mandarin) has been on the rise for years.

Challenges and the Road Ahead

Limits of the current Chinese soft power policy include imbalance of resources, legitimacy concerns regarding its political system, which has a unique structure that is poorly understood in much of the rest of the world, the lack of a coherent agenda, and the gap between an increasingly cosmopolitan and confident foreign policy and a closed and inflexible domestic political system. These limits are partly due to China's weaker domestic institutions, limited research capabilities, its (still) low level of education, and the complex feelings it arouses abroad among a global audience which is gradually becoming more aware of its rising economic importance. China has very few global name brands and a significant deficit in the trade of cultural products, even if it has become the factory of the world. Soft power is still a weak link in China's pursuit for stronger comprehensive national power.

The challenge for the growth of Chinese soft power is to create a set of values that would unite the population domestically and be convincing and attractive externally. Sinocised-Marxism does not have broad appeal. The key challenge is to identify which Chinese values have universal appeal and what generates passive soft power internationally. Up to now China has been part of a dazzling story of economic development (based on the 'Beijing Consensus', i.e. political authoritarianism plus economic liberalism, a term coined by American scholar Joshua Ramo, but not endorsed as such by the CCP or government officials), stability and the concept of harmony, based on traditional aspects of Confucianism. The task is to integrate, institutionalise and make these values operational.

Given the domestic problems that China must still overcome, there are limits to China's ability to attract others, but one would be imprudent to ignore the gains it is making. In this context, the Beijing Olympics were an important part of China's strategy to increase its soft power, even though only a partially successful tool. Both the internal (the Sichuan earthquake) and the international contexts (the uprisings in Tibet, the criticism for selling arms to Sudan) proved to be hostile. From the moment Beijing won the Olympic bid, the games have been closely linked with the situation in Tibet and China's lack of human rights. This was partially the result of Beijing's promise that hosting the Olympics would bring progress in China's human rights situation, but also of the media attention that human rights organisations and Tibet lobby groups attracted in the run-up to the event. The gains included the boosting of China's image as a powerful and capable country, with a rich culture, but in relation to normative issues, the Olympics seem to have done both harm and good. The opening ceremony's perfect organisation and cultural splendor dazzled the world, but could not hide the tight control over society and lack of full openness. Beijing seemed incapable of finding, despite the enormous amount of money invested in the event, the symbolic tools that could have conveyed the right messages to a predominantly Western audience.

Conclusion

It appears that a clear Chinese soft power strategy is still in its embryonic phase, despite the scrupulous efforts of the Chinese strategists to formulate various proposals. China's soft power approach lacks assertiveness. Nevertheless, Chinese diplomacy does suggest the possibility of a pattern of great-power politics as reconfigured by a non-confrontational competition over soft power. If this paradigm shift is to hold, a new global consensus transcending the polarised thinking of the 'Washington consensus' versus the 'Beijing consensus' will have to be negotiated.

The EU and China, as strategic partners, should undertake a deliberate effort to overcome the value distance and the cultural gap that still exists between them and to create a true *value* partnership that enhances the existing *interest* partnership; a long-term socialisation process is needed to create understanding in Europe of the Chinese way of thinking, in order to remove preconceived notions of China.

Given the signs of an emerging civil society in China, it would be productive to encourage and develop people-to-people diplomacy, including the growing presence of European students in Chinese universities and a stronger European cultural presence in China. It would also be useful to accelerate forward-looking research by launching major research programmes and facilitating the recruitment of a new generation of scholars; support the solid development of contemporary China studies in European universities; facilitate stronger cooperation between media channels; and surpass the intercultural stumbling blocks that impede (more) successful European business presence in China.

The Situation of Lawyers in the PRC
(April 2011)

Nicholas Bequelin
Senior Researcher on Asia, Human Rights Watch

Executive Summary

The reform of the legal system in the People's Republic of China is at a crossroads: promoted as a vital tool to foster economic growth and social stability, it is also constantly kept in check by a political system incapable of accepting challenges to its rule and fearful of allowing greater scope to the development of a civil society and loosening its iron grip on control.

This paper explores the ways in which a small but significant number of civil and human rights lawyers have been paying the price for the inherent contradiction between promoting a rules-based system while forbidding any attempt at putting into question the Party's actions and decisions.

These activist lawyers had represented the best hope for the progressive realisation of the broad legal entitlements promised to Chinese citizens, and their demise is part of a larger trend of turning away from legal reforms and the establishment of a rules-based system which guarantees a modicum of professional independence for the judiciary. Turning away from legal reforms means that the Party closes down what had been a major avenue of accommodation between state and society and raises the prospect of increased social instability in the future.

While China has never been kind to political dissenters and government critics, since preparation for the Beijing Olympics in 2008 began, a progressive clampdown on dissent has been taking place in the country, with dissidents, land and pensions rights protesters, ethnic minorities, human rights activists and human rights lawyers paying the highest price.

Several rounds of cyclical political tightening have culminated in an unprecedented crackdown launched in February 2011, following the North African and Middle Eastern protests and the preparations for a leadership transition in 2012, when President Hu Jintao and Premier Wen Jiabao will be stepping down.

This crackdown, which has come to the attention of the international community with the arrest of prominent artist Ai Weiwei, is marked by an exceptional number of arbitrary arrests and extra-judicial detentions of, among others, lawyers and human rights activists, and to greater censorship in the media and the Internet, with detentions and intimidations of journalists, editors and bloggers.

Main Points

- Human rights lawyers in China are under the most intense repression in years.
- Most prominent human rights lawyers have been disbarred, suspended, arrested or disappeared over the past five years.
- Legal reforms have been demoted in the name of 'protecting stability'.
- There is an increased use of extra-judicial tactics for political suppression.
- The government is showing a new hostility to the legal profession at large.
- The rise of the security apparatus will be a long-lasting challenge to legal reforms.
- The government is hollowing out international rule of law cooperation programmes.

Background Information

Since the start of the economic reforms in China that were launched at the end of the Cultural Revolution in 1978, the legal profession has been growing exponentially. At the beginning of the reform era China had no practising lawyers: today there are about 170,000. Of these, the vast majority devotes itself to commercial law, with a small but significant number active in a loosely defined movement that has taken the name of 'rights defence movement' (*weiquan yundong*). Contrary to classical political opponents and dissidents, the *weiquan* activists clearly inscribe their actions within the boundaries of the existing legal system and limit their goals to the realisation of rights and entitlements already enshrined in Chinese laws.

Taking rights seriously

Even though Chinese lawyers remain under the authority of the Party they play an important role even within the confines of a Chinese Communist Party (CCP)-dominated system, by virtue of being the most autonomous players in the judicial system. Indeed, the status of lawyers is an accurate way to measure the progress of the legal system and the adherence by the authorities, if not to the rule of law as such, at least to a rules-based system with a degree of predictability.

In fact, while constantly asserting the primacy of the Party's rule, the Chinese government in past decades has also vigorously promoted the idea of the primacy of the law, an ambiguity which has allowed space for a significant growth in legal institutions, including law schools, and to very active programmes of international cooperation with some of the best known legal scholars, institutions and universities from around the world. This has led to a significant rise in legal awareness both in the profession and in the population at large.

In spite of the lack of independence of the judiciary, the impossibility of bringing to court the Party and many government officials, and the use of the judicial system to punish political dissent (as in the case of Nobel Peace Prize laureate Liu Xiaobo), legal reforms have benefitted many ordinary citizens, and given activists concrete tools to promote and defend human rights. In parallel, the country's professional bar associations started to become increasingly more vocal in demanding greater institutional protection for their members.

From pioneers to victims

However, starting in 2005 the CCP, rattled by the perception that 'colour revolutions' had been spurred by international support to domestic civil societies, has been taking a gradual turn against increased autonomy of the legal profession. Over the years this has turned into a full-blown retreat on the part of the government and its commitment to rule of law reforms. The first victims of this changed state of affairs were several of the most outspoken legal activists, including lawyers Gao Zhisheng and the self-taught rural legal activist Chen Guangcheng (see profiles below), both of whom were harassed and unlawfully detained on various occasions starting in 2005.

The following year the environment became even harsher. The government introduced a campaign to promote 'socialist rule of law' highlighting the differences with 'Western' rule of law — in essence opposing the concept of judicial independence and advocating the subservience of legal work to Party authority and imperatives.

A new doctrine

In 2007 the government introduced a new doctrine by the name of the 'Three Supremes', which states that the will of the Party and the will of the people should override the importance of the written law in legal cases. During the National Conference on Political-Legal Work, held in 2008 by the central Political-Legal Committee that oversees the legal system, President Hu declared that 'In their work, the grand judges and grand procurators shall always regard as supreme the party's cause, the people's interest and the constitution and laws'.[16]

The impact of this doctrine has been widespread and far-reaching, subjecting all legal work to the Party's political imperatives. The once-promising field of legal aid, for instance, is increasingly being steered towards 'mediation', a process woefully inadequate to address disputes in which local power holders or government agencies are a party (such as abuses of power, illegal land grabs, forced evictions, unpaid wages or miscarriages of justice).

'Professionalisation' in the crosshair

Many observers had optimistically hoped that the Party was only trying to prevent the emergence of an opposition spearheaded by legal professionals, while non-politically sensitive aspects of law reforms, like commercial law, civil law and criminal law, would be left untouched.

However, in March 2008, the nomination of Wang Shengjun as head of the Supreme People's Court showed that the new doctrine was going to be felt in all legal fields. Wang, who had received no legal training prior to his appointment, is seen as a Party hard liner, and has reversed many of the reforms introduced by his predecessor, Xiao Yang, who had advocated professional competence and individual and collective judicial autonomy. Wang Shengjun started a far-reaching campaign to promote the Three Supremes, emphasising Party leadership and using the courts to foster economic development and social stability. Wang rejected his predecessor's call for the 'professionalisation of the judiciary', affirming that doing

---

[16] Jerome A. Cohen, 'Body Blow for the Judiciary', *South China Morning Post*, October 18, 2008.

so would only foster judicial independence and be contrary to the Three Supremes' directives.

Discouraging public interest litigation

Since the mid-2000s, several landmark articles in the Central Committee's theoretical publication, *Seeking Truth*, have denounced Western legal cooperation programmes as an attempt at subverting the Chinese legal system. The overt hostility to the mobilisation of legal mechanisms by civil society led to increased pressure on NGOs that had been promoting public interest litigation, with many being closed and disbanded.

The better-known cases involve the Open Constitution Initiative, or *Gongmeng* (accused of tax evasion over a Yale Law School grant), whose director, Xu Zhiyong, was detained for one month in mid-2009; the Women's Legal Research and Service Centre, whose registration was revoked, run by women's rights activist Guo Jianmei; and Aizhixing, a prominent HIV/AIDS anti-discrimination organisation whose director and founder, Wan Yanhai, was forced to flee the country in 2010.

Suspensions and disbarments

The authorities also started to manipulate more overtly the technical requirements lawyers have to submit to in order to renew their professional licenses each year, a move that has widely been perceived as a deterrent against accepting cases against the state. Thus, after 2008, the government for the first time applied denial of registration to large groups of *weiquan* lawyers. In 2010, the government took the unprecedented step of disbarring two prominent rights lawyers, Tang Jitian and Liu Wei.

Beyond the targeting of lawyers engaged in human rights work, and under the influence of the powerful Public Security Ministry, the government also took steps to block lawyers from becoming more active in criminal law. Revisions to the Law on Lawyers introduced in June 2008 included a new article (Article 37) that made lawyers liable for statements made in court that 'compromised national security, maliciously defamed others or seriously disrupted the court order'. Teng Biao, a *weiquan* lawyer currently disappeared (see case study below), described it at the time as 'a trap for lawyers'.

Deterring criminal lawyers

Another development seen by many as a direct attack against the legal profession was the arrest and sentencing of lawyer Li Zhuang in Chongqing in 2010. A criminal lawyer in Beijing hired for the defence of mobster Gong Gangmo, he was arrested by the police, tortured in custody to extract a false confession, and given two-and-a-half years in prison on charges of 'fabricating evidence' (Article 306 of the Criminal law). His lawyer, Chen Youxi, filmed his client showing signs of torture and retracting the confession. The trial ignored the evidence of torture and the retraction. The Supreme People's Court refused to reverse the verdict, indicating that criminal lawyers remain vulnerable at all times to judicial retribution by the investigating authorities under Article 306. In a recent twist, the judicial authorities in Chongqing have decided to reopen Li's trial, put more charges on him — and delay his release, scheduled for June 2011.

Rolling out a methodical crackdown

It is against this background that the Chinese authorities launched a comprehensive crackdown in February 2011, still unfolding at the time of writing. Human rights organisations have counted between 100 and 200 cases of detentions for advocacy across the country. Ten of China's top human rights lawyers have been arrested since mid-February and have not been heard from since.

Up to 50 people are facing prosecution for state security crimes and the loosely defined crime of 'inciting subversion', which includes criticism of the CCP. Writers, bloggers and critics have been intimidated. The campaign culminated with the arrest of Ai Weiwei — overtly on suspicion of 'economic crimes' in April 2011 — which sent the signal that anyone could be arrested, no matter how famous domestically and internationally (the European Parliament passed a resolution in support of Ai Weiwei in April 2011).

Increased recourse to extra-legal tactics

The methods employed by the authorities have changed. Instead of relying on short-term detentions and house arrests, the Public Security Bureau's No. 1 branch — the secret police in charge of 'domestic security' — has been making arrests on state security charges and using extra-judicial tactics such as disappearances, physical intimidation or beatings by plain-clothes thugs, and threats of torture and retaliation against family members and work associates. This shift to extra-judicial tactics was tacitly acknowledged by the authorities when a government spokesman warned on 3 March 2011 that 'the law was not a shield' for people 'creating trouble for China'.

A particularly dire aspect of the current crackdown has been the arrest and disappearance of the top human rights legal activists of the country. This move effectively deprived other people arrested later from being represented by experienced human rights lawyers and made the recourse to patently unlawful methods by the authorities easier.

The rise of the security apparatus

China's departure from the previous course of legal reforms may have long-term domestic implications. The emphasis on 'protecting stability' has considerably empowered the security apparatus (the public security as well as all the agencies in charge of social control, propaganda and censorship), whose budget is now estimated as equivalent to the armed forces budget. Although there are voices within the Party and the government who worry that undermining the legal system too much might ultimately create more social instability, an empowered security apparatus might act as an insurmountable opponent of rekindling legal reforms unless there is a clear reversal of policy after the leadership transition in 2012.

Policy Implications

The demotion of legal reforms in China's political agenda, the hostility against all active forms of public interest lawyering and against efforts to increase the autonomy of the legal profession present severe challenges to the EU's human rights diplomacy.

The Chinese government remains mostly indifferent to international pressures to respect its own laws and release those unlawfully detained, while reasserting that the country is 'ruled by law' and does not accept 'foreign interferences' in its internal affairs. Given this uncompromising attitude, international legal programmes and exchanges have long been seen as one of the most promising avenues for furthering the rule of law in China, if not directly, at least through the training of future generations of judges, prosecutors, lawyers, legal professionals and civil society leaders.

China's new political orientation away from legal reforms and the current drive to 'hollow out' existing cooperation programmes seriously undermine the prospect that legal cooperation may have any significant influence either on the course of legal reforms or on the gradual improvement of the human rights situation in the country. As many foreign practitioners based in China readily admit, the real *raison d'être* of many of these programmes is now that they are 'better than nothing'.

There are no easy solutions for the EU. Human rights is an important issue not just for its own sake, but also because Europe increasingly puts its credibility on the line when it defends human rights. China's readiness to engage in rule of law exchanges that are not artificially kept free of human rights issues is directly proportional to how much it feels external pressure on human rights issues. Therefore, increased public pressure is the best course to create the space to conduct meaningful human rights initiatives and support the legal profession in China.

Given that China has shown to be fundamentally indifferent to criticisms of human rights abuses when they are made at the EU level but not echoed by Member States, only greater internal cohesion of the EU Member States can yield the requisite changes. New mechanisms to coordinate human rights policy more effectively are essential.

Lawyer Profiles
Chen Guangcheng

Internationally known as the 'blind lawyer', Chen Guangcheng, born in 1971, is a self-taught legal counsellor who was operating from Shandong province, helping people navigate the complexities of the legal system and collecting evidence and materials for the cases brought forward to him. He is what is described in China as a 'barefoot lawyer', meaning a lawyer without academic training, but who acquired expertise through on the ground work.

His first politically sensitive cases started in 1998, when he helped peasants who had assets expropriated, and pushed for the rights of people with disabilities. The real trouble, however, commenced when he was asked for help on forced abortions and sterilisations by the Linyi (Shandong) municipal authorities. His research on this case revealed a systematic policy of physical abuse and severe intimidation of the less protected members of society in order to stick to the official birth rate targets, after some Shandong officials had been threatened with pay cuts and a freeze in promotions if they did not halt the population growth in their province.

In 2005 Chen tried to have the case accepted by a court in Beijing but was rejected. He then publicised his findings through the media and Internet, earning the ire of the authorities, who put him under house arrest together with his family in August of that year. He was disappeared in March 2006, and only charged three months later when he was formally detained. He was then sentenced to four years and three months in prison for 'intentionally damaging property' and 'gathering crowds to disturb traffic'.

His trial was widely condemned for being unfair and not respecting China's own laws, while those who tried to come to his support, including lawyers and friends, and the reporters who tried to cover the trial were regularly threatened, intimidated and beaten by thugs sent by the local authorities and police. His lawyers were detained and prohibited from entering the court. The ability of the local Linyi authorities to intercept whomever was coming from other cities to the town, even before they got off the train, suggests that the serious irregularities to this trial were approved also outside of Shandong.

Chen appealed, and was retried: but the sentence was upheld in 2007, and Chen was imprisoned. Released after serving his sentence at the end of 2010, Chen has been subjected to a particularly severe form of illegal house arrest, and both he and his wife have been repeatedly beaten. No visitors, including doctors, have been allowed, and Internet and phone services to and from the house have been disrupted. Security cameras guard the Chens' house, which is also flooded with light through the night. Tens of thugs are staging a round-the-clock surveillance in Chen's village, checking everybody's comings and goings. Chen managed to smuggle out a video of his harsh and extra-judicial home imprisonment, which was then posted on the Internet. As a consequence, Chen and his wife were badly beaten up, and the lawyers who attempted to have a meeting at a restaurant in Beijing to discuss ways to help him have been harassed. Several of the lawyers present, Teng Biao (see below), Tang Jitian and Jiang Tianyong, have been disappeared.

Gao Zhisheng

Gao Zhisheng, born in 1966 in Shanxi Province, is a former soldier. He passed the bar in 1995, after studying law by himself. He founded the Shengzhi Law Office in 2000, and was soon recognised by the Ministry of Justice as one of

China's 'top 10 lawyers'. He also received numerous accolades and recognitions both nationally and internationally (in 2007 he was awarded the Courageous Advocacy Award by the American Board of Trial Advocates), before being arrested and disappeared on various occasions. His whereabouts have been unknown since April 2010.

For years, Gao has been taking cases considered 'sensitive', defending Falun Gong members (a religious sect outlawed by the authorities), dispossessed peasants, underground Christians, victims of official corruption or medical cover-ups, other lawyers, etc. Gao is a classic example of a lawyer who has been turned into a dissident: as his cases were refused by the courts with increasing frequency, he became gradually more outspoken, talking to the foreign media, and writing open letters to the Chinese authorities criticising the human rights abuses he had witnessed. His activism soon brought dire consequences on him and his family: his house was put under surveillance, and in 2005 his young daughter was being followed on the way to school.

The year after, Gao was abducted, disappeared for more than a month, and beaten up while visiting Shandong. In December of the same year he was sentenced to four years in prison for 'subversion', with a five-year reprieve. His law licence was scrapped, and his law firm shut down. But after Gao described in detail the torture he was subjected to, the harassment only increased. In 2007, he was again kidnapped and tortured, using methods including electric shocks.

In 2009, his family decided to escape abroad, and reached the US through Thailand, where they asked for and obtained asylum. On February of the same year, Gao was again disappeared for a full year, then resurfaced to announce he would no longer be an activist, before being disappeared again. In January of this year, the Associated Press published an interview that had been recorded during Gao's brief reappearance, which was made under the understanding that the news agency would only release it in case of a new disappearance. In it, Gao detailed being subjected to torture and extra-judicial detentions.

As Gao prophetically said in 2005, 'you cannot be a rights lawyer in this country without becoming a rights case yourself'. The European Parliament has called for Gao's release on more than one occasion.

Teng Biao

A Beijing-based human rights activist and lawyer born in 1973, who received his PhD from Beijing University's Law School, Teng Biao is among those recently disappeared by the authorities. He took part in a meeting in a Beijing restaurant on 16 February 2011 to discuss how to help human rights lawyer Chen Guangcheng (see above) and was subsequently taken away by police a few days later. Also taken away on the same day were two other lawyers who had participated in the meeting, Tang Jitian and Jiang Tianyong, whose whereabouts are also still unknown. It is not the first time Teng has been detained: one of the founders of the Open Constitution Initiative (also known as Gongmeng, headed by lawyer Xu Zhiyong) in 2003, Teng is typical of those young lawyers whose interest in promoting respect for human rights and the rule of law puts them in a collision course with the Chinese authorities. In his career, mostly with the Beijing Huayi Law Firm, Teng has defended AIDS activists, Tibetan protesters, taken cases involving Falun Gong practitioners and cases involving peasants' land rights.

Teng Biao's first detention (which lasted several hours) was in 2006 in Linyi, Shandong province, where he went to attend the trial of fellow lawyer Chen Guangcheng. He was then detained in 2008, the year in which he signed Charter 08, the pro-democracy manifesto co-authored by Nobel Peace Prize laureate Liu Xiaobo. In March of that year, Teng Biao was kidnapped while on his way home. His kidnappers identified themselves as Beijing Public Security Bureau, and threatened him with dismissal from his teaching position at the China University of Political Science and Law, and a charge for subversion if he did not give up his activism. Forty hours later Teng Biao was released. The following month, he, and another 17 lawyers, offered legal assistance to the Tibetan protesters arrested after the uprising in Tibet, and shortly afterwards Teng Biao's licence renewal was denied. Also disbarred on the same occasion, and probably for the same reason, was fellow lawyer and activist Jiang Tianyong.

In 2010 Teng Biao was once again briefly detained, interrogated, beaten and threatened after he tried to visit the mother of legal scholar Fan Yafeng, who had been put under house arrest. Even after disbarment, Teng Biao kept being closely monitored by the security apparatus, with occasional house arrests ('soft detention' or *ruanjin*) during times that the authorities considered politically sensitive, like the anniversary of the Tiananmen crackdown in 1989. His dedication and activism has been recognised through many awards, both at home and internationally: in 2003 he was recognised as one of the 'Top Ten Figures in the Legal System' by CCTV (China Central TV) and also the Ministry of Justice. He also received the French Republic Award for Human Rights in 2007.

Cadre Training and the Party School System in Contemporary China
(October 2011)

Frank N Pieke

Professor in Modern China Studies, Institute for Area Studies, Leiden University

Executive Summary

- Training and educating administrative officials ('cadres') is a cornerstone of the socialist modernisation of the Chinese Communist Party (CCP) and the state.
- Cadre training takes place either in dedicated institutions, such as Party schools, or through collaborations, exchanges and commercial contracts with a range of local, national or international training providers.
- Cadre training serves two, somewhat contradictory, objectives — to cement ideological unity, and to improve professional competence. While the time devoted to ideology and policy in training classes has been declining for some time, many cadres continue to find training in these areas relevant, both in practice and to their career prospects.
- Cadres in China are better qualified and equipped for leadership than ever before, and it is arguable that China is now a state ruled by professional experts rather than revolutionary ideologues.
- The Central Party School in Beijing is a vital centre of ideological renewal for the CCP. Party schools conduct policy-oriented research, and occupy an

important space between more autonomous academic institutions and direct policy research taking place within administrative departments.
- The CCP leadership uses the Central Party School to spearhead ideological and policy innovation.

Introduction: Why Party Schools?

Chinese Communist Party (CCP) schools are more than mere remnants of China's Maoist past. The economic success of the reform policies since 1978 has made possible an ambitious programme of state building, through two interrelated processes. The growth of a market economy has created a robust revenue base for the administration. Linked to this, the transition away from comprehensive socialist economic planning has created a need for a state that regulates and enables orderly market operation and growth. As such, while the state arguably governs fewer areas of society, those areas it continues to govern are better managed than in the past.

Training and educating administrative officials ('cadres') is a cornerstone of the socialist modernisation of the CCP and the state. Cadre training takes place either in dedicated institutions, such as Party schools, or through collaborations, exchanges and commercial contracts with a range of local, national or international training providers.

Cadre training serves two, somewhat contradictory, objectives — cementing ideological unity, and improving professional competence. The former objective is a direct continuation of pre-reform Maoist practice; the latter developed since the early phases of the reforms begun in the 1980s. The time devoted to ideology and policy in training classes has been declining for some time. However, many cadres continue to find policy and (to a lesser extent) ideology relevant, as their employment and career prospects continue to depend at least in part on their approach to CCP doctrine. Although formal qualifications, performance and competence are now more important to promotion, the Chinese bureaucracy remains politicised along Leninist principles of centralism, discipline and orthodoxy.

Professional competence, the other aim of cadre training, addresses general management and leadership skills, in addition to specialised or vocational subjects, including economics, international relations and English. Increasing amounts of time are also devoted to the analysis and discussion of case studies, current events and research. Indeed, many classes spend considerable time on presenting and explaining the findings of research, and identifying how this research is relevant to administration. While there is considerable self-censorship, more experienced and respected lecturers will often point out the real problems caused by extant policy gaps identified in such research.

Training at a Party school is not only valuable because of the formal teaching provided — the opportunity to develop contacts among other cadres is equally important. Cadres learn much from one another through both formal and informal discussions, and the relationships formed during training courses are an important lubricant of the administrative system.

Much effort has been made in the last 20 years to strengthen the academic quality of teaching and research at Party schools. Nonetheless, while Party schools and other cadre training institutions are important sites of formal degree education, this role is gradually shifting to regular institutions of higher education. However, research, especially at higher-level Party schools, continues to contribute to policy making and evaluation.

The Central Party School in Beijing is a vital centre of ideological renewal for the CCP. Researchers, graduate students and high-level trainees experiment with ideological innovations and elaborations, often with the support of individuals or groups within the CCP leadership. Additionally, CCP leaders frequently test new ideas or policies by presenting them to audiences at the school. Party schools thus occupy an important space between more autonomous academic institutions and direct policy research taking place within administrative departments.

Organisation of Party Schools and Cadre Training

There are well over 2,000 Party schools in China. Party schools exist at all levels of the Chinese bureaucratic hierarchy, from the centre down to provincial, prefectural, county and township administrative levels. In addition, many larger state-owned enterprises, military organisations, and central government organisations will often run one or more specialised Party school of their own. Within each administrative area or institution, the local Party committee decides on annual cadre training plans including what courses will be taught at the local Party school(s). Specialised cadre training institutions include the schools of administration for high-ranking cadres who are not in charge of an organisation or department, and the academies of socialism that cater for leading cadres who are not members of the CCP. Cadre training plans may include specialised training programmes to be held at other institutions.

All Chinese cadres, even the highest leaders, are expected to undergo periodic training at an institution commensurate with their rank, place of service and position. The Central Party School trains cadres up to vice ministerial rank — higher ranked officials (including members of the Politburo) receive their training through special meetings, briefing sessions and conferences. The organisation department of the relevant Party committee selects candidates from the cadres under its jurisdiction, to participate in specific courses or programmes. Selection for training is usually a sign of success, as it indicates that the organisation department has a special interest in furthering the career of the individual concerned. Formally, cadres slated for promotion ought to undergo training first, but quite often training only happens after a promotion already has been made.

Cadre training organisations, Party schools, schools of administration and academies of socialism are fully integrated parts of the local administration. Usually, one of the local deputy Party secretaries is in charge of cadre training, and he or she also often doubles as pro forma head of the Party school. Indeed, cadre training is considered sufficiently important by the CCP that a member of the Politburo's Standing Committee is head of the Central Party School. When Hu Jintao became head of the Central Party School in 1993, this was one of the posts that ultimately allowed him to succeed Jiang Zemin in 2002. Xi Jinping's appointment as head of the Central Party School in 2007 seems to have followed this precedent. Xi has used this post to spearhead ideological and policy innovation in preparation for his likely assumption of the Party's top job in 2012.

Like most other elements of the Chinese administration, Party schools are not bound into a vertically integrated unitary organisation, but are part of a much more loosely organised 'system' without a direct chain of command. Although lower-level Party schools are coordinated and guided by higher levels, they are only directly answerable to the local Party committee of their administrative area. Funding is wholly derived from the local administration's cadre training budget. In addition, Party schools often raise their own income, for instance from courses and degrees offered outside their obligations laid down in the local cadre training plan. Party schools receive no funding from higher administrative levels or higher Party schools.

Marketisation and Diversification of Cadre Training

Since the mid-1990s, the CCP has fostered the proliferation of training institutions and diversified modalities of cadre training. As a result, Party committees have a much wider choice of training providers and types. Regular schools, universities and exchange programmes have acquired considerable market share, at the expense of the traditional Party schools. The curricula offered by these institutions usually lacks political content, and focuses instead on subjects such as management and leadership skills, economics, urban planning and law.

Nonetheless, even with respect to ideological and policy training, the market share of particularly lower-level Party schools has been seriously eroded. Many such schools have become defunct and exist in name only. Moreover, special training courses aimed at key personnel are increasingly entrusted to the Central Party School. Even more importantly, Party committees at both central and local levels have established new institutions, including the four new central cadre academies in Shanghai, Jinggangshan, Yan'an and Dalian, in a bid to increase competition even in higher-level administrative training. Recently, an attempt has been made to revive some defunct Party schools by making them branches of higher-level schools, but it remains unclear whether this has had any tangible effect on the availability of ideological and policy training.

Party schools have not been passive observers of this loss of market share. Rather, Party schools (particularly in the affluent and developed coastal regions) have entered the new market for commercial cadre training, themselves becoming diversified providers of higher education. The Central Party School, for instance, has opened a commercial branch that offers training courses for cadres who otherwise would not have been accepted into the school's regular courses.

The Effect of Changes to the Training System

Marketisation and diversification were originally encouraged in response to problems with Party schools. Sub-standard teaching and an ossified curriculum led to a lack of enthusiasm among trainees, and the perception that training was either a reward or an entitlement. Among the central leadership there has also been a consensus that conventional training has failed to deliver what it promised.

The response has been to invest more resources in cadre training, making China's administration arguably the most extensively trained bureaucracy in the world. It is undeniable that cadres in China are immeasurably better qualified and equipped for leadership than ever before. China is now a country ruled by professional experts rather than revolutionary ideologues.

However, problems with the CCP's approach to cadre training persist. There is a lack of information available on the efficacy of the different forms and modalities of training. There is thus little hard statistical evidence for the hypothesis that commercial courses at regular universities or abroad deliver better training than conventional courses at Party schools.

More fundamentally, even the potential benefits of training are overstated. Certain types of training might be an excellent way to impact specific practices and skills, or to identify promising new talent, but it is unrealistic to expect that training can cure systemic problems like corruption. Structural problems require structural solutions, and in this regard, training can only go so far.

The Role of Think Tanks in China
(December 2013)

Nicola Casarini

Senior Analyst, European Union Institute for Security Studies

Executive Summary

- China's think tanks have become an important means for foreign observers to follow developments and gain insights into the Chinese policy making system. Think tanks have unique knowledge of internal policy debates, in particular of dynamics occurring in the institutions which fund them.
- In China, there are no truly independent think tanks, although some do profess a certain degree of independence. The majority of think tanks operate within administrative hierarchies under either a State Council ministry, a Central Committee department, or one of the general departments of the People's Liberation Army (PLA) which provide funding to the think tank/research institute under their authority. They often flesh out some guidelines on the research topics to be pursued, and grant access to classified material that would otherwise be impossible to consult.
- The role of think tanks in China is to (i) provide analysis and advice to government officials and Chinese Communist Party (CCP) central structures; (ii) act as channels for information and intelligence gathering as well as for policy testing and dissemination; (iii) organise meetings with foreign experts to provide Chinese policy makers with information and feedback on official positions; (iv) carry specific messages and indications for foreign experts and policy makers; (v) meet foreign experts and officials with whom they are familiar in order to influence the policies of their governments and/or institutions *vis-à-vis* China.

- Among the think tanks focusing on international relations and foreign policy, the most influential is the China Institute of Contemporary International Relations (CICIR), followed by the China Institutes of International Studies (CIIS) and the Shanghai Institutes for International Studies (SIIS).
- Among the defence-related and military think tanks, the China Institute for International Strategic Studies (CIISS), the China Foundation for International Strategic Studies (CFISS) and the PLA Academy of Military Sciences (AMS) are the top institutes.
- Among the economic and political-economy think tanks, the Development Research Center (DRC) of the State Council, the China Center for International Economic Exchanges (CCIEE), the Institute of World Economics and Politics at the Chinese Academy of Social Sciences (CASS), and the National Economics Research Institute (NERI) are top.
- Research institutes at leading Chinese universities are increasingly becoming part of the think tank landscape. On international relations and foreign policy, the main ones are: the School of International Studies (SIS) at Peking University; the Institute of International Studies (IIS) at Tsinghua University; and the Center for American Studies (CAS) at Fudan University.

Policy Suggestions

- The EU has traditionally engaged with the more established CICIR and the CIIS. More attention should be paid to the SIIS and to the China Center for Contemporary World Studies (CCCWS), a small but increasingly influential think tank under the aegis of the International Department of the Central Committee of the CCP.
- The European External Action Service (EEAS) could engage further with the CIISS and the CFISS on Track II policy dialogues to advance the defence and military dimensions of EU–China relations.
- The EU could make more strategic use of think tanks and expertise available across Europe to further Track II policy dialogues with Chinese think tanks. This will allow collection of useful information and insight perspectives on Chinese policies to enable better development of a strategic approach *vis-à-vis* Beijing. Moreover, EU policy makers could consider triangular dialogues, e.g.

use expertise available in Europe to engage Chinese think tanks together with other research centres in the US and Asia in order to further discussion on issues of common interest.

The Role of Think Tanks in China

Since their emergence in the early 1980s, China's think tanks have become an important means for foreign observers to follow developments and gain insights into the Chinese policy making system. In 2007, the report of the 17th CCP Congress explicitly mentioned 'the role of think tanks' for the first time. This recognition and support from the authorities was indicative of the rapid development of think tanks as well as their expanding influence.

Chinese think tanks have unique knowledge of internal policy debates, in particular of the dynamics of the institutions which fund them. In China, there are no truly independent think tanks, although some profess a certain degree of independence. All operate within administrative hierarchies under either a State Council ministry, a Central Committee department, or one of the general departments of the PLA which provide funding to the think tank/research institute under their authority. They often flesh out some guidelines on the research topics to be pursued, and grant access to classified material that would otherwise be impossible to consult. A few think tanks have more than one line of institutional authority. The most prominent of these exceptions is the CICIR which is under the authority of the Central Committee Foreign Affairs Office (FAO) and the State Council Ministry of State Security. In general, Chinese think tanks/research institutes remain firmly embedded within vertically hierarchical bureaucratic systems.

The role of think tanks in China can be summarised as follows:

(i) They provide analysis to government officials and central structures of the CCP.
(ii) They act as channels for information and intelligence gathering as well as for policy testing and dissemination.
(iii) They organise meetings with foreign experts and officials to provide the Chinese policy making system with a steady stream of information and feedback on official positions and/or new policy directions.
(iv) They carry specific messages and indications for foreign experts and policy makers which often cannot be expressed through official channels and/or publicly.

(v) They use meetings with foreign experts and officials/policy makers with whom they are familiar in order to influence the policies of their governments and/or institutions *vis-à-vis* China.

The last two points have become increasingly important of late, as the Chinese government has increased its participation in Track II policy dialogues. As such it has better understood the utility of such venues for airing policy ideas and new initiatives and assessing the potential reaction of foreigners.

Chinese think tanks can be divided into three broad categories, according to the focus of their research:

- International relations/foreign policy think tanks.
- Defence-related and military think tanks.
- Economic and political-economy think tanks.

International Relations and Foreign Policy Think Tanks

(i) The **China Institutes of Contemporary International Relations (CICIR)** is one of China's oldest — and possibly most influential — think tanks conducting research and providing expertise on international affairs. Since its creation in 1965, it has served senior-level CCP leadership and has always been bureaucratically subordinate to the Central Committee Foreign Affairs Leading Group (FALG). The CICIR lies under the auspices of the Central Committee while being administratively and fiscally under the authority of the Ministry of State Security. CICIR's comparative advantages are:

a. its size — it is China's largest think tank on international relations and foreign affairs with around 400 staff;
b. its multiple sources of information and intelligence gathering; and
c. its bureaucratic proximity to the Foreign Affairs Office, the FALG, the Ministry of State Security and senior CCP leadership.

CICIR receives its money mainly from the Ministry of State Security, while the FALG is CICIR's main customer. CICIR uses a number of internal and classified channels to reach government audiences, and it publishes the influential journal *Contemporary International Relations* (*Xiandai guoji guanxi*). CICIR's expertise is wide-ranging, covering most international issues and regions of the world. CICIR was led until 2012 by Cui Liru, a well-known expert on US–China relations and a member of the Expert Committee of the Chinese MFA Foreign Policy Advisory Group. Since 2013, CICIR's President has been Ji Zhiye, a prominent expert on Russia–China relations and the post-Soviet space.

(ii) The **China Institute of International Studies (CIIS)** is the oldest of China's foreign affairs think tanks. It is the Foreign Ministry's think tank and is smaller than CICIR. The staff at CIIS consists of nearly 100 researchers and other professionals, including among their number senior diplomats. The CIIS staff also includes rotational assignments from the Ministry of Foreign Affairs. The latter increasingly uses CIIS expertise and has made the think tank the key Track II organisation to carry out exchanges for China. The President of CIIS is traditionally a diplomat. It is currently led by Qu Xing who previously served as Minister in the Chinese Embassy in France. The CIIS publishes the journal *International Relations Research* (*Guoji wenti yanjiu*).

(iii) The **Chinese Academy of Social Sciences (CASS)** is a huge organisation with ministerial status. It consists of over 30 research institutes with more than 3,000 full-time researchers and over 4,000 total staff. CASS carries out research across the whole spectrum of the social sciences and humanities. CASS is funded by the State Council and is led by Chen Kuiyuan, Vice Chairman of the Chinese People's Political Consultative Conference (CPPCC). CASS's eight regional studies institutes have substantial influence in China's policy making debates. In particular, the Institute of European Studies (IES) — headed until 2013 by Zhou Hong — and the Institute of American Studies (IAS) — headed until 2013 by Huang Ping, who is now the new head of the IES — are quite influential and able to provide policy advice to the top CCP leadership. However, CASS institutes lack the institutional channels to the top leadership that, for instance, CICIR enjoys. Instead, CASS researchers rely primarily on personal connections to transmit papers to senior policy makers.

(iv) The **Shanghai Institutes for International Studies (SIIS)** was established in 1960 and has maintained a strong research and analysis capability ever since. It is smaller than CICIR or CIIS, but the quality of its output is generally higher. The distance from Beijing also means that it is intellectually more free and able to produce analyses and policy proposals that vary from the standard policy line. SIIS specialises mainly in US–China and Asian affairs.

It has around 80 full-time staff members and lies under the administration of the Shanghai municipal government, from where it gets most of its funding. The SIIS has close relations with the top Chinese leadership in Beijing that originates from Shanghai. As such, its influence can vary considerably, depending on the composition of the Politburo and other senior-level bodies. It was led until 2012 by Yang Jiemian, the brother of former Foreign Minister Yang Jiechi (now a State Councillor). Since 2013, the SIIS President is Chen Dongxiao, a well-known expert on Chinese foreign policy, US–China relations and UN collective security.

(v) The **China Reform Forum (CRF)** is the think tank of the Party School of the Central Committee of the Chinese Communist Party from where it also gets its main funding. CRF research focuses on issues related to the development of China's reform and opening up policy as well as international affairs. CRF has around 100 staff made up of senior government officials, scholars and business executives in China. Since 2008, CRF's chairman has been Li Jing Tian, the Excecutive Vice President of the Party School of the Central Committee of the CCP. The CRF is quite influential, being very close to the School that prepares the top leadership.

(vi) The **China Center for Contemporary World Studies (CCCWS)** is the think tank of the International Department of the Central Committee of the CCP, from where it also gets its funding. It is under the direct authority of the CCP Central Committee and as such has good access to debates at the most senior Party level. The CCCWS was created a few years ago and today has approximately 25 staff of which around 10 are full-time researchers with PhDs from top Chinese and Western universities. The quality of research is very high and it is fast becoming one of China's best think tanks in the fields of international relations and foreign policy. It is headed by Yu Hongjun, Vice Minister of the International Department of the Central Committee of the CCP.

Defence-Related and Military Think Tanks

(i) The **China Institute for International Strategic Studies (CIISS)** is the foremost intelligence analysis think tank in the Chinese military. It is directly subordinate to the General Staff Second Department (intelligence) from where it receives its funding. Funded in 1979, the Chairman of CIISS is usually also the Deputy Chief of Staff whose portfolio includes foreign intelligence. The staff at CIISS consists of approximately 100 research personnel and includes both active-duty and senior retired intelligence officers, diplomats and scholars. It houses some of the best military analysts of the PLA. CIISS reports circulate to the General Staff Department and throughout the PLA senior leadership. The CIISS also acts as an important interface between the military intelligence apparatus and foreign experts. The current chairman of CIISS is Xiong Guangkai, formerly the PLA's deputy chief of staff.

(ii) The **China Foundation for International Strategic Studies (CFISS)** is under the aegis of the Second Department (Intelligence) of the PLA General Staff. Many of its staff members are active duty PLA colonels or generals, but there are also a number of retired diplomats and civilians. The CFISS is mainly funded by the PLA though it is also allowed to raise funds from the private sector through contract research. In practice, it mainly carries out research for the PLA and the Ministry of Foreign Affairs. The CFISS specialises on non-proliferation and disarmament issues, as well as American security policy and US–China relations. Over the years, this think tank has become a critical interface for military- and security-related exchanges between foreigners and the PLA. The CFISS is fairly involved in Track II policy dialogues and submits an annual year-end analytical report to the PLA. It is headed by General Pan Zhenqiang, a well-known strategist and military analyst.

(iii) Founded in 1958, the **Academy of Military Sciences (AMS)** is the national centre for military studies and the premier military research organisation in the PLA. It is directly subordinate to the Central Military Commission (CMC), but also receives direct assignments from the General Staff Department. The AMS conducts academic research on national defence, armed forces development and military operations, and the future of warfare. It provides advice and consults the Central Military Commission and the PLA General Departments, and coordinates academic work throughout the PLA. The AMS has around 500 full-time researchers who write reports for the military leadership, ghost-write speeches for top military leaders and serve as drafters of important documents like the *Defence White Paper*. It is headed by Lieutenant General Liu Chengjun.

Economic and Political-Economy Think Tanks

(i) The **Development Research Center (DRC) of the State Council** is a leading policy research and consulting institution directly under the State Council. Founded in 1981, its main functions are to undertake research on China's economic and social development, as well as reform and opening up. The DRC often serves informally as an independent check on the policy preferences of government departments. For instance, the DRC Research Department on Foreign Economic Relations provides feedback and analysis to the Ministry of Foreign Trade (MOFTEC). Being under the direct authority of the State Council (from where it gets its funding) allows DRC researchers — like the CICIR — to access inside information and channel their reports to China's senior-level government bodies. It has more than 500 staff and is headed by Li Wei, former Vice Chairman of China Banking Regulatory Commission.

(ii) The **China Center for International Economic Exchanges (CCIEE)** was founded in 2009 as a comprehensive association with the mission of promoting economic research and exchanges and providing consulting services. It operates under the guidance and supervision of the National Development and Reform Commission — which is its main client — and is registered in the Ministry of Civil Affairs from where it also gets part of the funding. Its influence is very high within the National Development and Reform Commission. With around 500 staff, it is headed by Zeng Peiyan, former Vice Premier of the State Council and a member of the International Advisory Council of the China Investment Corporation sovereign wealth fund.

(iii) The **Institute of World Economics and Politics (IWEP)** at CASS is one of the most respected economic and political-economy think tanks in China. IWEP is funded by the State Council and channels its reports, reference materials and publications to almost each department of the central government. IWEP has around 100 staff, with approximately 80 full-time researchers. It is headed by Zhang Yuyan. The Institute enjoys a very good reputation also outside China and publishes the influential journal *China & World Economy*.

(iv) The **National Economics Research Institute (NERI)**, part of the China Reform Foundation, NERI calls itself a non-governmental, non-profit research organisation, although its clients include many departments of the central government and the CCP. NERI provides policy advice to senior-level government bodies and analyses to the business community. It has around 80 staff and is headed by Fan Gang, one of China's most respected and influential economists and most active reform advocates.

Research Institutes at Top Chinese Universities

Research institutes at top Chinese universities are increasingly becoming part of the think tank landscape. This is due to the presence of some of the country's leading thinkers and strategists among their staff (most of them having gained previous experience in one or more of the think tanks listed above) and their growing reputation within senior-level policy circles. These research institutes are more and more committed to translating their academic findings into practical advice to policy makers as they compete for funding and recognition with established think tanks. The most important of these research institutes are:

(i) The **School of International Studies (SIS) at Peking University**. The Dean of SIS until 2013 was Wang Jisi, one of China's best-known experts on international affairs. SIS receives substantial funding from the government.
(ii) The **Institute of International Studies (IIS) at Tsinghua University**. IIS is headed by Yan Xuetong, a well-known thinker and strategist. IIS receives substantial funding from the government.
(iii) The **Center for American Studies (CAS) at Fudan University**. The Executive Dean of CAS is Wu Xinbo and the Vice-Dean is Shen Dingli. Both are well-known experts on US–China relations. The Ministry of Education and Fudan University provide financial support to the CAS.

Conclusion

China's think tanks have become an important element for foreign observers to follow developments and gain insights into Chinese policy making system. Think tanks have unique knowledge of internal policy debates, in particular of the dynamics in the institutions which fund them. The EU — in particular the EEAS — could make more strategic use of think tanks and expertise available across Europe to further Track II policy dialogues with Chinese think tanks. This would enable the collection of useful information and insight perspectives on Chinese policies so as to be better able to adopt a strategic approach *vis-à-vis* Beijing. For instance, the EEAS could partner with one or more of the established think tanks in Europe that have recognised expertise on China — e.g. Chatham House, the European Council on Foreign Relations, China Centre, the German Institute for International and Security Affairs (SWP), the Research Institute of the German Council on Foreign Relations (DGAP), Clingendael–Netherlands Institute of International Relations, the Finnish Institute of International Affairs, the Polish Institute of International Affairs (PISM), the Stockholm International Peace Research Institute (SIPRI) and so forth, or the EU Institute for Security Studies (EUISS) (the latter being overseen by the EEAS itself) — to further discussion with Chinese experts and officials on a certain topic of particular interest/concern ahead of important bilateral meetings (e.g. the yearly EU–China Summit, the high-level Economic and Trade Dialogue, the high-level Strategic Dialogue and so forth). Moreover, EU policy makers could consider triangular dialogues, e.g. use expertise available in Europe to engage Chinese think tanks together with other research centres in the US and Asia in order to further discussion on issues of common interest.

Public Consultations in China
(April 2012)

Jasper Becker
Author and Consultant

Executive Summary

- In recent years, China has become more open, providing much more public information about laws, regulations and law making.
- Starting with the introduction of village elections, China has tried out a wide menu of public participation mechanisms, including public hearings, technical seminars and opinion surveys.
- This has had an immediate impact on both environmental policy making and wage negotiations.
- Officials are much more aware of the need to prepare for and respond to public opinion.
- At present, the most interesting experiments have taken place in Chongqing and Shenzhen. China is open to further experiments in public consultation.

Introduction

For at least 25 years, China has tried out a wide menu of public participation mechanisms. These include public hearings, various open meetings (often called workshops), technical seminars with invited experts, publishing drafts for written comment, as well as more traditional means such as seeking input from relevant government agencies and organisations, site visits to talk with members of the affected public at the 'grassroots' level, and opinion surveys.

The on-and-off trials started with the introduction of village elections but the pace has picked up in recent years and shows interesting momentum. More can be expected following the 18th Party Congress. At the moment the most interesting experiments have taken place in Chongqing and Shenzhen.

Public consultation is the most visible part of an effort which Chinese leaders refer to as *tizhi gaige*, sometimes translated as 'political reform'. This is not be confused with *zhidu gaige*, meaning a switch from a single-party Leninist dictatorship with top-down 'democratic centralism' to a true multi-party democracy. The aim is to make the existing system work better and to give the actions of the Chinese Communist Party greater legitimacy.

This paper looks at:

- National People's Congress consultations.
- Public hearings.
- Workshops.
- Public consultation on environmental issues.
- Experiments in collective bargaining in Guangdong.
- Performance management.
- Experiments in direct elections.
- Public consultation on local budgets in Sichuan: Deliberative Polling in Wenling.
- Open recommendation and selection of officials.

National People's Congress Consultations

A 2008 State Council decision on strengthening administration in accordance with the law at the municipal and county levels emphasised the need to improve the public policy decision-making process by increasing transparency and public participation, including by means of written comments, expert meetings and through holding public hearings.

The State Council has also called for establishing and improving a feedback (*fankui*) system for government regulation. Several local governments are already regularly providing responses to the public comments they receive during administrative rulemakings. The adoption of the nationwide Open Government Information Regulations also requires the government to disclose a wide range of government-held information that was hitherto unavailable.

The National People's Congress (NPC) released only 15 draft laws for public comment between 1949 and the end of 2007. The published drafts included the 1954 and 1982 Constitutions, the 1998 Organic Law on Villager Committees and the 1998 revised Land Management Law.

After passage of the Legislation Law in 2000, the NPC began to use the Internet to publish drafts deemed to be of particular interest to the public, the first of which was the 2001 revision of the Marriage Law. The Property Law, one of the most controversial recent enactments, went through the first NPC reading in December 2002 and was not adopted until March 2007, after going through a 40-day public comment period in the summer of 2005 that drew over 11,500 comments.

The draft Labour Contract Law released for public comment in March 2006 received even more — almost 192,000 comments, 65% of which were from ordinary workers. These comments prompted major revisions to the draft that was ultimately adopted a little over a year later.

In April 2008, the NPC Standing Committee announced that, going forward, all drafts submitted to it for review and adoption will ordinarily be made public as a standard practice, observing that an open and transparent legislative process would better ensure the public's 'right to know, participate, express their views and supervise' and provide the people with a better understanding of new laws through participation in their formulation.

Most drafts are to be published for comment over the NPC website after the first reading, while those drafts believed to relate to the 'vital interests' of the public will also be carried in national media. The Standing Committee subsequently released drafts of all 15 laws that it considered in 2008, and has maintained to do so.

Moreover, each draft starting with the Food Safety Law, which was published for comment in April 2008, has been accompanied by an explanation of the reason for and major issues raised by the draft law. In some cases, this explanation also included specific questions on which the NPC wanted particular input.

Beijing was one of the first local governments to publish a draft regulation for comment, starting in the early 1990s with draft provisions on raising pet dogs, a topic that, like restrictions on fireworks, continues to provoke strong public interest. By the late 1990s, departments under the State Council such as the China Securities Regulatory Commission and the Ministries of Information Technology, Public Health, and Land and Resources also began to release selected draft departmental regulations for public input on their websites and in relevant newspapers.

Although the Shanghai Municipal People's Congress started releasing drafts of local legislation for comment earlier, the Shanghai government first experimented with public participation in administrative rulemaking. After May 2004, all draft government rules have been posted on the Shanghai government website, http://www.shanghai.gov.cn, as well as in local Shanghai newspapers, for public comment.

Although Shanghai has not promulgated any regulation mandating this practice, more than 50 draft rules had been posted by the end of 2008. Moreover, recent drafts have been accompanied by the drafter's explanation of the legal basis, need for and background on the proposed decision, in order to help the public better understand the purpose and content of the drafts.

The Guangzhou Public Participation Measures make the written comment procedure the heart of the public participation process and grant the right to participate to everyone, not just Guangzhou residents or Chinese citizens. Guangzhou has not only published all municipal government and agency rules for comment but is also applying similar procedures to policy making in land use and other areas and conducting active outreach through various kinds of meetings with associations, individuals and experts to discuss the drafts. While some drafts get zero or few comments, others, like a proposal related to raising pet dogs that elicited more than 5,000 comments during the preparatory stage, draw more public interest.

Following initial experiments by some central ministries and local governments, the State Council Office of Legislative Affairs (OLA) first released one of its own draft national regulations, on property management, for public comment in October 2002. The OLA gradually increased the number of drafts that it chose to make public each year. In March 2007, it published a notice to all State Council departments reporting agreement by the State Council leadership to establish a procedure for determining at the beginning of each year which draft laws and regulations should be made public for comment, and agreeing to publication of seven named laws and regulations for that year. As it turned out, the OLA released a total of 12 drafts in 2007.

In January 2008, the OLA announced in introducing its legislative plan for that year, that it and the central ministries would henceforth essentially abandon the test of whether legislation relates to the 'vital interests' of the public and would publish virtually all draft rules and regulations — other than those involving state secrets or national security — for public comment.

In line with this new policy directive, the State Council released 25 drafts, most of which were accompanied by a background explanation, for public comment in 2008. The State Council OLA, in announcing its 2009 legislative plan, encouraged expanding the scope of public participation to ensure the opinions of basic-level agencies and relevant industry associations and interest groups are heard. Within the first eight months of 2009, 45 central government agency and State Council drafts had been published for comment online.

The State Council OLA has also established and is working to improve a software program that collects, sorts and analyses the comments received, to make it easier to digest large numbers of public opinions. It is also working with provincial- and lower-level governments to upgrade their websites in order to provide more standardised and efficient notice and comment procedures. Unofficial estimates are that 27 of 31 provincial-level government OLAs (87%) have sought public input over the Internet, and 17 out of 50 central government ministries and organs have put out departmental rules through their websites as of July 2009.

Many local draft rules are now posted on the State Council OLA website — http://www.chinalaw.gov.cn — and on the central government portal website — http://www.gov.cn/zwhd/index.htm. The OLA plans eventually to establish an integrated nationwide information platform for providing written notice and comment capability for government rulemakings at all levels and for all agencies.

The Supreme People's Court has also on occasion held workshops to seek legal experts' input on their draft annual work reports and in 2003 started issuing selected draft judicial interpretations, which elucidate how laws should be applied, for public comment. The Court now has a column on its website, where it has posted 29 drafts that have gone through that process as of July 2009.

Public Hearings

Shenzhen has pioneered the *pangting* or audit system of inviting members of the public to sign up for the opportunity to sit in on legislative sessions and listen to the proceedings, a practice now regularly used by the National People's Congress (NPC) as well. These auditors are not permitted to take part in the discussion or ask questions, but are encouraged to submit written views about their observations, and suggestions for legislation.

The discretionary practice of holding legislative hearings was endorsed by the 2000 Legislation Law. This has been followed by implementing regulations on administrative rulemaking which provide some general guidelines on how all levels of government below the State Council itself should conduct public hearings.

If a government agency decides to hold a public rulemaking hearing, the organiser has to announce the relevant information at least 30 days in advance; the participants are permitted to raise questions and voice their opinions with regard to the draft; a written hearing record is to be kept; and the drafting unit is to carefully study the various opinions provided at the hearing. The drafting unit must also prepare a written explanation of the opinions expressed, and how they were dealt with, in the final draft to be submitted for approval together with the final draft of the rule. However, these regulations do not require public disclosure explaining how the public's opinions were handled or stipulate such matters as who can participate, when hearings should be open to the general public, and whether the hearing record should be publicly available. Moreover, implementing regulations under the Legislation Law did not provide comparable details on hearing procedures for use by the State Council and the People's Congresses.

Many provincial- and lower-level governments have embraced the idea of public hearings and have established their own local rules. By January 2006, 45 legislative hearings had been held by the standing committees of provincial People's Congresses on draft regulations and by mid-2008, 19 provincial-level governments and many large cities like Shenzhen, Harbin, Jinan and Dalian had promulgated administrative rules for hearings.

At the centre, the NPC and State Council have been cautious, aware of the difficulty of involving too many people in consultations. The NPC Standing Committee held its first and only public hearing to date in September 2005, on draft revisions to the Individual Income Tax Law. A hearing notice, accompanied by an application to speak on background information from the Ministry of Finance on the reasons for the proposed increase in the standard deduction, was posted online and carried in newspapers. Twenty representatives selected from 5,000 applicants spoke at the four-hour long televised and broadcasted hearing, after which the standard deduction was adjusted slightly higher. The NPC has promised to continue to experiment with public hearings but has not yet held a second hearing.

The State Council has not held any public hearings at all, despite encouraging other bodies to experiment, especially on proposals for imposing a licensing or permit requirement, or when a matter involves the 'vital interests' of the public. Ministries regulating areas of such areas like the Ministry of Land and Resources and the State Food and Drug Administration, have legislative and decision-making hearing procedures.

The first online legislative hearing tried out by Chongqing Municipality in November 2005 was an interesting experiment. This hearing was opened to questions and comments from the general public over the Internet, or by telephone to a special hotline, for two hours during which 80,000 web users visited the hearing webcast.

Workshops

Another method of public participation mentioned in the Legislation Law is the workshop (*zuotanhui*), to which affected government organs, social organisations, enterprises, experts such as legal scholars, and selected members of the public are called. These meetings can be run fairly flexibly, and held at different stages of the drafting process. Traditionally, the proceedings themselves are kept confidential to encourage participants to speak frankly. Both government departments and the People's Congresses use workshops to help ascertain preferences and resolve thorny issues. For example, the NPC convened over 100 workshops to discuss the hotly debated draft Property Law, which went through seven readings rather than the normal three.

Guangzhou Municipality requires at least one workshop for every agency rule-making under its 2006 Public Participation Measures, which are the first Chinese ordinances to regulate in some detail and mandate public participation for every rulemaking and at each stage thereof.

The Guangzhou Public Participation Measures introduced a new category of consultation literally called 'seeking opinions in an open manner' (*kaifangshi zhengqiu yijian*), which involves announcing and holding informal public meetings where any interested person can provide suggestions and comments to drafting officials.

This format, considered an innovation in China, has been adopted in the Hunan Administrative Procedure Act (APA) for use as appropriate, along with workshops, consultations (*xieshanghui*) and public hearings, to obtain public input on proposed major policy decisions.

Some localities are also experimenting with opening up executive government meetings for public observation and sometimes limited participation. Hangzhou in Jiangsu province started in 2008 to invite a few citizens to its executive government meetings that consider various actions, sometimes asking their input.

This 'government under the sunshine' practice of open meetings is also encouraged under Hunan's rules when administrative organs are considering matters involving the 'vital interests' of the general public.

Public Consultation on Environmental Issues

The state authorises public participation under the Environmental Impact Assessment (EIA) Law. It was promulgated in 2002 and came into effect in 2005. That year the State Environmental Protection Agency (SEPA), which has since become the Ministry of Environmental Protection, held a public hearing over a project to seal the eastern lake bed at the Old Summer Palace.

It was the first national public hearing on an environmental issue. For the first time, the EIA was released to the public. It also revealed the strong interest among Chinese Internet users or netizens. More than 200,000 articles about the project appeared on various websites and millions wrote about it. Only 120 people actually took part in the hearing but many of these were from NGOs which gave them stature and legitimacy. In the end the plastic lining of the water bed was largely replaced with clay.

The publicity storm generated by this small project led to the government suspending 82 large projects, mostly hydro-electric dams, which had not followed the EIA law's procedures. In 2006 the central government issued the Environmental Protection Administrative Hearing Regulation (Trial) to promote public participation in environmental guidance, including EIA processes. A new regulation on environmental governance transparency, the Environmental Strategic Planning Law which took effect in May 2008 gave a further boost.

The EIA Law has been instrumental in the growth and influence of environmental NGOs. There may be at least 354,000 at national and local levels. These range from charities to scientific associations, trade and business associations, cultural groups, professional societies and youth groups, but environmental NGOs are the most active in the political arena. They have actively raised the public's environmental awareness, supervised polluting enterprises and participated in environmental decision making and policy making.

One victory for conservationists has been the suspension of the construction of two major dams on the Jinsha River, a tributary of the Yangtze River. The dams at Longkaikou and Ludila were being built by two of China's largest power-generating companies — Huaneng Power and Huadian Power. Both had been started without environmental assessments or ministry approval. The ministry also suspended approvals for the two companies' other projects, except those involving energy-saving and pollution prevention measures. It also suspended construction projects in eastern Shandong province begun by a state-owned steel company because it had not submitted an environmental impact assessment. Another dam planned for the Tiger Leaping Gorge area was suspended after a public outcry in 2005.

In September 2009, 15 top academicians signed a joint letter to Premier Wen Jiabao expressing their concerns about a planned dam project which was included in a blueprint for the Poyang Eco-economic Development Zone. Poyang Lake is in Jiangxi Province. The central government approved the blueprint three months later, but the dam was ruled out. Instead, the province was asked to prepare scientific assessments on the potential impact. Jiangxi invited a collection of academics, including some of those who opposed the plan, to look into key aspects, such as how the dam would affect the water quality, wetlands and migrating birds. The studies funded entirely by the provincial government to the tune of RMB 10 m (EUR 1.125 m) were intended to provide scientific recommendations on whether the dam project should go ahead.

All six studies were completed in 2010, but the Jiangxi government did not make the complete reports public. Requests by several conservation groups to see the studies were turned down. The province also organised another environmental assessment for the Poyang Lake Development Plan, of which the dam is a major part, carried out by the Yangtze Water Resources Protection Institute, which is affiliated with the Ministry of Water Resources, and the Jiangxi Environmental Protection Institute. The joint report concluded that the plan 'will have both positive and negative effects on the ecology and environment, but there will be more good than harm'. It said the negative impact will be on migrating birds, aquatic animals and water quality, but added that this could be prevented by certain measures.

Urban planning, land use and major project decisions are other areas of great controversy. The Ministry of Land and Resources promulgated provisions in 2004 that require hearings on the formulation of rules and regulatory documents relating to land use, compensation for land takings and development projects. Continued experiments in this area led to the revised 2008 Urban and Rural Planning Law, which requires that draft urban and rural land use plans must be published for comment for not less than 30 days, the opinions of both experts and the general public must be sought through hearings, expert meetings and other channels, and those opinions must be considered and set forth in a report accompanying the draft plan submitted for approval.

Following large demonstrations in the southern city of Xiamen over plans to build a chemical factory in a suburban area, the Shanghai government responded to massive protests in January 2008 against an extension of a high-speed maglev train line by committing to do a better job of consulting the public on major projects. Residents had voiced concerns over noise, vibrations and possible electromagnetic radiation from the train system, some residents would have to be relocated to accommodate the new line, and homeowners living nearby feared the project would negatively impact property values.

Mayor Han Zheng promised to improve public opinion surveys, public notice of projects and public hearings, and make sure that citizens are effectively involved in major projects. The government eventually postponed the maglev extension while it conducted further studies. Mayor Han similarly announced in February 2009 a new system of prior consultation for major urban redevelopment projects, both to obtain agreement by a given percentage of affected residents to the project itself and at a second stage to obtain general agreement with the compensation and resettlement arrangements.

Experiments in Collective Bargaining in Guangdong

Wang Yang, while Party secretary of Guangdong Province from 2007 to 2012, responded to a series of damaging strikes by pushing for more collective bargaining. The Guangdong Provincial Federation of Trade Unions made Nanhai Honda a pilot site for collective bargaining after a damaging strike in 2010.

The enterprise union was restructured after the strike. The workers directly elected union team leaders, union committee members and a union vice chairman. On 1 March 2011, with guidance from the Guangdong Federation of Trade Unions, Nanhai Honda's workers and management signed a new collective contract raising combined wages and bonuses by an average of RMB 611 (EUR 76), a 33% increase.

Wang also pushed for a 'Democratic Management Act in Enterprises' and a 'Collective Wage Negotiation Act'. The current draft states that, where at least a third of an enterprise's workforce requests it, the trade union should call a democratic meeting among workers to choose delegates who will then bargain with the employer to arrive at collective wage agreements. When enterprises receive a letter of intent to collectively bargain for wages, they shall provide a written reply within 15 days. If, without good reason, they do not respond or do not arrange for negotiations, they may not revoke labour contracts because of union work stoppages or slowdowns. However, the draft also stated that when workers have not yet called for collective wage bargaining according to law, or during collective wage negotiations, they may not engage in work stoppages, slowdowns, or other excessive actions.

For those enterprises without trade unions, the local federation of trade unions should be responsible for guiding the workers in choosing their delegates democratically. Previous laws never gave workers the right to negotiate a collective wage agreement: the Trade Union Law (1992), Labour Law (1994) and Labour Contract Law (2007) simply handed the rights over to the trade unions.

If successfully enacted, the revised draft will provide a regular mechanism, distinct from the previous collective action mechanism, for the workers to demand a collective wage agreement and to defend their interests. It will restore to workers the right of collective negotiation, including the right to choose their delegates under the guidance of the trade unions, which will help workers to play principal role in future collective negotiations. Hong Kong business federations have waged a lobbying campaign both in Guangzhou and Beijing to scrap the revised regulations or water them down.

The Shenzhen Municipal Trade Union announced plans to negotiate and sign collective wage agreements at 550 enterprises in the city in 2011. This was followed by similar initiatives in towns and cities in Hunan, Hebei, Zhejiang and Shandong provinces. The All-China Federation of Trade Unions is running pilot programs in ten provinces and cities for enterprise union official wages to be paid by the higher-level union and not by the enterprise, as is currently the standard practice. If successful, the programme would be rolled out nationwide in 2012.

Performance Management

The Chinese government has been experimenting with ways to ensure that officials are judged not only by their superiors but also by the public. In other words, to ensure that officials 'look not only upward but also downward'.

In March 2008 former Premier Wen Jiabao stated that the government would introduce something called 'performance management' to evaluate the performance of civil servants. When Hangzhou introduced a 'Comprehensive Performance Assessment Scheme', half the credits came from public assessment. However by 'public' this meant members of the Municipal People's Congresses and People's Political Consultative Conference, as well as representatives of ordinary citizens, meaning 'scholars, businessmen, and journalists'.

A campaign inviting 10,000 people to assess the performance of government was also launched in Zhuhai, Shenyang and Nanjing. Nanjing sent out 8,438 assessment forms and received 6,373 responses. In addition, simplified questionnaires were sent to 23,400 residents. Ninety agencies under the municipal government were ranked in accordance with the results of the public assessment.

A Service Pledge scheme, a local initiative by the Yantai City of Shandong, was tried which was similar in intent to the UK's Citizen's Charter.

Experiments in Direct Elections

The Organic Law in Village Committees was launched in the late 1980s and since then there have been competitive elections in over 600,000 villages. However interest in direct village elections has worn off. The first township election was held in Buyun Township, Sichuan Province in 1998 but this was later declared illegal and unconstitutional.

More recently, Shenzhen has tried out direct elections for some local officials, creating a more independent judiciary and promoting greater openness and accountability with the Party. The plan, formally approved in June 2008, was concocted over three months by 24 specialised teams assigned by the Shenzhen Mayor to make Shenzhen 'a model for socialism with Chinese characteristics'. The local People's Congress has been given the power to supervise the local executive branch and be accountable to the people by allowing an expanding number of candidates to run in elections.

In Shenzhen three ordinary citizens began demanding access to budget information in 2006. They submitted requests to a dozen central governmental agencies and a dozen local governments, but were denied each time until in October 2008 the Shenzhen Department of Public Health permitted them to read the health budget. By the end of 2010, a third of 92 departments in Shenzhen had disclosed budget information.

Public Consultations on Local Budgets in Sichuan: Deliberative Polling in Wenling

In the fishing village of Wukan, Guangdong Province, villagers staged widely reported protests in 2011 because they believed officials had sold off their land to developers and failed to compensate them properly. Subsequently they were allowed to directly elect their own representatives.

A key concern across rural China is deciding what happens to the money when farmers' land is sold to developers. Villagers want adequate compensation and supervision of the funds.

In Wenling municipality, Sichuan, China has tested a new form of deliberative democracy (called 'democratic consultation') that allows local villagers to discuss local affairs and to make the local authorities more accountable and transparent.

The first democratic consultation meetings were carried out in Songmen township in 1999 and then in Xinhe and Zeguo township in 2005. The initial idea was to hold a public gathering for both cadres and locals to discuss public affairs rather than hold direct elections. In 2002, Wenling officials standardised the whole consultation process.

A participatory budgeting experiment conducted by local officials in Zeguo township of Wenling City (population of 240,000) was carried out in 2005. This technique was used to garner public feedback on a series of difficult budgetary allotment decisions for proposed infrastructure projects in the township. There were 30 potential public projects that year amounting to a total investment of RMB 137m (EUR 17.1m) while the government could only award RMB 40m (EUR 5m).

Of the entire population, 275 people were randomly selected to participate in surveys and deliberations taking part throughout the months of March and April. Participants filled out an initial questionnaire about their preferences and concerns, then attended a deliberative forum.

At the end of the process, the results of the poll were presented to the Zeguo's local People's Congress for further debate and deliberation by local politicians — a majority of whom voted to fund the top 12 projects ranked in the Deliberative Poll. After this, the local government adopted the Poll permanently and opted to open the entire budget to participatory feedback. The next step was to extend it throughout Wenling City.

Xinhe, another township in Wenling, tried to incorporate the democratic consultations within the existing political system by granting more power to the local

People's Congress. In 2005, Xinhe township leaders invited the People's Congress to discuss the annual budget draft and allow them to propose revisions. However, the local Congress was not elected by the villagers but appointed by superior officials. These reforms were not legalised and in 2007 Xinhe stopped further refinement of the participatory budget making.

These experiments were guided by Professor He Baogang of Deakin University and James Fishkin of Stanford University. These are just one set of a number of consultative and deliberative experiments that have taken place across China. For instance, in the Shangcheng district of Hangzhou city, a 'consensus conference', or 'consultative meeting' is held regularly once a month.

The first experiments started back in 1991, when the local People's Congress in Shenzhen set up a budget committee in which deputies had an opportunity to examine the budget. In 1998, Hebei province introduced sector budgeting, meaning that partial budgets were disclosed to the people's deputies of the People's Congress for examination and deliberation. In 2004, Huinan township in Shanghai also undertook an experiment in public budgeting.

Open Recommendation and Selection of Officials

This is a half-way house between a conventional Party nomination and congress ratification, and a direct election. It was first implemented in the Shizhong District of Suining Municipality in Sichuan and has since been tried out in 18 municipalities and 30 counties in Sichuan Province.

There are usually four steps in the whole open recommendation and selection process: application and qualification, written examination, and nomination. Qualified applicants, based on criteria of education (college degree at least), experience (administrative ranking requirement) and age (usually under 40), are recommended by the Party branch, a group of usually five villagers, or by the applicants themselves. The candidates are then cut down to six according to their grades in the written exam, covering economics, public administration, agricultural production, laws, science and history.

The finalists must then pass another oral exam, give speeches on predetermined topics in front of representative groups composed of Party members, government cadres, and People's Congress representatives, the candidates who receive the most votes from the representative group will win the position. Finally, the township

People's Congress approves the results and nominates the elected township head, while the higher-level Party committee addresses the Party secretary.

Conclusions

The CCP's enthusiasm for such experiments in reforms has waxed and waned over the years but it looks like the new leadership who will come to power at the 18th Party Congress will make a renewed push to deepen public consultation. In his last press conference Wen Jiabao announced the Party's determination to push through more political reforms. As such, China is open to learning from the experiences of other countries.

Chinese experts interviewed for this paper expressed very different views about what has been tried so far. Some were openly dismissive of their significance but others claimed that in the Chinese context a lot was being done and a body of experience had been accumulated.

We know from what happened to other areas that once the CCP has drawn its conclusions from such experiments, they could then be applied on a national scale.

The EU and its Member States could help by enabling more Chinese experts and Party advisers to travel around Europe observing local democracy at work at different levels of local government. That way they could gather their own ideas of what might work in China and then come back and try to get these tested in China. China could, for instance, explore the effectiveness of the UK's Citizen's Charter and the various experiments in the UK and other countries in e-democracy, or the different methods used by citizens to supervise the formulation of local budgets.

Clearly, the most innovative places in China are Shenzhen and Guangdong, and Sichuan and Chongqing, and the EU could try to foster relations with officials and academics in those places.

Section Three
Chinese International Relations

An Assessment of EU–China Relations in Global Governance Forums
(August 2012)

Giovanni B. Andornino

Assistant Professor of International Relations of East Asia, Department of Culture, Politics and Society, University of Torino

Executive Summary

China and the EU are both confronting a critical transition, whose outcomes will affect the mid- to long-term horizon of EU–China cooperation at the multilateral level. Beijing needs to reignite stalled institutional reforms at home, and strike a new balance between state intervention in the economy and market play to guarantee the sustainability of China's development. In Europe, the outcome of the euro crisis will determine how the material constitution of an increasingly two-speed EU shapes up and whether it can emerge as a more cohesive multi-level actor, addressing China's frustration with Brussels' seeming inability to act as a more autonomous 'pole' in international affairs.

With the recent financial crisis marking a systemic watershed, the EU should aim to create strategic space for engaging China in the remoulding of the institutional landscape of post-crisis global finance and trade. As the post-neoliberal era awaits definition, the EU has an opportunity to upgrade the profile of European discourses on economic governance and leverage Beijing's manifest interest in reforming the international monetary and financial systems. This would anchor China to a more legitimate international order, and provide constructive exogenous pressure for Beijing to implement difficult domestic reforms which can have global implications, including on key European economic interests.

The G20 is regarded both by China and the EU as a critical platform to generate political momentum for more effective global governance. Beijing has actively raised its profile from peripheral to core actor within the G20, as the forum fits several of its foreign policy priorities, including the enhancement of China's status, mitigation of external pressures and trust generation. For the EU the G20 is instrumental to increase internal cohesion and ensure that newly emerged and emerging countries perceive to have a stake in global governance. The EU and China share an ambition for the G20 to pursue sustainable global growth by encouraging diffuse domestic structural adjustments, fiscal consolidation in advanced economies and the restructuring of China's development paradigm to reduce global imbalances. Despite an apparent decline in effectiveness after 2009, the G20 has made progress in multilateral regulatory oversight through the Financial Stability Board. As the international financial system stabilises, it is now important for the EU to engage China in defining a post-emergency mission for the G20, and designing a new G20+ institutional formula with an agile permanent secretariat, coupled with a G20 advisory council of independent experts.

The EU can leverage the political capital arising from more robust leadership in the reform of Bretton Woods institutions to steer China's manifest interest in a more level international monetary playing field through joint contingency planning in preparation for a multipolar phase, to be followed by a new multilateral regime. Monetary and financial stability can be strengthened by China diversifying its currency portfolio and spreading risk: the EU can build on a strategic convergence of interests with China in this field by positioning the euro credibly as a global reserve currency and supporting the gradual internationalisation of the renminbi.

The EU and China are active participants in the WTO legal framework, reinforcing the role of the WTO dispute settlement system as a stand-in for incremental trade regulation. Pursuing a comprehensive negotiation of a Europe-wide agreement on investment with China, while deploying a comprehensive EU external public procurement policy would further encourage China to fulfil its obligations in the WTO and increase the staying power of free trade at a particularly critical juncture. This would create opportunities abroad and cut government costs at home both in Europe and in China and would be coherent with the EU's 2020

Strategy and China's 12th Five Year Programme, which converge on the strategic pursuit of green and sustainable growth based on an innovative economy.

Main Points

- Both the EU and China are facing a phase of critical transition domestically, whose outcomes will bear significant consequences on the mid- to long-term horizon of EU–China cooperation at the multilateral level.
- China has shown increasing frustration with the EU's seeming inability to emerge as a more unified, autonomous 'pole' in international affairs, but in the aftermath of the recent systemic crisis the EU can aim to create new strategic space for engaging China in the remoulding of the institutional landscape of the global financial and monetary systems.
- China has grown to regard the G20 as the most important multilateral global governance platform for economic and financial matters, and one coherent with several of its foreign policy priorities, including status enhancement, mitigation of external pressures, trust generation, and access to opportunities to become better acquainted with multilateral governance practices.
- The EU and China support the G20 to pursue sustainable global growth by encouraging diffuse domestic structural adjustments, fiscal consolidation in advanced economies, and the restructuring of China's development paradigm to reduce global imbalances.
- Despite an apparent decline in G20 performance since 2009, progress has been made in multilateral regulatory oversight through the Financial Stability Board; the EU should encourage China to support a more ambitious G20+ formula with an agile permanent secretariat, coupled with a G20 advisory council of independent experts.
- While EU–China cooperation in the IMF is affected by the over-representation of Member States and the non-representation of the EU itself, the EU should leverage the political capital arising from more robust leadership in the reform of Bretton Woods institutions (including relinquishing traditional European prerogatives over the office of IMF director and unilaterally renouncing a potential eurozone veto power) to steer China's interest in a more level international monetary playing field through joint contingency planning in preparation for a multipolar phase, to be followed by a new multilateral regime.

- Fundamentally aligned in support of free trade, the EU and China are active participants in the WTO legal framework, reinforcing the role of the WTO dispute settlement system as a stand-in for incremental trade regulation, which helps to preserve the overall staying power of free trade at the current critical juncture.
- Through an early concession of Market Economy Status and the de-linking of non-trade goals from trade negotiations, the EU should neutralise irritants with China and focus on an ambitious Europe-wide agreement on investment with China and on the development of a comprehensive EU external public procurement policy to induce the Chinese authorities to fulfil their obligations in the WTO by submitting a comprehensive Government Procurement Agreement, better aligning to international standards, and generally increasing market access for EU companies in China.

Introduction: Europe, China and Multilateralism

Both China and the EU are confronted by a pressing need to make good of the ambitious agendas for institutional reform that are being discussed in the run-up to the third plenary session of the XVIII central committee of the Chinese Communist Party (expected in November 2013),[17] and to the elections of the European Parliament in 2014, with the subsequent renewal of the leadership of the top EU institutions. Whether and how Beijing and Brussels achieve their goals domestically will affect prospects for enhanced cooperation between the two at the multilateral level.

The EU's profile as a global actor has been in a state of flux since 2009, when the coming into force of the Lisbon treaty coincided with the most severe financial crisis to hit Europe since 1929. The EU's capacity to play a strategically meaningful role at the international level in the future is thus fundamentally a function of its ability to carry out effective reforms on the domestic front today. The outcome of the euro crisis will determine whether the European project retains legitimacy in the eyes of its own public and how the material constitution of an increasingly two-speed EU shapes up. Failure would invalidate ambitions to leverage Europe's unique experience in sovereignty pooling to foster global governance practices

---

[17] The third plenary session was held in Beijing, November 9 to 12, 2013. It resulted in an extremely articulate "CCP Central Committee Resolution concerning some major issues in comprehensively deepening reform"; a full translation is available at: http://chinacopyrightandmedia.wordpress.com/2013/11/15/ccp-central-committee-resolution-concerning-some-major-issues-in-comprehensively-deepening-reform. Accessed 5 December 2013.

based on legalised frameworks of multilateral interaction. Success would graduate the Union past its security-preserving, market-enhancing credentials into a more cohesive multi-level political actor, boosting its credibility and influence at the international level.

The People's Republic of China (PRC) does not share the EU's normative commitment to multilateralism. Rather than viewing it as a tool to foster governance, Beijing mostly conceives multilateralism as a way to reproduce sovereignty, steering international order in directions that better reflect China's role and preferences, while constraining its foreign policy autonomy as little as possible. The Chinese notion of 'harmony' in international society is as much a rejection of conflicts that may derail China's development as a statement affirming the intrinsic legitimacy of political-economic models and values alternative to Western democratic liberalism. Having moved incrementally away from its non-aligned, sovereignist posture, the PRC today sees global challenges as becoming more prominent and security threats as increasingly integrated and volatile, in a context of global power diffusion. However, while the EU fears marginalisation in a world characterised by competitive multipolarity, Beijing favours the informal dynamics of great power concert diplomacy. Although the political transition in Beijing is unlikely to alter the course of China's foreign policy in the short term, there is growing consensus both inside and outside China that the PRC's political-institutional system is in urgent need of reform, while a new balance between state intervention in the economy and market play needs to be struck to guarantee the sustainability of China's development.

The PRC's frustration with the seeming inability of the EU to emerge as a more unified and autonomous 'pole' in international affairs, especially with regards to specific US desires, accounts for the relative loss of momentum in EU–China relations since the mid-2000s. Today, however, just as the dynamics generated by the financial crisis risk further denting the Union's profile as a meaningful partner at the multilateral level, the structural fragility of the global economic landscape offers strategic space for constructive engagement with China.

The G20: Catalysing Political Impulse to Enhance Global Governance

Established by the diplomacies of the US and major European countries, which remain the principal agenda setters, the G20 Leaders' Summit is one of the few multilateral forums where China has actively raised its profile from peripheral to core actor. Beijing has grown to regard the G20 as the most important multilateral global governance platform for economic and financial matters. As a forum operating by consensus to reform the global regulatory system, enhance surveillance and improve cooperation among the world's main advanced and emerging economies, the G20 fits several key foreign policy priorities of the Chinese government:

- It allows China to see its status as a newly emerged global power entrenched without being associated with the 'hegemonistic' aura of the Western-dominated G8.
- It preserves the strategic ambiguity of the PRC's profile as a world power that can choose to cast itself as merely the 'largest developing country' to mitigate external pressure and claim diplomatic affinity with developing nations.
- It reduces the risk of an undesired drift towards a G-2 or G-3 configuration of global governance practices, which would force China to abandon its cherished approach of 'keeping a low profile and acting proactively in a prudent, parsimonious way'.
- It facilitates a relatively hands-off learning process in an informal context where Chinese leaders can present China's positions and foster trust.

For the EU, which has its own seat at the G20 in addition to the four attributed to its largest Member States, the visibility and political weight acquired by the forum shapes a *de facto* dual system of global governance. It raises questions about its representativeness and how informal multilateral political impulse is translated into verifiable binding commitments. However, lack of consensus for substantial reform of the UN and other formal institutions, means that the G20 forum has become a critical proxy to ensure that newly emerged and emerging countries perceive to have a stake in global governance. This is especially true for China, whose self-awareness as the linchpin of the global economy has been nurtured by its participation at G20 meetings, fostering a more assertive posture that eschews past behaviour as a rule-taker.

Both the EU and China have benefited domestically from participation in the G20. EU coordination ahead of summits has improved, increasing its credibility as it takes advantage of the G20 platform to protect the euro while advancing a wider reform agenda for the global financial architecture. China has found in the G20 an ideal forum to move past its tendency to passively adapt to international norms or engage in preventive revisionism, honing its understanding of global governance practices. G20 recommendations also serve as an expedient external pressure to enhance the domestic political momentum for Beijing's economic reforms.

The performance of the G20 has appeared to suffer from a decline in effectiveness after the initial successes of 2009. Yet, although the *realpolitik* of national interests and significant industry resistance have slowed the pace of reforms, especially in the financial sector, substantial progress has been made in some areas of multilateral regulatory oversight through the efforts of the Financial Stability Board (FSB). The publication of the FSB's traffic lights scoreboard to track progress in the implementation of financial reforms has been endorsed by the G20 and offers reason for cautious optimism, as the degree of Member States' compliance with G20 recommendations has not been disappointing. The G20 decision at the recent Los Cabos summit to place the FSB on an enduring organisational footing, with legal personality, strengthened governance, greater financial autonomy, and enhanced capacity to coordinate the development and implementation of financial regulatory policies underlines the forum's commitment to a consistent implementation of financial reforms, which is essential to avoid the fragmentation of global financial system.

The EU and China share an ambition for the G20 to pursue sustainable global growth by encouraging diffuse domestic structural adjustments. This approach, in partial contrast to the US policy of quantitative easing, calls for fiscal consolidation in G20 advanced economies and a reduction of global imbalances through the restructuring of China's investment-/export-led development paradigm towards greater consumption. China's decision at Los Cabos to inject USD 43 bn (EUR 34 bn) in the IMF firewall set up to contain Europe's debt crisis is as much a reflection of Beijing's ambition to enhance its influence in Bretton Woods institutions, as it is proof of the stakes China sees for itself in the EU economy, in the euro as an alternative reserve currency to the dollar, and in the credibility of a (continental) European intellectual counterpoint to Anglo-Saxon neoliberal economic thinking.

With polemics on China's currency manipulation a politically induced irritant, and debates on how to define and monitor global imbalances a case of European division, risks of divergence between the EU and China at the G20 remain, but appear manageable and not of strategic significance. The two sides have a fundamental interest in preserving the efficacy of this platform. While at the height of the 2008–2009 crisis political momentum for enhancing the G20 hardly needed to be generated — as intense pressure was brought about by chaos in the financial markets and an immediate risk of systemic financial meltdown — with the global financial system now seemingly more stable, the urgency to define a post-emergency mission for the G20 has become apparent. This is a crucial debate in which the EU can leverage its unparalleled experience in multilateral governance to engage China in proposing that the G20 be cast — and reported about — as an incremental, drawn-out process with clearer mid-term ambitions.

Bretton Woods: Reforming the IMF into a 'Barking Watchdog'

EU–China cooperation in the IMF is fundamentally affected by the twin problems of the over-representation of Member States and the non-representation of the EU itself. These issues should be seen in the wider context of the forthcoming implementation of a quota revision that, despite lifting China to third-largest shareholder, penalises developing economies, preserves the US veto power, and allows the sum of EU Member States' quotas to far exceed that of BRICS countries. The Union's role in the IMF is further complicated by the fact that the EU combines a major exclusive competence on monetary policy for the eurozone with shared competences on economic policy at the EU27 level. Debate over structural reform of the Fund's voting shares — affected by a potential voluntary consolidation of eurozone states' quotas into a single seat — is thus a prime sphere for engagement between the EU and China.

If properly leveraged in the perspective of a more comprehensive revision of IMF governance mechanisms, the leadership shown by EU Member States in quota distribution could constitute a positive background for further engaging China. Beijing has made its commitment to Bretton Woods institutions manifest by sending extremely capable officials to operate in them, but also by arguing for increased representation for new economic heavyweights, and by offering ambitious proposals for the reform of the international monetary system.

In the latter realm, although European countries have long been tolerant of the 'exorbitant privilege' enjoyed by the US as the provider of global liquidity, concern has grown for the systemic distortions generated by Washington's reliance on monetary short-cuts to exit a financial crisis provoked by its own institutional failures in the first place. Although China has publicly offered a proposal to mitigate dollar centrality by enhancing the global role of IMF Special Drawing Rights — a healthy indicator of Beijing's willingness to stimulate rulemaking — the EU has not been keen to confront its transatlantic ally on this key front as of yet.

Chinese confidence in European leadership at the IMF, however, may be stimulated in other crucial areas. Given the euro's role as the only alternative to the dollar for its capacity to absorb Chinese liquidity, the EU has a natural shared interest with China in cooperating with the Fund to strengthen the single currency, while at the same time, cooperating to facilitate the internationalisation of the Chinese renmimbi beyond the current highly constrained set of purposes.

Secondly, both actors lament the IMF's failure to act as a reliable watchdog ahead of the 2008 global financial crisis. While China's rigidity on the definition and monitoring of global imbalances is matched by divisions within the EU on the same subject, both actors welcome greater institutional transparency at the Fund and an increase in its early warning and crisis-prevention capacity. The EU should further support China's request that the Fund promote professional training for personnel from developing nations to increase their ability to participate in IMF technical mechanisms.

While that of transforming the Fund into a truly independent, 'barking watchdog' is a profoundly political issue, the current economic and intellectual *milieu* favours ambitious structural reforms. Rather than witnessing the multiplication of veto power holders through a possible eurozone quota consolidation, the EU should publicly review the informal custom of having a European director of the IMF — a bargaining position unlikely to keep its salience for long — and invest its political capital to anchor both China and the US to a more level monetary playing field.

The WTO: Strengthening the Staying Power of Free Trade

A unique case among China's main international partners, EU–China relations do not owe their relevance to strategic or geopolitical calculus, but essentially to bilateral and international trade. The EU remains the world's largest exporter of manufactured goods and services, and the biggest export market for over 100 countries, including China. China's economic growth — and the overall stability of the Chinese polity — is in turn vitally dependent on exports (and imports, mostly from its own region). Brussels and Beijing thus fundamentally share a free trade agenda, a commitment reflected in Europe's leading role in General Agreement on Tariffs and Trade (GATT) and WTO negotiations, and, more recently, in China's seriousness about implementing the bulk of its WTO obligations in timely fashion.

In spite of this and the regularity of the dialogue between the two — during the annual EU–China Summit, EU–China High Level Economic and Trade Dialogue and sectoral dialogues — cooperation is declining, although by the law of unintended consequences this might work to the reinforcement of the WTO itself.

The weakening of political impetus for greater reduction of global trade barriers has become apparent in the continuing failure of the Doha round, but also in the perceived decline in support for free trade inside most advanced countries, most notably the US. As Washington and Brussels become more concerned about their trade deficits with China and global trade recovers slowly after the sharp contraction of 2009, divergences and competing interests with China gain traction among publics and policy makers.

The EU is finding it increasingly difficult to induce China to open various spheres of its economy to foreign investment, starting with the service sector. Beijing's peculiar national technical standards often function as non-tariff barriers further limiting access into the Chinese market, while incomplete protection of intellectual property rights, preferential treatment of domestic (and especially state-owned) enterprises, bureaucratic hurdles and a still-missing accession to the WTO Agreement on Government Procurement constitute severe obstacles to European business opportunities in the Chinese market.

Frustration with China's lack of progress helps explain the growing recourse to the WTO's dispute settlement system. After the initial grace period following China's accession in 2001, the cases debated are moving progressively closer to the heart of Chinese industrial policies and related domestic regulation. While operating on opposing fronts, however, China and the EU effectively participate in the WTO legal framework, thus strengthening the credibility of the WTO dispute settlement system, reinforcing the role of WTO panels and the Appellate Body as stand-in 'legislators' for incremental trade regulation, and augmenting the overall staying power of free trade in the current critical juncture.

The EU has so far appeared to have little capacity to counter the deterioration of the business environment in China. An early concession of Market Economy Status to China and the de-linking of normative, non-trade goals such as human rights, cultural diversity and sustainable development from trade negotiations could be employed to extract a set of 'WTO-plus' commitments to further open Chinese markets in investment and services.

Concluding Remarks and Policy Recommendations

While management of expectations remains important to maximise the impact of the EU's commitment to cooperating with China in global governance forums, it is essential that the Union upgrades the profile of European discourses on economic governance as the post-neoliberal era awaits definition. Depending on its future domestic developments, the EU can aim to create strategic space for engaging China in the remoulding of the institutional landscape of post-crisis global finance and trade. This would both anchor China to a more representative and legitimate international order, and provide constructive exogenous pressure for Beijing to implement vital domestic reforms with systemic implications.

Europe's experience in multilateral trust-building via the encapsulation of partners' interests is a key asset. Its finalistic approach, however, is at odds with Chinese culture at large, and specifically with Beijing's current perspective that an emerging power is best served by time-biding, free-riding behaviour. Greater intra-EU solidarity, substantive and perceived EU loyalty to global governance, and a new capacity to bargain hard on a lean, cohesive portfolio of key desired outcomes will place the EU on a stronger footing in preventing the erosion of global order.

The G20 has to date been one of the most successful instances of China's active participation in global governance forums. The EU should resist the widening of the G20 mandate to include overly ambitious development and climate agendas, given that unhelpful normative abrasion is likely to occur with China in these fields. Rather, the Union should leverage common strategic interests to cooperate with China in focusing the G20 agenda on the reform of the international financial and monetary systems. New codes of conduct and regulatory regimes for sovereign rating agencies would be a substantial first step forward to create the momentum for more ambitious measures, including in the definition of a regime for managing hot capital flows that can be the cause of extreme market volatility.

While the intergovernmental nature of the G20 summits at head of state level is an asset to be preserved, at the institutional level, the EU should encourage China to support a more ambitious G20+ formula. Here, the limitations currently imposed by the rotating chair system could be tackled through the establishment of an agile permanent secretariat, coupled with a G20 advisory council. While the secretariat would serve as a tool to avert risks of fragmentation and short-termism in the definition and pursuit of the G20 agenda, independent experts making up the advisory council would be tasked with strengthening intra-G20 peer-review processes, preventing their deterioration into 'peer protection' dynamics — which, in an age of intense interdependence, would be lethal to the G20 and to global interest at large. The council ought to be afforded a degree of concurrent authority over the G20 agenda with the freedom to make recommendation proposals and it should be guaranteed adequate media visibility. Both entities should be based in Asia to balance the Western-centric arrangements of other global institutions, with Hong Kong a potential candidate as host city.

The EU should further engage China's manifest interest in reforming the international monetary system. By relinquishing traditional European prerogatives over the office of the IMF director and unilaterally renouncing a potential eurozone veto power, the EU would make a powerful contribution to the reform of the IMF into a more independent, veto-free 'barking watchdog'. The Union should leverage the political capital arising from leadership in IMF reform to seek Chinese and US commitment to a more level monetary playing field in view of the gradual, relative decline of the US economy and of the dollar as the sole reserve currency. Specifically, the EU should engage China in contingency planning for an impending multipolar phase in the international monetary system, to be followed by a new multilateral regime.[18] The EU — and the eurozone in particular — should take the necessary political steps to position the euro credibly as a global reserve currency, including governance reforms, the streamlining of the eurozone external representation, and the creation of a eurobond market to supply reserve assets. China's efforts to progressively internationalise its currency through the development of an offshore market and the stimulation of re-denomination of Chinese trade should be supported.

Monetary and financial stability would be enhanced by increased Chinese investment in Europe, enabling China to diversify its currency portfolio and spread risk. This dynamic should be steered by the EU to translate into greater EU–China cooperation in bilateral trade and investment. The EU should neutralise irritants through an early concession of Market Economy Status to China and the de-linking of normative, non-trade goals from trade negotiations. It should further pursue

---

[18] M. Camdessus, A. Lamfalussy, T. Padoa-Schioppa, et. al., 'Reform of the international monetary system: a cooperative approach for the twenty first century', Paris, February 2011. Available at: http://global-currencies.org/smi/gb/telechar/news/Rapport_Camdessus-integral.pdf. Accessed 30 October 2013.

a comprehensive negotiation of a Europe-wide agreement on investment with China, which would improve the current patchwork of bilateral agreements to the benefit of both EU and Chinese investors. Contextually, it should finalise the development of a comprehensive EU external public procurement policy that includes mechanisms to encourage the EU's trading partners to start market access discussions where necessary. The objective should be to induce the Chinese authorities to fulfil their obligations in the WTO and submit a comprehensive Government Procurement Agreement offer that reflects public procurement realities (i.e. that a large proportion of China's public procurement is carried out at local levels and by state-owned enterprises). The EU should stress that GPA implementation would create opportunities abroad and cut government costs at home for China, while an agreement that encourages European investments into its economy would foster innovation and competition in China, in line with its 12th Five Year Programme.

China's Response to the US 'Return to Asia' Tour
(February 2012)

Andrew Small

Transatlantic Fellow, Asia Program, German Marshall Fund of the United States

Executive Summary

- President Obama's visit to the region in November 2011 was the first to take place under the auspices of the US 'pivot to Asia', a strategic orientation that was laid out by Secretary Clinton in her *Foreign Policy* article that month.
- While the articulation is new, much of the groundwork was laid in the last couple of years, and it builds on important initiatives that were launched under the previous administration. Moreover, central tenets of US strategy in Asia itself — the alliance system and the hedged approach to China — are long-standing.
- Yet the 'pivot' amounts to far more than a modest evolution in US policy. When seen in the context of the current challenges in the region and the broader shifts underway in US global posture, it is arguably the most significant American foreign policy development of the last decade.
- Regional anxieties about an assertive China have grown more acute, with rising concern about Beijing's willingness to escalate bilateral disputes and press its territorial claims. Yet the Chinese economy remains a major driver of growth for many countries in the region. China's neighbours have been nervous to see whether the US can steer an effective course between an accommodation with China that would leave them vulnerable to Chinese coercion, and a

confrontational relationship with Beijing that would create insecurity in the region and force them to choose sides.
- There have also been broader questions hanging over US policy in Asia. Some are more recent: will the US maintain the scale of its military presence in the region during a time of budget cutbacks? Others have a longer vintage: is the United States willing to play the diplomatic 'game' in Asia — investing energy in the emerging multilateral architecture and its long list of summits — or has it ceded that field? And is there a credible US trade and economic agenda to match the political and security one?
- The pivot is an attempt by Washington to provide convincing answers to these questions and it is doing so by way of a genuine strategic choice: a reduction in the US diplomatic, economic and security focus on Europe and the wider Middle East in order to maintain or upgrade commitments in Asia.
- The implications for the EU are wide ranging. In some respects, there are opportunities: US China policy is increasingly characterised by efforts to seek cooperation with other like-minded countries; the US also faces a growing need for burden sharing in parts of the world where its commitments are being reduced.
- Yet the challenges outweigh them. At present, Europeans are not seen as natural partners to the US in Asia, and avenues for consultation and EU influence in Washington on Asia policy are less extensive than with other regions. Moreover, Europe and the European periphery will simply command less US attention. There are already signs of US impatience: both that Europe is too slow to 'step up' in relieving the US on matters of security in its neighbourhood, and that the Europeans are clinging on to votes and seats in international institutions that the US would rather see go to emerging Asia.
- Naturally the EU will not want to set itself up in Asia as 'just' a US partner. It has its own distinct relationships, goals and policies. But the US will have a crucial role in shaping the future of a region that is central to European interests too. The EU should move quickly to take advantage of long-standing transatlantic affinities and mechanisms and position itself as one of Washington's principal counterparts when it comes to dealing with Asia.
- China's own response is still indeterminate. While undoubtedly unhappy at the direction of US policy, Beijing faces the problem that many of its potential actions only risk worsening its strategic situation. Chinese policy makers are

uncomfortably aware that it is China's own behaviour that has driven countries to seek closer security ties with the US and with each other, and understands that an ill-considered response will only deepen the perception that its rise is a threat.
- While China remains the most dynamic economic force in the region, it has not managed to convert that fact into a latent network of friends and allies of its own or any fraying of US alliances. Unless it is willing to risk escalating confrontation in the region, a period of rebuilding relationships with its neighbours may prove its only viable option in the short term.
- Early indications are that Beijing recognises this, and is acting on it. But it is also evident that a pattern of strategic competition between the US and China in Asia is becoming endemic, with important ramifications for European policy choices.

Introduction: Pre-Pivot

The essentials of US policy in Asia have been mostly consistent across the post-Cold War period, and arguably since the opening of relations with China. Economically, the US has played a leading role in pushing trade and economic linkages — bilaterally, regionally, and through drawing Asian states into the global trade and financial architecture. At the same time, concerns over China's intentions in the region have long been thought to require a hedging strategy, which, alongside a comprehensive engagement effort, necessitates a strong US security presence and a robust network of alliances.

The composition of the friendships and alliances has shifted over time. The Bush administration did much to enlarge the pool of US 'friends' in Asia, bringing Indonesia and Vietnam closer to Washington, and establishing the breakthrough US–India partnership. It also sought to move the regional security architecture beyond the traditional 'hub-and-spoke' model to encourage the expansion of ties between its allies. Simultaneously, despite early tensions over the downing of a US spy plane, Washington built a substantial framework of consultation and cooperation with Beijing, particularly during President Bush's second term.

Criticisms were levelled at US policy during this period: that it was dismissive of multilateral gatherings in the region (with Secretary Rice notably skipping the ASEAN Regional Forum (ARF) meetings in 2005 and 2007); overly focused on counter-terrorism in its early phase, and on North Korea in its latter phase; and insufficiently concerned with economic and trade relations. Its policy was at times unfavourably contrasted with a China that was heavily focused on economic interests, and adept at putting in diplomatic legwork with regional groupings. Nonetheless, in navigating the difficult balancing act of deepening its alliances while simultaneously maintaining a strong relationship with China, the Bush administration generally scored high marks in the region.

To describe the US as 'returning' to Asia therefore seems misplaced, and it is notable that it is a term most actively used by commentators and officials in China, who are keen to imply that the US role is fickle, provisional and unnatural. But the Obama administration was not above using a little of that rhetoric itself in dramatising some of its early moves. Both the Secretary of State and the President made symbolic early trips to the region. Washington took steps to address perceptions that the US was unwilling to put in summit face-time and unsupportive of the emerging multilateral architecture, most importantly by signing ASEAN's Treaty of Amity and Cooperation (TAC) and seeking membership of the East Asian Summit (EAS). It consolidated initiatives such as the India partnership that some feared may prove to be a one-administration shot. And it expanded the US focus on Southeast Asia, the source of most of the complaints about Washington 'neglecting' the region.

Much of this was occluded in public perceptions, however, by the other major focus of the Obama administration in Asia: upgrading bilateral relations with China. The view of some US policy makers was that by forging consensus with Beijing on areas of global concern and taking a relatively conciliatory stance on areas of Chinese sensitivity, it may be possible to erode the pervasive mistrust in the relationship. Meetings with the Dalai Lama and arms sales to Taiwan appeared to be slow-pedalled, attempts to find signature cooperation projects on climate change were launched, and US officials gave speeches on the subject of 'strategic reassurance'. The highpoint was supposed to be President Obama's first visit to China in November 2009, which saw the release of an unusually extensive joint statement spelling out an agenda for bilateral cooperation. Speculation about a new 'G2' in global affairs reached its peak.

Whether this approach would have worked in other circumstances is a moot point. With the economic crisis as a backdrop, China, rather than seeing US gestures as farsighted and magnanimous, treated them as symptoms of weakness and decline. Chinese assertiveness had already been fanned by the financial crisis, out of which it seemed to emerge as a relative 'winner'. The first year of the new administration confirmed an emerging view in Beijing that its strengthened position entitled it to demand more of other countries. The final months of 2009 acted as the denouement for this period in the US–China relationship. President Obama's visit to China played poorly in the US press, which contended that he had not been extended privileges that his predecessors received. Beijing seemed to pocket concessions from Washington while offering almost nothing in return. From bilateral economic issues to Iran sanctions, China rebuffed US requests virtually across the board. The culmination was the COP15 talks in Copenhagen, where Beijing managed to raise hackles not just with the substance of its position at the talks but with its almost insulting manner, which seemed to portend an ugly period of Chinese assertiveness ahead.

The US response was to push back, making it clear that China had misjudged the relative strength of its position. In rapid succession, Washington pressed ahead with arms sales to Taiwan and a Dalai Lama meeting at the White House, eliciting sharp responses from Beijing that went well beyond the usual pro forma complaints. Following the visit to Beijing in March 2010 by James Steinberg, Deputy Secretary of State, and Jeffrey Bader, Senior Director for Asian Affairs at the National Security Council, an agreement was reached for a mutually choreographed de-escalation of diplomatic hostilities, as well as progress on two issues of high US concern — currency revaluation and Iran. But this still-frosty accord was limited to the US–China relationship alone: the rest of the region saw continued manifestations of Chinese assertiveness throughout the year. After Japan arrested a Chinese fishing boat captain in September 2010, Beijing cut off rare earth exports, and demanded an apology even after his release. India saw a creeping escalation of pressure on border disputes. March 2010 saw some of the first references to the South China Sea being a Chinese 'core interest', on a par with Taiwan and Tibet. South Korea watched China give virtual *carte blanche* to North Korean aggression after the sinking of the Cheonan, a South Korean corvette, in March 2010, and the artillery attack on Yeonpyeong Island in November. But perhaps the symbolic low-point was the ARF meeting in July 2010, when, one by one, an array of Southeast Asian states raised their concerns about China's stance on the South China Sea issue — eliciting a fuming response from Chinese Foreign Minister Yang Jiechi that 'China is a big country and other countries are small countries and that is just a fact'.

The pattern of behaviour on all sides since the abortive effort at 'strategic reassurance' and the litany of incidents in 2010 has largely continued. While a fragile equilibrium has been maintained in US–China relations, including a successful visit to the US by Hu Jintao in January 2011, countries in the region have actively sought to upgrade relations with the US as a hedge against Chinese assertiveness. Those that were previously inhibited about expanding their own security capacities or developing intra-regional ties that might be seen as threatening by China, now perceive these steps to be necessary. The US has been ready and able to take advantage of China's missteps to shore up and expand its ties in Asia, as well as smoothing the way for developments such as a greater Indian role in the region and closer Japanese ties with a once (and still) reluctant South Korea.

Pivoting from the Greater Middle East

Several other factors provide the backdrop to the developments of late 2011. The first half of the year saw personnel shifts play a small role: the architects of the early phase of Obama's China policy stepped down, leaving a more alliance-focused team in full charge of Asian affairs. But more consequential has been the administration's changing attitude to the conflict once expected to be the defining issue for Obama's foreign policy. The administration's initial intentions to focus efforts on the 'right war' in Afghanistan (rather than the 'wrong' one in Iraq) resulted in proposals to launch a major counter-insurgency campaign there. Yet following an exhaustive review process across much of 2009, and disappointing results from its early counter-insurgency efforts, there was a growing sense that such a campaign would be doomed to failure — and a meaningless failure too, if the primary threat lay on the Pakistani side of the border. Struggles to achieve results in Afghanistan contrasted with the successes of an expanded programme of drone strikes and special operations raids in Pakistan. These were the tools of choice for those advocating a lighter US footprint in the region and a narrower focus on counter-terrorism.

Plans for a surge in Afghanistan were hence quickly matched by Obama with plans for a transition and drawdown of US forces — both being announced in the very same December 2009 speech. When combined with the conclusion of combat operations in Iraq, the stage was set for an end to what Assistant Secretary of State for East Asian and Pacific Affairs Kurt Campbell, described as a 'little bit of a Middle East detour over the course of the last ten years'. Even the Arab Spring did little to weaken that resolve. The Obama administration showed its determination not to get sucked into the Middle East at Asia's expense throughout its deeply ambivalent approach to NATO's campaign in Libya. Instead it stuck to the line advanced by then-new National Security Advisor Thomas Donilon, that the US was still 'overweighted' in the greater Middle East and 'underweighted' in Asia. When the Department of Defense in 2011/2012 found itself in the unusual position of having to make some brutal choices — as deficit reduction needs finally reached the door of a previously protected Pentagon — Asia was the only region clearly shielded from the multi-hundred-billion dollar blow.

Pivoting to Asia

Many of the arguments for the 'pivot' were pulled together in Hillary Clinton's November 2011 *Foreign Policy* article, 'America's Pacific Century': that the region is vital to America's strategic and economic future; that the US is vital to the security of the region; that this is a crucial period comparable to US engagement in the institution-building of post-war Europe; and that countries in the region wonder 'whether we are really there to stay' and 'whether we can make and keep credible strategic and economic commitments'. President Obama then put in motion various elements of the administration's strategy at the Bali EAS, the Asia-Pacific Economic Cooperation (APEC) Summit in Hawaii, and a visit to Australia that featured the announcement of a new US marine presence in Darwin.

However, several important points stand out beyond the case advanced in the article:

- The public diplomacy around the pivot serves to reassure states in Asia that are concerned about the future US commitment in the region, and pre-empt anxieties about the review of the US defence budget, while putting China on watch that the US will not play a declining role in its neighbourhood.
- There is an effort, through the Trans-Pacific Partnership (TPP), to demonstrate that Washington is at least cognisant of the need for a serious economic and trade component to its engagement with the region — and that China is not the only country that can make the weather in this respect. It also acts as a warning that China itself is in danger of missing out on this new phase of 'high-quality' trade deals due to its unwillingness to move sufficiently seriously on crucial issues ranging from state subsidies to intellectual property rights theft. In conjunction with the trade enforcement panel announced during the 2012 State of the Union address, it is clear that there will be an attempt to toughen up US China trade policy, especially during election year, and find ways to

navigate around China where possible — an economic 'hedging strategy' of sorts for the US in the region.
- With Obama's attendance at the EAS (the first by a US president) the US has signalled that — with the support of states in the region — it will now take an expanded role in shaping its new multilateral architecture rather than sitting on the sidelines. With the exception of a couple of delayed Presidential visits to Australia and Indonesia, the commitment from senior US officials to putting in time in the region, despite exceptional pressures at home, has been exemplary, and has acted as a statement of intent. Moreover, US support for 'open regionalism' will not be restricted to the US — other states such as India are being drawn into more active roles in the region too.
- US force numbers in the region will not necessarily be greatly increased, but they will be more dispersed. With the heavy concentration of forces in Japan potentially at long-term risk from China's expanding military capabilities, an expanded set of basing arrangements with other allies such as Australia and the Philippines, and a more robust presence in Southeast Asia, will be required (and largely welcomed by the countries in question).
- The sub-region that had previously received more modest levels of attention — Southeast Asia — will continue to benefit from an upgraded focus, as attested by rapidly improving ties with states in the region running from Myanmar/Burma (most dramatically) and Vietnam to Singapore and Indonesia.
- There is an effort by administration officials to stress that this is not 'all about China, but it is evident that one of the principal goals is to create a framework within which Beijing's choices are shaped. The hope remains that a more robust US stance in the region will lead not to confrontation but to an appreciation on China's part that it will best advance its interests through a more cooperative and magnanimous stance than it has adopted in the period since the global economic crisis.

China's Response

With China heading into its pre-Party Congress phase, this is not the moment for Beijing to mount a well-developed counter-play. Much of Chinese foreign policy is in something of a holding pattern and it will be 2013 before we are really able to see how China is seeking to position itself. More importantly, China has in many respects boxed itself in. The 'pivot' is as much the result of demand from other states in the region for a demonstratively strong US presence as it is a Washington-led initiative. Chinese efforts to retaliate against some of the countries that have been given US support will only accelerate these trends. It will take many years for China to patch up the diplomatic damage it has wrought with countries that include Japan, South Korea, India, Vietnam, Singapore and the Philippines. Those on the Chinese side counselling patience can point to the fact that economic trends continue to work in its favour — as neighbours become steadily more dependent on China for their economic growth, with increasing political consequences. But its economic weight does not seamlessly translate into leverage. Whether it is Myanmar/Burma or Japan, there is also a tendency for increased economic dependency to result in a push for diversification, and China is not the only potential source for growth in an economically dynamic region.

The actions taken so far by Beijing have been relatively constructive. It has acted to cool the South China Sea issue around which so much has hinged. Xi Jinping made a notably conciliatory speech in the lead-up to his US visit in February 2012. And there have been other small, positive developments, such as an unusually productive set of boundary talks between China and India. But there can be little doubt that the period ahead will see continued strategic competition in Asia. Beijing is not in any sense reconciled with the situation and this is at best likely to represent a pause in the process of pushing out on all fronts to try to ascertain what its growing power will yield. As one of China's most senior strategists noted in an interview with the author — 'the debate here is not about cooperation with the US. It is about assertiveness now or assertiveness later'.

Implications for the EU

- The ramifications for Europe are broad, spanning policy in Asia, relations with the US, and policy in other important regions of the world. Some of the implications are obvious but beyond the scope of this paper: reduced US military and diplomatic focus and presence in areas of vital interest to the EU will have a lasting impact; Europe commands less US attention now as a matter of course (except in the undesirable context of the eurozone crisis); European powers are starting to be seen as obstacles in the process of rebalancing seats and voting rights in global institutions — almost all changes that will come at Europe's expense.
- Some propose that the cleanest solution is an updated version of transatlantic burden sharing — Europe steps up in the regions where the US steps down.

positioning the EU as a vital facilitator for the 'pivot to Asia'. But in the short-term this is simply not seen to be taking place. In the defining recent example, European 'leadership' on Libya was perceived as an effort to drag the US into a conflict in which its stakes were limited, but where European states did not have the capabilities to run the military campaign without substantial US support. In the context of the European economic situation, there is virtually no prospect of Member States increasing their defence budgets as Washington hopes (even if, over time, a more integrated European defence capacity could remedy the problem without any budget expansion). In the short-to-medium term then, if the EU seeks to extend the transatlantic relationship to encompass the US 'pivot', the focus will need to be on establishing a more serious partnership on policy in the region itself.

- The EU does not have channels for consultation and influence in Washington on Asia that are as well-developed as those on other regions of the world, and this problem is going to become more acute unless serious steps are taken to remedy it. The older generation of US policy makers are Atlanticists whose careers have been defined by the Cold War. The emerging generations of Asia policy makers, a number of whom will be rising to the top slots in US foreign policy decision-making, do not necessarily have the same European exposure. There is no real instinct among the Asia policy community in the US of seeing Europe as a natural partner — it is perceived as a commercial actor in the region without major strategic interests, and the handling of the arms embargo issue in 2004/2005 has left a residue of mistrust.

- The one exception to this is trade, where EU and US officials have forged a close partnership in addressing a number of China-specific challenges. This should form the base for a more integrated set of transatlantic policy consultations on broader strategy in the region. The US is entering a period when it is seeking like-minded partners, especially when it comes to China policy. The EU should build out from trade policy to a wider process of collaboration on economic concerns spanning Chinese outward direct investment, state subsidies, public procurement, currency policy, and other associated issues. Both sides will be in a vastly stronger position in dealing with China if this can be translated into complementary positions.

- Other natural areas where cooperation can be extended include: values-based issues, such as human rights policy; responding to challenges posed by China's growing role in areas of the world outside its immediate neighbourhood, such as Africa and the Middle East; regional architecture issues; and support to other key states in the region, such as India and Indonesia, on matters ranging from

military capacity to trade access. Europe matters more to Asia than it is given credit for in Washington, but previous processes of consultation, such as the Asia-Oceania Working Party (COASI) *troika* meetings, have had little (or even at times detrimental) impact on perceptions there. A clear, effective agenda for cooperation from the European side would do a great deal more for the EU's positioning.
- Naturally the EU will not want to set itself up in Asia as 'just' a US partner. It has its own distinct relationships, goals and policies. But the US will have a crucial role in shaping the future of a region that is central to European interests too. The EU should move quickly to take advantage of long-standing transatlantic affinities and mechanisms and position itself as one of Washington's principal counterparts when it comes to dealing with Asia.
- EU policy in the region should also now assume an ongoing, and barely submerged process of strategic competition and hedging by the US, China and other Asian states. Europe's technology, trade relationships, arms sales and aid can all tilt the balance between different actors in consequential ways; the EU can gain leverage from this if it is willing to use these tools in an integrated fashion.

BRICS: A Cohesive Grouping?
(June 2012)

Sylvia Hui
Correspondent, Associated Press

Executive Summary

From improbable beginnings as a financial concept coined by investment bank Goldman Sachs, the BRICs — Brazil, Russia, India and China — have formed a loose organisation to push for a greater role for themselves and the developing world in the global financial and political order. Since 2009, the world's four leading emerging economies have met annually for formal leaders' summits to 'create conditions for a more just world order,' in the words of Russian President Dmitri Medvedev at the inaugural summit.

While the BRICs (which, since 2011, have adopted South Africa into the grouping, rendering the expansion BRICS) all aspire to a greater say in Western-controlled international economic and financial institutions, a lack of coherence among them has so far stopped the group from taking their demands very far. This paper will analyse the extent to which coherence among the group is achieved by considering the summit statements from all the BRICS leaders' meetings. It will also examine whether the BRICS have a joint stance on the EU, and discuss China's specific stake in and attitude towards BRICS. It argues that although the BRICS have achieved very little in real terms because of their differences, it has successively drawn attention to their cause in a worthy exercise of 'political marketing'.

Main Points

- From 2009 to 2012, the BRIC/BRICS grouping has used its summits to consistently lobby for greater influence and more decision-making powers for developing countries at international institutions such as the IMF. Despite the convergence of common interest, the summits have been largely symbolic, not substantive.
- The BRICS have succeeded, to some degree, in jointly pushing for IMF voting reform and diversifying the international currency system. They have also cooperated to take steps toward boosting intra-BRICS trade and building their own development bank.
- They have been much less successful in their political agenda, achieving no results in the stated aim of reforming the UN. They have, however, banded together to declare a broad joint position on Syria and Iran. Yet fundamental disparities and mutual distrust, especially regarding China, stand in the way of more meaningful accord.
- The BRICS summits have been reticent about Europe, although member nations have sought to put together a joint position on the eurozone crisis elsewhere. They have pledged funds but demand quicker IMF reform in return.
- China considers the BRICS one of several platforms where it could challenge the current world order, but is sceptical of its long-term potential.
- Despite many weaknesses, BRICS have shown considerable cohesion in pushing for the changes they want and drawing attention to their cause. For now the EU should maintain strong strategic relations with each of the BRICS. Engagement at the bilateral level remains key going forward.

Introduction

The term BRIC — an acronym for Brazil, Russia, India and China — was coined in 2001 by a Goldman Sachs economist to describe the four leading emerging economies expected to surpass today's largest economies by 2050. Together, the four nations account for more than 40% of the global population, and about a fifth of world GDP in 2011 — a jump from 16% in 2000. They are also among the ten largest accumulators of foreign exchange reserves. According to revised projections following the global financial crisis, Goldman Sachs forecast that the combined GDP of the BRICS may exceed that of the G7 countries by 2027, much sooner than initially believed.

Yet aside from large populations, increasingly influential economies, and a consensus on the need to change the power distribution in the world order, the BRICS nations have very little else in common. Fundamental disparities in their domestic political institutions, economic structure and challenges, and foreign policy priorities make cooperation a challenge, and the nations are further divided by numerous, barely concealed political and economic tensions and rivalries.

Despite such vast differences, the group began political dialogue in 2006 and met for its inaugural leaders' summit in 2009 on Russia's initiative. It has since met annually to coordinate their positions on international finance and politics. In 2011 China invited South Africa to join the group as a full member and the group thus became referred to as 'BRICS'. Although South Africa was supposed to represent the interests of Africa, not just itself, at the grouping, the expansion provoked much scepticism among observers who questioned why it was chosen among many other potential candidates with higher GDPs.

That the original BRICs came together at all owes much to the financial crisis, the challenges it posed, and the way it sharply highlighted the growing prominence of emerging economies. Brazil, Russia, India and China all emerged relatively unscathed compared to the battered US and western Europe; their common interest is to enhance their political clout on the back of their economic influence and check global reliance on the US. Indeed, so far the most significant and consistent aspect of the BRICS agenda has been calls to reform the international financial system to give more decision-making power to developing countries. In Chinese President Hu Jintao's words, cooperation among the BRICS represents a 'new model' of global economic cooperation that aims to create 'fair, just, inclusive' international financial systems. To this end, the group has proposed a number of plans in their summit statements, which will be set out in more detail below. The joint statements also put forth the group's stated desire to reform the UN as well as its views on international security and assorted other issues, although these have been much less coherent and too cautious to have real meaning.

The BRICS Summits

Since their inaugural summit in Yekaterinburg, Russia, in 2009, BRICs leaders have met for annual, formal summits in Brazil, China and India. The most recent leaders' summit was held in New Delhi in March 2012. Taken together, the joint statements resulting from these meetings consistently uphold the theme of calling for a more representative, less US-centric world order. The detail of how this could be implemented, however, is where coherence falls apart.

International economics and finance

Reform of the global financial system takes up the bulk of substantial proposals that the BRICS agreed on in their summit statements. Such proposals have been accompanied at every summit by consistent declarations from BRICS leaders blaming the West for lax financial regulation and venting joint frustration at the slow pace of reforms at the IMF. The BRICS have also coordinated specific demands and hashed out tangible goals. Foremost among these is the call for the World Bank and the IMF to adjust their quota systems to give more voting weight to developing countries, a reform agreed in 2010 by the G20. BRICS members, most notably Brazil, have repeatedly threatened to withhold additional BRICS funds requested by the IMF unless they gain a bigger say at the organisation. Meanwhile, the BRICS summits have also repeatedly urged for a more democratic process for electing the heads of international financial institutions, traditionally roles dominated by the West. Despite these demands, the BRICS failed to join together to back a candidate from the developing world to replace outgoing World Bank President Robert Zoellick in 2012.

A second and consistently repeated focus of the BRICS summits has been a call to move toward use of global reserve currencies other than the US dollar. Russia's Medvedev declared at the 2009 summit that 'there can be no successful global currency system if the financial instruments that are used are denominated in only one currency'. One of the most successfully developed proposals emerging from the past two summits was the agreement by all BRICS national banks to extend credit facilities in local currencies while conducting trade. Such measures are meant to reduce, over time, the groups' reliance on the dollar. In 2011's summit declaration the group also encouraged the IMF to expand its use of Special Drawing Rights (SDRs), a synthetic currency to transfer funds between member governments, although in the following year mention of SDRs was dropped.

Finally and perhaps most significantly, in their most recent summit the BRICS nations took further steps to formalise their grouping when stating that they would study the creation of their own development bank, funded and managed by BRICS and other developing countries, as an alternative to the US-dominated World Bank. While this was a breakthrough, no details about the shares of each country's voting rights or investment have yet emerged, and it is far from clear when — or whether — such a development bank may come into being.

Global governance and international politics

Since their first communiqué in 2009, BRICS leaders have proposed to reform the UN to make the body more effective, but this is one of the areas where the BRICS have had the least cohesion. On paper, all the joint statements called for making the UN — including the Security Council — 'more effective, efficient, and representative'. They also repeatedly declare the important role of India and Brazil (as well as South Africa after it joined in 2011) in international affairs, saying the BRICS 'understand and support' their aspirations to have a greater say at the UN.[19] However, so far none of them has put forward any details or proposals for how this goal may be achieved. It is clear that neither China nor Russia, both of which have permanent seats at the Security Council, are keen to extend their exclusive veto rights to any of the other BRICS.

In the past two years BRICS joint statements have widened their agenda to include political and security issues including the Arab Spring, Syria and Iran, reflecting the group's ambition to be seen as a politically coherent bloc. However, apparent coherence on paper often masks underlying disagreements. On Syria, for example, the 2012 joint declaration stated that BRICS leaders wanted a peaceful solution that respected Syria's sovereignty and supported a 'Syrian-led inclusive political process', despite India, Brazil and South Africa earlier supporting a UN resolution calling for Syrian President Bashar al-Assad to resign that China and Russia had vetoed. On Iran, the BRICS managed to jointly support its right to civilian nuclear energy and challenged the West's policy on Iran, stressing that dialogue was the only way to resolve the issue — a rebuff of any military plans by the West to curb Tehran's suspected nuclear activities.

BRICS declarations also include an array of other topics including the condemnation of international terrorism, concerns about food and energy security, climate change, urbanisation, and African development. However, these statements were more often than not overly broad and offered no concrete proposals. As such, they cannot be upheld as examples of meaningful convergence of views among the BRICS nations.

---

[19] See, for example, the Sanya Declaration in 2011 (paragraph 8):http://news.xinhuanet.com/english2010/china/2011-04/14/c_13829453_2.htm. Accessed 10 January 2014.

BRICS and the EU

The BRICS nations clearly consider Europe over-represented at the IMF, and have diverged from Brussels' strategy on Iran. But at the same time, each of the nations individually has important trade links with the EU, and all have a stake in ensuring the European sovereign debt crisis stays contained. Since 2011 BRICS have met outside their regular annual summits to attempt to put together a coherent stance toward the eurozone crisis. While these discussions captured the media's attention with prospects of so-called 'BRICS-aid', they largely fell flat because of significant divisions among the nations. In late 2011 Brazil initially signalled that the BRICS would lead an intervention to help the EU get out of the crisis, but a few weeks later it became clear that this was more rhetoric than reality following vocal opposition from China, Russia and India.

Both Beijing and Moscow told the media that Europe must present a clear strategy for rescuing its debt-ridden economies and find a solution for Greece before they would commit to increasing their eurozone bond holdings. China, which has individually been buying eurozone debt and has been vocal about helping Europe, signalled further that it wanted to be rewarded with official European recognition of China as a market economy. When the quartet met again in November 2011, ahead of the G20 summit in Cannes, India, Russia and Brazil appeared distinctly reluctant to contribute to the Europe rescue fund, indicating instead that they would give assistance through the IMF — but only in return for reforms at the institution. The BRICS 2012 summit declaration further disappointed when it failed to include any joint proposals for Europe; instead, it blamed market instability there for causing uncertainty in global economic growth and merely urged 'advanced economies to adopt responsible macroeconomic and financial policies'.[20]

Factors for Limited Cohesion

Many analysts see little potential for the BRICS to achieve a more coherent position or become a formal political grouping because of a long list of intra-BRICS political and economic disparities. India, Brazil and South African are vibrant democracies, Russia a declared democracy with strong authoritarian leanings, while China is an authoritarian power. As mentioned above, a joint vision about

---

[20] Paragraphs 5–6, Delhi Declaration, available here: http://www.cfr.org/brazil/BRICS-summit-delhi-declaration/p27805. Accessed 10 January 2014.

Security Council reforms is improbable given the permanent status of both Russia and China, as opposed to the long-standing aspirations of India and Brazil to gain a seat. In economics, too, bloc members hardly see eye to eye. Though all are dubbed 'engines of growth', China's dramatic growth rate is head and shoulders above the more modest development in the other BRICS; indeed, India's slowing growth rate in the past year has drawn alarm from investors, while South Africa's economic power is nowhere near that of any of the original quartet. Disparate economic structure also means the BRICS have competing priorities; for example, Russia is a huge exporter of energy, while China and India are the reverse. Further, intra-BRICS criticism of China's currency policy, especially from Brazil and India, has so far been swept under the carpet because of the scale of trade between the countries, but such disputes cannot be ignored for good. Finally, the group is rife with mutual geopolitical suspicion such as long-standing distrust between India and China over territorial claims and each country's relations with Pakistan.

Even the broad principles that the BRICS agree on in their communiqués are problematic on closer inspection. In most cases, such divergences of interest result from the fact that China is simply too powerful for the rest of the bloc. While all are critical of the dollar as a reserve currency and advocate a power shift from the US, China has by far the most vested interest on the issue; it has been cautious about proposals to encourage the use of SDRs as an international currency both because of its huge holdings in US dollars and bonds, and also because it considers the yuan the best contender to replace the dollar. Meanwhile, on the reform of IMF voting structure, any gains India may take home from the changes would benefit China even more, and India does not necessarily want to see reform that would increase the Chinese vote so dramatically. Finally, the agreed proposal to set up a BRICS development bank will face huge roadblocks not least because of intra-BRICS suspicion that China will take an overly dominant role and gain most from the proposal.

China's Stake and Attitude

As the dominant economic power among the BRICS nations, China has an ambivalent attitude toward the group. In general, Chinese observers believe the grouping has considerable potential, but are sceptical that it could overcome its many internal divisions to become a more formalised grouping in the long run. For Beijing, the BRICS is not the most important multilateral vehicle for global change, and it isn't the main focus of its multilateral activities. The G20 is, for now, the more prominent grouping by far. Still, there are benefits for Beijing. BRICS summits provide a forum for interaction with states that China has not always had good relations with. They also allow China to posture as a leading member of a group that, in Ambassador Zhang Yan's words, is 'the guardian of the interests of developing countries',[21] reassuring other developing nations, including India and Russia, that it is on their side.

The main benefit for China of participation in the BRICS process is that it provides a forum for Beijing to express dissatisfaction with the current global order and challenge it — or, as one official scholar insisted, not to overthrow the system, but to reform it by redistributing power within it to make it more representative. Like other organisations that China actively participates in, it is not a pre-existing grouping of countries established by the West based on liberal principles. Crucially, it is a forum that doesn't leave China as a lone voice of dissatisfaction but as part of a broader grouping that includes democratic states that are often seen more as allies of the West than enemies. This is thought to give greater legitimacy to calls for change than just acting alone, which risks raising the spectre of a 'China Threat' to the Western liberal world order.

While they might not be aired within BRICS summits, bilateral tensions and rivalries between China and India as well as Russia, and to a less degree Brazil, persist. Interviews with academics in Beijing who specialise in China's role in the global order in May 2012 revealed a largely sceptical view of the long-term future of BRICS given the various tensions among the member states. Beyond acting as a platform for the articulation of a common dissatisfaction and the discussion of issues of mutual interest, there is more that divides than unites among the BRICS. This view was echoed in a number of foreign embassies in Beijing, who saw BRICS as symbolic of a shift in global power, but a shift that sees the individual member states — rather than the BRICS collectively — as the key loci of power.

Chinese participation in the BRICS process should be viewed as part of a broader strategy of forming functional alliances with groupings that are not dominated by the West or overtly liberal ideas — blocs such as the Shanghai Cooperation Organisation, but also less formalised forms of cooperation like the Forum on

---

[21] Address at the Inauguration of Pre-BRIC Summit Preparatory Meeting by H. E. Mr. Zhang Yan, Chinese Ambassador to India, 2009:http://in.china-embassy.org/eng/embassy_news/2009/t562457.htm. Accessed 10 January 2014.

China-Africa Cooperation. In the process, China's leaders seek to not only push for change, but also to promote an idea of China as a global actor and a great power that behaves differently from the way previous great powers interacted with the developing world.

Conclusion

The BRICS' vocal criticisms of the developed Western economies reflect their growing confidence and ascendency in the world. But although they are united by a shared frustration about Western economic leadership in international organisations, especially amid the global economic downturn, the countries have not articulated any further shared vision or actionable objectives. Nonetheless, the EU should not dismiss the influence of the BRICS outright. Despite its many weaknesses, the grouping has shown considerable cohesion in pushing for the reforms they want — most powerfully by threatening to withhold much-needed funds — and as such, have succeeded in a kind of international political marketing for the member nations. It is too early to tell how the group may evolve and the EU should monitor its activities closely. For now, maintaining strong strategic relations with each of the BRICS at a bilateral level remains key.

China–Pakistan Relations
(August 2013)

Gareth Price

Senior Research Fellow, Asia Programme, Chatham House

Executive Summary

Pakistan and China have enjoyed a close relationship for decades. Political relations have remained strong regardless of political developments within Pakistan. Pakistan was one of the first countries to recognise China rather than Taiwan. The 1962 Sino–India War strengthened the relationship and, in 1963, Pakistan agreed to cede part of Kashmir to China. From Pakistan's perspective, opposition to India remains an important element in the relationship. But China's policy towards India appears to be less Pakistan-focused. Instead it is primarily driven by India's strategic partnership with the US.

China's policy towards Pakistan is clearly in its own self-interest; the infrastructure it is building in Pakistan (often by Chinese workers) is primarily intended to expedite the export of Chinese goods. But China is also aware that instability within Pakistan is a significant threat to stability in Xinjiang, and its defence cooperation is as much in China's direct interest as it is benevolent.

At both a government-to-government level, and in terms of Pakistani public opinion, China is seen as a more long-standing friend of Pakistan than the West. However, even if Pakistan sees the US as a fair-weather friend, while it remains reliant on US (and associated multilateral) financial assistance, and while the US remains in Afghanistan, Pakistan cannot publicly shift its primary alliance to China.

The strong political relationship contrasts with the economic and cultural links between the two countries. Cultural links are limited. While Chinese investment in Pakistani infrastructure is welcomed by Pakistan, trade flows are heavily in favour of China and Pakistan's textile sector has suffered because of Chinese competition since the ending of the Multi-Fibre Arrangement.

Main Points

- China's concerns about Uighurs, rather than India, underpin present-day defence cooperation with Pakistan. Counter-terrorism cooperation is deepening.
- China sees Pakistan as a gateway for its exports and is building up infrastructure links to ease access between Xinjiang and the Indian Ocean.
- China receives important political support from Pakistan, particularly in forums such as the Organisation of the Islamic Conference.
- Unusually for a developing country, Pakistan records a significant trade deficit with China. Its vital textile industry has suffered at the hands of Chinese competition.
- People-to-people and cultural links between the two countries are weak, but China benefits from positive public opinion within Pakistan. Unlike the West, China is seen as an 'all-weather' friend of Pakistan.

Background Information
Political Relations

High-level visits between the two countries are frequent. Underneath the positive statements lies a genuine desire to strengthen relations, notably in the field of defence. The extent of potential economic cooperation, however, is frequently over-stated. These two areas have been the primary focus of recent visits, as detailed below:

January 2011: China and Pakistan celebrate 60 years of relations with a series of events and visits to mark 'Friendship Year' to build on the signing of multi-billion dollar Memorandums of Understanding (MoUs) during Wen Jiabao's visit to Pakistan in December 2010.

May 2011: Pakistan's Prime Minister Yousuf Raza Gilani visits China on a four-day visit to commemorate 60 years of diplomatic ties between the countries. Visit was planned before the death of Osama bin Laden.

January 2012: Pakistan's Army Chief, General Kayani, visited China on a five-day trip. The visit took place at a time when US–Pakistan relations were strained in the aftermath of NATO killing Pakistani troops.

May 2013: Chinese Premier Li Keqiang visits Pakistan. Six of the jointly built JF-17 fighter jets escorted Premier Li's plane into Pakistani airspace. He was also awarded the Nishan-e-Pakistan, the highest award given by the Government of Pakistan for service to the country. Former President Hu Jintao was also given this award.

July 2013: Prime Minister Nawaz Sharif visits China. This was his first official foreign visit abroad. The focus of the visit was the 2000 km road and rail economic corridor linking Kashgar to Gwadar.

Arms Trade

China is the largest provider of military equipment to Pakistan; unlike Western countries, China is unlikely to impose military sanctions on Pakistan. Military cooperation in both conventional and non-conventional security is strengthening. The JF-17 combat aircraft is the most notable piece of military hardware that is jointly produced. Pakistan also purchases frigates and tank components from China and in recent years China has supplied an increasing amount of counter-terrorism equipment, such as explosive scanners, to Pakistan.

Military cooperation between China and Pakistan started in the 1960s when China began supplying arms to Pakistan and established a number of arms factories in Pakistan. The Karokoram Highway (connecting Kashgar with Pakistan) was justified as a means of allowing China to provide military aid to Pakistan. Both countries supported anti-Soviet fighters in Afghanistan during the 1980s. China's cooperation was driven by concern over India. From 1990, following the US imposition of sanctions on Pakistan, China became Pakistan's largest weapons supplier, and supplier of choice given Western history of imposing sanctions on Pakistan.

In 1979, a few months after it was set up CATIC (China Aviation Technology Import & Export Corporation) signed an agreement to export fighter planes to Pakistan. In 1986, CATIC signed an agreement with Pakistan to jointly develop the K-8 jet trainer, and the first six aircraft were delivered in 1994. The clearest example thus far of Sino–Pakistani cooperation is the JF-17 fighter jet project (JF standing for joint fighter), the 'flagship' of the two countries' partnership. The jointly funded project was launched in 1999, when CATIC signed a cooperation agreement with the Pakistan Air Force. Both countries contributed half of the cost, estimated at USD 150 m.

The design for the plane was finalised in 2001, and the maiden flight was held in 2003. The plane is part-built under licence in Pakistan. As of May 2013, Pakistan has showcased the fighter plane twice in China's International Airshow. The fighter planes also escorted Premier Li into Pakistani airspace during his visit. India had placed pressure on Russia not to sell engines to the joint fighter project, but after temporarily refusing exports, Russia finally agreed to provide the engines. The planes are to be armed with Chinese missiles following France's decision to refuse to sell missiles to Pakistan.

Counter-Terrorism Cooperation

Chinese concern over its Muslim Uighur population intensified in the 1990s. Following an Islamist uprising in the Chinese town of Baren in 1992, China closed the Karakoram Highway for several months, and in 1995 China hesitated to upgrade the highway for fear that it would increase the spread of radical Islamist ideology. Under pressure from China, Pakistan took a less tolerant approach to its own Uighur community, closing settlements in Pakistan and arresting and deporting Uighurs. Its approach to the Uighurs stands in contrast to its more ambivalent approach to the Afghan Taliban.

China's demand in return for acquiescence in the US invasion of Afghanistan was for the East Turkestan Islamic Movement (ETIM) to be proscribed; both the US and the UN have described the group as a terrorist organisation, a move that many in the US subsequently regretted since China used the ban to crackdown on peaceful religious activities. While China has been quick to publicise links between Uighur groups and Al-Qaida, many question the depth of these links.

China's security cooperation with Pakistan has deepened since 9/11. China expanded its counter-terrorism cooperation as a means of breaking links between Uighur separatists and Pakistan-based militant groups. It has also attempted to try to gain support within Pakistan (including from religious parties) on the issue of Muslim separatism in Xinjiang. In December 2001 General Pervez Musharraf, at the time 'chief executive' of Pakistan, visited Xi'an and called on Chinese Muslims to be loyal to the Chinese government. Pakistan's army also took steps to crackdown on Uighurs based in Pakistan's tribal areas, notably killing the leader of the ETIM, Hasan Mahsum, in 2004. A number of other Uighurs have been killed and extradited to China.

In 2004 China and Pakistan held their first joint anti-terrorism exercise, 'Friendship 2004', with about 200 soldiers from both sides participating. More than 400 troops took part in the second military drill, named 'Friendship 2006'. In 2008 China sold unspecified anti-terrorism equipment to Pakistan and the following year the two countries agreed to strengthen defence and counter-terrorism cooperation, and to build a comprehensive security strategy. This was reaffirmed during President Zardari's July 2010 visit to China. In the same month, the third joint anti-terrorism exercise was held ('Friendship 2010'). The drills were aimed at enhancing counter-terrorism capabilities and demonstrated the commitment to crackdown on the ETIM. Following the July 2009 riots in Xinjiang, Pakistan demonstrated its political value to China, endorsing China's strategy and using its influence to prevent the issue from being raised at the Organisation of the Islamic Conference.

China's counter-terrorism strategy within Xinjiang involves a dialogue with the two main Islamic parties in Pakistan, the Jamaat-e-Islami (JI) and the Jamaat-e-Ulema-e-Islami (JUI). The leaders of both parties have visited China since 2009, at the invitation of the Chinese Communist Party (CCP). Indian newspapers reported that the JI agreed not to support Islamist groups in Xinjiang (both parties continue to support the Taliban within Afghanistan). The leaders of both parties continue to express their support for Sino–Pakistan relations, and both parties have signed MoUs with the CCP.

China is believed to have warned Pakistan of plans by Uighurs to kidnap Chinese diplomats in Islamabad. A number of Chinese workers have been killed in Pakistan. Despite claims by both countries, the killings seem unconnected to Uighur groups. Several have been killed in Baluchistan, by Baluchi militants fearful of an influx of Punjabis, a likely by-product of Chinese construction of roads in the province. Others have been killed by Pakistani Islamists. Several Chinese workers were killed during the siege of the Red Mosque in Islamabad in 2007. Prior to the siege, Islamists had been attempting to enforce morality within the capital. In June they raided a Chinese-run health centre, a euphemism for a brothel, and kidnapped seven Chinese citizens.

Nuclear Trade

China played a major role in the development of Pakistan's nuclear weapon capability, as well as nuclear power. China provided nuclear technology to Pakistan for decades, and some reports suggest China conducted a proxy test for Pakistan in 1980. China claims to have ended support for Pakistan's nuclear weapons programme after it signed the Non-Proliferation Treaty (NPT) in 1992, although assistance is widely believed to have continued.

China signed a civil-nuclear agreement with Pakistan in 1986, since then it has supplied two nuclear power plants to Pakistan. China National Nuclear Corporation has announced plans to set up two additional reactors. The terms of the Nuclear Suppliers Group prevent the transfer of nuclear technology to countries, such as Pakistan, which have not signed the NPT. However, China claims that it agreed the deal prior to signing the NPT and thus is not beholden to its conditions. At the same time Pakistan has demanded a deal similar to the US–India civil nuclear deal to provide it with access to civilian nuclear technology. For now the issue is stalled.

Trade and Investment

There are significant discrepancies in trade and investment data between China and Pakistan. Sources from China tend to provide higher figures than those from Pakistan. According to Chinese customs data, the value of total bilateral trade between Pakistan and China in 2012 was more than USD 12bn. Both, however, make clear that, unusually for a developing country, Pakistan records a significant trade deficit with China. Pakistan's trade data is shown in Table 1, below.

Pakistan's exports primarily comprise raw materials, including ores, minerals and steel. Pakistan's exports of cotton cloth are increasingly important (demonstrating Pakistan's failure to compete with China in the production of ready-made garments).

Table 1. China–Pakistan export relations (millions USD).

	2010	2011	2012
Pakistan exports[a]	1,210	1,645	2,085
China exports[b]	3,283	4,144	4,277
Net inflow of Chinese private investment in Pakistan[a]	−3.6	47.4	126.1

[a]http://www.sbp.org.pk/ecodata/SBP-Exports-by-Selected-Countries.pdf. Accessed 21 January 2011.
[b]http://www.sbp.org.pk/ecodata/SBP-Imports-by-Selected-Countries.pdf. Accessed 21 January 2011.
Fiscal year (i.e. for 2010 refer to 2009/2010)
http://www.sbp.org.pk/reports/stat_reviews/Bulletin/2013/Jul/PakistanBalancePayment.pdf p. 140. Accessed 21 January 2011.
http://www.sbp.org.pk/ecodata/Netinflow.pdf. Accessed 21 January 2011.
http://www.sbp.org.pk/ecodata/NIFP_Arch/index.asp. Accessed 21 January 2011.

Pakistan has called on China to take steps to tackle the trade deficit, and has asked for tariff concession on around 270 product lines. It has also asked for assistance for training to produce higher-value items in sectors including textiles, jewellery and surgical equipment. China exports a range of cheap goods to Pakistan. Among the larger export items are arms, man-made fabrics, fertiliser and engineering goods. China and Pakistan have set an ambitious target of USD 15 bn for trade in 2011.

The investment figures given by Pakistan mask a range of Chinese investment for which no cash transfer takes place. These appear to include the construction of Gwadar Port in Baluchistan, and work building highways in Gilgit-Baltistan. China's military is also involved in construction projects, including the upgrading of the Karakoram Highway. The ultimate intention is to provide road and rail links from Xinjiang through to Gwadar Port. China is also involved in the construction of the 4,500-megawatt Neelam-Jhelum hydro-electric project in Kashmir.

In July 2010, China and Pakistan set up a joint investment company, intended as a conduit for investment in sectors including defence, energy, engineering and IT. China has helped modernise a number of state-owned facilities in Pakistan, notably in the defence sector. These include the Karachi shipyard and the Pakistan Aeronautical Complex.

China and Pakistan formed a strategic partnership in 1972. Chinese assistance is wide-ranging and expanding but the absolute amount of assistance is unknown. The relationship is predicated on Pakistan becoming a trade and energy 'corridor' for China. China funded the construction of a deep-water port in Gwadar, Baluchistan in a move seen as providing China with access to a deep-water harbour close to the Straits of Hormuz. In 2013 China also took over the management of Gwadar Port.

On occasion China has also provided Pakistan with monetary assistance. In 1996 China provided Pakistan with USD 500m in balance of payments support (which helped avert Pakistan from defaulting on its external debt until 1998). However, in 2008 when Pakistan's economy again neared default, China refused to provide cash assistance to Pakistan, forcing it to turn to the IMF for support. This reflects a growing Chinese focus on the provision of tangible rather than monetary assistance.

Regional Relations

Until around 1990 it was clear that China hoped to sustain animosity between Pakistan and India as a means of ensuring that India remained focused on Pakistan, rather than China, although there were limits to its support; China did not come close to intervening in the three wars between India and Pakistan. Since then China's approach is less clear-cut. In April 2005 China appeared to recognise Sikkim as an integral part of India. This peace-offering came at a time when India's relations with Pakistan were improving. But in 2006 the Chinese Ambassador to India restated (one week before the arrival of Hu Jintao in India) China's claim over the Indian state of Arunachal Pradesh. In recent years, relations between India and China have deteriorated further, with India taking exception to China's statement that Kashmir is a disputed territory. 2013 has also seen an escalation in incidents between Indian and Chinese border patrols in Ladakh.

Yet the correlation between the policy towards India of China and Pakistan is not clear-cut. Claims, particularly from US observers, that China seeks to undermine India by providing military assistance to Pakistan are negated by its actions in 2005, when its positive approach regarding Sikkim supported the rapprochement between India and Pakistan. The more recent deterioration in China–India relations would appear to owe more to China's concerns over growing US–India ties, India's own military modernisation and the continued presence of the Dalai Lama in India, rather than China's ties to Pakistan. That China's support for Pakistan causes consternation in Delhi is a by-product of China's relationship with Pakistan rather than the fundamental purpose.

China and Pakistan agreed in December 2010 to strengthen coordination on regional affairs, and particularly in relation to Afghanistan. China has growing commercial concerns in Afghanistan. China is fearful of any Taliban/Islamist presence bordering China, while Pakistan's policy is more ambiguous. China advocates the Shanghai Cooperation Organisation as one means of tackling Afghanistan, while Pakistan remains beholden to the current US-led strategy. But while China remains concerned about links between parts of the Pakistani state and the Taliban, it is more concerned that Pakistan continues to demonstrate resolve against Uighur groups within Pakistan.

The change of leadership in 2013 for both China and Pakistan will not significantly alter the nature of Sino–Pakistani ties. Both countries will continue to seek to strengthen diplomatic relations, boost trade and investment, and develop people-to-people ties. The announcement of a 'Kashgar–Gwadar' economic corridor and the Pakistan government setting up a special China cell in the Prime Minister's office is illustrative of this desire to deepen strategic relations. However, the lynchpin of this relationship depends on Pakistan being able to ensure that Chinese interests and investments in Pakistan are secure.

The Chinese Reaction to the March 2011 Earthquake and Tsunami and the Nuclear Aftermath
(April 2011)

Caroline Rose

Professor of Sino-Japanese Relations and Director of East Asian Studies, School of Modern Languages and Cultures, University of Leeds

Executive Summary

The earthquake and tsunami that hit northeastern Japan on March 11 2011 has had devastating consequences for the country. The ensuing nuclear crisis at the Fukushima Daiichi power plant has further exacerbated the situation, and powerful aftershocks continue to impact the northeast of the country, causing concerns about the safety of Japan's other nuclear power plants. China's response to the disaster was swift and effective, and was warmly received in Japan. While this will have a positive impact on the relationship between the two countries in the short term, it is unlikely that it will fundamentally alter the oft-troubled nature of their political and diplomatic interaction. The impact of the nuclear crisis on China's own nuclear energy policy may give decision makers pause for thought in the short term, but early indications suggest that the Japanese situation will not radically alter China's plan to pursue nuclear power as a means of sustaining the country's economic development and helping to satisfy its energy demands. The disaster has highlighted the need for bilateral, and East Asian, regional cooperation on nuclear safety and disaster prevention, which in turn would help to build confidence in the region. However, these discussions are very much in their infancy.

Main Points

- China's response to the crisis in Japan in the form of pledges of aid and assistance was rapid and warmly received by the Japanese government and people; this was China's first time to offer assistance to its neighbour and was offered in the spirit of returning one favour with another (with reference to Japan's assistance after the May 2008 Sichuan earthquake).
- Both governments stressed the long and friendly cooperative credentials of the China–Japan relationship, and the desirability of strengthening the strategic and mutually beneficial relationship.
- The limits to this rapprochement were soon revealed, however, when other ongoing issues re-emerged, albeit on the periphery. This indicates that the crisis has not had the effect of transcending perennial problems such as Japanese textbook content and territorial disputes.
- China announced the implementation of nuclear safety checks and halted approval for new nuclear power plants in the immediate aftermath of the Fukushima Daiichi disaster.
- In the longer term, it is unlikely that the nuclear crisis will radically alter the general direction of China's nuclear energy policy, which has been actively pursued since the early 2000s and has been identified as the best alternative to fossil fuels. Nonetheless, greater caution is emerging from China in relation to the safety aspects of the nuclear power industry and the need for robust systems.
- More broadly, the Fukushima crisis has highlighted the need for greater information sharing and cooperation on the development and management of nuclear energy in the region. East Asia currently lacks effective institutions and mechanisms, although the trilateral meetings between China, Japan and South Korea show promise.

Background Information

As the triple disaster unfolded in Japan, declarations of friendship and cooperation proliferated at both the official and popular levels in China. Messages of condolence were expressed at the highest level by then Chinese President Hu Jintao and Premier Wen Jiabao. A shared experience of natural disasters reinforced feelings of solidarity, and the Chinese press and Internet blogs commented on Japanese stoicism and resilience. Chinese pledges of assistance were immediate, expressed in terms of 'returning the favour after receiving one' in reference to Japan's help after the Sichuan earthquake. A Xinhua report (widely reproduced across the Chinese press) suggested that the mutual support and understanding born from cooperation in dealing with natural disasters ('the common enemies of mankind') had brought the Chinese and Japanese people closer together and 'perhaps even helped close old wounds'. At the popular level, sentiment was mixed, with some netizens welcoming the earthquake. This was by no means the mainstream view, however, which was marked more by sympathy and expressions of condolence and support. Japanese Foreign Minister Matsumoto Takeaki expressed gratitude on March 19 for China's messages of condolence and offers of emergency assistance. Using the standard terminology of friendship between China and Japan ('two countries separated by a narrow strip of water'), he stressed the need to forge ahead with the development of their strategic and mutually beneficial relationship.

Aid and assistance

The Chinese government made immediate offers amounting to RMB 30 m (USD 4.57 m) of material aid such as blankets, tents, emergency lights, followed by gasoline and diesel shipments, drinking water, rubber gloves, and training shoes. The Chinese Red Cross also donated RMB 6 m (USD 917,000) and numerous fundraising activities were organised across Mainland China and in Hong Kong Special Administrative Region. A 15-member Chinese rescue team was despatched to Ofunato in Iwate prefecture within two days of the earthquake and tsunami — the first overseas rescue team to reach the area. Chinese diplomatic staff in Japan made emergency arrangements for approximately 20,000 affected Chinese citizens who were either evacuated from the northeast of Japan to safer regions, or transported back to China. In the latter case, approximately 1,000–2,000 Chinese were flown back to China in the seven to ten days after the earthquake and tsunami.

Nuclear safety checks and monitoring

In the immediate aftermath of the announcements about the crisis at the Fukushima Daiichi power plant, the Chinese Ministry of Environmental Protection and the National Nuclear Safety Administration gave reassurances that the nuclear leaks posed no immediate threat to China. Nuclear safety checks of China's 13 nuclear power plants indicated that all were operating normally. The State Council announced on March 16 that it was temporarily suspending approval of nuclear power projects including those in preliminary stages of development. Nationwide radiation monitoring was implemented, in addition to the screening of Japanese imported goods. Reassurances about the lack of direct effect of radiation on China were regularly made in the press, but as the nuclear crisis continued into early April, Chinese concerns mounted over higher than normal radiation levels of some cargo arriving from Japan. As a precautionary measure, the government announced it would ban the import of farm produce and foodstuffs from some parts of Japan.

Policy Implications
Impact on Sino–Japanese relations

Initial concerns were expressed about the possible impact on trade between the two as a result of this disaster. Japan represents China's largest import market constituting 13% of China's total imports. In particular, Japanese joint ventures (especially in Tianjin, Dalian and Jiangsu) are expected to be affected due to shortages of component imports. For example, the Dongfeng Nissan factory in Hubei cut production due to part shortages. Exports in certain sectors (aluminium alloy for the auto industry) and from certain areas of China, for example Fujian and Shandong (agricultural products), are also expected to be negatively affected in the short term. The assessment of the Chinese Ministry of Commerce, however, is that the earthquake will have only a limited impact on Sino–Japanese trade overall. Economic relations will most likely revive gradually, in line with the recommencement of production in Japanese factories and Japan's own recovery. The possibility of cooperation between China and Japan on the reconstruction of northeastern Japan, which would boost both economies, was discussed at the preparatory meeting (held in Beijing in April) for the 7th annual Beijing–Tokyo Forum, which will be held in August 2011. Jointly organised by the China Daily and Japanese think tank Genron NPO, the Forum has become one of the more influential Track II organisations in Sino–Japanese relations, attended by government representatives, academics, business leaders, think tanks and the media from both countries.

At both the diplomatic and popular levels, the relationship has been boosted in the short term due to the expressions of sympathy and solidarity from China and the speed with which China offered its assistance. Although survey data is not yet available, this will help to create a certain amount of goodwill among the Japanese public and should improve China's image as reflected in the regular opinion polls that measure feelings of friendliness or closeness towards each other. Similarly, depending on how the Japanese government handles the nuclear crisis, perceptions of Japan in China may also improve, albeit temporarily, as they did shortly after the Sichuan earthquake. In the longer term, however, this will probably not be sufficient to dramatically alter the nature of the relationship which has been marked by inherent contradictions for much of the post-war period. There are occasional flare-ups often relating to Japan's perceived failure to acknowledge responsibility for the Second Sino–Japanese war of 1937–1945, and the deep popular sense among many Chinese of grievances from the war.

Perennial issues regarding the content of Japanese school textbooks and their largely benign treatment of Japanese behaviour during the 1937–1945 war, as well as activities around the disputed Diaoyu/Senkaku islands and East China Sea (ECS) (where both countries claim sovereignty), resurfaced within weeks of the disaster. The Chinese media, for example, reported in late March on the content of newly authorised Japanese junior high citizenship (civics) and geography textbooks, which contained more specific reference to Japan's assertion of its sole ownership of the Diaoyu/Senkaku islands, as well as Takeshima/Dokdo (which the Republic of Korea (ROK) claims) and the northern territories (which Russia claims). Initially, the press took the usual angle of reporting on the ROK's (generally more vociferous) protests to the textbook changes as a sort of proxy for China's own grievance on the matter. In early April, however, the Chinese Foreign Ministry made a 'solemn representation' on the issue, claiming China's 'indisputable sovereignty' over the Diaoyu islands.

In addition, Japanese vigilance over Chinese activities in the ECS has not declined in the wake of the crisis in northeastern Japan, with the Japanese government claiming that a Chinese helicopter had flown too close to a Maritime Self-Defense Force (MSDF) ship in the ECS. This elicited a response from the Chinese Foreign Ministry urging Japan to stop adversely affecting bilateral relations.

In both cases, this hardly reflects a new attitude of 'closing old wounds' as the official Chinese news agency Xinhua had optimistically suggested, but it would be unrealistic to expect such matters to be dismissed so lightly. The content of Japanese school textbooks has been on and off the diplomatic agenda between China and Japan since 1982; the textbooks authorised in 2011 were the first batch of new junior high social studies textbooks produced under a revamped national curriculum, itself informed by the revision of the Fundamental Law of Education (FLE) in 2006. Of particular concern in some Japanese and Chinese circles was the possible effect of a new FLE clause that referred to the need to encourage love of country in textbooks — seen as an attempt to instil greater patriotism in schoolchildren. The inclusion of references to the Senkaku islands as Japanese territory in textbooks from this most recent round of authorisation is interpreted as a sign by the Chinese government that Japan is becoming more assertive in its territorial claims. The timing of the press reports on the results of textbook authorisation was purely coincidental — the results are always released in late March, and often generate some media response in Japan, China and South Korea, particularly where major changes to textbook content have been anticipated.

Similarly, the incident regarding the Chinese helicopter in the East China Sea forms part of the rumbling dispute over territory and, reputedly, large gas and oil deposits, to which both China and Japan lay claim. The dispute escalated in September 2010 when a Chinese fishing boat rammed two Japanese coastguard ships, sparking a major diplomatic issue. Although this was more or less resolved after the Chinese skipper was released from Japanese custody, concerns remain, with the Japanese MSDF and coastguard regularly reporting on the activities of Chinese fishing boats and other vessels operating in the area. The latest incident thus forms part of an ongoing pattern of protest and counter-protest, which serves to keep the pot boiling on the ECS issue and demonstrates that the earthquake/tsunami and nuclear crisis could not keep such disputes off the agenda for very long.

Impact on Chinese Nuclear Energy Policy

While China is a relative latecomer to nuclear power (its first nuclear power station became operational in 1991 at Qinshan in Zhejiang province), rapid economic development and the concomitant increase in energy needs, particularly since the early 2000s, have meant that the development of nuclear power has become integral to China's energy strategy. Nuclear power is seen as an effective, sustainable and clean means of reducing China's reliance on fossil fuels and satisfying energy demands on which it relies for over 70% of its current needs. Thus a general consensus emerged within the policymaking community in China in the early 2000s on the need to expand nuclear power generation, albeit with differences of opinion on how it should be developed (the debate was split between those who favoured the development of indigenous technology and those who favoured importing advanced foreign technology — the latter view prevailing). The 10th Five Year Plan (FYP, 2001–2005) provided for the construction of eight new nuclear reactors, while the 11th FYP (2006–2011) was more ambitious, aiming to 'actively develop' nuclear power plants. The 12th FYP (2011–2015) remains committed to nuclear energy. 13 nuclear power stations are currently in operation in China, with 27 under construction, and a further 50 in the planning stage.

Early indications suggest that the Fukushima disaster has not produced a U-turn on China's plans for nuclear energy development. In the more critical analyses of Japan's situation, problems were attributed to the age of the Fukushima reactors or to design flaws at the plant. This lies in contrast to positive appraisals of China's nuclear energy industry in terms of its safety record, the use of advanced and safer technologies, and rigorous standards dictating the location of nuclear power plants (that is, away from active fault lines or areas that have previously recorded magnitude 6.0 earthquakes). By late March, the National Development and Reform Commission (NDRC), the government ministry in charge of economic planning, stated that while nuclear safety standards would continue to be reinforced, China's nuclear programme would continue.

In early April, however, the NDRC indicated that the use of nuclear power would be decreased, and solar power increased up to 2020, suggesting a slight adjustment in thinking about the relative weightings of the energy mix. In addition, some Chinese commentaries argue that lessons must be drawn from the Fukushima Daiichi situation in terms of location of plants, enhancing tsunami resistance (most of China's existing nuclear power plants are on coastal sites), and ensuring adjacent resources are adequate (for example, sufficient water supply if plants are to be built inland). Public opinion in China is not generally seen as an obstacle to the government's plans (possibly due to lack of awareness), but the potential for opposition should perhaps not be overlooked as Chinese people watch the Fukushima crisis develop and consider the potential risks to their own communities should new plants be sited locally (where consultation currently appears to be rather light-touch). While the Chinese media was quick to reassure its readership that there was no immediate danger in China from Japan's nuclear disaster and that China's own reactors were safe, subsequent reports about raised (though still 'extremely low') levels of radioactive iodine having been detected on some Chinese agricultural crops (spinach and lettuce), along with the ban on some foodstuffs from Japan, may raise greater awareness among the Chinese public about the hazards associated with nuclear accidents.

The Fukushima crisis has highlighted the need for greater cooperation not just between China and Japan, but across East Asia in terms of nuclear safety, information sharing and energy development. Criticisms were voiced by the Chinese, Russian and South Korean governments in early April about the lack of information from Japan in relation to the continued pumping of radioactive water into the sea. Raising concerns about marine safety in the region as a whole, the three governments called for prior notification and more accurate information from Japan.

Despite various attempts over the years to establish a regional organisation akin to the Association of Southeast Asian Nations or the EU, Northeast Asia still lacks a robust institutional framework to deal with the sorts of issues arising from the current disaster. Trilateral cooperation between China, Japan and the ROK on disaster prevention and nuclear safety was discussed at the foreign ministers' meeting in Kyoto on March 19 and is to be discussed further during the summit to be held in Tokyo in May, where the Japanese government has indicated it will share its experiences and lessons from the disaster. This would present a valuable opportunity to explore proposals for a much needed energy and safety infrastructure in the region — building, for example, on the work of the Asian Nuclear Safety Network, established in 2002 with the purpose of sharing knowledge and experience among nine Asian countries (including China, Japan and the ROK) with support from European partners and the US.

The trilateral summits between China, Japan and the ROK have become more established in the last two to three years, and have already yielded an agreement on food safety. If existing plans for proposed nuclear plants in all three countries were to go ahead, there would be upwards of 300 reactors in the region, with the bulk of these in China. Given the Fukushima Daiichi disaster and its impact across the region, the need for a more robust institutional framework in East Asia to deal with such events appears not to be lost on government leaders, and should be further encouraged by the EU.

This might be best achieved by lobbying either directly or via global nuclear energy governance mechanisms. In addition, leverage may be gained through individual EU (and non-EU) government and corporate links with China. China has sought technology transfer mainly from the US, Canada, France, Russia and Germany. In particular, the French company Areva has concluded contracts with the Guangdong Nuclear Power Corporation and has supplied technology to the Qinshan (Zhejiang) and Daya Bay (Guangdong) power plants, as have German and Spanish companies. Japanese companies have also entered the Chinese nuclear energy market, most notably US-based Westinghouse (purchased by Toshiba in 2006), which is involved in the construction of four plants using third generation technology, in addition to Hitachi and Mitsubishi Electric. China is still somewhat reliant on its international partners for technology transfer, safety training, education and operations management, though these skills are gradually being developed locally. In addition, its nuclear power plants are subject to international standards and inspections. But safety culture remains a concern, and an area in which the EU should lobby while China is still seeking international input to develop its nuclear energy sector.

China–Vietnam Relations on Maritime Borders
(October 2011)

Marianna Brungs
Associate Fellow, Asia Programme, Chatham House

Executive Summary

Vietnam's tolerance of the recent series of anti-China protests in Hanoi marked another chapter in the ongoing dispute between the two countries over maritime borders in the South China Sea. Vietnam used the protests to signal its discontent to China, but was careful not to unduly provoke its neighbour.

The South China Sea and its resources are under claim from all surrounding countries, with China claiming over 80% of the area. Growing Chinese assertiveness in the South China Sea and ASEAN over the past few years, combined with increasing domestic tensions within Vietnam, resulted in strained relations between the two countries in the middle of 2011. Following a shift by China to a more conciliatory approach, including the signing of Guidelines on the South China Sea with ASEAN, tensions between the two countries have eased somewhat. Vietnam and China are currently participating in both multilateral discussions through ASEAN, and separate bilateral talks.

Vietnam and China's relationship is based on a long history of asymmetric interaction and careful management. While Vietnam needs to manage domestic antipathy against China, overall political and military relations are robust, largely due to an extensive network of people-to-people contacts, particularly between the two Communist parties. Economic links are also considerable, but largely in China's favour, contributing to Vietnamese resentment. The South China Sea dispute and the significant trade imbalance are the primary political irritants in the relationship.

The prognosis for the current dispute is reasonably positive. Limited armed conflict through accidental or minor provocation is possible, given that both countries are boosting their naval capabilities and presence in the South China Sea. The most likely outcome, however, is some kind of negotiated agreement on development or joint management of resources. Vietnam and China's negotiation of their land border serves as a hopeful precedent. It is also feasible that China and ASEAN will agree on a binding code of conduct for claimants to the South China Sea ahead of next year's ASEAN Regional Forum, although the agreement may be largely ceremonial.

The international community has key strategic interests in ensuring the security of maritime routes in the South China Sea, given the large proportion of the world's trade that passes through the region. The US is the key international player on the maritime borders dispute and has urged the parties to move forward through collaborative, diplomatic processes. Vietnam and other ASEAN states support the use of the 1982 UN Convention on the Law of the Sea (UNCLOS) as a basis for resolving the dispute, but China has been reluctant to clarify its claims according to the system of maritime zones set out in the UNCLOS.

Over the next five years, Vietnam and China are likely to maintain a relatively robust political relationship, albeit with cycles of inflamed tensions and conciliatory measures. Economic integration is also liable to increase. On external relations, Vietnam is likely to seek to strengthen its position on the South China Sea *vis-à-vis* China by further drawing in ASEAN and key international players.

Introduction: The Recent Protests Regarding Maritime Borders

Protests are an unusual occurrence in Vietnam's controlled political environment. By allowing the series of anti-Chinese protests in Hanoi in autumn 2011 to continue for some time, Vietnam sent a strong signal to China about its determination to stick firmly to its claims over the South China Sea.

The weekly protests took place in Hanoi from early June to mid-August. They were initially held close to the Chinese Embassy, and then moved to the vicinity of Hanoi's central lake, Hoan Kiem, after the area around the Embassy was blocked off. Protest numbers were not large (generally only 50–100 participants at a time), but gradually shifted from being primarily students to a more diverse group of intellectuals, dissidents and religious leaders. The messages were nationalistic, focusing on China's alleged violations of Vietnamese territorial waters and harassment of Vietnamese boats and fishermen. While the protests were closely monitored to ensure they did not morph into broader anti-government displays, they provided an opportunity for the state to allow disaffected groups in Vietnam to 'let off steam' in a relatively controlled manner. Two larger anti-Chinese protests in June in Ho Chi Minh City, involving over 1,000 people, were quickly shut down by state authorities.

China was well aware of the protests and privately urged Vietnam to end them. Vietnam only closed the protests down after a wider range of disparate groups started uniting behind the anti-Chinese banner, and following further high-level discussions with China. Several protesters were arrested and detained briefly, but additional action by the authorities against those involved was limited. Momentum seems to have abated among activists on this issue, and it is unlikely that protests will resume without significant negative developments in the dispute.

Vietnam and China's Dispute over Maritime Borders: Further Context

In addition to Vietnam and China's multiple clashes over the South China Sea, parts of the area are also claimed by the Philippines, Malaysia, Brunei and Taiwan. As well as including crucial maritime trade routes and significant fish stocks, the South China Sea is believed to contain large oil and gas reserves. The two main sets of islands in dispute (along with their territorial waters) are the Paracels in the north and the Spratlys in the south. China controls the Paracels having seized them from Vietnam in 1974, although Vietnam and Taiwan continue to assert claims to these islands. China, Taiwan and Vietnam claim the Spratly Islands, with Brunei, Malaysia and the Philippines also claiming parts. Overall, China claims over 80% of the South China Sea, within a 'nine-dashed lines' map submitted to the UN Commission on the Limits of the Continental Shelf in 2009.

Increasing tensions

The most recent cycle of heightened tensions between Vietnam and China over the South China Sea began in 2009. States Parties to UNCLOS were required to lodge submissions to the UN Commission on the Limits of the Continental Shelf in 2009 on all claims to the continental shelf that extended beyond 200 nautical miles. China protested Vietnam's claim and tabled its 'nine-dashed line' map in response. China also increased its assertiveness in patrolling and claiming sovereignty over the disputed waters, including pressuring international extractive companies including BP, ConocoPhillips and ExxonMobil to pull out of projects with Vietnam in disputed areas by threatening retaliatory action against their interests in China.

At the same time, domestic pressure grew in Vietnam for increased assertiveness regarding the South China Sea, including criticism in Vietnamese social media that Vietnam had not been defending its claims forcefully enough. Anti-Chinese sentiment was exacerbated by China's regular harassment and detention of Vietnamese fishermen working in disputed waters. In addition, Vietnam finalised its difficult and lengthy land border demarcation negotiations with China at the end of 2008, allowing the state to shift its attention to the maritime dispute.

The concerns of Vietnam and other regional states over China's claims to the South China Sea were magnified by China's ongoing military expansion and efforts to increase its leverage in Southeast Asia more generally. To counter this, Vietnam and other ASEAN states strengthened their strategic relationships with the US, making it clear they would welcome the US's involvement in the South China Sea dispute. Vietnam also pushed for regional states to combine forces in multilateral discussions on the South China Sea through ASEAN, rather than engage in the uneven bilateral discussions preferred by China.

Highlighting the deterioration in relations, Vietnam publicly accused Chinese naval vessels of harassing Vietnamese fishing fleets in the South China Sea at the end of May 2011, as well as of cutting the exploration cables of a seismic survey ship.

China's shift in approach

In response to this growing regional concern, China shifted to a more conciliatory approach on the South China Sea to maintain its relationships and influence in the region. In July, China and the ASEAN states agreed on non-binding 'Guidelines for the Implementation of the Declaration' at the ASEAN Regional Forum (ARF).

The Guidelines reaffirmed the parties' commitment to the 2002 'Declaration of the Conduct of Parties in the South China Sea' between China and the ASEAN states. The Declaration outlined the parties' agreement to seek peaceful solutions and exercise self-restraint in relation to the disputed territories, and to work towards the adoption of a Code of Conduct. While the Guidelines are general and non-binding, they were seen as a positive diplomatic outcome that improved the political dynamics between China and concerned ASEAN states including Vietnam.

Vietnam–China talks

Vietnam currently has a two-track approach to negotiations with China on the South China Sea. As well as participating in the multilateral negotiations between ASEAN and China on the Spratly Islands and general principles on the South China Sea, it is undertaking bilateral negotiations with China. The bilateral talks were not made public until the start of 2011 and are assumed to deal with the Gulf of Tonkin.

The Current Status of Relations between Vietnam and China
Political relations

Vietnam focuses significant attention on China, and works hard to maintain its interests on key issues, such as the South China Sea, without souring the broader bilateral relationship. Vietnam's response to the recent protests presents a good example — Vietnam was careful not to overly provoke China, while sending a clear message about its level of discontent. However, while maintaining good relations with China, Vietnam also needs to manage domestic tensions. There are high levels of anti-Chinese sentiment within Vietnam, based on perceived political and economic interventions in Vietnam and a long history of Chinese dominance.

China also has a strong interest in maintaining the relationship. It needs to avoid direct conflict with Vietnam in order to maintain its claim of being a peacefully rising nation in the region, particularly given that Vietnam is an emerging regional strategic player, and a stronger and more robust player internationally.

Overall the relationship is healthy, and Vietnam and China publicly characterise their relationship in strongly positive terms. A key factor underlying this is the close behind-the-scenes ties that allow many issues to be resolved at an early stage. Vietnam and China have extensive people-to-people links across the Party, government and military, involving hundreds of official visits each year. Vietnam uses these well-established mechanisms to press its case on political issues involving China.

Economic relationship

In addition to maritime borders, the other key political irritant in the Vietnam–China relationship is the significant trade imbalance in China's favour. China is Vietnam's largest trading partner. Over the last decade, Chinese imports into Vietnam have grown exponentially compared to Vietnamese exports to China. In conjunction with an increase in two-way trade from USD 3,024 m in 2001 to USD 31,770 m in 2010, Vietnam's trade deficit with China ballooned from USD 189 m in 2001 to USD 19,096 m in 2010.

The large trade deficit has exacerbated Vietnamese resentment against China and is regularly mentioned in Vietnamese media. To offset the deficit and boost the economy, Vietnam has urged China to increase investment in Vietnam for some years. Public opinion in Vietnam, however, opposes increased Chinese investment and its side effects, including the influx of Chinese labourers, the poor environmental record of Chinese companies, and the potential for Vietnam to become overly economically dependent on China. This was highlighted by civil activism opposing Chinese bauxite mining in Vietnam's Central Highlands.

Military links

While Vietnam's military links with China are not as extensive as its political or economic ties, they are nonetheless healthy. The two states regularly exchange high-level military delegations, host annual defence security consultations, undertake military training exchanges, and participate in joint naval patrols in the Gulf of Tonkin. During the Vietnam–China Strategic Defence and Security Dialogue held in August 2011 in Beijing, Vietnam and China agreed to expand bilateral defence cooperation to new fields, and to increase communication between the defence ministries.

How Current Border Disputes could Evolve

While limited armed conflict is possible, the most likely outcome in the South China Sea dispute between China and Vietnam is some kind of negotiated agreement, due to the strategic interests of both states in avoiding conflict.

Military conflict

All-out naval engagement is unlikely, although it remains possible. China has significantly increased its naval capabilities, and is reluctant to compromise on territorial disputes. Vietnam has boosted its naval powers through orders for submarines, military frigates and anti-ship missiles.

Both sides, however, would have much to lose from military conflict. China would forfeit any claim to be a peacefully rising power, and would push regional states towards the US. Vietnam would likely suffer the loss of both its military power and the disputed territory.

Accidental provocation

Vietnam, China and other interested states have built up their naval presence in the South China Sea to bolster their claims to the area. The rapid growth in naval activities may lead to limited conflict through accidental or minor provocation. Continued Chinese harassment of Vietnamese fishermen and seismic survey vessels could also result in an escalated response by Vietnam.

Negotiated agreement

While much of their diplomatic relations happen behind the scenes, it appears that Vietnam–China relations over the South China Sea have improved since the heightened tensions earlier this year, and that bilateral discussions between Vietnam and China are moving forward, albeit slowly. Both states have been keen to emphasise publicly that the dispute will be dealt with in a constructive way through continued dialogue. China and Vietnam's land border agreement in 2008 indicates the real possibility of a negotiated outcome. Following 15 years of secret negotiations, the demarcation of the land border resulted in a reasonably fair deal for Vietnam, and major confidence building between the two states.

Nonetheless, even in light of reduced tensions, negotiations over the South China Sea are likely to be long and difficult, as the dispute is more sensitive and more players are involved. China will need to back down from its current claim to the majority of the area. Vietnam may also feel it can push harder, using its status as a stronger regional player.

One possibility is that Vietnam and China will maintain their existing territorial claims, and instead reach an agreement on development or joint management of resources. There is some precedent for this, including a previous agreement in 2005 (now expired) between the national oil companies of China, Vietnam and the Philippines for joint seismic testing.

The Role of the International Community

A large proportion of the world's trade passes through the South China Sea. While maritime routes have not yet been affected by the dispute, the international community has a strategic interest in ensuring the ongoing security of sea lanes.

As with broader East Asian security dynamics, the US is the key international player in the South China Sea dispute. At the 2010 ARF in Hanoi, following diplomatic requests from regional states, Hillary Clinton sent a strong message to China by stating that the US considered the South China Sea to be a matter of national interest, and declaring US support for a 'collaborative diplomatic process by all claimants for resolving the various territorial disputes without coercion'.[22] This statement helped to push China towards a more conciliatory approach on the South China Sea issue. Since then, the US has been attentive to the dispute, but has been careful to urge ongoing dialogue, rather than indicate support for Vietnam and other ASEAN states against China.

The role of the UNCLOS

Apart from Taiwan, all claimants to the South China Sea are parties to the UNCLOS, including China. While the recently agreed Guidelines do not mention the UNCLOS, they reaffirm the 2002 Declaration, in which the States Parties outlined their commitment to resolve territorial disputes in accordance with universally recognised principles of international law, including the UNCLOS.

Under the UNCLOS, states can claim sovereign rights to resources located within their maritime zones, which are in turn demarcated by the outer extent of the exclusive economic zone or the continental shelf. As UNCLOS does not deal with territorial sovereignty, claims to sovereignty over the disputed islands (and thus to the corresponding maritime zones) would need to be determined according to other sources of international law.

---

[22] Hillary Rodham Clinton, Secretary of State, National Convention Center, Hanoi, Vietnam, 23 July 2010, 'Remarks at Press Availability': http://www.state.gov/secretary/rm/2010/07/145095.htm. Accessed 12 Dec 2012.

Vietnam and other ASEAN states support the use of the UNCLOS as a basis for resolving the South China Sea dispute, particularly the provision that any claim to sovereign rights must be made on the basis of maritime zones derived from claims to land features. The Philippines has urged the competing claimants to take the matter before the International Tribunal for the Law of the Sea, but recognises it is unlikely that China will agree to this measure, particularly since China has exercised its right to opt out of the dispute settlement system for matters relating to maritime boundary delimitation.

In order for the competing claims to be assessed under the UNCLOS, China would need to clarify its claims according to the UNCLOS system of maritime zones, rather than its current unsupported claims to sovereignty over all areas within the 'nine-dashed line' map. While this is likely to reduce the coverage of China's claim and would be domestically unpopular, China also has a strong interest in maintaining the existing law of the sea regime, given its growing dependence on secure international shipping routes for trade and energy resources.

The Future Relationship between Vietnam and China over the Next Five Years

Vietnam is likely to increasingly use ASEAN to strengthen its regional clout, and as a useful counterbalance to China's influence. ASEAN solidarity, however, should not be taken for granted. China is likely to be able to weaken multilateral discussions through pressuring individual states, particularly those with no real interest in the South China Sea. In addition, if Vietnam considers it is able to get a better deal on South China Sea issues outside ASEAN, then it is likely to pursue bilateral negotiations.

Vietnam is also likely to seek to further internationalise the maritime dispute by encouraging other key states, including Japan, South Korea, India and the US, to increase their security presence in Southeast Asia. However, Vietnam will need to balance this carefully against exacerbating tensions with China.

Economically, Vietnam is likely to become increasingly integrated with China through investment and trade, given its geography, investment needs, and the increasing regional infrastructure of the Greater Mekong Sub-region. As Vietnam is unlikely to be able to overcome its trade imbalance with China through investment, it will need to expand its export access to the US, the EU and Japanese markets. On the military side, while separate military force modernisation will continue, it is likely that China and Vietnam will also strengthen military cooperation, given China's desire to continue to expand its influence in the region, particularly relative to the US.

Overall, the relationship between Vietnam and China is likely to remain relatively robust, albeit with ongoing cycles of inflamed tensions followed by conciliatory measures. Strong people-to-people links will play a significant role in ensuring ongoing dialogue and a negotiated resolution to the South China Sea dispute.

Patterns of China–Russia Cooperation in Multilateral Forums
(February 2013)

Neil Munro

Lecturer in Chinese Politics, School of Social and Political Sciences, University of Glasgow

Executive Summary

Multilateral forums vary not only in their participants but also in their purposes and the degree of constraint their decisions impose on members. This paper analyses patterns of China–Russia cooperation based on examples from three forums representing different levels of cooperation and different degrees of constraint. These forums are:

- The East Asia Summit (EAS).
- The Shanghai Cooperation Organisation (SCO).
- The UN Security Council (UNSC).

Strategic competition between the US and China in the Asia-Pacific region is growing. Although Russia is often assumed to favour China, its behaviour at the EAS and in other forums in fact reveals a variable position, depending on the issue. For example, Russia has failed to support China's demand that the Spratly and Paracel islands disputes should be resolved through bilateral negotiations between the claimants and has adopted a neutral position regarding China's dispute with Japan over the Diaoyu/Senkaku islands. In terms of wider strategic calculus, China and

Russia once stood together in opposition to US missile defence plans. Now Russia seeks to develop missile defence jointly with the US.

The SCO is at the heart of the China–Russia relationship. Although based on shared views of world politics, the SCO shows signs of internal tension due to political differences between Russia and China and China's superior economic performance. A notable outcome is that China has effectively broken Russia's monopoly on transportation networks for oil and gas in Central Asia. If Russia fails to diversify its sources of growth, it risks becoming unstable in the future. However, China–Russia energy cooperation is deepening, which may help to promote regional economic integration.

Russia and China still tend to unite to defend norms of state sovereignty and non-interference in internal affairs. To a large extent, this is a direct reaction to assertive Western foreign policies which they interpret as expansionist. In dealing with Iran, although the UNSC as a whole recognises the seriousness of the proliferation issue, no effective action has been possible in that forum because of China–Russia cooperation watering down proposed economic sanctions and pre-empting threats of military action.

China–Russia cooperation has been even more obstructive in preventing UNSC resolutions against countries accused of repression. Under the terms of their July 2001 Treaty on Good Neighbourly Friendship and Cooperation, the two states have agreed to oppose the use of force to intervene in the domestic affairs of sovereign states. Under the same treaty they have agreed to strengthen the role of the UN, and especially the responsibility of the UNSC for promoting international peace and stability. Joint adherence to the norm of non-interference reflects a fear of political instability at home and a suspicion that the West desires to foment democratic regime change worldwide.

Introduction

This paper identifies patterns of China–Russia cooperation within multilateral frameworks. Multilateralism implies coordinating national policies among three or more states. At a more substantive level, it involves coordinating behaviour on the basis of general rules applicable to all members. By adhering to such rules, states are able to pursue common goals. A discussion of China–Russia collaboration within multilateral frameworks requires consideration not just of the decisions made in multilateral forums but also a clear focus on the goals that these forums exist to promote and the degree of constraint they impose on their members.

Context

In recent years there has been a proliferation of multilateral forums involving Russia and China: in addition to the EAS, the SCO and the UNSC, there are the Six Party Talks surrounding the two Koreas, the World Trade Organization (WTO) which Russia finally joined in December 2011, various efforts to build free trade areas in Asia and the Pacific, and a range of summit formats that bring together different combinations of states in the region, the major emerging markets, industrialised countries and so on. For reasons of space, this paper will concentrate on three forums, representing different levels of China–Russia cooperation, different degrees of flexibility and constraint, and different issue areas, all with significant implications for the EU. These are the EAS, the SCO, the UNSC.

The EAS is a new forum for Russia. Its Foreign Minister formally participated for the first time in November 2011, along with the US President. Meeting annually since 2005, the EAS was founded by the ten countries of the Association of Southeast Asian Nations (ASEAN) plus China, Korea, Japan, Australia and New Zealand, with Russia attending as a guest. China showed some initial enthusiasm for a regional organisation focused on ASEAN+China, South Korea and Japan. However, after the membership expanded to include India, China welcomed its further expansion, perhaps as a means of ensuring that the format remained relatively 'powerless'. Like many other summit formats, the EAS operates by consensus and can generate resolutions of major political importance, but cannot make binding decisions. Of the three forums discussed here, the EAS has the broadest agenda and the least ability to constrain its members' actions.

The SCO originated in 1996 as the Shanghai Five, including China, Russia, Tajikistan, Kazakhstan and Kyrgyzstan. It was renamed in 2001 when Uzbekistan joined. It has a military dimension focused on 'anti-terrorist' exercises, a political dimension focused on the China–Russia relationship, and an economic dimension focused on energy cooperation and infrastructure development. Its stated purposes include strengthening relations among the members; promoting cooperation across a broad range of policy fields; and promoting security in the region, including efforts to create a 'democratic' and 'just' international order. Its decisions are made by a summit of heads of government which meets yearly.

At the heart of the SCO is the China–Russia relationship, governed by the July 2001 Treaty on Good Neighbourly Friendship and Cooperation, under which the two countries have agreed to cooperate *inter alia*: in advocating strict adherence to international law, opposing use of force to intervene in the internal affairs of sovereign states, preserving global strategic balance and security, promoting nuclear disarmament and preventing proliferation of weapons of mass destruction; and strengthening the role of the UN, especially the responsibility of the Security Council. The SCO has a mid-range ability to constrain its members' actions. However, especially since China failed to offer political support to Russia in its war with Georgia in 2008, Russia has been trying to maximise its influence in Central Asia through organisations overlapping with the Commonwealth of Independent States (CIS), of which China is not a member. Other problems in the relationship include allegations of espionage, the theft of weapons designs and the time taken to secure a deal over gas exports.

The UNSC is composed of five permanent members, Russia, China, France, the UK and the US, along with ten other countries elected for two-year terms by the General Assembly. Under the UN charter, the UNSC is responsible for maintaining international peace and security and member states are obliged to implement its decisions, which on substantive matters require at least nine affirmative votes, including those of the permanent five. It thus has the highest level of ability to constrain its members' actions.

Key Arguments
Geo-strategic considerations

China is in dispute with five of its neighbours in Southeast Asia over control of the Spratly and Paracel island groups and associated territorial waters in the South China Sea, and also with Japan over the Diaoyu/Senkaku islands in the East China Sea. A related issue is the US military stance in Asia more generally. The announcement by Barack Obama in November 2011 that the US would rotate 2,500 troops through Darwin, Australia, was seen as a response to escalating tension in the region. At the same time, the China–Russia strategic partnership is entering a period of flux. For example, at one time, China and Russia were united in their opposition to US missile defence plans, arguing that they would encourage a new Cold War, but Russia has since changed its tune, seeking to develop missile defences jointly with the US, and calling on China to enter into multilateral nuclear disarmament discussions. Russia fears that its own excessive nuclear stockpiles may eventually become obsolete, and has little to lose from reductions. China, by contrast, is seeking to narrow the technological gap with the US, and its nuclear capabilities are poorly understood.

At the EAS in Bali in November 2011, an important issue was whether to include security topics on the agenda, including the South China Sea dispute. China, whose claims are expansive, seeks to resolve the dispute bilaterally with much weaker neighbours. The US, supported by Australia, India, the Philippines, Malaysia, Thailand and Singapore, managed to secure the inclusion of the issue. Russia was among the other countries that talked about maritime security more generally, and only Myanmar/Burma and Cambodia supported China by not touching on it at all. Although Russia may seek material profit from regional rivalry, for instance by selling more submarines to Vietnam, its commercial ambitions in the region require secure and peaceful shipping lanes, as do those of the EU.

Similarly, Russia's position on the Diaoyu/Senkaku islands dispute has been firmly neutral. On a visit to Japan in October 2012, the head of Russia's Security Council, Nikolai Patrushev, said that Russia would not take sides in the dispute and that China and Japan must resolve it through dialogue. Analysts suggest that Russia may feel it has more to gain from helping to limit China's influence in East Asia than it has to lose by offending China.

Economic interests

China received only 6% of its oil from Russia in 2010. This was before the January 2011 opening of the Chinese spur of the East Siberia Pacific Ocean (ESPO) pipeline, which should deliver 300,000 barrels per day to China and make Russia China's third-largest supplier after Saudi Arabia and Angola. However, there are question marks over Russia's ability to deliver this amount, as East Siberia has been insufficiently explored. If East Siberia's reserves turn out to be disappointing, China and Europe could eventually become competitors for West Siberian reserves of oil and gas. Meanwhile, a pipeline connecting Turkmen gas fields to China across Uzbekistan and Kazakhstan has recently been completed, allowing the Central Asian States to reduce their dependence on Russian pipelines.

More than 70% of Russian exports to China are raw materials, while more than 50% of Chinese exports to Russia are technology based. While China has been moving steadily up the value chain, Russia is dangerously dependent on oil and gas.

China has the money and capacity to deliver needed infrastructure, and Russia has resources China needs. Their cooperation has the potential to become the core of regional integration processes. It is in the EU's interest that these processes should succeed and that Russia as a whole should become prosperous. Chinese proposals for high-speed rail-links to Europe are an example of the type of infrastructure which may be developed as a result. In addition, as argued by Keun-Wook Paik of the Oxford Energy Institute, projects based on the exploitation of Russian energy resources can help to wean China from its dependency on coal.

Non-proliferation and human rights

Both China and Russia emphasise multilateralism in their foreign policy concepts, including resolving conflicts within the UNSC framework. Both also recognise Iran's right to pursue nuclear enrichment as long as it complies with the International Atomic Energy Agency's regulations. Western diplomats complain about the role of Russian and Chinese cooperation in 'watering down' resolutions against Iran. In January 2012, China refused an appeal by the US to cooperate in implementing economic sanctions, and without Russian and Chinese support effective action under a UN mandate appears next to impossible. North Korea has set a baleful precedent. After more than a decade of fruitless negotiation and considerable expense in the form of aid to North Korea, its regime presented the world with a *fait accompli* with its first nuclear test in October 2006. India did the same in 1998.

China and Russia have repeatedly used a double veto against sanctions on countries accused of political repression. This includes Syria (October 2011 and February and July 2012), Zimbabwe (July 2008) and Myanmar/Burma (January 2007). In the case of Libya (March 2011), Resolution 1973 authorised all necessary measures to protect civilians, and Russia and China both abstained along with Brazil, India and Germany. Russian and Chinese acquiescence took consideration of Arab League support for a no-fly zone, but their attitudes to the action changed after it became clear that its purpose was to assist the rebels.

Russia and China's double vetoes of UNSC resolutions on Syria in February and July 2012 and their 'no' votes to the UN General Assembly (UNGA) resolution on 16 February 2012 marked a deepening rift with the West. The vote in UNGA (137 countries in favour, 12 against, and 17 abstained) showed that Russia and China were relatively isolated from the mainstream of world opinion, along with such 'anti-US' countries as Iran, North Korea, Cuba and Venezuela. While Russia and China have a shared position at the UN, their motives appear different. Although both countries endorse the principle of non-interference in the internal affairs of sovereign states, Russia is a long-standing ally of the Syrian regime, and has plans to build up an existing supply base for its navy in Tartus, while China's material interests in Syria are slight. China's main objection to the UNSC and UNGA resolutions was that these resolutions called on President Bashar al-Assad to step down, which meant taking sides in an internal dispute. Although both Russia and China sell arms to Syria, the amounts are small compared to their worldwide volumes.

The strength of China and Russia's opposition to even political interventions in Syria reflects their shared anxiety about regime changes initiated from below — the so-called 'colour revolutions' — which have occurred in former Soviet countries and North Africa. Both countries share a perception that even when no foreign military intervention occurs, these kinds of regime changes have been orchestrated with the participation of Western intelligence services. Analytical commentaries on both Russian and Chinese state-run television have alleged that the situation in Syria has been deliberately stoked up in order to provide an excuse for 'humanitarian' intervention.

Although neither country sees Syria as primarily a human rights issue, they would argue that interference in other countries' affairs in defence of human rights is unwarranted. Thus, Russia was among the 16 countries that boycotted the award ceremony for Liu Xiaobo's Nobel Peace Prize in December 2010. Firm Russian support for China's position in the UN Human Rights Commission (UNHRC) dates from 1995 and Russia helped China to foil US attempts to reform the UNHRC in 2005. It seems likely that only a significant liberalisation of the political climate in Russia or China would change their evolutionary view of human rights as an aspiration which must be balanced against the priority of political stability.

Conclusions

- The China–Russia strategic partnership is entering a period of flux. For example, at one time, China and Russia stood together in opposition to US missile defence plans. Now Russia seeks to develop missile defence jointly with the US. Neither country has supported the other in territorial disputes with neighbours.

- China has effectively broken Russia's monopoly on transportation networks for oil and gas in Central Asia. If Russia fails to diversify its sources of growth, it risks becoming unstable in future.
- The EU, Russia and China have a shared interest in deepening China–Russia economic integration as the foundation stone of a wider economic space spanning Europe and Asia.
- Although all UNSC members share common interests in pursuing non-proliferation, China–Russia cooperation has effectively thwarted effective action on this issue through the UNSC.
- Similarly, in the human rights field, China and Russia are solidly against intervention in the domestic affairs of sovereign states, for reasons related to their own political stability.

Competing Claims in the South China Sea: Assessment and Prospects
(July 2012)

Philip Andrews-Speed

Principal Fellow, Energy Studies Institute (ESI), National University of Singapore

Executive Summary

The South China Sea has great economic and strategic significance for East Asia and for the EU. These seas provide passage for some 30% of world seaborne trade. They also harbour substantial fish stocks and are believed to hold significant hydrocarbon resources. This large maritime region is host to several territorial and maritime disputes and the last two years have seen a number of stand-offs and skirmishes involving China, most notably with the Philippines and Vietnam. In response to what is seen as China's growing assertiveness, the other coastal states are strengthening their maritime forces and are going to considerable lengths to ensure that the US navy remains engaged in the region. The risk of armed conflict is increasing.

Three types of dispute require resolution in the South China Sea: (1) sovereignty over groups of islands, (2) the extent to which these islands generate extended maritime claims and (3) overlapping maritime claims. These disputes could be resolved through established international judicial procedures. While the outcomes of these procedures are impossible to predict, recent jurisprudence suggests that:

- Sovereignty over each of the disputed island groups might be divided between the respective claimants, rather than granted to just one claimant.

- The effect of these island groups on maritime delimitation would be minimised.
- The subsequent delimitation of extended continental shelves would remain a complex task.

However, East Asian states prefer to rely on direct negotiation rather than to submit disputes to third-party adjudication or arbitration. This creates a potential role for the EU to urge the parties to make progress in these negotiations in order to alleviate tensions and reduce the risk of armed conflict.

The first priority should be to encourage China and the other coastal states around the South China Sea proper to start negotiations to establish a number of joint development arrangements for hydrocarbon exploration and exploitation. These would provide a stable environment for investment to explore and exploit much needed energy resources and should help build trust between the parties.

The second priority should be to persuade the coastal states to follow international jurisprudence and reach a collective agreement that the disputed islands have minimal effect with respect to maritime delimitation. This would clear the way for the states to follow the procedures of the UN Law of the Sea to address the problem of overlapping extended continental shelves. The issue of island sovereignty could then also be addressed, but in a less inflammatory context.

Main Points

- The South China Sea has great strategic significance for East Asia and the EU, but is host to a number of unresolved disputes relating to islands and maritime territory.
- Recent events in this region show that inter-state tensions are rising. Limited armed conflict could arise unintentionally.
- The coastal states prefer to resolve disputes through direct negotiation rather than through the involvement of third parties (judicial or mediation).
- Two initial goals for these negotiations would be (1) the establishment of joint development arrangements for hydrocarbons, and (2) agreement that the disputed islands should have minimal effect on the delimitation of maritime zones.

Issues Examined by the Paper

This paper examines the competing claims over islands and maritime territories in the South China Sea. After presenting background information on the South China Sea and recent events, the paper provides an account of the principles of island sovereignty and maritime delimitation as applied to the South China Sea. It then examines the available mechanisms for dispute resolution and management and how they have been applied in this region. The paper concludes with an assessment of the situation, three scenarios and options for the promotion of collaboration between the coastal states.

Background to the South China Sea Disputes
Basic information

The South China Sea proper is a semi-enclosed sea stretching from Taiwan to Singapore and covering an area of about 3.5 m square kilometres. This paper will also cover parts of the wider South China Sea, specifically the Gulfs of Tonkin and Thailand. The ten coastal states of the wider South China Sea are (clockwise from the north): China, Taiwan, the Philippines, Malaysia, Brunei, Indonesia, Singapore, Thailand, Cambodia and Vietnam.

The South China Sea has great economic and strategic significance for East Asia and for the EU. These seas provide passage for some 30% of world seaborne trade. This trade includes ever growing quantities of oil, gas, coal and other raw materials going to China, as well as manufactured goods being exported from China, Japan and Korea. These seas also harbour substantial fish stocks and are believed to hold significant hydrocarbon resources. This large maritime region is host to several territorial and maritime disputes which date back to the end of World War II and the end of the Cold War. Some of the territorial disputes relate to groups of (mainly) uninhabited islands and expand the potential scope for conflicting maritime claims. Most controversial is the 'nine-dashed line' of China (and Taiwan) which appears to represent China's claim to historical rights and embraces nearly all of the South China Sea proper. Progress towards resolving these disputes is constrained by historical resentments and by entrenched views of sovereignty which have hardened over the last two decades.

Recent events

Recent incidents at sea involving Chinese and Philippine ships are but the latest encounters between China and its neighbours in the South China Sea. In June 2011 the Vietnamese government accused a Chinese fishing boat of deliberately cutting across seismic cables being dragged by a Vietnamese boat. China arrested two Vietnamese fishing boats near the Paracel Islands in March 2012. The latest incident resulted from the attempt by a Philippine patrol vessel to arrest Chinese fishermen believed to have been catching protected species in waters around the Scarborough Shoal that lies just 220 km from the Philippine Island of Luzon. Similar incidents have also been occurring in the East China Sea. Tensions have been raised further since late June 2012 by Vietnam's formal protest at China's invitation to foreign oil companies to bid for oil exploration blocks in the South China Sea. Vietnam claims that not only do that these blocks lie in their waters, but they also overlap with areas already licensed by Vietnam to foreign companies.

The significance of China

While the triggers for these clashes are most likely to have been fishermen with little knowledge of or respect for international maritime law, the speed and manner of escalation reflect long-standing tensions between the coastal states of the South China Seas. These tensions have been accentuated by the steady growth of China's economic, political and military power and by its consequent willingness to assert itself in the region, which in turn have provoked unease among its neighbours. While China can rightly claim that the actions of other coastal states have been provocative, its behaviour in these seas over the last few years reflects internal, often bureaucratic tensions between those institutions that wish to secure their own or the nation's economic and sovereign interests and the Ministry of Foreign Affairs, which wants to present China as a responsible international citizen. The net result is that irrespective of who in China is responsible for many of these incidents, the impact on the littoral states has been very clear. These states are strengthening their own maritime forces and are going to considerable lengths to ensure that the US navy remains engaged in the region. The risk of armed conflict is increasing, although none of the states seek such conflict.

Island Sovereignty and Maritime Delimitation
Key principles

The primary source of law relating to maritime delimitation is the United Nations Convention on the Law of the Sea (UNCLOS). The underlying principle is that the right to maritime territory derives from sovereignty over adjacent land, and this principle provides the basis for delineating a number of zones with different rights (see Table 1). As a consequence, two interconnected types of problem arise in the South China Sea: disputes about sovereignty over islands, and disputes over maritime delimitation.

Rocks and islands

Disputes over island features have three aspects:

- Which nation has sovereignty over the island? (Not a matter for UNCLOS.)
- Is the feature an island or a rock? (See Table 1.)
- What is the effect of an island on maritime delineation? (See Table 1.)

Four significant groups of island features exist in the South China Sea proper, of which three are disputed (see Table 2). Of these, the Spratly Islands occupy the most critical physical location and are claimed, in part or totality, by six countries. Taiwan has a military base on the largest of these islands (Itu Aba) and the Philippines occupies Pagasa Island. In 1992, China passed the Law on Territorial Sea and Continuous Zones which includes an explicit statement of sovereignty over all four features listed in Table 2. Very recently (June 2012), Vietnam passed a maritime law which asserts its sovereignty over the Paracel and Spratly islands.

Just as important as sovereignty, is the issue of whether or not these island groups can generate extended maritime claims. If they are capable of generating exclusive economic zones (EEZs) and continental shelf rights, then no continental shelf beyond the 200 nautical miles (nm) limit exists in the South China Sea proper. Conversely, extended continental shelf areas only exist in the South China Sea proper if the disputed islands are judged to be incapable of generating extended maritime claims. Most of the coastal states appear to hold the view that the effect of the island features should be small; but China takes the opposing view.

Table 1. Simplified definitions of terminology from UNCLOS.

Term	Simplified physical definition	Significance (selected) for coastal state
Island	Naturally formed area of land, surrounded by water, which is above water at high tide; and which can sustain human habitation or economic life of its own.	Provides a basis for determining territorial sea, contiguous zone, EEZ and continental shelf.
Rock	An island which cannot sustain human habitation or economic life of its own.	No EEZ and no continental shelf.
Base line for territorial sea	Low water line along the coast.	Provides starting point for definition of the various zones of rights.
Territorial sea	No more than 12 nm from baselines.	Full sovereignty over sea, air, seabed and sub-seabed.
Contiguous zone	No more than 14 nm from baselines.	Rights to exercise control relating to infringement of domestic laws.
Exclusive economic zone (EEZ)	No more than 200 nm from baselines.	Sovereign rights relating to the exploration, exploitation, conservation and management of natural resources (living and non-living). Jurisdiction over establishment and use of artificial islands and structures, over scientific research, and over marine environmental protection.
Continental shelf	Either the outer edge of the continental margin or 200 nm from baselines, whichever is further, and not further than 350 km (with exceptions), provided there is no overlap with neighbours.	Sovereign rights over the exploration and exploitation of mineral and non-living natural resources on seabed and in subsoil, and harvestable, stationary living organisms on or under the seabed.
Extended continental shelf (informal term)	That part of the continental shelf extending more than 200 nm from baselines.	As for continental shelf.

Table 2. Summary of main island groups in the South China Sea proper.

Name (Chinese name)	Number of features	Claimants	Occupancy
Spratly (Nansha)	150+	Brunei, China, Malaysia, Philippines, Taiwan and Vietnam	China, Taiwan, Vietnam, Philippines, Malaysia
Paracel (Xisha)	130	China, Taiwan and Vietnam	China
Macclesfield Bank (Zhongsha) and Scarborough Shoal (Huangyan)		China, Philippines	
Pratas (Dongsha)		Not disputed	Taiwan

The continental shelf and extended continental shelf

The most difficult types of maritime dispute to resolve are those which revolve around the definition of the edge of the continental shelf (see Table 1). A large amount of data has to be collected and a multi-disciplinary approach is needed. This requires technical expertise and financial resources and is highly subjective. To address this problem, UNCLOS established a UN Commission on the Limits of the Continental Shelf (CLCS), the role of which is to make a technical evaluation of the extent to which coastal states have followed the requirements of UNCLOS in establishing the limits of their continental shelves. It is not a dispute resolution body. Three submissions relating to EEZs and continental shelves have been made in the South China Sea proper:

- A joint submission by Malaysia and Vietnam (May 2009) which fixes the outer limits of EEZs and identifies a disputed area of outer continental shelf claims which lies to the southwest of the Spratly Islands. This led to formal protests from China and the Philippines concerning sovereignty over the different island groups.
- A submission by Vietnam (May 2009) covering an area lying to the north of the joint submission, just southeast of the Paracel Islands. Again this led to protests from China and the Philippines.
- A preliminary submission of Brunei (May 2009) indicating that it is likely to make a claim for some of the area covered by the joint Malaysia–Vietnam submission.

Dispute Resolution and Management

The options for dispute resolution include direct negotiation, a judicial court such as the International Court of Justice (ICJ) or the International Tribunal of the Law of the Sea (ITLOS), arbitration at the Permanent Court of Arbitration (PCA) or an *ad hoc* tribunal, and mediation, conciliation or good offices. Alternatively the parties can set aside the dispute and negotiate a joint development arrangement (JDA) to exploit the natural resources and establish other confidence-building measures.

Disputes over islands

In territorial disputes over islands, courts and tribunals look at the effective control and display of sovereignty by one (or more) parties before the dispute arose, and at the acquiescence to that control and display by other parties. The ICJ has also focused attention on whether the use of the island feature for generating extended maritime claims would have a disproportionate or inequitable effect. As a consequence, islands have been variously given full effect, half effect or partial effect, and have even been enclaved. The general trend is to reduce the effect of small islands on maritime claims. Three territorial disputes over islands in the wider South China Sea have been resolved at the ICJ, but none of these have involved China:

- Natuna Islands, Vietnam–Indonesia (2003). The court took into account historical arguments and final judgment was made on the basis of 'effectiveness' of control.
- Pulau Ligitan and Pulau Sipidan, Malaysia–Indonesia (2002). The ICJ concluded in Malaysia's favour as it had demonstrated a degree of administrative authority over the islands.
- Pedro Branca/Pulau Batu Puteh, Malaysia–Singapore (2008). The original title lay with Malaysia, but the ICJ ruled that sovereignty had passed to Singapore. In the related cases, the ICJ ruled that Middle Rock should remain with Malaysia, and that South Reef belongs to the state in whose territorial waters it lies, an issue that is still unresolved.

Maritime delimitation disputes

In deciding disputes over maritime delimitation, courts and tribunals look at the physical geography of the coast and tend not to take into account demographic, economic or security issues. In areas of overlapping territorial sea, the median line method is used unless historical rights or some other special circumstances dictate otherwise. All the coastal states of the wider South China Sea are signatories of UNCLOS, and only Cambodia has not yet ratified it. UNCLOS states that if a dispute arises and if bilateral negotiation fails, the parties are free to choose a dispute settlement mechanism. Conciliation is the mechanism proposed by UNCLOS. If this fails, the parties should take a judicial path through the ICJ, ITLOS or arbitration. Of these three, the ICJ has taken by far the greatest number of maritime delimitation cases, but none in the South China Sea.

With one exception (Singapore–Malaysia), the coastal states of the South China Sea have preferred to exclude third parties and to pursue settlement through negotiation. Examples of disputes resolved in this way include: the agreements between Indonesia, Malaysia, Singapore and Thailand over the Malacca Straits (1969–1973); agreements in the Gulf of Thailand between Malaysia and Thailand (1979), and between Thailand and Vietnam (1997); agreements in the southwestern part of the South China Sea proper between Brunei and Malaysia (1958), Indonesia and Malaysia (1969), and Indonesia and Vietnam (2003); and between China and Vietnam in the Gulf of Tonkin (2000).

In addition to the island disputes discussed in the previous section, three groups of maritime dispute remain unresolved in the wider South China Sea:

- Vietnam, Indonesia, Malaysia, Brunei and the Philippines all object to the nine-dashed line of China and Taiwan which overlaps the EEZs and shelf claims of these states.
- Bilateral overlapping claims and undefined boundaries in the South China Sea proper between Malaysia and Indonesia, Malaysia and the Philippines, and Vietnam and Indonesia.
- In the Gulf of Thailand overlapping claims involve Malaysia, Thailand and Vietnam, and bilateral disputes exist between Cambodia and Thailand, and Cambodia and Vietnam.

Other approaches to dispute management

Two other approaches can be and have been taken to manage, rather than settle, disputes in the South China Sea: JDAs and confidence-building measures. JDAs are commonly used around the world to allow two or more states to jointly undertake the exploitation of natural resources in disputed waters. Examples in the South China Sea are mostly restricted to the Gulf of Thailand and include the Malaysia–Thailand (1979) and Malaysia–Vietnam (1992) JDAs. The JDA between Vietnam and Cambodia (1982) has not yet been implemented and one between Cambodia and Thailand is under negotiation. In the South China Sea proper Brunei and Malaysia have agreed a revenue sharing area, and China, Philippines and Vietnam concluded a tripartite agreement in 2005 to carry out seismic exploration.

The major player in pursuing confidence-building measures has been the Association of Southeast Asian Nations (ASEAN) which issued a Declaration on the South China Sea in 1992 that emphasised the need to resolve disputes peacefully and to exercise restraint. Ten years later, ASEAN and China signed Declaration on the Conduct (DOC) of the Parties in the South China Sea. The DOC was followed by the ASEAN Dispute Settlement Mechanism in 2009 and the (very vague) Guidelines for the Implementation of the DOC in 2011.

Assessment
Key considerations

These disputes over island features and maritime delimitation could be resolved through established international procedures. The ICJ or an arbitral tribunal could resolve the disputes over the island features and decide on their effect. This would probably involve historical evidence for some of the Chinese, Taiwanese and Vietnamese claims. UNCLOS procedures could then be applied for maritime delimitation. While the outcomes of these procedures are impossible to predict, recent jurisprudence suggests that:

- Sovereignty over each of the disputed islands groups might be divided between the respective claimants, rather than granted to just one claimant.
- The effect of these island groups on maritime delimitation would be minimised.
- The subsequent delimitation of extended continental shelves would remain a complex task, but China's continental shelf would probably be restricted to the northwestern part of the South China Sea proper.

However, the record shows that East Asian states prefer to rely on direct negotiation rather than to submit disputes to third-party adjudication or arbitration. While direct negotiation has yielded agreements between many of the coastal states of the wider South China Sea, none of these agreements have involved China (with the exception of the Gulf of Tonkin) or have covered the central areas of the South China Sea proper. The lack of progress in this region reflects the complex combination of overlapping maritime claims and sovereignty disputes over islands, as well as the general lack of trust between China and the other coastal states.

Possible scenarios

Three scenarios can be envisaged:

- Business as usual. This scenario would see little change in the South China Sea proper. Rhetoric, bickering and skirmishing would continue. No JDAs would be established, and no territorial or maritime disputes would be resolved. The risk of escalation into armed conflict persists at a low level. In the Gulf of Thailand, the progress towards resolving disputes and establishing JDAs would continue at a slow pace.
- Joint development. In this scenario, the coastal states of the South China Sea proper follow the example of those in the Gulf of Thailand and make progress to establish JDAs. These attempts will be complicated by the probable need for multilateral and not just bilateral agreements. Such progress might lead to tentative steps being taken to address the island and maritime disputes through direct negotiation or, less likely, through third-party involvement.
- Rising tensions. Here the skirmishes increase in frequency and intensity, and eventually lead to limited armed conflict between opposing navies. Such conflict may not be deliberate central government policy of any of the countries around the South China Sea, but a combination of external provocation and domestic frictions might encourage the navy of one country to deliberately test the nerve of the other states.

Annex One: Historical Chronology (Selected Highlights)
Pre-20th century

Historical records form the basis for the claim of 'historical rights' over the islands of the South China Sea by a number of nations:

- The Chinese claim that their sailors were navigating the waters of the South China Sea 2,000 years ago and discovered these islands. Historical documents

and maps purportedly show that China discovered, surveyed, named and administered these islands over the succeeding centuries.
- The Philippines also base their claim over the Spratly islands on discovery.
- Although Vietnam claims to have ancient rights over the Spratly and Paracel Islands, currently available historical documents only support Vietnam's activity in these island groups since the 17th century. In the 18th and 19th century, Vietnam organised the exploitation of natural resources on and around the Paracel Islands.

Early 20th century

The early decades of the 21st century saw the first steps to formally address the issue of sovereignty:

- After the fall of the Qing Dynasty in 1911, China was unable to actively assert its sovereignty over these islands. In 1914 the nationalist government published the first map with the 'nine-dashed line' to show the extent of China's 'historical waters' and this practice has been continued by the communist government since 1949. Yet neither actor formally explained the significance of the line nor of the term 'historical waters'.
- The 1898 Spanish–American Treaty did not include the Spratly Islands within the Philippines.
- France occupied the Paracel Islands in the 1930s and then transferred them to Vietnam.

World War II

During World War II, Japan occupied the Spratly and Paracel Islands and controlled most of the South China Sea until pushed back by the USA.

1945–1970

The end of World War II ushered in a relatively quiet period during which sovereignty over island groups was unclear and individual nations were more concerned with domestic nationbuilding than with asserting claims.

- After the end of World War II, Japan withdrew from the South China Sea. Both the communist government of the People's Republic of China and the Nationalist

Republic of China government in Taiwan claimed sovereignty over the Paracel and Spratly Islands. But they were unable to assert their claims formally as neither was invited to the San Francisco Conference of 1951 at which Japan was obliged to renounce sovereignty over these two islands groups.
- The Philippines wanted to make a formal claim over the Spratly Islands in 1946 but were prevented from doing so by the US, who did not want to see conflict between the Philippines and the nationalist government of China.
- Vietnam did participate in the San Francisco Conference and issued a statement asserting its sovereignty over the Paracel and Spratly Islands, and occupied some of the Paracel Islands in 1951 together with French soldiers.
- In 1956 China occupied some other islands in the Paracel group. While the government of South Vietnam protested, the communist government of North Vietnam explicitly acknowledged Chinese sovereignty over the Paracel and Spratly Islands in 1956 and 1958.
- In 1956 a Philippine business man hoisted the national flag on several of the Spratly islands, claiming them for the Philippines. The following year the Philippine and US navies began conducting exercises in the area of the Scarborough Shoal and the Macclesfield Bank and in 1965 a lighthouse was built.
- In the 1950s, China's government was pre-occupied with Taiwan and did not actively pursue its claims in the South China Sea, but in 1958 its Declaration on China's Territorial Sea stated that the Pratas, Paracel and Spratly Islands and the Macclesfield bank belonged to China.

1970–1990

The 1970s were marked by the end of the Vietnam War, a major political transition in China, and the realisation that the South China Sea might contain large quantities of petroleum. These events triggered a rise of interest in asserting sovereignty over the islands of the South China Sea.

- The government of the Philippines formally confirmed its claim over most of, but not all of the Spratly Islands in 1971, a time in which it was taking the first steps to explore for offshore petroleum. China formally protested against the Philippine claim and reasserted its sovereignty over all the islands of the South China Sea. Diplomatic relations were re-established in the 1975 and neither side sought to escalate the dispute during the 1970s and 1980s.

- A sea battle over the Paracel Islands occurred between China and South Vietnam in 1974 which resulted in South Vietnam having to end its occupation of these islands. Despite this loss, South Vietnam enhanced its presence in the Spratly islands by issuing oil exploration licences. The new communist government of Vietnam occupied some of the Spratly Islands and reasserted its claim over the Paracel and Spratly Islands 1975.
- Vietnam's alliance with the USSR made China fearful of encirclement, but China limited its response to diplomatic measures and to building up its military presence on the Paracel Islands.
- Malaysia asserted its claim over some of the Spratly islands and from 1979 started occupying them. In 1984, Brunei claimed one of the islands.
- By the late 1980s Vietnam, Philippines, Taiwan and Malaysia each occupied different features in the Spratly Islands. After a battle with Vietnam in 1988, China established a military presence in the Spratly Islands and incorporated them and the Paracel Islands into Hainan Province.

1990–2005

The end of the Cold War and the progressive economic rise of China triggered a change in attitudes and behaviours in the South China Sea. UNCLOS came into force in 1994, and provided a new forum of the governments to pursue their claims. For the first time, ASEAN started to pay close attention to the South China Sea.

- In the early 1990s, the US reduced its military presence in the Philippines.
- China and Vietnam normalised relationships in 1991.
- In 1992 China enacted its Law of Territorial Sea and the Contiguous Zone which reasserted its claims over the islands of the South China Sea. At the same time the government expressed its interest in exploring for hydrocarbons. In 1995, China occupied the Mischief Reef in the Spratly Islands.
- In 1994, Vietnam reaffirmed its claim over the Paracel and Spratly Islands at its ratification of UNCLOS.
- The Philippines made its first formal claim to the Scarborough Shoal in 1997.
- In 1998 China enacted its Law on the Exclusive Economic Zone and Continental Shelf. This drew protests from the Philippines and led to disputes and skirmishes over the Spratly Islands and the Scarborough Shoal.
- ASEAN and China signed a Declaration of Conduct in the South China Sea in 2002. As a consequence, China, Philippines and Vietnam concluded a

tripartite agreement in 2005 to carry out seismic exploration in an area of the South China Sea.

Significance for the Legal Effect of the Islands

When adjudicating territorial disputes over islands, international courts and tribunals look at the effective control and display of sovereignty by one (or more) parties *before* the dispute arose, and at the acquiescence to that control and display by other parties.

In this respect, we can deduce from this chronological summary that international courts and tribunals *may* choose to focus on the period after the withdrawal of Japan in 1945 and before the 1970s when the disputes started to arise. *If* they take this approach, courts and tribunals *may* favour China and Vietnam in the Paracel Islands and the Philippines and China in the Spratly Islands, though proximity may strengthen the case of the Philippines in the Spratlys. The Scarborough Shoal and Macclesfield Bank remain unoccupied, but the Philippines *may* be favoured through displays of sovereignty.

All these cases will be complicated by the fact that other parties have, in general, not shown acquiescence. As a consequence, rather than assign sovereignty for an entire island group to one nation or another, an international court or tribunal *may* choose to sub-divide each island group between two or more claimants.

The ICJ has also focused attention on whether the use of the island feature for generating extended maritime claims would have a disproportionate or inequitable effect. As a consequence, islands have been variously given full effect, half effect or partial effect, and have even been enclaved. The general trend is to reduce the effect of small islands on maritime claims.

On this basis, an international court or tribunal *may* choose to assign only partial effect to the island groups of the South China Sea. As a consequence, the delimitation of maritime zones would then be based primarily on baselines drawn along mainland coastlines or around agreed archipelagos.

Annex Two: The Diaoyu/Senkaku Islands Dispute in the East China Sea

Names

Chinese name: Diaoyu Islands; Japanese name: Senkaku Islands.

Location

The eight uninhabited islands of this island group lie northeast of Taiwan and midway between the Chinese mainland and Japan's Okinawa Island.

Administration

The islands are currently administered by Japan.

Claimants

The islands are claimed by China, Japan and Taiwan, and are located towards the southwestern end of a 200-nm-wide disputed maritime area. The dispute over the maritime area arises because China claims the full width of the continental shelf which extends eastwards from China to about 50-nm west of the Ryukyu Islands of Japan. In contrast, Japan claims the maritime area up to the median line between Japan and China.

History

- Chinese written records of these islands date back to 15th century and illustrate the administration of the islands during the Ming and Qing dynasties.
- Japan formally annexed the islands in 1895 after the First Sino–Japanese War and this was confirmed by China in the Treaty of Shimonoseki in the same year. Japan retained effective sovereignty until 1945 when the USA took over control.
- The treaty of San Francisco in 1951 nullified the Treaty of Shimonoseki.
- In 1972, the USA handed the islands back to Japan, and since then they have been administered by the Mayor of Ishigaki. The islands are included in the US–Japan Security Treaty.

Chinese (and Taiwanese) arguments in support of their claim

- Historical arguments.
- A letter written in 1885 by the Japanese Minister of Foreign affairs stating that it was inappropriate for Japan to claim these islands.

- The Cairo Declaration of 1941 and the Potsdam Declaration of 1945 which limited Japanese sovereignty to the main islands of Japan.
- The occupation of the islands by the US had no relevance for the validity of different claims.

Political significance

The islands have become emblematic of unresolved historical differences between China and Japan dating back to Japan's progressive occupation of China which started in the 1931.

Strategic importance

Occupation of the islands by a military force could threaten China, Taiwan or Japan as well as sea lanes between Northeast Asia and the South China Sea.

Economic significance

The economic significance of the islands lies in the fact that they could generate extensive rights over the East China Sea, an area rich in fish resources and possible oil and gas resources, though only limited gas reserves have been proven to date.

Oil and gas development

In 1969 the UN published a report which suggested that significant reserves of oil and gas may lie under the East China Sea. During the 1970s China was self-sufficient in energy and saw no need to explore for these hydrocarbons nor to reach agreement with Japan over maritime delimitation. Minor skirmishes around the islands occurred from 1978 onwards, but both sides played down the dispute in order to further economic cooperation. Brief talks on joint hydrocarbon development were held in the mid-1980s, but led nowhere. Escalation of the dispute began in 1992 when the islands were named in China's Law on the Territorial Sea and Contiguous Zone. In 1996 China discovered reserves of gas in the Chunxiao field just 5 kilometres from the theoretical median line. This and other gas fields probably extend into waters claimed by Japan. China started to build production platforms on the Chunxiao field in 2006. After four years of negotiation China and Japan reached an informal agreement in 2008 to create a joint development zone, but no progress has been made to draft and implement a detailed agreement.

Significance for sovereignty over and effect of the islands

Following the arguments laid out in the context of the South China Sea, an international court or tribunal *may* choose to ignore events before the 20th century and even those before 1945, and rather to focus on Japan's administration of the islands since 1971. However, the picture is complicated by the number of international documents relating to Japan's sovereignty over islands in the East China Sea. The adjudicating body *could* decide to sub-divide the islands between China and Japan, and to limit their effect on maritime delimitation.

The Impact of the Arab Revolutions on China's Foreign Policy
(May 2012)

Ben Simpfendorfer
Founder, Silk Road Associates

Executive Summary

The Arab revolutions have presented a serious test for China's foreign policy at a time when the country is facing its greatest domestic challenge for nearly two decades.

That said, the Middle East is less central to China's foreign policy than it is to the foreign policy of both Europe and the US. In part, this is a matter of expediency given the country's still-developing foreign policy capabilities and the demands of other regions, in particular the US, Europe and Southeast Asia. The fact that China's reengagement with the Middle East is barely a decade old is another factor.

Moreover, the Arab revolutions have not seriously threatened China's oil security: oil imports from Egypt, Libya, Syria and Yemen account for just 5% of total oil imports. Nonetheless, there has been a 'tactical' change in China's foreign policy in the Middle East. Most important is China's engagement with opposition groups in armed conflict with the state. There is growing recognition that political regimes can and do change through conflict, and so opening dialogue with opposition movements can help to mitigate against risk.

The long-standing policy of 'non-intervention' remains intact as a strategic objective: most academics and officials will still privately and publicly declare their support for the principle. However, whether it can in fact survive the constant 'tactical' changes that have so far been evident in the Middle East is yet to be seen. But Chinese officials are certainly operating on the assumption of no change.

Europe should respond to China's tactical change in foreign policy. However, it is best advised to expect only a gradual evolution, rather than revolution, in policy. Engaging with China through multiple parties is critical, whether through embassies or academics. Engaging through non-public means is also important, to avoid putting officials or academics in the awkward position of conflicting with state policy and ensuring healthy debate between all sides.

Above all, consideration must be given to China's long-term domestic interests, as this is how the country's foreign policy is determined. To this end, the stability of existing regimes best serves China's interests for now. This would change only in the event of conflict between major oil producers, or a sudden shift in 'international' public opinion away from China's position.

Main Points

- China's policy of 'non-intervention' remains its strategic objective. Officials and academics will privately and publically declare their support for the principle.
- However, there is growing recognition that some 'tactical' flexibility is needed in order to respond to the fact that regimes can and do change.
- China's engagement with opposition movements in conflict with the state is one such example of 'tactical' flexibility, as previously the country dealt only with the ruling authorities.
- Nonetheless, the change is evolutionary, not revolutionary, and will not yet materially change the Middle East's outlook, or result in China abandoning its strategic policy of non-intervention.
- China's domestic interests remain central to the country's foreign policy and, in the Middle East, are best served by support for existing regimes.
- Europe must engage with change through multiple Chinese actors, while dampening expectations for significant short-term results.

Introduction

The Arab revolutions have presented a serious test for China's foreign policy at a time when the country is facing some of its greatest domestic challenges for nearly two decades: a leadership change as the fifth generation of leaders takes power; internal Party tensions with the fall of Politburo member Bo Xilai; and risks from an economy that is increasingly reliant on state-owned and heavy industrial-led activity.

However, observing this change is not straightforward to the casual observer. The influences on China's foreign policy are markedly different to those in Europe and the US — whether the result of China's status as a developing country, its short history as a participant in Middle East politics, its focus on economic security as opposed to political security, or its disinterest in political reforms. This also makes it difficult for Middle East observers to apply the same analytical framework to China's behaviour in the region as that used to understand the behaviour of Europe and the US.

A good example is the Israeli–Palestinian conflict. The fact that China has no powerful Israeli lobby (unlike the US) and no historical obligation to deal with the problem (unlike Europe) allows China to sit on the sidelines where possible. As a senior Chinese official once privately commented: 'Why should we get involved? Neither side is serious about finding a solution'.

The challenge is compounded by the fact that China's reengagement with the Middle East is arguably only a decade old and one largely based on commercial relations. There is little published material on the subject and what is available dates relatively quickly. Field research, rather than academic theory, is therefore the more appropriate way to understand the changes taking place.

With that in mind, this paper is written from two perspectives: first, as an Arabic and Chinese-speaking scholar of China's reengagement with the Middle East; second, and arguably more importantly, as a private sector participant in China's strengthening trade and investment relations with the Middle East, focused on acquisition, joint venture, and capital-raising opportunities between the two.

The Middle East in China's World View

It is popular to assume that the Middle East is a primary focus for China's foreign policy, just as it is for Europe and the US. That, however, is not the case. This might appear counterintuitive given that China's oil imports already account for half of domestic oil consumption, and the share is rising steadily. It is, however, a matter of expediency: China's foreign policy priorities are shaped by the country's still-limited foreign policy capabilities at least relative to the large developed countries and the realities of its geography.

The US as the world's major economic and military power is naturally a primary focus. Europe is also a focus given the region's similar economic power, albeit more 'diluted' military and political power. Korea, Japan, Russia and Southeast Asia, while individually less important, are still a key focus, whether because of shared borders, commercial relations, or historical disputes.

The upshot of this is that China's Middle East policy is often a 'residual' of its foreign policy in other regions, especially with respect to China's broader relations with the US. For instance, China's stance on Iran cannot be viewed in isolation, but rather against the backdrop of what China is simultaneously seeking from the US in Taiwan, the South China Sea, or even trade issues.

Three additional realities underscore its secondary position. First, China's long-standing policy of not intervening in the affairs of other countries has allowed it to avoid committing significant resources to dealing with the Middle East's most protracted problems, in contrast to Europe and the US: the Israeli–Palestinian conflict is the most obvious example with China playing a negligible role since its re-emergence over the past decade.

This comes in spite of the fact China has emerged as a strong trade partner of Israel, even importing large amounts of Israeli arms. Israel has lobbied China aggressively, especially through sponsoring students, academics and media to study and work in Israel. They form part of what is popularly called an 'Israeli faction', although this faction has only limited influence and cannot be compared to those in Washington.

In the Gulf, there was some criticism of China regarding the amount of aid paid for reconstruction of Gaza after fighting in 2009, which was a small fraction of the Gulf's aid for reconstruction of Sichuan after the earthquake in 2008. But the fact that the US remains a far larger and more partisan economic and political partner of Israel helps to deflect attention from China's relations with Israel.

Whether China can maintain this apparent neutrality is less certain, especially in the event of another Israeli attack on Gaza (or a neighbouring state). But its ability to 'avoid' the issue, for reasons cited above, mean observers should not assume that the Israeli–Palestinian conflict exerts the same pull over China's foreign policy in the Middle East as it does for Europe and the US.

Second, China's commercial relations with the Middle East are growing, but are nonetheless less significant than the Middle East's commercial relations with Europe and the US. Chinese exports to the Middle East reached USD 105 bn (EUR 82 bn) in 2011, just 4% of total exports, and considerably less than total exports to the US (USD 396 bn (EUR 310 bn)) and the EU (USD 381 bn (EUR 298 bn)), and not much larger than Korea (USD 82 bn (EUR 64 bn)).

Third, the Middle East is a relatively complex place for China's leadership to understand. Most Chinese are unfamiliar with the ethnic, tribal and sectarian complexities of the Middle East. There are also few Middle East scholars in China, particularly those that speak Arabic. Much of the Chinese-language academic research on the Middle East is thus heavily reliant on work by foreign scholars, especially from the US.

Chinese Middle East scholars and Arabic linguists who do travel regularly to the region and are able to work from original Arabic-language documents are too small in number to influence policy. The number of Arabic-speaking diplomats is larger, but they tend to spend unusually long periods in the Middle East, limiting their ability to influence policymakers in Beijing.

The combined effects of having a limited pool of Middle East specialists and a foreign policy that is often just a residual of foreign policy in other parts of the world mean that it is less clear which parties or interests are driving China's Middle East policy. This comes in sharp contrast to Europe and the US, where policy is centre stage of the political debate. This makes it difficult to observe changes in China's stance towards the region as there is no single department or official whose statements carry significant weight.

Nevertheless, it is possible to identify a number of actors that help shape Chinese policy:

- The individual views of Politburo members on the Middle East have the greatest influence on policy (for instance, the opening of a branch office of the China Development Bank in Cairo was an impromptu decision taken by Li Keqiang after his visit to the country).
- The Ministry of Commerce and state-owned construction companies looking to win deals in the region are also influential in the absence of a more unified political strategy towards the region.
- Lastly, the Foreign Ministry and academics in Beijing who regularly brief the senior leadership on events in the region.

An Evolutionary Change in Policy

China's foreign policy stance has evolved in response to the Arab revolutions. The change is evolutionary, not revolutionary, but has important implications.

In private conversations with academics and officials, it is typically argued that China's strategic policy of 'non-intervention' is unchanged. However, there have been 'tactical' changes in the country's approach to the Middle East. As China's Special Envoy to the Middle East, Wu Sike, argued in an editorial published in the *People's Daily* in May 2011, 'non-intervention is not equal to inaction'.

The most important of these changes has been recognition of opposition movements, especially those in armed conflict with the state. The Chinese state has historically avoided dealing with such movements for fear of setting a precedent by which foreign powers might deal with opposition movements in China. Two examples in Libya and Syria underscore this change.

In June 2011, the Chinese Foreign Ministry announced that the Libyan opposition movement was an 'important political force'. This was shortly followed by a visit by Mahmoud Jibril, the Chairman of the National Transitional Council, to Beijing in July. (The opposition Libyan movement was generally referred to in the Chinese media as a representative of the transitional government, rather than opposition force.) The pace of change in China's policy stance then further accelerated when Syria's unrest worsened during early 2012. Vice Foreign Minister Zhai Jun visited Damascus in mid-February, meeting with both the ruling regime and opposition movements. Earlier that month, Zhai had met a delegation from the National Coordination Committee for Democratic Change, a major opposition group, in Beijing.

The problem is relative perception. While these changes were significant to close observers of China's foreign policy, they meant little to Libyans and Syrians using Europe and the US as their foreign policy benchmarks. Instead, attention was paid to China's refusal to participate in military action against the Gadhafi regime, or vote against measures raised against Syria at the UN Security Council.

As a reflection of this, China has, anecdotally, found it difficult to restore commercial relations with Libya. There is anecdotal evidence from Libya whereby officials have refused outright to deal with Chinese firms (and Indian, for that matter), a major concern for those firms wanting to return to the country. (That said, this stance depends on individual cases, and the extent to which Libya has alternatives to Chinese firms.)

The irony is that China's relations with the previous regime were in fact relatively weak. Indeed, the former Libyan Foreign Minister, Musa Kusa, publicly accused China of having 'colonial interests' at a China–Africa Forum in 2009. But China's lack of support for sanctions and armed intervention against the regime in 2011 angered the Libyan opposition forces and suggested China was pro-Gadhafi.

China's Commercial Interests in the Middle East

Oil interests

China prioritises its own economic stability as the best means of safeguarding its social and therefore political stability. This belief was central to a massive policy stimulus made in response to the global crisis. It also influences China's engagement with the rest of the world, especially the large commodity producers concentrated in the developing world.

This suggests that China should prioritise its reliance on oil imports from the Middle East. China's domestic oil production has largely peaked, and marginal increases in consumption are supplied by imports. The Middle East is already supplying 52% of China's oil imports and 28% of total oil consumption, a figure that is forecast to rise gradually in the coming years. To put that in perspective, China's crude oil imports are worth 2.6% of GDP, compared with a figure of 0.8% of GDP in the US in the early 2000s, shortly before the Second Gulf War.

The disruption to Libya's oil supply was a warning signal of the potential risks to China. Libya supplied 3% of China's total oil imports pre-revolution, implying a physical disruption to supplies, alongside a price disruption as international oil prices soared to around USD 100 a barrel. The rise in prices compressed profit margins among Chinese manufacturers and drove gasoline prices higher for the middle class. That noted, the Arab revolutions have not resulted in a material disruption to supply: together, Egypt, Libya, Syria, and Yemen were worth 5% of China's total imports pre-revolution.

The bigger challenge for China then is potential conflict between Iran and Saudi Arabia. Together, the two supply 31% of China's total oil imports, not including the exports from Kuwait and the United Arab Emirates (UAE) that would be disrupted in the event that oil tankers are prevented from travelling through the Strait of Hormuz. China has unsurprisingly remained reluctant to take sides in cross-straits disputes for fear of antagonising either party.

Oil imports from Iran did fall in early 2012. It is unclear to what extent this reflects a variety of factors: the growing pressure of sanctions; the resumption of Libya's oil exports to China around the turn of the year, which made up half the loss from Iran; and worries about a reliance on Iranian supplies in the event of an

Israeli or American attack on Iran, among other reasons. This development is also still relatively new and we have seen oil imports from Iran fall to this level as recently as mid-2009.

The extent of China's support for Iran is also easily overstated. Academics talk of 'China being a strategic partner for Iran, but Iran not being a strategic partner for China'. The former Special Envoy to the Middle East, Sun Bigan, wrote in 2009 about concerns that Iran would strive for its 'maximum self-interest' and would be quick to sign agreements with Western oil companies in the event of any political settlement.

What is clear is that the politicisation of China's oil imports is a growing risk. Indeed, Arabic-language reports surfaced in March 2012 claiming that Saudi Arabia had lobbied for China's support for UN action against Syria through the promise of increased oil supply. (Much as Saudi Arabia was reported to offset any declining supply from Iran if China acted more firmly against Iran's nuclear ambitions.)

The reports are unsubstantiated and may be fabrications of the Syrian opposition, but they do reflect the growing ties made in the Middle East between the region's oil exports to China and the latter's growing importance to the Middle East's politics. It would not be a surprise to see such pressure grow in the long term, especially in the event of conflict between Iran and Saudi Arabia.

Still, oil supply and prices, while at risk, have not yet been dislocated to the extent that China's foreign policy towards the region might change significantly.

Non-oil interests

China's non-oil commercial relations with the Middle East have meanwhile flourished since the early 2000s, but are not yet motivation for the country to take a more activist position in the region.

First, the magnitude of trade with the Middle East, while growing, still accounts for less than 4% of China's total exports. This is similar to its exports to Africa (4%) and modestly smaller than exports to Latin America (6%). It is thus not significant enough to represent a material risk to China's export sector and social stability in the event of the region's export demand collapsing.

Second, Chinese workers have not flooded the Middle East as they have Africa. This owes to far tighter restrictions on the entry of foreign workers to most Middle East countries. Egypt, for instance, only permits one in ten workers on any single project to be foreign nationals. Temporary exceptions are only granted in hi-tech sectors where local labour supply is considered insufficient.

Libya and Algeria (and, to a lesser extent, Yemen) are obvious exceptions to the rule, and there were an estimated 35,000 Chinese workers in each country prior to the recent social unrest. Chinese state-owned firms have suffered large losses in these countries as construction sites were looted. And those losses may in part help explain the 'tactical' change in China's foreign policy towards Libya's armed opposition groups.

The other implication is that the region's social unrest has not exposed large numbers of Chinese workers to violence. Libya is again the clear exception. Yet, while Chinese nationals had an often harrowing time trying to evacuate the country, as armed groups occupied and ransacked many building sites, there were no serious attacks against Chinese nationals or loss of life.

Individual Chinese traders are present across the region. Reports surfaced in 2010 of Chinese traders leaving Dubai for cities across Iraq, attracted by the country's recovering demand and margins as high as 50%. Indeed, a short YouTube movie released in 2012 showed Chinese traders sponsoring a Shi'ite religious festival near one of Iraq's second-tier cities and embedding themselves within the local community. These individual traders are a risk for China's Foreign Ministry in the event that they are killed or kidnapped, but their limited numbers are unlikely to spark a sudden change in China's foreign policy.

Nonetheless, China's economic interests are large enough that the Ministry of Commerce plays an important role in the country's relations with the Middle East. It was Ministry officials that took the lead in coordinating with Chinese firms in Libya and providing aid to both Chinese nationals and Libyans. (It is common for academics to play down the importance of the Ministry of Foreign Affairs.)

That said, most of China's construction interests are in the Gulf region where the opportunities are significantly greater. There are over 50 Chinese companies in Saudi Arabia with a permanent presence and hundreds more in the UAE. The upshot is that the large bulk of China's economic interests have been largely unaffected with the exception of those in Libya and, to a lesser extent, Algeria and Yemen.

If Chinese firms start to lose commercial contracts in the Gulf as a result of China's stance towards Syria, the Ministry of Commerce might attempt to exert greater influence over China's foreign policy in the Middle East. So far, there are only rumours of this. Saudi Arabia will also be careful to avoid upsetting its largest oil buyer. However, such an event would likely have a material effect on China's stance.

The large state-owned firms also have the ability to indirectly affect China's relations with the region through their business practices. The best example of this was the reported attempt by a Chinese firm to sell arms to the Gadhafi regime in early 2011. The tendency to hire Chinese labourers also creates tensions with the local community, mainly in the Levant and North African regions.

China's Domestic Policies

China's domestic politics are a further restraint on the country's ability, and willingness, to act more decisively in response to the Arab revolutions, albeit a restraint that is often overlooked.

China's economy has reached an inflection point as imbalances in the composition of growth built-up over the past decade, but especially since 2008, have raised the risks of a sudden slowdown in growth. Coupled with worsening income inequalities, whether because of slow real income growth or rising food and house prices, this has raised the threat of serious social unrest.

Many of the complaints made by Middle East protestors about living costs and corruption thus resonated in China, and there was some fear among China's senior leadership of a spillover revolt. (In fact, Prime Minister Wen Jiabao, while speaking at the National People's Congress in 2012, went so far as to publicly deny a link between events in the Middle East and China's own challenges.)

China's large Muslim population is an additional reason for the state to avoid direct intervention in the Middle East. Official estimates put the population at 20 m, while unofficial estimates put it significantly higher. While tensions with the 8 m Muslim Uyghurs are long-standing, there are legitimate worries that intervention might shake the so far healthy relations with the 10 m Hui Chinese.

It is also easily overlooked that China's western provinces are bordered by a number of Muslim states, many host to extremist groups. Unlike the more geographically isolated US, Chinese academics have noted concerns about the trouble Muslim states could cause China in its own 'backyard' should the country intervene more forcefully in the Middle East and oppose long-standing regimes.

Implications for Europe

China's policy of 'non-intervention' remains in force. However, there has been a 'tactical' change in the country's approach to the Middle East. Whether that change is material enough to change the trajectory of other countries, or Europe's interests in those countries, is still far from clear. So far, the evidence from Libya and Syria is 'no'. Nonetheless, the change is sufficient to require a response.

With this in mind, a few points can be made with respect to Europe's engagement of China in the Middle East.

- China's engagement with opposition forces is not conducted for the same purpose as that of Europe and the US, for example, support for the principles of a multi-party democratic political system. It instead reflects a growing recognition that political regimes can and do change, and so opening dialogue with opposition movements in conflict with the state is a pragmatic means of hedging against this risk.
- China will rightly worry that as long as Europe and the US lobby more aggressively for regime change, they will be the greater beneficiary from such change. This discourages China from taking a more assertive stance in support of opposition movements in conflict with the state, as the benefits from such a stance are unclear, unless international opinion has firmly swung against the ruling regime (as in the case of Libya).
- China's domestic interests remain primary when considering the country's actions in the Middle East. Most important is China's economic security, especially its growing reliance on oil imports. To this end, the stability of existing regimes best serves China's interests, especially given that intervention by Europe and the US over the past decades have yielded limited results.
- Observers should be cautious about reading too much into small shifts in China's policy towards the region. The fact that its policy is a residual of China's interests in the rest of the world; the fact it has a shortage of Middle East expertise; and that the bulk of China's commercial interests are in the Gulf and largely unaffected, means policy changes so far are partly opportunistic and not necessarily a good guide to future behaviour.
- Europe should engage China's tactical adjustment in its foreign policy stance towards the Middle East. However, Europe should expect only a gradual evolution, rather than revolution, in policy. Forcing a faster pace of change is unlikely to yield results.
- First, and as a general rule, engaging with China through multiple parties is critical, in part owing to the diffuse nature of China's Middle East policies, but also the country's increasingly consensus-driven rule. Engaging through

non-public means is also important, to avoid putting officials or academics in the awkward position of conflicting with state policy and so ensuring healthy debate between all sides.
- Second, China is increasingly keen on being viewed as a responsible global power. This may tempt its leadership to play a more active role in the region given the importance of the Middle East to all the world's major powers. Europe should consider establishing whether China might join a group such as the Quartet on the Middle East; however, in the author's view, the chances of acceptance are small. Indeed, pragmatism will remain China's guiding rule, especially in a region where there are so many competing strategic powers (Europe, the US, Russia, Turkey, Israel and Iran). And, as long as China's interests remain mercantilist, trying to balance commercial relations with Iran, Israel and Saudi Arabia will further restrain the country's ability to take a more public position.
- Third, engaging China as a partner in plans for economic aid or post-conflict reconstruction would demonstrate that Europe's support for regime change is not an attempt to squeeze China's economic interests in the Middle East (a popular fear in China). It would also better suit China's interests to engage at an economic, rather than political, level, and so maintain its strategic policy of 'non-intervention'. That noted, it would be better to divide priorities so that China can at least appear to be acting independently of Europe, rather than propose joint-aid programs. To illustrate, the China Development Bank might make a direct loan to Egypt for highway construction, albeit after having coordinated with other European development banks on a list of construction priorities.
- Fourth, working with China's major oil suppliers, especially Saudi Arabia, as an indirect form of lobbying. This is especially important on the issues related to Syria and Iran, as Europe and Saudi Arabia share a similar stance on these two countries. It might be that such pressure is later publicly realised through the cover of the Arab League, but discrete bilateral lobbying through China's oil suppliers is the more immediately effective approach. However, it is important to point out that Saudi Arabia's interest in lobbying China aggressively is weakened by the fact that Saudi Arabia is as dependent on China's oil demand as China is dependent on Saudi Arabia's oil supply. This 'co-dependency' is strengthened by the fact the two sides are ideal partners in so far they both have

a preference for long-term oil contracts made between producers and final users.
- Finally, when observing China's changing foreign policy towards the Middle East, events in Syria are more important than those in Libya, owing to the greater complexities of the unrest. China's support for the armed opposition in Libya was more straightforward given Gadhafi's almost universal unpopularity in the Middle East. This is less true of Syria, especially given its Sunni–Shi'ite backdrop. Above all, consideration must be given to China's long-term domestic interests, as this is how the country's own domestic policy is determined, and, by consequence, foreign policy.

China and the Democratic People's Republic of Korea
May 2012

Amy Studdart
Program Officer for Asia, German Marshall Fund of the United States

Executive Summary

Although China is the Democratic People's Republic of Korea's (DPRK) main economic, political and diplomatic partner, the relationship between the two is tense and characterised by a lack of trust. As a result, China's leverage has only been useful insofar as it does not run counter to the regime's number one priority — its own survival. China has not been able to persuade the DPRK to carry out any meaningful and long-lasting economic reforms, and neither has there been any progress made on denuclearisation. This is largely because the regime in Pyongyang has been able to exploit the differences in the priorities of the members of the Six-Party Talks to its own advantage, gaining leverage through brinksmanship and keeping long-term solutions to the crisis on the peninsula elusive. While the emergence of a new leader in the DPRK may still provide a window of opportunity, the Unha-3 rocket launch has put any hopes of progress on the peninsula on hold, leaving the international strategy unclear and the possibilities of further crisis high.

Main Points

- China's political and diplomatic relationship with the DPRK is well established, as are its economic ties. China is currently the DPRK's main economic lifeline.
- The China–DPRK military relationship remains ambiguous, although there has been a trend towards greater Chinese support for the North Korean military.
- Nevertheless, China's leverage over the regime in Pyongyang remains limited. 'Self-reliance' (*Juche*) remains a key governing ideology of the North Korean regime and Chinese mistrust of their North Korean counterparts is high.
- The Six-Party Talks have been hindered by the conflicting priorities of its members. While the US is largely focused on using sanctions as a way to negotiate towards North Korean denuclearisation, China is not willing to use its leverage in a way that might compromise North Korean stability.
- Beijing has tried to use its leverage to encourage the regime in Pyongyang to follow the China model and open up economically without political reform.
- While the death of Kim Jong-il and the succession of Kim Jong-un may provide scope for a changed set of priorities in the DPRK, for the time being, it appears that the regime intends to steer the course set by Kim Jong-il.
- The lack of progress on finding a permanent solution to the crisis on the peninsula coupled with the succession of a provocative new leader, means that concerns about North Korean regime collapse are high. Although Beijing's steadfast commitment to stability means that this point has not yet been reached, it also means that there has been a commitment to maintaining the *status quo* rather than making progress on the North Korean issue.

An Assessment of China's Leverage in the DPRK

China and the Democratic People's Republic of Korea (DPRK) have a well-established political and diplomatic relationship, one that goes back to the start of the Korean War when, in 1950, China stepped in to defend the North. It has only become stronger in recent years: in the two years before his death in December 2011, Kim Jong-il went to China four times (three of which were official visits), while the only other foreign trip he made was to Russia, in August 2011. As the plans for Kim Jong-un's succession firmed up, in May 2010 his father took him to China for formal introductions and Beijing's public blessing. China has also been willing to put its reputation on the line internationally: after the sinking of the Cheonan in 2010 and the shelling of Yeonpyeong, a group of inhabited South Korean islands, in 2011, the Chinese response remained steadfastly committed to its 'two Koreas' policy, refusing to — at least publicly — take sides and condemn the attacker. In February 2012, China came under fire for its policy of repatriating North Korean defectors, transporting them across the border in the dead of night on buses with drawn curtains.

The economic ties between the DPRK and China are also extensive and present at every level: state-to-state, the private sector and the black market. Conservative estimates suggest that, despite UN sanctions, trade between the two countries has at least doubled since 2006, with China now accounting for between 60 and 80% of the DPRK's foreign trade. According to data from the Chinese Ministry of Commerce, bilateral trade for the first quarter of 2012 surged 40%. Chinese investment is also on the rise, as seen in the attempts to either establish or re-establish special economic zones (SEZs) in the DPRK, the most notable being the port in Rason. Less public efforts are also underway. Chongjin, one of the DPRK's biggest ports until the famine of the 1990s, is coming back to life. And the private sector is active too. On 27 April 2012 the Chinese Chamber of Commerce opened its first North Korean office in Pyongyang. While Chinese businessmen are reluctant to trust their North Korean counterparts, there is profit to be made and private partnerships are present in both the legal and the black markets. The DPRK's illicit cash products — whether drugs, people or counterfeit goods — find some of their main trade routes through, and many of their consumers in, Chinese territory. The restrictions placed on foreign travel and communication mean that there is a reliance on Chinese colleagues to facilitate both trade and connections with eventual consumers or middlemen suppliers. As a result, China is currently the DPRK's main economic lifeline.

With regard to military-to-military contact, there is at least the appearance of a strengthening relationship. In 2001 the two countries renewed the 1961 Sino–North Korean Mutual Aid and Cooperation Friendship Treaty, which includes a mutual defence pact, although there has been little evidence of practical military–military cooperation. However, China has systematically provided the military with resources, especially energy and food aid — something the broader international community has balked at. On 18 November 2011, China announced its intentions to increase military ties with the DPRK and made vague promises of greater exchanges between the two sides. In a DPRK military parade shortly after the Unha-3 rocket launch, a Chinese-made missile carrier was placed front and centre, despite UN sanctions on the transfer of military equipment to the DPRK. While the China–DPRK military-to-military relationship is currently an ambiguous one, it is clear that there is presently a trend towards greater Chinese support for the North Korean military — at least on the surface.

But despite the apparent closeness of the relationship, China's leverage over the regime in Pyongyang has been limited. In the last years of Kim Jong-il's reign, the level of Chinese involvement in the DPRK's economy made the country's elite acutely nervous. '*Juche*' (or 'self-reliance'), the governing ideology since Kim Il-sung founded the regime, has meant that successive North Korean leaders have staked their legitimacy on their ability to keep out foreign influence and avoid being a pawn in the games of the world's super powers, using the memory of prolonged colonial exploitation under the Japanese in the early half of the 20th century as a powerful reminder of North Korean suffering at the hands of outsiders.

Chinese strategists, for their part, were hardly filled with admiration for Kim Jong-il, and the assessment of Kim Jong-un seems to be even worse, with many voicing concerns about his inexperience and immaturity. Chinese businessmen suffer at the hands of North Korean counterparts who will not uphold their end of deals, to the point where the norm is to demand cash upfront in transactions. Mistrust is so endemic that when the Cheonan was sunk, some US, South Korean and Chinese officials and analysts privately believed that the regime had carried out the attack not as a threat to Seoul, but to embarrass and put pressure on Beijing.

Conflicting Strategies: Sanctions versus Economic Engagement

The Six-Party Talks, established in 2003, were originally primarily conceived as an effort in coordination. The guiding assumption was that all members of the talks — China, the US, South Korea, Japan, Russia and the DPRK — were not only necessary for working out a solution, but also ultimately shared the same mutually compatible goal, that of a denuclearised, unified and more stable peninsula. While this remains true, in reality, conflicting priorities of the various actors mean that there has been, and continues to be, very little room for progress. By and large, the US is focused on using sanctions as a way to negotiate towards denuclearisation, an outcome that the DPRK has made clear it will not accept. China, for its part, will not use its leverage in a way that might compromise North Korean stability and has instead attempted to convince the regime to follow its own model of economic reforms. South Korea has shifted between the two but never fully committed to either, instead moving from the progressive 'Sunshine Policy' of 1998–2008, to the more hawkish policies of the Lee Myung-Bak administration, with another shift possible as South Korea goes through its presidential elections later this year. The regime in Pyongyang has masterfully played these divergent interests off against each other, prolonging its own survival.

While it is debatable whether harsher sanctions outside of the UN are the right policy for advancing a resolution to the conflict with the DPRK, it is certain that, unless Beijing signs up, they are futile. When China has given its support, there have been instances where sanctions have had an economic impact on the regime. The most effective were the 2007 efforts against Banco Delta Asia, a small bank run out of Macao which held around USD 25m (EUR 19m) in North Korean cash reserves, and was also accused of aiding the regime in its money laundering activities. The sanctions dealt a real blow to the regime, tying up their reserves, but — more significantly — also putting a stop to many of the DPRK's financial operations and seriously disrupting the regime's access to international goods and services.

The effectiveness of these (and indeed all) sanctions in bringing about progress on the peninsula has been the subject of much debate, and there are real concerns — especially in Beijing — that increased sanctions may even be counterproductive. China has argued that although further isolating the regime might help weaken its hold on power, it will also encourage further antagonistic behaviour and re-entrenching the 'military first' policy it had pursued until late 2010/ early 2011. Beijing benefits from being able to keep an eye on the regime and from its ability to intervene if there are signs of instability and it has been unwilling to give that access up for the tougher public condemnations or sanctions that the US has called for, and that it does not believe will accomplish very much by way of real progress.

Instead, China has tried to use its leverage to encourage the regime to reform its economy and gradually open up. The advice to the North Korean regime has been that it should follow the China model, opening up economically without political reform. While, at least under Kim Jong-il, the DPRK has been willing to dabble in economic reforms, allowing spontaneous street markets to flourish on and off since 2002, letting citizens accumulate cash savings, freeing up regulations to allow for more robust tourism, and establishing a number of SEZs, many of the reforms have either not seen success or have been abruptly reversed. The currency reforms of 2009 essentially destroyed the markets and took away all of the savings that North Korean citizens had accumulated. Since then, markets and savings have been allowed to rebuild, but the threat of similar action remains. After years of trying, Beijing has made only moderate progress with its agenda. In private, Chinese officials and analysts voice tremendous frustration about the stubbornness of the regime.

The North Korean regime has consistently held a single priority: securing its own survival. It has been swayed from this course by neither the promise of financial enrichment, the starvation of its people, the honouring of political relationships or humiliation. China's economic reasoning has fallen foul of the regime's reliance on an unbending version of totalitarianism to keep control of both the elites and its population. Agreements reached between the US and the DPRK that include steps toward denuclearisation have been reversed by the regime's belief that its nuclear capabilities give it immunity against international intervention, a belief that has likely been reinforced by the fall of Saddam Hussein in Iraq, and now Muammar Gadhafi in Libya. While the death of Kim Jong-il and the succession which followed may still provide the scope for a changed set of priorities, the Unha-3 rocket launch and the voiding of the US–DPRK Leap Day Agreement suggests that — for the time being at least — the regime (regardless of who is in charge) intends to steer the course set by Kim Jong-il.

What Next?

In all quarters, there is now a significant lack of political will to seek solutions proactively. In China, the leadership transition later this year and the continued political turbulence over the fall of former Party secretary of Chongqing and Politburo member Bo Xilai has only served to strengthen Beijing's desire to see stability rather than push for change on the Korean peninsula. Were the DPRK to collapse, refugees would pour into China's northeastern provinces, and even nearby Beijing, on a scale that could put serious pressure on the country's infrastructure and slow the country's growth. US, and probably also South Korean, troops would move in to secure the DPRK's nuclear arsenal, bringing them uncomfortably close to Chinese territory. China, for its part, would need to deploy its own troops — at least to the Sino–North Korean border — to help stem the tide of refugees and to make a show of support for the regime, which, in a worst case scenario, could bring Chinese and US troops up against each other. Over the longer term, a collapsed DPRK would not only lose China an ally, but could end up as part of a peninsula unified on South Korean terms — terms which would involve democracy and a close relationship with the US, both of which are unappetising for an already nervous political elite in Beijing.

And South Korea, after having tried both engagement and the more hawkish methods of its current President, Lee Myung-Bak, is tired of investing energy in its neighbour. The peninsula has been split for 64 years, and the generations of people that remember a unified Korea, and whose families and friendships were split with the country, are dying out. Younger generations of South Koreans not only see unification as unimportant, they are wary of it, believing that the backward and poverty-stricken North will simply drag the South down and damage their futures. This transformation in national psychology has been visible in South Korea's parliamentary and presidential election debates, which — despite the death of Kim Jong-il — have made little mention of the DPRK, and have instead focused on a battle of ideas over the correct formulae for social welfare.

The Obama administration, for its part, is in a quandary. It had framed the Leap Day Agreement as a test of the new regime, an attempt to figure out whether or not a changed leadership would make for a changed set of North Korean priorities. In the first week of March, shortly after the Leap Day Agreement but before the Unha-3 launch, the US and the DPRK met to discuss the parameters and redlines of the deal they had, at least publicly, already reached. Kim Kye-gwan, the North Korean negotiator, detailed a conversation that he explained had taken place between Kim Jong-il and Kim Jong-un in the months leading up to the elder Kim's death, in which it had been decided that the DPRK would be willing to give up uranium enrichment and proliferation in exchange for food, investment and an improved relationship with the US, but that it would neither denuclearise nor agree to stop satellite launches until the country, and the regime, felt secure. This was not a deal that the US was willing to accept. Not only are promises to stop uranium enrichment and proliferation easy to turn back on (as the North Korean regime has proved time and time again), but it would also send a signal of tolerance to other would-be nuclear weapons states, seriously undermining the Obama administration's denuclearisation agenda. The result is that all sides are again at an impasse with no clear way forward in sight.

With no progress having been made on finding a permanent solution to the crisis on the peninsula, and with a new leader who has proven his willingness to be provocative and whose grip on power is unlikely to be a firm one, concerns about North Korean regime collapse are high. There is a great deal of nervousness about the lack of contingency planning talks between the Chinese, South Koreans and the US. Beijing has repeatedly rejected Washington and Seoul's requests for direct military-to-military conversations, conversations which stand in direct opposition to its alliance agreements with the DPRK and would be seen as seriously antagonistic in Pyongyang. While China's reasons for choosing not to engage in joint contingency planning are understandable, the absence of mutually agreed plans means that there is a real risk of confrontation. Beijing's steadfast commitment to stability means that this point has not yet been reached, but also means that — despite the big changes in the DPRK — there has been a commitment to maintaining the *status quo* rather than making progress.

Conclusions and Policy Implications

Over the longer term, Europe will face a choice between two opposing strategies:

- Economic engagement. More European economic engagement with the DPRK would be welcomed by both Pyongyang and Beijing, and may help stabilise the country and improve the lives of the North Korean people, but it could also prolong the life of the regime and give it the cash needed to create a more convincing nuclear threat. Although civilians have profited from the marketisation process in the DPRK, those who have most benefited most are the military (who have access to oil, vehicles and a wide network of contacts) and the traditional elites (who are able to solicit bribes from those carrying out any number of illegal economic activities).
- Economic isolation. The DPRK is more desperate than ever before for food and resources. Not only does Kim Jong-un desperately need to prove his ability as a leader, the North Korean people have been promised that the centennial celebrations of Kim Il-sung's birth, which took place in April 2012, would mark the start of a new and more prosperous future. At a point when the North Korean people are expecting improvements in their livelihoods rather than the constant decline that they have become accustomed to, it is possible that any

cuts to existing economic engagement would help to put pressure on the regime. Kim Jong-un also needs to prove to the elites that he is able to protect the DPRK from becoming overly reliant on China, so a reduction in the number of international actors that the regime is able to engage will weaken his grip. However, although further isolation would certainly weaken the regime, it would almost certainly precipitate provocations and increase instability on the peninsula.

One of the key questions is whether or not North Korean reliance on China will help or hinder European priorities on the peninsula. More European economic engagement would balance China's influence and afford more direct insight and leverage over the regime. But further economic isolation would give China a better hand in its relations with the DPRK, which — because of the historical relationship, political ties and the increased pressures it would put on the regime — could help force the regime to make more meaningful progress on reforms and opening up its economy.

For the moment, however, neither is a risk-free option. Not only is there currently no united international strategy, but China, South Korea and the US are all at the stage where they are having to reconsider their own individual strategies and priorities. Despite US claims that the Leap Day Agreement was a test of the new leadership in Pyongyang, it is still unclear whether Kim Jong-un will mean business as usual, opportunities for progress, or instability and potential collapse. Without greater clarity, there is little scope for decisive action, and Europe is left with few policy options.

However, Europe can take advantage of its own leverage to help an old ally — the US — and a new friend — South Korea — develop a coherent and realistic strategy and set of priorities *vis-à-vis* the DPRK. Europe has a lot to offer: at the time of writing, all of the EU Member States have some form of representation in Pyongyang; there are currently four EU Member States sitting on the UN Security Council; there is a well-established aid relationship with the DPRK; and Europe's relative neutrality means that it may be able to help relieve some of the tensions in the US–China relationship over DPRK policy. Europe is in a good position to help — but, at the moment, it is unclear what that help should look like.

Reappraising Chinese Engagement in Africa
(March 2012)

Ian Taylor

Professor in International Relations and African Politics, School of International Relations, University of St. Andrews

Executive Summary

- China is now Africa's most important bilateral trading partner.
- A polarised debate dominates the pros and cons of this engagement.
- Chinese involvement in Africa is driven by resource security concerns but also the search for new markets.
- Chinese policy in Africa does not follow an overarching grand strategy, despite what Beijing may claim or wish.
- The eclectic nature of Chinese actors involved in Africa is often outside the control of Beijing and at times their non-sanctioned behaviour threatens China's broad reputation.

Introduction

The increase in China's economic and political involvement in Africa is arguably the most momentous development on the continent since the end of the Cold War. The People's Republic of China (PRC) is now Africa's most important bilateral trading partner. Since the upsurge of interest in Africa (circa post-2000), the Chinese leadership has been enthusiastic in showcasing its country's engagement with Africa and publicising what it habitually describes as a relationship that 'has always been based on mutual benefits and win-win results' (*Xinhua,* May 15, 2007). In contrast, critics have claimed that, for the most part, Africa is exporting oil and other raw materials to China while importing cheap manufactured Chinese goods — an exchange remarkably similar to that of the colonial era. Indeed, the accusation that China is a new colonising power, exploiting Africa's natural resources and flooding the continent with low-priced manufactured products while turning a blind eye to its autocracies is at the core of most critiques of China's current engagement with Africa.

A key aim of Chinese involvement in Africa is resource security, but Beijing's entrepreneurs also seek commercial advantages. As China's economy has taken off, the search for more and more markets for Chinese exports has intensified and Africa is seen as a useful and profitable destination. Chinese imports into Africa — mostly low-cost and low-quality goods — have taken over the marketplaces in most African countries, as any visitor will attest. The impact on local economies of Chinese imports is becoming more and more apparent, leading to growing local resentment with concerns over 'unfair' Chinese competition.

However, in analysing Sino–African relations and the policies that shape and are shaped by them, we must always keep in mind that there are many Chinas and equally, many Africas. Thus the allegation, levelled by Western and African commentators alike, that China is colonising Africa is inherently misleading, based on the assumption that Chinese foreign policy in Africa follows an overarching grand strategy dictated by Beijing. Rather, it is at best acceptable to state that Beijing's policy makers have certain aspirations for specific facets of Sino–African ties. The most obvious example concerns China's state-owned oil corporations and their investments in African resource industries, which are clearly connected to the energy needs and domestic dynamics associated with China's rise. But even here, rivalries among energy companies point to the fact that the interests of one Chinese actor may not always coincide with those of another, be it state or private. Given the secrecy surrounding energy deals signed by Chinese corporations in Africa (which are by no means unique in this regard), untangling underlying impulses and motives can be extremely problematic.

Beyond the energy sector, rivalries among Chinese provinces, cities, municipalities, and/or individuals play themselves out on a daily basis in Africa and lay bare the myth of a monolithic China relentlessly pushing forward on some sort of 'trade safari'. Nuanced analyses of Sino–African relations transcend talk of a 'Chinese strategy' for Africa, which encodes fears of conflict with Western interests; equally, they recognise that Sino–African relations represent processes of globalisation not colonisation, involving the reintegration of China into the global economy — a project that has hitherto enjoyed the enthusiastic support of the capitalist West.

Commodities and Confusion

Where there is coherence in Sino–African relations, it is arguably based on several key aims of Chinese foreign policy. One is that Chinese corporations 'go global' and help ensure regime security in the process, namely by gaining access to crucial resources. A statement issued by the Chinese Ministry of Commerce explicitly posits Africa as 'one of the most important regions for carrying out our "go outward" strategy'.[23] The resulting hike in commodity prices has in itself been good for many of Africa's economies, although it is obviously uneven and dependent upon resource attributes. The coincidence of higher prices and higher production levels has propelled an increase in sub-Saharan Africa's real GDP, much of this linked to burgeoning Chinese demand. But the benefits are skewed toward select industries. South Africa provides iron ore and platinum, while the DRC and Zambia supply copper and cobalt. Timber is sourced from Gabon, Cameroon, Congo-Brazzaville and Liberia, while various western and central African nations supply raw cotton to Chinese textile factories. It is, however, oil that remains China's biggest commercial interest in Africa.

Indeed, China's growing dependence on imported oil has become a major concern for Beijing, and it is within the context of oil security that we might identify a strategic element to Sino–African relations. The pressure on state-owned oil corporations to engage in international trade is predicated upon a single-minded interest in the accessibility and dependability of foreign oil supplies. Policy analysts in Beijing connect the global political *milieu* to domestic energy security and feel that China is vulnerable until and unless it can diversify its oil sources and secure greater access to the world's oil supplies. Africa is an intrinsic — and possibly central — target of this stratagem. Thus Chinese policies regarding oil deals in Africa are driven by worries that there may one day be too little oil to meet worldwide demand and that the energy needs of foreign powers — in particular the US — will eclipse those of China. Any reasonable state administration in Beijing's position would encourage its actors to do what Chinese state-owned oil corporations are doing, namely defending the national interest.

---

[23] Quoted in Gu Xuewu, 'China Returns to Africa', *Trends East Asia*, No. 9., 2005.

Chinese oil companies have been vigorous in seizing opportunities long overlooked by more established actors. Granted, state-owned enterprises have an advantage over their private, commercial competitors; it has been alleged that they can, unbeholden to shareholders, outbid for major contracts by paying over the odds. In addition, because they are state-owned, China's national oil companies can work with the government in a neomercantilist fashion, making sweetener deals involving generous loans and/or infrastructure-development projects in return for oil. Lubricating commercial deals with extras was, of course, precisely what Western powers were doing in Africa long before China arrived on the scene, and prior to the ascendancy of neoliberalism.

Reputation at Stake?

A constant in both Western and African media outlets is how problematic Chinese companies are *vis-à-vis* labour rights, safety standards, pay levels etc. Here, Beijing is in a bind because even if Chinese policy makers earnestly seek to regulate Chinese business practices in Africa, their ability to do so is extremely limited. Indeed, the more China liberalises, the less easy it is to control private businesses domestically, let alone in far-off Africa. This is a major conundrum for the Chinese government, striving as it does to safeguard Beijing's image as a responsible power — but it is not unique to Sino–African relations. Chinese actors engaging in illegal behaviour are no more representative of Beijing's African policies than the bad practices of a British or US company are of London's or Washington's diplomatic objectives in Africa — or elsewhere, for that matter.

However, the world community still erroneously sees China as a centrally controlled, monolithic actor. This perception is arguably informed not only by longstanding tradition, predating 1949, but by Westerners broadly frustrated by their inability to impose their will on China. While the Chinese state is often viewed as a machine whose parts all mesh smoothly, in fact, the system of central control and coordination is largely a thing of the past. Closer to the mark is Kenneth Lieberthal's use of the term 'fragmented authoritarianism' to characterise the regime.[24] This *milieu* is only growing as China reengages with the global economy

---

[24] Lieberthal, K. (1992) 'Introduction: The "Fragmented Authoritarianism" Model and Its Limitations' in K. Lieberthal and D. Lampton (eds.), *Bureaucracy, Politics and Decision Making in Post-Mao China*. Berkeley: University of California Press.

under the conditions of *de facto* liberal capitalism and domestic trends spread overseas. However, for China this is a problem: if Shell engages in unsavoury activities in Nigeria's Delta region, no-one blames David Cameron or the British; no-one makes a direct link between Shell and 10 Downing Street. Yet if a Chinese corporation acts in an unscrupulous fashion in Africa, 'the Chinese' are instantly castigated, and the leadership is almost personally implicated.

Complicating this scenario is the fact that many of the Chinese-made products sold in African markets are brought to the continent not by Chinese but by African traders. There are now quite elaborate trading networks linking China and Africa, many centred in the southern province of Guandong, where a relatively large population of African entrepreneurs live and make deals. Indeed, in the city of Guangzhou, an estimated 20,000 Nigerians live and work. African traders have also long been established in Hong Kong, primarily at Chungking Mansions in Tsim Sha Tsui, where products from China are sold in large quantities to traders from across Africa, who ship their products via Chinese-owned cargo companies directly to Africa.

Here, the point is that Chinese traders are not simply flooding the African market with cheap Chinese goods; African actors are actively facilitating the inundation. We do not have estimates of the respective proportion of goods sold in Africa's markets by Chinese entrepreneurs to those sold by African traders, but information gleaned from various interviews and observations made in a variety of African marketplaces suggests that a large percentage was sourced and shipped by the latter. This is somewhat ironic given that many African trade unions and civil-society organisations lay the blame for the 'Asian tsunami' of cheap products squarely on 'the Chinese'. Even those who argue that trade between Africa and China is becoming colonial in character must admit that it is occurring with the active cooperation of many Africans themselves.

Overall, the balance sheet on Sino–African ties is arguably positive and the recent upsurge in Chinese activity holds a great deal of opportunity for the continent. Not least, it has spurred other external actors to take the continent's potential more seriously. Clearly, China is not the new imperialist in Africa. Although there are facets of Sino–African trade that fit the pattern usually described as neocolonial — for instance, the fact that Africa exports raw material and imports finished products — they are by no means unique. Rather, they characterise virtually all of Africa's bilateral trade relations and, according to many influential analysts, have their roots in the colonial period — when China was wholly absent from Africa. Viewed in this light, the notion that China's economic engagement with Africa should be totally different from that of other external actors seems unrealistic.

Furthermore, Chinese economic policies, if at times arguably neomercantilist, are fundamentally capitalist. The post-Mao Chinese leadership is thus doing precisely what the West wants it to do and yet is, on occasion, castigated for doing so in areas formerly held to be in the West's sphere of influence. Here, the growing concern about global energy supplies is particularly apt for explaining negative reactions to China's rise in Africa and elsewhere in the developing world.

This challenge is most often flagged in debates over governance, whereby Chinese engagement with Africa is arguably less positive, relating as it does to Beijing's non-interference policies and *de facto* hands-off approach to issues of human rights. It is, of course, true that such policies are long-standing and shape relations beyond Africa. What is more, they have a certain cachet when the alternative is presented by overweening powers bent on promoting particular economic and political agendas as universal truths. However, a middle ground — one that respects international society and recognises that borders cannot be used to shield miscreants from censure if and when they infringe upon basic rights to life, self-realisation and social development — is more appropriate. There is growing evidence that the Chinese leadership is approaching this middle ground, arguably spurred on by the damage to its reputation done by its relations with various dubious regimes. Chinese policies in Africa are in a complex process of evolution and Beijing policy makers realise that Chinese operations need security just as much as Western ones do, and that if they wish to facilitate the extraction of Africa's resources in order to keep China's economy going, they must ensure a safe operating environment and the protection of investments.

Summarising Sino-African Ties

If Sino–African relations could be reduced to their essence, three main points would stand out. First, China is not a unitary actor. This may seem elemental, but judging from a lot of the literature on Sino–African relations, it seems to have been overlooked. As the Chinese leadership has pursued its (admittedly uneven) post-Mao economic liberalisation policies, they have encountered increasing difficulties in controlling — or even keeping abreast of — the diverse activities in which various Chinese corporations and individual merchants are engaged overseas. Although major oil and other energy-based companies are probably under constant supervision (which rivalries may however complicate), the huge proliferation of small-scale traders operating in Africa, very often private individuals or families, is all but impossible to manage. Weak rule of law, endemic corruption and bureaucratic tendencies at every level of government means that the central leadership is in a perpetual and losing struggle to keep up with a surging economy, whether domestic or when it is projected overseas.

Chinese trade with Africa has become, in many ways, normalised, which is to say diverse, and involving multiple actors, rather than state-directed and state-controlled. Tracing production networks — the processes by which things are made and/or finished and delivered to markets — is increasingly complicated. This may be why so many analyses reduce relations between 'China' and 'Africa' to an almost bilateral level.

The second key point about Sino–African relations is that there has been a fair degree of scapegoating of China for its alleged negative impacts upon Africa. On close inspection, these allegations appear much less salient and accurate and are often balanced out in any case by positive impacts. For instance, Chinese construction companies are criticised for hiring only Chinese workers — even unskilled ones — so that infrastucture-development projects do not generate much local employment or promote skill acquisition. Yet while many Chinese are employed as unskilled casual laborers, local Africans often garner management and administration positions. Given the low skills base in much of Africa, it is unreasonable to expect a high proportion of the skilled jobs to be held by Africans in any case; Western corporations operating in Africa likewise tend to install expatriates at the management level, even after many years in country.

It is true that health and safety standards, as well as workers' rights and environmental issues, do not appear to be priorities for some Chinese companies. This is unfortunate and indefensible. But it reflects what is happening back home in China, where the leadership resolutely pursues the capitalist road to development. It is up to African states to regulate the activities of foreign companies and ensure that extractive operations do not destroy the local environment or deny African workers their labour rights. Unfortunately, many of Africa's elites post-independence have shown scant regard for their citizens' constitutional rights in general; it is doubtful that they will suddenly spring into action where Chinese investment is concerned.

Many of the criticisms of Sino–African ties point to Africa's domestic problems and then extrapolate to place the blame on 'China'. This is unreasonable.

The Chinese leadership may, however, be culpable for a non-interference policy that has negative implications for the human rights of Africans. But, as mentioned, Chinese policy is evolving. Although the Chinese have considered their approach to Africa to be benign, they are beginning to feel exposed by the intricacies of Africa's politics. Kidnappings in Nigeria, the murders of Chinese workers in Ethiopia, anti-Chinese riots in Zambia, a high-profile campaign against the Beijing Olympics over China's role in Darfur, and a threat by Darfurian rebels to target Chinese citizens — all of these have provided a steep learning curve.

This leads us to the third and final key point in our summary of Sino–African ties: that it is up to African leaders to manage their relations with China to benefit their own economies and citizens. Obviously, the internal structure of any given African state is all-important and varies widely across the continent. The fact that, for example, South Africa is a consolidated democracy by African standards accounts for the huge difference between the way Pretoria and, say, Sierra Leone deal with China. Fundamentally, Beijing's engagement with Africa is grounded in pragmatism, and so it is up to each African state to negotiate how and where it takes shape. China's abandonment of ideology for economic growth actually affords Africa greater room to manoeuvre — but Africa's elites must do so wisely. In some countries, they will. In others, however, predatory elites at the apex of neopatrimonial regimes, unconcerned with promoting development, will forfeit the chance to make the most of renewed Chinese interest in Africa. Chinese involvement in Africa offers up a wealth of opportunities for the continent, but only if Africa approaches them prudently. How Sino–African relations will play out in the years to come, which Africans and which Chinese will benefit or lose, and in which states and economic sectors, are questions for future studies on the multifarious nature of Chinese engagement with the continent.

Europe's Response

For the EU, an upsurge in Chinese interest in Africa poses important challenges. Not least is the way in which Europe thinks about Africa. European commercial and political preeminence in Africa can no longer be taken for granted. A constructive relationship with China (and other 'new' actors in Africa, such as Brazil and India) is absolutely essential. Brussels would be well advised to engage with Beijing whenever and wherever possible. It must be said that China is somewhat suspicious of such attempts at trilateralism, as are many African states (who relish the idea of a competition for their attention and favour). But Brussels must persist. If interaction with Chinese state officials at the Ministry of Foreign Affairs proves to produce limited results, the EU should seek engagement with both the Ministry of Commerce of the People's Republic of China *and* the corporations that have substantial investments in Africa. These all have the bottom line in mind and certainly do wish to safeguard their interests. All of these corporations have research arms who are crying out for help for critical policy analysis. However, the Chinese academic community's capacity to deliver sound policy advice is limited as very few academics do fieldwork and most tend to stick to the official state line. Helping to build Chinese academic and think tank capacity in African studies would be invaluable.

Identifying where and how Europe and China can work together in Africa will be substantially more productive than accusing China of undermining European interests and/or demonising Beijing's role on the continent. There are certainly some negative aspects of Chinese engagement in Africa, but on balance these are potentially outweighed by the positives if managed correctly by African states. If Brussels' key concern in Africa is to promote development, China should be welcomed as an important new partner, offering some new perspectives and as interested in stability as the EU.

China's Energy Policy Towards Central Asia
(April 2012)

Bobo Lo

Associate Fellow, Russia and Eurasia Programme, Chatham House

Executive Summary

- Energy has been at the heart of China's transformation from a peripheral presence in Central Asia to the region's leading economic actor.
- Chinese energy policy in Central Asia serves multiple purposes. In the first instance, it is designed to access the region's rich oil and gas resources. It is also key to promoting socioeconomic development and political stability in China's poorer western regions, and to strengthening bilateral relations with the Central Asian states.
- The Chinese approach towards regional energy cooperation is defined principally by a determination to acquire as much equity as possible. To achieve this, they are prepared to pay or lend generous sums that appear commercially unjustifiable, but which have longer-term economic and strategic logic.
- In pursuing their energy interests, the Chinese have adopted an integrated approach that involves the senior Party leadership, state-owned energy majors (such as the China National Petroleum Corporation) and financial institutions.
- Beijing's strategic ambitions in Central Asia remain relatively modest for the time being. Notwithstanding its prominent involvement in the Shanghai Cooperation Organisation, it does not seek to become the regional leader. It is

sensitive to concerns that others — Russia and the US, as well as the Central Asians — may have about a potentially dominant China.
- Nevertheless, China's emergence as a leading energy actor in Central Asia has transformed the regional environment. The former Soviet republics now have greater strategic choice than at any time since independence, while Russian influence has been significantly undermined. It is likely that as China's economic presence grows, it will become more politically assertive.
- The implications of China's expanding energy interests are almost entirely negative for the EU. EU Member States will find it more difficult to access Central Asian gas, while the Nabucco pipeline project is set to become a prime casualty. Western companies face ever stiffer competition from the major Chinese energy companies, and could be squeezed out over time.
- China's growing influence in Central Asia will also mean that local regimes will remain highly resistant to democratisation, the rule of law and Western principles of good governance.

China's Energy Strategy in Central Asia
Background

In just over a decade, China has grown from being a marginal presence in Central Asia into its leading economic actor. At the heart of this remarkable transformation is an energy policy that has not only produced major oil and gas deals, but also fundamentally changed the region's strategic outlook.

Curiously, this transformation has come about more by accident — or series of accidents — than design. Four factors, in particular, have been critical:

1. China's growing dependence on energy imports. Since it first became a net importer of oil in 1993, this dependence has increased dramatically as a result of the country's continuing industrial boom and the heightened demands for oil and other natural resources.
2. The rise in global oil prices after 1999. This underlined the importance of diversifying external sources of supply, all the more so given anxieties at that time about China's 'Malacca dilemma' — the vulnerability of sea lines of communication and the existence of potential choke-points.
3. Difficulties in Sino–Russian energy relations. Beijing's preferred choice in diversifying foreign imports — cooperation with Russia — became increasingly

problematic after 2003. Moscow's balancing act between Chinese and Japanese interests stalled construction of the East-Siberian Pacific Ocean oil pipeline, while a Sino–Russian gas supply agreement remained elusive due to disagreements over price. Frustrated by protracted delays, and Moscow's refusal to allow Chinese companies into the Russian energy sector, Beijing searched for alternatives. Central Asia's huge energy reserves made it an attractive alternative.

4. 9/11 and the American-led military intervention in Afghanistan. These events created a new set of realities in Central Asia. The strategic environment was no longer dominated by Russia, the long-time hegemon, but became much more open. This posed new challenges for Beijing, such as America's geopolitical and normative presence next to China's sensitive western regions. But it also offered opportunities, not least because Russia's position had been severely weakened. It became clear, too, that Beijing would need to rely on its own efforts to advance Chinese economic and security interests.

Chinese objectives

Beijing's energy policy in Central Asia encompasses a range of interests and objectives that extend well beyond the basic aim of accessing new oil and gas reserves:

- Central Asia is primarily important to China as a long-term source of natural gas. Although gas currently accounts for only 3% of national primary energy consumption, this share is set to rise to around 10% by 2020. The growing use of natural gas reflects the government's commitment to cleaner and more sustainable forms of energy, although China will remain heavily dependent on coal for some decades yet.

- The development and consumption of Central Asian gas is a key element of Beijing's 'Go West' strategy. This not only looks to meet energy consumption needs in western China, but also to promote socioeconomic development in these regions and bind them more closely to the rest of the country. The expansion of China's natural gas capacities is as much a political and security project as it is an economic objective.

- Central Asian oil is of niche rather than central importance to China's energy mix. The facts do not support the conventional wisdom that Beijing is seriously concerned about the safety of international sea lanes. In recent years, Chinese oil imports from the Persian Gulf and Africa have increased, both in absolute terms and as a share of the total — from 66% in 1999 to 77% today. Central Asia, specifically Kazakhstan, is a useful source of oil, with considerable potential for future growth. But for the time being it is only one of many external sources of supply, accounting for only 3% of Chinese oil imports in 2010.

- China's oil and gas projects in Central Asia are a critical component of its broader relationships with the former Soviet republics. Such projects represent the most effective means of portraying China as a key contributor to regional economic and security cooperation. They give substance to Beijing's rhetoric about 'win-win' solutions, and are intended to facilitate a neighbourhood of friendly states. In short, China's energy interests serve larger foreign policy and strategic goals, as well as more specific security objectives, such as containing ethnic Uighur nationalism.

China's Approach to Energy Cooperation in Central Asia

The approach of the Chinese government and state-owned companies such as China National Petroleum Corporation (CNPC) in Central Asia does not differ greatly from their *modus operandi* in other resource-rich, governance-poor regions of the world.

- Its principal feature is what has been called an 'equity approach'. The Chinese are not content simply with receiving contracted amounts of oil and gas, but aim to be active project partners. They acquire as much equity as possible, often by paying well above the odds and offering huge loans on generous terms. The logic is straightforward: direct ownership of resources is the best way of ensuring project efficiency and of securing reliable, long-term supply. It is the main reason why CNPC and other energy majors, such as CNOOC (China National Offshore Oil Corporation) and SINOPEC (China Petroleum and Chemical Corporation), have switched their focus to Central Asia away from Russia.

- The Chinese do not attach political conditions to loans and investments. Considerations of good governance, democratisation, the rule of law and human rights are moot. Beijing's message to the Central Asians, as it is to authoritarian regimes around the world, is that it is interested in doing business and little else. This attitude reflects, in part, the principle of 'non-interference' in Chinese foreign policy. But it is also informed by the belief that any attempt to introduce conditionality would jeopardise major deals. Indeed, Beijing has sought to make a virtue out of non-conditionality, contrasting it to the more intrusive and legalistic approach of the West.

- Chinese political leaders, energy companies and banks appear less concerned than their Western counterparts about value for money, given the vast sums that are lavished on various equity acquisitions and project loans. In reality, the Chinese simply have a different conception of 'value for money'. They are motivated in the first place by considerations of strategic (long-term) security of demand. Second, since Chinese objectives are as much political as commercial, the basis for assessing the cost–benefit balance is multifaceted. This is demonstrated by their energy cooperation with the two principal Central Asian resource economies, Kazakhstan and Turkmenistan.

- In 2005, CNPC paid what many industry pundits regarded as an exorbitant USD 4.18 bn (EUR 3.14 bn) to buy PetroKazakhstan. Beijing calculated that this acquisition would establish China as a major energy player in Central Asia, following on from CNPC's 1997 purchase of 60% of Kazakhstan's third-largest oil company, AktobeMunaiGaz (it now owns 85%). Subsequently, CNPC purchased 50% of MangistauMunaiGaz in April 2009, as part of a USD 10 bn (EUR 7.5 bn) loan-for-oil deal with Astana. Again, the motivation was less the commercial attractiveness of the company than the opportunity to consolidate CNPC's position in the Kazakhstan oil sector, where it is now the third-largest oil producer after the state oil and gas company, KazMunaiGaz, and Chevron. Finally, the completion in 2009 of the Atyrau–Alashankou oil pipeline extending from western Kazakhstan to Xinjiang province has tied the two countries more closely than at any time in their history. These various projects have not only strengthened the position of Chinese energy interests, which currently control about 25% of Kazakhstan's oil sector, but also boosted the political relationship, and helped legitimise China's expanding presence in Central Asia.

- Similarly, in Turkmenistan, Beijing's intimate involvement in developing the local gas industry has implications that go far beyond individual projects. The 30-year agreement to provide 65 bn cubic meters (bcn) of gas per annum (up from 30 bcm when the original agreement was signed in 2006); the 2007 production-sharing agreement for the exploitation of the Baktyyarlyk fields on the right bank of the Amu Darya; the China Development Bank's USD 4 bn(EUR 3 bn) loan for first phase development of the huge South Yolotan field, followed by an additional USD 4.1 bn (EUR 3.1 bn) for the second phase; and the construction of the Central Asian Gas Pipeline from Turkmenistan to China via Uzbekistan and Kazakhstan (at an estimated cost of USD 7.3 bn (EUR 5.5bn)) — all of these represent major steps in China's progressive domination of the Turkmenistan gas market. As a result of its involvement in these projects, Beijing's economic influence has penetrated deep into Central and West Asia, while its bargaining position over a possible long-term gas supply agreement with Russia has also been greatly strengthened.

- The Chinese adopt an integrated approach in pursuit of their energy interests. This brings together various actors — senior Party leaders, the energy majors (CNPC in particular), and financial institutions (China Development Bank, China Investment Corporation, China International Trust and Investment Corporation) — to promote China's diverse agendas in Central Asia. In the first instance, this means securing reliable access to the region's oil and gas resources. But just as important is the use of energy cooperation to develop closer political ties with the Central Asian regimes. This was exemplified by the decision in June 2009 to grant a USD 10 bn (EUR 7.5 bn) loan to the Shanghai Cooperation Organisation (SCO) to help its member states recover from the global financial crisis. There was no tangible economic dividend, but the loan was important in selling China as a good pan-regional citizen at a time when Russia, the US and Europe were preoccupied with their own problems. In these circumstances, it made sense to deploy a tiny portion of China's vast foreign currency reserves to enhance its economic and political influence in a strategically important region.

- It is important not to overestimate the extent of Chinese engagement in Central Asia. For the time being at least, Beijing's goals remain relatively modest. It does not seek to become the regional leader, and has shown little inclination even to assume a major role in security building. It has been quite active within the SCO, but mainly to promote China as a benign and constructive presence rather than out of any active desire to project power. Beijing remains sensitive to the concerns that other players — not only the Central Asians, but also Russia and America — may have about a potentially dominant China. It is keen to avoid unnecessary complications that might harm its political and security, as well as energy, interests.

Implications of China's Energy Presence in Central Asia

China's growing footprint has considerable implications for the region and beyond, although its full impact is yet to be felt.

- The most immediate outcome is that the former Soviet Central Asian republics enjoy greater strategic choice than at any time since their independence. Although they remain economically reliant on Russia, both for direct trade and as a transit country to Europe, they are in a far stronger position compared with a few years ago. For example, before the signing of the Sino–Turkmen gas agreement in 2006 Ashgabat had been obliged to sell its gas at discount prices to Russia, its sole customer. Today, however, it is able to turn to China, which has not only become its principal market, but also one which is more reliable and lucrative. The reorientation has not been as dramatic with Kazakhstan and Uzbekistan (which consumes most of its own gas), but even here there has been a pronounced shift. China's reentry into Central Asia after a hiatus of some two centuries has enabled Astana (in particular) and Tashkent to pursue more independent and multivectored foreign policies.

- By contrast, Russia has lost out substantially from the expansion of Chinese energy interests. It has seen the end of its monopsony over Turkmenistan's gas exports; its position in the Kazakhstani and Uzbekistani energy sectors has weakened considerably; its political and strategic influence in Central Asia is in long-term decline; and it now looks unlikely that Moscow will be able to finalise a long-term gas supply agreement with the Chinese on favourable (or possibly any) terms.

- The impact of Chinese energy activity in Central Asia on the Sino–Russian 'strategic partnership' has, however, been relatively limited. Moscow is uncomfortable with the erosion of its regional influence, beginning (but not ending) with the energy sector. On the other hand, it can still count on several enduring advantages: close inter-elite networks with the Central Asian regimes; long-standing economic, cultural and linguistic ties; and local fears about Chinese economic dominance. Crucially, too, the fact that Central Asia is a secondary priority of both Russian and Chinese foreign policy makes it easier to manage any bilateral tensions.

- Nevertheless, the news is not all good for Beijing. There is already significant anti-Chinese popular sentiment in Kazakhstan, while Central Asian elites are concerned about the increasingly unbalanced nature of economic relations. This is not confined to the energy sector, but is also reflected in worries about the influx of Chinese consumer goods and labour. On a more general level, the Central Asians do not wish to replace one regional hegemon (Russia) with another (China). They are mindful of the need to preserve their strategic independence by diversifying their foreign relations as far as possible.

Despite impressive progress over the past decade, the overall Chinese presence in Central Asia is still fairly modest and limited largely to the economic sphere. China remains a peripheral political and security actor, and has shown little desire to translate economic influence into more comprehensive power projection. However, as its energy interests expand, and the stakes increase, it may pursue a more active and multifaceted approach to the region. This could lead to increased frictions with smaller neighbours and major powers alike.

Implications for the EU

- The growth of Chinese energy interests in Central Asia is bad news for the EU in several respects. In the first place it will make it much harder for EU Member States to access Central Asian gas, principally from Turkmenistan. Moreover, if and when a trans-Turkmen gas pipeline is eventually built, much of the gas in the Caspian Sea area earmarked to go west will go to China instead. This would effectively kill off the EU's already struggling Nabucco pipeline project.

- Although Western companies are involved in a number of Central Asian oil and gas projects, the arrival in force of the Chinese makes their operating environment more problematic. Ashgabat has indicated that it would like to reach a long-term gas supply agreement with Brussels. But the EU's cumbersome decision-making processes, divisions between Member States, the scarcity of project finance at a time of economic crisis, and political conditionalities add up to a highly uncompetitive package. By comparison, China enjoys the advantage of being a unitary actor, with a proven capacity to develop and implement energy projects quickly, and without the constraints of democratic accountability and the rule of law.

- It is possible that Chinese companies may seek partnerships with European companies in order to access advanced technology. But more likely they will look to squeeze out Western interests, if necessary by working closely with the Russians, who have an obvious commercial interest in seeing Central Asian gas go anywhere but Europe.

- Finally, as Chinese energy interests consolidate and expand their presence in Central Asia, local regimes will continue to be highly resistant to democratisation, the rule of law and Western principles of good governance. EU attempts to promote such values in the region have been almost entirely ineffectual, a state of affairs that will not change anytime soon.

China and Latin America
(March 2012)

Rhys Jenkins

Professor of Development Economics, School of International Development, University of East Anglia

Executive Summary

Over the past decade, the People's Republic of China (PRC) has emerged as an important actor in Latin America, following its accession to the World Trade Organization (WTO) in 2001. The global financial crisis and the recovery in the region since 2009 has seen the role of China grow further.

The most significant aspect of China's involvement in Latin America has been the growth of bilateral trade which reached around USD 200 bn[25] (EUR 150 bn) in 2010. China is now an important trade partner for all large Latin American countries and is currently the top export market for Brazil and Chile. There are also now signs of increased interest in the region as a destination for Chinese foreign direct investment (FDI) which rose sharply in 2010, while a number of major loans have also been made to the region. Closer political relations between China and Latin America have in the main reflected the growing economic links between China and the different countries of the region with the exception of those Central American countries, the Dominican Republic and Paraguay, which continue to have diplomatic relations with Taiwan.

China's interest in Latin America is primarily driven by its growing demand for raw materials. This is reflected in the pattern of exports to China that are

---

[25] International Monetary Fund, *Direction of Trade Statistics* (Mimas, University of Manchester, 2012).

overwhelmingly made up of primary products and the sectors that have attracted Chinese FDI and loans (a general trend of Chinese overseas FDI globally). A second motive is to secure access to the Latin American market for Chinese exports of manufactured goods, which have grown rapidly since the mid-2000s. Politically, apart from its efforts to isolate Taiwan by getting countries to switch recognition to the PRC, China has maintained a relatively low profile in the region, following a pragmatic, rather than an ideological, course.

Closer economic ties with China have had differential impacts within Latin America. Exporters of a limited number of primary products in a few Latin American countries have benefited from growing Chinese demand and rising prices, while many manufacturers have faced increased competition from Chinese goods both at home and in their export markets. Attitudes towards China in different Latin American countries partly reflect the relative significance of these different interests. Chile and Peru have enjoyed substantial benefits from booming exports to China and both signed free trade agreements with China in 2005 and 2009, respectively. At the other extreme, Mexico has suffered from competition from Chinese imports both in its domestic market and in the US in industries such as garments, electronics and televisions, while exporting relatively little to China. Brazil and Argentina have a more mixed situation with industrialists complaining about unfair competition from imported Chinese products, while exporters have gained substantially. Relations with Brazil are particularly important for China as its most important trading partner in the region.

China's shares of both Latin American imports and exports are projected to overtake those of the EU by the middle of the decade. This does not mean that EU trade with the region will decline but could lead to increased competition. At present the EU's major exports to Latin America do not compete with China's, but there is considerable similarity in terms of the products which are imported. The most serious economic concern for the EU is therefore continued upward pressure on commodity prices and potentially greater difficulty in obtaining access to Latin American resources in the future. Politically, there is no reason to believe that China is having a negative impact in relation to EU interests in the region.

Main Points

- Relations between China and Latin America have grown rapidly over the past decade.

- The most significant aspect of the relationship has been trade which reached over USD 200 bn (EUR 150 bn) in 2010.
- FDI and other financial flows from China have been more limited but have grown rapidly over the past couple of years.
- China's interests in the region are primarily economic. The most important of these is to obtain raw materials; a second interest is market access for Chinese manufacturers.
- China competes with Taiwan for diplomatic recognition in Central America and the Caribbean, although this has become less intense since 2008.
- Chinese demand for raw materials has benefited primary product exporters.
- Latin American industrialists have faced increased competition from China in both domestic and export markets.
- Although China has a Latin America strategy, the region does not deal with China collectively, but at the level of individual countries. As a consequence, different countries within Latin America have been affected differently by China's expansion.
- Brazil is China's most important partner in the region.
- Among the larger Latin American countries, Mexico has the most difficult relations with China.
- Chile and Peru have benefited from substantial exports of minerals to China and have signed free trade agreements with China.
- China continues to maintain a relatively low profile politically in the region.
- China will overtake the EU in terms of its share of Latin American trade by the middle of the decade.
- The EU's main exports to Latin America are not currently threatened by Chinese competition.
- The EU and China import similar products from the region and this may lead to rising prices and reduced access for the EU in future.

Introduction: The Growing Presence of China in Latin America

Before 1970, the only Latin American country with diplomatic relations with the People's Republic of China (PRC) was Cuba. Although most South American countries and Mexico established relations with China during the 1970s and 1980s, economic links were relatively limited until the start of the millennium. Since then, particularly after China's accession to the World Trade Organization (WTO) at the end of 2001 and President Hu Jintao's visit to Latin America in 2004, economic relations have grown rapidly, paralleled by an expansion of diplomatic contacts. This led to the Chinese government publishing its first Policy Paper on Latin America and the Caribbean in 2008.

The most striking evidence of the growing involvement of China in Latin America is the increased level of bilateral trade. Between 2000 and 2010, Latin American exports to China and Hong Kong grew more than 15-fold to USD 77 bn (EUR 58 bn),[26] while imports to the region grew from less than USD 10 bn (EUR 7.6 bn) to almost USD 125 bn (EUR 95 bn). China's share of the total exports of 19 Latin American countries rose from 1.3% in 2000 to 9.1% in 2010, and was more than 15% in Cuba, Chile, Peru and Brazil. Over the same period, China's share of total imports to these countries increased from 2.5% to 14.1%. China is the top export destination for Chile and Brazil and the second most important for Argentina, Peru and Colombia. It is the top import supplier in Chile and the second most important in all the other larger Latin American countries. Three countries have sought to consolidate their economic links with China through signing free trade agreements. The first to do so was Chile in 2005, followed by Peru (2009) and Costa Rica (2010).

Chinese foreign direct investment (FDI) in Latin America lags a long way behind the growth of bilateral trade, but has grown rapidly over the past couple of years. There is no reliable comprehensive information on Chinese FDI in the region since investments are often made through holding companies located in tax havens or subsidiaries elsewhere, rather than directly from China. The UN Economic Commission for Latin America and the Caribbean (ECLAC) has estimated that China invested a total of over USD 15 bn (EUR 11 bn) in 2010 (making it the third most important investor in the region in that year) with a further USD 22 bn (EUR 17 bn) in the pipeline from 2011 onwards. Investment has gone mainly to Brazil, Argentina and Peru, all of which have strong trade links with China.

Loans, primarily from the China Development Bank (CDB) and the Export-Import Bank of China (China Ex-Im Bank), also grew rapidly at the end of the last decade. Again data is difficult to come by, but a recent *Inter-American Dialogue Report*[27] estimated that total Chinese loans to the region increased from USD 6 bn

---

[26] At the time of writing, USD 1 = EUR 0.76.

[27] K. Gallagher, A. Irwin and K. Koleski (2012), *The New Banks in Town: Chinese Finance in Latin America*, Washington DC, Inter-American Dialogue, available at: http://www.thedialogue.org/PublicationFiles/TheNewBanksinTown-FullTextnewversion.pdf. Accessed 10 January 2014.

(EUR 4.6 bn) in 2008 to USD 18 bn (EUR 14 bn) in 2009 and USD 37 bn (EUR 28 bn) in 2010, although indications suggest that they fell back to USD 13 bn (EUR 10 bn) in 2011. In 2010 China's loans to the region exceeded the total lent by the World Bank and the Inter-American Development Bank. More than half of Chinese loans to the region between 2005 and 2011 went to Venezuela, with Brazil, Argentina and Ecuador accounting for the bulk of the remainder.

Political relations between China and Latin America have followed closer economic links. Since the start of the millennium, China has signed 'strategic partnership agreements' with Venezuela (2001), Mexico (2003) and Argentina (2004), adding to an earlier agreement with Brazil (1993). There have been a number of high-level diplomatic exchanges with President Hu Jintao visiting Latin America on four occasions, while numerous Latin American presidents have visited China during the same period, some of them on more than one occasion. China is also becoming increasingly involved in multilateral fora in the region. After initial resistance, it was accepted as a member of the Inter-American Development Bank in 2008. It also has permanent observer status at the Organization of American States. China is a member of the East Asia-Latin American Cooperation Forum, established in 2001, and has also initiated a series of dialogues with regional organisations such as MERCOSUR and the Andean Community. Cultural exchanges with Latin America are also growing with 32 Confucius Institutes established since 2006 and growing people-to-people exchanges. There are 100 pairs of sister province and city relationships between Chinese and Latin American localities.

China's Key Interests in the Region

China's interests in Latin America are primarily economic and, with one notable exception (the issue of the diplomatic recognition of Taiwan), political relations with the countries of the region tend to reflect these economic interests. China's burgeoning demand for raw materials has been the primary driver of trade between Latin America and China. Over 70% of the region's exports to China are of primary products and over half of the remaining 30% are processed raw materials. As trade grew after 2000, the share of primary products in Latin American exports to China increased. The main products exported are copper ore and concentrates, soybeans and soy oil, iron ore, crude oil, refined copper and fishmeal.

The importance of securing raw materials is also reflected in the pattern of Chinese FDI in Latin America. The bulk of Chinese investment in the region is of the 'resource seeking' variety, focusing on oil and minerals. Unfortunately there is no detailed breakdown of Chinese FDI by sector in Latin America, but it is clear that oil, gas and mining have been a major focus for such investment. The UN ECLAC estimates that 92% of confirmed Chinese investments in the region were in natural resource extraction, primarily oil and gas. Ten of the twelve major mergers and acquisitions by Chinese firms in South America between 2002 and 2008 were in raw materials, energy and power. Major Chinese companies with investments in Latin America include Sinopec, China National Petroleum Corporation and China National Overseas Oil Corporation in oil and gas and Minmetals, Chinalco and Wuhan Steel in minerals.

Securing access to natural resources has also been an important factor in other financial flows from China to Latin America. Two-thirds of the value of the loans made since 2008 involve deals under which Latin American countries supply oil and it is estimated that China will receive around 1.5 bn barrels of oil over the next ten years. Some of the most high-profile examples include a loan of USD 10 bn (EUR 7.6 bn) from the China Development Bank to Petrobras in Brazil and a series of loans to the Venezuelan state oil company PDVSA. Other loans have been for mining, including one for naval transportation of iron ore to China, and for infrastructure development.

A second key Chinese interest in Latin America is its value as a market for the country's exports of manufactured goods. Although it does not represent as large a market as the US or the EU, accounting for only about 5% of total Chinese exports, China is keen to diversify its exports and the region represents a growing market. Although imports from China fell during the economic crisis in 2009, they recovered strongly in 2010 and buoyant growth in the region since then makes it a particularly attractive market at a time when both the US and EU are facing economic difficulties.

An important objective of Chinese diplomacy in the region has been to improve market access for Chinese goods. One way in which it has tried to do this is by obtaining 'market economy' status from Latin American governments.[28] This was one of the key objectives of the visit of President Hu Jintao to Latin America in 2004 and Brazil, Argentina, Chile, Venezuela, Peru and several Caribbean countries agreed to grant China market economy status at the time, although the necessary legislation has never been approved in Brazil.

---

[28] Market economy status is a WTO designation which affects the ease with which countries can apply anti-dumping measures. By achieving this status, China hopes that it will not be subject to so many anti-dumping actions. The EU still regards China as a non-market economy.

Although, as discussed earlier, Chinese FDI in Latin America has been largely focused on extractive industries, there has also been some Chinese investment in manufacturing, for example in textiles and electronics in Mexico and in consumer electronics and telecommunications in Brazil. Most of the Chinese FDI in manufacturing has been market seeking, i.e. to supply the domestic market, while investments to create export platforms to sell in third markets have been minimal. Whereas investment in oil and mining is dominated by large state-owned companies, FDI by manufacturing companies involves a wider range of firms in terms of ownership and size. Surveys of small and medium Chinese firms have found that FDI is often seen as a means of promoting exports, either of the firms themselves or of other Chinese firms.

Chinese loans to Latin America also help promote exports from China. Most are wholly or partly tied to purchases of Chinese products such as construction machinery, telecommunications or railway equipment. A USD 10 bn (EUR 2.6 bn) credit line to Argentina to purchase a train system, for example, will go directly to Chinese railway companies. In some cases, part of the loan has been denominated in Chinese yuan (e.g. half of the USD 20 bn (EUR 15 bn) loan to Venezuela in 2010 was made in yuan) thus ensuring that it is used for the purchase of Chinese goods.

It is often noted that half of the countries that continue to recognise Taiwan and do not have diplomatic relations with the PRC are in Latin America and the Caribbean. These include Paraguay, all of the Central American countries apart from Costa Rica, and the Dominican Republic. A third key strategic interest of the PRC in the region is to use its influence to try to isolate Taiwan diplomatically, although this has been emphasised less since Ma's election in 2008. Both countries have used aid in order to get diplomatic recognition from the smaller countries of the region. Trade and FDI flows between China and those countries which recognise Taiwan tend to be less, as might be expected, than with those countries with which they have diplomatic relations. In this case it seems that political considerations affect economic relations rather than the other way around.

China's Relations with Particular Latin American Countries

The economic interests of China in Latin America impact groups within the region differently. Exporters of primary products have benefited from growing Chinese demand for raw materials and rising commodity prices. On the other hand, the region's manufacturers have faced increased competition from Chinese goods, both in their domestic markets and for exports. As a result there have been complaints from industrialists about 'unfair' competition and pressure put on governments to restrict Chinese imports. These tensions play out differently in different countries, reflecting the extent of these impacts and the strength of the affected parties.

From China's point of view its most significant relationship in the region is with Brazil. The two countries embarked on scientific and technological cooperation signing the China-Brazil Earth Resources Satellite agreement in 1988, even before China recognised Brazil as a strategic partner in 1993. As co-members of BRICS, they meet regularly at an international level and Brazil is China's most important trading partner in the region and the most significant destination for Chinese FDI. Nevertheless, despite this friendly relationship, the growth of Chinese imports to Brazil has led to tensions, particularly with industrialists, and has resulted in a number of anti-dumping cases being brought against Chinese products.

At the other extreme, the most fraught relationship between China and a major Latin American country is with Mexico. This in part has an economic basis, since Mexico has a large trade deficit with China and, unlike Brazil and some other South American countries, has not been able to export to China on a significant scale. Mexico was the last WTO member to agree to China becoming a member in 2001 and kept very restrictive tariffs on some Chinese imports until December 2011. Other factors, including the Chinese government's decision to confine some Mexican tourists to their hotel in China during the swine fever outbreak and the visit of the Dalai Lama to Mexico, have further ratcheted up tension over the past couple of years.

Although not to the same extent as in Mexico, there have also been some tensions between Argentina and China, mainly around trade issues. Argentina has imposed anti-dumping measures and protectionist tariffs on Chinese imports and, allegedly in response, in 2010 China banned imports of soy oil from Argentina on the grounds that it contained high levels of a solvent.

The other country which China has recognised as a strategic partner in the region is Venezuela. Although growing, trade links with Venezuela are not as significant as those with Brazil or Argentina. It is however the largest recipient of Chinese loans in the region, most of which involve deals for oil, as noted above. China has sought to avoid getting drawn in to the anti-US rhetoric of the Chavez government in Venezuela. Given that China's key interests in Latin America are economic, it is not interested in provoking an unnecessary conflict with the US, preferring a more pragmatic strategy in the region, rather than allying itself with the more radical left wing government currently in power.

Chile and Peru have both signed free trade agreements with China and are key suppliers of primary commodities, particularly copper in various forms, and fishmeal from Peru. Both countries have enjoyed significant surpluses in their trade with China and public opinion towards China is favourable. Peru, relative to its overall size, has probably received more Chinese FDI than any other country in Latin America, particularly in the mining sector and these have given rise to some conflicts with mineworkers. However, despite this, overall relations have remained good.

Challenges for the EU

As already seen, China's share of Latin America's trade has increased significantly over the past decade. Projections made by ECLAC in 2010 indicate that China's share of both the region's imports and exports will overtake that of the EU by the middle of the current decade. While this does not necessarily involve a decline in the absolute level of trade between the EU and Latin America, it may well indicate increased competition. This depends on the extent to which the EU and Chinese trade with Latin America involve similar products.

Although it is no longer the case that Chinese exports are comprised mainly of traditional labour-intensive products such as garments, footwear and toys, there is nevertheless a significant difference between the types of products exported to Latin America from China and Europe. The top ten products exported from China are in the main electronic and electrical products, whereas the top ten from the EU are pharmaceutical products, vehicles and parts and non-electrical machinery. Only one product, apparatus for electrical circuits, boards and panels is amongst the top ten Latin American imports from both China and the EU.

The main imports from the region to both Europe and China are primary products. Of the top ten products exported from Latin America, as many as seven are among the top ten in both markets. These include oil, copper in various forms, iron ore, feedstuffs, oil seeds and pulp, and waste paper. This suggests that, at present, the main concern for the EU as far as China's growing involvement in Latin America is concerned comes in terms of competition for natural resources. This is, of course, not to rule out the possibility that in the not too distant future, the continued expansion of Chinese exports and the growth of technological capabilities in industries such as motor vehicles and machinery, will lead to intensified competition for the Latin American market.

Up to now the main impact of Chinese demand for raw materials has been to put upward pressure on prices, particularly of minerals. However, as seen above, Chinese firms are beginning to invest directly in exploration and production in Latin America and the Chinese authorities are providing financing in return for long-term supply contracts. Because the firms involved are almost all state-owned enterprises, there is a possibility that they will be required to give priority to supplying Chinese producers, making access for European buyers more difficult and more expensive.

There is no reason for the EU to fear the growing political influence of China in the region. While some governments may welcome the opportunity to diversify their trade and financial relationships that the growth of China provides, they are not about to replace existing links with either the EU or the US. Neither is China showing signs of wishing to challenge the US in its own 'backyard'; indeed, it has been keen to avoid confrontation. As an important trading partner and a major investor in Latin America, the EU will continue to play a significant role in the region, even while China's international links become more diversified.

Conclusion

The paper has highlighted that:

- China is becoming an increasingly important actor in Latin America, both economically and politically.
- Its main interests in the region are economic — Latin America is primarily viewed as a source of raw materials and, to a lesser extent, a market for Chinese exports.
- China will overtake EU as a trade partner for the region by the middle of the decade.
- Although EU trade with Latin America will continue to grow, competition with China for raw materials is likely to intensify.

China's 'Non-Policy' for Afghanistan
(February 2012)

Bernt Berger
Senior Fellow and Head of Asia Program, Institute for Security & Development Policy

Executive Summary

The future security situation in Afghanistan following the disengagement of the International Security Assistance Force (ISAF) due to take place in 2014 is one of the great uncertainties in China's foreign policy. In fact, Beijing has no defined policy that deals with the security situation inside Afghanistan. China has not interfered in Afghanistan's political development and has refrained from any direct involvement in the country's security affairs and cooperation with NATO. Instead, China has focused on the stabilisation of Afghanistan's neighbourhood. A stable regional environment may *inter alia* be conducive to the development of the country and possibly prevent Afghanistan returning to the role of a pawn in struggles between regional powers. Accordingly, China has promoted regional solutions for the mid-term development of Afghanistan in international forums.

So far China has exercised restraint in security affairs. Most of its own elementary security interests have been served by the US-led 'global war on terror' and intervention in Afghanistan, as well as cross-border missions into Pakistani territory. During confrontations of US and Pakistani military forces with Al-Qaeda and other Islamist groups, the leadership of militant Uighur separatist groups was entirely eradicated.

China has been a bystander in terms of direct engagement into Afghan security. Its main concern lies with the ongoing destabilisation of Pakistan, due to spillovers of militancy from Afghanistan and a fragmented, inefficient state system. Before the US reengagement in Afghanistan and Pakistan in 2001, Pakistan was Beijing's primary intermediary in dealing with Afghanistan. Beijing's policy makers still believe that Pakistan is key to the stability of the region.

Depending on the security situation in Afghanistan after 2014, China will mainly be concerned with two potential security risks:

- The possibility that a re-emergence of state-free regions could once more create safe havens for separatist militant mobilisation beyond China's influence.
- The possibility that the potential destabilisation of wider Central Asia could harm China's political and commercial interests.

In its multilateral engagement in Central Asia and the Shanghai Cooperation Organisation (SCO), Beijing has promoted a stable neighbourhood with existing security mechanisms. It has also started to engage in Afghanistan's economic reconstruction with risky investments that offer uncertain returns. In international forums such as the London Conference and Bonn II, it has consistently pushed this regional approach. The belief is that the stabilisation of the wider region surrounding Afghanistan:

- Helps to stabilise the country while preventing major external interference in its political development and internal power balance.
- Helps to prevent spillover of militancy into the neighbourhood.
- Reduces the need for extra-regional actors.

All in all China is the least problematic actor in the region and will most likely have a positive impact on the future of Afghan and Central Asian stability and development. Thus, for Europe, it is a likely partner in regional development. For this to happen, this would require:

- Following China's lead and considering the value of existing mechanisms such as the SCO.
- Defining issues of destabilisation as well as economic and development interests in the region and Afghanistan, and dovetailing them with the perception of needs by regional actors.
- Liaising with Beijing and creating channels of communication and cooperation within existing regional security mechanisms.

Main Points

- The future security situation in Afghanistan following the disengagement of the International Security Assistance Force (ISAF) due to take place in 2014 is one of the great uncertainties in China's foreign policy.
- Beijing has no defined policy that deals with the security situation inside Afghanistan. It has not interfered into Afghanistan's political development and has refrained from any direct involvement in the country's security affairs and cooperation with NATO.
- Instead, China has focused on the stabilisation of Afghanistan's neighbourhood. It has promoted regional solutions for the mid-term development of Afghanistan in international forums.
- In its multilateral engagement in Central Asia and the Shanghai Cooperation Organisation (SCO), Beijing has promoted a stable neighbourhood with existing security mechanisms. It has also started to engage in Afghanistan's economic reconstruction with risky investments that offer uncertain returns.
- China is the least problematic actor in the region and will most likely have a positive impact on the future of Afghan and Central Asian stability and development. Thus, for Europe, it is a likely partner in regional development.

Afghanistan: China's Strategic Blind Spot?

One of China's core priorities in security policy is the stabilisation of its immediate neighbourhood. Beijing has pulled out all the stops to achieve this goal by means of multilateral and bilateral diplomacy, as well as aid. In so doing, it has sought to break into new markets, gain access to resources, move forward with confidence building and maintain peace in its own periphery. Yet, despite its common border with Afghanistan and its significance for regional stability, Beijing has adopted a surprisingly passive approach towards the country.

China's reluctant engagement with Afghanistan does not come as a surprise. After the International Security Assistance Force (ISAF) Mission in 2001 brought peace enforcement under the aegis of NATO's leadership, China had little stake in the security and reconstruction of the war-torn country. Previously Beijing had engaged in the 'Six Plus Two Contact Group', a UN initiative of Afghanistan's neighbours plus Russia and the US. The group sought to achieve peaceful conflict settlement and combat illicit drug trafficking, and continued even after the Taliban had taken over the northern city of Mazar-e-Sharif and assumed full control over the country in 1998.

During the 1990s China was confronted with a first wave of separatist militancy and small-scale terrorist attacks in its northeastern province of Xinjiang. At the time, China had a justified concern about connections between the Turkestan Independence Party/East Turkestan Islamic Movement (TIP/ETIM) and Al-Qaeda, who were rumoured to have hideouts in Afghanistan. Beijing's security agencies thus used their links to Pakistani military intelligence to broker an agreement with the Taliban. Following this, Beijing received guarantees that no terrorist activity would originate from Afghan soil, even though anti-Chinese militants have been trained in Afghanistan under the auspices of Al-Qaeda.

After 2001, international efforts during the 'war on terror' served Beijing well. Although China provided full support to the US, it largely relied on third parties and had only limited ability to look after its security concerns itself. Nevertheless, between 2003 and 2010, US and Pakistani forces eliminated the leadership ranks of TIP/ETIM. Militant Uighur separatists have typically heavily relied on the support of other Islamist or pan-Turkic nationalist groups. After Al-Qaeda's demise in the region they were left without support and either had to integrate with sympathetic movements or go into hiding in small cells. In recent years the main militant threat to China comes from Pakistani soil and from within China.

On the whole China's concern for developments in Afghanistan has been lukewarm. The security situation along the short border has been stable. Geopolitical threats have not played a role since the Cold War when Beijing feared encirclement by the Soviet Union. Neither are there any signs that China regards Afghanistan as a strategic buffer between the regional powers. Yet, Afghanistan's stability is essential for the whole of Central and South Asia and therefore China's immediate Western neighbourhood.

What is at Stake for Beijing?

At present China does not face any organised militant threats from Afghan soil. Rather, it faces threats from separatist militant groups in northwestern China, although this remains at a low organisational level. Small cells inside China, returnees from Pakistan and instigation from cells based abroad are the main sources of violence on Chinese soil. The main motive of separatist militant assaults is to instigate social scission along ethnic lines and, to a much lesser extent, challenge the central state directly.

Beijing's biggest headache is an increasingly unstable Pakistan and increasing cross-border activity from Afghanistan aggravates this situation. Insurgent groups, such as the Haqqani network, operate on both sides of the border along Waziristan, one of Pakistan's Federally Administered Tribal Areas (FATA). These groups have erratic ties to the Pakistani military and its intelligence service and have at times deceived them. US disengagement from cooperating with Pakistan creates new challenges for China because Beijing is financially and militarily unable to pick up the slack.

Greater destabilisation from a weak government, a faltering economy and an increasingly uncontrolled military in Pakistan have led to greater risks for Chinese interests. Pakistan has also become an unpredictable partner in dealing with Afghanistan. So far China has regarded the military as a guarantor for stability in Pakistan that is efficient at dealing with insurgent groups. However, this image has lately started to erode. While the Pakistani military has, more than ever, sought to secure China's support, in 2011 Beijing started to seek closer consultations with Washington.

In the event that ISAF disengages from Afghanistan after 2014, China will be faced with a range of uncertainties. It is possible that a weak government in Kabul might become a pawn in the hands of regional powers, which could seek to impose their blueprint of a regional order. Such a development might weaken the government in Kabul to such an extent that it would need to employ considerable diplomatic resources, in order to counter these actions. Chinese interests are at risk in mainly two ways. Firstly, a weak Afghan government or even a failing state would once again provide state-free zones where anti-Chinese militancy could be organised. Secondly, a spillover of Afghan insecurity into its neighbouring Central Asian states would pose a risk for Chinese energy mid-stream operations, a range of infrastructure projects, and citizens. This is because, in recent years, Chinese companies have, with the help of intense diplomatic efforts, managed to get a foothold in Central Asian energy markets. China's energy security increasingly relies on the region and uninterrupted overland-pipeline operations. So far, Turkmenistan supplies approximately 50% of China's total gas imports. Kazakhstan only supplies 4% of China's total crude oil imports. Yet, in both cases numbers are on the rise, as China tries to diversify its supply away from Gulf States such as Saudi Arabia and Iran.

Overall and despite its concerns, China has factored out proactive security measures for Afghanistan. It stands to reason that Beijing will remain sitting on the fence until 2014. For the time being there is little scope for long-term considerations until NATO and Washington clearly define the terms of ISAF's disengagement. Nevertheless, China's multilateral and economic initiatives have started to make an impact.

Risky Direct Investments and Economic Reconstruction

China has gained attention for its successful bids in tenders for development of resources and, to a lesser extent, investment in infrastructure development in Afghanistan. For China, direct investment is the least controversial and most frictionless way of engaging in Afghanistan and can be regarded as a contribution to economic reconstruction. Early investment projects such as the Aynak Coppermine were risky in terms of security and offered little promise of returns. Newer oil projects might in the long run benefit Chinese companies but, for now, will only create revenues that will benefit Afghanistan's weak economy (if at all).

As early as 2007, the Beijing-based China Metallurgical Group (MCC) and Jiangxi Copper Co. won a bid for mining concessions in the so-called Aynak Coppermine in the southwest of Kabul. The state-owned company won the tender with a deal that involved a USD 3 bn direct investment. Yet, the investment is not only risky in terms of the security situation surrounding the project. The development of the mine is accompanied by the requirement of high expenditures on transport, a power plant and social infrastructure for over 8,000 workers, and around 30,000 indirectly employed people who will, for example, develop roads, hospitals, schools, mosques and water supplies.

Due to the lack of transport infrastructure, the MCC has engaged in a costly (estimated at USD 6 bn–7 bn) railway project along a north–south corridor, connecting Kabul and Mazar-e-Sharif, and the copper mine with Pakistan, Tajikistan and Uzbekistan. The project is also part of a planned wider regional railway network. In 2010 the MCC commissioned a feasibility study and announced that if the security situation were to deteriorate in Pakistan's border region, it would have consequences on the future of the project. Rumour has it that cases of corruption and underhand payments have also led the MCC to reconsider the whole project.

In December 2011 China's state-owned National Petroleum Corporation International Ltd (CNPCI) and the Afghan Ministry of Mines signed an agreement on the exploration of the three oil blocks in the Amu Darya Basin. The contract covers the tapping of new wells and extraction by the China National Petroleum Company International Watan (CNPCIW), a joint corporation under Afghan law between CNPCI and the local Watan Oil and Gas Company, where the former owns 75% of the share. The Watan Group is an (controversial) Afghan conglomerate that already cooperates with Chinese companies in the telecommunication sector and metal processing. Under the agreement, the CNPCI agreed to pay a 15% royalty on the gross sales revenue of oil for the lease of the blocs (according to Article 23, Afghan Hydrocarbon Law), 20% corporate tax and up to 70% of the net profit (depending on the quantity of produced hydrocarbons) as gain sharing to the Afghan State, represented by the Ministry of Mines.

The investment in Afghan oil is a risky undertaking, both in terms of expenditures and the unpredictable security situation. The expected net revenue for the CNPCI is low and the actual quantity and quality of crude oil is unknown due to incomplete geological data. In addition, viable infrastructure is lacking. It is possible that the CNPCI might be able to link potential oil production facilities with existing gas projects in Turkmenistan on the other side of the Amu Darya River; regardless, high expenditures for transport, housing and social infrastructure are inescapable.

All in all, economic engagement by Chinese companies in Afghanistan is marked by high risk and little returns. Yet, the investments also possess a dual security dimension. Economic development, increasing state revenues, development of social infrastructure and reduction of unemployment may contribute to greater stability in Afghanistan. However, in the face of uncertainties regarding the security situation after 2014 and its related threats to Chinese subjects, it appears more likely than not that companies will eventually start to move out of Afghanistan again.

China's Multilateral Engagement

Beijing has taken part in a range of international initiatives in dealing with the future of Afghanistan and is regionally involved by virtue of its Shanghai Cooperation Organisation (SCO) membership. So far the SCO has served China's economic and security interests well. Yet, with regard to regional security affairs (including Afghanistan and a greater role for the SCO) Beijing has been noncommittal to international demands. Instead it has primarily used international forums to push its own security interests and principles related to the future of Afghanistan. During recent conferences Beijing highlighted what it believes to be the central role of regional solutions. However, it remains unclear whether this emphasis on a regional framework means anything more than restricting the influence of external actors. In the eyes of Beijing's policy makers, the current *modus operandi* of the SCO serves its preferred approach for stabilising the region. Yet, what has changed is that Beijing has shifted the organisation towards the centre of international attention.

Beijing's timely 1996 campaign for a regional initiative in Central Asia, namely the Shanghai Five and later the SCO, served its security interests well. Not only was it possible to resolve border disputes with Russia and the newly independent Eastern European states but, later, the campaign served as a framework for intelligence sharing, confidence building and military-to-military contacts. In 2005, the SCO–Afghanistan contact group was established as a consultation mechanism for proposals on cooperation between the SCO and Kabul and, in 2011, Afghanistan requested full observer status during the SCO Astana summit, receiving support from Russia. Decision makers in Beijing have not been pleased by these developments. From their perspective, greater Afghan participation has the potential to overburden the SCO with security issues, which may sideline Beijing's own goals within the forum. Current priorities lie with greater bilateral economic integration with SCO member states, thereby buttressing regional development and stability.

The SCO provides a platform that includes the most important Central and South Asian neighbours of Afghanistan such as China, India, Pakistan, Iran and Russia. Thus, it theoretically forms an ideal framework to reconcile conflicting approaches and stabilise Afghanistan in a common effort. Yet China, not to mention the other powers, will neither get involved in regional power struggles nor deviate from its bilateral approach. So far for Beijing, regional multilateralism has never meant integrating its partners nor being conducive to their mutual relations. Rather it is a means for trust building and establishing bilateral political and economic ties. In contrast to its regional approach, China has moved the SCO into the centre of attention even outside the region.

On the international stage Beijing has been more proactive and accommodating. In December 2001, Beijing approved the UN Security Council Resolution 1386 and thus co-authorised the establishment of ISAF. During the London Conference on security, development and international support for Afghanistan in early 2009, Chinese Foreign Minister Yang Jiechi adopted a determined stance and most of China's proposals are reflected in the *Afghanistan Compact* that was adopted during the conference. The measures suggested by Beijing included:

- Enabling the Afghan government to take up responsibility for safeguarding the security of the country.

- Rendering support for the implementation of the Afghanistan National Development Strategy.
- Improving governance capacities by providing training to government officials, including among others, those in diplomacy, economy and trade, medical and healthcare, finance, tourism, agriculture and counter-narcotics.
- Enhancing coordination and cooperation to integrate, complement and reinforce the international community's efforts, particularly at the regional level among neighbouring countries under the leadership of the UN. Beijing also suggested the creation of a security belt around Afghanistan set up by its neighbours.

During the Bonn II Conference in December 2011, China joined Russia, Iran and Pakistan's opposition to a new framework for regional security and cooperation (including permanent US bases) that had been discussed at the Istanbul Conference earlier the previous month. Foreign Minister Yang Jiechi emphasised that the role of the SCO and other international organisations/mechanisms should be brought into full play in Afghanistan. However, he remained vague about how this idea could be practically implemented. Yet, the message implied that China prefers regional solutions without interference from what it regards as external actors.

Conclusion: Implications for European Policies

So far the main concern regarding China's approach towards Afghanistan and its possible future engagement has rested with NATO. However, the EU and China share a range of economic and security interests and acceptable modes of cooperation need to be established by both sides. Nevertheless, there are issues: divergences exist in their expectations of how regional actors should get involved in the reconstruction and future stabilisation of Afghanistan. They also need to overcome China's set priorities and its reluctance to fully engage in its Western neighbourhood.

However, there is little to worry about Beijing's intentions in Afghanistan. Compared with other regional players such as Iran, Pakistan, Turkey or even India, who could use Afghanistan as a proxy battleground for regional power struggles, China is the least critical actor. Dealing with China in Afghanistan and its neighbourhood requires greater understanding of how China perceives the challenges that it needs to confront in the short-to-mid term. It also involves Beijing's main security concerns in Pakistan. Pakistan is the weakest link in the stabilisation of Afghanistan's neighbourhood and its 'outside–in' approach. Although Beijing is not keen to let third parties interfere into its close but onerous relationship with Pakistan, it will not be able to maintain economic and social stability in that country alone. Recent moves by the EU to lift tariffs on Pakistani textile products as a contribution to bolster Pakistan's economy are welcome. Yet, with greater engagement, Europeans might confront the same challenges as China: economic engagement mostly benefits Pakistan's small ubiquitous circle of elite families and is hardly effective in stabilising the country. For this reason, closer exchanges with Pakistan and consideration of its role in regional stability are necessary.

Beijing should be taken seriously regarding its demands for a greater role for existing regional mechanisms made at the Bonn II Conference. It will resist any approach that its decision makers perceive as interference into its regional ties. However, there needs to be more clarification and debate with regard to the role of the SCO in particular, how it seeks to deal with arising issues and what kind of capacities are needed. The question is how a stable Central Asia can help to stabilise Afghanistan and not the other way around; how possible negative developments in Afghanistan after 2014 might impact on the stability of Central Asia. The Organization for Security and Cooperation in Europe (OSCE), which is gaining observer status at the SCO, and Track I–II dialogues are neutral but effective channels to establish common interests and approaches between wider Central Asia and Europe.

In sum:
- With regard to Afghanistan's future, China is the least problematic regional actor.
- Beijing has proven readiness to take up responsibility within a self-defined framework of action.
- So far, Chinese engagement includes stabilisation of the neighbourhood by means of economic development, regional security mechanisms and economic reconstruction inside Afghanistan.
- Cooperating with China on Afghanistan-related security issues means to cooperate and promote existing security mechanisms in terms of capacity building. However, China needs to explain more explicitly what kind of channels of cooperation it has envisioned.

China–Burma Relations
(March 2012)

Marianna Brungs
Associate Fellow, Asia Programme, Chatham House

Executive Summary

China–Burma (Myanmar) relations are underpinned by strategic interests and geographic realities. China has been an important source of political and economic support for Burma. In return, China has been given access to Burma's abundant resources, and an ability to use it as a strategically important entry point to the Indian Ocean.

While several key challenges lie ahead, including the upcoming 1 April 2012 by-elections, the speed and breadth of the recent political and economic reforms in Burma under Thein Sein's government have been remarkable. Following earlier efforts to engage the Burmese regime, the US was quick to respond to Thein Sein's reform programme with support and encouragement. The Secretary of State visited Burma in December 2011, and full diplomatic relations with Burma were restored in January this year.

Burma's reforms and improved relations with the US present an interesting challenge for China. The reforms are likely to lead to greater stability and economic development in Burma — a common goal for China and the US — but threaten China's economic and political dominance in its neighbour. China is also suspicious of the motives underlying the US's engagement in Burma, in the context of the US's broader strategic shift to Asia.

Although China has sought to increase its influence in Burma for strategic and economic reasons and Burma turned to China for protection during its international isolation, China's ability to contain Burma has been limited due to Burma's strong sense of nationalism and independence.

Chinese media reports on the general reform process and US engagement have focused on issues concerning stability and economic development, rather than on the shift towards a more democratic system. On matters such as the suspension of the Myitsone dam and the US 'pivot' towards Asia, coverage tends to be more critical, and raises concerns about the potential impact on China's political and economic interests in Burma and the wider region. Censure tends to be focused on the US, rather than Burma.

While Burma's reforms do appear genuine, the underlying motivations are not clearly known. Burma's concern about over-reliance on China, and a desire to reassert and leverage its independence are likely to be key factors. The military regime may also have decided that reform was necessary for the ongoing survival of Burma and for the military to be able to retain some form of control.

The Burmese government is keen to engage with the EU among others. In determining next steps, the EU should consider how to help foster sustainable reform and development in an independent Burma. The EU's development assistance should be provided as rapidly as possible, and the EU should support Burma in protecting its economy and environment from being swamped by competitive foreign investors.

Main Points

- China has been an important source of political and economic support for Burma. In return, China has been able to access Burma's abundant resources, and to use it as a strategically important entry point to the Indian Ocean.
- Following earlier efforts to engage the Burmese regime, the US was quick to respond to Thein Sein's reform programme with support and encouragement. The Secretary of State visited Burma in December 2011, and full diplomatic relations with Burma were restored in January 2012.
- While Burma's reforms will result in a more stable and prosperous neighbour, China is concerned about the potential impact on its economic and strategic interests.
- China's ability to contain Burma has been limited due to Burma's strong sense of nationalism and independence.
- Chinese media reports on the general reform process and US engagement tend to focus on issues around stability and economic development. Reporting is more critical when Chinese interests are directly affected.

- The reforms are likely to have been prompted by Burma's concern about over-reliance on China. The reforms may have also been intended to ensure the survival of Burma and to enable the military to retain some form of control.
- In determining next steps, the EU should consider how to help foster sustainable reform and development in an independent Burma.

Introduction: China–Burma Relations Before the Recent Reforms

As with a marriage of convenience, relations between China and Burma have been underpinned by strategic interests and geographic realities. While China is a dominating neighbour, it has been an important source of political and economic support for Burma.

Political relations

From 1988 until the recent reforms, Burma increasingly relied on China's support to shield it from international pressure and mitigate its growing isolation. In the UN Security Council, China protected Burma from punitive measures by blocking meaningful discussion, softening the language of resolutions and exercising its veto. Burma was able to circumvent arms embargoes by the US and EU by turning to China for military hardware and technical assistance.

On China's side, Burma has a strategically important location between South Asia, China and Southeast Asia. Accessing the Indian Ocean through Burma provides China with a strategic presence in the Indian Ocean, boosting its ability to compete with India, as well as enabling access to alternative shipping routes to the congested and strategically vulnerable Straits of Malacca. These trading routes could also help to open up China's less economically developed western provinces. For this reason, China is developing several ports along Burma's coast on the Bay of Bengal, and building highways through Burma linking these ports to Rangoon and the Chinese interior.

Economic interests

During its international isolation, Burma relied heavily on China for trade. The balance of trade is significantly in China's favour, and imports from China have grown exponentially over the last few decades. China has also provided significant development assistance to prop up the regime, including loans and grants.

In return, China has had access to Burma's abundant resources to boost its own growth and meet its energy requirements. To extract these resources, China has invested billions of dollars into infrastructure projects, including more than USD 20 bn into a planned high speed rail line, and more billions into oil, gas and hydro-electric power projects, including a planned oil and gas pipeline to transport energy resources to China's cities.

Recent Improvements in US–Burma Relations
The recent reforms in Burma

The remarkable speed and breadth of political and economic reform in Burma over the past six months is well known. While the November 2010 elections were condemned as flawed by the international community, due to vote rigging, other fraud and voter intimidation, the elections did result in the dissolution of the military regime's ruling body, the State Peace and Development Council (SPDC) and the convening of President U Thein Sein's nominally civilian government in March 2011. Although Thein Sein's government consists primarily of retired senior military officers with close links to the former military regime, Thein Sein — originally seen as a regime flunky — has led a wide-ranging reform programme since coming to power.

Political reforms include the release of hundreds of political prisoners since mid-2011, ongoing negotiations with armed ethnic groups, electoral and media law reform, and reaching out to pro-democracy leader Aung San Suu Kyi. While many of the proposed reforms are still to be implemented, Aung San Suu Kyi believes Thein Sein is genuine in his desire for change. Her party, the National League for Democracy (NLD), will contest by-elections on 1 April 2012 to fill seats departed by parliamentarians who became ministers. On the economic side, Burma is working to modernise and open up its economy, including improving its banking and foreign exchange systems, and talking more openly about the need to address high levels of corruption.

While the reform process has considerable momentum and will be difficult to reverse, the road ahead will not be easy. The April by-elections will be the first real test and the government is well aware of the close international scrutiny surrounding the democratic nature of the elections. Other challenges include continuing conflict with ethnic groups, and huge capacity gaps in the ability of the government to implement the proposed reforms.

Given the broad nature and speed of the reform process, Burmese dissidents and the international community initially questioned the sincerity of Thein Sein and his reform agenda. These concerns have now abated somewhat, as the evidence indicates that Thein Sein and key figures in his government are genuine in wanting to implement reforms that will lead to greater stability and development in Burma, including boosting its international engagement. The underlying motivations and the extent of the government's desire to move towards participatory democracy, however, are still not clear.

The US response: improved US–Burma political relations

The US was quick to respond to Thein Sein's reform programme with support and encouragement. Since 2009, the Obama administration had been looking for opportunities to increase engagement with the military regime. They considered that the Bush administration's policy of sanctions and isolation had not succeeded in improving conditions in Burma, and had only made the regime more resentful towards the US and more closely aligned to China. They wanted to create US influence in Burma, including on issues such as its relationship with North Korea, and to boost support for moderate factions. More broadly, hostile relations with Burma had obstructed the US's ability to redevelop and strengthen its relationship with the Association of Southeast Asian Nations (ASEAN).

Initial outreach efforts from late 2009, including regular visits by senior US State Department officials, did not meet with much success. These efforts, however, meant that the US could move quickly when Thein Sein's reform programme started to take shape, including the appointment of a Special Representative and Policy Coordinator for Burma in August 2011.

Aung San Suu Kyi's meeting with Thein Sein in August 2011 and her subsequent endorsement of his sincerity opened the way for the Secretary of State's visit to Burma in early December 2011. During this visit, Clinton said the US wanted to assist Burma in its reform efforts if these maintained momentum. On 13 January 2012, Clinton announced that the US intended to 'meet action with action', and would restore full diplomatic relations with Burma.

The US has maintained its sanctions regime against Burma, and its next steps will depend on how the April by-elections are conducted. If the elections are seen as free and fair, the US is likely to find ways to provide significant financial and technical assistance. While the current policy of engagement and support for Burma has bipartisan support, removing the sanctions requires congressional approval, which will take some time. The current conditions of this include continued political reform and reconciliation with the ethnic minority groups.

Chinese Perspectives on Improved US–Burma Relations

For China, Burma's reforms and improved foreign relations present an interesting challenge. On one hand, the reforms are likely to lead to greater stability in a strategically important neighbour. On the other hand, Burma is shifting itself out of China's orbit, threatening China's economic and political dominance in Burma. China is also suspicious of American motives, within the broader context of the US's very public strategic 'pivot' to Asia.

Greater political and economic stability in Burma

Stability in Burma is a common goal for China and the US. China has had long-standing concerns about the military regime's economic and political mismanagement, including activities such as diverting significant resources to building the new capital in Nay Pyi Taw. US assistance in promoting stability in Burma would allow China to focus more on maximising the value of its economic and strategic interests.

On the economic front, China's ability to do business in Burma and maximise the returns from its large investments has been hampered by the lack of economic development and adequate institutions, as well as significant corruption and other failings in governance. China has been required to provide massive financial assistance to Burma to shore up the regime and maintain stability.

Politically, China needs a stable neighbour, particularly in the border regions. While China would not encourage full autonomy for Burma's ethnic groups, given the precedent this would provide for ethnic groups on its own side of the border, reconciliation between the Burmese government and Burmese ethnic groups would reduce the pressure on China from ongoing conflict and refugee flows.

At the national level, it is likely that China would be willing to deal with whichever government is in power. China's ambassador was the first to congratulate Aung San Suu Kyi following the NLD's landslide victory in the 1990 elections. Aung San Suu Kyi has emphasised publicly her desire to maintain good relations with China.

The threat to China's economic dominance in Burma

While it may lead to greater stability, the opening up of Burma's economy will threaten China's ability to maintain its substantial influence in Burma's economic development. Increased engagement by Burma with the US and others is likely to lead to greater competition for access to Burma's natural resources, and closer scrutiny of the environmental and social impact of Chinese investment.

Currently, the US, EU and others still maintain economic sanctions against Burma. However, these will be reviewed and potentially removed if the April by-elections go smoothly and the reform momentum continues. While some Western corporations are still cautious about the investment climate in Burma, cancelling the sanctions is likely to generate much greater interest in economic opportunities in Burma. An influx of investors is likely to push up the price that China is required to pay to access resources.

Chinese investment in Burma, particularly in the extractives sector, has a poor reputation for ignoring adverse effects on the environment and failing to promote wider economic and social development. There have been allegations of forced labour and other human rights violations. More broadly, China's support for the military regime is still resented by many in the Burmese population. China was seen as propping up an authoritarian and abusive regime in return for access to large swathes of Burma.

Public resentment towards China, and a greater choice of investment partners, has already impacted on Chinese interests. In September 2011, in a statement highlighting Burma's reduced reliance on China, Thein Sein suspended China's large Myitsone dam project, stating that the dam was contrary to the will of the people. The hydro-electric project would have spanned the Irrawaddy River, and was a key project for the former military regime. It was financed and led by China Power Investment, a state-owned Chinese company, and was due to deliver electricity to southern China. While problems with the dam had been discussed with China, the decision to suspend the dam was reportedly not communicated to China in advance.

While Burma made some effort to assure China of its ongoing friendship following the suspension, it is unclear whether China is willing to accept the decision. There are reports that China recently started a public relations campaign in the area around the proposed dam. Chinese media coverage on the dam suspension continues to be negative.

Greater US political influence in Burma and the region

The US's increased engagement with Burma is part of a broader strategic shift towards Asia. In November 2011, Obama announced that the US was a 'Pacific power' and would be strengthening its presence in the Asia-Pacific. A US strategy document released in January stated that the strategic shift would be aimed at countering China's growing influence in the region.

The US has, publically and privately, made it clear to China that its increased engagement in Burma is aimed at supporting reform, rather than targeting China, and is in the best interests of both the US and China. Despite these diplomatic efforts, sections of the Chinese leadership see improved US relations with Burma as part of a broader 'containment' strategy by the US against China. China recognises that Burma highly values its independence and is unlikely to become a US puppet. China, however, is still concerned about the possibility of a US-dominated neighbour, particularly one with such strategic importance. Burma's declared shift towards a democratic system will also undermine China's championing of socialist market ideology in Southeast Asia.

Chinese containment of Burma

While China has sought to increase its influence in Burma for strategic and economic reasons and Burma turned to China for protection during its international isolation, China's ability to contain Burma has been limited.

As discussed later in this paper, China's leverage over Burma was not extensive even at the height of Burma's isolation. China was well aware that the military regime could cause significant headaches for China by blocking resources or causing increased unrest along the border and was not willing to risk its investments or border stability by overly pressing the regime on key issues.

Although Burma is conscious of its neighbour's enormous economic and military might, it has a strong sense of nationalism and independence and would be willing to sacrifice much to maintain its independence. In an effort to strengthen its autonomy, Burma has also worked to leverage its strategic geographic location and natural resources, for example, by leveraging China against India.

Chinese Media Perspectives on Improved US–Burma Relations

Official Chinese media coverage of developments in Burma reflects the perspectives outlined above. Media reports on the general reform process and US engagement have tended to focus on issues around stability and economic development, rather than on the shift towards a more democratic system. On matters such as the suspension of the Myitsone dam and the US 'pivot' towards Asia, coverage tends to be much more critical and raises concerns about the potential impact on China's political and economic interests in Burma and the wider region. Censure tends to be focused on the US, rather than Burma, perhaps because China is now competing to maintain its influence in Burma and cannot be overly critical of its neighbour.

Media reports on progress towards development and stability

Official Chinese media outlets (such as the *People's Daily*, the Chinese Communist Party's newspaper; and Xinhua News Agency, the official press agency of the Chinese government) have regularly reported on Burma's reform process and increasing international engagement. While the democratic nature of some reforms is mentioned, changes are generally presented as progress towards stability and development, rather than towards a more democratic political system.

Chinese government spokespeople officially welcomed Clinton's December 2011 visit to Burma and the resumption of full diplomatic relations, and said that China was 'glad' to see more contact between Burma and the US. Media reports have also covered other senior visits to Burma by the US and Western countries, as well as ongoing developments in Burma, such as preparations for the by-elections, the release of political prisoners, and Aung San Suu Kyi's campaign trail. There has also been regular reporting on the progress of negotiations with armed ethnic groups, indicating China's interest in border stability.

Reporting of high-level visits between Burma and China has largely emphasised the ongoing close bilateral ties and cooperation between them. Statements of support have also emphasised stability and development, including phrases such as: 'China supports Myanmar to walk on the development road which accords with its national conditions'[29] and 'China supports Myanmar's development path and will continue to back the country's efforts to maintain national stability and development'.[30]

Voicing Chinese concerns

Opinion pieces on the suspension of the Myitsone dam project and the US's broader strategic shift into Asia have criticised the US and raised concerns about the potential impact on Chinese interests in Burma and Southeast Asia. While not necessarily representing official government policy, opinion pieces generally reflect the views of some in the Chinese leadership.

The official statement on Burma's decision to suspend the Myitsone dam said that 'Relevant matters that have emerged during the implementation of the project should be properly settled through friendly consultations between the two sides'. Opinion pieces complained that Chinese interests had been 'stamped on', and speculated that the US was behind the decision, or had supported groups opposing the dam. Further reporting noted that this move 'sent alarming signals', and that China would need to invest more diplomatic effort in protecting the rights and interests of its companies investing in emerging markets.[31]

---

[29] Zhong Sheng, 'China takes frank, open stand on Myanmar issue', *People's Daily Online*, 6 January 2012. Available at: http://english.peopledaily.com.cn/90883/7698554.html. Accessed 12 December 2013.

[30] Mo Hong'e, 'China to cement cooperative partnership with Myanmar', *Xinhuanet.com*, 24 February 2012. Available at: http://news.xinhuanet.com/english/china/2012-02/24/c_131428158.htm. Accessed 12 December 2013.

[31] *Global Times*, 'Myanmar tips balance but not too far', 30 November 2011. Available at: http://www.globaltimes.cn/DesktopModules/DnnForge%20%20NewsArticles/Print.aspx?tabid=99&tabmoduleid=94&articleId=686381&moduleId=405&PortalID=0. Accessed 12 December 2013.

Ding Gang, *Global Times*, 'Myanmar cautious of US enticements', 30 November 2011. Available at: http://www.globaltimes.cn/content/686484.shtml. Accessed 12 December 2013.

Hu Yinan and Zhang Yunbi, 'China vows backing for firms investing abroad', *China Daily*, 6 January 2012. Available at: http://china-wire.org/?p=18099. Accessed 12 December 2013.

Opinion pieces have also voiced concern about the US's underlying reasons for engaging with Burma, in the context of its broader strategic shift towards Asia. By isolating and encircling China, some articles have argued that US engagement could threaten China's strategic interests in Burma, including access to the Indian Ocean. More positive reports note that China–US cooperation could be a common goal, if the US respects China's legitimate interests in the region.

Burmese Perspectives: Concern About Over-Reliance on China

While the motivations underlying Burma's reforms are not clearly known, Burma's concern about over-reliance on China, and a desire to reassert and leverage its independence are key factors. The military regime may also have assessed that reform was necessary for the ongoing survival of Burma and to maintain some form of military control.

Burmese mistrust of China

Burma prioritises independence and has a strong resistance to foreign intervention. While Burma sought and relied on China's protection during its international isolation in order to survive, it resented its dependence on China and remained suspicious of China's strategic intentions, even with wide-ranging cooperation. Many of the senior military officers in the regime fought against the Chinese-supported Communist Party of Burma (CPB) in the 1940s, and were well aware of China's more recent support for armed ethnic groups on the border, aimed at providing a counterbalance to the military regime.

The Burmese leadership has also been concerned about China's economic dominance in Burma, fearing that Burma was becoming an economic colony. As mentioned above in this paper, there is a significant trade imbalance between the two countries and Burmese markets are dominated by Chinese goods. China is also the largest investor in Burma by a sizeable margin. While some key figures in the former military regime have a personal financial interest in the *status quo* and close association with China (due to corrupt commercial deals), they have not yet been able to derail the reform process.

Burma also understands the value of its strategic location and rich resources. Reliance on China has limited Burma's ability to leverage these advantages, though it has been relatively successful in using India as a counterweight to China. One important benefit of greater engagement on the international stage will be an increased ability to leverage its strengths with other global powers, including the US, Japan and others.

Reforming to survive

Before the reforms, it was fairly clear that Burma had fallen far behind its neighbours. Its economy was in tatters, and there was a serious prospect of further large-scale social unrest, given the level of anger and hostility towards the regime. In order to be able to access necessary technical and financial assistance without increased dependence on China, Burma needed to reengage at the international level and, in particular, utilise the resources of international financial institutions, blocked by US sanctions.

Key figures in the former military regime may have decided to give some ground and implement economic and political reforms, rather than risk continued build-up of popular resentment and potentially destabilising uprisings that could topple the regime. In this case, it is possible the regime drew broad lessons from the Arab Uprisings.

These considerations may have helped push some of the more hard-line military figures to accept the reforms, particularly since Thein Sein's government still operates under the restrictive 2008 Constitution which enshrines power for the military. The extent to which the current Burmese government will be willing, and able, to move towards a more democratic and participatory system through constitutional reform is still to be determined.

Conclusion and Policy Recommendations

While the US and international financial institutions are key targets for Burma, the Burmese government is also keen to reengage with the EU and EU Member States. There have been numerous high-level visits from the EU and Member States over the past few months, including the EU Aid Commissioner Andris Piebalgs, a European Parliament delegation, UK Foreign Minister William Hague, French Foreign Minister Alain Juppé and German Development Minister Dirk Niebel.

The EU removed visa bans against some former regime figures in early February 2012 and announced that it would review the rest of the sanctions, including further visa bans, asset freezes and the arms embargo on 23 April 2012, following the by-elections. Piebalgs also announced EUR 150m in assistance to Burma.

In determining next steps, the EU should consider how to help foster sustainable reform and development in an independent Burma. To consolidate these early stages of reform and ensure they result in tangible benefits, the EU's development assistance should be provided as rapidly as possible, in close coordination with other donors.

The EU should also support Burma in protecting its economy and environment from an influx of competitive foreign investors, including assisting it to develop appropriate environmental, legal and social safeguards. It would not be in the long-term interests of Burma or the EU if the Burmese economy was flooded with investment before it developed the absorptive capacity to ensure that finance is used productively and sustainably.

Burma's suspension of the Myitsone dam project, and the recent cancellation of a 4,000 megawatt coal-fired power plant, part of the USD 58 bn Thai-led Dawei project, shows that the government is willing to consider the social and environmental impact of investments and is not afraid to stand up to its neighbours. The EU should seek to involve China in the development of these safeguards and emphasise the common goal of sustainable long-term development and stability in Burma.

China and Southeast Asia
(April 2012)

David Camroux

*Associate Professor and Senior Researcher,
Sciences Po, Paris*

Executive Summary

- In April 2012, several incidents in the South China Sea underlined some of the tensions in China–Southeast Asia relations.
- China and Southeast Asia are complex entities. China can be conceptualised in three ways: namely, as a conventional nation-nation and even an imperial construct; as a regional actor; and as a global power. It is the tension between these three 'Chinas' that is at the heart of its relationship with the ten countries of Southeast Asia.
- Southeast Asian countries are themselves incredibly diverse. They are comprised of very different levels of economic development, with different belief systems and political regimes, ranging from authoritarian to vibrant democracies.
- Chinese soft power has not had the desired results in the Association of Southeast Asian Nations (ASEAN, founded in 1967) countries: while these countries do pay attention to China, China has been unable to attract its southern neighbours to its governance model.
- From a Southeast Asia perspective, a series of 'asymmetrical bilateralisms' is a salient way to describe the region's relationship with China.
- Drawing upon the traditional Southeast Asian version of a 'middle power' approach, the countries of Southeast Asia are involved in a soft hedging, or balancing, strategy in relation to China.

- China has now become a key player in Southeast Asia's *de facto* economic regionalisation. However, not all the consequences are seen as positive.
- China has been less successful in imposing its *de jure* institutional regionalisation since the creation of the East Asia Summit, which includes India, the US, Russia, Australia and New Zealand.
- Moreover, China's peaceful rise has prompted the pivot of US foreign relations back to Asia, which Southeast Asian countries welcome as the ultimate security guarantor.
- Strategic balancing and soft hedging in Southeast Asia has opened up a space for a stronger European presence. However, this is conditional on Europe remaining united in its actions.
- The EU needs to develop a clear strategy and communicate clearly both in word and deed its commitment to Southeast Asia.

Introduction

If one were to seek a metaphor for the relations between China and Southeast Asia, reference to clichéd jokes about (wealthy) mother-in-laws may be a useful starting point. Firstly, as with a mother-in-law, the people of Southeast Asia have no choice in having such a large and powerful neighbour. Secondly, it is often considered better to have a wealthy mother-in-law, from whose riches one can benefit than one who requires support. Finally, the further away one resides from her, the more comfortable one is about her existence. Thus, views of Chinese power in Jakarta are significantly more sanguine than those found in Hanoi.

The confrontation between the Philippines Navy and Chinese fishing vessels and surveillance craft (from one of the five poorly coordinated agencies with this responsibility) in the Scarborough Reef area of the South China Sea in April 2012 would seem to confirm the appropriateness of this metaphor. This incident occurred during the same week that Vietnam dispatched a small group of monks to the disputed Spratly chain in order to reinforce its territorial claim. It not only highlighted the potential for conflict in a maritime area of major significance for international trade, but also expressed a heightened wariness among China's immediate neighbours about the latter's ostensibly benign intentions. This concern is exacerbated by the opacity of Chinese decision-making and doubts about who is ultimately in control. Both of these factors are embedded in the nature of the Chinese polity.

Hydra-Headed China and a Multiple Southeast Asia

An examination of China's relations with the countries of Southeast Asia and, for that matter, their regional organisation, the ASEAN, requires an understanding of the complexity of the two entities concerned. China may be a single nation state but it can also be considered a region state or an imperial construct in which the interrelationship of its (domestic) parts impact on its relations with its southern neighbours. Secondly, it is a regional actor that operates in diverse regional contexts — Northeast Asia, Central Asia and Southeast Asia — in which the latter is merely one of several that requires attention. In this regard, there is a general sentiment[32] that China's relationship with ASEAN is of secondary importance to involvement, say, in the Shanghai Cooperation Organisation (SCO). Indeed, Beijing not only houses the secretariat and determines the agenda of the SCO, but the organisation also deals with domestic issues of crucial importance for the Chinese regime, namely the control of secessionist movements, the integrity of borders and access to the vast energy resources necessary to fuel the Chinese economy. Thirdly, as the world's second-largest economy, China is a global power in a multi-nodal world in which its regional action in Southeast Asia is already inscribed within its domestic–foreign relations nexus.

As for Southeast Asia, it is undoubtedly one of the most diverse regions in the contemporary world: Singapore has a GDP superior to most EU Member States while countries such as Laos and Burma/Myanmar are among the least developed countries in the UN. Thriving Southeast Asian megacities, such as Bangkok, Jakarta and Singapore, provide tangible demonstrations of the Asian Economic Miracle, but they coexist with much poorer rural heartlands where, on average, 70% of the population still live. This diversity is not merely economic; the five or six major religious and philosophical traditions — Buddhism, Christianity, Confucianism/Taoism, Hinduism and Islam — are present to varied degrees in the ten countries of the region and these belief systems impinge on the political cultures and polities concerned, ranging from absolute monarchy in Brunei to the present dysfunctional democratic system in Asia's first independent republic, the Philippines. Between these two extremes are soft authoritarian regimes (Vietnam, Laos and Cambodia), soft or semi-democracies (Malaysia and Singapore), and assertive, if problematical,

---

[32] Ascertained through interviews by the author's Sinologist colleagues with Foreign Ministry officials and think tank specialists in Beijing.

democracies (Indonesia). There are also countries undergoing forms of political evolution, such as Burma/Myanmar (formerly in the hard authoritarian category), and Thailand, which oscillates between soft authoritarian and soft democratic norms, whose trajectory is unclear at this point in time. Finally, despite their membership of one regional association (ASEAN), the classical geographical distinction between mainland/continental Southeast Asia (Vietnam, Laos, Cambodia and Burma/Myanmar) and maritime/island Southeast Asia (Malaysia, Singapore, Brunei, Indonesia and the Philippines) remains salient. Indeed, it is argued below in this paper that one of the consequences of an increasingly assertive Chinese role in Southeast Asia is the accentuation of divisions between the two.

Tributary Relations and Asymmetrical Bilateralisms

The elites of all ten Southeast Asian countries share a common challenge, namely, coping with a large neighbour to the north, the only 'civilisation to form itself a nation'.[33] Of course this situation is not new, and neither is the imbalance in the relationship. In his seminal work written in 1968,[34] eminent American sinologist John Fairbank argued that traditional Chinese foreign relations were characterised by sinocentrism and a sense of superiority over non-Chinese people. The result was a series of tributary relations in which the monarchs of various Southeast Asian polities went to China to acknowledge Chinese suzerainty by paying tribute to the Chinese emperor. By showing respect in such a way, the polities to the south were allowed virtual autonomy.

One way of interpreting China's relations with Southeast Asia today is to suggest that there is a renewal of this type of relationship in which China assumes what the Chinese elite regard as its 'rightful' place at the centre of Asia. Indeed, the pageantry that accompanies the regular visits of Southeast Asian political leaders to Beijing is designed to stress, at best, fraternal ties and, at worst, a relationship of subordination. Today, Chinese scholars and officials tend to argue that China has never been an expansionist power in Southeast Asia: the millennium of Chinese

---

[33] These words were spoken by John Fairbank in 1968. The author's own interviews conducted over the years in various parts of Southeast Asia underline the fact that this is *the* overriding geopolitical and geo-economic challenge in the region.

[34] John Fairbank (ed.), *The Chinese World Order: Traditional China's Foreign Relations* (Harvard University Press, Cambridge Massachussets, 1968).

occupation of what is today northern Vietnam being the exception that proves the rule. The stress in today's official Chinese rhetoric on its 'peaceful rise', 'harmonious society' and being 'good neighbours' is a contemporary expression of benevolent paternalism. The reform era in China since the mid-1980s has been accompanied by increasingly sophisticated Chinese efforts to reassure its southern neighbours through various forms of what has been described as 'soft' power, i.e. cultural diplomacy (e.g. the creation of Confucius Institutes), development assistance, investment, dialogue within the context of regional organisations, etc. However, ostensible Chinese soft power needs to be unpacked.

Soft power involves three elements, namely, attentiveness, persuasiveness and attractiveness. While China's rise and increasing political and economic power has undoubtedly focused the *attention* of elites in Southeast Asia, this has not necessarily been translated into an ability to *persuade* them to accept, for example, the so-called 'Beijing Consensus' — in other words, that illiberal governments are a prerequisite for economic growth. On the contrary, since the Asian Financial Crisis of 1997, seen by most analysts as marking the beginning of the new Chinese posture as a responsible regional actor concerned with the well-being of its southern neighbours, political trajectories in Indonesia, Thailand and, today, Burma/Myanmar have moved away from authoritarianism. Moreover, outside the city-state of Singapore, where two-thirds of the population are of Chinese origin, it is difficult to find public intellectuals who are attracted by the virtues of the Chinese model. Just below the surface of public opinion in Southeast Asia is a visceral, reflexive sinophobia, fuelled during the colonial period and today nurtured by dependence on/resentment towards the business elites of Chinese origin who are preeminent in most Southeast Asian economies. While the most recent riots against ethnic Chinese in Southeast Asia occurred in Indonesia in 1998 (accompanying the fall of the Suharto regime), interviews conducted throughout the region over several years underline the ease with which politicians can generally designate a Chinese scapegoat to maintain their popular support.

If we move away from the sinocentric view of a tributary relationship and instead conceptualise it in terms of the asymmetrical relations between China and the Southeast Asian countries, two indigenous metaphors are helpful. The first, from mainland Southeast Asia, is the Burmese expression of *pauk-phaw,* which can be translated as 'kinsfolk', and implies a relationship between a younger sibling and his elder brother. The second, from maritime Southeast Asia, is a concept developed by Indonesia's first Vice President, Mohammad Hatta (in 1947), *mendayung antara dua karang*, loosely translated as 'rowing between two reefs'. Both concepts imply a level of 'actorness' on the part of Southeast Asian political elites. China may proclaim itself to be a leader of the Asian peoples, echoing former Chinese Premier Zhou Enlai at Bandung in 1955, but 'followership' can also be a tactical choice. Learning from the time of King Mongkut and King Chulalongkorn in Siam in the latter half of the 19th century (who maintained their country's independence, in part, by playing the French against the British), Southeast Asian political elites have, since independence, adopted a strategy of soft hedging, balancing one power against another. By dividing the region into two hostile camps, the Cold War rendered such a strategy unworkable; however, with its end, this strategy has come to the fore once again.

Since the end of the Cold War and the entry of Vietnam (1995), Laos (1997), Burma/Myanmar (1997) and Cambodia (1998) into ASEAN, we have seen a second strategy in relation to China (and the West) reinforced; namely, strengthening the Association as a regional organisation — symbolised by the adoption of the ASEAN Charter in November 2007, which for the first time gave it a legal personality. The implementation of the ASEAN Free Trade Agreement which will lead to the establishment of an ASEAN Economic Community in 2015 is designed to increase intra-ASEAN trade from its present low of 25%. According to ASEAN's jargon, this is designed to keep it 'in the driver's seat' of regional integration in Asia and the Pacific. China's strengthened role in Asia's regional economic integration and its own regional policies potentially call that central role into question.

China's Relations with Southeast Asian Countries and ASEAN: The Economic Dimension

A key question underlying this report concerns the nature of Asian regional integration. In the literature on comparative regionalism, a distinction is often made between *de facto* economic regionalisation and *de juré* institutional regionalisation. China is impacting on both in Southeast Asia but, given the importance of geoeconomics in relation to geopolitics, it has particularly impacted the former. In the trade area the impact is profound. Trade between China and Southeast Asia grew from about EUR 8 bn in 1994 to EUR 180 bn in 2008, falling slightly in 2009 as a result of the global financial crisis. For all of the ASEAN countries combined, this trade has been balanced on average. However, the overall figures hide important discrepancies in trade between the member countries who export raw materials and energy sources, such as Indonesia and Laos, and who have trade surpluses. This recent massive increase in trade is partly a result of the China–ASEAN Free Trade Agreement established in 2010. This agreement provided an 'early harvest' programme for the poorer countries of Southeast Asia, which acted as a sweetener for the trade deal. However, since 2010 trade flows have started to shift to the benefit of China.

China has also become an investor in Southeast Asia, providing some EUR 38 bn of investment in 2008. However, one should note that this is a mere 2.6% of China's total stock of investment overseas and, moreover, some 80% of these investments are in Singapore, largely in financial services. When it occurs, Chinese investment outside of this area is above all designed to meet the needs of the Chinese domestic market. This is the case for dam building in Laos, Cambodia and Burma/Myanmar which is designed to provide electricity for the Chinese market. Unlike the Japanese, the Chinese have not yet developed vertical production networks in Southeast Asia and, at present, Chinese companies buy components from these countries to be assembled in China itself. For the middle income countries of Southeast Asia, notably Malaysia and Thailand, this is a long-term worry. However, as China continues its industrialisation and modernisation process, benefiting the poorer regions in its western interior, these imports from Southeast Asia will find themselves in competition with domestically produced components. The long-term outcome may well result in trapping the middle income countries in the *status quo*, in contrast to South Korea and Taiwan who have managed to emerge with their own innovative industries.

Moreover, forms of *de facto* economic regionalisation could potentially have the effect of dividing ASEAN between its mainland and island members. Propelled by the Chinese government, and with the support of the (Japanese-led and partly Western-financed) Asian Development Bank (ADB), the Greater Mekong Sub-Region has become the most dynamic part of Southeast Asia. Nominally its membership includes Cambodia, Laos and Myanmar as well as the two southern Chinese provinces of Yunnan and Guangxi. The ADB has contributed a third of the approximate USD 11 bn (EUR 8.4 bn) worth of infrastructure investment since 2000, the lion's share of the remainder coming from China. In Burma/Myanmar alone the Chinese invested some USD 8 bn (EUR 6 bn) in oil, gas and hydro-power in 2010 and had agreed to USD 80 bn (EUR 61 bn) in investment projects in Cambodia. On the ground, these forms of economic integration will see mainland

Southeast Asia, Yunnan and Guangxi served by a Chinese-sponsored, integrated network of high-speed rail connections, pipelines and highways by 2020. Given that these networks will by-pass the poorest and least developed areas in order to provide new openings for Chinese trade outside of Southeast Asia, the local benefits are debatable.

China's Relations with Southeast Asia: The Political Dimension

With the benefit of hindsight, China has been less successful in imposing its own concept of *de juré* institutional regionalisation. While China had a privileged position in relation to ASEAN at the ASEAN +3 Forum, this position had to be shared with Korea and Japan — yet another example of the hedging strategy of its southern neighbours. In 2005, this Forum saw itself being overshadowed by the creation of the East Asia Summit (EAS) involving ASEAN +3, India, as well as Australia and New Zealand. As a result China sought to complete the negotiations for an East Asian inner circle (i.e. ASEAN +3) in which China would be the main player through a China–ASEAN Free Trade Area. However, six years later in November 2011, the East Asia Summit saw the admission of the US and Russia to balance China's role.

While the Chinese may still remain cautious concerning regional institutionalisation, since the first EAS in 2005, their view of multilateralism has evolved to the extent that they are no longer pre-occupied with excluding the US from the region. Within China, many analysts and policy makers recognise that an international order requires multilateral norms and must be inclusive. Moreover, the kind of weak regional integration that the EAS represents — that is, one bereft of institutionalisation — is seen in Beijing as another convenient way of organising Chinese multilateral action within Asia. In other words, the Chinese have encouraged regional widening in order to undermine any regional institutional deepening. Some authors have highlighted the re-emergence of the concept of *tianxia* ('All Under Heaven') in Chinese foreign relations discourse as a reflection at the multilateral level of the ideal of a harmonious society traditionally applied to the Chinese domestic context. This is not to suggest that the objective of a sinocentric regional order or a new form of tributary has fallen by the wayside. Rather, these objectives have been subsumed under a global commitment to multilateralism within the international environment. The consequence is a reformulation of

Chinese foreign policy in terms of multiple levels of multilateralism in which the various pan-Asian, Asia-Pacific and Eurasian relationships are placed in an evolving hierarchy. In this hierarchy Southeast Asia is not a priority despite the rhetoric of a special relationship.

Conclusions

As argued above, the Chinese regime's efforts to export the notion of a harmonious society to characterise its good neighbour relations with Southeast Asia have only partly been successful. Despite claims regarding the benevolence of Chinese soft power, it has only taken a couple of maritime incidents in the South China Sea and the increasingly strident and arrogant language of Chinese diplomats to arouse, once again, a certain wariness in Southeast Asia *vis-à-vis* China. ASEAN ambassadors have expressed concern, also heard elsewhere, that an increasingly nationalist and confident younger generation in China will push an otherwise trustworthy regime towards taking provocative actions with its neighbours, in order to strengthen its own domestic legitimacy. In addition, the People's Liberation Army's element of civilian control means that it has the capacity for action inimical to the aim of good neighbourly relations vaunted by the Chinese Communist Party leadership. While the expression 'arms race' would be misguided — most Southeast Asian countries, with the exception of Singapore and Burma/Myanmar, spend less than 2% of their GDP on defence — within their limited budgets, the increased allocation for air and maritime equipment by Southeast Asian nations is designed to counter the threat provided by the significant increase in Chinese military power in the last decade. The encouragement or, at least benign acquiescence, in the strengthening of the US military presence in the Asia-Pacific must also be seen in this light. Indeed, contrary to the expectations of some pundits, China's rise has not been to the detriment of the US but rather has set the stage for a strengthened American presence in East Asia.

Internally, economic relations with China are raising questions. The cancelling of the Chinese-funded Myitsone Dam project on the Irrawaddy River by the new semi-civilian government in Burma/Myanmar in September 2011 is significant. This cancellation was justified by the new Burmese President, Thein Sein, on the grounds that it was made under pressure from the public. A counter example is provided in the case of Cambodia, where a corrupt authoritarian regime is secretly selling off large tracts of protected areas and national parks to Chinese interests.

In this process, thousands of peasants and fishermen are being dispossessed of their land and livelihoods with little compensation. The implication is clear, many aspects of the Chinese presence in Southeast Asia feed off the weakness of states and the absence of strong civil societies.

Implications for Europe and the EU

Through the practice of soft-hedging alluded to above, a space has opened for a strengthened European role in Southeast Asia. Such a role, however, is dependent on Europe remaining united in its approach and not allowing internal competition to detract from a common front. To state the obvious, the EU does not have a Seventh Fleet floating around in the Pacific and, in other words, cannot *directly* contribute to the security of the countries of Southeast Asia. However, it can *indirectly* do so in four ways:

1. The US 'pivot' to Asia will mean that, by default, Europeans will have to take greater responsibility for their own defence. In other words, the time for a strengthened Common Foreign and Security Policy has arrived and a more united security front will legitimise the EU's presence overseas.
2. The EU needs to support the ASEAN members in making sure, for example, that the resolution of territorial disputes in the South China Sea are addressed multilaterally and not bilaterally so as to avoid a significant power advantage to China.
3. The EU should provide continued support (through technical assistance, etc.) to ASEAN in order to enable it to strengthen its own regional organisation.
4. By engaging in trade and investment that respects the people and environment of Southeast Asia, Europe can act as an alternative partner to a China, which is perceived as rapacious and predatory, particularly in the weaker Southeast Asian nations. The recent agreement on sustainable forest products between the EU and Indonesia (worth EUR 800 m annually) provides an example of how Europe can parlay its market power in a way that is mutually advantageous. An EU that has resolved its own economic problems will also be in a position to play this balancing role, for example, through its participation in the ADB. As they continue to emerge, the countries of Southeast Asia can provide opportunities for European countries through the need to build infrastructure and develop the service sector. The regulatory and political economy dynamics in

these countries are certainly more favourable to European business than a one-party state like China.

A three-fold strategy is required from Europe. Firstly, it must offer continued support for ASEAN and help it to achieve the objectives of the ASEAN Charter. In this regard, the decision of Catherine Ashton, the EU's High Representative, to attend the EU–ASEAN Summit for the first time is welcomed. Secondly, as the European External Action Service strengthens its delegations and creates new ones (such as that announced in April 2012 in Rangoon), it should commit to a concomitant strengthening of country action programmes. Negotiations for individual Preferential Trade Agreements with Vietnam, Malaysia and Singapore should be accelerated. Thirdly, the only Southeast Asian country to be a member of the G20, Indonesia, should be offered a strategic partnership with the EU (like those with the three Northeast Asian countries) and be cultivated as a potential coalition partner in global governance.

China's rise and the American return to Asia provide a window of opportunity for a reinvigorated European role in Southeast Asia. For this to occur, European elites need to rise beyond a Manichean 'dragon bashing' or 'panda hugging' obsession with the People's Republic. A good start would be to look at China through the eyes of our potential Southeast Asian partners: as both a threat and opportunity.

The Changing Politics of Nepal
(January 2013)

Gareth Price
Senior Research Fellow, Asia Programme, Chatham House

Executive Summary

- China's influence in Nepal is growing. Its investments are increasing, more Chinese tourists are visiting Nepal and more Nepalese are travelling to China for studies. However, its influence remains secondary to that of India. More important are Nepalese attempts to play a 'China card' to counter Indian influence.
- China's main point of influence would appear to be in relation to Tibetan refugees, which have declined in number in recent years. However, whether this is primarily because of Chinese pressure, or whether it reflects a Nepalese desire to garner goodwill with China is less clear cut.
- China clearly resents Western, and particularly US, politicians visiting Nepal and criticising China. At the same time, some Nepalese are concerned that Nepal's own interests are secondary to Nepal's utility as a stick to beat China.
- Nepal's politics remains in flux; neither of the main political parties wants an election to be held while their opponents control the government. The most likely path forward would be for a well-respected member of civil society to become Prime Minister and oversee elections though for now there is no domestic consensus on this.
- India has a much greater influence on Nepalese politics and economics. At periods during which India's control appears to be on the wane, Indian commentators frequently focus on China's influence.

- The EU and its Member States have less leverage over developments in Nepal than India and China. While there is goodwill towards European support for Nepal's post-conflict development, there are concerns that focusing on the rights of specific communities may work to entrench or exacerbate divisions within the country.

Introduction

In recent months Nepal's political situation has been nebulous. The Federal Democratic Republican Alliance (FDRA) government led by the Prime Minister, Baburam Bhattarai, is a coalition of Maoists and parties representing Madhesis (people from the southern plains of Nepal). The Constitution has lapsed and there is no elected parliament. The last election was held in 2008; the parliament converted itself into a Constituent Assembly charged with drafting a new Constitution within two years. Since then Nepal has had a succession of governments. The Constituent Assembly was dissolved in May 2012.

The Constitution itself remains unfinished largely because of disputes over the nature of federalism to be introduced. An election was scheduled for 22 November 2012 but this was not held: some opposition parties blamed the government for unilaterally delaying the election, but the electoral commission argued that in the absence of a Constitution there were no workable provisions to enable a vote. Nepal's political parties agreed to hold elections for a new Constituent Assembly within six months of 22 November.

However, the interim Constitution does not have provisions for the election of a second Constituent Assembly. This means that the president will have to amend the interim Constitution.

At present, the opposition Nepali Congress (NC) and the Unified Marxist Leninist (UML) party are unwilling to agree to an election unless they are leading the government. The FDRA instead wants them to join their government, led by Bhattarai. The NC and UML believe that the FDRA's reluctance to accept a new Prime Minister demonstrates that it does not intend to hold an election. The Maoists believe that if the NC's Sushil Koirala becomes Prime Minister, he will not hold elections. All parties fear elections run while their opponents are in government and are fearful of public reaction following the prolonged infighting in Kathmandu. The political stalemate has impacted upon policy making. In recent years budgets have been passed late, reducing funds for development projects.

The absence of parliament also means that the judiciary is understaffed since new appointments cannot be made.

There is increased scepticism over whether a general election can be held before May 2013. The main political parties have become more blasé about breaking the president's deadlines as more deadlines have been missed. The president's attempts to get the parties to form a consensus government have failed. The only plausible solution appears to be some form of interim government, led by a trusted non-political individual from civil society. On 3 January Bhattarai indicated that he would stand down if a neutral government were to take over. He suggested that Daman Nath Dungana (a lawyer and former speaker of parliament) or Devendra Raj Pandy (a former civil servant and finance minister, and now civil society activist) would be suitable neutral replacements. For now the Nepali Congress and UML rejected the proposal but in time this may well be the way forward. In the longer term, Nepalese politics is recalibrating into a leftist grouping led by the UCPN and a centrist grouping led by the Nepali Congress.

Over the past few years, China appears to have encouraged Nepal to take a more hard-line approach towards Tibetan refugees. The number of Tibetan refugees arriving in Dharamsala, India has fallen sharply: between 2004 and 2007 12,000 refugees arrived, but between 2008 and 2011 this figure fell to just 2,500. This partly reflects restrictions inside Tibet and along the Chinese border with Nepal following the 2008 riots in Lhasa.

However, Nepal has also been accused of cracking down on Tibetan refugees. According to diplomatic cables from the US released by Wikileaks, Chinese security forces have bribed Nepalese police to return Tibetans. Some reports suggest that Chinese security forces operate on the Nepalese side of the border. Previously, under an informal agreement with the UNHCR, Nepal had allowed Tibetans to pass through Nepal en route to India. Western criticism of Nepal's treatment of Tibetans has increased in recent years and the US has been particularly vocal on Nepal's need to respect the rights of Tibetan refugees. However, although there have been a few well-publicised instances in which refugees have been returned, there is little concrete evidence that this reflects a coherent policy.

Nonetheless, Nepal's attitude towards Tibetans has clearly become less welcoming in recent decades. Following the 1959 annexation of Tibet by the People's Republic of China, Nepal welcomed Tibetan refugees (around 20,000 Tibetans currently live in Nepal). In 1989 it stopped accepting additional refugees (prompting the 1990 agreement with the UNHCR allowing transit to India). In 1998

Nepal stopped issuing 'refugee identity certificates' to Tibetans, barring many Tibetans from attending school, applying for jobs or opening bank accounts. And in 2010 Nepal confiscated hundreds of ballot boxes during the election for the Tibetan Prime Minister in exile.

This shift clearly coincides with an increase in Chinese assistance for Nepal. In 2007 China began construction of a railway connecting Lhasa with the Nepalese border town of Khasa. In 2011 China pledged USD 20m (EUR 15m) in military assistance, and in 2012, during a visit by Chinese Premier Wen Jiabao, China pledged USD 119m (EUR 89m) in aid. China has promised to provide assistance in the construction of a 'dry port' on the border and, in April, Nepal cleared a Chinese firm to construct a USD 1.6bn (EUR 1.2bn) hydro-electric plant (see below). There are also increased numbers of Chinese tourists; namely, Chinese volunteers teaching Mandarin and Nepalese students studying in China.

In the absence of detailed evidence relating to Tibetans being repatriated to China, some commentators believe that Western criticism of Nepal risks confounding the situation. China is obviously sensitive towards the issue of Tibet; its ambassador to Nepal in 2011 was widely quoted as having said that Nepal was 'turning into a playground for anti-China activities'.[35] The postponement (from December 2011 to January 2012) of Wen Jiabao's visit to Nepal was interpreted as a means of putting pressure on Nepal to maintain a hard line on Tibetans. China's concerns with the issue of Tibet stem not just from concern at foreign interference in China's domestic politics, but at an increasing recognition of Tibet's importance as the source of many of China's rivers.

Aside from pressurising Nepal over Tibet, China's role in the domestic politics has been relatively restrained. Of greater relevance has been the decision by various Nepalese politicians, ranging in recent years from the former king to Maoist leader Pushpa Kamal Dahal, to play the China card, to counter Indian influence.[36] Generally, China has rebuffed such manoeuvers. However, in recent years, as Nepal has become beset by political uncertainty, China appears to have attempted to deepen its understanding of, and contact with, Nepal. While this was initially focused on combatting Tibetan expression, of late this has shifted

---

[35] See, for instance, http://www.telegraphnepal.com/headline/2011-10-17/intl-forces-escalating-anti-china-activities-in-nepal:-amb-houlan.html. Accessed 10 January 2014.

[36] For instance, King Gyanendra turned to China for arms during the civil war after the US, UK and India refused to supply arms.

into concerns about Nepal's domestic political trajectory particularly in relation to the controversial issue of federalism.

According to reports, a senior Chinese official recently relayed concerns about the dangers that a federal system could pose to Nepal, stating that China would prefer a unitary Nepal. If a federal system were adopted, according to this official, it should not be ethnically based. This statement has been interpreted in several ways:

- China may be concerned at the prospect of having to engage multiple power centres along its border.
- China may fear that 'ethnic' states in the north could be used as bases for Tibetan unrest.
- China may perceive that politicians from indigenous groups would be pro-Western.[37]
- China may feel that ethnically based federalism could increase the power of Madhesis (people that live in the Terai lowlands of Southern Nepal). China may perceive the Madhesis to be pro-Indian.
- Alternatively, the official may simply have been reflecting China's own preference for a unitary government or indeed have been misquoted or misunderstood.

China's intervention (whether intended or not, this is how it has been interpreted in Nepal) risks polarising Nepal between those that support unitary government and those that are opposed, most notably the Prachanda-led Maoists and marginalised social groups such as the Madhesis and Janjatis. India, meanwhile, is more sanguine about the introduction of a federal system in Nepal, given its own history of linguistic-based federalism.

Nepal has long felt the need to balance the interests of its two giant neighbours. Nepal's unifying king described Nepal as 'a yam between two boulders'. While there is currently some concern over China's growing influence, this needs to be seen in a context within which many Nepalese believe that India has designs to take over the country or to guide its policies. Following its independence in 1947 India took over the British role of directing most of Nepal's political and economic

---

[37] Many development agencies have concentrated their efforts on marginalised ethnic groups. Within Nepal there is a debate over the extent to which this focus on ethnicity has worked to strengthen ethnic identities within Nepal in recent years.

development. India trained Nepalese troops and Indian military personnel were stationed along Nepal's northern border from 1951 to 1969.

While arguments that Indian intelligence agencies were involved in the royal palace massacre of 2001 may appear conspiratorial, they are widely believed in Nepal. Events such as the 1989–1990 Indian blockade of India are not forgotten (this blockade related to a dispute over transit and trade treaties, but many Nepalese believe India was irked by Nepal's 1988 decision to purchase Chinese weapons). India also blockaded Nepal in 1962. Compared to this, many are sanguine about China's role.

In economic relations, too, there is a clear tilt towards India. Two-thirds of Nepal's trade is with India; just 10% with China. This reflects the close relationship between India and Nepal, as well as the easier logistics of trade with India than China. In the 1950s India helped to build up Nepal's infrastructure, including better access between India and Nepal. Under the 1950 India-Nepal Treaty of Peace and Friendship, citizens of both nations are treated equally in matters of business, jobs and property ownership. This dependence on India has made anti-Indian sentiment a basis for Nepalese nationalism. Many Nepalese work or study in India although the numbers are deeply contested. The lowest estimate of Nepalese refugees is 589,050, the figure provided by Nepal's 2001 census. Most surveys suggest a figure in the range of 2–3 m. The highest estimates, generally given by Indian commentators, are in the field of 12 m.

At times, and notably in the mid-1990s under the 'Gujral Doctrine', India has taken steps to improve its image in its smaller neighbours, including Nepal. India is proud to have developed most of Nepal's infrastructure in the 1950s. In part because of a perceived increase in Chinese influence, India is again reverting to a policy of 'non-reciprocity'. In October 2011 India provided Nepal with a USD 250m (EUR 187m) concessional line of credit for infrastructure projects. The agreement was signed in tandem with a bilateral investment promotion and protection agreement.

China and Nepal are currently negotiating a similar investment agreement. The Chinese deal goes further than the India deal, however, and seeks to protect prior investment, and to ensure full protection and security for Chinese investments. While Nepal has objected to some elements of the deal, given its need for investment it seems likely to acquiesce soon. China has also increased its development assistance and expressed an interest in developing Pokhara airport. China pledged USD 750m (EUR 562m) assistance to Nepal during Wen Jiabao's visit to

Kathmandu on 14 January 2012. He also suggested that China might spend more than USD 5 bn (EUR 3.4 bn) on infrastructure development in Nepal. Meanwhile more Chinese tourists are visiting Nepal, and more Nepalese students are being educated in China.

Chinese investments in Nepal are also growing. In February 2012 a Chinese firm, China Three Gorges International, was awarded the USD 1.6 bn (EUR 1.2 bn) West Seti hydro-power project, in the far west of Nepal. Under the agreement, Three Gorges will own 75% of the 750-megawatt project, with the remainder owned by the Nepal Electricity Authority. The project is intended to begin in 2014 and be completed by 2019. The primary consumer will be Nepal, although any surplus may be exported to India. Nepal faces a severe power shortage and this is the largest single investment project in Nepal. However, while Chinese interest in Nepal is clearly growing, for now Indian investment remains far more substantial.

Nepal did not put the West Seti bid out to tender, leading to complaints about irregularities. Eventually, after Three Gorges threatened to pull out, a parliamentary committee approved the project. Among the changes recommended by the committee were that Three Gorges stake was diluted with a 10% stake given to local residents and a 14% stake given to domestic industrialists and other residents. The project had originally been awarded to an Australian company, Snowy Mountain Engineering Corporation in 1997. This contract was cancelled in 2011 on the grounds that the project had not started. While it is estimated to have hydro-power capacity of 43,000 megawatt, actual production is around just 650 megawatt. Indian-run projects such as Upper Karnali and Arun III have stalled, in part because of protests by Maoist cadres.

Both India and China stress their non-interference in the internal affairs of Nepal. China has stated its interest in working with India to develop Nepal on a trilateral basis. China's ambassador has stated that 'China is also willing to work with India to jointly support Nepal to realize stability and prosperity, and promotes mutual beneficial cooperation among our three countries'.[38] While these statements may be partly rhetorical, they also serve to undermine the image of Nepal as a hotbed of competition between its neighbours.

While the UK and the US have some influence in Nepal, this is dwarfed by that of India and China. Nepal is a significant recipient of support from the UK's Department for International Development (DFID). DFID has pledged GBP

---

[38] See, http://np.chineseembassy.org/eng/EmbassyInfo/asaa/t972600.htm.

331 m (EUR 400 m) between 2011 and 2015. The UK has pledged to create 230,000 jobs through private-sector development, build or upgrade more than 4,200 km of roads, improve sanitation for 110,000 people and help 4 m Nepalese to cope better with natural disasters and the impact of climate change. The UK has also contributed USD 5.7 m (EUR 4.3 m) to the Nepal Peace Trust Fund to implement the 2006 peace accord and support grass-root peace initiatives. British leverage has also stemmed from the continued use of Nepalese soldiers in its Gurkha regiments.

The US government has provided more than USD 1 m (EUR 0.75 m) to the ministry of peace and reconstruction and the UK has pledged an additional USD 20 m (EUR 15 m) to support the Nepal Peace Trust Fund (NPTF) and the UN Peace Fund for Nepal over the next four years. It has also signed a Trade and Investment Framework Agreement with Nepal and, in September 2012, it removed the Maoists from its list of terrorist organisations. Both the US and UK have stressed the need to improve the investment climate in Nepal while the US has particularly stressed the benefits for Nepal of greater regional connectivity. However the US is also happy, by and large, for India to take the lead role in the smaller countries of South Asia.

Other donors to the NPTF include Norway, Switzerland, Finland, Denmark, Germany and the EU. In total, donors have contributed around USD 50 m (EUR 37.5 m) to the NPTF, while the government of Nepal has contributed around USD 100 m (EUR 75 m) to the fund which is intended to implement programmes under the 2006 Comprehensive Peace Accord. The largest item of expenditure relates to the rehabilitation of former combatants.

Indian concerns about Chinese influence in Nepal are not dissimilar to concerns about Chinese influence in Bhutan. In the case of Bhutan, India is even more influential: Bhutan's economy has boomed on the back of hydro-electricity sales to India, from projects constructed by India. From 1949 to 2007 Bhutan agreed to be guided by the advice of India in relation to foreign policy; in the 2007 friendship treaty, this was revised so that the two countries 'shall cooperate closely with each other on issues relating to their national interests. Neither government shall allow the use of its territory for activities harmful to the national security and interest of the other'.[39]

---

[39] 2007 Indo Bhutan Friendship Treaty. Available at: http://www.satp.org/satporgtp/countries/india/document/papers/indiabhutan.htm. Accessed 10 January 2014.

While there was widespread Indian concern of some deepening of Bhutan's relations with China following a meeting between the Chinese premier, Wen Jiabao, and Bhutan's Prime Minister, Jigme Yoser Thinley, in mid-2012, this would only mark a slight dilution of Indian dominance over Bhutan. For now Bhutan does not even have diplomatic relations with China. It is widely believed that India scuppered Bhutan's attempts to forge diplomatic relations in 2012. Like Nepal, Bhutan does not allow the Dalai Lama to enter.

Policy Recommendations

- Recognise that Nepal's politics remains in flux; even if short-term challenges regarding constitutional issues can be surmounted, there is no consensus regarding the future trajectory of the country;
- Reports of Chinese influence in Nepal relate primarily to developments within Nepal; the greater the turmoil, the greater the focus, particularly from India and the US, on Chinese activities. The longer that Nepal remains in political turmoil, the greater is likely to be the focus on Chinese 'interference'. Given that Nepalese politics are undergoing a period of realignment, this is likely to be the case.
- China's main concern regarding Nepal relates to Tibetan refugees rather than political influence *per se*. Given Nepal's recurrent attempts to use China to balance Indian influence, whatever party is in power in Kathmandu is unlikely to take steps to irk China particularly in relation to Tibetans.
- China is concerned that the issue of Tibetan refugees can be used as an entry point for foreign (Western) intervention in its external affairs. However, the underlying relevance of Tibet is that it is the source of most of China's water.
- The EU and its Member States have less leverage over developments in Nepal than India and China. While there is goodwill towards European support for Nepal's post-conflict development, there are concerns that focusing on the rights of specific communities may work to entrench or exacerbate divisions within the country.
- Increased Western 'intervention' in Nepal is likely to encourage greater Chinese 'intervention'. While the US government is keen for Nepal to remain in India's sphere of influence, China resents frequent comments by US politicians visiting Nepal regarding Tibet. There is a broader concern within Nepal that the interests of Nepal are secondary to Nepal's utility as a stick to beat China.

China and Russia's Competition for East and Southeast Asia Energy Resources

(May 2013)

Philip Andrews-Speed

Principal Fellow, Energy Studies Institute (ESI), National University of Singapore

Introduction

The aim of this paper is to provide a brief review of the engagement of China and Russia in the energy and mineral resource sectors of East and Southeast Asia, and to assess the extent to which political or economic competition exists in respect of these resources. The paper is structured as follows:

- China and Russia's relations in the region.
- Contrasting energy and resource strategies.
- Sino–Russian energy and resource relations.
- Chinese and Russian resource activities in Southeast Asia.
- China and Russia in DPRK.
- Looking to the future: conflict or cooperation.

China and Russia's Relations in the Region

Russia and China are two global resource powers. They are global political and economic powers in their own right, and both play a major role in international energy and resource commodity markets. Russia is the world's largest producer of oil and of gas, is a treasure house of mineral resources, and has ample supplies of water for hydro-electricity. The downside of this endowment is Russia's continuing dependence on the energy and minerals industries for 10–15% of its GDP and on the energy industry for about two-thirds of its export earnings. In contrast, China has become a major importer of natural resource raw materials over the last ten years, despite its own considerable resource endowment. It is the world's largest importer of oil; at times is the largest, or one of the largest, importers of a wide range of commodities such as coal, iron ore, copper and zinc; and is a rapidly growing importer of gas. These supplies of energy and mineral raw materials have provided vital support for China's infrastructure-led economic boom over the last ten years or so.

China has been steadily increasing its political and economic engagement with countries across East and Southeast Asia since the end of its diplomatic isolation in 1978, and especially since the 1990s. This engagement has both strategic and economic dimensions. The strategic objectives include the security of the sea lanes in the East and South China Seas through which most of China's large and growing quantity of imports and exports flow, as well as the need to counterbalance the USA's long-standing military and strategic commitments in the region. Central to this latter objective has been China's long-standing support for North Korea (DPRK). China plays a critical role in the economy of East and Southeast Asia through trade in manufactured goods and, increasingly, energy and raw materials, and through outward and inward investment flows. In support of these strategies China's government has steadily deepened its relations with the Association of Southeast Asian Nations (ASEAN) as well with its individual member states.

The Soviet Union and the Russian Federation have consistently paid much less attention to East and Southeast Asia than has China. With the exception of the Soviet Union's support of the new communist government in China during the 1950s, the political and economic attention of the government in Moscow has been directed predominantly to Europe in the west and, to a lesser extent, to Central Asia in the south. The main priorities for the Soviet Union in the east were to maintain the DPRK as a buffer against US encroachment and to use Vietnam as a naval base for the protection of sea lanes. The newly formed Russian Federation also neglected the region and only slowly woke up to its economic and strategic importance after Putin took over from Yeltsin as President in 2000. Since then a combination of factors have encouraged the Russian government to expend effort on eastward-directed diplomatic and economic engagement: greater domestic political stability; a stronger economy and improved policy coherence; the need to promote economic growth in eastern Russia; the growth of demand for energy and other raw materials in East Asia; deteriorating political and economic relations with the EU; and, more recently, the economic crisis in Europe. Two important priorities for Russia today are the search for markets for oil, gas, other commodities and manufactured goods in the Asia-Pacific, and, like China, to counterbalance US engagement in East Asia. A further priority is the rapid opening of the Arctic Ocean as a potential trade route. Russia's deepening engagement with the DPRK is an important part of Russia's regional strategy.

In addition to their separate bilateral relations with individual states in Southeast Asia, both China and Russia have formal diplomatic relations with the Association of Southeast Asian Nations (ASEAN), and are members of the Asia-Pacific Economic Cooperation (APEC), the East Asia Summit (EAS), the Asia-Europe Meeting (ASEM), and the ASEAN Regional Forum. In the context of Central Asia, both China and Russia are members of the Shanghai Cooperation Organisation (SCO) and both participated in the Six-Party Talks relating to the DPRK.

Despite this growing engagement across the region, both China and, to a lesser extent Russia, continue to experience tensions in their relations with certain individual states that arise from a combination of unresolved historical issues and specific territorial disputes. In China these actual or potential disputes involve most of the littoral states of the East and South China Seas. Russia's main dispute is with Japan.

Contrasting Energy and Resource Strategies

Russia and China have contrasting energy and resource strategies on account of their quite different balances between supply and demand, though one priority unites them — the desire to retain state control over key assets and resource flows for both political and economic reasons.

China

As a growing net importer of energy and mineral raw materials, for China, the key priority is security of supply. Government strategies involve maximising domestic production of oil, gas, coal and mineral resources, building good relations with the governments of energy and mineral-exporting countries, diversifying sources of imports, constructing import pipelines for oil and gas imports from neighbouring states, and placing increasing emphasis on energy and resource efficiency in the domestic economy. In addition, the government and its state-owned companies are constructing strategic stockpiles of oil and selected minerals, and greater attention is being paid to sea-lane security in the East and South China Seas and in the Indian Ocean.

Domestic oil production has almost reached a plateau due to the limited size of the remaining reserves, but natural gas production continues to rise rapidly and may be further enhanced by shale gas in due course. The production of coal is not limited by resource availability but by increasing costs for transportation, a desire to limit pollution, and by intensifying shortages of water in the coal-producing regions of north China. Although China has large resources and production of many mineral resources, it imports about half of its annual requirement of crude oil, iron ore, copper, lead and zinc, and is a significant importer of other minerals such as aluminium, cobalt and manganese, and a growing importer of coal and natural gas.

In addition to direct actions to enhance supply security, China's government provides explicit political and economic support to state-owned energy and mineral companies that want to invest overseas. Nevertheless, the primary driver for this overseas investment comes from the companies themselves as they seek opportunities for assets, revenues and profits outside their own country. This is for the simple reason that the opportunities abroad are often more attractive than those at home and may be essential to the long-term success of the companies. Government support primarily takes the form of low-interest loans from state-owned policy banks. In some cases this is complemented by diplomatic support, which may involve aid, trade and other forms of investment. The government provides this support because this overseas investment is in line with the industrial policy to promote the internationalisation of large state-owned enterprises in selected sectors, because it provides employment and tax revenues, and because a belief exists that these investments enhance security of supply. At the same time, China's government can use these investments to raise its diplomatic profile in the respective countries and regions.

In terms of investment and trade, Southeast Asia plays a relatively small role in China's global energy and mineral resource strategies on account of the relative paucity of its endowment, but its significance arises from its proximity to China and its location astride key sea lanes. Of particular importance to China in recent years has been the rising (but still speculative) expectations of the existence of substantial oil and gas resources beneath the South China Sea.

Russia

One of President Putin's top priorities during his first two terms as President (2000–2008) was to regain control for the state over the energy sector, especially the oil and gas industries. This objective has largely been met, and Rosneft, Transneft and Gazprom now dominate the domestic oil and gas sectors. A further priority was to use the gas resources of Eastern Siberia to support domestic economic development for this relatively backward region of the Russian Federation. Thus, the government gave Gazprom a monopoly over all gas exports and BP's plans to develop the Kovytka field for the export of gas were foiled. A final priority for the energy sector has been to develop new markets and export routes in East Asia for its huge reserves of oil and gas. This has been easier to achieve for oil than for gas, for oil is a more fungible commodity than gas and the transportation infrastructure cheaper to build.

Russia has ready markets for oil in East Asia, notably, Japan, China and South Korea (ROK) which are all highly dependent on the Middle East for oil imports. Not only that, but they pay an 'Asian premium' for Middle East oil. As a consequence, Russia constructed the East Siberia-Pacific Ocean (ESPO) oil pipeline to the Pacific coast with a branch to northeast China. The branch to China has been operating since late 2010 and in 2012 delivered 15 m tonnes of oil to China. The main line to Kozmino on Russia's Pacific coast was completed in December 2012 and brings the total export capacity of this pipeline to 80 m tonnes, though full use of this capacity will depend both on demand for the oil and on the rate at which production can be raised in East Siberian oil fields.

Russian interest in exporting natural gas eastwards dates back to the mid-1990s when intergovernmental agreements addressed the issue of exporting gas and electricity from Russia to China, and production sharing contracts were signed with foreign oil companies to exploit the gas fields off the shores of Sakhalin. While gas from the latter fields could be and has been exported as liquefied natural gas (LNG) and sold on international markets, gas sold to China would depend on that country's ability and willingness to pay an acceptable price, as well as on Russia's ability to develop sufficient gas reserves and construct the necessary pipelines. In particular, Russia has wanted China to pay a price equivalent to that paid by its European customers. As of April 2013, no agreement on price has been reached.

Like China, the Russian government supports overseas investment by its state-owned energy and resource companies, but the scale of activity is much smaller on account of the abundance of domestic resources remaining to be exploited and a shortage of funds. With respect to nuclear energy, Russia's priority appears to be to export the technology as part of its wider drive to diversify its economy and exports away from dependence on natural resources.

Sino–Russian Energy and Resource Relations

Despite the 'strategic partnership' proclaimed by Presidents Jiang and Yeltsin in 1996 and the Treaty of Friendship signed in 2001 by Presidents Jiang and Putin, economic engagement in the form of trade and investment has grown only slowly, despite the obvious complementarity in respect of energy supply. The total value of trade in 2012 was USD 88 bn, with most of Russia's exports taking the form of energy (mainly oil) and other raw materials. China's potential economic importance to Russia is greater than *vice versa*. Deep distrust of China persists in Russia, including an often irrational fear of a mass migration of Chinese to Russia's empty spaces in the east. Cross-investment in energy infrastructure has been further constrained by regulatory and pricing issues.

Building on the momentum created by the diplomatic rapprochement, an agreement was signed in September 2001 for Yukos and CNPC to collaborate to construct an oil export pipeline from Angarsk in Eastern Siberia to Daqing in northeast China. This project was first suspended and eventually abandoned in 2005 after the nationalisation of Yukos assets. Although oil exports from Russia continued by rail, in its determination to put in place an overland import pipeline, China's government switched its attention to Kazakhstan and constructed a pipeline which was commissioned in 2005. Only in 2008 was agreement to construct an oil export pipeline from Russia finally reached (the ESPO pipeline, see above), with China providing a USD 25 bn loan to the Russian oil companies, to be repaid in oil. During President Xi Jinping's visit to Moscow in March 2013, Rosneft agreed to triple the annual quantity of oil piped to China. This will require further loans from China.

The slowness of the Russians to conclude a deal also drove China to look east for an overland import pipeline for gas. A Memorandum of Understanding was signed in 1994 to draw up plans for a gas pipeline between the two countries. In 2003 BP, CNPC and the Korean Gas Corporation published a feasibility study for a pipeline to bring gas from the Kovytka field through China and under the Yellow Sea to the ROK. The proposal was undermined by the Russian government's new energy strategies and BP was later forced to relinquish its interest in the Kovytka field. As a consequence of this delay, China turned to the vast gas resources of Turkmenistan. An agreement was signed in 2007 and by the end of 2009 gas was flowing from Turkmenistan to Shanghai. Russia's slowness to conclude a gas supply deal with China has its roots in changes to domestic energy priorities and in Russia's quest for a 'European' price from China. At the meeting in March 2013, Russia committed to supplying China with gas from Eastern Siberian gas fields, but the exact route and price have yet to be agreed. The parties' claim that the deal will be finalised by the end of 2013 will probably be dependent not just on agreement being reached on price but also on the provision by China of a USD 25 bn loan to Gazprom.

Other interactions between China and Russia in the energy field include the supply of hydro-electricity and coal from Russia to China and a limited extent of cross-investment in different energy fields such as oil and gas exploration, oil refining and nuclear power.

Despite these frustrations in the field of energy transactions, they do not seem to have undermined the otherwise strong overall diplomatic relations between the two countries. In many respects the two governments have similar attitudes to international institutions for governing energy and natural resources. While they see certain advantages to be gained by joining or cooperating with organisations such as the World Trade Organization (membership) and the International Energy Agency (cooperation), both Chinese and Russian governments seek to limit outside interference in the governance of their domestic energy sectors. An institution such as the Energy Charter Treaty, with its emphasis on transnational investment and transit, is unlikely to attract full membership of either party until their domestic energy industries and policies are substantially reformed. They are both founder members of the Shanghai Cooperation Organisation, but energy does not feature prominently on the agenda of this security-focused group.

Chinese and Russian Energy and Resource Investments in Southeast Asia

There is no comparison between China and Russia in the scale of investment in energy and mineral resources in Southeast Asia. With the exception of Vietnam and Cambodia, China's investments in this region are one or two orders of magnitude greater than those of Russia in terms of funds deployed or committed and are much more diverse. In addition, most of the agreements for investments by Russian companies have been made in just the last two years, with a few dating back to 2008 or before. In contrast, many Chinese investments date back ten years or more, with a few (oil and gas) originating in the mid-1990s

Chinese energy and mineral companies are investing in every country in Southeast Asia, with the apparent exception of Timor Leste (but Chinese companies are active in other sectors there). They are active in the extractive industries of oil and gas exploration and production, mineral production and, to a much lesser extent, coal mining. Investment in these extractive industries is greatest in Indonesia and Myanmar; Indonesia on account of the scale of its resource endowment and Myanmar on account of its proximity to, and diplomatic relationship, with China. China imports growing amounts of gas and coal, and declining quantities of crude oil from Southeast Asia.

Its own domestic energy sector has given Chinese companies great experience in the construction and operation of hydro-electric dams, both large and small. These companies are deploying their skills and funds in nine countries across the region, most notably in Vietnam, Myanmar and Laos, where hydro-electricity is seen to hold the key to economic development. However, this dam building, along with the construction of large dams in southwestern China, is causing significant controversy in the region on account of the disruption to the livelihoods of those living near and downstream of the dams, and because some of the electricity is to be sent to China. China's nuclear power companies appear not to be investing overseas, but rather are focusing their attention on building new capacity at home.

The activities of Russian companies are very modest in comparison to the tens of billions of dollars invested or committed by Chinese companies, and appear to be limited to just four countries: Vietnam, Cambodia, Myanmar and Indonesia. Vietnam remains the key regional partner with two Russian 1 gigawatt nuclear power plants contracted to start construction over the next two years and two others under discussion. In the oil and gas sector, Lukoil, Gazprom and TNK-BP (now Rosneft) hold offshore exploration and production licenses. A Russian company is constructing a 1 gigawatt hydro-electric dam in Cambodia.

Myanmar has significant resources of uranium, some of which are exploited as a by-product of gold mining. In 2007 Russia agreed to build a nuclear research centre in Myanmar. This project was soon suspended due to civil unrest in the country, but the training of Myanmar nuclear engineers in Russia has taken place. Russia appears to be trying to rebuild this relationship. In Indonesia, discussions are reported to be in progress relating to nuclear power and to oil and gas exploration, but no firm contracts appear to have been signed.

China and Russia in DPRK

China and Russia have been key strategic and economic allies of North Korea since its creation in 1945, not least during the Korean War from 1950 to 1953. Until 1990 the Soviet Union played the greater role in providing economic support to the DPRK, but after the collapse of the Soviet Union China has taken the lead in this respect. In 2011 China accounted for 74% of the DPRK's total international trade (exports and imports totalling about USD 6 bn), while Russia accounted for just 1.5% (USD 130 m).

Energy trade between the DPRK and China is substantial, given the small size of the DPRK's energy sector. Since the year 2000, China has supplied just over 500,000 tonnes per year of crude oil to the DPRK. This, together with small but unknown quantities of oil imported from Russia by rail, supplies nearly all of the DPRK's crude oil demand, as its domestic crude oil production is very small.

Using this crude oil, the DPRK's oil-refining capacity provides about 70% of the country's annual consumption of refined oil products. The balance is imported from several countries. China continues to be the largest supplier to the DPRK of refined oil products with 86,000 tonnes of diesel and gasoline in 2012; the importance of these supplies rose markedly after the cessation of the Six-Party Talks in 2009 reduced the total imports by more than 50%. Russia also supplies refined oil products to the DPRK. In February 2013, China provided no crude oil to the DPRK, although it is not known whether this was in reaction to DPRK's nuclear test.

In return for the oil supplies, the DPRK exports significant quantities of coal to China. In 2010 this amounted to 4.6 m tonnes, or possibly about 20–25% of the DPRK's annual production. The growth of coal exports to China has been facilitated by the arrival of Chinese coal mining companies. A minor amount of two-way trade in electricity from hydro-electric dams takes place across the border between China and the DPRK. The DPRK has significant non-energy mineral resources and recent years have seen Chinese mining companies investing in iron, copper and gold mines. China also provides the country with iron, steel, machinery, vehicles and other manufactured products.

In addition to oil and food, Russia provides the DPRK with wood, pulp, fertilizer and iron and steel but, as indicated above, the scale of Russia's trade with the DPRK is but a fraction of China's. In 2011, the Russian government started to display a growing interest in deepening economic engagement with the DPRK. This culminated in September 2012 when Russia wrote off 90% of the DPRK's USD 11 bn debt and declared that it would invest USD 1 bn in energy, healthcare and educational projects. One of the energy projects was to be a pipeline to take gas from the Sakhalin gas field in the Russian Far East to the ROK, transiting across the DPRK. Similar proposals exist for railway lines. These recent steps by Russia have been part of its wider strategy for East Asia, but the timing can be traced to the recovery of the Russian economy after the 2008 financial crisis and to the change of regime in the DPRK.

In recent years, explicit cooperation between China and Russia in matters relating to the DPRK has been relatively limited. Both countries were founder members of the Tumen River Area Development Programme (TRADP), which was launched in 1993 and transformed into the wider Greater Tumen Initiative (GTI) in 2005. The TRADP involved Russia, China, DPRK, ROK and Mongolia, whereas the DPRK is not participating in the GTI. Like the TRADP, the GTI is focused on the economic development of the Northeast Asia region, with energy cooperation as one of the priorities. Both Russia and China took part in the Six-Party Talks which ran from 2003 to 2009, along with the US, Japan, ROK and DPRK.

Looking to the Future: Conflict or Cooperation

China and Russia share significant strategic interests, most notably the desire for stability on the Asian continent and a resentment of the US presence on their eastern flank. Both governments have enough challenges at home and with other neighbours, without the need to disrupt the relationship with their largest neighbour. The importance of this relationship was highlighted in March 2013 by President Xi Jinping choosing Moscow for his first overseas visit as President.

Compared with Russia, China has had much longer and deeper political and economic relations with almost all the nations of East and Southeast Asia, with the exception of the DPRK and Vietnam. Combined with the nature of its energy and resource strategies, this has allowed its companies to gain a relatively strong position across Southeast Asia. Nevertheless, in countries such as Indonesia and Malaysia, which have been open to foreign investment for decades, China is still a minor player. Only in those countries which have just recently opened their doors to foreign investment have Chinese companies managed to build a relatively strong competitive position.

In contrast, Russia and Russian companies are latecomers to energy and mineral resources in East and Southeast Asia, with the exception of Vietnam. The scale and quantity of investment is negligible, though this may grow quickly depending on the availability of funds. They, and companies from other countries, will certainly face competition from Chinese companies. In some cases the outcome of this corporate competition will be decided by the scale of the political and financial capital expended by the governments behind the state-owned companies. In other cases, it may be decided by the host governments in their quest to balance the external political and economic influence of foreign governments, most especially China, the US and Russia.

This recent interest shown by Russia in Southeast Asia is part of a growing realisation that the wider East Asia region is of strategic and economic importance to the country. This is reflected in Russia's closer engagement with the DPRK and participation in regional organisations. This timing coincides with the USA's 'pivot to Asia' as well as with China's increased assertiveness in the East and South China Seas. In this respect, there certainly exists a degree of geopolitical competition in East Asia between these three powers, but energy and mineral resources are not the focus of the competition.

That being said, China has clearly been using its quest for energy and mineral resources as a diplomatic tool in parts of Southeast Asia, as well as elsewhere. To date it has encountered relatively little concerted opposition from outside powers, with the exception of the close attention paid by the US to the South China Sea. Russia may have chosen to deploy energy as a diplomatic tool, but it lacks the financial resources and the import requirement to act as a serious competitor to China in this or most other regions of the world. Further, a lack of familiarity with the region, host governments and host companies means that Russian companies struggle to identify economic interests shared with Southeast Asia.

In the short term, while resources may not become a source of competition in themselves, they could become a serious irritant to Sino–Russian relations if, for example, the activities of Russian oil and gas companies in offshore Vietnam expand into disputed waters.

In the longer term, were Russia willing and able to press ahead with investments in the developing countries of Southeast Asia in which China has significant interests — such as Cambodia, Laos and Myanmar — diplomatic tension between these two powers could rise, especially if China saw Russia as forcing its way into China's 'backyard'. Similar opportunities for tension exist in North Korea in the absence of effective coordination between China and Russia.

Conversely, the likelihood that China and Russia would or could collude to create separate spheres of influence in the region's resources appears low at present:

firstly, because Russia is far behind China in its engagement, with the exception of Vietnam and possibly of the DPRK; secondly, the skills, interests and financial capacities of their energy and mineral companies differ to such a significant degree that the companies themselves are likely to seek different types of commercial opportunities; and thirdly, because most host governments in the region resent over-dependence on a single actor and seek to balance the external powers.

The main point of entry for the EU in this arena would appear to relate to this last point. In its diplomatic engagement with the governments of Southeast Asia, the EU should encourage the efforts of these governments to balance the external powers and prevent over-dependence on any one of them. The potential role of the EU on the Korean Peninsula would appear to be rather limited.

Section Four
The Chinese Economy

The Liberalisation of Chinese Financial Markets
(September 2012)

Vilem Semerak

Researcher, Institute for Democracy & Economic Analysis (IDEA), Center for Economic Research & Graduate Education-Economic Institute (CERGE-EI)

Executive Summary

Despite China's rapid development and modernisation, several aspects of its financial system remain unchanged: (i) the system remains centred around banks, (ii) the Communist Party still uses the sector as one channel for achieving control over the economy, and (iii) banks are still seen by many as a way to support state-owned enterprises and local economic interests. Previous reform experience shows that this hidden role of the financial sector remains crucial and giving up this valuable instrument of control is difficult. However, a genuine need for full reform exists. The current system has negative effects on both welfare and the structure of the economy, and it also inhibits China's ability to shift focus towards domestic demand and cope with macroeconomic imbalances.

Any reforms to the Chinese market are likely to be slow, and there will be faster changes in the external appearance of the system than in its real internal mechanisms. The resulting system is likely to preserve a strong reliance on banking, a dominant role for domestic financial institutions, and at least some indirect control of the official structures that deal with the allocation of capital. European financial business working in China will find it easier to succeed in sectors that are less directly linked to state control (e.g. consumer lending) and in operations linked to the activities of other European companies in the Chinese market.

Main Points

- While the Chinese system has experienced rapid modernisation and expansion, many of its features still differ from those of a pure market economy.
- The Chinese financial system is, and will remain, bank-centred. Both the stock market and bond market will play a secondary role in the external financing of companies.
- Banks have also played an important role in the portfolio of instruments which the Party uses in both official policies and the individual agendas of its influential members.
- There is empirical evidence supporting the claims that the current financial system has distortive effects and influences that are negative to both the welfare of Chinese citizens and the structure of the Chinese economy.
- While the need for reform definitely exists and the proposals of many Chinese officials are genuine and well-intended, real progress is likely to be constrained by power-related factors and is likely to be slow.
- In spite of gradual opening up and internationalisation, the Chinese banking market is likely to remain dominated by domestic financial groups.
- Opening up will occur faster in sectors which are less relevant for control over economy.
- European banks and other financial institutions may find interesting opportunities in China in innovative products, especially in services for European companies in the Chinese market.
- Chinese banks will be more active abroad (including the EU), especially if the liberalisation of the Chinese financial market continues.

Introduction

Proper evaluation of the current and future development of the financial architecture of the People's Republic of China (PRC) is of utmost importance for European policy makers and companies. This is both because of its relevance for the future growth and macroeconomic stability of the PRC, as well as what it reveals about the internal political dynamics of the country and the ambitions of its elites, especially during the current period of transition to a new generation of leaders (expected to take place in late 2012).

This paper focuses on four main questions, mainly from the perspective of the banking sector: what are the prospects for further deregulation and financial liberalisation in the PRC?; how is liberalisation related to macroeconomic efficiency and stability of the country?; how is the process related to the capital (financial) account opening of the country?; and what is the relevance of this for European institutions? By financial deregulation and liberalisation we mean greater access for foreign (or new) financial institutions in the Chinese financial markets, as well as changes in the regulation of intermediation channels (e.g. caps on interest rates for depositors) and influence of various administrative bodies on the allocation of capital.

Financial Architecture of the PRC

Theorists analysing empirical data often find that 'things are not what they seem to be'. This cliché is very true for the Chinese financial system which, on the surface, appears to resemble the systems of many developed market economies but, below the surface, has internal logic and dynamics that remain very idiosyncratic.

Chinese financial architecture: external appearance

The Chinese financial system has undergone dramatic changes since 1978, both in terms of structure and regulation, and in terms of the sophistication and size of its main institutions. Having started with a model inspired by the Soviet Union's central planning system, which had a very passive and subsidiary role for financial markets (which only existed in the form of banking intermediation), since 1978 the PRC has introduced a traditional banking system, opened official stock markets and reintroduced bonds. While most traditional channels of direct financing and intermediation are present, the resulting system still heavily relies on banking intermediation. The dominance of the banking sector in external financing is nothing unusual *per se* (it is common even in developed countries like Germany and Japan), and moreover both China's stock market and bond market appear to be very dynamic and receive a lot of attention at home and abroad.

Chinese banks have managed to dominate the rankings of the world's largest banks over the past 15 years. In 1999, there were no Chinese banks listed among the top 20 world banks by market capitalisation, but by 2009 China had five banks listed in the top 20, three of which took the top three positions (Industrial and Commercial Bank of China (ICBC), China Construction Bank (CCB) and the Bank of China (BoC)). Results for late 2011/early 2012 show a similar pattern: four Chinese banks are in the global top 20 by capitalisation with ICBC and CCB ranked in first and second place, respectively. Their position is slightly weaker in terms of total assets, where ICBC only ranks eighth, but the PRC still has four institutions in the global top 20. No other emerging country in history has achieved anything similar.

The Chinese banking system also seems to be highly liquid and stable — although it needed assistance with its non-performing loans (NPLs) in the 1990s, recent official statistics show that both the volume and share of NPLs had declined during 2006–2010 and profits were increasing. Chinese banks accounted for 29% of global profits in the banking industry in 2011. Chinese banking appears very colourful thanks to a high number of bank and bank-like institutions (top three wholly state-owned banks, five equitised commercial banks, 92 local banks under control of local administrations, 12 Chinese joint-stock banks, a fully private bank), which also includes 185 foreign banks from 45 countries. It also successfully keeps up with modern trends — ranging from the modernisation of the regulatory environment (Basel III) to mobile banking or even microfinance-oriented institutions in rural regions.

China's equity market(s) also appears to be a success story. Since the inception of stock markets in Shenzhen and Shanghai in 1990, the extent of stock trading reached and then exceeded the typical dimensions for the most developed market economies, much higher than in European transition economies. Outside of China's two stock markets, many joint-stock companies are also listed in Hong Kong. Initial public offerings (IPOs) of shares, especially for state-owned enterprises (SOEs), are popular and occur much more frequently than in transition countries; futures trading (including stock index future trading) and short selling exist and authorities (namely, the China Securities Regulatory Commission) have tried to regulate the market to fight against insider trading. Foreign investors have been allowed to invest in A-shares within the Qualified Foreign Institutional Program (QFII) since 2002. In short, the symbols of the market economy seem to be alive and well-established in China.

The Chinese bond market emerged with the issuance of government bonds in 1981 and currently consists of the inter-bank bond market and the exchange market. Its role has been increasing, even though its total role in external financing remains low (because most of the traded bonds are government bonds and central bank notes). However, innovations and growth of the market continue — in June 2012, for example, China opened a high-yield junk bond market. Bonds are important for the possibility of a more intensive international role for Chinese currency, in particular the so-called 'Dim Sum' bonds (RMB denominated bonds issued offshore) which were introduced in 2007. The issuance of these bonds reached around EUR 10 bn in 2011.

The financial markets are regulated and supervised in a way that is reminiscent of standard market economies. The China Banking Regulatory Commission (CBRC), China Securities Regulatory Commission (CSRC) and China Insurance Regulatory Commission (CIRC) are each responsible for their respective fields. Chinese authorities and officials also publicly declared the need for further change and opening repeatedly, even in official documents such as the 12th Five Year Programme.

Capital Market in PRC: Below the Surface

The institutions that we tend to believe epitomise market forces seem to work slightly differently in China. Stock markets and bond markets are very good examples of this paradox. Important Chinese companies remain under the control of the Chinese Communist Party (CCP), which means that their control is never really traded in stock markets, despite the fact that their shares are tradable. Buyers of shares are thus allowed to 'contribute' their funds during an IPO and can participate in the profits. The role of foreign investors under the QFII regime (relevant for investing in A-shares) remains limited — while their quota was increased to USD 80 bn (EUR 65 bn) in April 2012, their share remains below 0.8% of market capitalisation.

Even the formation of the Shenzhen and Shanghai stock markets can be viewed as an attempt to channel market forces under supervision of the centre, rather than real decentralisation. Bond markets are fairly unique too — most of the bonds are held until maturity and are never really traded. Most importantly, state-controlled entities are often found on both sides of the transaction.

Banking also remains fairly specific. Firstly, the state maintains significant direct control (more than 90% of banking sector assets are majority state-owned). Secondly, their liquidity and financial stability is achieved by excessive regulation of the banking market in the form of ceilings on interest rates for deposits and floors on rates for borrowers. The interest rate ceilings together with the lack of alternative forms of investment mean that Chinese depositors' high savings are used as a convenient liquidity cushion for the banking sector. Last but not least, the banking sector is very concentrated, with the top state banks forming an oligopoly, surrounded by numerous weaker and much less influential entities. All this means that banking is fairly unlikely to function efficiently and play its basic economic role (i.e. efficient allocation of capital).

The CCP thus preserves a substantial degree of control over the financial system. While some experts consider this to be an omission or relic of the past which will disappear with further reforms, others find this feature a part of a deliberate design serving several purposes. Most importantly, it provides the authorities with a comfortable instrument for direct economic interventions, such as the 2009 credit boom; and with guaranteed and cheap financing to preferred companies and project. Very importantly, this type of governance can act as a vital stabilising mechanism with respect to dealing with debt problems of e.g. provincial governments. Negotiating and arranging debt roll-overs or write-offs is therefore much easier and gives the authorities power that their European counterparts do not have. Sacrificing these powers for the sake of long-run efficiency is quite a challenging decision in the current turbulent environment.

While the current system is thus very different from traditional centrally-planned finance in its external appearance, its function has more similarities. In spite of its profits and growth in assets, banking in particular remains part of the system that is assumed to play an accommodative role — providing finance for projects which central or local (depending on the balance of power) authorities consider important and guaranteeing a substantial degree of softness to the budget constraints of public and semi-public institutions.

Determinants of the Financial Architecture in the PRC

The financial system of the PRC has in recent years been formed by seven key factors, outlined below. Given the path-dependency that is typical for large economic and political systems, most are likely to remain stable in the near future. Together they imply that: (i) the Chinese financial system needs further reform and opening up, (ii) many officials are aware of this necessity, (iii) despite reform, the Chinese system is likely to remain different from the financial systems of developed countries, and (iv) consideration should be given to factors that could slow down and dilute the necessary steps for reform.

1. *The character of Chinese economy*

The Chinese economy is still that of a less-developed country and faces significant problems with information asymmetries and a large share of the population without extensive experience of financial markets. In this environment, economies of scale in information acquisition and processing are important and lead to reliance on more indirect and concentrated forms of financial intermediation. Consequently, the dominant role of banking remains likely to prevail. There is nothing wrong with this *per se* — bank intermediation has the potential to be more efficient in this kind of environment.

However, China has also been described as 'over-banked' because of the sector's unusually high share of credits/assets to GDP. It would therefore be unreasonable to expect expansion of the whole sector at rates that significantly exceed the growth of the country's nominal output; instead we are likely to see a gradual structural change and modernisation in this sector.

2. *WTO membership and the opening of the Chinese market*

Access to the Chinese market was very selective before its accession to the World Trade Organization (WTO). China basically only allowed foreign banks to conduct foreign currency business in selected cities. When entering the WTO in 2001, China committed to fully opening its banking sector to foreign competition by 2006. This pledge has played a very positive role, as it seems to have motivated China to assist its four large state-owned banks with their huge stock of NPLs accumulated during the 1990s and recapitalise them in a relatively standard way.

However, market excess remains asymmetric and foreign banks still face a number of requirements which do not apply equally to foreign and domestic banks. The market share of foreign banks remains low (about 2%) and their ability to attract clients is limited as they are required to maintain a 75% ratio between loans and deposits while being subject to the same interest rate regulation as domestic banks (i.e. they cannot offer higher returns to depositors). There is also a three-year waiting period to which foreign bank branches are subject before being eligible to submit their application for the RMB license. It is also difficult for foreign banks to attract deposits because of their significantly less widespread branch network.

3. *Changes in banking regulation in other countries (Basel III)*

In sharp contrast to increasingly negative opinions on the attractiveness of foreign financial systems, the PRC seems to be one of the most enthusiastic supporters of the Basel III regulation. Although the CBRC has been granted some flexibility in this respect, these steps are expected to improve the transparency and stability of Chinese banking. As a by-product, the environment and regulatory requirements could become better for dealing with foreign institutions.

4. *Long-run efficiency considerations*

There is a vast macroeconomic literature that focuses on the efficiency of financial institutions (especially with respect to the allocation of capital and growth). Some theoretical models suggest that impediments to the efficiency of allocation lead to biased growth, meaning that the economy is likely to achieve sub-optimal results. Similar outcomes can be derived from microeconomic models that consider the effects of soft budget constraints. This may result in lower growth, waste in the form of investing scarce capital into sectors with low or no returns, and redistribution of wealth. If these theoretical insights are true, how can we reconcile the lack of motive for efficient behaviour observed with the fast growth of the Chinese economy?

A relatively high part of China's economic growth has been based on total factor productivity (TFP) improvements. The ability to generate high TFP growth differentiates the Chinese case from traditional centrally planned economies and suggests that Chinese growth could, at least to some extent, be sustainable even with distorted financial markets. However, there is a price to pay, as impressive growth rates require even more impressive investment ratios. Some commentators suggest that China would have been able to generate equally impressive growth with a much lower rate of investment; a significant proportion of investment made between 1978 and 2008 was in the less efficient state sector, which has a rate of return close to zero. The country's inhabitants thus paid a fairly high price for the inefficiency of financial institutions. Households (especially those without access to forms of saving outside of bank accounts with capped interest rates) have been subsidising growth. Inefficiencies in the financial system have therefore restricted China's ability to rely on domestic demand and increased its dependence on external demand, as well as its reliance on the industrial sector at the expense of services.

Three main factors have so far prevented greater adverse effects on the growth and stability of the Chinese economy. Firstly, China has started from a very low base, i.e. from a situation where many kinds of investment could lead to relatively high positive returns. Consequently, errors in allocation might have had less pronounced macroeconomic effects. Secondly, the Chinese economy was in the process of overcoming a development gap — achieving fast growth is easier when a country is only just returning to its potential (and when efficiency can be increased with the help of imported technologies). Finally, suppressed demand at home has been overshadowed by China's reliance on external demand. All of these factors are likely to be less reliable in the coming years. Consequently, the continuation of financial sector reform is necessary if China is to sustain fast and balanced growth in future.

5. *Short-run economic factors*

The current structure of the financial sector and its regulation are also indirectly responsible for both real estate bubbles and for the occasional outbursts of inflation seen in recent years. Further liberalisation should bring additional benefits in the form of more balanced and stable development.

However, while Chinese banking as it currently stands is not ideal, it can appear 'good enough' to a non-economist decision maker, especially when official numbers are compared with the troubles faced by many developed countries in the Economic and Monetary Union (EMU).

There are two additional reasons which can dilute the determination for further reform:

- The effects of the build-up of debt of provincial governments since 2009. While this development vividly demonstrates the weaknesses of relying on the financial system as the main instrument of control and stimulation (and as such it theoretically should support the need for reform), the risks related to the current exposure can convince the Party to prefer the *status quo*. Having control over both debtors and creditors substantially increases the chances that the debt problem can be contained without the escalation faced by several EMU countries.

- The financial crisis also dramatically reduced the attractiveness of both US and European financial systems and reinforced the self-confidence of Chinese political elites. The 'don't show me any failed models' mentality has therefore become a key factor which could undermine the efforts of foreign pressure for further reforms.

Therefore, from the perspective of some Chinese elites, there may be (i) other more pressing issues for reform, such as high (and increasing) inequality and the need for an efficient pension system, and (ii) reasons to be cautious. Political and social stability are seen as more important than the efficiency of allocation of capital.

This means that there is still the opportunity to carry out reform before it becomes truly urgent, and this is most likely one of the motives for several recent pro-reform proposals and speeches made by representatives of the People's Bank of China (Zhou Xiaochuan) and government (Wen Jiabao). But opportunity does not mean necessity. Ample evidence from other countries shows that reforms addressing long-run issues tend to be postponed until the situation becomes critical, especially if the necessary steps are viewed as politically costly. The current extremely positive statistics associated with Chinese banks, in combination with the perceived failures of the financial systems of many other countries, may thus prove to be a mixed blessing.

6. *Inherent logic of power and control*

The logic of power and control has been, and will most likely remain, the single most influential factor in discussion over the future structure of reforms. While close relations between top business leaders, banks, and political elites are common in many countries, these relations reach a special level in China. Most importantly:

- The state/CCP officially controls SOEs;
- The state/CCP controls the top banking institutions and has the power to negatively affect SOEs and local administrations;
- Many influential CCP members have relatives who enjoy high positions in SOEs and banks.

Contacts and influence are thus important for stabilising one's position in both business and the Party structure. Although this tangle presently has a relatively stable form, any deeper changes could necessitate a more complicated strategic game. Liberalising financial markets and increasing the role of independent foreign entities in the market could thus be politically risky, as it could restrict the ability for individuals to use this channel to gain support from others in the network. The third feature means that when the opening of Chinese markets is discussed, the interests of the strong domestic incumbents are extremely well represented in debates over future policies.

While it is theoretically possible that the Party could use existing channels or open new ones in order to exercise at least some influence over foreign banks, which could reduce the Party's fear of losing control over the financial sector, such strategies are still more risky than sustaining the *status quo*.

7. Capital account, external macroeconomic equilibrium and the internationalisation of the RMB

While the Chinese balance of payments may be very appealing to mercantilists, excessive accumulation of foreign exchange is a symptom of macroeconomic disequilibrium and creates problems for the central bank. The most appropriate response to this macroeconomic dilemma would be a combination of a change in the exchange rate regime (transition to floating, which is gradually being implemented) with increased convertibility of the RMB. The latter feature in particular is directly linked to the liberalisation of the financial sector and is also a prerequisite for an increased international role for the RMB.

Liberalisation and Deregulation: Future Trends and Opportunities

Chinese policy makers know that reform is needed (especially in the long run) and have taken (often costly) steps signaling their determination to liberalise the sector (for example, through recapitalisation of top banks — ABC received RMB 130 bn (almost EUR 13 bn) in 2008). However, adoption of further steps is selective and gradual. True liberalisation will only succeed if those in power are strong and act to maximise the long-run welfare of the country regardless of the effects on their own position, or if elites find an alternative mechanism which allows them to do without control over finance. It is unclear whether any of these factors apply to the current

PRC and even more unclear how the new administration will behave as it strives to stabilise its position in a potentially complicated macroeconomic environment.

A sudden real change in the way that Chinese financial markets operate is therefore unlikely and we should instead expect a sequence of gradual and partial (sometimes superficial) changes through which the CCP attempts to deal with problems without sacrificing too much, or are related to issues that coincide with the interests of the top players. It is therefore logical to expect that the Chinese capital market will still depend on banking in the future and that the fundamental features of Chinese banking (such as the importance of political factors and dominance of local banks) will change only very slowly. In short, the Chinese financial sector will change in an evolutionary and not a revolutionary way.

Implications for European financial institutions

The aforementioned factors (especially point six) mainly apply to banking because of its vital role in financing companies. Other parts of financial services that are less important for control over the economy are less likely to be viewed as sensitive and are therefore more likely to enjoy faster liberalisation. This can be verified by the relative success of foreign institutions in the insurance market and in consumer credit.

The assumed gradualism of deeper changes together with the tradition of 'bird cage economics' suggest that real restrictions on the activities of foreign banks are likely to be reduced slowly and perhaps unequally, for example, through regional economic experiments. Such opportunities should definitely be embraced by foreign companies — while they will not bring substantial market shares at the national level, they will help them improve their knowledge of the environment.

The restrictions mentioned under point one, together with the fact that China has been able to finance existing high investment rates from domestic savings, imply that useable strategies for the expansion of foreign banks remains limited.

However, there seem to be three main opportunities for expansion in the activities of European banks in China:

- Financial innovations, i.e. innovative products, especially products focused on niche markets which have not caught the interest of current market players. One successful example of this approach involves consumer credit and the

successful market entry of PPF Group N.V. with their Home Credit project. Future opportunities may include foreign currency accounts for Chinese citizens, though this requires further changes in regulation.
- Focus on supplying services to foreign enterprises and nationals active in China. In the past, a similar mode of expansion has been used by, for example, Japanese banks during their expansion abroad. The obvious competitive edge of European banks lies in knowledge of their clients and in trust related to confidentiality of information.
- Alliance (joint venture) with a local partner (often inevitable because of regulatory requirements) in which the European partner can base its position on reputation (brand) and experience.

At the same time, European banks should be ready for future attempts of Chinese banks to expand abroad. While such ambitions have been to some extent suppressed by economic factors so far, related policy measures have been announced and Chinese banks are becoming increasingly active. Future expansion of such activities depends on similar factors as financial liberalisation — as long as the banks are required to play the role of a cushion or support mechanism for provincial governments and key companies, the scope for their foreign expansion may be limited. Reforms of the Chinese financial market therefore not only open the market for European companies, but they can also indirectly open new opportunities for Chinese banks in the EU. We can expect that such activities would be primarily focused on (i) acquiring market skills, expertise and information, (ii) trade financing — here it would form part of wider effort to increase the share of Chinese companies in the value chain of exports of Chinese commodities to Europe.

Conclusion

Although theoretical economists express their concerns about the long-run effects of the state-managed banking sector on the efficiency of allocation of capital and the microeconomic efficiency of companies, it seems that other (political and power-related) factors are likely to prevail and that the current system will only see slow change. We can therefore expect that the dominant role of banking and the small role of foreign competition in the financial market of the PRC will be preserved.

While nominal barriers to foreign activities may be reduced and foreign entities will be able to increase their participation in Chinese financial institutions, their real role in Chinese markets is unlikely to increase fast. Liberalisation will be faster in sectors that are less directly related to control over the economy (insurance, consumer credit). In banking, however, the nature of current regulation restricts the set of usable strategies. While the share of foreign banks in the Chinese market (and related profits) will become more diverse in future, it is unlikely that the Chinese market will become as dominated by foreign financial institutions as the markets of the transition economies. At the same time, the EU should expect attempts at either market entry or merger and acquisition activities by Chinese banks (and sovereign investment funds) as well.

Table 1. Global top 20 (ranked by market capitalisation).

Rank within sector	2008		2009		2010		2011		2012 sec. quarter	
	Company	Country	Company	Country	Company	Country	Company	Country	Company	Country
1	**Indl & Coml Bank of China**	**China**	**Indl & Coml Bank of China**	**China**	**Industrial & Commercial Bank of China**	**China**	**Industrial & Commercial Bank of China**	**China**	**Industrial & Commercial Bank of china**	**China**
2	HSBC	UK	**China Construction Bank**	**China**	**China Construction Bank**	**China**	**China Construction Bank**	**China**	Wells Fargo	USA
3	**China Construction Bank**	**China**	**Bank of China**	**China**	Bank of America	USA	JP Morgan Chase	USA	**China Construction Bank**	**China**
4	Bank of America	USA	JP Morgan Chase	USA	JP Morgan Chase	USA	HSBC	UK	HSBC	UK
5	**Bank of China**	**China**	HSBC	UK	HSBC	UK	Wells Fargo	USA	JP Morgan Chase	USA
6	JP Morgan Chase	USA	Wells Fargo	UK	Wells Fargo & Co	USA	**Bank of China**	**China**	**Agricultural Bank of China**	**China**
7	Banco Santander	Spain	Banco Santander	Spain	**Bank of China**	**China**	**Agricultural Bank of China**	**China**	**Bank of China**	**China**
8	Citigroup	USA	Mitsubishi UFJ Financial	Japan	Citigroup	USA	Bank of America	USA	Bank of America	USA
9	Wells Fargo	USA	Bank of America	USA	Banco Santander	Spain	Citigroup	USA	Common wealth Bank of Australia	Australia

(*Continued*)

Table 1. (Continued)

Rank within sector	2008		2009		2010		2011		2012 sec. quarter	
	Company	Country	Company	Country	Company	Country	Company	Country	Company	Country
10	Mitsubishi UFJ Financial	Japan	Itau Unibanco	Brazil	BNP Paribas	France	Itau Unibanco	Brazil	Citigroup	USA
11	BNP Paribas	France	Royal Bank Canada	Canada	Itau Unibanco	Brazil	Banco Santander	Spain	Royal Bank Canada	Canada
12	Intesa Sanpaolo	Italy	Bank of Communications	Canada	Royal Bank Canada	Canada	Royal Bank Canada	Canada	Toronto-Dominion Bank	Canada
13	Unicredito Italiano	Italy	Westpac Banking	Australia	Commonwealth Bank of Australia	Australia	BNP Paribas	France	Mitsubishi UFJ Financial	Japan
14	BBVA	Spain	BNP Paribas	France	Westpac Banking	Australia	Commonwealth Bank of Australia	Australia	Westpac Banking	Australia
15	Sberbank of Russia	Russia	Commonwealth Bank of Australia	Australia	Mitsubishi UFJ Financial	Japan	Sberbank of Russia	Russia	Banco Santander	Spain
16	Royal Bank of Scotland	UK	Credit Suisse	Switzerland	Barclays	UK	Toronto-Dominion Bank	Canada	US Bancorp	USA
17	**China Merchants Bank**	**China**	Intesa Sanpaolo	Italy	Sberbank of Russia	Russia	Westpac Banking	Australia	Itau Unibanco	Brazil

(Continued)

Table 1. (Continued)

Rank within sector	2008 Company	2008 Country	2009 Company	2009 Country	2010 Company	2010 Country	2011 Company	2011 Country	2012 sec. quarter Company	2012 sec. quarter Country
18	Bank of Communications	China	**China Merchants Bank**	**China**	Toronto-Dominion Bank	Canada	Bradesco	Brazil	ANZ Banking	Australia
19	UBS	Switzerland	BBVA	Spain	Lloyds Banking Group	UK	UBS	Switzerland	Sberbank of Russia	Russia
20	Royal Bank Canada	Canada	Toronto Dominion Bank	Canada	Credit Suisse Group	Switzerland	Bank of Nova Scotia	Canada	Bank of Nova Scotia	Canada

Sources:
Financial Times Global 500 – 2012, FT, July 18, 2012 (data for 2008–2009)
Financial Times Global 500 – 2011, FT, June 26, 2011 (data for 2010)
Financial Times Global 500 – 2010, FT, June 24, 2011 (data for 2011)
Financial Times Global 500 – 2009, FT, May 29, 2009 (data for 2012)

Table 2. Banks in global top 20 by country (ranked by market capitalisation).

	2008		2009		2010		2011		2012 sec. quarter	
	Country	# of banks in top 20	Country	# of banks in top 20	Country	# of banks in top 20	Country	# of banks in top 20	Country	# of banks in top 20
1	China	5	China	4	USA	4	China	4	USA	5
2	USA	4	Canada	3	China	3	USA	4	China	4
3	Italy	2	Australia	2	UK	3	Canada	3	Australia	3
4	Spain	2	Spain	2	Australia	2	Australia	2	Canada	3
5	UK	2	UK	2	Canada	2	Brazil	2	Brazil	1
6	Canada	1	USA	2	Brazil	2	France	1	Japan	1
7	France	1	Brazil	1	France	1	Russia	1	Russia	1
8	Japan	1	France	1	Japan	1	Spain	1	Spain	1
9	Russia	1	Italy	1	Russia	1	Switzerland	1	UK	1
10	Switzerland	1	Japan	1	Spain	1	UK	1	France	0
11	Australia	0	Switzerland	1	Switzerland	1	Italy	0	Italy	0
12	Brazil	0	Russia	0	Italy	0	Japan	0	Switzerland	0
Total		20		20		20		20		20

Sources:

Simple regrouping based on the original tables from FT Global 500:

Financial Times Global 500 – 2012, FT, July 18, 2012 (data for 2008–2009)

Financial Times Global 500 – 2011, FT, June 26, 2011 (data for 2010)

Financial Times Global 500 – 2010, FT, June 24, 2011 (data for 2011)

Financial Times Global 500 – 2009, FT, May 29, 2009 (data for 2012)

Investment Provisions in China's Free Trade Agreements
(February 2012)

Christopher M Dent

Professor of East Asia's International Political Economy, East Asian Studies, University of Leeds

Executive Summary

China has become one of the world's most active free trade agreement (FTA) protagonists. Having signed deals with nine partners, it is now negotiating with a further five, and it has begun proposals with a number of other states. China has also become a major overseas investor, as articulated in the Chinese government's 'going out' strategy. This has been driven primarily by the resource demands of China's economy. The investment rights provisions in many of its more recent FTAs reflect China's changing investment interests. Having shifted from its almost exclusive concern with attracting inflows of foreign direct investment (FDI), the central government now seeks to protect the outward FDI of Chinese enterprises.

This paper explores the relationship between investment provisions in China's newer FTAs and its overseas investment interests in general terms. This exploration is further enunciated through three case studies on China's FTAs with Pakistan, New Zealand and Peru. These FTAs contain substantive investment rights provisions.

While FTAs have become an important mechanism by which China protects its overseas investments, it remains unclear how significant these provisions will become in future, and how China will negotiate investment provisions in agreements with larger trade partners.

Introduction

The relationship between foreign direct investment (FDI) and China's economic development is complex and multi-layered, particularly since China not only attracts large inward flows of FDI, but has now itself become a major overseas investor. Free trade agreements (FTAs) most recently signed or currently being negotiated by Beijing have sought to protect the investment rights of Chinese enterprises, and have become a key component of Chinese foreign policy. More generally, FTAs have significantly shaped today's regional and global trade diplomacy landscape, expanding in number from just 16 in 1990 to over 300 by the end of 2011. FTAs are international treaties containing enforceable provisions that cover various trade-related policy areas. The growth of FDI flows and deepening functional linkages between trade and investment have made investment chapters in FTAs ever more important. The inclusion of stronger investment rights in these agreements has been hitherto largely championed by developed country powers such as the EU, the US and Japan, who have sought to protect the commercial interests of their multinational corporations. When China began to pursue FTAs in the early 2000s, China negotiated provisions that only permitted investment *cooperation* rather than investment *rights* — many of China's 'strategic' industries (for instance, telecommunications and energy) remain off-limits to foreign investors. However, more recent agreements with Pakistan, New Zealand and Peru show a growing orientation towards an investment rights approach, as Chinese outward FDI has expanded.

China's FTA Policy and the 'Going Out' Strategy

China developed its FTA policy after gaining accession to the WTO in 2001. Initial basic agreements were signed with the Special Administrative Regions of Hong Kong and Macao in 2003. These were soon followed by agreements with the Association of Southeast Asian Nations (ASEAN), Chile, Pakistan, New Zealand, Singapore, Peru and Costa Rica. Beijing is currently in negotiation with a number of other trade partners, including Australia, the Gulf Co-operation Council (GCC), Iceland and Norway, and is engaged at the study or proposal stage with others.

China's initial FTAs were typical 'developing country' agreements, having more limited policy scope and depth of legal obligation compared to comprehensive 'developed country' style agreements. This is not surprising given that FTAs generally mirror a state's politico-economic development and commercial interests. The main motives behind China's FTA policy have been to:

- Expand exports and diversify export markets.
- Reduce costs to Chinese consumers and producers.
- Strengthen China's diplomatic relations and geopolitical position, both regionally and globally.
- Attract inward FDI to key sectors, particularly those sectors integrated into international production networks where elimination or reduction of component and finished product tariff rates can reduce network operating costs.
- Improve productivity in domestic industries, enabling Chinese brands to become more globally competitive.
- Secure better access to foreign natural resources.

This last motive has grown in importance as China's international investment interests have expanded. The 'going out' strategy was launched in 1998, and aimed to encourage Chinese enterprises to increase their overseas investments, further internationalising Chinese economic interests and recycling China's accumulating foreign exchange reserves. This strategy has been embedded in the nation's Five Year Plans, and China's outward FDI has risen exponentially, from just USD 3 bn in 1991 to USD 35 bn in 2003. Over time, securing access to foreign natural resources to sustain China's economic development has become the defining feature of its 'going out' strategy. Energy and mining presently account for around two-thirds of China's outward FDI.

China and Foreign Investment Rights

Inward FDI has played a vital role in China's economic development and reform process, and Beijing has, as of February 2012, signed 90 bilateral investment treaties (BITs) to help maintain the mass flow of foreign investment into the country. Like FTAs, BITs can vary significantly in scope and nature, and are designed, like FTA investment chapters, to protect the rights of foreign investors. Generally speaking, while BITs normally contain an investor-state dispute resolution mechanism, the provisions and legal enforceability of BITs — especially older ones — are much weaker than the comprehensive investment chapters of FTAs.

China has been signing BITs since the early 1980s. However, most of these were negotiated in the 1990s and early 2000s, and driven principally by nations with investment interests in China rather than *vice versa*. It is telling that the last BIT China negotiated was in 2006, the same year that it signed its FTA with Pakistan, the first country with which it brokered a substantive investment chapter. The three countries to date that Beijing has signed FTAs with substantive investment chapters are also well established BIT partners with China: New Zealand, Pakistan and Peru. We may therefore deduce that the FTA investment chapters in question were able to provide additional value beyond that currently offered by the BITs, which are still in force. Furthermore, the apparent switch from BITs to FTAs in the mid-2000s corresponds with the previously noted sharp growth in China's outward FDI levels.

Table 1 outlines key investment chapter provisions found across China's FTAs with Pakistan, New Zealand and Peru. Brief explanations of these sections are provided below:

- *National treatment*: investors from other parties are to be afforded the same treatment as domestic firms, in accordance with the principle of non-discrimination.
- *Most-favoured-nation (MFN) treatment*: investors from other parties are to be afforded treatment no less favourable to investors of any third state.
- *Fair and equitable treatment, full protection and security*: commits parties to providing full legal protection to investments and investors from the other parties, to the extent normally provided within the host party's territory.
- *Prohibition of performance requirements*: prohibits host parties from imposing performance criteria (for example, exports quotas or local content requirements) on foreign investors.
- *Expropriation*: prohibits the host party state from confiscating or nationalising the assets of foreign investors.
- *Compensation for losses*: compensation is provided to foreign investors should they suffer losses owing to the event of war, national emergency, insurrection, riot or other similar events in the territory of the other party, in accordance with the national and MFN standards.
- *Subrogation*: application of full subrogation insurance rights to foreign investors in the host party territory.
- *Transfers*: guarantees the right of foreign investors to freely transfer their investments and returns held in host party territory to overseas locations.
- *Transparency*: each party is required to publish international agreements pertaining to investment to which it is a party.

Table 1. Length of investment rights provisions in China's FTAs.

Provisions	Pakistan (2007) Word Count	New Zealand (2008) Word Count	Peru (2010) Word Count
Definitions	244	415	331
Objectives	—	93	—
Scope and Coverage	—	299	391
Promotion and Protection of Investment	133	48	74
National Treatment	195	54	124
Most-Favoured-Nation Treatment	—	226	216
Non-Conforming Measures	—	119	82
Fair and Equitable Treatment, Full Protection and Security	—	169	177
Prohibition of Performance Requirements	—	41	—
Expropriation	136	348	104
Compensation for Losses	83	85	78
Subrogation	123	154	123
Denial of Benefits	—	103	89
Transfers	172	629	229
Transparency	—	18	—
Dispute Settlement	609	1,027	974
Communications (Consultations, Meetings, Contact Points)	83	55	85
Committee on Investment	—	84	—
Essential Security	—	—	78
Taxation Measures	—	—	416
Other Obligations	80	—	55
	1,858	**3,967**	**3,626**

- *Dispute settlement*: these provisions provide recourse for foreign investors where a host state has allegedly failed to uphold the investment rights granted by the FTA.
- *Taxation measures*: these provisions impose special rules and exemptions concerning taxation laws.

These provisions are enforceable through recourse to the FTA's dispute settlement mechanism, and are the most extensive treaty-based protection Chinese overseas investment interests. Indeed, almost all of the above provisions extend protection beyond the WTO's 1994 Trade-Related Investment Measures (TRIMs) agreement, to which China is a signatory.

Case Studies on China's FTAs with Pakistan, New Zealand and Peru

The policy choices that States Parties make when concluding FTAs with others may seem neither obvious nor rational. Traditional theories of international trade suggest that agreements with large and similarly structured economic partners yield the greatest potential 'trade creation' welfare gains. However, states with which China has signed FTAs with substantive investment rights provisions to date — Pakistan, New Zealand and Peru — are not themselves significant recipients of Chinese outward investment or even important trade partners. This illustrates that economics is just one of many factors influencing FTA partner selection. As discussed below, Pakistan was chosen largely for geo-strategic reasons. New Zealand and Peru were meanwhile chosen as small, 'politically easy' and flexible negotiating partners. In addition, all three offered China a foothold in three separate regions — South Asia, Oceania and Latin America — consistent with the global spread approach of China's FTA policy. Investment and trade in natural resources also comprises a significant part of China's relations with all three nations.

Pakistan

Pakistan is viewed by China's leadership as geo-strategically significant given its littoral location on the Indian Ocean and Persian Gulf sea lane zones, and its middle-power status in the South Asia region. In November 2003, China and Pakistan signed a 'sub-FTA' preferential trade agreement, focused on trade in goods. Subsequent full FTA talks ran parallel with another key initiative, namely China's joint venture with Pakistan to develop deep water port and other infrastructural facilities at Gwadar. The port serves two key purposes. First, it provides the option of transporting oil and other resources from the Middle East and Africa overland into West China rather than having to take a long maritime route through US navy-patrolled waters and the narrow 'chokepoint' Malacca straits. Second, Gwadar will be the first overseas base for Chinese naval ships, located close to strategically important sea lanes. The development of Gwadar's port has been made possible by large-scale Chinese state investment. Chinese investment interests in Pakistan's oil, gold, raw cotton and other natural resource sectors have also grown, accompanied by investments in transportation, energy and communications infrastructure — part of China's usual 'bundle' of development aid and state-directed FDI. The Haier-Ruba Economic Zone (HRZ), situated near Lahore, also hosts a growing number of Chinese firms, and was China's first Overseas Economic and Trade Co-operation Area. The investment rights provisions contained in the China–Pakistan FTA are, at least from Beijing's perspective, primarily to protect China's strategic resource-based and military-related investments in Pakistan. In future FTA review processes, we may expect Beijing to push for the inclusion of the same kind of security clauses found in the later-negotiated China–Peru FTA, due to rising security concerns affecting foreign investors in Pakistan. In August 2011, the China Kingho Group — the nation's largest private coal mining enterprise — pulled out of a huge USD 19 bn investment deal reportedly due to the spate of bombings in Pakistan's major cities.

New Zealand

Representing China's first FTA signed with a developed country, its agreement with New Zealand has the longest chapter on investment rights of the three FTAs. China's investment interests in New Zealand are still on a relatively small scale, yet broad in scope. They are currently fast growing and possibly of some long-term strategic importance in key sectors. The China–New Zealand FTA feasibility study report, produced in 2004, noted that Chinese investments were spread over a number of industries, including forestry, commercial construction, property, meat processing, electronics, fish farming, tanning, light manufacture, hotels and tourism. Having the highest level of FDI in China of the three FTA partners, New Zealand was keen to have an investor-state dispute settlement mechanism that was as strong as possible and, in addition, strong provisions on investment transfers and expropriation clauses (see Table 1). These provisions are likely to establish baseline precedents on investment rights for other developed nations currently negotiating FTAs with China.

From a long-term strategic perspective, China's investment interests in New Zealand are likely to centre on the food security-related sectors of agriculture, food processing and biotechnology. China faces many food security challenges and an increasingly prosperous society has led to burgeoning demand for high protein food products. New Zealand is a major exporter of livestock and dairy products (these account for over 20% of New Zealand's exports), and has one of the world's most technologically advanced food sectors. Furthermore, the nation's pasture management, herd improvement, sustainable fishing and product processing methods have already attracted considerable Chinese interest. Chinese investment in biotechnology research joint ventures with New Zealand firms could potentially lead to increased crop yields in China's agriculture sector.

Certain high-profile Chinese investments in New Zealand have revealed a pattern of adverse attention, founded on often irrational fears that a 'rising China' is undermining the West. When Chinese company Bright Dairy purchased the Canterbury-based milk processor Synlait in May 2011, this move raised product quality and health issue concerns among the New Zealand public. New Zealand Prime Minister John Key countered this by stating that it did not matter where the investment came from, and that it created new jobs. Interestingly, there was little public outcry when Chinese firm Haier bought a 20% stake in one of New Zealand's highest-profile firms, the household appliance manufacturer Fisher and Paykel, two years earlier in 2009. More recently, when the New Zealand government approved the sale of 16 dairy farms to the Shanghai Pengxin Group in January 2012, this raised local anxiety about 'land grab' tactics. This was a relatively small-scale investment, and no such concerns were expressed when similar and larger investments by European and American firms had been made previously. Furthermore, notwithstanding the 'prohibition of performance requirements' provisions in the New Zealand-China FTA, Pengxin independently agreed to some performance requirements, including that milk products would be processed by a New Zealand-owned company and that New Zealanders would manage and operate the farms. In September 2011, it was reported that the state-run Chinese Development Bank was looking to make a USD 2.4 bn investment in Auckland's inner-city rail loop and second harbour crossing, with a possible expansion into other infrastructure projects across New Zealand. This could be an indication that the investment provisions of China's FTA with New Zealand are making Chinese investors more confident in expanding operations into a wider range of New Zealand markets and sectors, beyond traditional resource sectors.

Peru

Of the three FTA partners under consideration, China's economic relationship with Peru is arguably the most resource-oriented of all. In 2011, over 80% of Peruvian exports to China were concentrated in just four commodity sectors: copper (and copper products), iron, lead and fishmeal. Copper is an essential material in the production of electronic goods. The growth in Sino–Peruvian commodity trade helped China surpass the US by the third quarter of 2011 to become Peru's most important trade partner. A growing number of large-scale Chinese investments in Peru's mining and energy sectors have become the backbone of this rapidly growing trade relationship. To date, Chinese enterprises have invested USD 1.2 bn in Peru's mining operations and they have made pledges to invest a further USD 11 bn in forthcoming years, centring on five key projects:

- Shougang's USD 1.2 bn investment to expand its iron mine operation at Marcona, first established in 1992.
- Chinalco's USD 2.2 bn investment plan to further develop its Toromocho copper and zinc mines.
- China Minmetals and the Zijin Mining Group's USD 1.44 bn investment in the Rio Blanco copper mine.
- Jiangxi Copper's USD 2.5 bn investment to develop the Galeno mine in Cajamarca.
- Nanjinzhao's USD 2.5 bn to develop a new mineral field at Pampa de Pongo.

It has been estimated that Chinese firms will account for around a quarter of all anticipated domestic and international investments in Peru's mining sector over forthcoming years. However, notwithstanding ambitious plans to further deepen China's investment relationship with Peru, Chinese firms have been confronted with local unrest arising from labour strikes, community relocations and conflicts with illegal drug producers. This unrest has, on occasion, led to violence. While not facing the same scale of security concern as in Pakistan, Chinese investors have been mindful to take measures to protect their investments, working with the Peruvian government. The inclusion of special security-related clauses in the investment chapter of the China–Peru FTA reflects these concerns, and provides the legal basis for taking such measures. Similarly to the New Zealand FTA, there is a provision on 'Fair and Equitable Treatment, Full Protection and Security', and additionally, exclusive to the China–Peru FTA, a provision on 'Essential Security' that may be broadly interpreted to protect the essential security interests of investors in accordance with UN norms. The substantive dispute settlement mechanism embodied in the agreement also gives Chinese firms recourse to compensation where their investment interests are not being sufficiently protected in accordance to Peru's FTA commitments.

Conclusions

China has become one of the world's most active FTA protagonists. It is also now a major overseas investor, a role driven primarily by the resource demands of

China's burgeoning economy. The investment rights provisions in many of its more recent FTAs reflect China's changing investment interests, from an almost exclusive concern with attracting inflows of FDI to now protecting the outward FDI of Chinese enterprises. We have explored the relationship between investment provisions in China's newer FTAs and its overseas investment interests in general terms and also in relation to case studies on three FTA partners — Pakistan, New Zealand and Peru. While the Chinese government is currently in FTA negotiations with more important resource-exporting trade partners, these talks have made little progress of late, and it is unclear whether they will ultimately succeed.

Securing FTAs with strong investment provisions protecting Chinese investments may prove more difficult where the trade partners concerned have strong investment interests in China, and will therefore push for full reciprocity. Taking the ongoing FTA talks with Australia as an illustration, the Chinese government is unlikely to give Australian firms the same investment rights in China's domestic mining industry (currently off-limits to foreign investors) as Beijing itself seeks to secure for Chinese enterprises in Australia. Likewise, China is finding FTA negotiations with the GCC on investment rights difficult, as many resource sectors are state-owned or state-controlled. Some GCC countries are also nervous about China's growing financial power. Thus, while FTAs have become an important mechanism by which China protects its overseas investments, it remains unclear how significant FTAs will be in future, when China will have to negotiate with larger and more powerful trade partners.

Bond Issuance by Local Authorities in China
(February 2012)

Vanessa Rossi

Independent Consultant

Executive Summary

China's fiscal and monetary expansion, heavily used to promote growth in 2009–2010, has had important repercussions on government finances, particularly for local authorities that were at the forefront of the surge in expenditure. Local government deficit spending, largely hidden at the time, appears to have accumulated to at least RMB 10.7 tn (EUR 1.3 tn) between 2009 and 2010. This was only made possible through substantial financial support in the form of both bank loans, and covert 'irregular borrowing' (borrowing through investment vehicles set up to bypass the Budget Law enacted in 1994, which forbade local authorities from running deficits and issuing debt).

Borrowing through investment vehicles has not only obscured the scale of local government debt but also fuelled (perhaps exaggerated) concerns over hidden risks. The possibility of a slump in the property market has only exacerbated these concerns and fear of instability. Property has provided key collateral for loans and local government revenues have been boosted by land sales. Land sales now appear to have come to a standstill in those regions worst affected by the cooling of the real estate sector.

Although central government debt remained steady at about 17% of GDP from 2008 to 2011, incorporating the recent surge in local authority borrowing into official statistics probably implies that total government debt of all forms has more than doubled, reaching 45–50% of GDP at the end of 2011. While China is clearly a long way from crisis levels of debt, such a rapid swing in public sector finances, amid revelations of unexpectedly high debts and irregularities in local authority borrowing, and in the context of current international financial conditions, has served to alarm many observers. This may even threaten China's sovereign debt rating.

However, these financial problems are being addressed. For instance:

- Local authorities acted to combat irregularities and reduce debts during 2011. Moreover, borrowing may have been exaggerated in certain cases by misinterpretation of financial accounts;
- Some banks have extended loan repayment dates, and the central government has cracked down on loans for new projects;
- Key authorities were given permission in a pilot project in autumn 2011 to raise funds through bond issues guaranteed by the central government. By the end of 2011, RMB 22.9 bn (EUR 2.8 bn) appeared to have been raised by four regional governments at yields of 3–3.5% (a rate in line with central government bonds but around half the rate on bank debt); and
- With spending constraints in place, coupled with new avenues of funding, local government finances should begin to decouple from the property market. This should bring spending more closely into line with non-property related revenues and funds.

The landmark decision by the central government to allow local authority bond issuance represents an important break with the 1994 Budget Law. It shows the central government recognised both the heavy financial burden on local authorities, and the need to limit financing of debt through costly short-term loans. If this pilot project is expanded, then the growing government debt market may have further important implications for China's position in the global financial system.

The effects of the issuance of bonds by local authorities may include:

- The opportunity for local authorities to reduce interest costs on debts incurred during 2009–2010, and delay repayment for at least the duration of the bonds (typically three–five years). This would relieve payment pressures despite more sluggish growth in the economy and government revenues.
- An improvement in transparency regarding local authorities' financial dealings and debt levels. This would bolster market confidence.

Introduction: The Rise in Local Authority Debt

In response to the global financial crisis, China embarked on a rapid expansion in government spending accompanied by an equally significant relaxation in bank lending. China's fiscal package, initially intended to comprise 13–14% of GDP over 2009–2010, was accompanied by a rise in total bank loans from RMB 30 tn at the end of 2008 to RMB 55 tn by the end of 2011. In 2009 alone, bank lending grew by more than 30%.

Of the three-year increase of almost RMB 30 tn in lending, one-third to one-half was lent to local government investment vehicles, implying that the two-year fiscal stimulus started in 2009 was roughly double that initially intended, or more if additional local authority land sales are included. The true consolidated budget deficit for China was thus not the modest 1–2% reported for the last three years. It reached over 12% of GDP in 2009, and only fell to about 3.5% in 2011 thanks to strong economic growth. In spite of the present brake on spending, the government may find it hard to cut the total 2012 deficit below 2% (not alarmingly high but still about double previous estimates for the deficit).

This effort did successfully raise GDP growth rates from around 6 to 6.5% in late 2008 and the first quarter of 2009, to between 9 and 12% from mid-2009 to the end of 2011. Domestic demand rose sharply and the gains generated more than offset large losses in exports during the global recession. However, growth peaked in the first quarter of 2010, when GDP growth over the previous 12 months reached an average of 12.1%. Growth rates have since fallen, with GDP up by just 8.9% in the last quarter of 2011 and 7.8% for 2012 as a whole.

While the stimulus was successful in raising both the pace of growth and global confidence, the scale of China's expansionary policies was arguably larger than required to offset the risk of recession and achieve non-inflationary growth rates of 8.5–9% in 2009–2010. A much smaller stimulus could have sufficed. In fact, the substantial surge in growth arguably overheated the Chinese economy, while extremely rapid loan growth brought fears that the boom would transform into a flood of high-risk debt and defaults. Concerns about escalating debt levels heightened in 2011 as the clampdown on bank lending restricted borrowers' potential to top-up loans as a means of masking repayment problems. The sharp slowdown in global trade and in the Chinese economy in late 2011, combined with rapid cooling in China's property and construction sectors, only added to these fears.

While property developers, companies with extended borrowing and the banking sector have been key areas of concern, local authorities were also exposed to rising risks. Speculation over the scale of local government borrowing began to emerge in the international press in 2011, and some details were officially released by China's Audit Office during the second half of 2011. In particular, it was confirmed that outstanding borrowing by local authorities had surged to RMB 10.7 tn at the end of 2010, with irregular debts assessed at RMB 531 bn. Yet private analysts (in particular Moody's) continued to suggest that a further RMB 3–4 tn rise in local government debt was likely. By early January of 2012, the audit office announced that around half the irregular debts had been cleared during the course of 2011. Nonetheless, the worrisome revelations of the scale of local authority debt had already served to turn the spotlight on the threat posed by such borrowings, both in terms of potential repayment difficulties and a possible escalation in central government debt.

This crisis also highlighted divisions between local and central government policy priorities, revenue sharing and access to funding. Excluding operations undertaken via investment vehicles, funding for local government expenditure has derived largely from tax revenues and from land sales (the latter equivalent to around 40% of total spending). Now land sales look set to provide a much lower contribution.

Tensions Between Local Authorities and the Central Government

There is clearly a widening divergence between the policy goals of local authorities — the promotion of economic activity, large-scale projects and regional development — and those of the central government. The central government, having initially encouraged a spending surge, has become increasingly concerned about over-investment, the build-up of excess capacity and hidden debt risks. The central government started to direct banks not to permit lending to local authorities or their non-commercial investment vehicles for new infrastructure projects (with some exceptions including the new national priority of affordable housing). It also reined in the property sector, further restraining local government funds and development plans. These constraints are putting a brake not only on investment and GDP growth rates but also on local government autonomy.

In turn, local authorities are concerned at their low tax retention rates, the rising cost of social policies for which they shoulder the financial burden, and the constraints on investment imposed by the central government. Since the mid-1980s, when local authority and central government spending were roughly equivalent in scale, local authority spending has risen at a far faster pace — by 2000, it was more-or-less double that of central government, and today it is about four-times greater. Roughly one-third of reported budget expenditure is on education, social safety nets, pensions and medical costs. Yet the revenues at the disposal of local authorities remain at a similar level to those of the central government. Thus, the central government's relatively lower spending levels have left it with small budget deficits, but for local authorities, the gap between spending and revenues has had to be met largely by land sales (amounting to as much as 40% of the overall budget), which could prove unsustainable in the future especially if the property sector slumps.

Another issue typically raised by local authority leaders both historically and more recently (in the context of their deficit spending), is the amount of tax revenues paid over to the central government. Local authorities see their low retention rates as unfair, and a major reason for them having to find alternative funding (and thus becoming reliant on land sales). The central government's major source of revenue (over 50%) is the return of VAT and consumer tax receipts, with local authorities pocketing only about 20% of these revenues. In contrast, local governments keep about 75% of business and corporate taxes. Income taxes are more equally divided but typically account for less than 10% of total government revenues: roughly 30% of government revenues come from business and corporate taxes, and almost 40% from VAT and consumer taxes.

Rising revenues and limited responsibility for expenditure other than defence (about a third of the reported central government budget) have enabled China's central government to maintain low deficits and a very modest level of debt, with total official borrowing reported to be in the range 16–18% of GDP (currently about RMB 7–8 bn). And very little of this debt is borrowed abroad (less than 1%), while the central bank now holds external wealth of 3.2 tn US dollars in the form of foreign exchange reserves.

Many analysts note the potential for central government debt to approximately double if the central authorities have to absorb all debts built up by local authorities over the last three years and take responsibility for some deficit spending, especially if property markets and therefore land sales remain weak.

Combining official figures for local authorities' outstanding debt (quoted at RMB 10.7 tn at the end of 2010) together with estimates of additional hidden borrowing (possibly worth an additional RMB 3–4 tn) and the central government's outstanding debt of RMB 7–8 tn implies that total government borrowing may be as high as RMB 20–25 tn, that is, about 45–50% of GDP. And ongoing budget deficits could be 2–3% of GDP rather than the 1–2% previously expected.

However, if the central government were to effectively guarantee all local authority borrowing, the possible risk of official bank bailouts would probably be ruled out, eliminating this second perceived threat to government finances. Overall government debt would still remain manageable, especially in light of relatively high economic growth rates.

Although concern over a debt disaster in China looks exaggerated, the debt scare could imply that sharp curbs on government borrowing (especially the crackdown on local government project financing) will remain in force. If these persist in the longer term, they may lead to a permanent slowdown in both the rate of investment and GDP growth. Thus a shift towards more restrictive fiscal policy and lower long-run growth projections — rather than a debt crisis — may be the most likely downside scenario to emerge from the local authority debt scare.

China's Savings Structure and its Implications for Bond Issues

China's bank deposits are massive, reaching around RMB 81 tn (RMB 83 bn including foreign currency deposits) at the end of 2011, almost double GDP (RMB 47 tn in 2011). These deposits are still rising strongly at just under 15% per annum. Other financial assets include bonds (less than 20% of GDP) and equities (with the stock market capitalisation[40] displaying considerable volatility, varying from the current, unusually low, valuation of around 50% of GDP, to a more normal 100% of GDP during past peaks). With low foreign participation, most of these assets, worth in total about two-and-a-half times GDP, are held by Chinese investors.

Official external wealth, largely held by the central bank in the form of US, European and other government bonds, reached USD 3.2 tn at the end of 2011. Private external wealth is likely to be higher than officially recognised, thanks to

---

[40] Calculated as the combined valuation of the Shanghai and Shenzen stockmarket capitalisations, as quotes on the stock exchange websites.

Table 1. A comparison of China's financial asset holdings versus a hypothetical schema for the future (estimates in RMB tn).

	Value	Potential value	
	End 2011	2013	2015
RMB bank deposits	81	95	110
Equity market capitalisation	23	45	70
Government bond market	8	15	25
Total financial wealth	112	155	205
Compared with:			
Annual GDP	47	59	73
Financial wealth as a % of GDP	238	263	280

long-term leakages of capital out of the country — the total could well be more than USD 1 tn.

The structure of China's domestic financial system is clearly 'bond-light' (and bank deposit 'heavy') compared with other large markets, where as much as 60–100%[41] of GDP is typically held in government bonds alone. In total, it is common for about 25–30% of financial wealth to be invested in the form of bonds, compared with current holdings in China of less than 10%. Comparison with other economic blocs would suggest that Chinese savers might reasonably hold a lower proportion of financial wealth in bank deposits and as much as 50–60% of GDP in government bonds. But this can only occur if more government bonds are made available to savers either directly or through investment products such as pension funds and insurance policies.

Table 1 presents a potential scenario for China's asset markets, demonstrating how asset holdings could begin to shift over the next few years to 2015 if the government were to gradually convert local authority debt into government bonds over this period. Such a shift in the structure of wealth is unlikely to happen quickly, but it is important to consider the potential for such a change in China's financial markets and its implications. It is certainly viable to envisage a larger bond share in wealth, although yields could increase slightly (towards 4%, *ceteris paribus*) and new issues would need to be timed carefully to avoid market volatility.

The structure of assets and savings in China, with substantial holdings of highly liquid bank deposits, necessarily affects China's economic and financial stability.

---

[41]Shares have risen during the crisis and Japan's government bond market is now around 200% of GDP.

In the late 1990s, many feared that poorly performing Chinese banks, weighed down by non-performing loans, might suffer from bank runs. However, these failed to materialise as bank deposits were backed by government guarantees and bailouts. This threat remains, and concerns over a possible mobilisation of the large pool of liquid savings may also be an important factor holding back the full opening up of the capital account (thus preventing full exchange rate liberalisation).

If China were to liberalise fully the capital account, however, private savers would be able to freely transfer funds out of the country into foreign investments. Some portfolio diversification would be expected — and considered normal given (officially) low private holdings of wealth abroad. Capital inflows from abroad would likely also rise.

However, large holdings in liquid bank accounts in China could turn a moderate outflow into a flood of money moving overseas — with highly disruptive consequences for both China and recipient countries. These holdings should therefore be better anchored in domestic savings instruments before the capital account is fully opened.

A flood of money from China would only add fuel to the carry trades that have emerged in recent years — which have already been heavily criticised for their (politically and economically) destabilising effects.

From the Threat of a Debt Disaster to New Opportunities in World Markets

So far, most of the public discussion about China's financial trends has focused on the threat posed to China's stability and growth. However, more positive outcomes are possible. For example, the property sector in particular and bad debts in general would become less of a threat if confidence in the growth outlook improves. The currently weak stock market would also see rapid price gains, adding to both positive sentiment and prosperity.

The property market will continue to benefit from rapid urbanisation. While problems undoubtedly remain, the market may be less over-supplied and over-priced on a nationwide basis than some analysis suggests — the number of housing units built each year (7–8 m) remains commensurate with the needs of expanding city populations and replacement requirements.

Official recognition of the status of migrants into urban areas might provide a further boost to the property market (although chiefly at the bottom end of the market) although local governments would incur higher annual social costs.

However, local authorities could obtain loans to develop affordable housing, benefiting the construction sector.

A firm property market would help restore confidence in local authority finances and the viability of development projects. What currently appears as a serious debt risk could quickly become a minor incident in public sector finance. In addition, the move to permit local authorities to issue bonds (guaranteed by the central government) could be turned into a benign shift in China's savings trends and bond market presence. Bond issues could become part of an important restructuring into long-term investments and away from highly liquid bank deposits.

Government bonds bear much lower interest costs than rates on bank loans (6.5% or more), commensurate with the maximum rate on savings deposits (typically less than 3.5%, which is below recent consumer inflation rates of 4–5%). Thus bonds offer benefits both for local authorities doing the borrowing (reducing interest costs) and for private and institutional investors seeking a steady yield on their savings.

Expansion of this new segment of the government bond market compares favourably with the high-risk informal banking sector, both in terms of transparency and regulation. Nevertheless, the informal banking sector appears to have attracted sizeable funding from private investors hungry to earn higher returns but not necessarily appreciating the risks involved.

From the central government's perspective, encouraging households and companies to lock away more of their cash in relatively secure long-term government instruments will help reduce the risk posed by a large pool of liquid savings, both for the domestic financial system and, as capital flows move towards full liberalization, for balance of payments and exchange rate stability.

Is China Moving Towards a Debt Crisis or a Strengthening in its Influence on the Global Financial System?

Sharply conflicting views about the scenarios that might emerge from the present situation in China have been presented. The indicators that might point to which path China is following include:

- Economic growth: will this remain high enough to prevent rising unemployment and a serious property crash? If growth remains below 8%, concerns will certainly increase.

- Property markets: will prices and activity rates stabilise or could there be a collapse amongst those property developers with poor financial backing?
- Revelations of bad debts: are concerns set to wane or may there be a further flow of bad news on hidden debts and non-performing loans?
- Local authority funding: can an expansion of local authority bond issuance succeed in improving debt management, transparency and interest costs without stressing the bond market? Alternatively, if bond issuance stalls, will bank lending restrictions ease enough to avoid local authority bankruptcies?

The next six to twelve months should reveal important trends that will probably dictate the direction of China's economy, finances and policies over the next decade. If bond issuance remains small scale, then the local authority bond market will be merely a minor diversion in the history of China's emerging financial system. However, there is the potential to turn this situation into the beginnings of a major shift towards the development of a larger, more liquid government bond market that would have important, positive, implications for future development of China's financial markets and currency.

The Role of Shadow Banking in Chinese Business
(June 2012)

Sandrine Lunven

Quantitative Economist, Thierry Apoteker Consulting s.a.s

Main Points

- The informal lending market in China has expanded in recent years with tightened credit conditions. However, off-balance-sheet activities are not a new phenomenon in China.
- The size of informal lending is hard to measure but estimates generally provide a range between RMB 2 tn (EUR 0.25 tn) and RMB 18 tn (EUR 2.2 tn) for 2011 (i.e. from 2% to 38% of GDP).
- The expansion of the Chinese shadow banking system is related to financial repression: (1) negative deposit rates have prompted savers to find higher-yield investments outside the formal lending sector; (2) few alternatives are available, residential property being the best option. To fund this, many households and small and medium enterprises (SMEs) had to turn to underground finance; (3) an increase in the reserve requirement ratio has led to large and unsatisfied demand for credit, particularly from households and SMEs.
- Much shadow finance is actually driven by or through the major state banks (bankers' acceptances, letters of credit, designated loans) and some estimates state that 90% of shadow lenders are state-owned. Many of the state-owned enterprises that benefitted from official loans at low rate have also started to engage in the lending business (ChinaMobile, Cofco, PetroChina, BaoSteel, etc.).

- The informal lending market is mostly localised in the eastern provinces of China, particularly in Wenzhou (Zhejiang), Hongzhou (Zhejiang), Nanjing (Jiangsu) and Shenzhen (Guangdong).
- The biggest risk in shadow banking lies with the property market. Estimates show that this sector attracted around 60% of the informal lending market and the government has yet to try and contain speculation in this sector.
- Chinese authorities have already undertaken various regulations to restrain the development of the informal lending market, for instance, by increasing access to the formal lending market for households and small and medium eneterprises (SMEs).

Introduction: The Chinese Financial System

With China's rising economic and financial role at the international level and the success of its economic development, researchers and observers have increasingly focused on understanding the complexity of China's financial system and the way the People's Bank of China (PBoC) conducts its monetary policy.

According to the statutes of the PBoC, the goals of its monetary policy include maintaining the stability of its currency, thereby promoting economic growth. To achieve this objective, a group of intermediate targets has been set. These include the level of aggregate money supply, domestic loan growth, exchange rate stability, and a non-legally formulated target of maintaining profitability of state-owned banks.

Since 2000, the PBoC's record in terms of inflation performance has been rather remarkable. Despite being a country that is officially non-inflation targeting, China is thought to have achieved a substantial fall in inflation persistence since the end of the 1990s. China has also made an effort to maintain relative monetary policy independence, while often quasi-pegging its currency to the dollar, and trying to regulate capital flows in order to get around the well-known Mundell's incompatibility triangle. Basically, this trilemma states that the following three phenomena cannot coexist in a country: fixed currency, autonomous monetary policy and free capital movements.

To achieve its goals, the PBoC has used a large range of monetary instruments, such as regulated interest rates on bank deposits, open market operations, required-reserve ratio (RRR) interest on required and excess reserves, credit quota and 'window guidance' (this term is used to describe central bank pressures on financial institutions to stick to official guidelines). However, the PBoC controls interest rates in a way that has led to significant financial repression. The PBoC does not set interest rates based on the marginal return on capital but fixes them at an articially low level to encourage growth and to prevent 'hot money'.

As defined by Nicholas Lardy,[42] financial repression in China is represented by the low and sometimes negative real return on deposits. Since 2002, various periods of steep negative real deposit rates have been observed. Indeed, the PBoC has been reluctant to increase the deposit rates in line with the pace of inflation for fear of attracting even larger speculative inflows. In addition, the Chinese strategy to keep interest rates low has driven investments thanks to the low cost of capital.

To control the pace of Renminbi appreciation, the government has intervened in the foreign currency market and has very frequently used open market operations (through central bank bill issuance) and reserve requirement ratio to drain liquidity. Both types of sterilisation clearly constrain banks and impose a kind of tax as the interest rate on required reserves and on three-year central bank bills (1.62% and 3% respectively at the end of 2011) is far below the nominal one to three years lending rate (6.65% at the end of 2011). Based on recent academic research, this implicit tax on banks has increased since 2007, particularly in 2008 and 2010. In 2009, the easing monetary policy period, characterised by a loosening in credit quota and a cut in regulated interest rates, explained the slowdown in the implicit tax burden.

So, one consequence of the Chinese strategy to control the pace of the appreciation has been an increase in financial repression, constraining and taxing banks, households and corporates, which has contributed to the expansion in unofficial channels of credit — the so-called shadow banking system (*dixia jinrang*).

The Rapid Expansion of the Chinese Shadow Banking System

There is a lack of consensus defining the exact meaning of the term 'shadow banking'. Referring to the Financial Stability Board's (FSB) definition, the shadow banking system can basically be described as 'credit intermediation involving entities and activities outside the regular banking system'.[43] This term started being

---

[42] N. R. Lardy, 'Financial repression in China', Peterson Institute for International Economics, September 2008.

[43] Financial Stability Board, 'Shadow banking : scoping the issues, a background note of the financial stability board', April 2011.

used widely in the run-up to the recent financial crisis, reflecting an increased recognition of the importance of entities and activities structured outside of the regular banking system. This includes non-depository banks and other financial entities such as investment banks, mutual funds, hedge funds, money market funds and insurers, who typically do not fall under banking regulations. In other words, shadow banking is a term which includes both the off-balance-sheet activities of banks as well as credit created by other companies.

Economists' concern with the expansion of the shadow banking system is not just focused on China. Prior to the 2008–2009 financial crisis, the size of the shadow banking system in the US was estimated to be significantly larger than that of the formal banking sector. Moreover, off-balance-sheet activities are not a new phenomenon in China; companies and individuals have always lent money to each other. However, for the most part, the massive increase seen in this type of activity in recent years has been driven by tightened credit conditions in China (notably due to increasing inflation and the formulating housing bubble).

Basically, three main reasons explain the recent expansion of the shadow banking system in China, all of them related to the rise in financial repression:

- First, China's high level of saving (around 51% of GDP in 2011). Multiple periods of negative real deposit rates have led to a substantial incentive for savers to find higher-yield investments outside the formal banking system.
- Second, regulated lending interest rates at low levels, credit quota and quantitative controls on bank reserves have resulted in a large unsatisfied demand for credit (except in 2009). Basically, banks have prioritised loans to state-owned enterprises (SOEs) leaving households and small and medium enterprises (SMEs) with little access to the formal market, forcing them to turn to the informal lending market.
- Third, there are few investment alternatives for Chinese households and SMEs. Of these alternatives, real assets, such as residential property, are a good option and this has resulted in the rapid acceleration of property prices in urban areas in recent years. To fund these investments, householders and SMEs have had to fall back on underground finance, which is willing to lend well above the benchmark rate.

As a result, Chinese households and SMEs are willing to borrow in the informal market at interest rates at least twice or triple the official one-year lending rate (which was around 6.5% in 2011) rising to as much as 60–70%, according to

Credit Suisse. The lack of transparency and the complexity of monitoring the informal lending market make it difficult to manage.

How Large is China's Informal Lending?

Estimates regarding the size of informal lending in China provide very different results, mostly dependent upon the definition used. The estimates of different sources range from RMB 2 tn (EUR 0.25 tn) to RMB 18 tn (EUR 2.2 tn) in 2011, equivalent to around 8% and 38% of GDP. GaveKal Dragonomics' estimation of RMB 17 tn (EUR 2.1 tn), reveals that informal lending in China may have accounted for over 40% of new credit creation in 2010 and 2011 Q1-Q2, making it a potential challenge for Chinese banking regulation. However, Credit Suisse's reported estimation of around Rmb 4 tn (EUR 0.5 tn) does not cause alarm for China.

Total Social Financing (TSF), a broad central bank measure of liquidity in the economy, reached a peak of RMB 14.3 tn (EUR 1.8 tn) in 2010. However, the concept of social finance is not perfectly analogous to shadow banking. Basically, the indicator includes all the funds raised by entities in China's real economy during a certain period, such as loans of local and foreign currencies, entrusted loans, bank acceptance bills, corporate bonds, equity financing, foreign direct investment and foreign debt.

To go into detail, we take reference from the estimate of GaveKal Dragonomics. In their definition, three main types of credit are considered: (1) loans from financial institutions that are not banks, (2) credit arranged by banks that does not appear on their balance sheets, such as designated or entrusted (i.e. company to company) loans, letters of credit and bankers' acceptances and (3) loans made entirely outside the formal financial system, by private money lenders or individuals. Their estimates show that shadow banking increased by 69% in 2010 and 20% and 2011 H1.

Major Actors of the Shadow Banking System

The list of actors who play a role in informal lending business is quite long: banks, guarantee companies, pawnshops, investment guarantor companies, SOEs, entrepreneurs and individuals.

- Most of China's commercial banks participate in informal lending by offering services that do not fall on their balance sheets. The most important financing

instrument is a bankers' acceptance, a short-term credit instrument created by a non-financial firm and guaranteed by a bank. They usually arise in the course of international trade. Designated loans have also been frequently used in recent years, through which banks arrange loans from one company to another.
- In general, shadow banking lending operations proceed through an intermediary, a guarantor. In most cases, they are companies (often subsidiary companies of SOEs) but they are also sometimes connected with banks. Some estimates state that 90% of the shadow lenders are state-owned. Credit Suisse's estimate suggests that about 60% of lending in the informal market is ultimately funded by banks through various channels (for instance, lending to SOE parent companies), 20% by private entrepreneurs and about 20% by individuals.
- SOEs, which benefit from official loans at low rates, started to engage in lending due to a lack of compelling investment opportunities. Many SOEs have separate financing arms. For instance, in 2011, China Mobile announced the establishment of a finance company to lend out money at higher rates; China Railway Group and China's food giant Cofco have similar lending operations. PetroChina has an asset managemement arm, a trust bank, a commercial bank as well as an internal finance unit.
- Trust companies are an important source of finance outside of the traditional banking system. They serve as a third arm that links financial institutions and wealthy individuals. Basically, trusts purchase loans from banks, take them off the balance sheet and then sell these loans to other financial institutions or private borrowers. Baosteel Group has a 98% stake in Fortune Trust, one of the largest trust firms, while Hunan Valin Iron and Steel Group has a 49% stake in Huachen Trust.

Most of China's commercial banks (including the big four state banks) play a key role in the expansion of shadow finance, accounting for 65–70% of total outstanding credit in 2010 and 2011 through bankers' acceptances, letters of credit and designated loans. Trust loans have also boomed in recent years, even though they still represent just a small share of total credit. Basically, banks move part of their loan portfolios off their books by repackaging them as wealth management products (WMPs), the maturity of which can range from several days to several years. These totalled around RMB 3.8 tn (EUR 0.5 tn) at the end of 2010 according to the China Trustee Association. Private lending represented around 20% of the shadow banking system in 2010–2011.

Challenges for Authorities and Risks for Business

In 2011, growing concern regarding the expansion of shadow banking was in part fed by the debt crisis that hit Wenzhou city in southeastern Zhejiang province (which ranks among the top five cities in China in terms of highest amount of disposable income). Indeed, large debt issues have led to 29 bankrupt businesses in the city and even suicides by entrepreneurs. The blame has fallen on the shadow financing system. Even though the system has existed for a long time, it has grown rapidly, particularly thanks to borrowing by Chinese SMEs. The Wenzhou People's Bank estimates that 90% of families and 60% of businesses are involved in the private lending market, amounting to RMB 110 bn (EUR 14 bn; 38% of its 2010 GDP). The annual interest rates for a private loan could be as high as 100%, almost 15 times China's benchmark lending rates.

Credit Suisse estimates that the size of the informal lending market in 20 major Chinese cities equals around RMB 2.8 tn (EUR 0.35 tn). Among these cities, the informal market is most developed in the east China region (Jiangsu, Zhejiang and Fujian). More precisely, Nanjing, Hangzhou and Wenzhou are the cities with the biggest informal lending market, representing 39%, 43% and 38% of GDP respectively. Shenzhen (Guangdong province) is also a city with a very developed shadow banking system, representing 35% of GDP in 2010 and 20% of loans.

What are the Major Potential Risks?

- A property market correction presents the first risk. The real estate market has been the best destination for money loaned from the informal system (accounting for around 60% of informal lending). However, worries about price expectation grew as the government tried to contain speculation. If property prices fall sharply, private property companies will be most exposed although SOEs will also be affected.
- A potential liquidity shortage would represent a risk for deposit-taking institutions, particularly if shadow banking continues to develop and attract savers.
- A potential economic slowdown coupled with inflationary pressures could reduce expected investment yields and could deteriorate credit quality.

The development of shadow banking in China could represent a serious challenge for banking regulation. To discourage the development of the shadow banking system, the PBoC and the China Banking Regulatory Commission (CBRC) undertook various regulations in 2011, such as requiring banks to move certain off-balance-sheet assets back to their books by year end 2011.

In May 2011, the CBRC issued a guideline to instruct Chinese banks to boost their credit to small business operators and to tolerate a higher ratio of bad loans (a term generally used to describe unsecured loans) relating to SMEs. To address the credit crisis in Wenzhou city, the government imposed an upper limit on the interest rates that private non-bank lenders can charge borrowers. Under this special administrative measure, private non-bank institutions can only offer loans if the rate of interest does not exceed four times the benchmark lending rate. Premier Wen Jiabao has urged Chinese banks to provide preferential financial credits to support SMEs by reducing lending costs and eliminating unnecessary fees.

Conclusion

Many economists argue that the development of underground finance could force the Chinese government towards monetary policy normalisation and further interest rate liberalisation, especially on the deposit side, where rates are currently subject to a cap. If this takes place, it could be a signal of significant risks to come. In many countries, interest rate liberalisation has been followed by a banking crisis a few years later — a point the IMF made in its recent assessment of China's financial sector.

It is worth noting that the shadow banking phenomenon is not a new phenomenon in China — companies have always lent money to each other and this has contributed to the dynamic economic growth seen in several provinces in the few past years. However, the debt crisis in Wenzhou city (one of the richest cities in China) and the large increase in the size of the informal lending market has increased concern. All agents, banks, SOEs and SMEs, play an important role in the informal lending market but any instability and potential risks would mostly affect SMEs, which are highly dependent on this kind of financing. Bearing this in mind, a European business investment strategy would be more secure focusing on SOEs, which already have access to the formal market.

However, following the debt crisis that hit Wenzhou city, the PBoC and the CBRC have undertaken various regulations to promote increasing support for SMEs. This switch should allow for a more healthy and fair financing system. In addition, a decrease in systemic banking risks in China would reduce the potential global impact on European business in terms of their trade and investments in China.

Family Businesses in China
(September 2011)

Anonymous

Executive Summary

Family businesses in China are hard to distinguish from 'privately owned enterprises'. The exact size of the family businesses sector is thus unknown but holds a vast pool of capital in private hands, despite being largely restricted to the economy's less regulated sectors. Beijing has introduced a number of reforms to try and encourage the private sector in recent years but its impact has so far been limited. While Beijing wants to encourage a larger role for private equity, it must also protect the interests of the Chinese Communist Party's (CCP) 'commercial face', the state-owned enterprises (SOEs).

Main Points

- China has a vast surplus pool of capital in private hands which cannot leave the country and yet cannot be invested in most sectors of the economy which remain dominated by SOEs.
- On the mainland, Chinese family businesses have never regained the status they enjoyed prior to 1947, when the Kuomintang began nationalising most industries. Most feel they never will, as long as the CCP remains in power. Wealthy families remain extremely nervous and feel that they are vulnerable targets for the CCP or corrupt local officials. Many worry that they will be accused of making their money illegally or avoiding taxes.

- The central government hopes to redirect investment away from the overheated property sector by opening up more sectors to private enterprise. However, few feel that it will succeed.
- In the countryside, central government wants to reform banking and make credit more available to rural entrepreneurs. In the hi-tech sectors, Beijing has announced policies such as the '36 clauses' for the non-state economy, to support private enterprise in certain favoured sectors.

Introduction: What is China's Private Sector?

There is no agreed definition of China's private sector and, in practice, it is hard to separate 'privately owned enterprises' from 'family businesses'. Some claim that the private sector accounts for 70% of GDP and 160 m jobs. According to the All-China Federation of Industry and Commerce, private companies now account for 74% of China's enterprises. The total registered funds of the private sector reached RMB 19 tn by the end of 2010, with an average growth rate of 20.1% year-on-year and an accumulated growth rate of more than 150% over the past five years.

Other commentators have argued that the private sector is actually half that size, employs 60 m, and is both starved of capital and excluded from the most important economic sectors by SOEs, whose power has been inflated by the post-2008 stimulus program. At present, the private sector only plays a role in 41 of 80 domestic industries, while foreign capital has investment in 62 sectors. The top 500 national strong companies are SOEs.

The private sector accounts for only about 40 of the 1,600 Chinese companies listed on the domestic and overseas stockmarkets and their combined market capitalisation is less than 3% of the total. Further, less than 10% of credit goes to private enterprises which pay much higher interest rates than SOEs.

- A recent report by Bain Capital put the number of rich Chinese with assets of over RMB 10 m at 320,000 in 2009. Another report said China has 60,000 people with a personal wealth exceeding RMB 100 m.
- Bain says the total value of investable assets held by individuals in China in 2008 equaled RMB 38 tn. It said over half of China's wealthy are clustered in Guangdong, Shanghai, Beijing, Jiangsu and Zhejiang. In order to spread their

risk, nearly 80% of Chinese high net worth individuals (HNWIs) would like to further diversify their investment portfolios. At present, Hong Kong is the major destination for Chinese HNWIs' offshore investments.
- Unlike other offshore markets, more than half of the capital in Hong Kong is used for investing in local assets like Hong Kong stocks, property and insurance.
- Many of China's wealthy also travel in organised buyers' tours to invest in property in Vancouver, Singapore, California and other parts of America.

A Brief History of the Role of Family Businesses in China

In Republican China (1911–1948) family-owned businesses created and owned China's largest commercial enterprises. Family-run companies like the Wuxi-based Rong (or Yung family) sprang up with dominating roles in textiles, shipping, banking, insurance, milling, property, railroads and retail sectors. Many businessmen started off as compradors for foreign companies but were considered patriotic because they competed successfully against foreigners — above all, the Japanese, who dominated the textile industry (then the region's most important industrial and export sector). The Chinese industrialists benefitted from numerous nationwide boycotts of foreign goods. In the 'golden era of the Chinese bourgeoisie', they were independent, self-regulating and widely admired. By comparison, SOEs like coalmines, railways, cotton mills or shipping lines performed poorly.

After 1945, the Kuomintang (KMT) began to nationalise the private sector and to appropriate their gold and foreign currency savings. Even before the Communist takeover in 1949, many family businesses had fled, settling in Hong Kong, Taiwan, North America and South America. Hong Kong owes almost all of its prosperity to the influx of Shanghai money and entrepreneurs after 1949 and much the same can be said for Taiwan. From Hong Kong, the Shanghainese expanded around the region establishing factories in export processing zones — setting up first in Taiwan, then in countries all over the region, and finally in Africa, the Caribbean and Central America. They exploited the textile quota system, the absence of trade unions and taxes in these enterprise zones, and from cooperation with Japanese firms who were forced to go abroad to escape the strong Yen and quota restrictions.

Members of the old Shanghai capitalist families who stayed behind were persecuted and then slowly rehabilitated after 1979. Rong Yiren of the Yung family once again became the richest private individual in China (and Vice President after 1979). Deng Xiaoping brought back former Shanghai capitalists and gave them leading roles in newly established hybrid ventures like CITIC or Everbright in which the children of top Party officials and Shanghai capitalists were given leading roles.

Although few Shanghainese ended up in Southeast Asia, many poor Chinese emigrated there in 1911–1948 from Guangdong, Fujian and Zhejiang provinces. They would often undertake menial work such as tapping rubber trees on plantations in Malaysia. The descendants of those who did well are known today as the 'coolie billionaires'. These overseas Chinese dominate the economies of countries like Thailand and Indonesia.

As a consequence, a strong entrepreneurial tradition took root in the Yangtze Delta region, especially in towns like Wuxi, Shanghai, Nantong, Ningbo, plus former treaty ports like Wenzhou, from which many emigrants went abroad in search of work. Families established factories making garments, buttons, jewellery, small plastic toys, etc. They set up private banks and lent money to each other or borrowed from relatives living abroad. In the Mao era from 1949 to 1976, 'capitalist' provinces like Jiangsu, Zhejiang, Fujian, Guangdong were deprived of state investment but after 1980 they quickly prospered despite recurrent political campaigns against capitalists that lasted until 1995. These are now the richest areas in gross terms and per capita in China.

Generally speaking, most experts who talk about China's private sector mean these 'Wenzhou'-style entrepreneurs. Although they have a passing resemblance to the Shanghai capitalists of the Republican era, there are profound differences. The Shanghai capitalists who flourished from 1900–1949 were major league industrialists dominating key sectors with access to capital from major banks, who incorporated their firms and listed them on the Shanghai stock market, then the largest in Asia. The larger enterprises had branches or outlets around the country and created famous brands. In contrast, the Wenzhou entrepreneurs are excluded from the stock market and ignored by state banks. Although they are very wealthy, they cannot enter the 'commanding heights' of the economy which the Party reserves for itself.

Many of the Wenzhou entrepreneurs became involved in the textile industry. As they expanded, they employed millions of temporary migrant workers from the interior because this meant that they did not have to pay the same social and pension charges as the state-owned textile and garment factories that folded in the 1990s.

These family-run businesses remain under the thumb of the Party. This is largely because industrialised countries missed a vital opportunity to strengthen the independence of the private sector when the international trade in textiles was regulated by the Multi-Fibre Agreements. Instead of allocating import quota licenses directly to 'private-owned' factories, the US and the EU delegated that power to Chinese government industry organisations. The Party wielded the whip over these family companies by issuing export quotas and export tax rebates.

The Party used this power to rebuild the state-owned textile sector, move it out of Shanghai and other old industry centres, re-equip new modern factories with modern machinery, and discard all of the old pension liabilities that came with older enterprises. China now has the world's largest textile industry which controls more than half the world's textile trade. This industry is once again dominated by massive state-run enterprise subsidised by low cost bank loans from state banks.

In the last 15 years, the private sector has been squeezed out of textiles and has had to concentrate on the low-capital intensive garment sector, which employs around 4 m of the 20 m employed in textiles. With the abolition of quotas, the margins in this sector have dropped considerably from around 20% to just 2 or 3%. Rising labour costs, and higher commodity prices are forcing the garment businesses to relocate to the interior, or to Vietnam, Cambodia or Bangladesh. Many have closed down.

Many of these 'Wenzhou'-style businesses have expanded into other sectors but in general they have invested their capital to speculate in commodities, shares and, above all, in property. Since China privatised property after 1998, many of these individuals have made larger profits from property than from manufacturing and building up national service businesses — the property boom has seen property price rises of 300–600%. Many are very keen to invest their capital abroad but are deterred by capital controls.

Peasant Entrepreneurs

When calculating the size of the private sector, some estimates include peasants, i.e. anyone living off the proceeds of farming a small plot, growing staples or cash crops. After 1979, these individuals were allowed to start small enterprises selling agricultural 'side products' like fish, eggs or fruit in markets. Many peasants also opened small businesses such as restaurants, repair shops, building companies and other enterprises. This was allowed provided there were not more than ten workers. In the 1980s, many became quite rich and ploughed their capital into building new houses providing a boost to the construction sector. In the last 20 years, peasant incomes have stagnated, partly because they were not given land tenure and could not mortgage or sell their land, nor could they obtain operating capital from the rural banking sector. This is now being addressed by the government, which is beginning to give tenure to peasants in some places and is destined to become the norm in China.

In practice, many families in rural China will have members working the land, working in local enterprises or running a market stall, or working in the cities as a migrant worker.

Rural Enterprises

Xiangzhen Qiye or TVEs (township and village enterprises) are rural enterprises that were set up by officials in villages, small towns, counties and former people's commune administrations. Some of them started off in the 1970s when they secretly undertook work for SOEs in Shanghai. Most were financed by rural credit banks or cooperatives. They constitute the largest group of small and medium-sized enterprises in the country. Some of them are factories which went bankrupt under state management and were sold off. Many are now substantial enterprises which are involved in every sector from mining to steel-making or even aeronautics. For example, half of China's coal is produced by mines outside the planned state sector. The state has tried to close all of these down by merging them with half a dozen big coal mining enterprises, but high prices have meant that the private or collective coal mines are still running. Many Wenzhou businessmen have invested in these.

Another group of enterprises in the private sector sprang up in the 1990s when the state-sector was down-sized and many subsidiary enterprises owned by SOEs — shops, kindergartens, car fleets, hotels, orchestras, etc. — were privatised. State workers were therefore often suddenly transferred from the state to the private sector. In addition, all bureaucracies — even the ministry of foreign affairs and the People's Liberation Army — had also to set up private enterprises to absorb the large numbers of laid-off pen-pushers and demobilised soldiers.

In general, statistics on these SOEs are obscure or misleading. Some of these enterprises are truly privately owned and managed but more are controlled by local Party committees or relatives of Party officials.

Private Equity

There is now a large group of valuable hi-tech firms set up by professors and returning students in new sectors of the economy often to do with software, online sales, mobile telephones and the like. The private equity industry is now flourishing in China — some claim it is one of the largest in the world. Many of these like Baidu, Alibaba, or Tencent, have listed abroad. Out of the 500 start-ups listed abroad almost all have listed in America and few in Europe.

The National Development and Reform Commission got the ball rolling in 2006 and 2007 by approving the formation of ten industrial private equity (PE) funds. But after the government unleashed the stimulus package in late 2008, funds took off by tapping the abundant supply of stimulus cash sitting in the accounts of SOEs and local governments. The nation's 105 RMB-based PE funds raised nearly RMB 86 bn in 2010. Some of these have listed start-ups on China's NASDAQ called ChiNext. In the last two years, the average PE investment stock price has risen to more than 15 times the price–earnings ratio.

New Government Policies

As the stimulus program wound down in 2010, the government hoped that the private sector would take the lead in creating jobs and redirect capital away from the overheated property section.

The May 2010 'Measures for Encouraging and Guiding the Healthy Development of Private Investment' better known as the '36 clauses for the non-state-owned economy' promised to open up more sectors of the economy to private investment, including banking, education and public services.

An official from the National Reform and Development Commission claimed the 'new 36 clauses' represent the State Council's 'first comprehensive policy document aimed at the development, management and regulation of private investment' since 1979. But all the observers interviewed for this paper thought the policy would be so difficult to enforce that it would have little impact — at best, these individuals believed its effect would only be gradually felt over the next decade.

'The policy will be so difficult to enforce that I am afraid it will only exist on paper,' said one interviewee. 'State-owned companies dominate industries like telecommunications, railways and finance. It is doubtful that new private companies can compete. It remains to be seen how many barriers to private capital they remove. It is a real test of the government's commitment to reform.'

The state released the first version of these 36 clauses five years ago. However they did little to strengthen the development of the private sector. On the contrary, SOEs have actually strengthened their grip over the economy and have been encouraged to push private investors out of many sectors like coal, oil, steel, aviation, etc. Their access to the lion's share of multi-trillion dollar lending has even enabled them to take over the real estate industry which hither to was one domain where private investment thrived.

Between 2005 and December 2008, the State Council added four supplementary documents to the original '36 clauses'. In addition, central ministries and commissions tacked on 38 documents, and every province and city around the country also added their own — too many to be counted. Some measures, even those tightly bound to government interests, failed to eliminate systematic barriers to the development of the private economy.

The latest version of the 36 clauses covers six sectors and 18 industries. Detailed measures and supplements are expected to follow. The sectors listed are communications, telecommunications, energy, basic infrastructure, municipal public services, industrial science and technology of national defence, low cost housing construction (supported by the government), financial institutions, logistics, cultural, education and sports development, media and social welfare, and so on.

Beijing certainly wants private equity to play a bigger role but it also wants to continue protecting the interests of the SOEs which are more or less the commercial face of the CCP. This has led to conflicting opinions. For example, in the oil sector, soon after the policy was announced, The *Shanghai Securities News* quoted Zhao Youshan, President of Petroleum Circulation Commission of China Commerce Federation, saying that 'some of the biggest private run petroleum related enterprises immediately began researching how to exploit the "New 36 Clauses" to take part in the oil exploration. Six private firms have for the first time been given the green light to take part in building the strategic oil reserve by relevant government authorities. And that was the direct result of implementing the "New 36 clauses".'

But in the same paper Chen Shunsui, President of Guangdong Provincial Petroleum Industrial Association admitted that 'it would be difficult for the private investment to take part in the oil and gas exploration work in the near future[...]

There is almost no room left for the private sector in this sector.' Guo Haitao, a researcher at the China Strategic Energy Research Centre said that 'the policy allows private funds to invest in oil and gas exploration in theory, but in practice, it is still a question mark on whether that could be realised.'

Private Banking

Encouraging private investment in listed banks and rural financial institutions is part of a new State Council initiative to support private enterprise in the countryside since 2005. Among other things, it permits injections of private capital to establish financial institutions and encourages private investment in township and village banks, leasing companies and rural credit cooperatives. The government has also vowed to loosen limits on private investment in other financial institutions. Local loan companies, for example, now have a chance to restructure and rise to the level of full-blown financial institutions. But some analysts have warned that, if bank start-up and supervision requirements do not change, much of the financial sector will still be off-limits to private capital.

The 2005 policy made private involvement possible in regional joint-stock banks and credit cooperatives. And private enterprises that met certain conditions were allowed to offer intermediary financial services. According to the All-China Federation of Industry and Commerce (ACFIC), private investment accounted for only 9.6% of the sector's investments in 2008. Small and medium-sized companies cannot obtain loans because there are so few private banks. Restrictions on sponsors for establishing banks and inadequate regulatory enforcement at local levels are still the main barrier restricting private inroads in the financial industry. However the latest guidelines stress, for the first time, that 'no explicit ban means access', while listing six major areas for private investment, including financial institutions.

The China Banking Regulatory Commission (CBRC) began promoting rural banks and other types of new rural financial institutions in 2006 but approved only 172 new rural financial institutions between March 2007 and the end of 2009. CBRC followed up last year with a plan called the Overall Work Arrangement for New Rural Financial Institutions for 2009–2011, which called to set up 1,294 new rural financial institutions nationwide within three years. These were to include 1,027 town and village banks, 106 credit companies and 161 rural fund cooperatives. Of the 382 institutions scheduled to open during the first year, only 50 got off the ground.

Last year, the CBRC also released Temporary Guidelines for Small Loan Companies Restructuring into Rural Banks, which said small loan firms could become rural banks. But it stipulated that a commercial bank must be the majority or sole shareholder. In addition, eligible firms had to be debt-free, more than three years old, and have sustained profitability for two previous fiscal years. The State Council also loosened a requirement that says a major shareholder in rural banks must come from institutions in the banking sector. Currently, the largest shareholder in village banks must be a bank with at least a 20% stake. The 20% requirement may be lowered to 10% soon in one province, Inner Mongolia. In practice this has meant that only banks could be the founders or major shareholders at a new rural bank. Private capital could only be a minority shareholder, at best.

Conclusions

- Although China now has a very mixed economy, similar to those in established market economies, its private sector is marked by certain features. Most of the sector consists of family-owned businesses that have gravitated towards less regulated sectors, such as property and services. It tends to be concentrated either in the quasi-illegal low-cost end of the spectrum, or the very new hi-tech sectors at the other end.
- These firms invariably employ migrant workers from the countryside and try to escape the costly and burdensome employment regulations and taxes increasingly imposed on urban workers in foreign or state-run sectors. They also often flourish by avoiding intellectual property rights payments, flaunting environmental laws, child labour laws, planning laws etc. This means they rarely invest in brands or develop their own manufacturing or marketing know-how.
- Even so many of the private enterprises are very different from what they were 30 or 20 years ago. They are increasingly well run and managed by better-educated managers who employ a workforce with expectations different from the earlier generation.
- The efforts by the private sector to invest in aviation, oil, coal, banking, textiles etc. have been thwarted by determined opposition of the state sector. Despite the government's new policies to encourage private investment, many family businesses are skeptical and they doubt they will ever be allowed to prosper in China.

- Many businesses operating in China are increasingly geared towards the domestic consumer market and building up transnational outlets, rather than focused on exports as in the past. Here, however, they are at a disadvantage from the larger state-sponsored enterprises or foreign-managed ventures that are quickly creating nationwide giant retailing or beverage and food chains which now compete successfully against family-run restaurants and shops.

Where does China Stand in the Eurobond Debate?
(October 2011)

Vanessa Rossi

Independent Consultant

Executive Summary

China, along with many other observers, has stressed the need for the eurozone to propose, and fully commit to, a clear solution for the debt crisis and recapitalisation of vulnerable banks. Without this, there will be considerable reluctance on the part of China — or, indeed, any foreign investor — to participate in fundraising exercises for bailout countries or for those states whose bond markets have come under pressure.

To be successful in encouraging foreign investor participation, at the lowest possible yields, any vehicles used for fundraising must meet external criteria, including:

- Transparent and readily understood guarantees. Even complexity regarding the planned 2013–2014 changeover from the European Financial Stability Facility (EFSF) to a permanent European Stabilisation Mechanism (ESM) may sow doubts about long-term valuations of investments and raise the risk premium.
- A choice of structure and duration that meets investor preferences — for example, Asian investors tend to use short-term bond issues (three-year maturity or less). This may imply seeking a wide range of advice (for example, from Asia-based financial experts) on how to best target certain investor groups.
- A feasible timetable and scale of bond issuance that will suit the most important external investors.

- Sensitivity analysis. This could help improve terms and conditions, as the guarantee levels provided could be eased without significantly raising the interest rate offered to investors.

Introduction: Perceptions of the Background to the Crisis and the Risks Created by Small Fragmented Markets

The eurozone has suffered severe reputational damage, firstly from the eruption of the periphery debt crisis, and secondly from the continued high level of uncertainty regarding how the crisis will end. Rightly or wrongly, most foreign observers see this as a complicated internal debate within the eurozone in which they cannot, and do not wish to, play a role. However, external investors are willing to consider injecting funds on a normal commercial basis — that is, by assessing any issues offered to the market according to their own cash flow positions, the perceived risk profiles of the investment vehicles offered, and in comparison with the alternative investments available.

So far, the damage has not reached the German Bund market, but it has notably raised the premium on France's debt (and threatened the government's AAA credit rating). The fallout has certainly reached Italy and Spain — despite the fact that these states are yet to request bailout programmes, and despite their efforts to contain fiscal risks.

For Asian fund managers, and other potential investors, the periphery debt crisis has been especially confusing and tiresome as it has required greater information-gathering and analysis of the indebted small economies, which hold little intrinsic interest. This also highlights the inefficiency of raising funds through such small markets, even in periods of robust economic growth.

In the years immediately prior to the global financial crisis, the prevailing assumption was that eurozone bond yields could, and should, converge more closely because the most important differential risks had been eliminated by currency union, and the possibility of debt crises and defaults was virtually ruled out. Yet, even in this optimistic period, foreign investor participation (from outside of the EU) in the small, periphery markets was low — there was effectively a two-tier market of 'senior' and 'junior' partners (the former including Germany and France, and the latter Portugal and Greece). This was indicated by the relatively large concentration of eurozone bonds that remained within the eurozone banking system, creating a heavy exposure that has reduced confidence in the strength of Europe's banks.

Arguably, if the eurozone's peripheral states had been able to raise money in a consolidated 'eurobond', or 'junior euro' market, this might have marginally reduced the risk premium compared to the large eurozone bond markets. More importantly, however, it would have encouraged participation among a wider range of investors, critically spreading risks that have instead fallen heavily on the eurozone banks and compounded the debt threat. In fact, consolidation of 'senior euro' sovereign debt into a deeper, more liquid single market might also have reduced its risk premium.

Today's Calls for Consolidated Bond Markets

Calls for the creation of a single eurozone sovereign debt market, in part to capture the benefits of a 'large market'-effect and a more diverse investor base, were already active before the sovereign debt crisis broke. However, such calls have escalated in tandem with the crisis. Most proponents see this as a long-term target that would improve the functioning of the eurozone sovereign debt market — to create a true rival to US treasury bonds. Others believe that it should also be considered in the short run, as a possible way out of the crisis.

While a fully unified sovereign debt market would almost certainly be impossible in the near term, requiring as it would a change to the Lisbon Treaty, the EFSF has been interpreted as a precursor to a single eurozone bond market. While this fund is currently tasked with the very limited job of supporting the Greek, Irish and Portuguese bailouts, within the terms of the present Treaty, it could act as a vehicle for a more strategic and substantial move towards a consolidated debt market for all eurozone states otherwise struggling to access capital markets at acceptable rates of interest.

Proponents typically point to either the unification of the eurozone's national bond markets, or the development of a segmented market with varying levels of guarantees for investors — for instance, blue bonds backed by the eurozone, and red for 'top up' nations borrowing above prudential guidelines that would provide only national guarantees. Other suggestions generally involve senior versus junior markets consolidated either as geographic groupings or as types of issues.

Certainly, the use of eurozone-backed bond issues as a means of funding Member States in financial difficulties is already introducing a substitution effect from the most seriously malfunctioning national markets to a new market category for distressed Member States. And these developments may well appeal (on commercial terms) to external investors, including China.

A unified eurozone bond market: designing issues to suit investor preferences

Proponents of a unified eurobond market typically take inspiration from the US model — as they point out, average eurozone debt levels are not worse than that of the US economy but the US government bond market trades at low yields, similar to those of the German bond market. In fact, prudent Sweden typically has to pay almost the same interest costs on its debt as the US and Germany — providing an even better example of the penalty of being a 'small' market (only part of which might be explained by its non-euro status).

In addition, there is likely to be an even greater propensity for investors to require a higher premium on 'small country' debt in cases of increased default risk or currency uncertainty — and premium increases are likely to be non-linear. In contrast, large liquid markets (for example, the US sovereign debt market) continue to benefit simply from their size and management expertise.

While the price of a bond (which determines the spot interest rate) reflects a matrix comprising currency and default risks relative to other countries, it also includes technical factors, such as size and liquidity of the market. These latter factors will affect the premium or discount demanded by investors versus bonds otherwise accorded exactly the same default and currency status.

Unlike the eurozone, the US sovereign debt market benefits from its strong federal debt guarantee, and confidence in the dollar as an unchangeable single currency. The eurozone cannot present such strong credentials — in part because of its short history, but also because of the fragmented nature of its sovereign bond markets and governance structures. Thus, it will continue to suffer from additional interest costs.

Expanding the EFSF presents a practical means of testing investor interest and gradually growing the 'stability bonds' (or 'junior') market. Pricing, and the need for guarantees, can be assessed and adjusted over time according to improved information and liquidity in the market.

A comparison can be made with the successful development of the offshore Renminbi market in Hong Kong since mid-2010, which has grown from a very low base, with early issues bearing relatively high coupons, to a market worth over USD 25 bn (2011) and with coupons now typically ranging between 50 and 200 basis points. This success has occurred despite the market being composed of fragmented small issues from a variety of corporate and official borrowers. Fragmentation was offset by promotion of the 'umbrella view' of the 'single' Renminbi offshore market.

Funding Costs, the Investor Base and the Structure of Issues

Since the Greek debt crisis broke in early 2010, European opinion has typically been highly critical of the behaviour of financial markets and investors. There have been many vocal complaints about the soaring costs of borrowing for countries in financial distress and other highly indebted Member States — and relatively little interest in the problems facing investors. Complaints have also been stirred by the gaping differential between the high interest rates that troubled debtors might have to pay in the open market and the very low rates seen in the German Bund market and outside of the eurozone (e.g. in the US and UK). Escalating interest costs add to financial distress and to the difficulties of reducing public sector deficits and debt, potentially creating a vicious spiral. In these circumstances, the appeal of a single market is clear — it would presumably enable all eurozone states to access funding at low interest rates.

However, this analysis ignores the fact that the degree of success (and interest rate level) of any bond issues depends not only on the issuer, but also on the appetite of potential investors in light of their risk assessments, technical requirements and investment schedules.

Given the increased funding requirements of almost all advanced economies, net inflows of funds from foreign investors are particularly important. Eurozone investors will be the largest single bloc of contributors to funding eurozone government debt — but they will also diversify bond holdings across the major global markets. Eurozone savings alone will thus be insufficient to meet all its funding requirements.

Investors from other advanced countries will also diversify their holdings, and while they will purchase eurozone debt, the scope to increase net holdings is presently very limited given the substantial funding requirements of most of these nations. Indeed, simultaneously high debt levels across developed states have created greater competition for funds.

The net balance of capital to meet the eurozone's funding needs will have to come from the savings surplus countries — primarily from Asia and the oil-producing economies. Of these, China has the largest savings surplus, typically generating around USD 200–300 bn per annum in new external investments, which add to a massive existing stock of foreign exchange reserves held abroad (largely in the form of US bonds). These reserves were reported to have reached USD 3.2 tn by the end of September 2011. Japan and other Asian states in surplus form the second-largest bloc of net foreign investors.

Investment from Asia, and particularly from China, is therefore critical and might dictate the success or failure of efforts to meet the enlarged funding needs of governments throughout the developed world.

There has already been some 'courting' of Chinese investment, but it appears that China does not want to undertake any special, high profile, role in European debt markets, although it has participated, and will continue to participate, in each bond issue on its own merit. It has notably added its voice to calls for a commitment to clear solutions to the sovereign debt crisis.

China's Present Position as an International Investor

Certain inferences may be made regarding China's current financial position and its international investment policies and preferences. It is likely that:

- The build-up of foreign exchange reserves by the People's Bank of China (China's central bank) reflects a parallel build-up of foreign government bond holdings, chiefly in US Treasury bills but also including European government bonds.
- As the scale of Chinese investment has increased, investment has started to shift into sovereign wealth funds, largely to expedite the diversification of the portfolios managed — for example, into shareholdings that would not be suitable for a central bank foreign exchange reserves portfolio.
- While expressing unease about the impact of a weaker dollar on US investments, the People's Bank has had little choice but to continue holding most of its funds in US bonds. Most estimates suggest that as much as USD 2 tn of China's reserves are held in US dollar investments, with over USD 1 tn held in Treasury bonds.
- Holdings in the eurozone bond markets may amount to less than USD 1 tn. This has resulted, in part, from the small size (relative to China's investment appetite) of Europe's fragmented sovereign debt markets, the largest of which are only valued at around USD 2–2.5 tn each.

Conclusion

China will continue to see more of its wealth managed abroad and will be keen to seek an appropriate balance of international investments. However, its current sovereign debt portfolio is probably underweight in eurozone assets. This points to a significant opportunity to raise participation and inflows of capital to the eurozone, but it also highlights Europe's past failure to substantially deepen the involvement of foreign investors from across Asia and other emerging markets. More efficient fundraising may require greater attention to key investors' preferences in term of offerings and, over time, the development of a eurozone bond market structure that is better suited to being fully competitive with that of the US. As global economic and financial power continues to shift, towards Asia in particular, this will influence external investment flows and opportunities, impacting inevitably on capital market structures and the cost of capital. Europe must look ahead and adapt to the changes implied.

Innovation in China
(June 2012)

Alice Rezková

Research Fellow, Association for International Affairs (AMO), Prague

Executive Summary

Is China a 'copycat nation' or is it becoming a true innovator that will surpass the West? With China's achievements rising in terms of number of patents, scientific articles and university graduates that question becomes increasingly relevant. Nevertheless, it is generally assumed by Western analysts and politicians that China cannot catch up with its Western counterparts in the field of innovation. Many Western politicians and businessmen would like to keep the 'designed in Germany, manufactured in China' label indefinitely. But they must recognise that Chinese leaders are determined to overcome growing social and environmental problems through technological advances, and for the country to become a world leader in innovation.

Many myths exist about China's technological progress based on statistics and, without deeper analysis, one could conclude that China is starting to catch up with Western nations. Indeed, some Western leaders have expressed concern regarding China's impressive statistics and growth rates over the past few decades. However, aside from the fact that Chinese statistics may not necessarily be all that reflective of reality, China's performance can be interpreted differently, as this paper presents.

Chinese firms are excellent at mastering fairly basic technologies, but they still struggle to design and manufacture reliable and sophisticated technologies. In part this is due to a business culture which excels at speed of production and lowering costs, but has had less experience with the kind of highly complex products expected in Europe and North America. Further evidence from patent statistics suggests that research and development (R&D) activity carried out in China tends to be more process-based rather than cutting-edge research. However, China is currently intensively investing into building solid research platforms in experimental development. Therefore, sooner or later, China will have to be considered a relevant innovation player in many fields.

China currently invests major resources in R&D with the goal of becoming a global innovation leader. The EU should closely follow this development and support scientific collaboration with China. However, it should take care not to get caught in the race for highest number of patents, scientific articles and university graduates. The European comparative advantage lies in a broader concept of innovation. It excels in true innovations that bring breakthrough changes in business, technology, institutions and society.

Main Points

- China currently allocates considerable resources towards building a strong R&D platform in order to become a major player in innovation. It is already gaining momentum in electronics and telecommunication equipment and is developing its potential in pharmaceuticals and alternative energy.
- Chinese institutes have been oriented toward achieving statistical success, although the situation is slowly changing. They want to change their model in future to become more quality-oriented.
- Many countries are afraid of closer scientific collaboration with China because of persistent problems with intellectual property rights protection. However, scientific cooperation with China should be supported by European researchers.

Introduction

To understand the Chinese approach towards innovation, one should be aware that China now ranks second in terms of global R&D spending, accounting for 12% of total global expenditure. As a nation, China invests 1.6% of its GDP and plans to increase this figure to 2.5% by 2020. Universities and science parks are springing up around the country and China now graduates more engineers and scientists than the US.

However, turning China from a 'world factory' to an 'innovation nation' requires time and a strategy. The Chinese government is well known for its long-term planning approach that influences all aspects of its economy, with innovation and R&D being no exception. The National Program 2006–2020 for the Development of Science and Technology in the Medium and Long Term envisages technology-oriented growth focused on energy, water supply and environmental technologies. The plan aims (1) to develop key technologies within IT and production, (2) to catch up with other countries in biotechnology and (3) to speed up development in space and aviation technology.

The Program contains three main features:

- Increasing R&D expenditures to 2.5% of GDP.
- Strengthening domestic innovative capacity and reducing dependency on foreign technology.
- Establishing the business sector as the main driving force of the innovation process.

The Program is complex in its coverage, and its priorities are also reflected in successive Five Year Plans. However, despite these efforts, China is still not an innovation leader and there remains a lot of uncertainty whether it can actually become one.

This paper analyses Chinese elite thinking on innovation. It describes and explains myths that are commonly linked to Chinese development in innovation — namely, that China cannot become a leader in breakthrough innovations; China is innovative because it scores highly in patent statistics; and that Western countries should protect their innovation knowledge from China.

What is 'Innovation' and What is its Meaning in the Chinese Context?

In order to understand whether true innovation exists in China, it is necessary to define innovation in broad terms. Although there are many definitions of innovation, for the purpose of this paper, the OECD definition[44] will be used. This is

---

[44] OECD/Statistical Office of the European Communities, *Oslo Manual: Guidelines for Collecting and Interpreting Innovation Data, 3rd Edition: The Measurement of Scientific and Technological Activities* (OECD Publishing, Luxembourg, 2005).

primarily for its broad reach that helps us to better explain Chinese efforts in the field of innovation. This definition sets out four criteria by which innovation can be measured:

- Product innovation. An innovative product or service that is new or significantly improved. This includes significant improvements in technical specifications, components and materials, incorporated software, user friendliness and other functional characteristics.
- Process innovation. Process innovation involves a new or significantly improved production or delivery method. This includes significant changes in technique, equipment and/or software.
- Marketing innovation. Marketing innovation entails a new marketing method involving significant changes in product design or packaging, product placement, product promotion or pricing.
- Organisational innovation. Organisational innovation introduces a new organisational method in a firm's business practices, workplace organisation or external relations.

The OECD/Eurostat definition is very precise in pointing out various aspects of innovation. It is broad enough to encompass a new electronic device and a drug curing cancer, as well as improvements in product processes and methods. The Chinese Academy of Sciences defines innovation as a 'complex process of value creation, including scientific and technological value, cultural value, economic value and social value, concerning activities ranging from scientific discovery, technological invention, and business model innovation'.[45] While Chinese elites share this broad view, in reality the official attitude is more practical and oriented primarily towards technological advancement and patentable ideas.

Myths Related to Innovation in China

Myth 1: China cannot become a world leader in breakthrough innovation

China's developing potential to become an innovation leader is intimidating for western elites. Can China really replace western countries in the field of

---

[45] John Kao, 'China as an innovation nation', *CNN*, September 2011.

innovation? For now, the answer is 'no'. However, China is currently investing huge resources into creating a domestic environment that is favourable for innovation.

Most of the country's R&D funding is channelled into (government) research institutes. Cooperation between business and academia has not yet exploited its full potential in this R&D, probably because the research is already heavily supported by the government. Most of the funds in higher education are also focused on applied rather than basic research (project and result driven). Foreign funding represents just 1.3% of total R&D expenditure, most of which flows directly into Chinese businesses.

Chinese firms currently excel at mastering basic technologies although they still struggle to design and manufacture reliable and sophisticated technologies. They still lack the knowledge to build high-end products in terms of technology and user design. Instead, they tend to focus on innovations aimed at improving business processes, increasing speed of production or lowering costs. Nevertheless, Chinese firms have started to invest most of their R&D resources into experimental development, which could enable them to improve these areas and succeed in Western markets in future. However, it is difficult to analyse how advanced the Chinese actually are in their innovation attempts because statistical data cannot offer a full picture and empirical evidence does not indicate a consistent pattern.

There is currently a lot of cooperation among Western and Chinese researchers. China's large funds help to attract top-ranking scientists from all over the world to research in China. Approximately 30% of total industry funds are aimed at hi-tech technology, out of which over 60% flow into electronic and telecommunication equipment development. In terms of patents, China has a high number of applications in pharmaceutical, communications and electronics, but the proportion of applications it submits in the food chemistry sector is much higher than elsewhere.

Any discussion about Chinese innovation usually involves the issue of quality. Even though China's outputs score highly in many fields, they can be found lacking in quality. The number of Chinese publications in top journals provides one measure of the quality of Chinese scientific research. In 2009, Switzerland had the highest rate of high quality publications on a per capita basis among OECD and BRIC countries, followed by Sweden and Denmark. In terms of absolute numbers it was the US that published the highest proportion of scientific articles in top journals, followed by the UK. Overall, China produced the second-largest number of publications worldwide after the US. Only a small proportion of Chinese publications made it in to the top global scholarly journals (although Chinese contributions have been steadily rising). This could indicate quality issues with Chinese outputs, although may partly be because Chinese scholars publish in Chinese journals with which Western scientists may be unfamiliar.

Myth 2: China is innovative because it scores highly in patent statistics

Since 2000, the number of patent applications in China has grown rapidly. The country's 391,777 patent applications in 2010 placed it second globally, just behind the US. At a superficial level, the increase in Chinese patent applications over the past ten years could be analysed as a positive outcome of China's increased R&D investments. However, there may also be other reasons for this development.

China has marked increasing its competitiveness in innovation as a very high national priority. In order to achieve its goal, the government has announced an ambitious incentive program that supports companies, universities and individuals through the patenting procedure. The government also offers to cover a substantial part of the patent application costs. In October 2010, *The Economist*[46] reported that Chinese companies producing large numbers of patent applications are eligible for tax reductions of 15% to 25%. In addition, although not an official rule, professors in charge of a project that results in a patent application are more likely to retain their tenure. Even regular employees and students can more easily convert their rural *hukou* (residence permit) into an urban residence permit as a reward for submitting a patent application. In response to the government, some companies now offer rewards to employees that come up with a patentable idea. It is not uncommon to see advertisements for patent application writers who offer their services on the Internet.

China's successful hunt for patents has yielded stunning numerical results. But it is important to note that the quality and sophistication of Chinese patents is not comparable to other global players. Moreover, 65% of Chinese patent applications were refused in 2010. Statistics show that foreign subjects also play an important role in the Chinese innovation process — more than 41% of the granted patents were awarded to foreign residents, suggesting that Chinese innovation is already fairly collaborative. However, the US and the EU also grant a significant proportion

---

[46] Anon, 'Patents, yes; ideas, maybe', *The Economist*, October 2010.

of their patents to foreign residents (51% and 47% respectively) and Chinese researchers do not appear to be very active overseas, where they fill less than 5% of all applications.

Myth 3: Western countries should protect their innovative knowledge

Chinese entrepreneurs very often take inspiration from the ideas of others. An old Chinese proverb states that 'to steal a book is an elegant offence', a remark that is still valid in China. However, the Chinese government is aware of the perils of infringement on IPR particularly in the case of development of hi-tech industries. The government continues its struggle to improve IPR protection and improvements can already be observed, particularly in protection of trademarks and patents.

Because of the Chinese approach towards the protection of IPR, technology transfer and research cooperation in China can be a risky move for foreign firms. As a result, Western countries will need to make a conscious decision whether or not they want to be part of the very dynamic Chinese development in innovation. China is emerging as a new player in R&D and should be considered a partner for collaborative research that could create mutual benefits for the global community. For example, many pharmaceutical patents result from research involving Chinese traditional medicine, which often involves collaboration with Western medical researchers. With regard to collaboration on scientific articles, the strongest links are often made in partnership with the US. Most EU Member States are yet to develop scientific connections that are comparable to those of the US.

Chinese Investments into the EU Energy Sector
(February 2013)

Hinrich Voss

Lecturer in International Business, Centre for International Business, University of Leeds

Executive Summary

- Chinese firms invest little in Europe's energy sector. China's energy-related outbound investments into Europe are under-represented compared with its global average.
- Energy-related inward investments from Russia, the US and other extra EU27 investors dominate over those from China, according to European data. This and the previous point indicate that the potential for investment from China is commensurately greater.
- One reason for the low value of Chinese investments in the EU energy sector is the relative lack of endowments in energy-related resources across the European economy. This means that Chinese firms can only engage in equity deals within the EU27 to acquire access to oil and gas resources outside Europe, thus accounting for the low value of investments within the EU itself.
- While Chinese renewable energy companies have to date invested little in Europe, these firms are most likely to drive Chinese investments in Europe's energy sector in the future. This is because of the EU's renewable energy policy focus (cf. 'Europe 20-20-20'[47] to generate 20% of energy from renewable

---

[47] European Renewable Energy Council, 'Renewable Energy Technology Roadmap 20% by 2020' (EREC, Brussels, 2012).

energy sources by 2020). It is also the case that the private ownership (i.e., non-state-owned) of Chinese firms in the renewable sector will act as a force to reduce animosity towards inward investment from China. Private firms are globally competitive, and therefore promise to bring product and process innovation to the EU without invoking perceptions of Chinese government control and influence.
- EU–China cooperation in the field of renewable energy should be further pursued during the sixth Energy Dialogue to support the transition of the Chinese and European economy to a low-carbon one. This should include the attraction of direct investment and capacity building in the EU.
- However, uncertainties in how European energy policies will develop during the current economic situation act as a deterrent for Chinese investments. Predictable and stable implementation of policy goals will enable Chinese investors to assess and develop business cases for investing in production facilities in Europe.
- Reinstalling confidence in the growth prospects of the EU economies is crucial, particularly the reduction of uncertainties around the prospects of the eurozone. Sovereign debt problems and related governmental fiscal retrenchment negatively affect the attractiveness of the EU for Chinese investments in the energy sector, given that energy investments seek stability in revenue streams from investments.

Chinese Investments into the European Energy Sector

China's foreign direct investments (FDI) abroad have grown at a sustained high rate over recent years, and understandably have attracted much attention from advanced economy governments. This paper provides the context surrounding Chinese energy-related investments in the EU and assesses the benefits and risks to the EU from these investments.

Statistical overview of Chinese FDI in the European energy sector

China's global outward foreign direct investment has risen over the last decade from an outward FDI stock value of EUR 45.6 bn (in dollar terms USD 57 bn) in 2005 to EUR 306 bn (USD 425 bn) in 2011.[48] Over the same time period the share of investments that can be attributed to energy-related activities remained stable at about 16%.[49] Aggregate Chinese direct investments across the EU of 27 Member States (EU27) have increased faster than its global investments. The value of Chinese FDI stock in the EU27 increased more than 20-fold, from EUR 0.6 bn (USD 0.8 bn) in 2005 to EUR 14 bn (USD 20 bn) at the end of 2011. Unfortunately, a breakdown by industry and host country is not available from Chinese sources. If a comparable share of energy-related activities were to take place in Europe, we should witness Chinese investments of the order of EUR 2 bn (USD 3 bn).

However, according to data from Eurostat and the Heritage Foundation,[50] these figures have not borne out. By 2010, the latest year for which Eurostat reports a breakdown by industry, the stock of China's energy-related investments in Europe accounted for 2%, or EUR 0.1 bn, of all Chinese investments in Europe.[51] The Heritage Foundation reports that energy-related deals were worth EUR 12 bn (USD 17 bn) between 2008 and 2012 in the EU27, or 6% of China's global energy deals.[52] That is to say that, from a Chinese perspective, investments in the EU energy sector are under-represented in comparison to the global total. This is of little surprise given the emphasis that is placed by the Chinese government in developing and supporting national oil companies (NOCs) and through them, access to oil and gas supplies. The minor importance given to energy-related investments is mirrored on the European side. Chinese investments accounted for 0.1% of all inbound (i.e., from outside the EU27) energy-related investments by 2010. The largest beneficiary of this modest investment was Denmark.

It follows from these macro statistics that energy-related acquisitions in Europe should be few. Between 2005 and the end of 2012, Chinese firms completed

---

[48] USD terms are converted to EUR terms using the period average official exchange rate.

[49] This figure is calculated from the broad sectors 'mining' and 'production and supply of electricity, gas, and water'. Data for more narrowly defined sectors are not available from Chinese sources.

[50] Heritage Foundation, 'China Global Investement Tracker'. Available at: http://www.heritage.org/research/projects/china-global-investment-tracker-interactive-map. Accessed 25 January 2013.

[51] This figure is calculated from the sectors 'extraction of crude petroleum and natural gas; mining support service activities', 'manufacture of coke and refined petroleum products', and 'electricity, gas, steam and air conditioning supply'. Data for more narrowly defined sectors are not available from European sources. Country-level data are not available for all EU27.

[52] The Heritage Foundation reports Chinese deals worth USD 52 bn across all sectors in the EU27 between 2006 and 2012.

33 energy-related equity acquisitions in Europe.[53] Of these deals, the majority (22 out of 33) of the energy-related equity acquisitions across the EU27 were found in the oil and gas industry. Sinopec and PetroChina have been most active with six and five deals, respectively. Other companies such as Sinochem, Oriental Energy, and China National Overseas Oil Corporation have been active to only a minor degree. Although deals in the oil and gas industry dominate, not all of these deals involve assets located within the EU27. Seventy percent of these acquisitions include the transfer of oil and gas exploration rights from European firms to Chinese ones for assets outside the EU. Examples of such deals are the acquisition of Tullow Oil's (UK) exploration rights within parts of Uganda by a group of investors linked to CNOOC in 2010, and PetroChina's acquisition of a 40% stake in an oil and gas exploration and production block in Qatar — acquired from GDF Suez SA, France.

While deals are executed directly from China, they may also be executed by overseas subsidiaries of Chinese companies. An example of this is the acquisition of coal mining and exploration company Caledon Resources PLC, UK, by Guangdong Rising (Australia) Pty Ltd, a subsidiary of a Guangdong based company.

In addition to the acquisitions in Europe, Hanemann and Rosen[54] reported a total of 49 greenfield investments over the period 2000 to 2011; 45 of these were in renewable energies.

The main Chinese energy-related firms active in Europe

The main Chinese actors in the oil and gas, wind, solar, electricity grid and coal sectors are introduced in this section.

Oil and Gas

The key participants in the oil and gas sector are the NOCs PetroChina, Sinopec and CNOOC. PetroChina, China's largest NOC, has been involved in five successful equity deals worth in excess of EUR 4 bn (USD 5 bn) in the EU27 since 2005.

---

[53] OneBanker, Thomson Reuters. Available at: http://banker.thomsonib.com (2013).

[54] T Hanemann and DH Rosen, 'China Invests in Europe', Rhodium Group, June 2012. http://rhg.com/wp-content/uploads/2012/06/RHG_ChinaInvestsInEurope_June2012.pdf. Accessed 25 December 2012.

Most of its activities have been focused on acquiring non EU-owned upstream assets in countries such as Canada, Syria (Syria Shell Petroleum Dvlp BV), Kazakhstan (PetroKazakhstan), and Qatar (GDF Suez SA-Qatar Oil Block 4), from Europe-based firms. PetroChina also purchased a 50% interest in refineries in Scotland and France from UK-based INEOS, in 2011.

Sinopec has executed six deals in Europe since 2005 worth in excess of EUR 13 bn (USD 17 bn). It has been acquiring entire companies, plus considerable equity shares, in European oil and gas exploration and production companies, or their subsidiaries. Most notably, it acquired a 49% interest in Talisman's operation in the British North Sea in 2012. The single largest deal was the acquisition of Repsol YPF Brasil SA from Repsol (Spain) for EUR 5 bn (USD 7 bn) in 2010. Sinopec has an office in London dedicated to their African and trading operations.

CNOOC's deals involve energy assets in countries outside the EU27. In 2012 it acquired jointly with Total (France) explorations rights from Tullow Oil (UK) in Uganda. It coordinates its Africa operations through its office in London, UK, and in February 2013, CNOOC was given permission from the Canadian government to acquire Nexen for EUR 11 bn (USD 15 bn).

Wind

Goldwind, Sinovel, and MingYang are among the world's ten largest wind energy producers[55] and share a strategy to step up their presence in the European market over time. Goldwind and Mingyang each have credit lines of more than EUR 3.6 bn (USD 5 bn) from the China Development Bank for their international expansion.[56] Privately owned Goldwind has been the majority owner of Vensys Germany since 2008. Vensys produces wind turbines for the European and international markets in Germany. Vensys and Goldwind GmbH are currently financing a Chair in Wind Energy, with a EUR 2.5 m endowment, at the University of Applied Sciences, Saarbrücken, Germany.

Sinovel, a wind turbine manufacturer, first announced in 2011 a deal (publicised again in mid-2012) with Greece's Public Power Corporation (PPC) for the

---

[55] P Clark, P, 'GE breezes past Vestas in wind market', *Financial Times*, 11 February 2013. Available at: http://www.ft.com/cms/s/0/a4615f70-7440-11e2-80a7-00144feabdc0.html#axzz2KhD8alng. Accessed 21 January 2013.

[56] L Hook and P Clark, 'China's wind groups pick up speed' *Financial Times*, 15 July 2012. Available at: http://www.ft.com/cms/s/0/fb4bc872-c674-11e1-963a-00144feabdc0.html#axzz2KhD8alng. Accessed 21 January 2013.

development of onshore and offshore wind farms of 200–300 megawatts each.[57] Also in 2011, Sinovel struck its largest overseas contract in Europe, worth EUR 1.5 bn, with a 1 gigawatt project in Ireland. In February 2012, two 3-megawatt advanced wind turbines were installed in Sweden as demonstration projects. In Romania, Sinovel has an agreement to deliver 1,200 megawatt in wind turbine capacity for the Project Dobrogea, and is said to be considering opening a production in partnership with local company Faur. As part of this expansion, Sinovel is recruiting business development managers for its offices in Bucharest, Hamburg, London, Paris, Sofia and Warsaw.

China's largest power equipment producer, *Dongfang Electric Corporation*, has capabilities in wind turbine manufacturing and one office in Italy. *MingYang* maintains a R&D office in Denmark.

Solar

Noteworthy solar energy companies are Yingli Solar, Suntech and Trina. Yingli Solar, a private manufacturer of solar panel modules, announced the establishment of its regional headquarters in Switzerland in October 2012 and has sales offices across Europe. The subsidiary Yingli Europe is primarily engaged in the sale and marketing of photovoltaic (PV) products and relevant accessories in Europe. Yingli Italia and Yingli Spain have the same responsibilities for their respective domestic markets while Yingli Greece caters for Greece, Cyprus, the Balkans and the Middle East. Europe accounted for 90, 83 and 62% of Yingli's global revenues over the years 2009–2011.

Suntech has its European headquarters, Suntech Europe Ltd, in Switzerland and has a representative office in Munich. Its European activities include the supply of panels to the Pozohondo Solar Farm (5.1 megawatts), Spain, and the Stuttgart Trade Fair (3.8 megawatts). To date, no manufacturing base has been established in Europe.

Trina Solar has an established sales network in Europe, with offices in Derby, Madrid, Milan, Munich and Prague. It supplied 23 megawatts of solar modules to Italian solar plant operator Enerqos Spa in 2010. It has a contract to supply panels worth a total of 20 megawatts to four projects in Germany and the UK, under a

---

[57] P Clark, 'China breezes into European wind power', *Financial Times*, 1 July 2011. Available at: http://www.ft.com/cms/s/0/9aac531e-a40c-11e0-8b4f-00144feabdc0.html#axzz2KhD8alng. Accessed 21 January 2013.

cooperation agreement signed with PV system supplier Abakus Solar, and a further 61-megawatt capacity in an unrelated German project.

Electricity Grid

In February 2012, State Grid, the largest electricity grid operator in China, spent EUR 387 m to buy a 25% stake in Portugal's national power grid company Redes Energéticas Nacionais (REN), becoming its largest stakeholder. REN is active in Europe as well as in Africa and South America. State Grid also unsuccessfully attempted to acquire a stake in Spanish Red Electrica. Through its Portuguese operation, State Grid has become involved in the development of the Irish offshore grid.

Coal

The activities of China's state-owned coal companies in Europe are mainly restricted to trading. Chinacoal is exporting through its subsidiary China Coal Overseas Development Co., Ltd to eastern Europe, among other markets. Datong Coal Mine Group Co. set up a trading subsidiary with a capital of EUR 3 m (RMB 30 m) in 2010 with a branch office in Europe. The most significant activity in this sector is China Huadian Engineering's signing of a memorandum of understanding to build a 600-megawatt coal-fired power plant valued at EUR 1 bn in Romania.

The drivers of Chinese investments in the European energy sector

The majority of Chinese energy deals in Europe take place within the oil and gas industry sector. For these deals there is a clear focus on the acquisition of access to natural resources that will serve China's economic growth and are generally carried out by state-owned enterprises, i.e. NOCs. Through these investments NOCs will at times also gain access to advanced technologies. Investments in the renewable energy sectors and the energy grid form part of market development and are focused on the exploitation of the firms' competitiveness. In all relevant deals, Chinese firms have secured a foothold in Europe. The development of REN and Vensys illustrates this approach.

Goldwind started collaborating with Vensys in 2003, developing a megawatt-class wind turbine and agreeing to produce and distribute Vensys turbines under license in China. Goldwind and Vensys are both actively developing new technologies. According to Espacenet, which collects patent applications globally, Vensys has applied for seven patents and Goldwind for 64. An interesting observation is that Vensys applied last time in 2009. In 2008, Goldwind acquired the majority share of Vensys. Through this capital injection, Vensys was able to move from a technology developer who licences its technologies to a developer and manufacturer. Through Vensys, Goldwind bought subsidiary companies that produce converters and variable propeller systems for Vensys, expanding its access to key technologies. To date, Vensys turbines with a capacity of more than 13,000 megawatts have been installed globally (as of Dec 2012) — of which 11,657 megawatts are installed in China by Goldwind. In 2012, Wu Gang, CEO at Goldwind, stated that the European market will be served and further developed through its German affiliate Vensys. Goldwind recorded a global turnover of EUR 1.4 bn (RMB 11 bn) in 2012.

The State Grid Corporation of China (SGCC), ranked as the seventh-largest corporation in the world with a turnover of EUR 192 bn (USD 260 bn) in 2011 in Fortune Global 500, became a co-owner of Redes Energéticas Nacionais when it privatised in 2012. As an outcome of this relationship, the China Development Bank agreed to a EUR 800m loan to REN and REN signed an agreement in February 2013 with the China Electric Power Research Institute (CEPRI; representing State Grid International Development (SGID), a wholly owned subsidiary of SGCC), to establish a R&D centre in Portugal; SGCC's first overseas R&D centre. According to Espacenet, SGCC is the stronger technology partner in this relationship: CEPRI has applied for 123 patents globally and State Grid for more than 2,000; none is registered for REN. SGCC has expertise, *inter alia*, in ultra-high voltage (or high-voltage, direct current; HVDC) power lines which can be used in the development of smart grids and the transmission of renewable energy across the grid. SGID and REN also signed an agreement to set up a consulting firm in Brazil to provide consulting services regarding grid technology, engineering design, equipment selection, and electricity regulation in 2013. This follows from the partial acquisition agreement in 2012 in which both sides agreed to jointly explore the Brazilian market.

Risk and benefits attached to Chinese investments

China's energy-related acquisitions of European firms tend to involve assets that reside outside of the EU27. Sinopec, for example, acquired oil and gas exploration rights from European firms in Brazil, Kazakhstan and Russia. PetroChina has secured rights in Canada and Qatar. These deals have no immediate impact on the European economy as they neither develop nor destroy existing firm linkages. However, disposing these assets, which have potential strategic value for the energy security of the EU, could have long-term consequences.

CNOOC's acquisition of Nexen has secured it direct access to oil and gas assets in the British North Sea, specifically to the Buzzard, Ettrick, Blackbird and Scott/Telford fields which deliver about 112,000 barrels-of-oil-equivalent per day (boe/d) across them.[58] Nexen's investment in the Golden Eagle development in the North Sea will contribute about 26,000 boe/d once in full operation.[59] Nexen is also active in shale gas extraction: in Poland it has a joint venture to explore ten concessions with an estimated 185 tn cubic feet of recoverable resource. It is at this stage unclear how CNOOC plans to continue with the European developments started by Nexen.

The European policy framework towards Chinese investments in the energy sector

A cornerstone of European energy policy is its resolve to generate 20% of its energy from renewable sources and reduce greenhouse gas emissions by 20% by 2020. In order to achieve these goals, the current European Energy Commissioner, Günther Oettinger, stated that by 2020 investments of about EUR 1 tn will be required in the European energy sector. In other sectors, European wind and solar initiatives will be supported with investments of EUR 22 bn. Further support for renewable energy sources has traditionally come from the feed in tariffs (FITs). The European policy consensus on these energy policies can provide an attractive business environment for foreign investors as they deliver certainty of return on

---

[58] Nexen, Shale Gas — Growth Plans, 2013. Available at: http://www.nexeninc.com/en/Operations/ShaleGas/GrowthPlans.aspx. Accessed 21 January 2012.

[59] Nexen, Conventional Oil & Gas — UK North Sea, 2013. Available at: http://www.nexeninc.com/en/Operations/Conventional/UKNorthSea.aspx. Accessed 21 January 2012.

investment. A recent study by Ernst & Young[60] reported that France, Germany, Italy and the UK exhibit significant underdeveloped renewable energy sectors, despite the existing extensive investment record. In principle, Europe should be a promising and predictable market for Chinese investors. However, this has been undermined by: the policy adjustments to the FITs in a number of European countries in reaction to the current financial and economic crisis within Europe; the slow policy progress in individual Member States; and erratic policy implementation in other markets. Uncertainties in how policy goals may be implemented and enforced will distract Chinese investors and push them to markets that may have less ambitious goals but are more predictable and less competitive.

Policy Recommendations for the EU

- The predictable and stable implementation of EU policy goals regarding energy will enable Chinese investors to assess the European market more accurately and, on this basis, develop stronger business cases for investing in production facilities within Europe.
- The sixth Energy Dialogue should be used as an opportunity to advance EU–China cooperation in the field of renewable energies, including joint development projects. It should promote the attraction of direct investment to the EU, as well as capacity building, in the renewable energies sector.
- The renewable energies agenda has a double benefit. Because investment in renewables tends to add to capacity, Chinese investment should help Europe reach its targets here. This is in contrast with non-renewable energies, where inward investment is more likely to involve acquisition of existing capacity and is thus of lesser benefit.
- Reinstalling confidence in the growth prospects of the EU economies is crucial, particularly the reduction of uncertainties around the prospects of the eurozone. Sovereign debt problems and related governmental fiscal retrenchment negatively affect the attractiveness of the EU for Chinese investments in the energy sector as energy investments seek — and are particularly sensitive to — stability in revenue streams from investments.

---

[60] Ernst & Young, Renewable Energy Country Attractiveness Index, August 2012, Issue 34. Available at: http://www.ey.com/GL/en/Industries/Cleantech. Accessed 21 January 2012.

Chinese Overseas Acquisitions: The Nokia Siemens/Motorola Case
(July 2011)

Marc Laperrouza

Senior Research Associate, Swiss Federal Institute of Technology (EPFL), Lausanne

Executive Summary

In 2010 Nokia Siemens Networks announced its intention to buy the wireless network equipment assets of Motorola Solutions. The deal was blocked by Huawei, the leading Chinese telecommunication equipment manufacturer. The dispute stemmed from an agreement dating back to 2001 under which Motorola resold some of Huawei's gear outside of the US.

Huawei's slogan 'We see beyond telecom' may be a tribute to its technological competence and marketing savvy. The firm's ambitions have ignited the US government's suspicions that it may have links with the Chinese military. These alleged ties have derailed a series of technological acquisitions the Shenzhen-based telecommunication equipment manufacturer intended to make in the US. Whether the target of the acquisition is a start-up or a large player, whether the technology is broadband networks or cloud computing, Huawei seems to be finding the Committee on Foreign Investment in the US on its acquisition path.

Main Points

- A number of Chinese firms are proving to be formidable competitors to established telecommunications equipment manufacturers. They nonetheless

struggle to gain a foothold in certain markets (e.g., USA and India) for security and intellectual property concerns.
- Huawei as well as other national champions with global ambitions are learning to play the game of intellectual property rights both in markets and in courts.
- China's Anti-monopoly Law is impacting the merger and acquisitions conducted by multinational firms in China and abroad. The duration of review can become a real issue for merging parties.
- In addition to its established industrial policy, the Chinese government is likely to respond in a *quid pro quo* manner to protectionist measures encountered by its national champions abroad.

Case Background

In July 2010, Nokia Siemens Networks (NSN) announced its acquisition of the wireless network equipment assets of Motorola Solutions (MSI). The deal was subsequently approved by both US and EU regulators but it did not close at the time for two reasons. First, Huawei sued MSI and NSN on the grounds that MSI had not provided adequate assurances that Huawei's technology and intellectual property (IP) would not be leaked from MSI to NSN — Huawei had been a Motorola OEM/private label manufacturer for wireless equipment since 2000. Huawei wanted the deal to exclude any equipment based on GSM (Global System for Mobile Communications) and UMTS (Universal Mobile Telecommunications System) technology standards. It claimed that it developed, designed and sold technologies, and other products, to Motorola which resold them under its own brand. Huawei alleged that, through cooperation, Motorola obtained confidential information on Huawei's products. Following MSI's acquisition by NSN, Huawei feared that its confidential information would be transferred to the latter. Viewing NSN as a direct competitor, Huawei sued to prevent the information transfer under the conditions proposed by NSN. A US Federal District Court granted Huawei's request for a preliminary injunction. One of the reasons behind Huawei's lawsuit is that the deal with Motorola would have pushed NSN well ahead of Huawei in the network equipment market, whereas the rivals are currently neck-and-neck for second place (behind Ericsson).

Second, the Chinese Ministry of Commerce's (MOFCOM) anti-monopoly bureau took its time to grant anti-trust approval. In March 2011, the bureau extended its review of the bid for another 60 days. MOFCOM consulted both telecommunication operators and network equipment suppliers over NSN's planned acquisition of Motorola's assets. Under this consultation, Huawei informed the regulator that it opposed a completion of the deal as long as its dispute with Motorola was unresolved.

The sale finally went through in April 2011. MSI agreed to dismiss Huawei as a defendant in the legal dispute over misappropriated IP, while Huawei agreed to allow the transfer of its commercial agreements with MSI to NSN for a one-time fee, and to provide NSN with access to confidential information in order to support and service Motorola networks already deployed on Huawei hardware.

The Huawei Puzzle

With sales in 2010 of CNY 185.2 bn (EUR 19.9 bn[61]), a year-on-year increase of 24.2%, Huawei is without doubt the leading Chinese telecommunication equipment manufacturer. Its products are found both at home and abroad. Its 2010 sales revenue from overseas markets amounted to CNY 120.4 bn (EUR 12.9 bn), up 33.8% from the previous year. In other words, Huawei sells twice as much abroad as in China, indicating its drive to capture markets and take established multinational equipment manufacturers head on.

If one is to believe the firm's annual report, the Shenzhen-based firm invested CNY 16.5 bn (EUR 1.8 bn) in R&D in 2010, an increase of 24.1% year-on-year. More than 50,000 employees (46% of the total workforce) are currently engaged in R&D. Twenty research institutes have been established across the world including the USA, Germany, Sweden, Russia, India and China. They are complemented by a number of joint innovation centres with leading telecommunication operators. At the end of 2010, Huawei had cumulatively filed 49,040 patent applications (of which 3,869 were patent applications in China, 8,892 were international patent applications under the Patent Cooperation Treaty, and 8,279 were overseas patent applications). Of the 17,765 authorised patents granted, 3,060 were overseas patents. Huawei's presence is also increasingly felt in international standardisation groups. By the end of 2010, the firm was a member of 123 standards organisations, including 3GPP, IETF, ITU, OMA, NGMN, ETSI, IEEE and 3GPP2. In 2010, Huawei also increased its patent portfolio in the US, either by purchasing patents (e.g. from the network equipment maker Avici Systems) or by filing for patents based on its own technology.

---

[61] Exchange rate as of June 14, 2011: EUR 1 = USD 1.43 and EUR 1 = CNY 9.30.

While customers express great satisfaction with Huawei's products, the firm's relentless expansion abroad means that it has encountered a number of political obstacles — its ambitions have ignited the US government's suspicions that it may have links with the Chinese military. The company has consequently had to renounce several deals in the US, having to back out on the grounds of national security and IP. Huawei's bid for US broadband network software maker 2Wire was rejected even though it was significantly higher than the winning bid in monetary terms. It also tried to buy equipment maker 3Com with US-based Bain Capital in 2007, but the plan was blocked by the US government's Committee on Foreign Investment in the United States (CFIUS) over concerns that Huawei had ties to the Chinese military. Huawei also sought to acquire assets from Nortel but lost to Sweden's Ericsson on questions of IP rights infringement. Similarly, when the Shenzhen-based firm set out to supply telecom equipment to Sprint Nextel, some senators were concerned that this might create substantial risk for American companies and possibly undermine national security. Finally, in May 2010, the Chinese firm paid USD 2 m (EUR 1.4 m) to acquire the staff and IP of 3Leaf Systems, a start-up working on cloud computing (i.e., the pooling of multiple server resources). Pentagon officials took the unusual step of asking the company to retroactively clear the deal with the CFIUS. On top of this, Huawei has also faced significant difficulties in penetrating the strategic accounts of other countries — for instance, reports of the recent tie-up between Huawei and the Bangalore-based Indian Institute of Science once again raised security concerns.

As the firm is not listed on any stock exchange, and given the opaqueness of firm ownership in China, it is extremely difficult to formally establish how close Huawei actually is to the Chinese government and military. According to its annual report, Huawei Technologies Co., Ltd is a wholly owned subsidiary of Shenzhen Huawei Investment & Holding Co., Ltd. The latter is solely owned by its employees without any third parties (including government bodies) holding any of its shares. In any case, informal connections to the Chinese military or any agency matter as much as formal ownership when it comes to security concerns. Strong relationships between firms and military agencies are not unheard of in Western countries in particular when it comes to telecommunication systems.

Protectionism Abroad and at Home

One of the reasons why the NSN–MSI deal took so long is that, in order to comply with anti-monopoly regulations, Motorola needed to gain approval from the governments of nine countries and regions where it had assets, including the US, the EU, China, Brazil and Japan.

Chinese Anti-monopoly Law (AML) took effect on 1 August 2008. It has served mainly as a mechanism to block or attach conditions to large mergers. Under AML, companies with annual turnovers of RMB 10 bn (EUR 1.1 bn) globally and RMB 400 m (EUR 43 m) in China, or combined turnovers of USD 2 bn (EUR 1.4 bn) in China, must get anti-trust approval for a proposed deal from the Chinese government. Once MOFCOM is satisfied that a submitted filing is complete, it conducts a review (commonly referred to as a Phase I review) for up to 30 calendar days. If MOFCOM identifies serious issues to consider further, it may notify the concerned parties before the end of the 30-day deadline that it will be conducting an extended (Phase II) review. Where no such decision is conveyed to the parties during the Phase I period, approval is deemed to have been provided at the end of 30 days. Where MOFCOM notifies the parties that it will conduct a Phase II review, this review must be completed within 90 calendar days (although the deadline may be extended up to an additional 60 days, if the parties consent, the submitted documents are inaccurate or require further verification, or relevant circumstances significantly change after the initial notification). Accordingly, MOFCOM's formal review process in relation to notified deals can last up to 180 days. In China, enforcement agencies are granted much greater power than those in Western countries and their actions are not usually subject to effective judicial review. A number of multinationals have complained about the slow pace and transparency of the evaluation and review process. In the case of Panasonic's takeover of Sanyo, the ministry accepted the filing four months after the company first lodged its file.

In principle, MOFCOM has exclusive jurisdiction over merger control in China. Extraterritorial jurisdiction will only be conferred on the Chinese competition authorities should the transaction have the potential to exert negative influence on competition in China. The current regime departs from the previous system, in place prior to the AML's entry into force, in which MOFCOM shared responsibility for merger review with the State Administration for Industry and Commerce. The Chinese anti-monopoly bureau is gaining influence in global mergers and acquisitions. It has set conditions for big transactions, including a requirement that Pfizer divest its Chinese swine vaccine business as part of its acquisition of Wyeth and an anti-trust probe that led to the block of Coca-Cola's bid for China Huiyuan Juice Group in 2009.

Conclusion

Whether they are Japanese, American or European, disputes over IP are a normal component of business for multinational companies (MNCs). The Nokia Siemens/Motorola case illustrates a new trend, i.e. Chinese firms are taking IP issues to court. The lawsuits that Huawei and ZTE (a rival Chinese telecommunication equipment manufacturer) recently filed against each other on the grounds of IP infringement indicate that the battle for IP does not solely pitch Chinese firms against MNCs. However, a deal running against the interests of a firm considered a domestic innovation powerhouse — at a time when China was promoting the development of domestic technology through its 'indigenous innovation' programme — was bound to draw attention from the government. In fact, MOFCOM has repeatedly complained that the US government is using the CFIUS process as a pretext for damping Chinese investment in the US. Not surprisingly China has recently unveiled its own foreign investment review process.

The case also signals that a number of Chinese firms are building valuable intellectual assets and will go to great length to defend them. In fact, one could argue that past litigation (e.g., with Cisco) directly stimulated the formulation of Huawei's IP rights strategy to 'protect and utilize autonomous IPRs, respect IPRs of others, improve core competence and strongly support global product strategy'.[62] The strategy is central to keep enhancing Huawei's brand and to move away from its low-cost vendor image.

Finally, the case highlights a number of points regarding Chinese firms venturing abroad. First, when Chinese firms have established IP rights under Chinese law and contracts with parties in the US or elsewhere, it is important for them to understand the scope of their IP rights under all of the potentially relevant legal regimes. Second, claims for preliminary injunctive relief before national courts can be critical to the outcome of a dispute, even where a contract provides for private arbitration. Huawei made the point that it would be futile to wait for an arbitral tribunal to form because the potential infringements may have already caused irreversible harm before the tribunal was appointed. In other words, overseas courts can help Chinese firms protect their legitimate rights in their overseas dealings.

---

[62] Xue, Lan, & Liang, Zheng. (2010). Relationships between IPR and Technology Catch Up: Some Evidence from China. In H. Odagiri, A. Goto, A. Sunami & R. R. Nelson (Eds.), *Intellectual Property Rights, Development, and Catch-Up* (Oxford University Press, Oxford).

In summary:

- Huawei has emerged as a serious competitor in the market for telecommunication equipment. Having cut its teeth in emerging markets, it is now in a position to offer products of high quality and at very competitive prices to established telecommunication service providers. Firms like British Telecom are rolling out some of their next-generation networks with Huawei products.
- Some Chinese firms are starting to put IP and the rights that come with it at the centre of their business strategy. While investing large amounts in R&D, Chinese telecommunication national champions are on the lookout for technologies that complement their offerings.
- Chinese firms are getting more astute at navigating the legal system abroad; while distinct, the reciprocal lawsuits and the protracted review by MOFCOM of the NSN acquisition illustrate the ambitions of Chinese national champions and the backing they can get from the state.
- All types of onshore and offshore mergers, equity and asset acquisitions, and other arrangements that involve companies acquiring control (including joint ventures) could be subject to merger reviews in China; business deals directly or indirectly involving Chinese national champions (like Huawei) have a high chance of attracting the attention of government officials.
- The Chinese anti-monopoly bureau may not represent a true barrier to global mergers and acquisitions (M&A), but it is difficult to predict how the Chinese government will behave whenever a national champion is affected by the deals; companies planning mergers or acquisitions should plan their transactions with MOFCOM's review in mind; high-level exchange between China and the EU on M&A review procedure may ease transactions by providing more transparency.
- So far Huawei seems to have faced less resistance deploying its activities in Europe than in the US or India; this may however change if the firm embarks on 'sensitive' IP acquisition from European firms or research institutions.

The Chinese Middle Class
(September 2012)

Paul French
Author

Executive Summary

The Chinese middle class is a relatively new phenomenon having only really begun to seriously emerge in the late 1990s. This middle class has been a result of a growing white-collar employment market, continued urbanisation,[63] a decade of annual wage rises of (on average) 7%,[64] and the opening up of a private property market and a sustained period of overall economic growth for China.

It is this urban, educated, white-collar middle class that has primarily been the main driver of the expansion of China's booming domestic retail consumption market in the last five years. The success of a wide range of European companies from luxury brands such as Louis Vuitton and Chanel, to mid-market fashion brands such as Zara and H&M, as well as food and beverage and car companies is largely due to the growth and spending tastes of the middle class.

The growth of the middle class has been encouraged, and to an extent, 'subsidised' informally by the government to help achieve the target of 'rebalancing' the economy towards greater consumption. In this sense the middle class is an

---

[63] According to a May 2012 survey by Chinese survey company QQ and UK market researchers Mintel, while most of the middle class are second-generation urban residents, 32% grew up outside of cities.

[64] According to the brokerage CLSA Emerging Markets, over the past decade, real urban incomes have risen by 151%.

active economic agent but is not highly connected in a sociopolitical sense around various causes.

However, the middle class, while the major driver of consumption and discretionary spending, does have concerns. These are primarily around social security issues at present — healthcare and pensions being paramount. In an online poll conducted by China's largest Internet portal in 2007, Sina, 50% of respondents in the middle class income bracket expected to have to fund their own pension entirely and only 20% believed that they would be able to rely partially on the government pension scheme.

Concerns over the future costs of pensions and healthcare among a middle class with ageing parents and children could turn into anger at the government for lack of sufficient provision. Similarly, issues of self-protection arise when considering anything that threatens their property or assets — be this infrastructure, development projects or environmental degradation.

Finally, middle class self-protection has also become a more politicised theme as witnessed by middle class anger at the recent spate of food scares.

Main Points

- The Chinese middle class is, at the present time, ostensibly an economic class rather than a political one, that is to say that its main drivers are economic advancement in order to gain greater personal/family levels of security and self-protection.
- The middle class is fulfilling the role of driving the expansion of the consumption economy. This is helping to 'rebalance' China's economy though this may become less significant as China's economy slows, wage growth is more restrained and the cost of living/inflation rises (referred to by Premier Wen Jiabao as China's 'uncaged tiger').

Introduction: Defining the Chinese Middle Class

In 2012 Chinese middle-income households constituted 13.4% of total urban households in China, or approximately 30 m households.[65] This is equivalent to

---

[65] Research from the Shanghai-based market research company Access Asia and the journal *China Economic Quarterly*.

approximately 100 m people. However, this number grows somewhat when grey income is factored in — money that is gained neither through salary nor declared to the tax authorities. Although it is hard, if not impossible, to quantify this significant sum it does mean that the actual number of households with incomes at a level considered to be middle class will be higher than official numbers state.

China's middle class is overwhelmingly, if not totally, urban based. In 2012, China had a total of 421.4 m households nationwide, both urban and rural, and 221.4 m urban households (close enough to half to show the roughly 50% urbanisation rate in China at the moment).[66] While the Chinese middle class now represents 13.4% of urban households, it represents only approximately 7% of total Chinese households. This shows that there are still considerable opportunities for growth; the differentiation in growth rates between urban households and middle class households shows that, although urbanisation is now clearly slowing, the number of existing urban households and families moving into the middle income bracket is growing healthily.

A number of factors allow the middle class to enjoy the possibility of home and asset ownership as well as disposable income on relatively low salaries. These include 'grey income', as well various effective 'subsidies' by the state, including low personal taxation rates, a degree of social security cover and insurance, centrally subsidised prices on key items such as food staples and petrol, low public transport costs and low service costs (due to the pool of low-cost labour provided by ongoing urbanisation).

A snapshot of the current urban middle class in China would define them as follows:

- A minimum personal income of RMB 7,000 (EUR 844) per month in tier 1 cities; a minimum RMB 5,000 (EUR 603) per month in tier 2 cities.
- A minimum family income of RMB 15,000 (EUR 1,809) per month in tier 1 cities; a minimum of RMB 10,000 (EUR 1,206) per month in tier 2 cities.
- Professionally overwhelmingly white-collar office workers in either state or private business (and government), self-employed or small and medium enterprise (SME) owners.
- Educated at college level or above.
- Invariably property owners and most likely to be car owners.

---

[66] China's National Bureau of Statistics (NBS).

Drivers of Middle Class Growth

Significant rural-urban migration has driven rapid growth of the middle classes. A third of the middle class grew up outside of the cities where they now live, which shows the importance of urbanisation to the growth of China's middle class.

Additionally, China's traditionally high savings rate has allowed the new middle class to acquire property, assets and consumer goods as well as travel regionally and internationally. However, what are referred to as 'savings' are actually a more complex issue. Indeed the term 'savings' is really a misnomer and the persistently high savings rate is effectively a form of self-taxation. The high savings rate (which is highest among the middle income group in China at between 20–50% of gross salary)[67] means that families do have significant reserves of disposable wealth, which must often be used in old age, and for healthcare and emergencies in the absence of a fully functioning universal welfare state.

Property ownership is a major cornerstone of the foundation of the Chinese middle class and 50% already own their properties outright.[68] The rise of the Chinese middle class is almost synonymous with the opening up of China's property market to private buying and selling in the late 1990s. Property ownership is a major way in which the middle class has been able to grow as continued urbanisation has allowed more new urbanites buy their own homes. With the government's 2012 decision to significantly expand low income housing construction, more Chinese than ever before will become new home owners — the central government's targets are for 5 m affordable apartments to be built by end of 2012, with a goal of reaching 36 m units by the end of 2015.

Crucially the Chinese middle class is working hard to pay off their mortgages as quickly as possible which, when achieved, frees up cash for discretionary spending. With 50% of the Chinese middle class already in ownership of their properties outright and new legislation preventing multiple purchasing of properties for speculation, this will free up additional money for future spending.

---

[67] QQ/Mintel 2012 Survey, included in Paul French, *Consumer Lifestyles: China's Middle Class*, June 2012, Mintel International.

[68] QQ/Mintel 2012 Survey, included in Paul French, *Consumer Lifestyles: China's Middle Class*, June 2012, Mintel International.

The Middle Class and Consumption

Beijing's stated long-term economic policy goal is to 'rebalance' China's economy by encouraging more consumption to offset the traditional reliance on the export economy and inward investment. The middle class is obviously key to this aim and is the major driver of most mid- to high-end consumer markets including cars, electronic appliances (both white goods, such as washing machines, refrigerators, freezers and cookers, and brown goods, such as televisions, home entertainment systems, DVD players), luxury goods and fashion, as well as imported food and beverage products (a key area for European companies).

The Chinese middle class consumer is demanding and, while willing to spend, looks for quality and innovation. Ownership of smartphones among China's middle class is almost universal[69] and they are the heaviest users of China's fast emerging e-commerce market.

However, one potential risk with this fast growing period of consumption is that while growth was initially cash-based it is now increasingly credit-driven, as Chinese banks and consumers discover various forms of credit — mortgages obviously, but also loans, hire purchase and credit cards. 43% of China's middle class now have one credit card and 52% more than one.[70] More worryingly, according to China's Central Bank, since 2010, the six-month overdue credit card debt rate has risen by more than 14%.

The Middle Class and the Environment

Concern for the environment appears to be rapidly becoming a key middle class concern. Middle class Chinese have shown themselves to be increasingly supportive of grass-roots environmental movements with both money (donations) and time (volunteering). The range of issues is obviously broad — air, water, earth quality as well as species protection, waste and industrial pollution.

---

[69] 95% according to QQ/Mintel, included in Paul French, *Consumer Lifestyles: China's Middle Class*, June 2012, Mintel International.

[70] QQ/Mintel 2012 Survey, included in Paul French, Consumer Lifestyles: China's Middle Class, June 2012, Mintel International and backed up by similar numbers from MasterCard's own research.

Additionally, the middle class has become more vocal on issues that it feels directly affect it or its assets. This is effectively another form of self-protection — maintaining a good property resale price can be as important as hygiene. And here the middle class has uncharacteristically been quite vocal in complaining and protesting. Examples have included the demonstrations in Shanghai around extensions to the maglev train (a project involving several EU-based companies) and its proximity to properties and potential detriment to the health of residents nearby and the Xiamen PX case, a controversial petrochemical project that began in 2007 in southern China that was halted after a series of unprecedented demonstrations, mostly by middle class people.

Mr Pan Yue, a Vice Minister within China's Ministry of Environmental Protection, told the Western media in the aftermath of the Xiamen PX case, 'The Xiamen PX Project is not a victory of people's opinion, but manifested a systematic problem. It shows the demands of the middle class on the environment. It shows the relationship between the environmental assessment, middle class and the environment.'[71] It seems the Party has recognised middle class concerns about the environment.

Middle Class Self-Protection Strategies

Self-protection strategies can take many forms — educating children overseas (often in Europe); closely reading packaging labels; going organic; not buying goods in sectors where fakes and tainted products are common, such as infant formula or pharmaceuticals; buying goods overseas when travelling ('arbitraging'); and seeking out imported food, beverage and other products, considered to be of a higher standard than local equivalents. This is a trend that European manufacturers are able to take advantage of in many areas. For instance, European brand household chemicals are considered more effective in promoting hygiene and killing germs, thereby 'protecting' families.

Much of this activity has been the result of middle class fear of tainted products following repeated scandals around infant formula, milk and numerous other products that have become popular with middle class consumers.

Some of these self-protection strategies can seem innocuous — for instance the rise in Fairtrade products, organic food and official certification of products.

---

[71] Geall, S. (ed), *China and the Environment: The Green Revolution* (Zed Books, London, 2012).

Chinese consumers, when they can afford it, are trading up to 'organic' and 'green' produce as a potential way to self-protect — 80% are willing to pay more for organic and 87% more for 'green' products.[72] Similarly there is the small emergence of a Fairtrade movement in China too which consumers appear willing to pay more for; though this is at an extremely nascent stage at present. European manufacturers and brands potentially involved in food scares could, at best, find themselves with PR problems in China and, at worse, legal action taken against them. However, there are opportunities for European organic and green food concerns as well as local and regional certification bodies to become more involved in China's troubled food sector.

Conclusion

The Chinese middle class has arrived and is still growing and developing. Its future growth will not be a repeat of the last decade as China's economy slows, wage growth tapers off, the country's demographics fundamentally shift to an older weighted society and urbanisation slows. A slowing economy may have some detrimental effects on the middle class — wage growth combined with a rising cost of living and added inflationary pressure may curtail spending at the least, but could also lead to a rise in unemployment, mortgage defaults, credit non-repayment and a 'debt overhang' at worse. Ensuring that European banks with exposure to major Chinese lenders are aware of this scenario will be important for long-term planning.

Ultimately the growth in both middle class numbers and middle class spending will increasingly come from tier 2 cities, as wealth filters outwards from the coastal cities in China promoting social movement upwards. This will take some time, particularly in an economy with more restrained growth rates, but China's society and consumer base should start to look more diamond-shaped (a few rich, a few poor and most people in the middle) rather than its current more pyramidal shape. This should be encouraging news for European brands across the board from cars and luxury goods, to everyday items (soap, shampoo, diapers, etc.) and fashion, as more middle class shoppers enter the consumer market.

However, growing middle class incomes combined with greater asset ownership, notably property ownership, have the potential to politicise the urban middle class

---

[72] QQ/Mintel 2012 Survey, included in Paul French, *Consumer Lifestyles: China's Middle Class*, June 2012, Mintel International.

to look beyond consumerism and asset attainment. The potential growth of this politicisation will possibly be affected by one, or a combination, of the following:

- While presently the Chinese middle class is driven primarily by economic objectives — acquisition of property, financial savings and assets in order to provide security and self-protection — it is increasingly starting to realise that certain political ends are necessary to ensure this protection.
- Primary among these political goals are improvements in the legal system to protect assets, primarily personal property, savings and small businesses. But this political engagement is starting to move into areas that can be characterised as Nimby-ism ('not in my back yard') such as industrial project planning permission (i.e. Xiamen PX), infrastructure planning (e.g. maglev extensions close to housing compounds) and general environmental degradation that threatens the ability to self-protect (e.g. water and air quality).
- The middle class has also shown itself to be particularly sensitive to 'scares' that may threaten it — for instance food scares.
- Members of China's middle class may not yet be fully aware of their shared concerns and values — Nimby-ism, environmentalism, concerns over food scares and economic growth, etc. However, they do have the ability to connect up various campaign issues if they wish through almost universal access to means of communication such as smartphones and the Internet.

Policy Implications

The EU needs to be aware that the key consumer group driving growing consumption of European products and services in China is the new emerging middle class. This middle class consumer group is highly aware of the origin of the imported products/services that they purchase and increasingly look to self-protect through buying products perceived to have high production and safety standards. Therefore, a Europe-wide effort to persuade the Chinese middle class consumer that European standards are high in terms of product safety and reliability could be beneficial. Convincing the Chinese middle class consumer of this should yield a strong brand image for 'Made in Europe' products and ultimately sales.

Middle class Chinese parents are increasingly keen for their children to study abroad; after the US, the UK is second choice, with non-English speaking Europe third. The EU should be aware that this desire to study abroad continues to grow and that much of the decision-making process about where to study is often based on ease of access to visas. It is generally agreed that Australia has become a more desirable overseas study location of late due to easy visa issuance; European border control authorities need to see Chinese students as a key group of visa applicants.

The EU should also appreciate the growing global spending power of the Chinese middle class as it travels abroad and increasingly shops overseas. Europe is a target destination for aspiring middle class Chinese shoppers and they are keenly aware of both visa limitations in some markets (e.g. the UK), as well as the ability to claim tax back when leaving the EU (allowing them a significant discount on mandatory high luxury taxes in the PRC).

As demonstrated above the emerging middle class is becoming increasingly concerned about a number of issues that could lead them to become more politically engaged than at present. Primary among these are the environment and its potentially adverse impact on health and lifestyle. Additionally the other set of issues that are of most concern to the emerging middle class are social welfare issues, in particular healthcare and pensions. Beijing is aware of this discontent and is keen to seek advice, often from European countries and the EU, on potential alternative funding systems for healthcare and pensions.

Tax and Pensions in China
(May 2012)

Stuart Leckie and Rita Xiao
Stirling Finance Ltd.

Main Points

- As China's age structure evolves it is facing the serious challenge of an expanding retired population supported by a shrinking working population. This has been further exacerbated by rapid urbanisation, uneven economic development and an imbalanced sex ratio for new births. In response, the Chinese government has introduced several pension reforms.
- Urban pensions:
    - In 1997, State Council Document No. 26 was issued, aimed at transforming an overly generous pension system into a three-pillar model, broadly in line with the World Bank. The current pension system follows a revised five-pillar template.
    - All state pensions enjoy tax exemptions on pension contributions, investments and benefits.
- Enterprise annuities:
    - An enterprise annuity (EA) plan is a voluntary defined contribution scheme with funded individual accounts that both employer and employees can contribute to.
    - Compared with the compulsory state pension plan, EAs have not achieved their expected growth since establishment. The lack of a uniform tax policy applied at the national level has slowed the rate of EA development.

- China is still too reliant on the state pension system. A 'partial TEE' tax mode (for definition, see Table 1, below) has been suggested for EA development by pension experts.
- Commercial pensions:
  - Commercial pensions are a voluntary supplementary pension system provided by licensed insurance companies.
  - In 2009, these group pensions were granted the same treatment as EA plans whereby employer contributions within 5% of total employee payroll are tax deductible. However, as with EA plans, commercial pensions offer no explicit tax preferences for employees in the pension contribution, investment and benefit process.
- Rural pensions:
  - Serious rural pension reform began in late 2008, following the central government's promise to cover the entire rural population with a viable pension system by 2020.
  - The basic rural social pension pool will be fully supported by the government. The government will also contribute towards supplementary individual accounts.
  - As with the state urban pension, the new rural pension scheme will enjoy tax exemptions on pension contributions, investments and benefits.
  - Nevertheless, the rural system remains far behind the urban system in terms of benefits and current assets.

Table 1. Simplified tax modes and their effects on pension development.

Tax modes*	EEE**	EET	TET
Pension contribution	Tax exempt	Tax exempt	Taxable
Pension investment	Tax exempt	Tax exempt	Tax exempt
Pension benefit	Tax exempt	Taxable	Taxable
Effect on pension development	Very strong impetus	Strong impetus	Some disadvantage
Example	State pension in many developed countries	US 401(k)	Commercial pension in Portugal

*Tax policy modes: E — Tax exempt; T — Taxable.
**Three letters in the acronym stand for tax policies in the three pension segments: the 1st E for pension contribution, the 2nd E for pension investment, and the 3rd E for pension benefit.

- Pensions for expatriates:
    - 2011's new Social Insurance Law requires expatriates to participate in all five social security programmes — pensions, medical insurance, work injury insurance, unemployment insurance and maternity payments. Only German and South Korean expatriates are exempt because their countries have bilateral treaties with China on social security provision.
- In light of the success of the recent EU-China Social Security Cooperation Project, further cooperation could be explored through:
    - Broadening the investment scope for state pensions.
    - Developing EA and commercial pensions with more preferential tax modes.
    - Facilitating the synthesis of central and local policies regarding social tax on expatriates.

Introduction

The sixth national population census revealed that the total population of mainland China reached 1.34 bn people by the end of 2010, of whom 13.3% were aged 60 or above. As the country's age structure evolves, China is facing a serious challenge — a shrinking working population supporting a rapidly expanding retired population. The so-called 1–2–4 phenomenon, which stands for one child, two parents and four grandparents, is becoming increasingly apparent in China.

The Chinese government is fully aware of these issues and has introduced several pension reforms. Pensions, as an elastic public good, are often heavily influenced by government tax policies, relating to three segments: 1) pension contributions — whether employees' and employers' contributions are deductible before paying income/corporate tax; 2) pension investment — whether investment income and capital gains are taxed; and 3) pension benefits — whether employees are tax exempted when benefits are paid either by lump sum or regular annuities. Conventional international tax modes for pension systems are summarised in Table 1.

This paper aims to outline the pension systems in China, *vis-à-vis*:

- The urban pension system.
- Enterprise Annuities (EAs).
- Commercial pension business.
- The rural pension system.

Demographic Dynamics

The one-child policy became effective in China in the late 1970s. Without this, estimates suggest that China's population would now be around 1.7 bn, i.e. 350 m greater than the actual current population. This low fertility policy led to a lower child dependency ratio and a higher working age to total population ratio; however, China now faces an ageing population and deteriorating dependency ratio as severe issues.

The country's population reached 1.34 bn at the end of 2010. The proportion of young people aged 14 or below has decreased from 27.7% to 16.6% in the past two decades, while the population aged 60 or above has increased from 7.7% to the current level of 13.3%. This trend is expected to continue according to EU projections. Furthermore, an imbalanced sex ratio for new births (currently 118 baby boys born for every 100 girls), rapid urbanisation and economic development inequality across the nation are posing significant challenges for China's pension systems.

Urban Pension System

The urban pension system was originally principally applied to state-owned enterprise (SOE) employees, who received a pension after retirement equal to 80–90% of final salary. In July 1997, State Council Document No. 26 was issued, aimed at transforming the overly generous SOE system to a three-pillar model, broadly in line with World Bank recommendations. In order to address certain limitations, including the separation of the social pool pension from the individual account pension and full funding of the latter, Document No. 42 was issued in December 2000.

Under the influence of the World Bank's revised five-pillar pension template, Table 2 sets out a summary of the current urban pension system using Chinese terminology. Contributions of around 20% and 8% of employees' monthly salaries are paid to Pillar Ia and Pillar Ib respectively, and in return these two mandatory state pension components theoretically provide the average urban retiree with 20% and 38.5%, respectively, of the average final monthly salary after a working lifetime of 35 years. Contributions are subject to a cap of 300% of local average city pay for the previous year. The current retirement ages as stipulated by the law are 60 for men, 55 for white-collar women and 50 for blue-collar women.

With legacy SOE pensions and the pay as you go (PAYG) structure designed for Pillar Ia, current cumulative pension assets are largely derived from individual accounts (IAs), which have experienced exponential growth. Indeed, it is estimated

Table 2. China's five-pillar urban pension system.

Pillars (WB)		Chinese terminology	Contributions	Benefits	Funded status
	Zero	Zero: Minimum guarantee (Di Bao)	N/A	Basic cost-of-living allowance	From government
State	I	Ia: Mandatory Social Pool Old Age Pension	ER*: 20% of salaries (regional differences exist)	Monthly pension based on average local monthly wage, indexed individual wage and years of employment	Pay as you go (PAYG)
	II	Ib: Mandatory Individual Account (IA) Pension	EE*: 8% of salary	Monthly pension of 1/139 of IA balance at the time of retirement provided at least 15 years' contributions are paid	Should be funded
Private	III	II: Voluntary Enterprise Annuity (set up by eligible employers)	ER; EE	Lump sum or annuity benefit	Funded
		III: Other Voluntary Benefits, e.g. Insured Group Pension Plans	ER; EE	Lump sum or annuity benefit	Funded
Private & State	IV	IV: Family support; subsidised healthcare and housing	N/A	Varies	From government or family

*ER — employer; EE — employee.
Source: Stirling Finance Research.

Table 3. Investment scope.

	Equities/linked products	Financial/corporate bonds	Government-bonds/ deposits
Pillar Ia (state)	—	—	100%
Pillar Ib (state) (IA)	—	—	100%
Pillar II (EA)	< 30%	< 50%	> 20%
Pillar III (non-EA)	< 20%	< 20%	< 100%

Source: Stirling Finance Research.

that the total cumulative balances will amount to RMB 4.5–6 tn (EUR 0.5–0.7 tn)[73] in year 2020 and RMB 10–11 tn (EUR 1.2–1.3 tn) by 2030.

In terms of investment scope, Pillar Ib assets (and Pillar Ia, if any) are limited to bank deposits and government bonds, with an average return claimed to be around 2% p.a. in the past 10 years. EA plans, however, are allowed more flexible investment scope (see Table 3).

Urban pension benefits are increased each year, usually by an amount between price inflation (averaging 2.1% p.a. in the last decade) and earnings escalation (typically 10–12% p.a.).

Regarding tax treatment, all state pensions (Pillar Zero, Ia and Ib) use the EEE mode, meaning that all three segments in the state pension system enjoy tax exemption. To illustrate, mandatory pension contributions are tax deductible for both corporations and individuals, while investment returns and pension benefits (both lump sum and annuities) are tax exempted. However, any voluntary contributions above regulatory limit and the pension benefits derived therefrom are not tax deductible.

Enterprise Annuities

An EA plan is a voluntary defined contribution scheme with funded, individual accounts, and both employers and employees can make contributions. Contributions by the enterprise are limited to a cap of 8.33% of the employee's annual wage, i.e. one-twelfth of the previous year's wages. From the SOEs' perspective, an EA is an opportunity to bring replacement rates back up towards the 80–90% level.

---

[73] At the time of writing (24 April 2012), the exchange rate was EUR 1 = RMB 8.30.

EA funds are required to be set up under trust in accordance with China's Trust Law, through an unbundled model comprising of Trustee, Administrator, Investment Manager and Custodian. Two batches of 58 licences in total were awarded to 38 institutions in 2005 and 2007, with RMB 281 bn (EUR 33.8 bn) accumulated EA assets being held under trust as at the end of 2010. Regarding investment performance, EAs have achieved reasonable returns in recent years, with 3.4% in 2010 and an annualised return of 6.06% averaged over the last six years.

Compared to the compulsory state pension system, EA plans have not achieved the expected growth since establishment. Moreover, since tax deductibility should be a principal incentive for employers to offer EA plans, the lack of a uniform tax policy applied at a national level has initially slowed the rate of EA development. In December 2009, the tax regulation for EAs was finally codified by the State Administration of Taxation (SAT), but is still sub-optimal. Accordingly, employer contributions to an EA plan within 5% of total employee payroll can be deducted from profit before corporate tax. However, an employee's contributions are not tax deductible and indeed employer's contributions are treated as a separate income source for the employee and hence are subject to personal income tax.

Moreover, there is no explicit tax preference in respect of EA pension investments or benefits. In practice, investment income and capital gains are accumulated tax free, while the tax treatment for pension benefits varies according to provincial regulations. As a result, significant imbalances exist geographically and among enterprises, impeding EA development in the past several years. However, it has been suggested by Chinese pension experts to adopt a 'partial TEE' mode for EA plans, with employees' pension contributions not attracting tax relief.

Commercial Pension Business

A commercial pension is a voluntary supplementary pension system provided by licensed insurance companies. As at the end of 2010, there were more than 50 group pension insurance business entities offering a wide variety of group pension and individual annuity products. Five specialised pension insurance companies have been set up to provide both EA insurance and group pension insurance, namely, Ping An Annuity Insurance, Taiping Pension, China Life Pension, Taikang Pension & Insurance, and Changjiang Pension Insurance. Due to significant competition from EA plans, the size of group pension assets has declined since 2005.

Compared with EA plans, group pension products enjoyed no tax preference initially, causing many former supplementary group annuities to convert to EA plans. In 2009, the tax regulation enacted by the SAT finally granted group pension insurance the same tax treatment as EA plans: employer contributions within 5% of total employee payroll are tax deductible. Also as with EA plans, there is no explicit tax preference for employees in the pension contribution, investment and benefit process. However, the insurance indemnity can be tax exempted for individual annuity.

Rural Pension System

The rural population of China has just reduced to under half of the total population, resulting from a strong rural-to-urban migration trend: young people from the countryside move to the cities and often settle as urban residents. This trend leaves the rural elderly vulnerable to losing their main historic pillar; namely, family support.

In late 2008, serious rural pension reform finally began after the central government's official promise to cover the entire rural population with a viable pension system by 2020. Rural residents aged 16 and above, who are neither students nor currently participating in the state pension system as urban workers, are eligible to join the rural system on a voluntary basis, with pension payments starting from age 60 irrespective of gender.

As illustrated in Table 4, the basic social pool pension will be fully supported by government, providing no less than RMB 55 (EUR 6.6) per month for each individual, on an unfunded basis. For individual accounts, the government will

Table 4. China's new rural pension system.

Terminology	Contributions	Benefits	Funded status
Basic Social Pool	100% from government budget	No less than RMB 55 (EUR 6.6) per month	Unfunded
Individual Account	*Individuals*: RMB 100/200/300/400/500 (ranging from EUR 12.0 to EUR 60.2) per year *Government*: No less than RMB 30 (EUR 3.6) each year *Other sources*	Monthly pension benefit of 1/139 of IA balance at pension age assuming at least 15 years' contribution; otherwise, lump sum payable	Funded (accumulated in accordance with 1-year bank deposit rate)

Source: Stirling Finance Research.

contribute no less than RMB 30 (EUR 3.6) per year while individuals choose to contribute between RMB 100 (EUR 12.0) and RMB 500 (EUR 60.2) annually, at RMB 100 (EUR 12.0) intervals. Moreover, as an incentive to participate in the new scheme, rural residents who are already 60 can immediately receive the basic social pool pension benefit provided that their children participate in the new system and make contributions into their individual accounts. Regarding tax treatment, the new rural pension system has adopted the EEE tax mode, the same as the state urban pension.

Pension for Expatriates

On 1 July 2011, China's new Social Insurance Law came into effect, requiring expatriates to participate in all five social security programmes, namely, pension, medical insurance, work injury insurance, unemployment insurance and maternity payments. Under this new law, Germany and South Korea are the only countries whose expatriates are exempt, due to bilateral treaties with China on social security provision. However, only five local governments have released their implementation rules and significant disparities exist. For example, although Chinese nationals from Hong Kong, Macao and Taiwan are explicitly excluded by central regulation from paying social insurance contributions, Chengdu and Suzhou are enforcing mandatory contributions through local implementation rules.

Conclusion and Implications

To conclude, China has achieved great progress with pension reforms during the last two decades, but major concerns still remain:

- Facing demographic challenges, China has established a multi-pillar pension system for the urban sector. Accumulated state pension assets are experiencing exponential growth, facilitated by EEE preferential tax treatment. However, unsatisfactory investment returns pose a huge challenge for long-term pension assets.
- China is still too reliant on the state pension system, while both EA plans and commercial pension business have not achieved expected growth. Currently these supplementary plans lack preferential tax treatment, and a 'partial TEE' tax mode has been suggested for EA development by Chinese pension experts.

- The new rural pension has just started, and is expanding rapidly with government support. However, there is still a huge gap between the two systems and the benefits and current assets of rural systems cannot be compared to the urban position.
- Geographic disparities exist in China regarding social security, private sector pensions and tax treatment for expatriates.

In light of the success of the recent EU-China Social Security Cooperation Project, further cooperation could be explored regarding tax and pensions in China.

- More pension investment expertise could be introduced by the EU, to help diversify China's state pension investment channels and grow the assets. The average investment returns for these accumulated assets, at only 2% p.a., should be compared with the three different types of inflation in China, namely, price inflation (5.4% in 2011), wage inflation (averaging between 10–12% p.a.) and asset inflation (e.g. 15–20% p.a. for residential property).
- Preferential tax policies should be utilised in the supplementary pension sector as a stimulus to accelerate growth. It is strongly recommended that an EEE or EET tax mode be introduced for both EA business and commercial pension insurance, exemplifying the US 401(k) scheme.
- More cooperation could be explored regarding expatriates' pensions. Apart from Germany, more countries should seek bilateral treaties with China on social security provision, and to facilitate synchronising the process among central and local policies.

Waste Management in China
(March 2012)

Anonymous

Executive Summary

China's waste management problem is important to the EU because it is linked to a number of global issues (environmental damage, greenhouse gases and public health) and it represents commercial opportunities for EU companies. China also continues to be a destination for EU waste.

Integrated and sustainable waste management seems to be a long way off for China. The Chinese authorities face a very significant set of challenges including the volume of waste, rapid growth in consumption, rising costs and ineffective implementation of policy. There is urgent need for progress given the detrimental impact waste has on the environment, energy efficiency, the economy and people's health. Conversely, successful action could have a very positive impact. Waste volumes are forecast to continue increasing so the challenge of decoupling economic growth and materials consumption is significant.

Due to fast-growing waste volumes and the struggle to manage pollution and harmful health impacts (for example, dioxins from incineration), waste management remains a sensitive area with Chinese policy makers, and increasingly the Chinese people. Discussions regarding policy, data and programmes are therefore not straightforward.

Current policy initiatives and budgets, even with the increased focus on waste in the 12th Five Year Programme, do not look adequate to address the challenges.

This is compounded by the number of ministries and levels of government that need to act cohesively, and a lack of enforcement at regional and local levels. It is not clear whether strategic thinking has a long enough timeframe and is done in sufficient depth.

Effective engagement with the EU would probably be welcomed by China, and could provide valuable assistance across a number of disciplines, categories of waste and organisations.

EU collaboration should focus on types of waste and aspects of waste management which are more dangerous, more polluting, will grow dramatically and which, if treated effectively, could deliver energy-saving and environmental benefits. Ideally, this would mean agreeing engagement in areas of greatest impact, e.g. hazardous waste, municipal solid waste and industrial waste. There is good experience in certain Member States which can be shared. Co-funding might be an option, at least with the Chinese providing in-kind support. The EU will need to appoint a combination of Chinese project management and waste management expertise — officials working together with external resources.

To maximise impact for the EU, an approach involving a range of organisations and support for business is recommended (although there are risks with intellectual property rights). This should be coordinated and project managed by an external project team (under EU direction) to identify cross-cutting issues, realise synergies and maximise impact. To ensure effective and successful delivery, this would ideally be jointly planned and monitored with the Chinese side.

Main Points

- This document focuses on solid waste, providing a background summary of the estimated volumes, treatments, future drivers and challenges.
- Recent and emerging policy is considered together with the estimated national budget and highlights of some recent initiatives. The picture is one of an incomplete policy framework, variable implementation and patchy enforcement.
- The number of government departments involved, together with the dynamics between them, makes the task of improving national and local waste management that much greater.
- A range of foreign companies are involved in waste management, but it appears that many have not found this a straightforward process, even when compared to other areas of foreign involvement in China.

- It is likely to require careful negotiation and patience, but EU engagement could play a valuable role in assisting China in this field.

Background/Context
Types and quantities of waste

This document focuses on solid waste (rather than aqueous or gaseous). In China, solid waste is classified in three categories and generates the following estimated annual volumes:

- Industrial solid waste (ISW), mainly from mining and steel, 2 bn tonnes (t).
- Municipal solid waste (MSW), 250–350 m t.
- Hazardous waste (HW), 15 m t.

By comparison, total EU waste generated is 3 bn t (of which 100 m t is hazardous).

It is currently a challenge to find accurate, up-to-date estimates for many important measures of waste. There is a possibility that more useful estimates based on recent academic surveys and analysis may be released in the future.

Treatment of waste

- Waste separation remains a great challenge although schemes have started to be implemented in major cities.
- Reports regarding recycling rates indicate mixed messages. Anecdotally, anything which generates a margin is taken away by recycling companies (state-run and private), suggesting high recycling rates.
- Landfill remains the dominant means of disposal for 60% of the remaining MSW collected in China. A further 25% is dumped, and 13% incinerated (there are plans to increase this to 35%).
- In the EU, on average, 42% of MSW is recycled, 38% goes to landfill, and 20% is incinerated.

A high proportion of the MSW collected in China is organic or 'catering' waste (circa 50%), apparently offering opportunities for 'waste to energy' (WTE) treatment, mostly through incineration. There were plans to more than double the number of plants to 148 during the past Five Year Plan period 2006–2011 (there were 93 at the end of 2009). The economics and implementation of the expansion in incineration have since been challenged — this is explored in more detail below.

Macro drivers

Key macroeconomic trends are expected to continue in China: sustained growth in the economy, including industrial production, urbanisation (now over 50%), and growing consumption. These trends will all continue to drive unprecedented increases in the quantity of waste generated, placing significant demands on the emerging waste management processes and infrastructure.

The scale of the challenge

A comprehensive World Bank report was written in 2005 (we are not aware of anything as comprehensive that has been written since). It identified issues and recommendations for waste management in China, a number of which are still valid today:

- China surpassed the US as the world's largest waste generator in 2004.
- By 2030, MSW from China's urban areas was forecast to increase by 150% to 480 m t, more than twice the amount estimated to be generated in the US over the same period (the total China figure could potentially reach 600 m t; these estimates implied circa 250 m of MSW in 2010).
- In 2002 over 1 bn t of ISW was generated in China (over five times the amount of MSW). The figure for HW was 10 m t.
- All aspects of the waste management system were undergoing wholesale change. It was established that China needed to move up the 'waste management hierarchy', promoting waste minimisation, reuse and recycling, over other waste disposal methods.
- 1,400 new landfills were expected by 2025 (circa 1,000 already existed in major cities).
- China could face an eight-fold increase in the waste management budget by 2020.

- Increasing waste incineration from the then figure of 1% to a targeted 30% would at least double global ambient dioxin levels (a highly toxic persistent organic pollutant (POP)).
- Continuing challenges included increasing coverage, environmental requirements, cost-effective service delivery, 'brownfield' sites and sludge disposal.
- A number of critical issues were identified, including: information availability, decision-making processes and institutional arrangements, operating facilities, financing, private sector involvement and carbon financing.

Bearing in mind consistent growth in China's GDP, and the likely associated increase in MSW per capita, if China does not significantly improve its waste management, it seems quite possible that the 600 m t estimate for MSW in 2030 could be too low.

For hazardous waste, management and measurement are focused on industrial sectors (although they probably significantly underestimate the quantity); there is little or no management system for household hazardous waste.

Existing legislation

Legislation, regulations and guidelines in China have been growing but compared to the EU, there is still much to do both in terms of the central framework and local implementation, measurement and enforcement.

Some of the key legislation and regulations include:

- Laws:
    - Environmental Protection Law (1989).
    - Environment Pollution Caused by Solid Waste (amended in 2004).
    - Cleaner Production Promotion Law (2002).
    - Circular Economy Promotion Law (2008).
- Administrative regulations:
    - Hazardous waste.
    - Medical waste.
    - E-waste.
- Department rules: hazardous waste, municipal waste, recyclable waste, waste import/export.
- Local regulations.

Current Policy
Policy initiatives

Issued last year, the 12th Five Year Programme (FYP), running from 2011 to 2015, reflects increasing concerns in terms of energy security, energy efficiency and energy utilisation, together with a greater focus on the low carbon agenda, recycling, pollution control and safety, and protection of the environment. Specifically, the FYP gives greater attention to waste management and recycling.

As part of the development of a 'circular economy', and intensifying environmental protection, the programme encourages:

- Strengthened regulation (including on heavy metals, hazardous waste and soil pollution).
- Accelerated construction of waste treatment facilities.
- Upgraded waste separation, recycling systems and recovery of renewable resources.

With sustained pressure on China's level of greenhouse gas (GHG) emissions, effective management of MSW could offer a modest but not insignificant reduction in GHG, as well as offering a positive economic impact and more energy efficient growth.

In spring 2011, the State Council approved proposals by 16 ministries to strengthen the work of urban waste management companies, allowing treatment of perhaps 80% of urban refuse. A month ago, the Ministry of Environmental Protection (MEP) issued its own plan for the next three years; one of the nine major objectives is to achieve a significant improvement in the control of pollution arising POPs, hazardous chemicals and waste.

In terms of other recent developments and targets:

- 35 landfill gas (LFG) utilisation projects had been completed and commissioned throughout mainland China by the end of 2010, reducing methane and GHG emissions.
- Recently, a target of building 1,200 sewage plants in the next five years was set, with a combined treatment capacity of 46 m t.
- By 2015, the comprehensive utilisation rate of ISW is targeted at 72% and the urban household MSW treatment rate at 80%.

- An extensive survey has been undertaken over recent years by the China Society for Environmental Sciences (CSES); the data from this will hopefully allow more rigorous policy making and implementation.

There is also growing recognition that certain types of waste require particular attention, for example hazardous waste, medical waste and e-waste, with more detailed regulations and guidelines gradually being published.

National budget

In terms of China's investment in waste treatment facilities, certain estimates have recently been reported. China Solid Waste Net estimated RMB 170 bn (EUR 20 bn) during 2011–2015 — more than double the amount invested in the previous five years. Standard Chartered Bank estimated that investments in municipal waste treatment will quadruple to RMB 286 bn (EUR 34 bn) for central, provincial, local and private sector spend. These sources therefore imply a cost of RMB 34–57 bn (EUR 4–7 bn) per annum.

The 2005 World Bank report estimated a required annual spend of circa RMB 115 bn (EUR 14 bn) by 2010, apparently double the current estimated budget.

Comment

Given the wider objectives which the MEP has to address, including pollution reduction and the safety of drinking water, realistically only limited resources can be allocated to solid waste management. However, the effective management of waste can in itself make an important contribution to these key objectives. It is not clear whether the extent of the growing challenges is fully understood in government or if sufficient priority is being given to addressing them. The number of ministries and levels of government involved exacerbates the problem.

There are arguments that the rate of increase in waste volumes starts to decrease as an economy matures and waste management improves. Some estimates suggest that this may occur around 2020–2025 in China's case although it may be premature to rely on this scenario. The World Bank states that a planning horizon of 25 years is needed for waste management although, again, it is not clear whether the planning period and system is sufficiently robust.

The increase in incineration and WTE plants is understandable given pressures on landfill, but concerns exist about this expansion. For example, it can be unclear whether suitable pollution controls are effectively put in place resulting in concerns about the level of dioxins and the extent to which coal or oil is being used.

International waste markets are increasingly interconnected, for example, through the export of EU and US recyclable waste for processing in China, with its resultant problems.

It is understandable that policy implementation takes time, however in certain respects China could learn from other countries and consider more accelerated development, potentially advancing more quickly than some developed countries have done.

The Role of Central and Local Government

Central government provides the policy framework for waste management, largely driven by the National Development and Reform Commission (NDRC), Ministry of Finance (MOF), MEP and Ministry of Housing and Urban-Rural Development (MOHURD, formerly the Ministry of Construction). This leaves significant responsibilities for provincial and municipal government to determine local policy and ensure effective implementation.

The number of government departments involved in aspects of waste management, at national, provincial and local levels, increases the challenge of ensuring integrated policy and implementation. There seems to be considerable variation in policy, standards and enforcement, including funding, responsibilities and transparency. This is coupled with issues and sensitivities, such as corruption and unemployment levels as a result of closing down unregulated waste management companies.

The proportion of funding for waste management from central budgets is not known at this stage. It is also unknown how squeezed these budgets may become at the local level, given local government funding constraints.

Can pilot city provinces play a role?

Five cities and two provinces will reportedly set caps on GHG emissions in preparation for the launch of local carbon markets. These will set 'overall emissions control targets', submit proposals on how to hit the targets, and establish a dedicated fund to support the project. In addition, 100 other entities are to organise their own regional CO_2 emissions trading platforms.

The State Council has approved an implementation plan drawn up by Guangdong, China's biggest CO_2-emitting province, to cutting carbon intensity by 20%. As part of addressing the environmental agenda, it is understood that Guangdong is actively considering waste management issues and opportunities.

Entities Already Involved in Waste Management

A range of entities are involved in waste management:

i) *Companies*

The increase in a national pilot programme announced last year reportedly triggered the development of a large number of 'waste recovery' companies. These are estimated by one source to be around 100,000 in number, providing jobs for 18 m people, reportedly with the potential for revenue to grow at 30% annually. These are both state-owned and private entities; many of the latter are believed to operate illegally without regulation.

Registers of companies with environmental or waste handling permits are sometimes published by officials, particularly for hazardous waste. A number of foreign waste processing companies are already active or considering the market, for example, Veolia and Safetykleen.

Elements of the waste management industry have become increasingly interconnected commercially. For example, high proportions of certain types of waste are now exported from developed countries to China for processing, and Chinese companies have acquired some European companies in their supply chain.

ii) *Government*

As outlined earlier in this report, the Chinese government has given greater attention to developing waste management policy over recent years, including examples of cooperation with other countries, particularly where technology transfer is involved (for example, with Japan and Germany).

Local government departments and related agencies are increasingly active: various specialist institutes, foundations and trade associations exist, all of which can play a role in supporting effective engagement. This may be directly related to waste management, but also in areas of environmental science, energy efficiency, etc.

iii) *Non-government organisations*

NGOs are also in evidence. Arguments regarding incineration, for example, have been strongly put forward and are relatively highly publicised. As a minimum, they give local populations a chance to air their views. Local NGOs have been supported by overseas NGOs.

iv) *Multilateral agencies*

Organisations such as the World Bank have in the past played an important role in identifying issues and recommendations.

Prospective Cooperation with the EU

The prospects for cooperation will depend largely upon effective engagement and sufficient resources from the EU (including funding, technology, expertise and capacity building), and the receptiveness or otherwise of various players on the Chinese side. We understand that relevant funds have already been earmarked by the EU. Hopefully the Chinese will at least commit to providing in-kind support (for example, offices, accommodation and subsistence etc.). The EU will need to appoint a combination of Chinese project management and waste management expertise — officials (from the EU and Member State agencies) working with external specialist resources.

Possible future scenarios from the Chinese perspective include:

i) Active international cooperation from China to learn best practice and transfer technology with a number of partners, including the EU. This would allow a range of cooperation options to be more fully explored and tested.

ii) A preference to work with the US and/or Japanese, rather than EU. At one level, if the results are good, this may be acceptable from some perspectives. However, relations could be complicated by other tensions in bilateral relationships (for example, in commercial or foreign affairs) and would leave EU companies and other players marginalised.

iii) The Chinese go their own way, perhaps selectively accepting loans, incentives and technology.

Areas of collaboration

If the key players in China are engaged effectively, the prospects for cooperation with the EU and real progress could be significant. There are a number of levels at which collaboration could take place:

i) *Government/Agencies*

Overall coordination would be at the EU-level (for example, managed by DG Environment and through the Environment Sector Dialogue, with a cross-ministry group on the Chinese side). Due to capacity and the need for more specific and focused engagement, projects would probably be better driven at the level of Member States. Such assistance could include exchanges of staff and expertise to support areas such as planning, drafting legislation, guidelines, standards, policy, management models, and measurement and targets at a central and regional level.

To accelerate the process and maximise impact, coordination with other relevant groups (listed below) would be important, for example the EU Chamber of Commerce Working Group for the Environment.

ii) *Academic, science and research*

Greater cooperation could be funded in these areas, including sharing course content, collaborative case studies and research, preferably with a practical bias.

iii) *Think tanks, journalists and NGOs*

Similarly, further regular analysis of future scenarios, underlying issues and human rights would better inform the debate about how best to allocate resources and determine priorities. Organisations such as 'Green Beagle' in Beijing and the World Wide Fund for Nature (WWF) have been active in this area. Waste pickers are very substantial in number (one estimate indicates 3.8 m people) and could be an important community group.

iv) *Promoting commercial opportunities*

Engagement by EU waste management specialist companies could be more actively encouraged and facilitated, for example through trade and investment promotion. This would lead to more sharing of technology and know-how through consultants, contractors, etc. As always, care would need to be taken over the protection of intellectual property rights.

It is worth noting that collection methods vary from one country to another in terms of the range of vehicles, transfer stations and treatment plants. The Japanese or US experience and technology may be more readily applicable in certain cases.

'Exporting' solutions and technologies does not always work — local adaptation is likely to be needed. Anecdotally, some foreign firms have found it slow and difficult to penetrate certain markets partly due to market access issues. Local investment may be an important step.

Trade associations can play a role in helping to facilitate engagement and identify opportunities, such as the International Solid Waste Association and, at the country level, organisations such as the Chartered Institute of Waste Management in the UK.

Conclusions

- Realistically, integrated and sustainable waste management seems to be a considerable way off in China.
- The Chinese authorities face a very significant set of challenges in terms of scale, cost and effective implementation.
- If they are unsuccessful or too slow in achieving progress, the negative impacts should not be underestimated — in terms of the environment, energy efficiency, the economy and public health. Equally, the benefits of concerted, successful action could be very positive.
- In a number of respects, there needs to be a change in attitudes and behaviour regarding waste management, both among officials and much of the Chinese public. Related issues include the need for transparency and to build public trust, for example, with the building of new incinerators.

EU Policy Implications

- There is a real need and opportunity to actively work with China on waste management.
- EU entities will need to approach waste management with an open mind. They will need to recognise the progress China has made, understand evolving policy and challenges, treat China as an equal partner, and adapt their response. For example, over-ambitious environmental targets and timeframes may be counterproductive.

- To maximise impact for the EU, a combined approach across a range of entities seems likely to have the greatest impact. This should be coordinated and project managed to identify cross-cutting issues, realise synergies and maximise impact. Ideally, this would be jointly planned and monitored with the Chinese side.
- EU collaboration should focus on types of waste and aspects of waste management which are more hazardous, more polluting, will grow dramatically and which, if treated effectively, could deliver energy saving and environmental benefits. A prerequisite will include genuine agreement on effective, close working by the key players on the Chinese side. Ideally, this would mean agreeing engagement in the areas of greatest impact, across:
    - Hazardous waste.
    - Municipal solid waste.
    - Industrial solid waste.
- It is understood that a reasonable budget for collaboration has been created by the EU. Specific programmes and projects need to be identified and agreed. A useful start to cooperation might be a workshop which seeks to honestly and openly discuss the challenges and 'cultural' issues at play.

Section Five
Chinese Social Issues

Social Unrest in China
(November 2011)

Jude Howell

Professor, Department of International Development, London School of Economics

Executive Summary

According to most accepted measures, social unrest — which ranges from individual acts of protest to large-scale collective action — has increased in China since 2006. Social stability is a top priority for Chinese Communist Party (CCP) leaders. The contradictory impulses of the Chinese Party-state in dealing with social unrest point to deep-seated pathologies of governance, which will need to be addressed both to ensure social stability and sustainable processes of democratic institution building. This paper examines the nature of social unrest in China. It reflects on the availability of regular and reliable statistical information. It analyses the different types of unrest, the major trends over the last four years and the causes underpinning unrest. It considers the threat posed by recent unrest to the central leadership and concludes with key recommendations for the EU.

Statistical information on social unrest is incomplete, fragmented and irregular. Such information is considered politically sensitive and the CCP tightly controls the reporting of social unrest. Definitions of social unrest are imprecise, making comparisons across time difficult.

The main types of social protest relate to forcible evictions, land seizures, labour disputes, ethno-religious grievances, corruption and abuse of power, excessive use of state force and discrimination against migrants. Social protest has taken the form of strikes, riots, protests, individual suicides, bombing and petitioning.

Several trends in social unrest can be observed over the last four years. Social unrest is rising on all fronts. Most social protest is geographically limited, uncoordinated and spontaneous. The new generation of migrant workers are more organised, vocal and better educated and there is some evidence of demands for workers' elections of representatives, independent trade unions and participation in collective bargaining. Online media has become an important channel for exposing social injustices, government corruption and for venting frustration by disgruntled netizens, aggrieved workers and urban citizens with grievances against the local public officials. The CCP is trying to expand its repertoire of measures to deal with unrest, making greater use of conciliation and mediation to address grievances emerging out of rapid economic development.

The main causes of social unrest are rapid economic development, rising inequalities and unmet expectations; lack of independent, legitimate and effective channels for resolving conflict; lack of government accountability and transparency; and absence of independent watchdog organisations.

The CCP fears social protest that is coordinated on a nationwide basis and is suspicious of destabilisation by external actors. Continuing rapid economic development, high growth rates and tight controls over society mean that the CCP is not on the brink of collapse. However, there is always the element of the unpredictable in the conjuncture of events.

Main Points

- Statistical coverage of social unrest is fragmented, incomplete and irregular. The extent of social unrest is underestimated in official figures.
- The main types of social unrest relate to labour disputes, forcible evictions, land seizures, ethno-religious grievances, government corruption and abuse of power.
- Social unrest has been increasing over the last four years. Most protests are locally confined, spontaneous and uncoordinated. A new generation of migrant workers is more organised, vocal and demanding than their parents' generation. However, there is no enduring movement leadership or organisation around labour or other issues, or sustained emergence of political opposition groups.
- Online media play an increasingly important role in venting anger, exposing government corruption, and providing a channel for free expression. The CCP

continues to harass social activists and tighten controls over the media and Internet, with new directives to increase censorship issued in October 2011. It is devoting increasing amounts of resources to social stability.
- Social unrest is caused by political, institutional, economic and social factors. These include growing resentment at inequalities; indignation at social injustices and government corruption; increasing access to the Internet enabling the rapid mobilisation of alternative opinion and analysis; lack of effective, legitimate and independent institutional channels for resolving conflicts and grievances.
- The CCP is highly sensitive to social unrest. High economic growth and the CCP's tight control over communications and society make it unlikely that the CCP is about to collapse. Nevertheless, as seen in the Middle East, unpredictability and contingency should not be underestimated.

Introduction

Social unrest, ranging from individual acts of protest to large-scale collective action, has increased in China over the last four years. Social stability is a top priority for CCP leaders. This paper examines the nature of social unrest in China. It reflects on the availability of regular and reliable statistical information. It analyses the different types of unrest, the causes underpinning it, and the major trends over the last four years. It considers the threat posed by recent unrest to the central leadership and concludes with key recommendations to the EU.

Assessing the Extent of Social Unrest: Statistical Challenges

The statistical information on social unrest is incomplete, fragmented and irregular. Such information is deemed politically sensitive and is thus veiled in secrecy. The Ministry of Public Security from 1994 up to 2005 has occasionally released information on social unrest. For example, the Ministry reported that there were 87,000 'public order disturbances' in 2005 compared with only 10,000 such incidents in 1994. There have since been sporadic reports from different sources within China of 90,000 mass incidents in 2006, 127,000 in 2008 and 180,000 in 2010, pointing to a substantial increase in social unrest.

It is likely that figures that are released underestimate the extent of social protests, not just because of the difficulties of aggregating data but also because there are incentives that encourage central and local governments to under-report the extent of unrest. Added to this, the government has issued directives to the media not to report on mass incidents and intervenes to control the Internet and any publicity about other kinds of unrest. Data on particular kinds of protests such as religious, environmental, labour and land-related grievances have to be gleaned from local newspaper publications, academic studies, and external, issue-based monitoring agencies such as environmental networks, overseas religious organisations and labour monitoring non-governmental organisations (NGOs).

It is thus not easy to compare changes in social protest over time or neatly distinguish the issues driving protest. For example, not only are the definitions of 'mass incidents' and 'public order disturbances' unclear, but there is also confusion as to whether 'mass incidents' are a sub-set of 'public order disturbances' or whether the two terms are interchangeable. The term 'mass incidents' makes a statement about the large-scale character of an event, while 'public order disturbances' could include anything from mobs and riots to gambling or organising churches, according to Criminal Law.

Types of Social Unrest

The types of social unrest and the causes underpinning them have become increasingly complex and varied in the reform decades. In the past four years, social unrest has surfaced around several key issues, including ethno-religious grievances, labour disputes, house demolitions, land seizures, environmental concerns, discrimination against migrants, corruption, and police brutality. Social unrest has taken the form of more radical types of action including large-scale strikes, riots, protests, attacks on government buildings, sleep-ins, individual suicides and bombings, to more established forms such as petitioning.

Social unrest related to ethnic grievances has occurred in Inner Mongolia, Tibet and Xinjiang. In May 2010, following the killings of two Mongolian herders involved in separate protests against coal companies, there was large-scale unrest in Mongolia, spreading to six counties and cities. The geographical spread of the unrest was unusual as the majority of protests remained local. While this was the first major unrest since the 1980s, there have been sustained protests, demonstrations and riots in Tibet and Xinjiang over the last four years.

The issues sparking unrest in these two border provinces are complex, involving a combination of demands for greater autonomy and independence, grievances around religious freedom, discrimination against minorities, and the excessive use of force by Chinese security institutions. In March 2008, around the time of commemorations of the 1959 Tibetan Uprising, a series of protests, riots and demonstrations took place in the Lhasa region, spreading for the first time to monasteries outside of the Tibet Autonomous Region. Following the deaths of two Uyghur migrants in Guangdong province in March 2009, serious protests erupted in Xinjiang, leading to around 200 deaths and over 1,700 injured. Urban centres in both regions have a visible, military presence. Controls on the Internet and access to websites remain tight, while travel to the region by foreign journalists is severely restricted, limiting informational flows about unrest.

Labour disputes have risen steadily over the last three decades. Following the promulgation of the 2008 Labour Contract Law, the number of lodged disputes has risen significantly. This is because labour activists and aggrieved workers saw the new law as giving them further legitimacy and armoury in pursuing their claims. For example, in 2007, 350,182 cases were accepted by the labour dispute arbitration authorities, compared to around 50,000 in 1996 when figures were first reported. This almost doubled by 2008 to reach 693,645. Though this dropped to 602,600 in 2010, the total number of cases accepted by both mediation and arbitration committees rose to 1,287,400, suggesting that more cases were being settled through mediation. Statistics on labour-related protests such as strikes, demonstrations and sit-ins are not made public and many of these remain unrecorded. The suicides of 13 workers at a Foxconn plant in Guangdong province in 2010 attracted considerable domestic and international media coverage. Subsequent increases in wages at Foxconn prompted workers at other factories to press for wage rises. Strikes for higher wages at a Honda factory in May 2010 triggered disputes along the supply chain. The central government put pressure on local governments to raise local minimum wages, but the main driver for this was the shift in development strategy away from export-dependency towards boosting domestic consumption, rather than addressing labour grievances per se.

Apart from unrest related to ethnic grievances and workplace disputes, social protests have also occurred around issues of discrimination against rural migrants, land seizures and industrial pollution. Land seizures and subsequent demolitions of property by local government entities were the main source of social unrest in 2010. This has included individual protests at forced evictions from housing to much larger and often violent protests by villagers against government seizure of land.

Trends in Social Unrest in the Last Four Years

- Social unrest has been increasing on all fronts. Most social unrest remains isolated and protests are largely uncoordinated. There is little horizontal organisation between protestors in different regions and there are no alliances between protestors addressing different types of grievances. The CCP fears any coordinated, large-scale action similar to the 1989 Democracy Movement.
- There is growing suspicion of the motives of international foundations, NGOs and think tanks and concern that foreign governments are seeking to destabilise the government. The CCP thus watched the outbreak of the Arab Spring in 2011 with trepidation and responded aggressively to thwart a 'jasmine revolution' in China.
- There is a new generation of migrant workers born in the 1980s and after, who are more vocal, more organised, and better educated than the preceding generation of workers. Though most protests centre on economistic demands, some recent protests have included demands for independent trade unions, election of worker representatives and worker participation in collective bargaining.
- Workers who have played a leading role in strikes tend to move on to other factories and keep a low profile in order to reduce the risk of being singled out as 'trouble makers' by public security. Their participation in protest is thus temporary and fluid, making it difficult to build an enduring labour movement that draws on accumulated experience. Similarly, state repression constrains the development of enduring movement leadership around the environment, social justice or land issues, or the sustained emergence of political opposition groups.
- There is some anecdotal evidence of a rise in impromptu, often violent, mass incidents sparked by relatively minor incidents. In June 2011, for example, the alleged manhandling of a young pregnant Sichuanese street vendor in a county in Guangdong province sparked three days of mass rioting, leading to significant damage to government property.

- Online media such as the microblogging site Weibo, chat forums, and message boards such as QQ have become an important channel for venting anger, disseminating information, organising, and for exposing government corruption and abuse of power. China now has more than 300 m netizens, who are becoming increasingly sophisticated at evading controls over the Internet and at using online media to draw attention to corruption, inequalities and social injustices. The CCP is highly concerned about the potential influence of the Internet, which allows citizens to communicate autonomously and rapidly, providing an alternative source of knowledge and information. In the last four years it has continually adopted measures to close websites, control access to certain information by blocking words such as 'jasmine', 'democracy', 'Tiananmen', and to put pressure on Chinese and foreign Internet providers to practise self-censorship.
- An emerging phenomenon is that protests are aimed not just at seeking redress or the proper implementation of laws, but also at influencing policy, as seen in the environmental protests in Xiamen in December 2007 and Dalian in August 2011, which respectively prevented the construction and operation of paraxylene plants.
- The CCP is becoming more sophisticated in its handling of social unrest as it moves away from a singular repressive approach towards a broader repertoire of responses involving greater use of mediation, arbitration, conciliation and accommodation of grievances. However, social unrest that is deemed to threaten the stability of the regime such as ethno-religious, separatist protests in Xinjiang and Tibet, democracy activism, coordinated action across provinces, or protests timed around significant events continue to meet with fierce repression such as clampdowns on the Internet and media, detention of dissidents and activists and state-supported violence. Indeed the Party-state will take preventive measures to stymie protests, such as detaining social activists and blocking the Internet, in the run-up to international events such as the Olympics and in anticipation of any uprisings, as occurred with online calls for a 'jasmine revolution' at the time of the Arab Spring of 2011.
- In the last four years there has been increasing harassment of social activists, human rights lawyers and outspoken critics — the case of the internationally renowned artist, Ai Weiwei, being a key case in point.
- The government's growing concern about social unrest and its impact on social stability is reflected in the increasing amount of resources devoted to maintaining

domestic stability. In 2010 the Ministry of Finance reported that expenditure on internal security rose 15.6% compared with 2009 to RMB 548.6 bn (more than the RMB 533.5 bn spent on national defence), with plans to increase this even further in 2011.

Reasons for Social Unrest

The reasons for growing social unrest are multiple. Some of the main economic, social, institutional and political factors are noted below.

- The rapid pace of economic development has led to a diversification of social interests, more complex class structures, increasing income and regional inequalities, and unmet rising expectations, fuelling frustration and resentment. China's growing middle-class is becoming increasingly vocal and dissatisfied with controls over information, the lack of government accountability and the effects of environmental pollution on their quality of life.
- There is a lack of institutional channels for resolving conflicts in a context of transition from a planned economy and society to a market economy. Existing channels for resolving disputes are inadequate and new systems and mechanisms that are being put in place are incomplete. For example, though the long-established citizen petitioning system is well used, government agencies only address around 0.2% of lodged complaints. Similarly, although there is an Administrative Litigation Law, citizens face difficulties in redressing their grievances through this law because of a lack of legal representation, corruption, Party and government interference in the courts, fears of retribution, and official resistance.
- Perverse incentives introduced by the cadre responsibility system lead cadres seeking to achieve their social stability targets to use force in response to social unrest rather than creating more long-term institutional mechanisms for resolving conflict. The situation is compounded by the lack of independent judicial and political institutions, independent intermediary organisations, or independent civil society watchdog organisations.
- Increasing access to the Internet has enabled protestors and critics to mobilise opinion rapidly around individual grievances and injustices. The Internet has thus created an alternative site of knowledge, organising and resistance.

Evaluation of Threat to Central Leadership

The most dangerous threat to regime maintenance in China is coordinated protest across regions and across different types of grievances that challenge the legitimacy of the CCP. However, China's high economic growth rates coupled with its tight control over nationwide protest make it unlikely that the CCP will collapse imminently. Nevertheless, it is important not to underestimate the force of the unpredictable. Middle East analysts were not able to predict the Arab Spring of 2011 and its global consequences, nor were China-watchers able to predict the rise of the democracy movement in 1989.

The CCP's fear of destabilisation from abroad coupled with pressure on local government cadres to ensure social stability and economic growth will cause the state to continue to respond in contradictory ways, at times unpredictably and erratically. In the near future, we can expect the central Party to continue to adopt measures to appease public opinion and address grievances such as anti-corruption campaigns, promoting collective bargaining, using public tribunals to consult with urban citizens, reducing the scope for administrative discretion, emphasising 'social harmony', and easing restrictions on welfare-focused civil society groups. However, such measures will be offset by continuing bans on political publications, restrictions on reporting, controls over the media and websites, arbitrary extra-judicial detention of social activists and human rights lawyers, and tight control over rights-promoting civil society organisations.

Conclusion

The key findings of this paper are as follows:

- Social unrest in China has continued to increase over the past four years.
- The main issues driving social unrest are land seizures, working conditions, environmental pollution, regional autonomy and corruption.
- The prime causes of social unrest relate to rapid economic development, increasing income, social and regional inequalities, unmet rising expectations; a lack of legitimate, effective and independent social and political institutions for channelling, mediating and resolving grievances; lack of government accountability and transparency along with endemic systemic government corruption; and the absence of independent, civil society watchdog groups.

- The CCP is likely to expand its repertoire of accommodating responses to social unrest but this will be gradual, piecemeal and specific to particular threats that are interpreted as not regime-destabilising. The use of repression to address social unrest will continue, as local governments fail to establish longer-term mechanisms of conflict-resolution and as central Party leaders remain suspicious of 'hostile external forces' set to destabilise China.
- China's stability and economic growth is important for Europe's economic recovery and prosperity. The EU thus has an interest in China developing more sustainable and effective means of managing social grievances and in moving towards a more democratic style of politics.

The Recent Labour Unrest in China and the Politics of Handling Collective Mobilisation by the Party-State
(October 2011)

Eric Florence

Researcher, Centre d'Etudes de l'Ethnicité et des Migrations (CEDEM), University of Liege

Executive Summary

Since the mid-2000s, there has been a continuous increase in the number of labour conflicts in China. The 2010 waves of labour unrest are unprecedented, with more than 100 strikes occurring in the car and electronics industry in the Pearl River Delta, following the May–June strike at a Honda Factory in Foshan.

Since the adoption of the much-debated Labour Contract and Labour Dispute Conciliation and Arbitration Laws in 2008, workplace unions have become increasingly subordinate and subservient to the local governments, the Party committees and tribunals or other judicial institutions. From the mid-2000s, there has been an increasing radicalisation of workers' demands.

The recent unprecedented waves of mobilisation have not brought about any kind of institutionalisation of genuine independent representation of workers in the workplace. The Party-state is not likely to allow the existence of independent unions or even to fundamentally release its grip on the organisation and representation of workers in enterprises in the near future. The Party-state is very much likely to do its best to channel, control and co-opt any grassroots organisation within factories that emerge.

The EU can help to institutionalise some of the results of the recent labour mobilisations in China by:

- Urging European companies with plants in China to implement workers' training programmes, improve workers' representation, and run genuine collective-bargaining processes.
- Drawing on novel ways of collaboration with the Chinese government, All-China Federation of Trade Unions (ACFTU) and (when possible) the growing network of non-governmental organisations providing services to workers.

Main Points

- Since the mid-2000s, China has witnessed an increase in 'mass incidents'.
- These collective movements have started to radicalise as protestors have become more articulate and better educated. Protestors now have greater capacity to externalise their actions among the wider public and increasingly mobilise across class lines.
- The Party-state's reaction to such collective action is highly influenced by its desire to maintain a high pace of economic growth while also preserving social stability.
- The passing of the Labour Contract Law and labour dispute Conciliation and Arbitration Law in 2008 have done little to work in workers' favour. They have made workplace unions increasingly subordinate to local governments.
- The demand for democratically elected workplace representation has become a key issue for workers since 2006. This is upheld by a continued distrust of official workplace unions and government institutions.
- The Party-state is unlikely to allow the existence of independent unions or release its grip on the representation of workers in enterprise. It is wary of maintaining control over representation and collective mobilisation in the workplace and social space in general.
- As long as Chinese workers continue to experience a huge chasm between promises contained in new legislation, policies and rhetoric, and their daily experience of indignity in the workplace, labour unrest will continue to grow.

Introduction

This paper focuses on the post-mid-2000 labour unrest in China and the ways in which it was handled by the Party-state and branches of the All-China Federation of Trade Unions (ACFTU) in southeastern coastal China, i.e. the Pearl River Delta (PRD) in Guangdong province. This choice has been dictated by the fact that for the last three decades, the PRD has been the major powerhouse of export-led economic development in the country. This area also has the highest concentration of manufacturing enterprises and (mainly rural) workers (around 25 m of them in the PRD alone). It is also the location of the most frequent occurrence of labour unrest, including the collective action which triggered the summer 2010 wave of unrest.

Increasing Labour Conflicts

According to official statistics, at the national level, China has witnessed an increase in 'mass incidents' (defined as an 'unauthorised gathering of more than 20 people') from around 10,000 such incidents in 1994 to 74,000 in 2004. Since then, the categorisation of incidents has changed and no coherent or comprehensive data has been released. This renders comparisons between different periods problematic. According to unofficial estimates though, there may have been more than 120,000 national 'mass incidents' in 2008, which would entail a 70% increase when compared with 2004. For 2009, Chinese scholar Yu Jianrong estimated that there were around 90,000 such incidents, out of which one-third are estimated to be labour-related. According to a January 2008 estimate released by the Agence France Presse, at least one strike involving more than 1,000 workers occurred daily in the PRD in 2007. According to one Shenzhen-based NGO, from March to December 2010, more than 1 m workers have been involved in around 1,000 strikes across the whole country. In the automobile and electronics sector alone, more than 100 strikes occurred in the PRD in the aftermath of the Honda Plant strike.

Major Features of the Recent Wave of Collective Mobilisation

In order to better apprehend the major features of the recent wave of strikes, it is important to consider the characteristics of earlier occurrences of collective labour mobilisation. An important body of scholarship shows that the early strikes of the 1980s were small in scale (often limited to a single factory or a department in a factory) and that workers tended to mobilise along regional lines. It was rare for formal demands to be expressed. From 1993–1994 onwards, a gradual increase in the collective dimension of protests, networking across different factories, the expression of formal demands and the length of strikes was recorded.

If these were the growing trends from the early 1990s onwards, collective movements started to radicalise and to grow in scale from the mid-2000s. The major features of these movements may be summarised as:

- *Workers involved belong mainly to the second generation of migrant workers* who are more individualistic, have a higher level of education, a better knowledge of the law, are more radical in their demands and have stronger experience of social exclusion.
- *Greater scale and radicalisation of strikes*: one can see from the Internet postings which circulated during and after the strikes that workers are able to articulate their demands by mobilising elements of labour legislation and Party ideology as well as core elements of their collective identity as a marginalised group;
- *Protestors have much greater capacity to externalise their actions* via a variety of means such as blogs, microblogs, etc. For instance, during the May 2010 Honda Plant Strike, the use of new technologies enabled very fast circulation of information among workers, but also between workers, the media and lawyers, as well as people specialised in the protection of labour rights who could react instantly. Similarly, it has become increasingly popular for videos of events to be posted on the web by protesters;
- *Protesters are increasingly able to mobilise across class lines* of skilled or semi-skilled personnel and often collectively participate in actions.

Legal Developments and the ACFTU

The increase in labour-related conflicts and abuses of workers' rights from the 1980s onwards represented a real challenge to the legitimacy of the Party-state. On the one hand, these conflicts represented mounting threats to social stability. On the other hand, the sheer assault on workers' rights contradicted the very ideological tenets of a Party whose founding legitimacy still partly rested on the rejection of exploitation and the representation of the interests of the working class. Following the passing of the 1994 Labour law, 2008 was marked by the adoption of the Labour Contract Law which aimed chiefly at formalising the employment of workers and making sure that they signed contracts. The labour dispute Conciliation and Arbitration Law was also promulgated in January 2008. However, this law left a number of issues unsolved and left out the notion of 'bargaining'. There was no reference to strikes or work stoppages in either the Labour or Arbitration Laws. The 2007–2008 reforms of ACFTU have led to workplace unions becoming more and more subordinate and subservient to the local governments, the Party committees and tribunals or other judicial institutions.

In the context of the 2008 economic and financial crisis, which provoked massive factory closures and sacking of workers in the PRD (often accompanied by non-payment of wages by these companies), provincial and local governments reacted swiftly by ordering that a brake be put on the implementation of the protective provisions contained in the national Contract Law, for example, implementing minimum wages. At the same time, however, in the face of growing conflict and unrest related to massive factory closures in 2008, local governments often tended to compensate non-payment of wages by paying such wages directly to workers instead of the employers in order to maintain social stability. What stands out clearly here is the paramount importance of the twin core principles of rule of the Party-state and how much they influence both the local governments and ACFTU's actions, i.e. maintaining a high pace of economic growth and preserving social stability.

Workplace Representation Demands During the Recent Wave of Workers' Collective Actions and How the Party-State Dealt with Them

The general context which preceded the unprecedented 2010 wave of labour collective actions is marked by two contradictory trends. On the one hand, thanks to the action of a variety of official, semi-official and unofficial organs (labour bureaus, legal advisors, NGOs, the media, legal clinics, citizens' agents, etc.), a new generation of workers has become increasingly aware of labour legislation. As a result, workers' expectations in matters of labour rights have also grown. However, on the other hand, as local governments take a series of pro-capital measures in the context of the 2008 economic crisis, these workers have become increasingly frustrated by their daily experience of the non-implementation of legal provisions and by the long-standing abuse of their rights. Hence, the non-fulfillment of legal and rhetorical promises has increasingly helped to fuel social anger. If Mary Galagher was right when she argued that the Party-state's attitude towards workers has been chiefly 'preemptive and paternalist', aiming at 'helping workers so as not to empower workers',[74] the scholarship on collective action in the PRD in the second half of the 2000s points to a radicalisation of workers' demands, to the more interest-based nature of these demands and to their better organising capacity.

Several analysts and commentators have noted that none of the 2010 collective actions were linked to the formal process of collective negotiation attached to the 2008 Contract Law. Therefore, the nature of these actions basically constituted 'independent labour activism'. Such demands were still rare in the early 2000s, but from the mid-2000s on, there has been a growing, although modest, trend towards workers demanding democratically elected workplace representation. This trend started to become clear from 2006 and has since become a major demand in many of the 2010 waves of mobilisation.

In this last round of mobilisation, workers actually endeavoured to face management and engage in real negotiation and bargaining. This kind of genuine grassroots activism should not be mistaken with unionisation which would declare itself completely autonomous from the Party-state or from any Party-state sanctioned organisation such as the ACFTU. Most workers and activists are aware that such a public statement of full autonomy would most likely entail retaliation from the Party-state — as the rare formation of independent unions in the past has shown. What most workers have demanded is a democratically elected union, which would then have to register at the higher-level formal union.

In order to apprehend the demands from workers for genuine workplace representation, one should note that most investigations in factories of the PRD point to the alarming and conspicuous void left by workplace unions in foreign invested enterprises. Anita Chan, who has been researching labour relations in South China for almost 30 years, commenting on the recent spate

---

[74] Mary Gallagher quoted in 'China's rulers 'well aware' of labor's leverage and political potential', *Democracy Digest*, 29 April 2011. Available at: http://demdigest.net/blog/chinas-rulers-well-aware-of-labors-leverage-and-political-potential/. Accessed 10 January 2014.

of mobilisation made this assessment in a January 2011 *China Journal* paper: '(...) the workplace union in the private factories in the PRD are worse than weak, in the factories where they do exist they are an integral part of factory management'.[75] If this judgment sounds radical, it is fully evidenced by both scientific and press reports published over the last 20 years. The most recent investigation into the conditions of labour in PRD factories pointed to the deep distrust which workers showed for the official trade union within enterprise. This distrust and the firm belief that the union could not play any kind of meaningful role and offer support to workers actually influenced their mode of protest and demands to negotiate directly with the management, without any imposed ACFTU or local government interference. This distrust in the government institutions is probably one of the main and long-standing features of migrant workers' conditions and collective identity, and it has been singled out continuously in scientific scholarship since the end of the 1980s.

Some of the journalists who covered the 2010 collective protests noted the change in attitude of local government and singled this out as a sign of watershed change. They noted that local governments had started to take a more pro-labour stance in labour conflicts and had distanced themselves from their earlier chiefly repressive attitude, which considered any labour collective mobilisation a threat to social stability. Drawing on insiders' investigations into these collective actions, however, I hereafter show that the extent of such a change needs to be qualified.

The main rationale of local governments seems chiefly to be to endeavour to contain any labour unrest through a large array of means, ranging from negotiation to intimidation to repression (it is often the case that these means are combined by local governments in their management of strikes or work stoppages; for example, material concessions may be accorded to protesters, while leaders are often arrested and sentenced). If there is a legal void in defining whether strikes are legal or not, they are still often perceived as threats to social stability. The ways in which local governments will react to mobilisation will depend on a variety of factors and may change over time or even within the course of one single labour conflict (it may be conditioned by the scale, social visibility of the movement, by the economic

---

[75] A. Chan, 'Strikes in China's Export Industries in Comparative Perspectives', *China Journal*, January 2011, Issue 65, p. 27–51.

and social conjuncture, the power of entrenched coalitions of interests between local governments and investors, etc).

In-depth studies of labour relations show that from the mid-2000s, the Labour Protection and Social Security Bureau had tended to progressively take a more pro-labour stance. But studies which take a historical perspective such as that of Chris-Chi Chan show that gains obtained by workers through their mobilisation were quickly counterbalanced (with the tacit approval of governments — evidenced by maintenance of an extremely low rate of labour inspection personnel in the PRD, around 1/20,000 workers, equivalent to levels in 1999) by continuous endeavours by the management to intensify production, which in turn was a major factor generating collective mobilisation by workers. This last feature remains pivotal in accounting for waves of labour protests in the Pearl River Delta in 2010 and early 2011. On the whole Chan's study shows that the Party-state is torn between, on the one hand, standing on the side of enterprises and protecting the environment for investors and, on the other, pacifying labour relations by putting pressure on factories to raise wages and improve conditions and social welfare.[76]

While in quite a number of reported cases in the 2009 and 2010 protests, governments did not quell the movements and workers managed to obtain wage increases or other demands regarding social benefits or overtime payments from their companies, in numerous other cases, local governments used the usual mix of intimidation and repression to put pressure on workers, threatening or sacking them if they did not resume work, or hiring other workers to replace them.

By providing insights into the most famous strike which occurred in May and June 2010 at a Honda plant in Foshan, one may get a better grasp of the complex ways that the Party-state handles labour protests.[77] This strike lasted for 17 days (which is exceptionally long) and involved 1,800 workers, 80% of whom were interns from technical schools and 20% were formal employees. The strikers had made public four formal demands. These were: 1) a wage increase of RMB 800; 2) seniority subsidy; 3) a better promotion system; 4) democratic reform of the

---

[76] Chan, Chris-Chi, *The Challenge of Labour in China. Strikes and the Changing Labour Regime in Global Factories* (Routledge, Abingdon, New York, 2010).

[77] See for instance several chapters of C. Scherrer (ed.), *China's Labor Question* (Rainer Hampp Verlag, Munchen Mering, 2011). Available at: http://www.global-labour-university.org/fileadmin/books/CLQ_full_book.pdf. Accessed 10 January 2014.

workplace trade union. The violence which was inflicted on workers acted as a turning point in the attitude of the local government. While it initially sided with the management, after the violence became public via videos, it started to back some of workers' demands. In the end, an agreement was reached on wage increases. At first sight, the government has shown a remarkable degree of tolerance during the movement, even allowing a renowned Beijing legal scholar to act as mediator between the parties. The formal demand for genuine workers' representation was still resisted by the management in 2011 and legal activists who took part in the mobilisation were intimidated by the police in the PRD and in Beijing. Therefore, as Hui and Chan have argued, what appeared at first sight to be a path-breaking change in the way the local government dealt with the protests may, on second thoughts, be considered chiefly an effort to contain the potential extension of the collective movement and, once again, to prioritise social stability and economic growth.[78]

Conclusions

Can the wage increases gained by some workers through their recent participation in collective action be seen as a sign that the balance of power between workers and enterprises is starting to change? If such a change is taking place it needs to be qualified. Evidence from the past shows us that newly designed legislation — often declared 'ground-breaking' at the time — has often brought unexpected results that have further fuelled workers' discontent. This paper has stressed that, during times of economic crisis and when pressure is exerted by powerful coalitions of local governments and companies, the Party-state has often swiftly adapted some of its policies in favour of enterprise. The recent unprecedented wave of collective action by workers has not brought about the institutionalisation of genuine independent representation of workers in the workplace.

The evidence put forward in this paper tends to show that the Party-state is not likely to allow the existence of independent unions or even to release fundamentally its grip on the organisation and representation of workers in enterprises. The recent wave of labour mobilisation has urged the Party-state and ACFTU to

---

[78] Pun, Ngai and Huilin Lu (2010), 'Unfinished Proletarianization: Self, Anger, and Class Action among the Second Generation of Peasant-Workers in Present-Day China', *Modern China,* September 2010 36: 493–519.

push forward issues of collective negotiations instead of going ahead with its counterproductive logic of individuation of labour disputes. The Party-state has been alerted to the urgency of improving the representational function of the ACFTU and is very much likely to do its best to channel, control and co-opt any grassroots organisation within factories in the near future. In the context of the recent Arab revolutions, the Party-state is indeed very wary not to lose what is still one of its basic and self-defining prerogatives, the control over representation and collective mobilisation in the workplace as well as in social space in general.

Chinese workers are becoming increasingly radical in their demands, more determined and better organised in their collective actions. As long as they keep experiencing a huge chasm between the promises contained in new legislation, policies and rhetoric, and their daily experience of indignity, labour unrest will keep growing. In this respect, a key question to consider is the extent to which, and how, the Party-state will alter the deeply entrenched power balance and politico-institutional and legal arrangements which have allowed extremely rapid accumulation and economic growth for the last two decades, but which have also generated alarming social unrest.

Further Reading

Chan, Chris-Chi and Pun Ngai, 'The Making of a New Working Class? A Study of Collective Actions of Migrant Workers in South China', *The China Quarterly*, 198, June 2009, p. 287–303.

China Labour Bulletin, 'Going it Alone, The Workers' Movement in China', *China Labour Bulletin Research Report*, 2009. Available at: http://www.clb.org.hk/en/files/share/File/research_reports/workers_movement_07-08_print_final.pdf. Accessed 10 January 2014.

China Labour Bulletin, 'Protecting Workers' Rights or Serving the Party: The way forward for China's trade unions', *China Labor Bulletin Research Report*, 2009. Available at: http://www.clb.org.hk/en/files/share/File/research_reports/acftu_report.pdf. Accessed 10 January 2014.

Hui, Sio Leng, 'Understanding Labor Activism: The Honda Workers' Strike', in Christoph Scherrer, *China's Labor Question* (Rainer Hampp Verlag, Munchen, Mering, 2011) p. 133–152. Available at: http://www.global-labour-university.org/fileadmin/books/CLQ_full_book.pdf. Accessed 10 January 2014.

Pun, Ngai, Chris-Chi Chan, and Jenny Chan, 'The Role of the State, Labour Policy and Migrant Workers' Struggles in Globalized China', *Global Labour Journal*: Vol. 1: Issue 1, 2010, 132–151.

Si, Luoqi, 'Collective contracts but no collective bargaining', in Christoph Scherrer, *China's Labor Question* (Rainer Hampp Verlag, Munchen, Mering, 2011), p. 133–152. Available at: http://www.global-labour-university.org/fileadmin/books/CLQ_full_book.pdf. Accessed 10 January 2014.

Urbanisation, Rural-to-Urban Migration and Housing in China
(April 2012)

Bettina Gransow

Professor of Sinology, Freie Universität Berlin

Executive Summary

In 2011, for the first time ever, more than half of China's citizens were living in cities. Against the background of rapid urbanisation, it has become increasingly difficult to provide affordable housing for lower-income families. A hike in property prices has also exacerbated the problem by making housing unattainable for even middle-income groups.

Urbanisation in China is largely driven by rural-to-urban migration. The strategic approach to urbanisation in the 12th Five Year Programme (2011–2015) is to channel rural migrants away from megacities and big cities and into small and medium-sized cities. Yet in marked contrast to this approach by the Chinese government, it is the megacities and big cities that rural migrants are primarily attracted to. The influx of migrants into urban metropolises remains an ongoing and increasing trend despite the various measures and policies instigated by the Chinese government to try and control it.

There are two main scenarios for promoting urbanisation reform: the first scenario would target the administrative hierarchy for cities, redirecting more resources to small and medium-sized cities to enable them to provide more and better services (including housing) and to attract more investment and migrant workers. This approach could turn out to be very costly and time-consuming. The second scenario would open up the megacities and big cities to the migrants who already reside there. This would require the provision of affordable housing and essential public services. Both scenarios imply a redistribution of resources from urban *hukou* (housing registration) holders in first-tier cities, either to smaller cities or to migrants within the megacities who would thus become classified as urban citizens. The need for a more inclusive approach toward migrants in the city becomes even more urgent in view of recent development strategies that place a priority on expanding the domestic market and strengthening domestic consumption as part of a structural reorientation of the Chinese economy.

Due to internal migration, there has been a marked increase in the demand for low-rent urban housing. This demand has been reinforced by the following factors: 1) a growing tendency for entire families to migrate; 2) greater expectations by second-generation migrants to stay in the cities; 3) a growing number of young graduates from colleges and universities who wish to stay in big cities even with meagre incomes; and 4) a growing number of former peasants who have lost their land. Despite being seen as an important attempt toward solving the problems for low and middle-income families in urban areas, the government's affordable-housing programme (outlined in the 12th Five Year Programme) has raised concerns regarding its potential negative impact on affordability in general. Informal housing units will be replaced by fewer affordable-housing units that might still be out of reach for most migrants in urban areas either because they are ineligible for the programme or because they lack sufficient financial means to pay the higher rent (compared with the costs of informal housing). Other concerns include the fiscal risk for local governments, eligibility criteria and fair distribution for different types of affordable housing, and the quality of construction.

Since 2010 the Chinese government has introduced various policies to curb speculation and excessive gains from property transactions, which have led to lower prices for most players. Controls on the housing market conflict with the interests of most players at the local level such as early buyers, potential home buyers, developers and local governments, but they nevertheless help to promote widespread construction of affordable housing. They thus have the potential to meet the essential needs of lower and middle-income citizens and migrants if — and only if — the many challenges associated with implementing the programme are mastered.

To ensure the effectiveness and fairness of the affordable-housing programme, it is crucial to have clearly defined targets and eligibility criteria. For this purpose, a comprehensive social assessment of the government's affordable-housing programme is needed that focuses on different groups of migrants and their respective housing needs. It should also cover questions of household registration as well as access to public services and social security.

With increasing numbers of people moving from rural to urban areas in search of a better life, China and Europe face the common challenge of ensuring sustainable urbanisation. National and local governments have to provide better public services, including affordable housing, to a growing number of city residents. An exchange on the challenges, experiences and prospects of affordable-housing programmes and on redevelopment in the context of urbanisation and migration could help facilitate and deepen the dialogue between China and the EU on sustainable urbanisation and its economic, social and environmental implications.

Main Points

- While the Chinese government is seeking to channel rural migrants into small and medium-sized cities, rural migrants themselves are primarily attracted to megacities and big cities.
- Due to internal migration there has been a marked increase in the demand for low-rent urban housing.
- The Chinese government has launched an ambitious affordable-housing programme to build 36 m units of affordable housing over the five-year period, 2011–2015.
- It is feared that the programme may have a negative impact on affordability because some informal housing units will be replaced by fewer affordable-housing units that might still be out of reach for most migrants.
- Government housing interventions will probably have a limited effect on the *rate* of urbanisation in China because only a very small part of the affordable-housing programme targets low-income families.
- The two scenarios for promoting urbanisation focus on either big/megacities, or on small/medium-sized cities. Both scenarios imply a redistribution of resources away from urban *hukou* holders in first-tier cities, with the latter scenario probably more costly and more difficult to put into practice.
- Central government control conflicts with the interests of most players at the local level such as early buyers, potential home buyers, developers and local governments, but is promoting widespread construction of affordable housing.

Recommendations

- An exchange on the challenges, experiences and prospects of affordable-housing programmes and on redevelopment in the context of urbanisation and migration could help facilitate and deepen the ongoing dialogue between China and the EU on sustainable urbanisation and its economic, social and environmental implications.
- To ensure the effectiveness and fairness of the affordable-housing programme, it is crucial to have clearly defined targets and eligibility criteria. A comprehensive social assessment of the government's affordable-housing programme is recommended as a precondition for greater dialogue.

Introduction

In 2011, for the first time ever, more than half of China's citizens were living in cities. According to projections from the Development Research Center of the State Council, in 2020 the urbanisation rate will be as high as 60%. A further 325 m people are expected to move to urban areas within one generation. Against the background of rapid urbanisation it has become increasingly difficult to provide affordable housing to lower-income families, particularly since a hike in property prices from 2003 to 2008 exacerbated the situation by making housing unattainable even for middle-income families.

In light of the commitment by the 12th Five Year Programme (FYP) to increase the rate of urbanisation in China, this paper will examine the effects of China's rapid urbanisation on the domestic demand for housing, with particular reference to affordable government housing. It will examine how government housing interventions will impact the rate of urbanisation in China, and consider alternatives ways of achieving this. It will also consider how central government control of the housing market conflicts with local demand.

China's Rapid Urbanisation and the Strategic Approach of the 12th FYP

Urbanisation in China is largely driven by migration processes. This consists primarily of internal rural-to-urban migration. According to the 2010 population census, the total population of 1.34 bn people consisted of 665.57 m urban and

674.15 m rural residents, or 49.68% and 50.32%, respectively. The total number of migrants, who were defined in 2010 as persons staying for more than six months in locations other than the towns (townships or streets) listed on their household registrations (*hukou*), was 261.39 m. Of this number, 39.96 m had a current residence different from the location on their household registrations but in the same city. This leaves 221.43 m people who can be classified as belonging to the migrant population. This figure is 83% higher than that in the 2000 population census, which recorded 117 m persons at different locations from their household registrations.

The strategic approach to urbanisation in the 12th FYP aims to channel rural migrants away from megacities and big cities toward small and medium-sized cities. While it argues the case for steadily allowing rural migrant workers to become urban residents, it repeats the mantra of urban development espoused in China since the 1990s:

> Megacities need to keep their population within reasonable bounds; large and medium-sized cities need to strengthen and improve population management and continue to make full use of their important role in absorbing the migrant population; and small and medium-sized cities and small towns should relax conditions for outsiders to become residents based on their particular condition.[79]

In marked contrast to the Chinese government's approach to urbanisation, rural migrants are primarily attracted to the megacities (特大城市) and big cities (大城市). Despite the government measures and policies to control migrant flows, the influx of migrants into the urban metropolises represents an ongoing and increasing trend. In 2009, 63.3% of the migrant workers in China were employed in big and medium-sized cities of prefecture level (地级市) or greater, with 9.1% in municipalities (直辖市), 19.8% in capital cities (province level 省会城市), and 34.4% in prefecture-level cities. These data show that China's urbanisation process is dominated by megacities and big cities, with the fastest population growth being seen in cities with more than 2 m inhabitants. When

---

[79] English Section of the Central Document Translation Department of the Central Compilation and Translation Bureau, trans., *The Twelfth Five-Year Plan for National Economic and Social Development of the People's Republic of China*. Beijing: Central Compilation & Translation Press, 2011, pp. 90–91.

considering the impact of urbanisation on Chinese domestic demand for housing, it is necessary to differentiate between the real urbanisation process of migrants voting 'by their feet' (based on spontaneous and largely market-driven factors) and the government's strategic approach of channelling migrants into smaller cities (which emerged and were shaped in reaction to this spontaneous development).

Impact of China's Rapid Urbanisation on Domestic Demand for Housing

Due to the continuous rise in rural-to-urban migration, there has been a marked increase in demand for low-rent urban housing. Demand by migrants in the city for different types of housing is determined to a large degree by the types of jobs they obtain and only a certain number therefore rent on their own. Migrants and their housing can be roughly divided into the following categories:

- Construction workers, who make up a large proportion of male migrant workers and who generally sleep in barracks at the construction sites.
- Factory workers, both male and female, who are usually housed in company-owned dormitories.
- Household workers who are accommodated in private households.
- Migrant labourers whose place of work is also where they live.
- Migrants with privately rented housing, often employed or self-employed in small shops, small-scale production enterprises, the restaurant and service sectors, or employed in cleaning, peddling or similar occupations. In other words, they usually hold informal jobs. These rural-to-urban migrants rent on their own and frequently live in *urban villages*.

As evident in figures from the Ministry of Public Security, demand by migrants for private housing has shown a continuous increase in recent years. Between 1998 and 2008 the number of migrants who lived in independently rented housing rose from 11.35 m to 57.2 m. In percentage terms, this represents a rise from 28% to 49%. These figures clearly show the rapid increase in low-priced accommodation for migrant workers in the cities. Based on urbanisation tendencies and the distribution of migrants in cities of different size, the demand for affordable housing will be particularly strong in megacities and big cities.

Growing demand for inexpensive housing is expected to be amplified by at least four developmental tendencies:

- The increasing and normal tendency for entire families to migrate as migration periods lengthen.
- Higher expectations by second-generation migrants (born in the 1980s) to stay in the cities and become permanent urban citizens compared with first-generation migrants.
- A growing number of young graduates from colleges and universities who (often from a rural background) have difficulty in finding a decent job after graduation, but want to stay in the big cities and therefore also seek minimum-rent housing.
- A growing number of 'land-less peasants' (失地农民), namely those who have lost their land due to acquisition of a number of investment projects.

Without an effective means to integrate these newer groups of migrants, social tendencies toward polarisation and alienation in urban centres can very easily intensify. Affordable-housing programmes could help with such problems, but only if implemented in a prudent manner.

Housing Reform and the Affordable-Housing Programme

China's housing reform started during the 1980s when a few cities began liberalising their housing markets by removing rental subsidies and selling public housing on the open market. In 1988 these new housing measures were taken up at the national level, which effectively shifted the responsibility for providing housing from the government to the market. In 1994 and 1998, the State Council strengthened the housing reform by introducing two directives, one on a market-based housing rental system and the other on a housing provident fund (住房公积金, compulsory housing savings system providing subsidised loans to employed homebuyers). These reforms led to a significant increase in the level of privately owned housing, but created problems in providing housing for lower-income families. Local governments neglected the supply of low-rental housing, and fewer than 3% of lower-income families were living in low-rental housing before 2006.

Housing prices in most Chinese cities rose rapidly and created a large group of urban residents in the 'sandwich stratum' (夹心层), i.e. those who are neither able to afford private housing nor eligible to apply for public housing (公共住房). One of the reasons behind the property boom was the introduction of an open-tender system for residential and commercial land sales in 2002. To generate higher returns, local governments favoured the sale of land to private over public residential developers. These actions were supported by an evaluation system for measuring the performance of local officials that was based on local GDP growth rates. This in turn resulted in a climate that allowed speculators to drive property prices upwards. In response, the State Council established a general framework for a new public housing system in 2007, including fundraising recommendations for local governments other than land sales, such as acquiring funds from local budgets, collecting rent from lower-rental housing and deriving income from the housing provident fund. That same year the home ownership rate reached 82.3% in urban China. However, housing affordability has become a major issue, particularly in large cities.

Against the background of the global financial crisis in 2008–2009 and the continuous rise in housing costs, the Chinese government allocated 10% of China's RMB 4 trillion (USD 486 bn) economic stimulus package to the construction of low-income housing, the modernisation of dilapidated housing and other measures to improve housing conditions. Building on this (and again as an economic stimulus), the Chinese government has launched an ambitious programme to provide affordable housing to qualified families. This programme calls for 36 m units of affordable housing to be built within five years (2011–2015). When completed, the programme is expected to cover 20% of the country's urban housing supply. In 2010 China started to construct 5.9 m government subsidised flats, and in 2011 some 10 m affordable-housing units should have been built, including 4 m for people in rundown areas, 2.2 m public-housing rental units and 2 m limited-price houses (the latter two options for middle-income earners who cannot afford to buy on the commercial market), and 1.6 m government-subsidised low-rental units. Central government funding for building affordable houses has increased from RMB 5.1 bn in 2007 to 16.8 bn in 2008, 47 bn in 2009, 80.2 bn in 2010, and RMB 152.2 m in 2011.

Different cities have created different policies to navigate the central government's social housing policy. While, for example, Chengdu has launched a pioneering reform of its household registration system that allows tens of thousands of migrant workers living in the city to enjoy the same social benefits (including housing benefits) as their urban counterparts, megacities such as Beijing and Guangzhou are opening up public housing to migrants without a substantial reform of their household registration systems. In Beijing where 7 m migrants make up more than a third of the capital's population of 19.6 m (2010), as of December 2011, non-*hukou* holders may now also apply for public-rental housing. But while very clear criteria are in place for applications by Beijing *hukou* holders, the criteria for applicants without *hukou* remain vague, and individual district and county governments will stipulate additional requirements based on their specific situations and housing availability. In Guangzhou there are two public housing options: government-administered for *hukou* holders, or society-based (without the *hukou* restrictions). The government is responsible for the 'sandwich stratum' as their main target group; for these *hukou* holders the rent should be at least 40% of the market price. For public housing without *hukou* restrictions for which migrants can also apply (certain restrictions such as a specified period of previous city residence, stable employment etc. are still held under consideration), the rent should not be higher than 80% of the market price. In both cities, non-*hukou* holders seeking to apply for public-rental housing, cannot own property in the city.

Concerns about the Affordable-Housing Programme

A variety of concerns have been raised regarding the government's affordable-housing programme. These include:

- The fiscal risk for local governments.
- The eligibility criteria for different kinds of affordable housing and a just distribution system.
- The quality of construction.
- Rent inflation caused by enforced upgrades following large-scale demolition of urban villages.

Fiscal risks for local governments

With only RMB 152.2 bn invested by the central government, local governments will have to contribute most of the estimated RMB 1.3 tn (EUR 149 bn) for financing the 10 m low and middle-income housing units. This will entail a high fiscal risk for local governments, which will have to borrow and might face difficulties in paying off their debts. This is because they will have to provide developers of affordable-housing projects with land essentially free of charge, i.e. they cannot use the auction of land use rights which is normally their main source of income. In addition, the governments will bear an ongoing obligation to pay for property maintenance and repairs.

The eligibility criteria for different kinds of affordable housing and a just distribution system

As confirmed by the Minister of Housing and Urban-Rural Development, Jiang Weixing, there are loopholes in the programme's management — illustrated, for example, by the fact that some well-off residents of affordable-housing units can be seen driving around in luxury cars. One suggestion is to establish a national information system covering personal housing assets in order to lay the foundation for a fairer distribution system. The lottery system used previously should be replaced by a waiting list of eligible people. Each city — and sometimes even each city district — is establishing its own eligibility criteria for affordable housing. The question of how to integrate migrants into the programme poses particular difficulties, affecting both the balance between the low-income urban population and the rural migrants in the city, and the question of institutional responsibility for the programme's different target groups.

The quality of construction

The poor quality of building construction has led to complaints by people who have been resettled due to redevelopment. Several reasons lie behind the concern that the quality of affordable housing might be poor. Because the developers of affordable housing are only permitted a 3% profit margin, quality may suffer as a result of efforts to save money during construction. Another factor is the time pressure facing contractors to finish their work. Moreover, insufficient numbers of skilled workers might be involved in the project, due either to financial restrictions or a shortage of these workers. Either eventuality could lead to poor quality of construction. However, it should be noted that poor quality of construction is also a problem for the construction of commercial-sector properties due to the speed and scale at which buildings are built.

Rent inflation

As part of the affordable-housing programme, residents of dilapidated urban housing will be resettled in public-rental housing. This may have an unintended negative impact on affordability. As in most urban renewal projects, demolition of this (mainly informal) housing will mean losing the majority of lowest-rent housing stock. Rural migrants often live in the urban villages which have become targets of demolition and renewal. In contrast to the local urban *hukou* population, they do not receive any compensation when forced to move out. Most of them will probably not be eligible for the affordable-housing programme, either because they do not meet the criteria or because they lack sufficient means for the rent. This means that the affordable-housing programme would have the effect of enormously increasing the demand for affordable housing by the lowest-income groups.

Government Housing Interventions and their Impact on the Rate of Urbanisation

Government housing interventions will probably have a limited impact on the *rate* of urbanisation in China. For one thing, only a very small part of the affordable housing programme targets low-income families (in 2011 no more than 1.6 m affordable-housing units out of a package of 10 m units) and this will have to be shared among poor urban *hukou* residents and migrant non-*hukou* residents. In addition, the megacities and big cities which are the preferred destinations for rural migrants all have strict regulations in place that control and restrict the influx of migrants (even if they are not very effective). Under these conditions, the formulation of eligibility criteria for migrants seeking to participate in the affordable-housing programme might turn out to be another instrument for channelling them to the small and medium-sized cities.

The incongruity between official Chinese urbanisation policy that attempts to channel migration streams into small and medium-sized cities and the economic incentives that attract ever greater numbers of rural migrants to mega-urban areas is, to some extent, related to the role of the cities in the Chinese administrative hierarchy. In the course of the reform process, ever more cities received extensive right of autonomy. This has doubtless contributed substantially to China's economic rise. Yet despite considerable decentralisation, the hierarchical nature of the top-down polity remains. Only first-tier cities are in a position to provide the best public services. Because of their higher rank these cities can gain more resources through administrative means. With more resources, public welfare benefits increase for urban *hukou* holders. The urban elite might worry that their living environment and access to public welfare benefits will erode as migrants in the city are granted full citizenship rights. The same economic mechanisms attracting rural migrants to megacities are causing their exclusion from costly public services. This has resulted in the emergence of a predominantly informal migration regime including informal housing, employment, schooling and healthcare.

Two Scenarios for Promoting Urbanisation

Given this situation there are two main scenarios for promoting urbanisation reform: the first scenario would target the administrative hierarchy of Chinese cities and redirect more resources to small and medium-sized cities, enabling them to provide more and better services (including housing) and to attract more investment and migrant workers. That would mean adjusting the existing administrative and management system of cities in line with priorities of the government's urbanisation strategy. This approach could turn out to be not only very costly, but would also require a considerable amount of time, basic changes to the existing city management system and, if successful, would probably result in rapid growth by these small and medium-sized cities.

The second scenario would be to open up megacities and big cities to the migrants who already reside there and enable them to become urban citizens without excessively high hurdles. In this case it would be necessary to build on and carefully upgrade the existing informal economy and infrastructure and to provide affordable housing and essential public services. Both scenarios imply a redistribution of resources away from urban *hukou* holders in first-tier cities — either to smaller cities or to rural migrants living in megacities and big cities who would thus be classified as urban citizens and consumers. The need for a more inclusive approach to migrants in the city becomes even more urgent in view of recent development strategies that place priority on expanding the domestic market and strengthening domestic consumption as part of a structural reorientation of the Chinese economy. A precondition for enabling migrants to settle in the cities, including the big and megacities, consists of greater attention to securing the wages of migrant workers, as well as their social welfare and housing. The main question then would not be how to prevent migrant workers from placing a strain on the urban infrastructure, but how to prepare the physical and social infrastructure needed to receive them as new urban citizens.

How Central Government Control of the Housing Market Conflicts with Local Demand

Since 2010 the Chinese government has introduced various policies to curb speculation and excessive gains from property transactions. Measures include rules that prohibit residents from buying more than a certain number of properties, higher transaction taxes, and an increase in the supply of flats for poorer people. Shanghai and Chongqing have launched a trial property taxation system with the aim of cooling down the housing market. The central government's property market policies are leading to lower prices for most players.

The importance of cooling the property market was reiterated by Premier Wen Jiabao in early February 2012. The main aims here include 1) returning housing prices to a reasonable level; and 2) promoting long-term, steady and sound development of the property market (thus avoiding a burst in the housing bubble). The recent decline in house prices confirms that the policies are working. But at the local level there are various protests and attempts to reverse them. Early buyers in Beijing and Shanghai have been protesting and asking for refunds. Potential home buyers are anticipating further price drops and delaying their plans to purchase a flat. Local governments of third-tier cities are trying to ease or even break the state's tightening policies. For example, in October 2011 the third-tier city of Foshan in Guangdong province allowed families to buy an additional dwelling and to trade houses that had been owned for more than five years. But the policy was halted within 12 hours after it was announced. The city of Wuhu in Anhui province announced in February 2012 that home purchasers would receive subsidies for an entire year if these homes were smaller than 90 m^2, purchasers of smaller homes would receive an even higher subsidy and all buyers would be exempt from deed tax. This policy was suspended within three days, and the central government seems unlikely to loosen its rigorous real estate policies in the short run.

Land Acquisition in China
(July 2012)

Staphany Wong
Independent Researcher and Translator

Executive Summary

In this study, land acquisition refers to government acquisition of farmland from farmers (with compensation), changing the land use and then leasing it to developers. The large price gap between compensation and lease rates has created enormous profits for local governments. This has provided essential ground for China's industrialisation, which has led to nearly double-digit average annual GDP growth over the past ten years. Urbanisation continues to occur and the urban population is expected to reach 1 bn by 2030.

Following three decades of land acquisition, 40–50 m farmers have become landless urban residents and 3 m more are joining them each year. The majority report a decline in living standards following land acquisition. Currently there is no appeal mechanism for farmers to challenge land acquisition decisions imposed by local governments. The village collective, the owner of the farmland, is governed by the village committee and Party village branch. Driven by political and economic interests, these governing bodies often sacrifice ordinary villagers' rights to fair compensation and resettlement.

The abolition of agricultural taxes in 2006 has, on the one hand, helped to ease the burden on the agricultural population; however, it has also led local governments to intensify land acquisition in order to generate revenue. Land lease prices have rocketed in recent years, earning an average of RMB 9.1 m (EUR 1.13 m) per hectare (ha) of land transferred in 2011. Motivated by enormous profits, land acquisition has become a hotbed for corruption.

The compensation scheme for farmers who lose their land offers a very low rate, which comes to a maximum of 30 times the average output value three years preceding land expropriation. Older farmers with less skills are likely to find it difficult to enter and compete in the urban job market. There has recently been a rise of mass protests in China, estimated at 200,000 in 2011. 50% to 65% of these are related to land acquisition.

The central government, while acknowledging the unfairness, corruption and social conflicts surrounding land acquisition, finds itself in an awkward position, as its fiscal budget is heavily supported by the tax contributions of local governments. Land revenues account for approximately 40% of local government tax revenues.

The EU has little influence on China's land acquisition. Yet it is in its interests to stay informed of developments, particularly in relation to food security issues and for promoting corporate social responsibility (CSR) of European companies. The EU should be more vocal when human rights abuses surrounding land acquisition take place. This should be made on the basis that these abuses are creating increasing levels of contention and conflict in society, which may well become unmanageable and is already expensive to police and control.

Main Points

- Land ownership and land usage rights are divided in China. Rural households are entitled to use an allocated piece of arable land, but the village collective, governed by the village committee and the local Party branch, dictate land use.
- Driven by business and political interests, local governments above the village-level have intensified land acquisition across China. The scale and speed of this intensification has been impressive, but the current procedure is not transparent and includes no appeal mechanism for members of the affected rural population.
- The compensation scheme is outdated and the rate paid to affected farmers is low. Farmers are often not entitled to citizen social security packages, even though they have become landless and forced to settle in the city. These factors have contributed to massive social unrest in China.
- Some recommendations have been made by civil society groups hoping to see fairer distribution of profits from land acquisition between farmers and local governments and ease the scale of social unrest. However, very few of these have been carried out.

- The central government has repeatedly tried to address these problems but seems reluctant to carry out fundamental land ownership reform, as land acquisition provides 40% of its taxes revenues from local governments.
- The EU should pay more attention to this issue as China's land acquisition could have a large impact on global food security and investment from European companies in China.

Introduction: Land Acquisition in China

Industrialisation and urbanisation as the driving force

Land acquisition has come hand-in-hand with China's economic development. China started its 'Open Door' policy in 1978 and, throughout the 1980s and 1990s, infrastructure building and industrialisation were prioritised in the state's Five Year Plans. As a result, much rural land was allocated to serving this purpose. Throughout the 21st century, this trend has continued — China's fast rate of annual GDP growth (almost double-digit), has further increased the pace of industrialisation, fuelling demand for land, and the scale and pace of China's urbanisation has continued at an unprecedented rate. The total urban land area was 2.3 million km^2 in 1990, but by 2005 had expanded to 2.6 million km^2. 24,727 km^2, an area a tenth the size of the UK (or a half of Slovakia), is added as urban land each year.

In terms of population, between 1990 and 2005, the urban population grew from representing 22% of the total population, to 44%. It is estimated that two-thirds of the Chinese population will become urban residents by 2025, totalling 1 bn by 2030. In order to feed the needs of industrialisation and to accommodate the growing urban population, land acquisition is expected to continue, if not speed up, in the foreseeable future.

Land use rights and ownership

In China, urban land is owned by the state. Rural land is distributed equally to all rural residents who are allowed to farm on this land or, under certain conditions, can transfer the land to others for agricultural use. The right to use land is separate from land ownership and farm land remains owned by village collectives, governed by the village committees and the village's Party branch.

The two concepts of land acquisition

Land acquisition in China involves two concepts, land requisition (*zhengyong*) and land expropriation (*zhengshou*). The 2004 constitutional amendment defines land requisition as a temporary act that usually takes places in an emergency and in the public interest. During land requisition, the collective retains ownership of the land, which will eventually be returned with adequate compensation. Land expropriation involves a change in land ownership from the collective to the state, with payment of compensation. The state, often represented by local governments, converts the usage of the land and leases it to developers for between 40 to 70 years. As a change of ownership is involved, land expropriation requires approval from the State Council in accordance with the Land Administration Law (LAL).

The Scale of Land Acquisition

Impacts on the rural population

The 2011 China Land and Resources Report reveals that the transfer of land use from agricultural purposes to land for development projects has increased from 406,000 ha in 2006 to 612,000 ha in 2011.

In terms of population affected, the Chinese Academy of Social Sciences' 2011 report on China's urban development reveals that 40–50 m farmers have lost their land so far. In addition, more than 3 m farmers are losing their land each year, which will affect 110 m farmers by 2030. In a recent survey, 60% of landless farmers interviewed say that they now suffer from financial difficulties and 81% say they are worried for their future. However, in a minority of cases, adequate compensation has been offered to farmers via schemes offering pensions or long-term rental fees to farmers and there have also been reports of farmers voluntarily giving up their land in the belief that 'planting the field has no future'.

Threats to China's food security

China's Ministry of Land and Resources has warned that the misappropriation of farmland has brought the country dangerously close to the so-called 'red line' of 296 m acres (19.7 m ha) of arable land that is needed to feed a population of 1.34 bn. To combat the misuse of arable land, the Ministry has started to engage in a number of activities: it now uses satellite imagery to spot abuses; has launched a fresh crackdown on illegal land use since 2011, targeting golf courses, hotels and villas in particular; and claims to have punished Party officials (2,078 in 2010) in several high-profile cases regarding this matter.

The Procedure of Land Acquisition and Loopholes

The motivations of local governments

As required by the LAL, any individual or unit that needs land for construction purposes must apply to use state-owned land. Therefore, for any proposed development project in a rural area, land ownership must first be acquired by the state, when it can then be leased to the developer. This practice creates room for local governments to make enormous profits, acquiring the farmland cheaply from farmers and leasing to developers at a much higher rate.

Apart from land conveyance fees, during land acquisition, local governments are often able to collect other taxes, such as farmland occupation tax, land use rights fees, etc. This has enabled local governments to cash in on land acquisitions, which has particularly been the case following the abolition of agricultural taxes in 2006. In many circumstances, local governments are shareholders in the investment plan, or officials and their families hold senior positions at the corporate involved. This gives an additional strong incentive for local governments to acquire farmland as cheaply as possible.

The Constitution stipulates that land acquisition can only be carried out in the 'public interest', yet this term is not clearly defined. Research conducted in 2010 shows that more than 80% of land acquisition is motivated by commercial interests, rather than in the public's favour. When a local government acquires farmland, it often has no clear development project in mind and instead offers the land at auction. The local governments may try to justify their actions by arguing that the land conveyance fees generate income to finance urban development and that this promotes employment and exports, as seen, for example, in the special economic zones (SEZs). SEZs, which are mostly built on former farmland, experience two to three times higher GDP growth than the national average and act as the driving force behind the ever-growing national GDP.

The imbalance of power between villagers and the local governments

Affected villagers are required to follow the decisions, terms of compensation and relocation plan that have been devised by the local government without their prior consent. Some even report that the local government has leased their land to developers, without informing or compensating them. Currently, there is no appeal mechanism for farmers to overthrow the land acquisition decision, although farmers might negotiate better terms of compensation through the village committees, protest or by hiring lawyers.

Only the State Council, China's version of a Cabinet, can revise local government land acquisition decisions. By law, the acquisition of basic farmland or arable land of more than 35 ha must be approved by the State Council. However, in order to avoid this, it is common practice for local governments to divide the land into smaller areas for the acquisition process. As indicated in the *2011 China Land and Resources Report*,[80] other than 2009, between 2006–2011 local governments transferred more land per year than the State Council. In some years, two-thirds or more of land transfers are carried out by local governments.

Power structure at the village level

As the governing body of the collectives, village committees and local Party branches are responsible for negotiating on behalf of villagers, in order to reach deals on land ownership transfer. The village committee is elected every three years by villagers aged over 18 years and is responsible for mediating civil disputes, maintaining social order and reporting popular opinion and proposals to the government. The local Party branch is appointed by the higher-level Party Committee every five years to exercise leadership according to the Party Constitution. There is no restriction on the frequency of a member being re-elected and re-appointed and it is not unusual to find village chiefs and Party secretaries who have taken office for decades. Vote buying is also reported as common practice.

---

[80] Available at http://www.mlr.gov.cn/zwgk/tjxx/201205/P020120516305280627517.pdf. Accessed 12 December 2013.

Low level of democracy and transparency in village governance

In terms of power structure, the local Party branch tends to lead, ratifying decisions made by the village committee, although very often the Party chief and the chairperson of the village committee are the same person. Individual farmers are often excluded from the negotiation process for compensation and resettlement. The cadres at the village committees and Party branches have a track record of conspiring with local government and business to seize farmland. This is especially the case with local Party branches, as the political careers of cadres are in the hands of their supervisors — namely, those in the upper echelons local governments — who often push for deals to be finalised. Their involvement in embezzling, intercepting and withholding farmers' compensation has frequently been reported.

The Central Government's Stance

The fiscal structure between central and local governments

Land leases account for about 40% of local government revenues. The fiscal relations between the central government and the provincial governments are a complicated matter. Local governments (from village governments to provincial governments) fund 80% of the country's public spending but are required to hand over half of their tax revenues to the centre. For poorer provinces, the handouts received from the central government fill the gap or even exceed their own contributions, but the more developed provinces are cash cows for central government funds. For example, in 2010, Guangzhou city government, the capital of Guangdong Province, handed over RMB 210 bn (EUR 26 bn) to Beijing — nearly two-thirds of its total funds collected from local taxes (RMB 338 bn (EUR 42 bn) in total).

The challenge for central government

Both the size and market price of land transfers have increased in recent years. In 2011, the total land sales price reached RMB 3 tn (EU 370 bn). In 2006, the average transfer price for each ha was RMB 3. 5 m (EUR 0.43 m) but by 2011, this had increased to RMB 9.1 m (EUR 1.13 m). Despite the high inflation rate in China, the price hike is significant.

On the one hand, the Chinese media and Premier Wen Jiabao have openly criticised the loopholes that exist regarding the land acquisition procedure, acknowledging the unfair compensation scheme and its linkage to social unrest. However, on the other hand, they have not pressed local governments to alter their land acquisition practices. Over the past few years, legal experts have discussed the fact that China needs to revise or even create a new land acquisition law that better defines 'public interest' and reforms the compensation scheme. However, no draft or timeline has been announced at the time of writing (July 2012).

The Compensation Scheme
Calculation method

There is no market price for rural land in China, as there is only one buyer, namely, the state. Article 51 of the LAL states that different standards and levels will be applied to major projects of national interest, enabling local governments to exercise their administrative power by underpaying farmers in the 'national interest'.

According to the LAL, total compensation should include land compensation fees, compensation for above-ground buildings and other attached objects, and compensation for crops on the land. Land compensation fees range from six to ten times the average output value three years preceding land expropriation. Resettlement fees should be calculated according to the agricultural population to be relocated and should be four to six times the average output value three years preceding the expropriation. The standards can be determined by local governments, but the combined total of land and relocation compensation should not exceed 30 times the average output value three years preceding the expropriation. The Ministry of Land and Resources also recommends that local governments subsidise expropriated farmers if the legal maximum compensation cannot restore their original living standard.

Low compensation in implementation

With the 30-fold average annual output value as the ceiling and no legal minimum limit on compensation, local governments tend to offer compensation that is lower than the ceiling price. Looking into this further, if the farmland is cultivated, compensation will be made according to the output value of crops. However, in the past two decades, a large number of farmers have become migrant workers (estimated at 250 m in 2011) who leave behind their farmland to look for jobs in the city. If the land of these farmers is not attended by their families, resulting in little or no crop output in the previous three years, their compensation payment would be seriously distorted should their land be expropriated. Despite this, migrant workers are not eligible to receive urban social security packages and have no rights to remain in the city once they are out of a job. (This is due to the urban–rural dual system, known as *hukou*.) Because many migrants plan to eventually return to their home villages, often returning to farming as part of a retirement plan, if their farmland is acquired without proper compensation, or even without them being informed, many migrant workers lose their basic social safety net.

Unfair basis for calculating the compensation

Even when legal maximum compensation is paid, farmers still do not receive a fair price given that grain prices in China are kept artificially low. For decades, national policy has meant that grain prices have been heavily controlled to ensure that adequate cereal grain supplies can be provided to urban residents at low and stable prices. It is not just the price of farming products which are affected and the market price of land for urban use should also be considered here.

Obstacles from fiscal structures

For national projects that are handled separately by the State Council, such as large or medium-sized water conservancy and hydro-electric projects or pipelines for natural gas, compensation comes directly from the state although the amount varies between the provinces. Due to the fiscal structures of central and local governments, funds are allocated downward to lower levels of governments, from state, to provincial, municipal, county and finally township levels. A portion of funds is retained at each level of government, namely for public goods and services. By the time payments have trickled down to farmers, they receive only one-quarter of the initial compensation.

Different forms of compensation

The majority of compensation is offered in cash settlements. On average, a household receives compensation of RMB 76,271 (EUR 9,469), which is only enough to cover basic needs for three to four years in rural areas. Although cashing this in may be an attractive option for farmers, without healthy investment channels, high inflation and long-term planning, the compensation would run out in just a few years. Moreover, a significant percentage of them cannot compete in the tightening urban labour market, given their age and skill level. In a 2010 study of Hunan Province, 60% of landless farmers say that re-employment is their biggest concern and 30% cannot find jobs. Only 34.3% of farmers report that their livelihood has improved after land acquisition. Voices from civil society have started lobbying for welfare provision for those affected by land acquisition, such as urban housing, medical insurance, pensions, low-income allowance, etc., to be included in the compensation package in future.

Some pilot projects, held as part of land acquisition reform, were introduced throughout the 2000s. These included the compensation of elders (men over 60 and women over 50 years old) with monthly social security payments for a certain period of time (around 15 years or so) and the entitlement of the middle-aged population to receive social security payments after their retirement. Some have adopted a rent-based approach, in which farmers can receive annual rents, instead of a one-off lump sum. This is equivalent to their average output value over the previous three years and adjustments are made every few years according to inflation and agricultural product price changes. However, these pilot projects have only taken place in a few prosperous cities, such as Shanghai, and cover only a small number of affected farmers.

Hukou for the landless farmers

When farmers lose their land due to land acquisition, their identity as part of the rural population very often remains unchanged. Their resettlement and new employment might be in cities, but without the relevant citizen residence, they are not entitled to participate in urban social security schemes. This means that education and medical services become comparatively more expensive for them and they are not entitled to retirement benefits or basic safety net protection. Discrimination against migrants and conflicts between migrants and citizens are also on the rise.

The 2011 Social Security Law entitles landless farmers to enrol in a new social security system. Yet it remains doubtful how many farmers will be willing and able to pay the premium for their pension.

Social Conflicts Related to Land Acquisition

Continuous rise of conflicts

According to a lawyer specialising in demolition and resettlement cases, half of the disputes in China relate to collective land acquisition. Another researcher, Yu Jianrong of the Chinese Academy of Social Sciences, estimates that since 1990, 65% of large-scale protests, also known as 'mass incidents', in rural areas involved land disputes. Rural land disputes are reportedly starting to spread from the eastern coast to the less developed western part of the country. Yu has calculated that, over the past 20 years, governments have seized 6.7 m ha of rural land and deprived farmers of RMB 2 tn (EUR 250 bn) in compensation, because local governments often compensate much less than the market price for the land.

No appeal mechanism available

Currently there is no systematic appeal system for farmers to voice their concerns or opposition to land acquisition and very few can afford lawyers. It has become normal for farmers to stage sit-in protests, road blockades and, in some extreme cases, even commit suicide to protest against forced demolition and land seizure.

Wukan protest as an example

The village of Wukan, in southern China, provides one example of how intense and violent the tension regarding land acquisition can be. Having already protested against land acquisitions for several years, in 2011 villagers in Wukan alleged that village officials had sold their farmland without informing or compensating them. They only noticed the land sales when the developers started construction work. The deal reportedly generated RMB 1 bn (EUR 12 0 m) for 400 ha of land, which was pocketed by officials. During the protests, one village representative was abducted by police and died in police custody shortly afterwards. His death led to an uprising in the village in December that year and caused the upper level of government to call an election for a new round of village committee members in early 2012.

Land rights defenders

Thugs have reportedly been hired by local governments and developers to silence land rights defenders. A recent case occurred in Fujian Province on 12 June 2012, when a farmers' representative was attacked by thugs who injected him with toluene. He died two days later in hospital and his body was forcibly taken away by police after his family demanded a public investigation.

The State Bureau for Letters and Visits (the highest-level petitioning bureau in Beijing) is overrun by landless farmers on a daily basis. Farmers travel from the countryside, hoping to have their cases heard. Yet, provincial governments have been accused of hiring people in Beijing to abduct petitioners and to force them back home, or send them to 'black' jails. Human rights organisations have documented allegations of torture and mistreatment in these facilities.

Right to organise not protected

Freedom of association and the right to organise are not respected in China. Farmers who choose to try and defend their rights are often accused of 'mobbing and disturbing social order', which is a criminal offence. The police also hold the power to place these 'offenders' in 're-education through labour' — an imprisonment lasting up to three years that does not require any legal proceedings.

Recommendations

As social conflicts have increased in scale and number in recent years, academia and civil society have concerned themselves with ways to improve the land acquisition procedure to make it fairer and more transparent. In order to avoid these abuses, 'public interest' needs to be well defined and central government needs to start reviewing cases closely. An effective appeal mechanism that works independently from local governments should be introduced to assist farmers in reviewing the motivation for land acquisition, compensation terms and distribution of compensation.

Democratisation and transparency are key for land acquisition reform to help keep check on corruption, collusion between officials and business, and abuse of police power. Farmers should be consulted on when, where, for what purpose and at what price their farmland will be acquired. Their rights to organise should be respected.

The compensation level should be increased to market price level to fairly compensate farmers and make their lives sustainable. The compensation methods should be diverse, taking the farmers' age, skill level and employability into consideration.

China's Food Security
(August 2012)

Robert Ash

Professor of Economics with reference to China and Taiwan, School of Oriental and African Studies

Executive Summary

- China's post-1978 record in protecting its basic food security is impressive. With only 7% of the world's arable land and 8% of its water supplies, its output of staple cereals (rice, wheat and corn) has been sufficient to meet the basic needs of a population that constitutes around one-fifth of the global total.
- Pursuit of food security requires China to meet two challenges: first, eliminating hunger among 120 m poor farmers. In order to fulfil this task, farmers will be required to produce more grain for *direct* consumption. The second challenge involves meeting the dietary aspirations of an increasingly affluent population that seeks to consume more meat, poultry, fish, fruit and dairy products. In order to meet their needs, an increasing premium is being placed on grain farmers to produce grain for *indirect* consumption (i.e. to feed pigs, poultry, etc.).
- Since 1979 (the start of the 'Reform Era'), staple food production has shown quite a strong positive trend. In particular, the period from 2008 to 2011 has seen successive bumper crops, taking total and per capita cereal production to record levels in 2011. But past fluctuations in production make it unwise merely to extrapolate from this performance in predicting future output growth.
- The Chinese government has for many years sought to maintain 95% self-sufficiency in staple foods. Cereals apart, China has already found it impossible to meet its soyabean requirements (mainly needed for feed) from its own

- supplies. In recent years soya imports have risen explosively, making China the largest purchaser in international markets.
- In addition, China is now at a tipping point in terms of meeting its corn requirements (mainly needed for feed, but also biofuels). In the last few years China has shifted from being a net exporter to becoming a net importer of corn. Imports will continue to rise, albeit not on the same explosive scale as soyabeans.
- Looking ahead, rising incomes and changing diets will dictate a greater involvement for China in other international food markets. These include pork, milk and dairy products, and some fresh fruits.
- China's size suggests that its increased engagement in international grain markets will have potentially significant implications for global food security by squeezing available staple food supplies, and by leveraging international prices at a time when they are already under severe pressure.
- In its efforts to generate sustained food output growth into the future, China faces difficult policy challenges. Resource (especially land and water) constraints are already severe, and will intensify. There is evidence too that farm chemicals are being used wastefully, and that marginal returns to further chemical fertiliser use are diminishing or have become negative.
- Central to China's future food security strategy is the need to maximise returns from relevant scientific and technological research. Pay-offs from advanced research promise to have the greatest impact. China has invested heavily in genetically modified (GM) crops and will continue to do so. At the same time, it has taken a cautious stance on GM technologies. In November 2011, the Chinese government announced that it would suspend commercialisation of GM rice and wheat for up to ten years. Significantly, however, this suspension did not apply to GM corn, commercialised use of which could be endorsed by 2020.
- Recent years have seen rapid growth in EU–China agricultural trade. The EU27 is the third largest market for Chinese farm products; China is the EU's fifth-largest such market.
- As China's population becomes more affluent, increased demand for high-value products (e.g. wine, meat and dairy products) will offer favourable commercial opportunities for EU producers. The ability of the EU27 to export staple foods, such as wheat and corn, will be severely constrained, at least until EU enlargement incorporates countries such as Ukraine and Belarus.

Recent Performance

- China's grain output has trended upwards during the last three decades. In 2011 the grain harvest recorded a fourth successive record level. Meanwhile, per capita grain production was also at an historic peak.
- However, analysis of China's output performance since 1979 reveals sharp fluctuations, with periods of positive growth contrasting with periods of negative growth. From this perspective, it would be unwise to extrapolate from the most recent past and assume that the momentum of strong output growth will automatically be maintained into the future.
- In recent decades, expanding sown areas under corn and soyabeans have contrasted with contracting areas under rice and wheat. This pattern of change reflects the increasing premium placed on growing grain for animal feed.
- The most encouraging aspect of China's recent performance is that per hectare yields of all staple food crops have risen. However, it is significant that recent years have seen such growth slow for all such crops.
- To date, except for soyabeans, China's involvement in international staple food markets has been minimal. In general, since 1980 it has been a net exporter of rice and (until recently) corn, and a net importer of wheat.
- In the last five years, China has shifted from being a significant net exporter of corn to becoming a significant net importer. This is set to become a permanent feature of China's agricultural foreign trade.
- Cereals and biofuel crops are not the only commodities traded by China. Today, oilseeds dominate its food imports, as 20 years ago cereals did. But as dietary patterns have changed, so too the import share of vegetables, fruit, meat and dairy produce has also risen significantly.
- In the last five years, China's overall balance on its food trade account has shifted from surplus into deficit (totalling more than EUR 220m in 2010).

Outlook

- The principal drivers of future food demand in China will be rising incomes and demographic change (above all, urbanisation).
- Growing affluence will be reflected in a continuing shift from a grain-based diet to one based on higher consumption of animal protein (meat, poultry and dairy products), as well as of fish and fruit.

- The most important consequence of the changing pattern of food demand will be to place a higher premium on the need for feed grain to meet the anticipated rise in demand for meat and dairy produce.
- With arable and sown areas already under severe pressure, the key to future grain output growth lies in generating sustained increases in unit area yields. The recent slowing in cereal and soya yield growth throws into sharp relief the urgency of this task.
- There is a consensus view within and outside China that maintaining 95% self-sufficiency in staple foods will become unsustainable. Authoritative Chinese projections indicate major declines in self-sufficiency rates for corn, soyabeans, edible oils and dairy products in the coming decades.
- Declining domestic food self-sufficiency will have serious foreign trade implications for China. The biggest burdens will be carried by the two main feed grains — soya and corn.
- US Department of Agriculture projections suggest that China's soya imports will rise from 53 m tonnes to 90 m tonnes between 2011 and 2022. During the same period, its imports of corn are expected to increase from 3 m to more than 18 m tonnes.
- China's extra soya imports during the next decade are projected to account for 80% of expected growth in *global* soya imports, while its incremental corn imports will absorb some 45% of global corn import growth.
- Chinese imports of some meat, fruit and dairy products are also set to increase. Pork imports, in particular, are expected almost to double by 2021.

Policy Issues

- Land and water shortages seriously threaten to constrain future food output growth.
- China's arable land base has declined significantly under the impact of post-1978 reforms, although the rate of decline has slowed sharply in recent years. A mandatory target under the current Five Year Programme (2011–2015) is that the arable area should be maintained unchanged at 121 m ha.
- Pressures of industrialisation and urbanisation will make it difficult to fulfil this target. If it is fulfilled, it will be at the cost of bringing less fertile, reclaimed land into cultivation, with a consequent fall in average yields.

- Farmers currently enjoy land use, but not land ownership rights. The introduction of a free land market would facilitate the emergence of more efficient, larger-scale farms. Although current official orthodoxy continues to oppose such an initiative, land consolidation is starting to take place through transfers of land use rights, and will accelerate.
- China faces serious water shortages, which are acute in parts of the North China Plain, where much of China's wheat and corn is produced.
- The South–North Water Transfer Project seeks to redirect water from southern China to the north, though many doubt the wisdom of this huge and costly engineering project. Water conservation and the introduction of more rational water charges are also high policy priorities.
- Policy initiatives notwithstanding, it seems inevitable that farmers will continue to face serious water shortages for the foreseeable future.
- Increased applications of farm chemicals show signs of running into negligible, even negative marginal returns. Their use has also had deleterious environmental consequences. Future policy priorities will be to raise the efficiency of fertiliser use through the greater use of compound fertilisers.
- Scientific and technological progress is central to maximising China's domestic food security. The Chinese government is investing heavily in advanced research, including development of GM technologies.
- China currently ranks sixth in the world in terms of its GM crop acreage. However, it lags well behind leading GM crop growers, such as the US, Brazil and Argentina.
- The Chinese government is taking a cautious stance on endorsing the commercialisation of GM rice and wheat. However, there are signs that commercialisation of GM corn may be less restricted.

Implications for the EU

- Bilateral EU–China agricultural trade has grown rapidly in recent years, and China is now the fastest-growing market for EU farm products.
- The EU27 is the third-largest export market for Chinese farm products, and China's fifth-largest source of agricultural imports.
- Food security considerations will help shape the EU's future export trajectory *vis-à-vis* China. In particular, growing affluence will generate increases in demand

- for European high-value food products (e.g. wine, meat and dairy produce), as well as for organic foods.
- Bilateral trade in cereals and other staples will, however, be severely constrained by existing patterns of food production and foreign trade in China and the EU.
- The embrace of major cereal producers, such as Ukraine and Belarus, within an enlarged EU would, however, offer significant cereal export opportunities.
- Cooperative programmes, taking advantage of EU research and experiential expertise, promise to facilitate sustainable food output growth and diversification in China.
- Enhancing China's food security-related capabilities through such cooperation will help meet China's needs, and simultaneously serve EU and wider interests by mitigating the detrimental impact on prices and global food security arising from a major increase in China's involvement in international markets.
- China's search for food security also offers major commercial opportunities to EU agrifood companies. Such opportunities are not confined to food production, but extend to a wide range of ancillary activities across the entire food supply chain.

Introduction: China's Food Security

For many years, a priority goal of Chinese government economic policy has been to maintain 95% self-sufficiency in staple foods. To date, China has largely succeeded in fulfilling this objective. In more than three decades of reform, only one year saw cereal imports exceed 5% of total domestic output, and China has frequently been a net cereal exporter. The only staple crop for which the 95% target has not been met is soyabeans, of which China has become by far the largest importer in the world.

China's record in protecting its basic food security is a remarkable one. With only 7% of the world's arable land and 8% of its water supplies, it has produced sufficient cereals (rice, wheat and corn) to meet the basic needs of a population that constitutes about one-fifth of the global total. There is, however, growing evidence that China may have reached a tipping point. In addition to soya imports continuing to rise to record levels, 2009–2011 have seen a sharp increase in corn imports that have pushed China's trade balance in cereals firmly into deficit. Maintaining adequate food supplies from domestic sources will prove increasingly difficult in the years ahead, as China's population becomes more affluent. As excess demand emerges, China's involvement in international grain markets will increase. To what extent such involvement will affect food prices and destabilise international markets should be a matter of major concern to Western governments and the corporate sector.

Context

The problem of food security poses one of the most profound challenges facing the world today. In 2011, the UK Government Office for Science's report on 'The Future of Food and Farming'[81] noted that 925 m people throughout the world suffered from absolute hunger, while a further 1 bn people endured 'hidden hunger' through lack of vital micronutrients, such as vitamins and minerals. Ironically, another 1 bn people were 'over-nourished' — susceptible to ill-health and disease as a result of over-consuming.

In many ways, China is a microcosm of global nutritional conditions. The poverty-alleviation impact of more than three decades of GDP growth averaging almost 10% per year is unprecedented in human history. The incidence of hunger has fallen dramatically during the last three decades, and China is one of few countries — perhaps the only one — certain to fulfil the Millennium Development Goal of halving the incidence of hunger between 2000 and 2015. Yet absolute poverty has not yet been eliminated in China, especially in the countryside, where in 2012 more than 120 m rural Chinese were officially classified as falling below the poverty line. In absolute terms China is second only to India in terms of the number of people affected by under-nourishment (129.6 m, 2006–2008). These under-nourished are overwhelmingly farmers, living in remote inland (especially western) regions of China. Relieving them of the threat of hunger is the most elemental food security challenge facing the Chinese government today.

By far the greater food security challenge facing China reflects the increasing *affluence* of its urban population, as well as of growing numbers of rural residents. Sustained income rises have already facilitated major dietary adjustments through changes in both the level and also the structure of food consumption. Higher incomes have enabled hundreds of millions of Chinese to shift to a more diversified

---

[81] *The Future of Food and Farming*, 2011, Department for Business, Innovation & Skills. Available to download from https://www.gov.uk/government/news/the-future-of-food-and-farming

diet, characterised by the consumption of more meat, poultry, fish, fruit and dairy produce. The less favourable consequences of growing affluence have also started to emerge. The healthy nature of the traditional Chinese diet, characterised by low intakes of fat, oil and sugar, has long been recognised. But since the 1980s, changing work and lifestyles have encouraged a sharp rise in consumption of less healthy snack foods, alcohol, soft drinks and fast foods. Obesity now affects more than 100 m in China, compared with fewer than 20 m in 2005. Almost 10% of the population has diabetes — almost the same as in the US (the corresponding figure for the EU is around 7%).

Part of the burden on Chinese farmers is to produce more grain for direct consumption by those who are still hungry. But the shift towards a more varied diet based on higher consumption of animal protein has placed an increasing premium on the production of grain for *indirect* purposes: above all, to provide more feed for pigs, poultry, cattle, etc. Between 1980 and 2011, the amount of corn used for animal feed relative to total domestic output rose from 43 to 68%; for wheat, the corresponding increase was from 3 to 19%. The explosive rise in soya imports too reflects burgeoning demand for livestock feed.

In its pursuit of food security, China faces major production and distribution challenges. Recent output growth has been impressive, but in the face of resource and environmental pressures, significant rises in yields will be necessary to maintain the momentum of such growth. The distributional (including logistical) challenge is also formidable. Estimates of national Gini coefficients show that in the mid-1980s China was one of the most equal societies in the world. Subsequently, steadily widening gaps in income distribution have made it one of the most unequal. As for logistics, although state grain storage capacity has expanded considerably in recent years, large-scale investment is needed to further extend and improve storage facilities, especially at local levels. Meanwhile, the burden on rail transport to ship grain from producers to consumers is immense. In 2010 China's railway system carried 97 m tonnes of grain over an average distance of 1,802 km.

A recent plan issued by the Ministry of Agriculture seeks to achieve 100% self-sufficiency in rice, wheat and corn during 2011–2015. This target will be difficult to fulfil, as domestic grain supplies come under increasing pressure to generate increasing amounts of animal feed to grow meat and dairy products to meet changing dietary tastes. If it is not met, China's increased involvement in international grain markets will have significant implications for global food security at a time when food prices are already under severe pressure.

China's Recent Grain Performance

The recent output performance of China's grain sector has been impressive.

Despite significant fluctuations (most recently, in 2000–2003), total and per capita grain production has displayed quite a strong positive trend. In 2011 China achieved a record grain harvest (571 m tonnes). This generated a record per capita level of grain production of 424 kg of raw grain per head — a figure that is almost 25% higher than the 400 kg benchmark considered sufficient to provide for a diet offering significant intakes of animal protein, as well as carbohydrates.

Recent grain output growth has been impressive, rising by 3.6% per annum between 2003 and 2011, although during 1998–2003, the corresponding figure was strongly negative (a drop of 3.4% per annum). Much of growth post-2003 is therefore by way of recovery from the previous severe downturn in output. Moreover, although China has enjoyed a run of four successive record harvests since 2008, the previous (1998) per capita peak was only re-attained and surpassed in 2011. It would be unwise to extrapolate from the experience of the last few years and merely assume that the momentum of strong output growth will be maintained into the future.

Output growth reflects changes in area and yields per hectare. Analysis of China's experience during the last three decades reveals that the sown area under rice and wheat has declined, while that of corn and soya has expanded. But yields of all four crops have increased. This yield performance is encouraging: China faces severe resource constraints, and increases in yields offer the firmest basis for continued increases in output.

China's Foreign Trade in Staple Foodstuffs

Since 1980 China has been a net importer of wheat, a net exporter of rice and, until recently, a net exporter of corn. In general, China's foreign trade in grain has hitherto had only a minor impact on international cereal markets. However, the potential impact of China on such markets is huge. In 2004, for example, as output declined, China was forced into international wheat markets in order to offset the depletion of domestic stocks. As a result, within a single year China shifted from being a net wheat exporter to a net importer, becoming the largest purchaser of wheat in the world.

To date, the most dramatic example of China's impact on international food markets is that of soyabeans. Until the mid-1990s, China was a net exporter of soyabeans. But since 1996 burgeoning demand for protein meal by the livestock sector has forced China into international soya markets on a dramatic scale, growing by more than 30% annually. China is now easily the largest importer of soyabeans in the world, accounting for more than 60% of global trade. US Department of Agriculture (USDA) projections made in 2009 indicated that of an additional 20.9 m tonnes of soya expected to be traded from 2009–2019, China would absorb almost 18 m tonnes (86%).

In the coming years, the most significant influence on China's foreign trade in staple foodstuffs will be the changing demand–supply balance for corn. China's recent record in producing corn is impressive. Since 1978, not only has the sown area under this crop expanded by more than 60% — in part, by shifting cultivation out of rice and wheat — but yields have also doubled. As a result, total output of corn doubled between 1978 and 1995, and thereafter increased by a further 72%. In 2011 total production was 191 m tonnes, accounting for 38% of total output of all three cereals (rice, wheat and corn) — a rise of 10% in little more than a decade.

The rapid increase in corn production in recent years reflects the need to meet the inexorable rise in demand for meat and dairy produce. Corn is by far the most important source of animal feed — though recent years have also seen a rapid rise in the use of wheat for feed — as well as being the basis of biofuel (ethanol) production. About 70% of corn supplies are now allocated to feed.

Thanks to booming domestic output growth, for many years China was a net exporter of corn. But between 2006 and 2011 China shifted from being a net exporter of 5 m tonnes of corn to being a net importer of 4 m tonnes. As increasing excess demand emerges in China, imports of corn are set to continue to rise, placing further pressure on international markets.

For most of the last 30 years, China's food trade balance was in surplus. Since 2007, however, a growing deficit has emerged, reaching around 2,000 m RMB (c. EUR 223 m) in 2010. Meanwhile, changes in the composition of food imports offer a revealing perspective on the shifting dynamics of China's search for food security. Since 1990 the share of cereals in China's total food imports has fallen from more than half to less than 10%. Offsetting this contraction has been a huge rise in the share of oilseeds: from 8% to almost 50%. The remaining balance is accounted for by vegetable oil (18% of all imports in 2010); fruit and vegetables (9%); and meat (6%).

Future Trends
Outlook for food demand

Growing affluence in China has generated continuing rises in demand for grain, but increasingly for indirect uses — above all, to feed animals and generate meat and dairy products. Before the 1970s, the dominant shaping influence on food demand was population growth. Today, the principal drivers are income growth and urbanisation. Under the current 12th Five Year Development Programme (2011–2015), some 40 m farmers are expected to move into the urban sector; in the same period, rural and urban per capita incomes are targeted to rise by 7% per annum.

The general direction of future changes in food demand is clear, although quantifying such changes is very difficult. Chinese demand projections confirm that as incomes continue to rise and urbanisation accelerates, the shift towards more varied diets, based on higher intakes of meat, fish, fruit and dairy products, will intensify. The biggest rise in demand will be for dairy products (with milk expected to rise six-fold by 2050). But major increases will also take place in the demand for seafood (up an expected three-fold), meat, poultry and fruit. Meanwhile, demand for rice and wheat will gradually decline. Implicit in these projected changes are large increases in demand for feed grains.

Hitherto, dietary changes have been most pronounced in the urban sector, where incomes have risen most rapidly. However, income growth in rural areas will become an increasingly important determinant of food demand in the future. Wealthy urban families are approaching — and in some cases, have already reached — capacity limits in terms of food consumption. As income rises among poorer households, mostly concentrated in the rural sector, begin to accelerate, their spending on food will also increase *pari passu*. Central to estimating grain requirements is the ability to assess future levels of meat demand. Since 1990 meat consumption has more than doubled to reach around 50 kg per head. How rapidly demand will continue to rise will depend on income growth and changes in tastes and diet (the latter influenced by government and popular attitudes to the dangers of the increasing incidence of obesity). Even the most conservative projections suggest that meat consumption will grow by around 30% in the coming decade (to reach 65 kg by 2020) — and some posit a figure as high as 55% (almost 80 kg). By 2030, meat consumption is expected to have reached between about 75 and 95 kg per head. With good quality grazing land already under severe pressure, meeting future demand for meat and dairy produce will require securing adequate supplies of feed grains to grow pig and cattle herds. Generating such supplies is likely to be beyond China's domestic production capacity, making it increasingly dependent on imports of corn, soyabeans and cassava.

Outlook for domestic food production

With arable and sown areas under severe pressure, the key to future grain output growth in China lies in securing continuing increases in per hectare yields. China's record in generating yield growth is not unimpressive. But it is revealing that estimates for all four major grain crops — rice, wheat, corn and soya — all reveal a slowing in yield growth since 2000. A consensus view is emerging that future food output growth will be increasingly constrained, and that China's pursuit of 95% self-sufficiency in staple foods will be progressively more difficult to sustain in the coming years. Compared with projected increases in demand, planned rates of output growth for edible oils, meat, fish and dairy produce contained in the 'National Modern Agriculture Development Plan, 2011–15' (published by the State Council in January, 2012)[82] look distinctly modest. It is telling too that estimates made by the Chinese Academy of Sciences (CAS) indicate that under a baseline scenario, with technological development and agricultural investment rates held unchanged at 2004 levels, self-sufficiency rates for wheat, corn, edible oils, sugar, some meats and dairy products would all decline to 2020. Indeed, the CAS projections suggest that by 2050 self-sufficiency rates for corn, soyabeans, edible oils and dairy products will have fallen to 71%, 38%, 58% and 79%, respectively.

Outlook for foreign trade

The trade implications of demand and supply projections are likely to be quite profound. The biggest burdens will be carried by feed grains — soya, corn and cassava.

While China is expected to remain a net exporter of poultry and to play a minor role in beef trade, its imports of pork are projected to increase quite significantly in the coming decade (up from 415,000 to 807,000 tonnes between 2010

---

[82] National Modern Agriculture Development Plan (2011-2015), 2012, State Council. Available at https://www.gov.uk/government/news/the-future-of-food-and-farming

and 2021). If such projections are correct, China's share of global trade in pork will rise from 9% to more than 11% during the same period. Recent years have also seen a sharp rise in imports of milk and milk products — a trend that is likely to continue, especially if concerns about the safety of domestically produced dairy products persist. In addition, imports of some fresh fruits may be set to rise. Finally, there has been a steady trend increase in fishmeal imports since the 1980s to meet the burgeoning needs of aquatic producers.

Policy — Opportunities and Constraints

Beijing faces difficult policy challenges as it seeks to maintain a high level of domestic food security.

Land

The contraction of China's arable land base — under way since the late 1950s — accelerated sharply during the 1980s and 1990s, although the rate of decline has slowed markedly in recent years. One of the few mandatory targets contained in the 12th Five Year Plan is to keep the arable area unchanged at 121 m hectares. Pressures of industrialisation, urbanisation and infrastructural construction will make it difficult to meet this target, even if illegal land grabs can be controlled. In any case, fulfilment of the target conceals an important *qualitative* dimension, as losses of fertile land in eastern coastal regions are offset by cultivation of new, but less fertile land in northwest China (where most reclamation takes place). In other words, hidden within an unchanged arable land base is an implicit output loss. Meanwhile, the grain sown area is expected to contract — by 3% decline from 109.9 to 106.7 m ha (2010–2015), according to some projections. This anticipated decline throws into sharp relief the need to increase land productivity (yields per ha) to maintain continued output growth.

Another major challenge reflects the tension between decentralised, small-scale farming and agricultural modernisation based on larger, more mechanised and more efficient farms. Because of the ideological imperative of retaining collective ownership of arable land, farm operators in China possess only contractually based land use rights. In addition, concern that land consolidation will deprive millions of farmers of their ultimate form of social security has impeded the introduction of a free land market that would facilitate the creation of larger farms. For the time being, the government remains unwilling to sanction the institution of individual land ownership rights. Recent regulations have, however, made land transfers easier, as a result of which the profile of land use is changing. Significant land consolidation has, for example, recently taken place in parts of northern and south-western China. The economic desirability of increasing the scale of farming applies to livestock husbandry, as well as crop cultivation. Thus, by 2015 China seeks to expand large-scale dairy cattle and pig farming by significant margins.

Water

Lack of water — especially the existence of acute *regional* shortages — is another huge challenge for China. The North China Plain — China's 'grain basket', where much of its wheat and corn is produced — is severely deficient in water, thanks to excessive use of surface water supplies and the depletion of natural underground aquifers through over-pumping. Since the early 1980s the area affected by over-pumping of water in this region has more than doubled to some 200,000 km^2, and in some areas the water table is falling by two metres a year.

Farming currently accounts for about two-thirds of total use. It will still account for half in 2030. Less than half of the total arable area is effectively irrigated, and physical shortages are exacerbated by inefficiency in the use of water. Farmers' high demand for water is driven in part by their high dependence on flood irrigation, which is often wasteful. By contrast, sprinkler and drip-irrigated farms account for less than 5% of total demand for wheat, corn, vegetables and oil crops. By 2030 excess water demand will exceed 200 bn cubic metres — the equivalent of one-third of total water supplies in 2010.

China's solution to its water shortages is a gigantic engineering project, known as the South–North Water Transfer Project, is intended to redirect vast amounts of water from the Yangtze River in the south to the Yellow River in the north. Although this is well under way, its wisdom is increasingly being questioned — on economic, social, geological, environmental and ecological grounds. Many would argue that a more effective approach is through water conservation and the introduction of more rational pricing policies.

Farm chemical use

China's record in chemical fertiliser use is mixed. Increased applications over the last half-century have contributed greatly to increased land productivity. But in more recent years, marginal returns from further increases have declined — and in some areas have become *negative*. There is evidence too of wastage of agricultural chemicals, with unused fertilisers and pesticides left in fields, often seeping into surface or sub-surface water, with serious environmental consequences.

China still leads the world in its use of nitrogenous fertilisers. These account for more than 40% of total domestic fertiliser consumption. In 2005–2006 per hectare applications of nitrogen were three times the world average (for pesticides it was twice the average). Despite a recent surge in the use of compound fertilisers, their share of total consumption (32%) is still far below that of advanced countries, such as the US and UK (around 80%).

Future policy will focus on reducing nutrient inputs and increasing the efficiency of fertiliser use. One priority is to build on recent trends by applying more compound fertilisers for cereal production; a second is to increase the use of bio-chemical-inhibitor, slow-release fertilisers, especially for high-value cash crops, such as fruit and vegetables.

Application of science and technology

Scientific and technological progress is central to China's pursuit of food security. In some areas, China has already made significant progress. For example, it has invested heavily in developing GM technologies (planned investment is estimated at USD 2,930 m, 2008–2020 (approx. EUR 2,330 m)), and its GM crop acreage ranks sixth in the world. For the time being, however, China's 3.7 m hectares of GM crops — mainly cotton, but also papaya, tomatoes and sweet peppers — are insignificant compared with the corresponding acreage in the US, Brazil and Argentina. In the face of concerns about safety, the government has proceeded cautiously, and in late 2011 it announced that it was to suspend commercialisation of GM rice and wheat for between five and ten years. Significantly, however, it endorsed the continued development of corn breeding technology, and observers have speculated that GM corn commercialisation be approved before 2020.

Future priorities for agricultural scientific R&D include development of plant and animal germplasm resources, and of plant-breeding science and technology; promotion of biotechnology research; research into water-saving and energy-saving farm practices; and the development of more sophisticated agricultural chemicals. A fundamental underlying goal is to use long-term scientific R&D in order to accommodate the needs of a more sustainable agriculture in China.

Implications for the EU
Foreign trade

Recent years have seen strong growth in EU–China agricultural trade, and China has become the fastest-growing major market for EU farm products. Since 2005, EU27 agricultural exports to China have increased by almost 26% per annum, while annual growth of imports has been 9.4%. As a result of surging exports, which have more than doubled since 2009, not only has bilateral farm trade reached a record high, but in 2011 the EU's previous deficit in its agricultural trade with China was transformed into a surplus (EUR 408,000 m).

The importance of agriculture in bilateral trade is captured in the finding that the EU27 is now the third-largest export market for Chinese farm products, while the EU is China's fifth-largest source of agricultural imports. The EU's single most valuable export product is wine, which now accounts for about one-quarter of all EU exports to China; next in importance are milk and dairy products, and pork. The composition of exports reflects the changing nature of Chinese diets under the impact of rising incomes (see above). EU farm imports from China are dominated by intermediate and final products (for example, China is the EU's most important source of processed vegetable imports, worth EUR 674 m in 2011).

Food security will be a major factor governing future EU exports to China. In particular, growing affluence among wider sections of the Chinese population seems certain to generate further significant rises in demand for high-value farm products, such as wine, meat and dairy products, all offering favourable opportunities for European producers. Changes in taste among urban Chinese consumers also offer good prospects for EU exports of organic food products, which rose by 25% in 2011. However, the EU's capacity to supply basic food commodities to China — above all, grain (including soyabeans) — will remain severely constrained. In 2011 wheat was the only cereal grain exported on a significant scale from the EU. For the foreseeable future, the focus of cereal import demand from China will be corn — as a product of which the EU is also a significant overseas purchaser, with net imports of around 2 m tonnes in 2011. There seems little prospect of the EU27 emerging as a supplier of corn to China — at least until enlargement incorporates major corn producers (e.g. Ukraine and Belarus) in the EU. As for soyabeans, China and the EU will also continue to be competitors in international soya markets: in 2011 purchases of soyabeans (including soyabean meal), worth EUR 4,700 m, accounted for 11% of all EU27 agricultural imports.

Agricultural cooperation

The EU–China Dialogue on Agriculture was established in 2005. The six meetings that have since taken place have facilitated enhanced mutual understanding and laid the foundation for strengthened cooperation in key areas of shared concern affecting agriculture. From the beginning, food security and related issues — for example, food safety and the environmental implications of changing dynamics of food demand and supply — were identified as core issues. Most recently of all, in June 2012 China and the EU signed a 'Cooperation Plan on Agriculture', designed to give a new impetus to ongoing discussions. Among the priority areas identified for future cooperation were food security, organic farming and food safety.

Other institutional initiatives that promise to enhance EU–China cooperation include the 'Task Force on Food, Agriculture and Biotechnologies' and the G20 'Action Plan on Food Price Volatility and Agriculture' (both launched in 2011). The EU has rich expertise and experience, which can be harnessed to help formulate policies designed to facilitate sustainable output growth and diversification across all branches of food farming activities in China — cereal and other forms of crop cultivation, livestock husbandry and fisheries. As a matter of urgency, the EU should maximise the opportunities inherent in the existing institutional framework to pursue constructive collaboration with China.

Collaboration also has a commercial dimension, and China's pursuit of food security offers a host of opportunities for foreign companies. The global economy is dominated by firms in high-income countries. Agriculture is no exception. To take one example, just three firms account for about 70% of the global market share in farm equipment manufacturing. Major global companies, including European agrifood companies (e.g. Bunge, Danone, Nestlé SA, Nutreco, Unilever, etc.) have a significant and expanding presence in China. Opportunities for profitable collaboration are by no means limited to sectors *directly* related to food and agricultural production. Rather, they embrace a large range of ancillary activities and extend across the entire food supply chain, linking producer, distributor and retailer, and consumer. As such, they embrace infrastructural construction, transport provision, processing, retail distribution, finance, storage, food hygiene and food safety, as well as production. It is revealing that China has only one agriculture-based company in the Fortune Global 500 list — COFCO (China National Cereals, Oil and Foodstuffs Corporation), which is ranked 393rd in the latest list.[83] Moreover, in the face of competition from multinationals, its share in international trade in grain and edible oils has declined. In terms of revenue, profits and assets, it lags well behind its global rivals. COFCO's own Chairman has described his company as a 'small fish in a big pond'.

COFCO's experience is revealing. It highlights the fallacy of believing that, as a source of supposedly 'low-technology' products, agriculture is a sector in which Chinese firms can more readily compete on the global stage. The truth is that not only do farming practices increasingly embody high technology, but so too does the entire value chain of the agrifood business. Organising, developing and realising the benefits of this value chain are huge challenges for Chinese firms. No less a challenge is that of creating trusted global brands.

---

[83] Fortune Global 500, 2012. Available at http://money.cnn.com/magazines/fortune/global500/2012/

Suggested Further Reading

On EU–China Relations

Kerry Brown (ed.), *China and the EU in Context* (Palgrave Macmillan: Basingstoke, 2014).

Stanley Crossick and Etienne Reuter (eds.), *China-EU: A Common Future* (World Scientific Publishing, Singapore, 2008).

Fei Liu and David Kerr (eds.), The *International Politics of EU-China Relations*, British Academy Occasional Papers (Oxford University Press/British Academy, Oxford 2007).

Robert S Ross (ed.). *US China EU Relations: Manaing the New World Order* (Routledge, London, 2010).

David Shambaugh, Eberhard Sandschneider and Zhou Hong (eds.), *China-Europe Relations: Perceptions, Policies and Prospects* (Routledge, London, 2007).

On Chinese Domestic Politics

Michael Barr, *Who's Afraid of China: The Challenges of Chinese Soft Power* (Zed Books, London, 2011).

Richard Baum, *Burying Mao: Chinese Politics in the Age of Deng Xiaoping* (Princeton University Press, Princeton, 1996).

Zhiyue Bo, *Chinese Elite Politics: Governance and Democratization* (World Scientific, Singapore, 2010).

Kerry Brown, *Ballot Box China* (Zed Books, London, 2011).

Kerry Brown, *Hi Jintao: China's Silent Ruler* (World Scientific, Singapore, 2012).

Kerry Brown, *Contemporary China* (Palgrave Macmillan, Basingstoke, 2013).

Li Cheng, *China's Leaders: The New Generation* (Rowman and Littlefield Publishers, Lanham MD, 2001).

Jonathan Fenby, *The Penguin History of Modern China* (Penguin, Harmondsworth, 2008).

Joseph Fewsmith, *China Since Tiananmen*, 2nd Edition (Cambridge University Press, Cambridge, 2008).

Richard McGregor, *The Party: The Secret World of China's Communist Party* (Penguin, Harmondsworth, 2011).

Frank Pieke, *The Good Communist: Elite Training and State Building in Today's China* (Cambridge University Press, Cambridge, 2009).

Tony Saich, *The Government and Politics of China*, 3rd edition (Palgrave Macmillan, London 2010).

David Shambaugh, *The Communist Party of China: Atrophy and Adaptation* (University of California Press, Berkely, 2009).

Vivienne Shue, *The Reach of the State: Sketches of the Chinese Body Politic* (Stanford University Press, Stanford, 1986).

Teresa Wright, *Accepting Authoritarianism: State Society Relations in China's Reform Era* (Stanford University Press, Stanford, 2010).

Keping Yu, *Democracy is a Good Thing; Essays on Politics, Society and Culture in Contemporary China* (Brookings Institute Press, Washington DC, 2008).

Chinese Society

Jingqing Cao, *Along the Yellow River: Reflections on Rural Society* (Routledge, London, 2006).

Guidi Chen and Wu Chuntao, *Will the Boat Sink the Water: The Life of China's Peasants* (Public Affairs, New York, 2006).

Gloria Davies, *Worrying About China: The Language of Chinese Critical Enquiry* (Harvard University Press, Cambridge Massachussets, 2009).

Elizabeth Economy, *The River Runs Black: The Environmental Challenges to China's Future* (Cornell University Press, New York, 2005).

Xiaobo Liu, *No Enemies, No Hatred: Selected Essays and Poems* (Harvard University Press, Cambridge Massachussets, 2012).

Qiusha Ma, *Non-Governmental Organisations in Contemporary China: Paving the Way to Civil Society* (Routledge, London, 2005).

Jonathan Watts, *When a Billion Chinese Jump: Voices from the Frontline of Climate Change* (Faber, London, 2011).

Guobin Yang, *The Power of the Internet in China: Citizen Activism Online* (Columbia University Press, New York, 2009).

Chinese Economy

Bruce J Dickson and Jie Chen, *Allies of the State: China's Private Entrepeneurs and Democratic Change* (Harvard University Press, Cambridge Massachussets, 2010).

Karl Gerth, *As China Goes, So Goes the World: How Chinese Consumers are Transforming Everything* (Hill and Wang, New York, 2011).

Yasheng Huang, *Selling China: Foreign Direct Investment During the Reform Era* (Cambridge University Press, Cambridge, 2005).

Yasheng Huang, *Capitalism with Chinese Characteristics: Entrepreneurship and the State* (Cambridge University Press, Cambridge, 2008).

Barry Naughton, *The Chinese Economy: Transition and Growth* (MIT Press, Cambridge Massachussets, 2006).

Peter Nolan, *China and the Global Economy: National Champions, Industrial Policy and Big Business Revolution* (Palgrave Macmillan, Basingstoke, 2001).

Peter Nolan, *China at the Crossroads* (Polity Press, London, 2003).

Jean C Oi (ed.), *Going Private in China: The Politics of Corporate Restructuring and System Reform in the People's Republic of China* (Asia-Pacific Research Center, Stanford, 2011).

Chinese International Relations

Rosemary Foot and Andrew Walter, *China, the United States and Global Order* (Cambridge University Press, Cambridge, 2010).

M Taylor Fravel, *Strong Borders, Secure Nation: Cooperation and Conflict in China's Territorial Disputes* (Princeton University Press, Princeton, 2008).

James Millward, *Eurasian Crossroads: A History of Xinjiang* (Columbia University Press, New York, 2008).

Robert S Ross, *China's Security Policy: Structure, Power and Politics* (Routledge, London, 2008).

Xuetong Yan, *Ancient Chinese Thought, Modern Chinese Power* (Princeton University Press, Princeton, 2011).

Index

9/11, 151

Academy of Military Sciences, 94
'A Digital Agenda for Europe' initiative, 17
Afghanistan, 133, 150–152, 155, 234, 251–260
    National Development Strategy, 259
Africa, xviii, 137, 141, 208, 332, 357, 384, 386
    African traders, 227
    China–Africa Forum, 206
    engagement with China, 223–231
    Forum on China–African Cooperation, 146
ageing population, 409
agriculture, 333
aid, 138, 157, 158, 180, 247, 253, 297
    military aid, 150
Ai Weiwei, 57, 72, 76, 437
Aizhixing, 75
al-Assad, Bashar, 143, 181
All-China Federation of Industry and Commerce, 356, 363

All-China Federation of Trade Unions, 442, 443, 445–447, 449, 450
All-China Women's Federation, 39
Al-Qaeda, 151, 251, 254,
Anhui, 464
anti-dumping, 248
anti-dumping measures, 246
Anti-monopoly Law, 391, 394
Arab League, 180, 212
arable land, 477, 489
Arab Spring, 133, 143, 272, 436, 437, 439, 450
Argentina, 244–248, 481, 491
arms embargo, 7, 9, 137, 273
arms sales, 138
arms trade, 150
Ashton, Catherine, 8, 284
Asia-Europe Meeting, 296
Asian Development Bank, 280, 283
Asian Financial Crisis, 278
Asian Nuclear Safety Network, 163
Asia-Oceania Working Party (COASI), 138
Asia-Pacific Economic Cooperation, 134, 296

Asia-Pacific region, 175, 268, 282, 296
Association of Southeast Asian Nations, 131, 163, 165, 166, 168, 169, 173, 177, 192, 196, 265, 274, 276, 277, 279–284, 295, 296, 328
  ASEAN +3, 281
  ASEAN Regional Forum, 130, 132, 166, 168, 296
  Charter, 279, 284
  Dispute Settlement Mechanism, 192
  Economic Community, 279
  Free Trade, 280
  Free Trade Agreement, 279
  Guidelines on the South China Sea, 165
  Hanoi 2010, 172
  Treaty of Amity and Cooperation, 131
Aung San Suu Kyi, 264, 267, 269
Australia, 135, 177–179, 275, 281, 328, 336, 405
authoritarianism, 278
authoritarian regime, 276, 282

Baluchistan, 152, 154
banking sector, 345
  bank loans, 337, 339
  Chinese banks, 312, 322, 344
  European banks, 320, 321
  foreign banks, 316, 319, 320
  in China, 309–322, 338, 340, 361
    Central bank, 401
  Japanese banks, 321
  rural banks, 363, 364
Bank of China, 312

Beijing, 108, 356, 459, 464
  consensus, 69, 70, 278
  Olympics, 69–71
  Public Security Bureau, 81
Belgium, xv
Bhutan, 292, 293
bilateral disputes, 128
bilateral investment treaties, 329, 330
bilateral relations, 7, 296
bilateral trade, 244
bin Laden, Osama, 149
biofuel, 478, 479, 486
biomass power, 27
biotechnology, 333, 375
'black' jails, 476
black market, 216
bond market, 366, 368
  central government bonds, 338
  local authority bond issuance, 337
Bo Xilai, 44, 203, 219
Brazil, 139, 141, 142–146, 180, 230, 241–248, 387, 388, 394, 481, 491
Bretton Woods institutions, 116, 117, 121, 122
BRICS, 122, 139, 140, 141, 145, 146, 147, 248, 377
  2012 summit declaration, 144
Brunei, 167, 185, 189, 191, 192, 196, 276, 277
Budget Law, 337, 338
Bulgaria, xv
bureaucracy, 229
  bureaucratic systems, 90
Burma/Myanmar, 135, 136, 179, 180, 261–273, 276–280, 282, 301, 304

Bush, George, W., 130, 131
business
    European business, 284

cadres, 82–87, 110, 438, 439, 471
    cadre responsibility system, 438
    cadre training, 82–87
Cairo Declaration, 199
Cambodia, 179, 185, 191, 192, 276, 277, 279, 280, 300, 301, 304, 359
Cameron, David, 227
Campbell, Kurt, 133
Canada, 163
capitalism, 228, 229
Carbon Capture and Storage, 31
Caribbean, 246, 247, 357
censorship, 77
Central Asia, 176, 178, 179, 182, 232–240, 252, 255, 258, 260, 276, 295
Central Asian Gas Pipeline, 237
central government, 340, 345, 413
    debt, 340, 341
    revenues, 341
    spending, 341
centrally planned economies, 316
Central Military Commission, 46–48, 67, 94
Central Party School
    Party School of the Central Committee, 93
central planning system, 311
cereals, 477, 479
Chengdu, 414, 459
Chen Guangcheng, 73, 78, 81

child labour laws, 364
Chile, 241–244, 246, 249
China Aviation Technology Import & Export Corporation, 150
China Banking Regulatory Commission, 95, 313, 363, 364
China Center for Contemporary World Studies, 89, 93
China Center for International Economic Exchanges, 89, 95
China Construction Bank, 312
China Development Bank, 205, 212, 237, 244, 246, 384, 387
China Foundation for International Strategic Studies, 89, 94
China Institute for International Strategic Studies, 89, 93, 94
China Institute of Contemporary International Relations, 89–91, 95
China Institute of International Studies, 89, 92
China Insurance Regulatory Commission, 313
China International Trust and Investment Corporation, 237
China Investment Corporation, 237
China Metallurgical Group, 256
China National Cereals, 494
China National Offshore Oil Corporation, 235
China National Overseas Oil Corporation, 246, 383, 384, 388
China National Petroleum Corporation, 232, 235, 236, 246, 299
China Petroleum and Chemical Corporation, 235

China Reform Forum, 93
China Reform Foundation, 95
China–Russia relations, 175–182
   energy cooperation, 176
      Treaty on Good Neighbourly
         Friendship and Cooperation, 176,
         178
China Securities Regulatory Commission,
   312, 313
China Society for Environmental
   Sciences, 422
China's rise, 63, 64, 130, 334
China Threat, 146
China–Vietnam Relations, 165–174
Chinese Academy of Sciences, 376, 488
Chinese Academy of Social Sciences, 56,
   89, 92, 95, 468, 475
   Institute of American Studies, 92
   Institute of European Studies, 92
   Institute of World Economics and
      Politics, 89, 95
Chinese Chamber of Commerce, 216
Chinese Communist Party, 13, 14, 19,
   35, 37, 39, 51–54, 56, 65, 73, 82, 83,
   86–88, 90, 99, 112, 152, 203, 309,
   313, 314, 318, 355, 362, 431–433,
   436–440, 457
   Central Committee, 93, 118
      Central Comittee Foreign Affairs
         Leading Group, 91
      Central Comittee Foreign Affairs
         Office, 90
   Central Secretariat, 51
   Chinese Foreign Ministry, 206
   Chinese Ministry of Commerce, 391
   Communist Party Committee, 57

Foreign Ministry, 205, 209
   International Department of the
      Central Committee, 89
   Ministry of Commerce, 205, 209,
      231, 394, 395, 396
   Ministry of Environmental
      Protection, 105, 421
   Ministry of Finance, 103, 423
   Ministry of Foreign Affairs, 92, 94,
      186, 231, 360
   Ministry of Land and Resources,
      468, 472
   Ministry of Public Security, 433
   political reform, 60
   State Council, 361, 363, 364
   United Front Department, 51, 55,
      57
Chinese Development Bank, 334
Chinese domestic market, 280
Chinese economy, 315–317, 339, 453
   consumption economy, 398
Chinese elite, 4–6, 11, 56, 57, 60, 64,
   318, 319
Chinese energy companies, 233, 240
Chinese financial markets, 309–322
   bond market, 310–313
   deregulation, 311, 319
   reforms, 317
   stock market, 310, 312, 313
Chinese firms, 229, 247, 250, 256, 257,
   301, 321, 327, 328, 333, 335, 356,
   377, 390, 395, 494
   private enterprises, 381
Chinese goods, 11, 246, 247, 248, 271
Chinese households, 399
   urban households, 399

Chinese imports/exports, 224, 248–250, 263, 295
    soya imports, 478
Chinese investment, 267, 291, 395
    in Europe, 382
    in the EU energy sector, 380–389
    investors, 342, 389
Chinese leadership, 91, 37, 227–230, 232, 268, 270, 282, 439, 440
    Chinese leaders, 5
    leadership transition, xv, 203
Chinese manufactured goods, 224, 239, 242, 295
Chinese military, 390, 393
Chinese military power, 282
Chinese outward direct investment, 137
Chinese People's Consultative Conference National Committee, 51
Chinese People's Political Consultative Conference, 39, 51–62, 92, 109
    Chair's Council, 59
    Committee for Handling Proposals, 58
    National Committee, 54, 56, 59
    National Committee plenary session, 58
    Political Consultative Conference, 52
    Standing Committee, 57, 59
ChiNext, 361
Chirac, Jacques, 9
Chongqing, 44, 76, 98, 99, 104, 112, 219, 464
civil activism, 170
civil servants, 109
civil society, xiii, 71, 75, 283, 285, 287, 438, 439, 466, 474, 476

Clean Development Mechanism, 31
clean energy sources, 18
climate change, xvii, 13, 18, 26, 28, 131, 143, 292
    national climate change programme, 24
    negotiations, 31
Clinton, Hillary, 128, 134, 172, 265, 269
cloud computing, 390, 393
coal, 24, 26, 28, 30, 180, 185, 297, 300, 302, 362, 364, 383, 386, 423
    coal mining, 333
    consumption, 24
    energy consumption, 27
    mining, 301, 360
    mining companies, 302
    power plants, 24, 26, 28, 273
coastal regions, 86
Cold War, 137, 178, 185, 196, 223, 254, 279
collective bargaining, 107, 108, 432, 436, 439
Collective Mobilisation, 441–450
Colombia, 244
colonialism, 224, 225, 278
Commonwealth of Independent States, 178
Communist Party of Burma, 271
Communist Youth League, 55
competition policy, 13
Confucianism, 68, 69, 276
Confucius Institutes, 64, 66, 68, 245, 278
Constitution, People's Republic of China, 42, 45–48, 52–54, 100, 469
consumption, 398, 416, 419, 484, 487
    retail consumption, 397
COP15, 132

Copenhagen Accord, 25, 30
Copenhagen Climate Change Summit, 25
corn imports/exports, 478
corporations, 225
    corporate social responsibility, 466
corruption, 45, 57, 63, 87, 210, 229, 256, 264, 266, 355, 423, 431–434, 437–439, 465, 466, 476
Costa Rica, 244, 247, 328
counter-terrorism, 130, 133, 149–152
Cuba, 181, 243, 244
Cultural Revolution, 52, 72
Cyprus, 385
Czech Republic, xv

Dalai Lama, 52, 131, 132, 155, 248, 293
Dalian, 86, 103, 159, 437
debt, 338
    debt crisis, 342, 345
defence expenditure, 341
democracy, 220, 230, 265, 437, 439
democratic consultation, 110
democratic parties (*minzhu dang*)
    3 September Society, 62
    Chinese Association for the Promotion of Democracy, 61
    Chinese Democratic Association for National Construction, 61
    Democratic League of China, 61
    Justice Party, 62
    Kuomintang's Revolutionary Committee, 61
    Peasant and Workers Democratic Party, 62
    Taiwan Democratic Autonomous League, 62

Democratic People's Republic of Korea, xvii, 130, 180, 181, 214–222, 265, 294–296, 302, 303–305
    defectors, 216
    Sino–North Korean Mutual Aid and Cooperation Friendship Treaty, 216
democratisation, 233, 235, 476
    democratic reform, 448
demographics, 6, 16, 403, 406, 408, 414
    demographic change, 479
Deng Xiaoping, 52, 358
Deng Yingchao, 53
Denmark, 292, 377, 382, 385
denuclearisation, 214, 215, 217, 219, 220
Department for International Development (DFID), 291
dependency ratio, 409
developing economies, 20
developing world, 16
development assistance, 278, 290
development gap, 317
Diaoyu/Senkaku islands, 160, 175, 178, 179, 197
digital technology, 13, 17
diplomacy, 253
    cultural diplomacy, 278
diplomatic relations, 262, 265, 269, 293, 300, 301, 329
direct investment, 256
disaster prevention, 156
dissent, 71
dissidents/dissenters, 71, 167, 265, 437
    disappearances, 72–81
domestic interests, 213
domestic reforms, 116

domestic stability, 438
Dominican Republic, 241, 247
drug trafficking, 253
Du Qinglin, 51

East Asia-Latin American Cooperation
    Forum, 245
East Asia Summit, 131, 134, 135, 175,
    177, 275, 281, 296
    Bali 2011, 179
East China Sea, 160, 161, 178, 186, 197,
    199, 200, 295–297
Eastern European states, 258
East-Siberian Pacific Ocean oil pipeline,
    234, 298
East Turkestan Islamic Movement, 151,
    152
e-commerce, 17, 401
economic aid, 212
Economic and Monetary Union, 317
economy, 244, 247
    economic and trade relations, 131
    economic development, 266, 267,
        274, 329, 406, 432, 467
    economic engagement, 221, 222,
        228, 302
    economic growth, 12, 13, 15, 230,
        296, 339, 342, 367, 386, 397,
        404, 416, 439, 440, 442, 445, 449
    economic reconstruction, 256
    governance, 115, 125
    integration, 11
    liberalisation policies, 228
    reforms, 214, 218
    sanctions, 180
Ecuador, 245

e-democracy, 112
education, 13, 16, 17, 64, 66, 84, 111,
    303, 341, 361, 362, 404, 444, 474
elections, 109, 220, 261, 264, 265, 267,
    269, 273, 285–288
    electoral reform, 46
    village elections, 109
Electoral Law, 40, 41
elites, 219, 221, 222, 230, 277–279
    Chinese elites, 311
    political elite, 220
    western elites, 376
emerging markets, 372, 396
emissions
    control, 18
    trading scheme, 24, 29
    targets, 24
    CO_2, 29
employment, 18, 463, 469
energy
    consumption, 28
    cooperation, 177, 237
    efficiency, 12, 24, 424
    energy policy, 232–240
    energy sector, 224, 380–389
        Electricity Grid, 386
        solar energy, 385
        wind energy, 384
    imports/exports, 233, 294–305
    markets, 255
    resources, 180, 184, 276, 294–305
    security, 26, 143, 225, 255, 388
    technology, 27
entrepreneurs, 224, 227, 357
    Chinese entrepreneurs, 379
    Peasant Entrepreneurs, 359

rural entrepreneurs, 356
Wenzhou entrepreneurs, 358, 360
environment, 229, 402, 405, 421, 436
    environmental damage, 416
    environmental degradation, 404
    Environmental Impact Assessment
        Law, 105
    laws, 364
    movements, 401
    protection, 18
        Environmental Protection Law,
           420
ESPO pipeline, 299
ethnic groups/minorities, 39, 41, 56, 72,
    264–266, 269, 271, 289
ethnic minorities, 39, 56, 72
European Union, xiii–xviii, 3–20, 23–32,
    70, 78, 89, 96, 115–127, 129, 136,
    137, 139, 140, 144, 163, 164, 177, 179,
    180, 182–185, 230, 231, 233, 239, 240,
    242, 243, 249, 250, 262, 263, 267, 272,
    273, 275, 283, 286, 292, 296, 305, 310,
    322, 328, 359, 367, 378, 381, 382, 388,
    389, 391, 394, 396, 405, 415, 416, 418,
    420, 423, 425–427, 431, 433, 440, 442,
    454, 466, 467, 482, 484
    Common Foreign and Security
        Policy, 283
    counterweight to the US, 9, 11
    DG Environment, 426
    enlargement, 9
    EU–China, 115, 117, 119, 123
        agricultural trade, 478, 481, 492
        Dialogue on Agriculture, 493
        Economic and Trade Dialogue, 97,
           124
        EU–China relations, xiii, 3, 89,
           115–127
        Social Security Cooperation
           Project, 408, 415
        EU–China Summit, 10, 97, 124
    EU producers, 478
    Europe 2020, 12–20, 116
    European Commission, xiv, 6, 7
    European Council, 7
        President, 8
    European External Action Service,
        xiv, xv, xix, 4, 8, 89, 96, 97, 284
    European Parliament, 8, 44, 76, 80,
        118
    High Representative, 8
    institutions, 118, 311
    Member States, 78, 233, 239, 272,
        276, 379
    Presidency, 6
euro, 10, 11, 120, 121, 123, 126
eurobonds, 144, 366–372
    eurobond market, 126
European companies/firms, 310, 388,
    396, 401, 402, 416, 466, 467
European Financial Stability Facility, 366,
    368, 369
European identity, 4, 8
European Renewable Energy Council,
    380
European Stabilisation Mechanism, 366
Europe China Research and Advice
    Network, xiii–xv, xviii
eurozone, 10, 122, 123, 126, 136, 144,
    366–372, 381
    bond market, 371, 372
    sovereign debt market, 368

eurozone crisis, xvi, 115, 118, 140, 144, 296, 371, 389
    debt crisis, 366, 367
    Greek debt crisis, 370
    Irish and Portuguese bailouts, 368
exchange rate liberalisation, 344
exchange rate stability, 345
exclusive economic zones, 172, 187–189, 191
Export-Import Bank of China, 244
export markets, 329
exports, 204, 247, 357, 469
extractive industries, 247, 301
extra-judicial tactics, 76, 77

failing state, 255
Fairbank, John, 277
Falun Gong, 80, 81
farmers, 465–477, 489
    grain farmers, 477
federalism, 289
Federation of Trade Union, 55
feed grains, 487, 488
feed-in tariffs, 388, 389
fertilisers, 481, 490, 491
financial reform, 19, 121, 309
financial services, 280
Financial Stability Board, 116, 117, 121
Finland, 292
fiscal policy, 342
Five Principles of Peaceful Coexistence, 67
Five Year Plan, 14, 162, 329, 375, 419, 467, 489
Five Year Programmes, 23, 30, 37

Five Year Programme, 2006–2010, 30
Five Year Programme, 2011–2015, xiv, 12–20, 24, 26, 28–30, 58, 117, 127, 162, 313, 416, 421, 452, 453, 480, 487
food
    food/agricultural production, 477, 493
    prices, 484
    safety, 493, 494
    scares, 402–404
    security, 143, 333, 466, 467, 477–494
foreign direct investment, 10, 65, 241–249, 303, 327, 328, 330, 333, 336, 381, 382
foreign exchange reserves, 9, 31, 140, 237, 329, 341, 370
foreign investors, 262, 273, 330, 370
foreign workers, 208
fossil fuels, 29, 157, 161
France, xv, 66, 92, 163, 178, 194, 367, 384, 389
free trade, 124
    free trade agreements, 242–244, 249, 327–336
Fudan University, 89, 96
    Center for American Studies, 89, 96
Fujian, 358, 475
Fukushima triple disaster, 18, 156–164
futures trading, 312
Fu Ying, 5, 49

G7, 140
G8, 7, 120

G20, 3, 7, 20, 116, 117, 120, 121, 125, 126, 142, 146, 284, 493
    Cannes Summit, 144
    G20+, 116, 117, 125
    Summit, 119
Gao Zhisheng, 73, 79
gas, 237, 239
    Central Asian, 233
    gas supply agreement, 238
    imports/exports, 255
    natural gas, 234, 297, 298, 473
    shale gas, 297, 388
GDP, 17, 140, 141, 225, 276, 339
GDP growth, 24, 342, 465, 483
General Agreement on Tariffs and Trade, 123
genetically modified (GM) crops, 478, 491
    GM technologies, 481
geo-economics, 279
geopolitics, 279
Georgia, 178
Germany, xv, 7, 69, 163, 180, 292, 311, 367, 369, 373, 384, 385, 389, 392, 408, 414, 415, 424
Gilani, Yousuf Raza, 149
Gini coefficients, 484
global economic governance, 15
global financial crisis, 8, 10, 15, 18, 115, 123, 131, 140, 141, 207, 237, 241, 279, 318, 339, 367, 445, 446, 459
global financial system, 121
global governance, 115–127, 284
    global governance forums, 125
globalisation, 6, 224
    speed, 6

global powers, 272, 274
    global resource powers, 294
global reserve currencies, 142
global trade, 339
'go global' policy, 225, 327, 329
government bonds, 411
'Go West' strategy, 234
grain, 484
    feed grain, 480
    prices, 473
    production, 479, 485, 488
grassroots activism, 446
Greater Mekong Sub-Region, 173, 280
Greece, 144, 367, 368, 385
green development, 18, 24, 26
Green Economy, 23–32
green energy, 16, 30
    targets, 27
green enterprises, 26
greenfield investments, 383
greenhouse gases, 23, 26, 416, 423
    emissions, 18, 388, 421
    emissions targets, 24
    global emissions, 26, 28
green technology, 12, 13, 17, 20, 23, 24, 31, 32
Guangdong, 99, 107, 112, 356, 358, 383, 424, 435, 436, 443, 464, 471
    Federation of Trade Unions, 107
Guangxi, 281
Guangzhou, 101, 104, 108, 227, 459, 471
Gulf Co-operation Council (GCC), 328, 336
Gulf of Thailand, 191–193
Gulf of Tonkin, 169, 170, 185, 191, 193
Gulf States, 255

Gulf War, 207
Guo Moruo, 52
Gwadar Port, 154

harmonious society, 19, 63, 68, 278, 281, 282
healthcare, 302, 398, 400, 405, 463
High Level Economic Dialogue, 13
High Level Strategic Dialogue, xvi
high net worth individuals, 357
hi-tech sector, 208, 356, 361, 364, 379
Hong Kong, 36, 42, 54, 56, 108, 158, 227, 244, 312, 328, 357, 369, 414
    Basic Law, 42, 50
housing, 452–464, 474
    affordable housing, 453, 454, 458–463
    housing reform, 458
    informal housing, 453
Huawei, 390–393, 395, 396
Hui Chinese, 210
Hu Jintao, 66–68, 72, 85, 133, 141, 150, 155, 157, 244–246
hukou, 378, 453, 459, 460, 462, 463, 473
human rights, xvi, xviii, 7, 44, 63, 67, 70, 78, 81, 124, 137, 181, 182, 228, 230, 235, 426, 466, 476
    activists, 72
    extra-judicial detentions, 72
    human rights diplomacy, 77
    human rights organisations, 76
    lawyers, 72
    violations, 267
Hunan, 474
Hundred Flowers Movement, 52

Hungary, xv
hydro-electricity, 295, 300, 301, 473
hydro-power, 18, 27

Iceland, 6, 328
imports/exports
    agriculture, 479, 482, 485, 486, 488, 492
income inequality, 210
Independence Party/East Turkestan Islamic Movement, 254
India, 16, 131–133, 135–137, 139, 141, 143–146, 148, 150, 151, 155, 173, 177, 179, 180, 230, 258, 259, 269, 272, 275, 281, 285, 286, 288–290, 292, 293, 391, 392, 483
    Sino–India War, 148
    US–India, 130, 155
Indonesia, 130, 135, 137, 185, 191, 277, 278, 280, 283, 284, 301, 303, 358
Industrial and Commercial Bank of China, 312
industrialisation, xvi, 280, 465, 467, 480, 489
industrial sector, 317
inflation, 317
informal economy, 463
innovation, 6, 17, 373–379, 392, 395, 401
insurance market, 320
integration, 6–8, 10
intellectual property, 392
    intellectual property rights, 32, 124, 134, 364, 374, 379, 391, 393, 395, 396, 426
Inter-American Development Bank, 245

International Atomic Energy Agency,
    180
International Court of Justice, 190–192,
    197
international currency system, 140
International Energy, 300
international financial and monetary
    systems, 20, 115, 122, 125, 126, 141
international financial institutions, 142
international governance system, 12
international institutions, 129
international maritime law, 186
international markets, 478
International Monetary Fund (IMF), 117,
    121–123, 126, 140, 142, 144, 154,
    241
    Special Drawing Rights, 142
    voting reform, 142, 145
International Security Assistance Force
    (ISAF), 251, 253, 255, 256, 258
international trade, 32, 225, 332
International Tribunal of the Law of the
    Sea, 173, 190, 191
investment agreement, 290
Iran, 132, 140, 143, 144, 180, 181, 204,
    207, 208, 212, 255, 258, 259
Iraq, 133, 209, 219
    war, 9
Ireland, xv, 44, 385
Israel, 212
Israeli–Palestinian conflict, 203, 204
IT, 375
Italy, xv, 367, 385, 389

Jamaat-e-Islami, 152
Jamaat-e-Ulema-e-Islami, 152

Japan, 69, 132, 133, 135, 136, 156–164,
    173, 175, 177–179, 185, 194, 195,
    197–200, 204, 217, 234, 272, 280,
    281, 296, 298, 303, 311, 328, 370,
    394, 424, 427
    China–Japan relations, 156–164
    China–Japan–South Korea relations,
        163
    China–Japanese War, 160–198
    US–Japan Security Treaty, 198
Japanese firms, 357
Jasmine Revolutions, xvii, 201–213
Jiangsu, 356
Jiang Zemin, 43, 53, 67, 68, 85, 299
Jia Qinglin, 53
judiciary, 41

Karakoram Highway, 150, 151, 154
Kashmir, 148, 155
Kazakhstan, 177, 179, 235–239, 384,
    388
Kim Jong-il, 215, 217–220
Kim Jong-un, 215, 217, 220–222
Korea, 204, 281
    China–Japan–South Korea relations,
        163
    Korean Peninsula, 305
    Korean war, 302
Kuomintang, 52, 355, 357
Kyrgyzstan, 177

labour
    labour disputes, 431, 432, 434, 435
    Labour Dispute Conciliation and
        Arbitration Law, 441, 442
    strikes, 335

Labour Law, 108
    Labour Contract Law, 108, 435, 441, 442, 445
    labour market, 474
    mobilisation, 449
    movement, 436
    Protection and Social Security Bureau, 448
    rights, 226, 229, 444, 445
    supply, 208
    unrest, 441–450
land
    acquisition, 458, 465–476
    disputes, 475
    landfill, 418, 419, 422
    land grabs, 431, 432, 434, 435, 439, 489
    land rights, 81
        land ownership rights, 490
    land use rights, 461, 469, 481, 489
    sales, 337, 339, 340, 341, 459
    tenure, 360
Land Administration Law, 468, 469, 472
Laos, 276, 277, 279, 280, 301, 304
Latin America, 208, 241–250, 332, 357
lawyers in the PRC, 71, 72, 437, 439, 470, 475
    human rights lawyers, 71, 75–77
    Law on Lawyers, 75
leadership transition, 77
Lee Myung-Bak, 218, 220
legal aid, 74
legal and regulatory environment, 13
legal system of the PRC, 71, 73
    legal reforms, 71, 77
Legislation Law, 102, 103, 104

Leninism, 83, 99
Libya, 133, 137, 201, 206, 207, 209, 219
Li Changchun, 67
Li Jianguo, 39
Li Keqiang, 60, 150, 151, 205
Ling Jihua, 51, 55
Li Peng, 43
Li Ruihuan, 53
Lisbon Treaty, xiv, 4, 8, 9, 118, 368
Liu Xiaobo, 181
Li Xiannian, 53
Li Zhuang, 76
loans, 237, 241, 242, 245–248, 264, 297, 337, 359, 401, 425
local government, 314, 321, 337, 414, 447, 449, 460, 465, 466, 469–473, 476
    autonomy, 340
    debt, 317, 337, 340, 342
    loans, 345
    revenues, 341

Macao, 36, 54, 56, 218, 328, 414
    Macao Special Administrative Region Basic Law Committee, 50
Macclesfield Bank, 189, 195, 197
macroeconomics, 310, 317, 320
Malacca Straits, 191
Malaysia, 167, 179, 185, 189, 190, 196, 276, 277, 280, 284, 303, 358
Malaysia–Thailand, 192
manufacturing industry, 16
Mao Xinyu, 59
Mao Zedong, 52
marine safety, 163
maritime disputes, xv, 165–174, 183–200
    dispute resolution, 185

Maritime Self-Defense Force, 160, 161
market access, 13
market economy, 310, 438
Market Economy Status, 118, 124, 126, 144
marketisation, 221
mass incidents, 436, 442, 443, 475
mass protests, 466
Ma Ying-jeou, 247
media, 5, 144, 226, 362, 434, 435, 437, 439, 445
   censorship, 72, 433
   Chinese media, 5, 67, 68, 157, 160, 162, 206, 262, 268, 269, 270, 434, 472
      China Radio International, 64, 67
   online media, 432, 437, 438, 444
medical services, 474
Medvedev, Dmitri, 139
megacities, 276, 452–454, 457, 462, 463
Member States, xiii–xvi, xix, 112, 286, 368, 370, 389, 417, 426
MERCOSUR, 245
mergers and acquisitions, 322, 391, 394, 396
   Chinese Overseas Acquisitions, 390–396
Mexico, 242, 243, 245, 247, 248
microblogs, 444
middle class, 207, 438
   in China, 397–405
Middle East, xviii, 129, 133, 134, 137, 201–213, 298, 332, 385, 433, 439
middle income countries, 280
middle power, 274, 332

migration, 344, 454
   migrant workers, 360, 432, 435, 436, 444, 447, 452, 457, 472, 473
   rural-to-urban, 452–464
   second-generation migrants, 458
militancy, 252, 254
military, 262
   assistance, 288
   cooperation, 174, 216, 217, 221
   intervention, 181
   Military Court, 48
   Military Procuratorate, 48
   regime, 265, 267, 271
mineral production, 301
mineral resources, 302
minimum wage, 18
mining, 247
Minister of Finance, 41
Ministry of Agriculture
   Ministry of Agriculture, 484
Ministry of Justice, 79
Ministry of State Security, 91
minority groups
   minorities, 435
missile defence, 176, 181
modernisation, xvi
money laundering, 218
Mongolia, 303, 364, 434
Motorola Solutions, 390–396
multilateral forums, 177
multilateralism, 176, 180, 258, 281, 282
multinational enterprises/companies, 391, 394, 395
multipolarity, 9, 68, 119
Musharraf, Pervez, 151

Muslim population in China, 210
Muslim separatism, 151

Nanjing, 109
National Committee, 55
    China Committee on Religion and
        Peace, 55
    China Economic and Social Council,
        55
    China Institute of the Theory of
        the CPPCC, 55
National Conference on Political-Legal
    Work, 74
National Coordination Committee for
    Democratic Change, 206
National Development and Reform
    Commission, 95, 162, 361, 423
National Economics Research Institute,
    89, 95
national interest, 225
nationalism, xiv, 262, 269, 290
National League for Democracy, 264,
    267
National People's Congress, 13, 14, 24,
    25, 35–38, 40–45, 47, 49, 52, 54, 55,
    99, 102–104, 210
    Chairman of the Standing
        Committee, 36, 38, 42–45
    China–Europe parliamentary
        relations group, 44
    Finance and Economic Committee, 38
    Foreign Affairs Committee, 38
    Report on the Work of the
        Government, 37
    Standing Committee, 35–42, 45, 47,
        55, 100, 103

National Program for the Development of
    Science and Technology in the Medium
    and Long Term, 375
National Reform and Development
    Commission, 361
Natuna Islands, 190
natural disasters, 157, 158, 292
natural gas, 26
natural resources, 224, 246, 249, 262,
    264, 267, 269, 271, 295, 300, 329, 332
naval activities, 171
neoliberalism, 226
neomercantilism, 228
Nepal, 285–293
netizens, 105, 158, 432, 437
new 36 clauses, 361, 362
newly emerging economies, 15
New Zealand, 177, 275, 281, 327, 328,
    330, 332–334, 336
nine-dashed line, 167, 168, 173, 185, 194
Nobel Peace Prize, 181
    Liu Xiaobo, 73, 81
Nokia Siemens Networks, 390–396
non-fossil energy, 23, 25, 27, 30
non-governmental organisations, 105,
    425, 426, 434, 436, 442, 443, 445
    environmental, 105
non-intervention/non-interference, 176,
    181, 202, 204, 205, 228, 230, 236,
    291
non-performing loans, 312, 315, 344, 346
non-proliferation, 94
    Non-Proliferation Treaty, 153
non-tariff barriers, 124
North Atlantic Treaty Organization, 133,
    149, 251, 253, 256, 259

North China Plain, 481, 490
Norway, 292, 328
nuclear
    disarmament, 178
    energy, 143, 162, 164
    nuclear energy policy, 156, 157
    nuclear threat, 221
    power, 18, 27, 30, 152, 161, 300, 301
    power plants, 156, 163, 164
    test, 180
    weapons, 152, 153
Nye, Joseph, 65

Obama, Barack, 9, 128, 131–134, 178, 220, 265
Office of Chinese Language Council International (Hanban), 68
oil, 26, 203, 207, 221, 233, 245, 247–249, 257, 332, 362, 364, 423
    companies, 229
    crude oil, 301, 302
    global oil prices, 233
    imports/exports, 207, 208, 211, 224, 235
    oil producers, 202
        oil-producing economies, 370
    oil security, 201
    oil supply, 207, 212
    prices, 207
    security, 225
    state-owned oil corporations, 226
Oil and Foodstuffs Corporation, 494

oil and gas, 182, 185, 199, 232, 234, 235, 237, 246, 264, 280, 294–305, 362, 380, 382, 383, 386
    deals, 233
    exploration, 388
    oil and gas exploration and production companies, 384
oilseeds, 479
oligopoly, 314
Olympics, 6, 437
one-child policy, 409
Open Constitution Initiative, 75, 81
Open Government Information Regulations, 99
opposition movements, 211
Organisation for Economic Co-operation and Development (OECD), 375–377
Organisation of the Islamic Conference, 149
Organization for Security and Cooperation in Europe (OSCE), 260
Organization of American States, 245

Pakistan, 133, 145, 148–155, 252, 254–256, 258, 259, 327, 328, 330, 332, 335, 336
    Federally Administered Tribal Areas, 255
Pan Zhenqiang, 94
Paracel Islands, 167, 175, 178, 186, 187, 189, 194–197
Paraguay, 241
Party Congress, 135
    18th Party Congress, 99
Party schools, 82–86
    Central Party School, 82–86

patents, 27, 374, 377–379, 392
    patent applications, 392
    patent applications in China, 378
peaceful rise, 278
Pearl River Delta, 443, 445–449
Pedro Branca/Pulau Batu Puteh, 190
Peking University, 89, 96
    School of International Studies, 89, 96
Peng Zhen, 42
pensions, 318, 341, 343, 398, 405, 406–415, 468, 474
    cwwommercial pensions, 407
    expatriate pensions, 408, 414
    government pension scheme, 398
    reforms, 408
    Rural Pension System, 407, 408, 413
    state pension system, 414
    urban pension system, 406–410
People's Bank of China, 318, 371
People's Congress, 36, 39, 40, 103, 104, 109–112
    elections, 40
    People's Congress system, 41
    Shanghai Municipal People's Congress, 101
People's Liberation Army, 36, 39, 88, 90, 94, 282, 360
    Academy of Military Sciences, 89
    General Staff Second Department, 93, 94
people-to-people links, 70, 149, 165, 169, 245
Permanent Court of Arbitration, 190
Peru, 242–244, 246, 249, 327, 328, 330, 332–334, 336
PetroChina, 383, 388

pharmaceuticals, 249, 374, 402
    pharmaceutical patents, 379
Philippines, 135, 136, 167, 172, 173, 179, 183, 185, 187, 189, 191, 192, 194–197, 276, 277
pipelines, 179
    East Siberia Pacific Ocean (ESPO), 179
planned economy, 438
planning laws, 364
Poland, xv, 388
policy making, xvi, 90, 96, 105
    environmental policy making, 98
policy of 'no interference', 8
Politburo, 85, 93, 203, 205
    Standing Committee, 53, 85
political economy, 283
political reform, 19, 99, 203, 215, 218, 261, 264
political stability, 181, 182
pollution, 297, 401, 421, 435, 438, 439
    pollution reduction, 422
population growth, 16
Portugal, 367, 387
post-conflict reconstruction, 212
post-neoliberal era, 115
Potsdam Declaration, 199
poverty, 18
    European Platform Against Poverty, 18
Preferential Trade Agreements, 284
private enterprises, 399, 424
    family businesses, 355–365
private equity industry, 361
private sector, 94, 216, 292, 415, 420
Procuratorate, 41
    Chief Procurator, 41

proliferation, 220
propaganda, 77
Property Law, 42, 104
property ownership, 400, 403
property sector, 337, 338, 340, 341, 344, 345, 356, 359, 361, 464
protectionism, 20
protests, 166, 167, 436, 437, 439, 444, 448, 449, 475
provincial-level government, 102
public engagement, xv
public health, 416
public hearings, 103
public opinion, 439
public participation, 98, 99, 104
    Guangzhou Public Participation Measures, 101, 104
    Hunan Administrative Procedure Act, 104
public procurement, 137
public sector finance, 345
Public Security Ministry, 75
public services, 453, 454, 463, 473
Pulau Ligitan, 190
Pulau Sipidan, 190
Putin, Vladimir, 295, 298

Qiao Shi, 42
Qing Dynasty, 194
quantitative easing, 121

Ramo, Joshua, 69
rare earth exports, 132
realpolitik, 121
recycling, 418, 419, 421

reform, 268, 269, 271–273, 318
    constitutional reform, 272
reform and opening up, 95, 314
refugees, 219, 266, 290
regime change, 181, 202, 211, 212, 221
regional integration, 279, 281
regionalism
    economic regionalisation, 275, 279, 280
    institutional regionalisation, 275, 279, 281
regional security mechanisms, 252
regional stability, 253, 260
renewable energy, 24, 30, 383, 386, 387, 389
    projects, 31
    renewable energy investments, 26
    sources, 27
    target, 27
renminbi, 116, 123, 319, 369
research and development (R&D), 16, 17, 20, 374, 375, 377, 385, 387, 392, 396, 491
Rice, Condoleezza, 130
risk, 201, 211, 222
Romania, xv, 385, 386
rule of law, xvi, 73, 78, 81, 229, 233, 235, 239, 240
rural population, 41
rural residents, 414, 483
rural-to-urban migration, 400, 413
Russia, 139, 141–146, 151, 163, 175–182, 204, 212, 215, 217, 233, 237–239, 253, 258, 259, 275, 281, 294–305, 388, 392
    Sino–Russian relations, 294–305

Index 517

sanctions, 180, 217, 218, 265, 272
    economic sanctions, 267
    military sanctions, 150
San Francisco Conference of 1951, 195, 198
Sarkozy, Nicolas, 6
Scarborough Shoal, 186, 189, 195–197, 275
Schroeder, Gerhard, 9
science and technology, 13
scientific collaboration, 374
sea lanes, 172, 199, 234, 295, 297, 332
secret police, 76
security, 234, 260
    architectures, 130, 137
    economic security, 203
    political security, 203
    resource security, 224
    risks, 252
self-censorship, 437
service sector, 13, 16, 19, 124, 283, 457
    international trade in services, 20
Shandong, 58, 78–81, 106, 159
Shanghai, 43, 86, 93, 101, 107, 111, 300, 342, 356, 358–360, 402, 464, 474
    stock market, 312, 313, 358
Shanghai and Shenzhen Stock Exchanges, 56
Shanghai Cooperation Organisation, 146, 155, 175–178, 232, 237, 252, 253, 257–260, 276, 296, 300
Shanghai Institutes for International Studies, 89, 92
Sharif, Nawaz, 150
Shengzhi Law Office, 79
Shen Yueyue, 39

Shenzhen, 98, 99, 102, 103, 109, 112, 312, 313, 342
Sichuan, 99, 109–112
    earthquake, 157, 158, 160, 204
Singapore, 135, 136, 179, 185, 190, 191, 276–278, 280, 282, 284, 357
sinocentrism, 277
Sinopec, 246, 383, 384, 388
sinophobia, 278
Sino–Turkmen gas agreement, 238
Six-Party Talks, 214, 215, 217, 296, 302, 303
skilled jobs, 229
Slovakia, 467
small and medium-sized enterprises, 360, 363, 399
social activists, 433, 437
social exclusion, 444
social injustices, 433, 437
social instability, 77
Social Insurance Law, 414
socialist democracy, 41, 55
socialist market ideology, 268
social justice, 436
social safety net, 473
social security, 399, 414, 415, 454, 466, 473, 474, 489
Social Security Law, 474
social security systems, 19
social stability, 431, 437, 439, 442, 444, 445, 447, 449
social unrest, xvii, 210, 272, 301, 431–440, 450, 466, 472
    mass incidents, 434
    public order disturbances, 433, 434
social welfare, 220, 362, 405, 448, 463

soft power, 59, 63–65, 69, 70, 274, 278, 282
  public diplomacy, 66, 67
solar power, 27, 162
South Africa, 139, 141, 143–145, 225, 230
South China Sea, xv, 132, 136, 165–174, 178, 179, 183–200, 204, 274, 275, 282, 283, 295–297, 304
Southeast Asia, 131, 132, 135, 168, 173, 178, 201, 204, 268, 274–284, 294–305, 358
South Korea, 69, 132, 133, 136, 157, 160, 161, 163, 173, 177, 185, 204, 217–222, 280, 298, 299, 303, 414
sovereign debt crisis, 4, 9, 10
sovereign debt rating, 338
sovereign investment funds, 322
sovereignty, 119, 143, 172, 173, 176, 183–185, 187, 188, 190, 192, 194, 195, 197, 200
sovereign wealth funds, 371
soyabeans, 477, 479, 480, 486, 488, 492, 493
Spain, 367, 384, 385
Special Drawing Rights, 145
special economic zones, 216, 218, 469
Spratly Islands, 167, 169, 175, 178, 187, 189, 194–196, 197, 275
stability, 269, 270, 273, 318, 344
  political stability, 296
staple foods, 478–480, 488
State Bureau for Letters and Visits, 476
State Council, 37, 38, 46, 48, 88, 90, 92, 95, 99, 101–103, 159, 421, 424, 458, 459, 468, 470, 473
  Development Research Center, 89, 95
  ministers, 37

Ministry of State Security, 90
Office of Legislative Affairs, 101, 102
State Councillors, 37
State Grid Corporation of China, 387
state-owned companies/enterprises, 84, 124, 209, 226, 232, 247, 250, 256, 267, 297, 304, 309, 312, 318, 355–357, 359–362, 386, 409, 411, 424
  national oil companies, 382, 383, 386
  state-owned energy companies, 386
state subsidies, 134, 137
stock markets, 311
Straits of Malacca, 263
strategic dialogues, xvi
strategic partnership, 284, 299
  agreements, 245
Sunshine Policy, 218
Sun Yat-sen, 52
super powers, 217
Supreme People's Court, 36, 38, 42, 46–48, 74, 76, 102
Supreme People's Procuratorate, 36, 38, 47, 48
sustainability, xiii
sustainable development, 23, 26, 124
sustainable growth, 17
Sweden, xv, 369, 377, 385, 392, 393
Switzerland, 6, 292
Syria, 140, 143, 180, 201, 206–209, 384

Taiwan, 10, 36, 44, 54, 131, 132, 148, 167, 185, 187, 189, 195, 196, 198, 199, 204, 241–243, 245, 247, 280, 357, 414
Tajikistan, 177
Taliban, 151, 152, 155, 253

tariffs, 248, 260
tax, 406–415
    social tax, 408
technology, 6, 138
telecommunication, 247, 257, 362, 374, 390, 392, 393, 396
Teng Biao, 75, 79, 80
territorial disputes, 128, 171, 172, 183–200, 283, 296
terrorist activity, 254
textbook issues, 157, 160, 161
textile industry, 149, 358, 359
    Multi-Fibre Arrangement, 149
Thailand, 179, 185, 191, 277, 278, 280, 358
Thein Sein, 261, 264, 265, 267, 272, 282
think tank, xiii, 88–97, 159, 231
    Defence-Related and Military, 93
    Economic and Political-Economy, 95
    International Relations and Foreign Policy, 91
Third Plenum, 118
Three Supremes, 74, 75
Tiananmen, 53, 54, 81
Tibet, 10, 44, 55, 70, 81, 132, 287, 288, 293, 434, 437
    1959 Tibetan Uprising, 435
        Tibetan refugees, 285, 287, 288, 293
        Tibetan unrest, 289
total factor productivity, 316
totalitarianism, 219
tourism, 19, 218, 259, 285, 291, 333
township and village banks, 363
township and village enterprises, 360
Track II dialogue, 89, 91, 94, 96

Track I–II dialogues, 260
trade, xvii, 10, 153, 170, 204, 208, 216, 227, 243, 245, 247–250, 263, 271, 279–281, 290, 297, 302, 327–336
    anti-dumping, 6
    barriers, 124
    deficit, 124
    international trade, 275
    negotiations, 118, 124, 126
    policy, 6, 137
    trade deal, 280
    traders, 227
trade union, 108, 357, 432, 436, 447, 449
    All-China Federation of Trade Unions, 108
    Trade Union Law, 108
    workplace unions, 441–450
transatlantic partnership, 9
Trans-Pacific Partnership, 134
trilateralism, 230
Tsinghua University, 89, 96
    Institute of International Studies, 89, 96
Turkestan, 254
Turkey, 212, 259
Turkmenistan, 236–239, 255, 300

Uighur, 149, 151, 152, 155, 210, 435
    nationalism, 235
    Uighur separatists, 151, 251, 254
unemployment, 15, 257, 345, 403, 414, 423
united front, 52, 53, 54
United Kingdom, xv, 44, 69, 178, 288, 291, 292, 370, 377, 384, 385, 389, 404, 405, 467, 491

United Nations, 3, 93, 120, 140, 141,
    143, 151, 176, 178, 180, 181, 199,
    208, 216–218, 253, 259, 276, 335
  Economic Commission for Latin
    America and the Caribbean, 244,
    246, 249
  General Assembly, 180, 181
  Human Rights Commission, 181
  Security Council, 3, 7, 143, 145,
    175–178, 180–182, 206, 222, 263
  Security Council Resolution, 258
  UN Commission on the Limits of
    the Continental Shelf, 167, 189
  UN Convention on the Law of the
    Sea (UNCLOS), 166, 167, 172,
    173, 184, 187–189, 191, 192, 196
  United Nations Framework
    Convention on Climate Change, 25
  UNHCR, 287
United States, 4, 6, 8, 9, 66, 69, 80, 90,
    97, 119, 122–124, 126, 128–138, 141,
    142, 145, 148, 163, 166, 168,
    171–173, 176, 178, 179, 181, 194,
    195, 198, 201, 203, 204, 211, 212,
    215, 217–222, 225, 226, 233, 237,
    246, 248, 250, 251, 253, 254, 259,
    261, 263, 265–270, 272, 275, 281,
    282, 285, 287, 288, 291–293, 295,
    303, 318, 328, 359, 369, 370, 372,
    374, 377–379, 390, 391–395, 404,
    427, 481, 484, 491
  bonds, 371
  engagement, 269, 271, 296
  navy, 183, 186
  pivot, 262, 266, 269, 283, 304
  treasury bonds, 368

US dollar, 11, 121, 123, 126, 142,
    145
US pivot, 9, 128–138
US–China, xv, xvii, 92–94, 132,
    134, 271
US–India, 130, 155
US–Japan Security Treaty, 198
USSR, 196
Urban and Rural Planning Law, 106
urban citizens, 432, 439, 453, 458, 464
urban development, 469
urban infrastructure, 464
urbanisation, 143, 344, 397, 399, 400,
    403, 406, 409, 419, 452–465, 467,
    479, 480, 487, 489
urbanisation of Chinese society, 41
urban planning, 106
urban residents, 413, 465, 467, 473
Uzbekistan, 177, 179

van Rompuy, Herman, 8
Venezuela, 181, 245, 246, 248
veto power, 123, 126, 180
Vietnam, 130, 135, 136, 165–174, 179,
    183, 185, 186, 189, 191, 192,
    194–197, 275–279, 284, 295, 300,
    301, 303–305, 359
Vietnam–China Strategic Defence and
    Security Dialogue, 170
village collective, 465, 467
village committee, 470, 475
village elections, 98

Wang Shengjun, 74
Wang Yang, 107
war on terror, 251

waste
    hazardous waste, 417, 418–420, 422, 424
    industrial waste, 417–421
    municipal solid waste, 417–421
    waste management, 416–428
    water conservation, 481, 490
Weibo, 437
welfare state, 400
Wen Jiabao, 7, 72, 106, 109, 112, 149, 157, 210, 288, 290, 293, 318, 398, 464, 472
Wenzhou, 358, 359
    rail crash, 45
western regions, 232, 234, 263, 280
Women's Federation, 55
Women's Legal Research and Service Centre, 75
World Bank, 142, 245, 406, 409, 419, 422, 425
World Trade Organization, 116, 118, 123, 124, 127, 177, 243, 246, 248, 300, 315, 328, 331
    Agreement on Government Procurement, 124
    Doha round, 124

World War II, 185, 194
Wu Bangguo, 36, 43
Wukan, 110, 475

Xiao Yang, 74
Xi Jinping, 60, 85, 136, 299, 303
Xinjiang, 148, 149, 152, 236, 254, 434, 437

Yang Jiechi, 93, 132, 258, 259
Yangtze, 105, 490
yuan, 145, 247
Yunnan, 281
Yu Zhengsheng, 51, 53

Zhang Dejiang, 36, 38, 44, 49
Zhang Qingli, 55
Zha Peixin, 44
Zhejiang, 356, 358
Zhou Enlai, 52, 279
Zhu Rongji, 43
Zimbabwe, 180
Zoellick, Robert, 142
Zweckoptimismus, 11